FLYING HIGH

TUSCANY

FLYING HIGH

WHITE STAR
PUBLISHERS

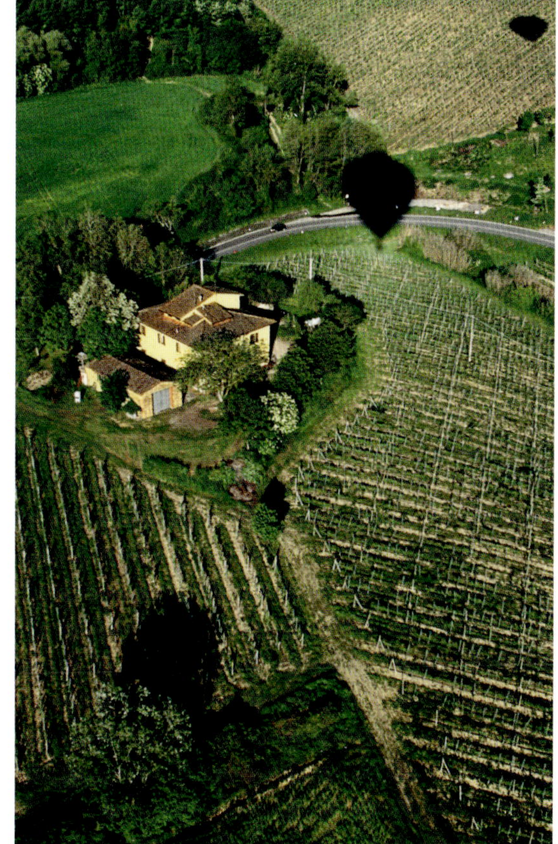

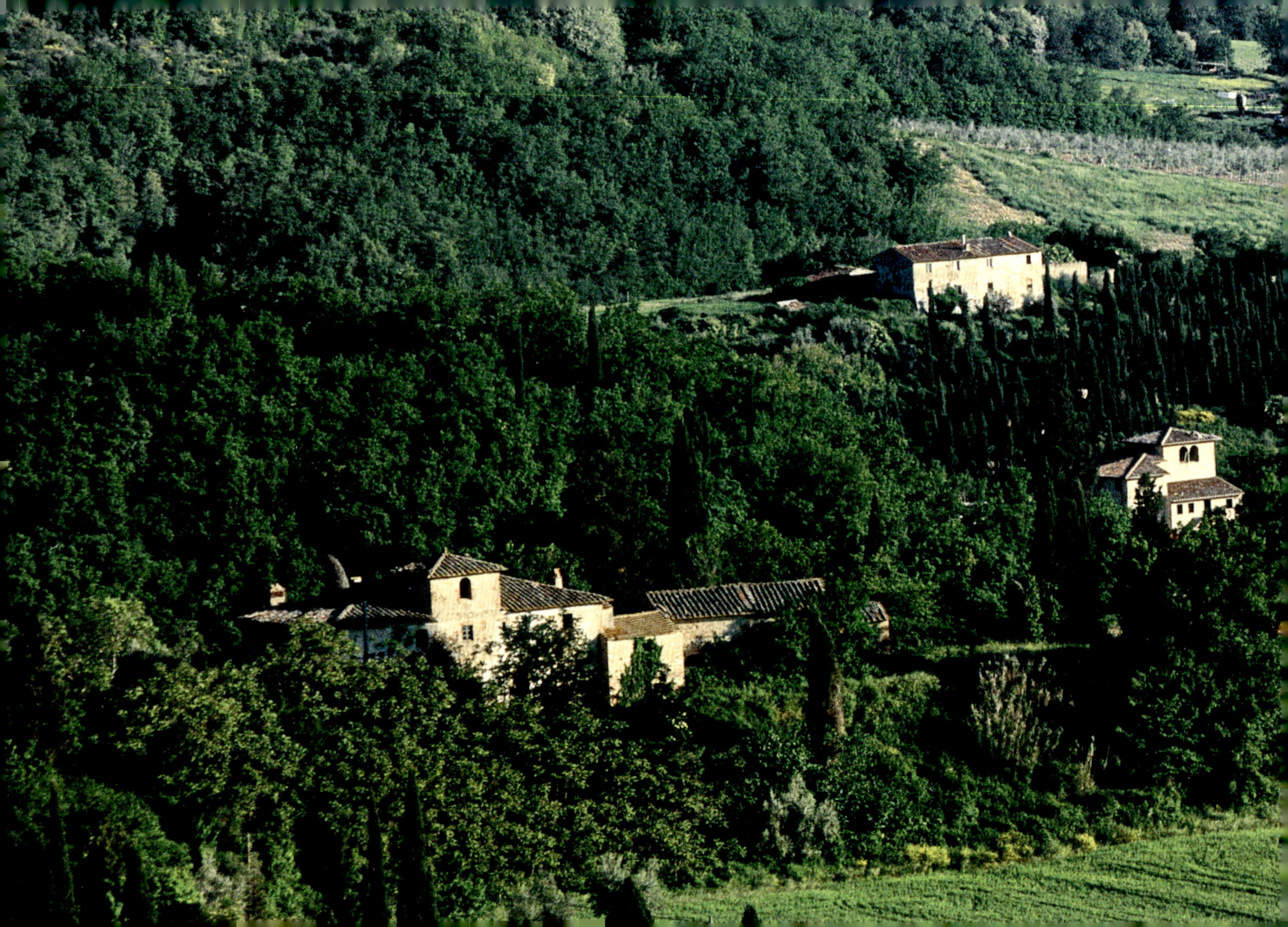

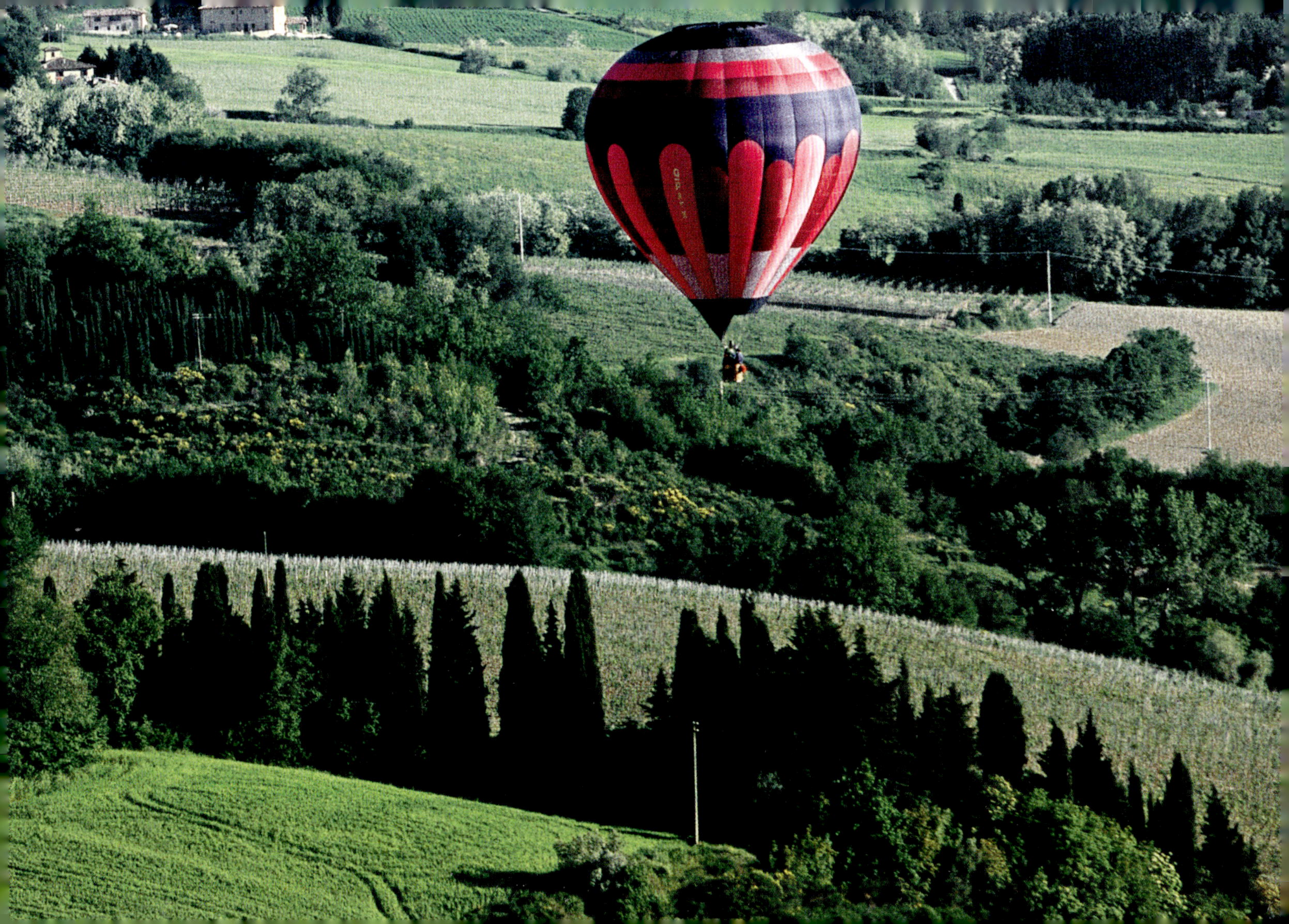

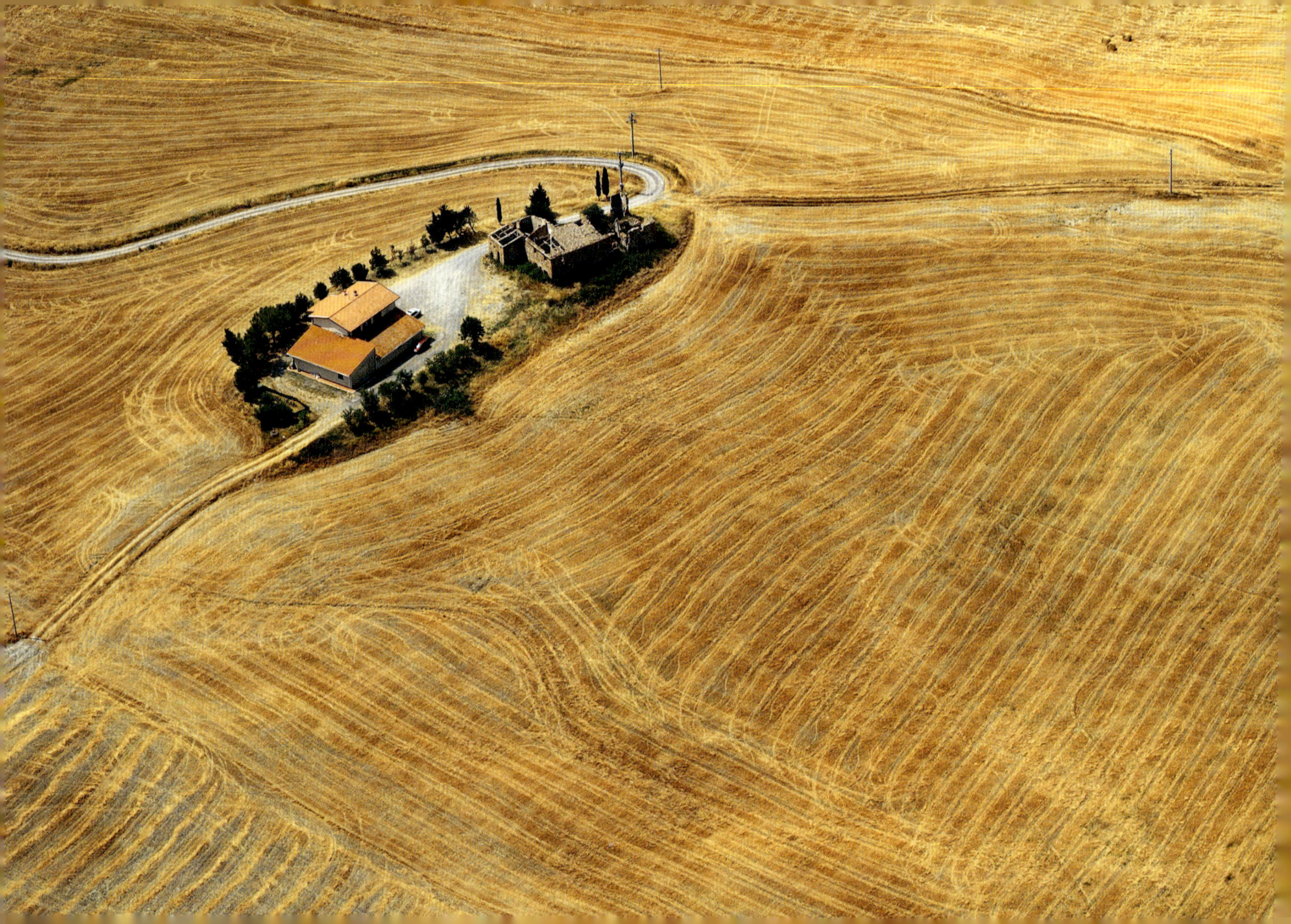

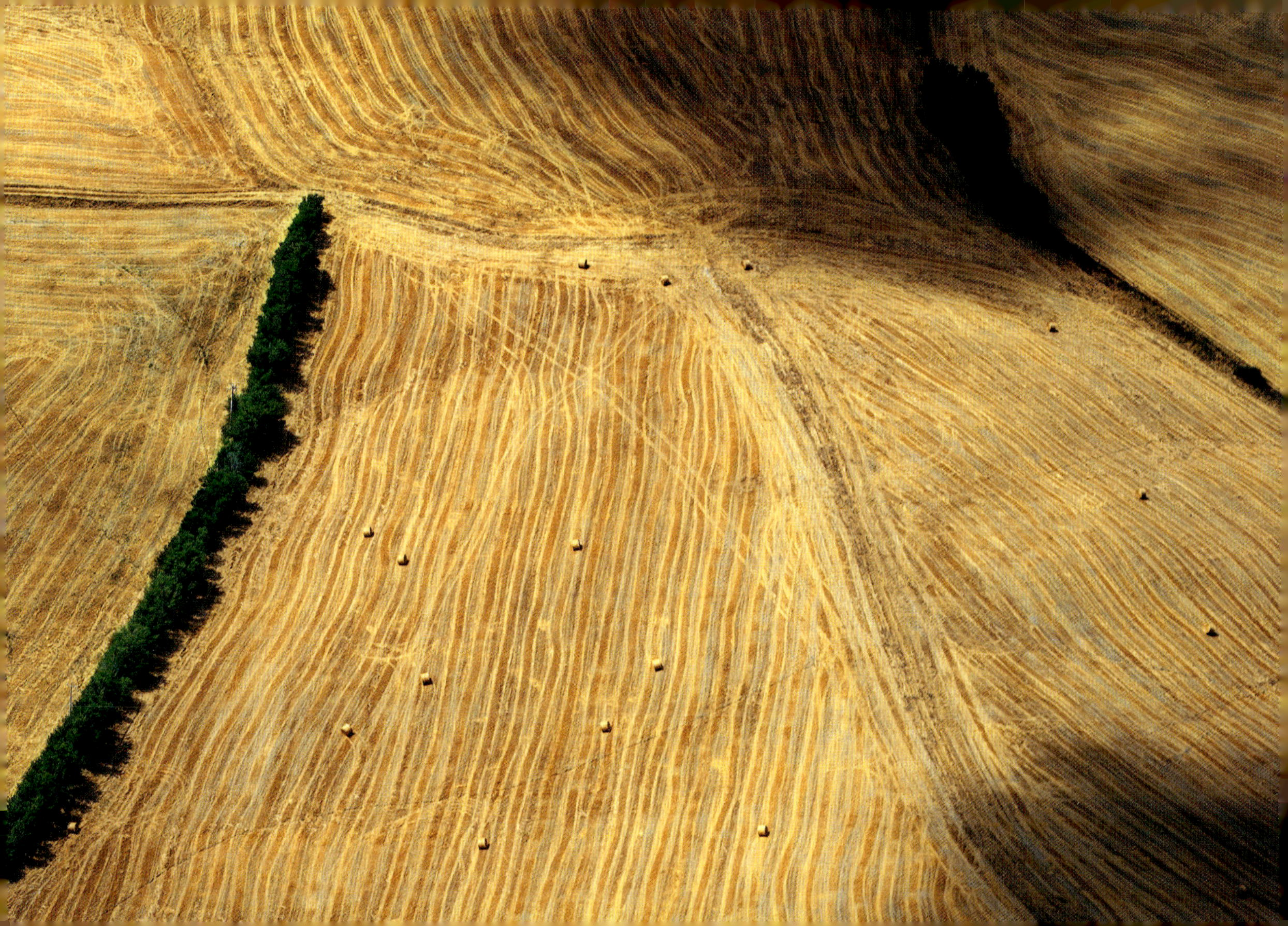

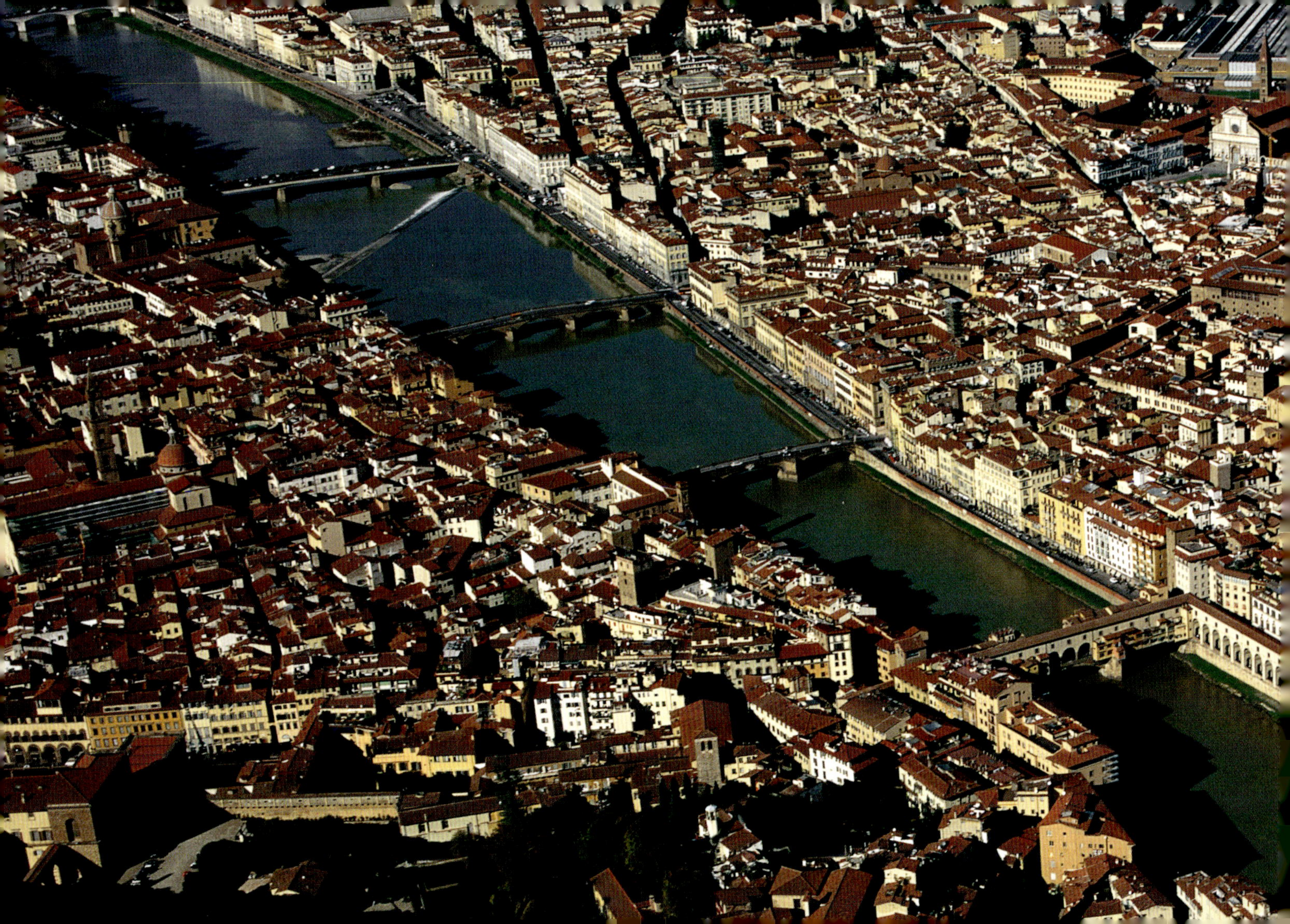

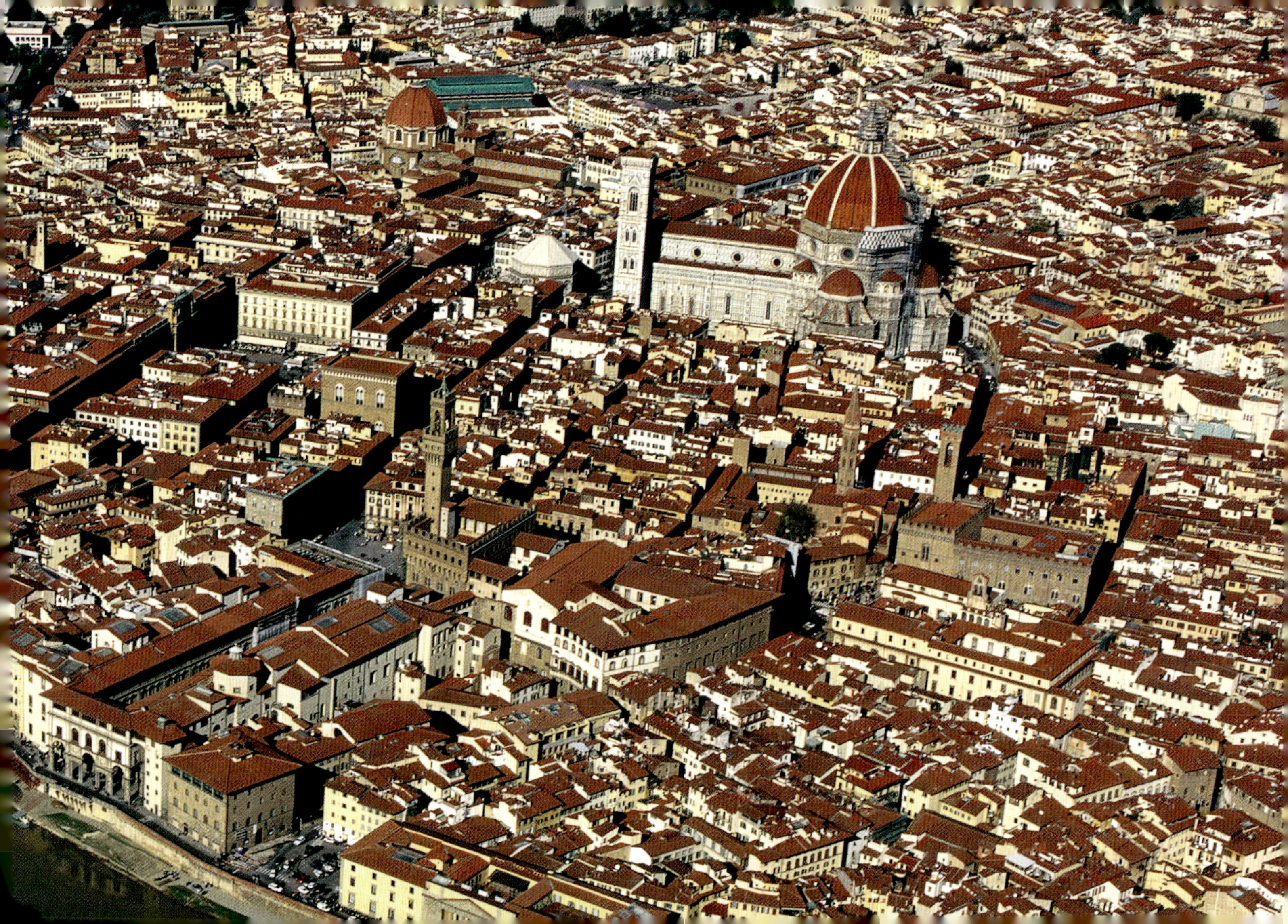

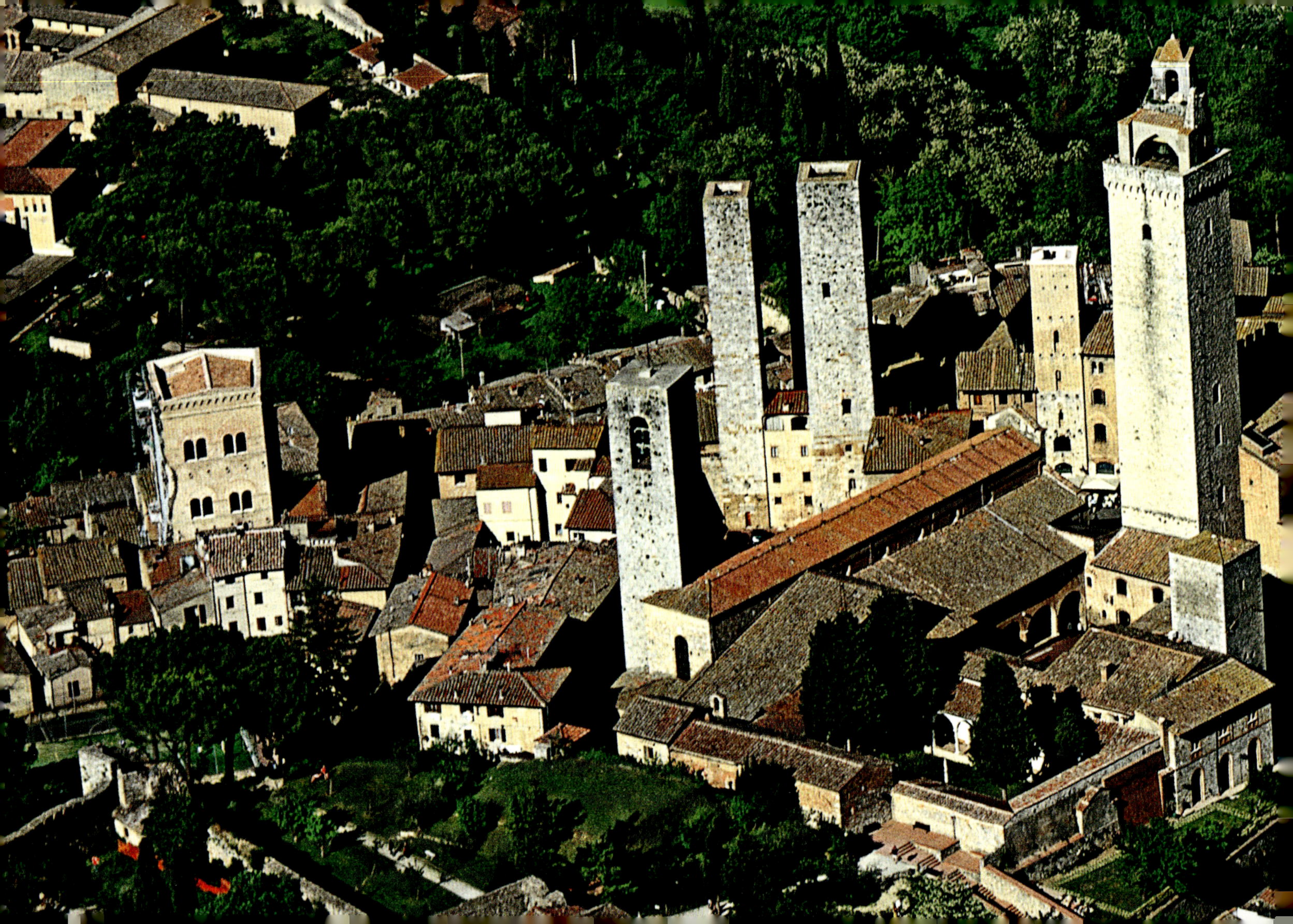

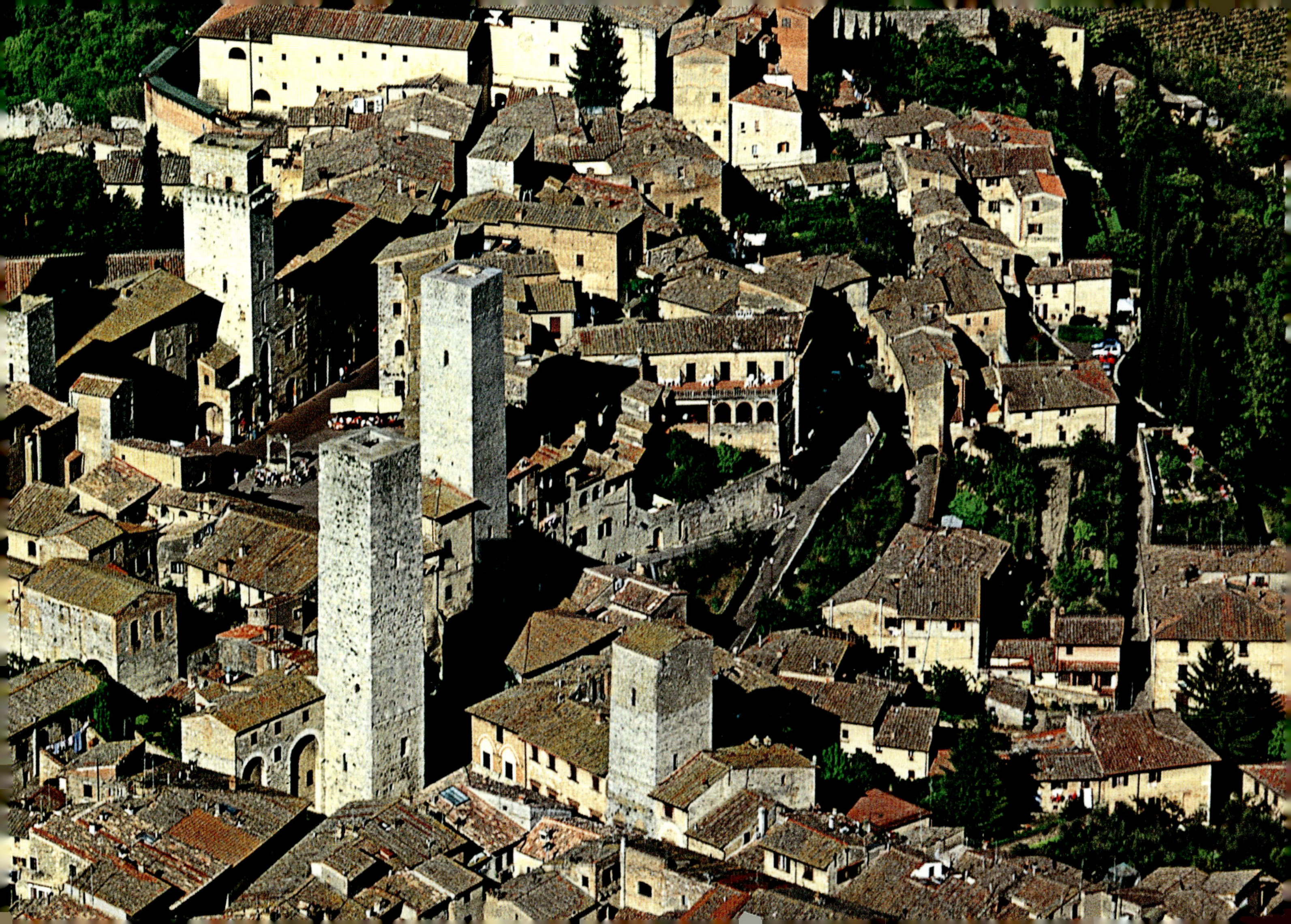

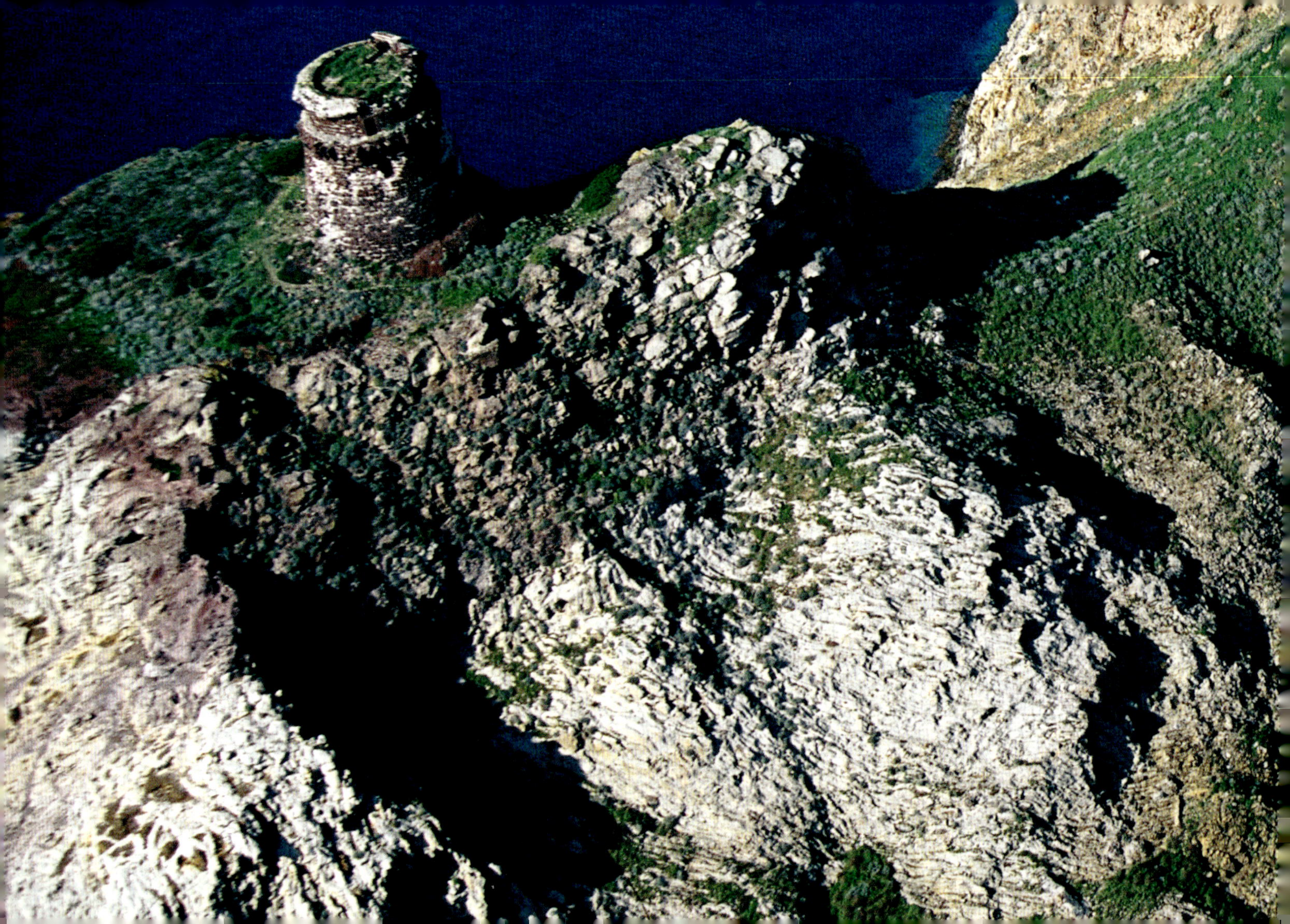

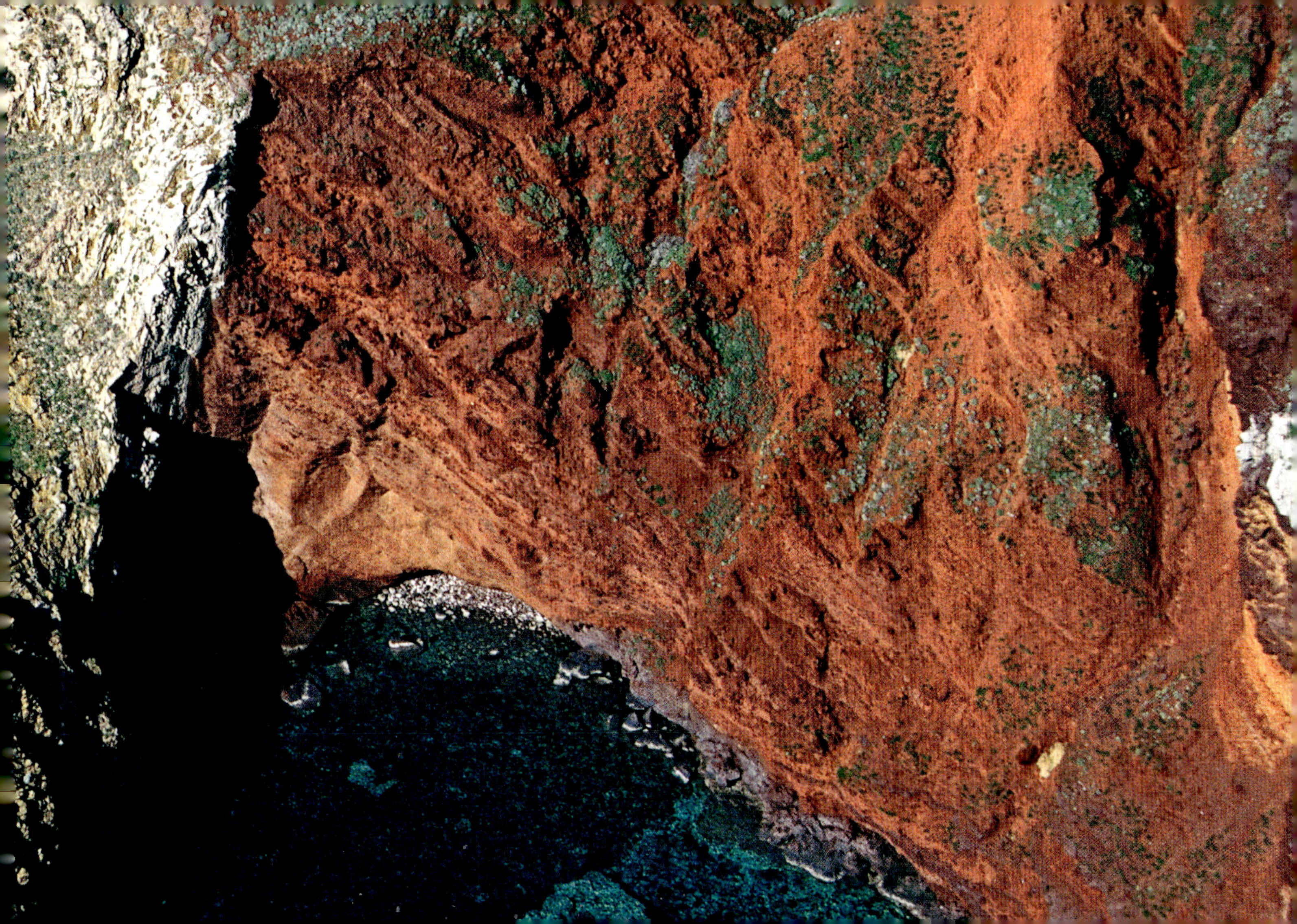

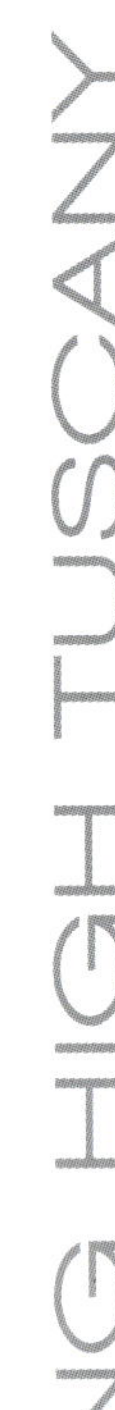

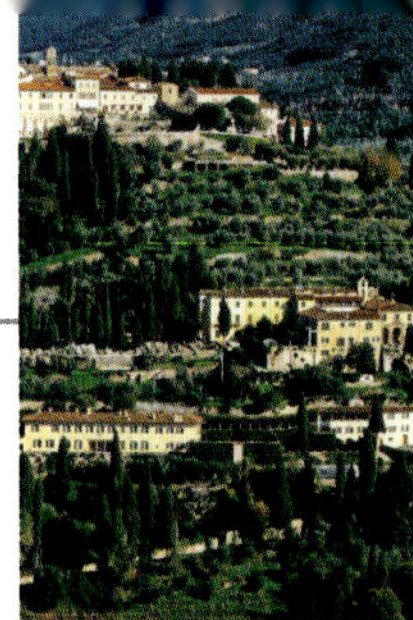

PHOTOGRAPHS

Antonio Attini

TEXT

Renzo Rossi

PROJECT EDITOR

Valeria Manferto De Fabianis

GRAPHIC DESIGN

Paola Piacco

Via Candido Sassone, 22-24
13100 Vercelli - Italy
WWW.WHITESTAR.IT

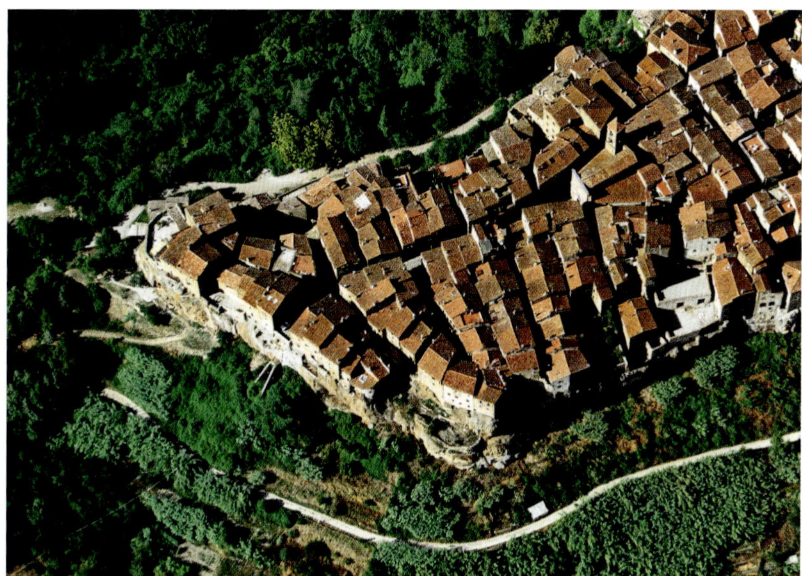

Translation: Maresa Moglia

ISBN 88-544-0131-5

Reprints: 1 2 3 4 5 6 10 09 08 07 06

Printed in China
Color separation: Fotomec, Turin

1
Extensive vineyards cover these hillsides in Tavernelle, Val di Pesa.

2-3
To fly over Val di Pesa in a hot air balloon is a fantastic trip in the heart of Chianti.

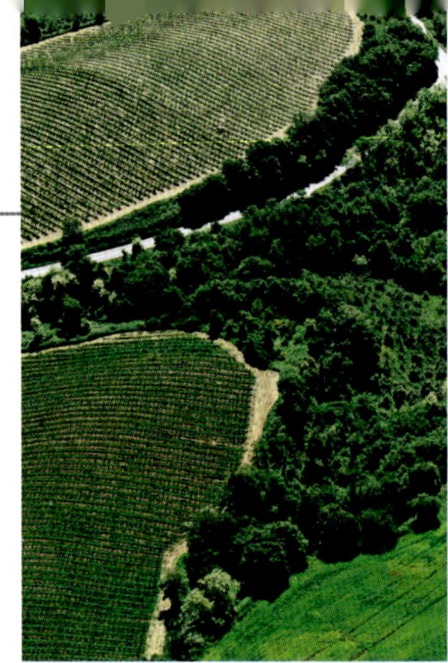

Contents

4-5
After the harvest, the fields around Arezzo seem like velvet.

6-7
The Arno and Florence: the flowing water and the tide of history.

8-9
The towers of San Gimignano dominate the hills of Val d'Elsa.

10-11
Capraia is one of nature's pearls: time seems to have come to a stop.

12
Fiesole is an elegant residential small town on the hills overlooking Florence.

13
Pitigliano: ancient, magical Etruscan village.

14
The fields carved out of the irregular, forested hills of Chianti have strange shapes.

15
Piazza del Campo and the Torre del Mangia are Siena's jewels.

FLYING HIGH TUSCANY

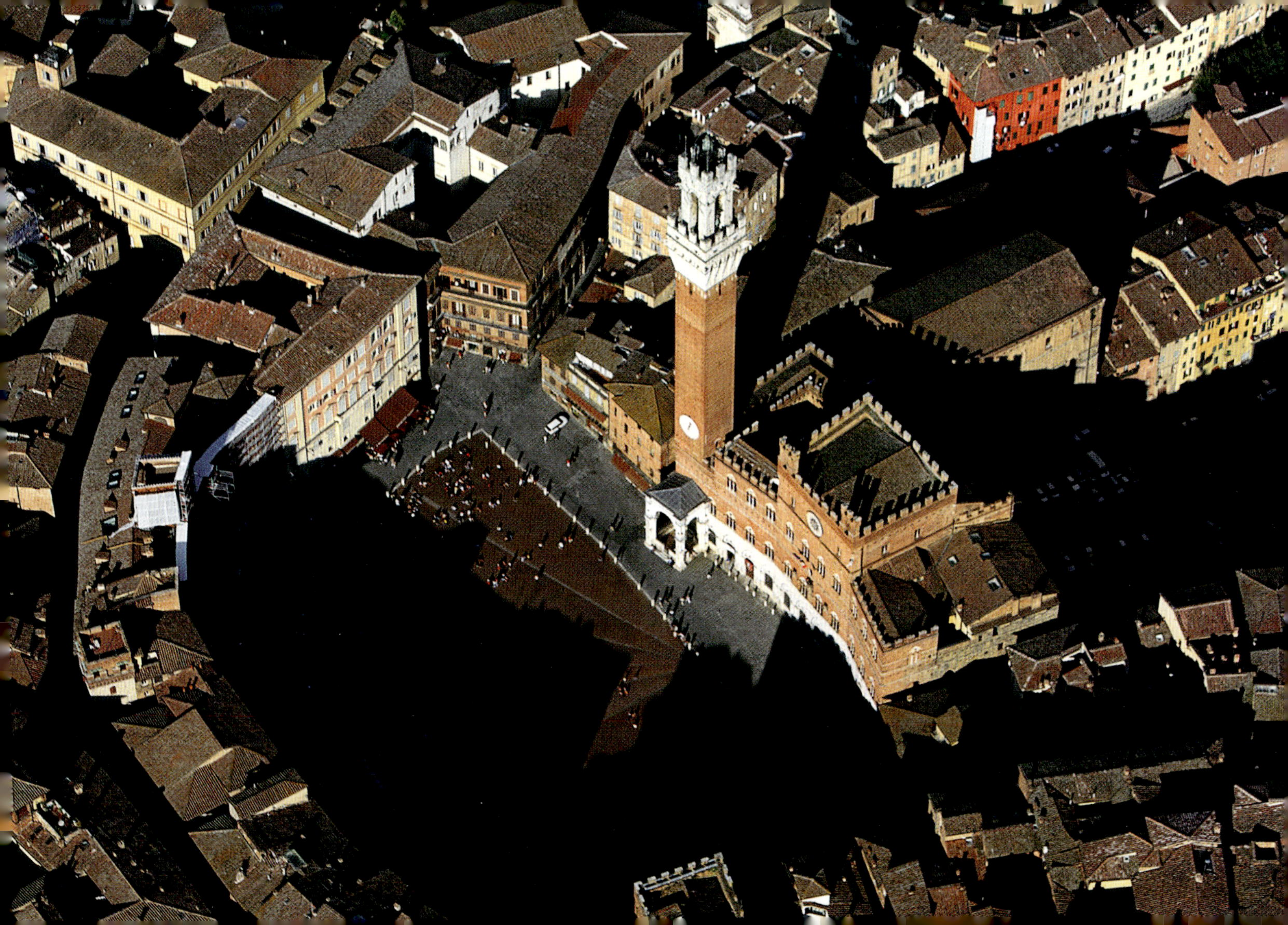

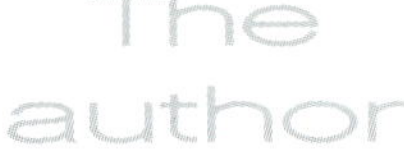
The
author

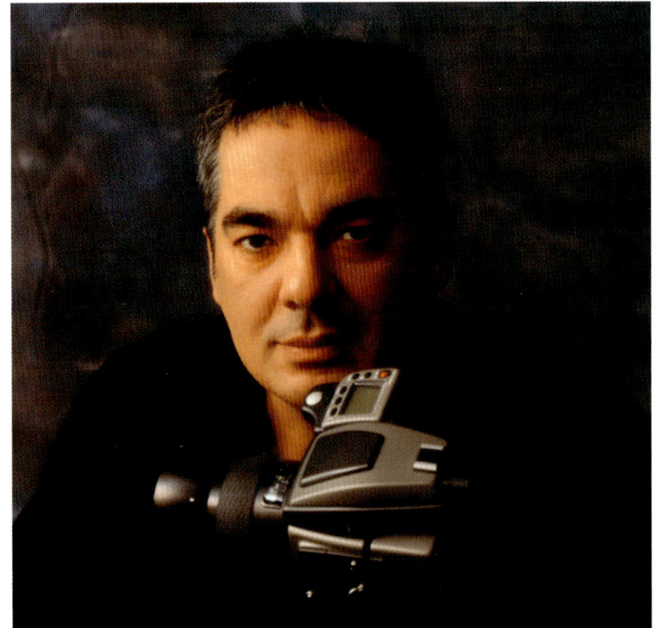

ANTONIO ATTINI WAS BORN IN TURIN IN 1960 AND HAS PRODUCED NUMEROUS PHOTO REPORTS IN EUROPE, AFRICA, ASIA AND AMERICA, WHICH HAVE BEEN PUBLISHED BY THE WORLD'S LEADING TRAVEL MAGAZINES. HE HAS WORKED WITH WHITE STAR PUBLISHERS SINCE 1989, TAKING THE PHOTOGRAPHS FOR NUMEROUS VOLUMES BELONGING TO THE *COUNTRIES OF THE WORLD, THE WORLD FROM THE AIR* AND *PLACES AND HISTORY SERIES*, AND ALSO CONTRIBUTING TO THE CREATION OF MANY OTHER PRESTIGIOUS WORKS. HE HAS BEEN A MEMBER OF THE KODAK GOLD CIRCLE SINCE 1994, WITH THE STANDARD OF EXCELLENCE. IN RECENT YEARS HE HAS SPECIALIZED IN AERIAL PHOTOGRAPHY, SHOOTING FEATURES FROM THE SKIES OF AMERICA, EUROPE AND AFRICA. HIS BOOKS INCLUDE *IRELAND FROM THE AIR, AMERICA FROM THE AIR, CHICAGO FROM THE AIR, HAWAII FROM THE AIR, HIGH ABOVE NEW YORK, HIGH ABOVE SAN FRANCISCO* AND *IRELAND FLYING HIGH*, ALL PUBLISHED BY WHITE STAR AND ALREADY TRANSLATED INTO TEN LANGUAGES. THESE WORKS WERE RECENTLY JOINED BY THE HANDSOME VOLUME, *ITALY FROM ABOVE*, ALSO PUBLISHED BY WHITE STAR.

18-19
Stone-built houses surrounded by typical Mediterranean vegetation are quite common along the San Vincenzo coast, in the province of Livorno (Leghorn).

20-21
Inhabited since the Paleolithic Age, Massa Marittima is now a charming medieval city near Grosseto.

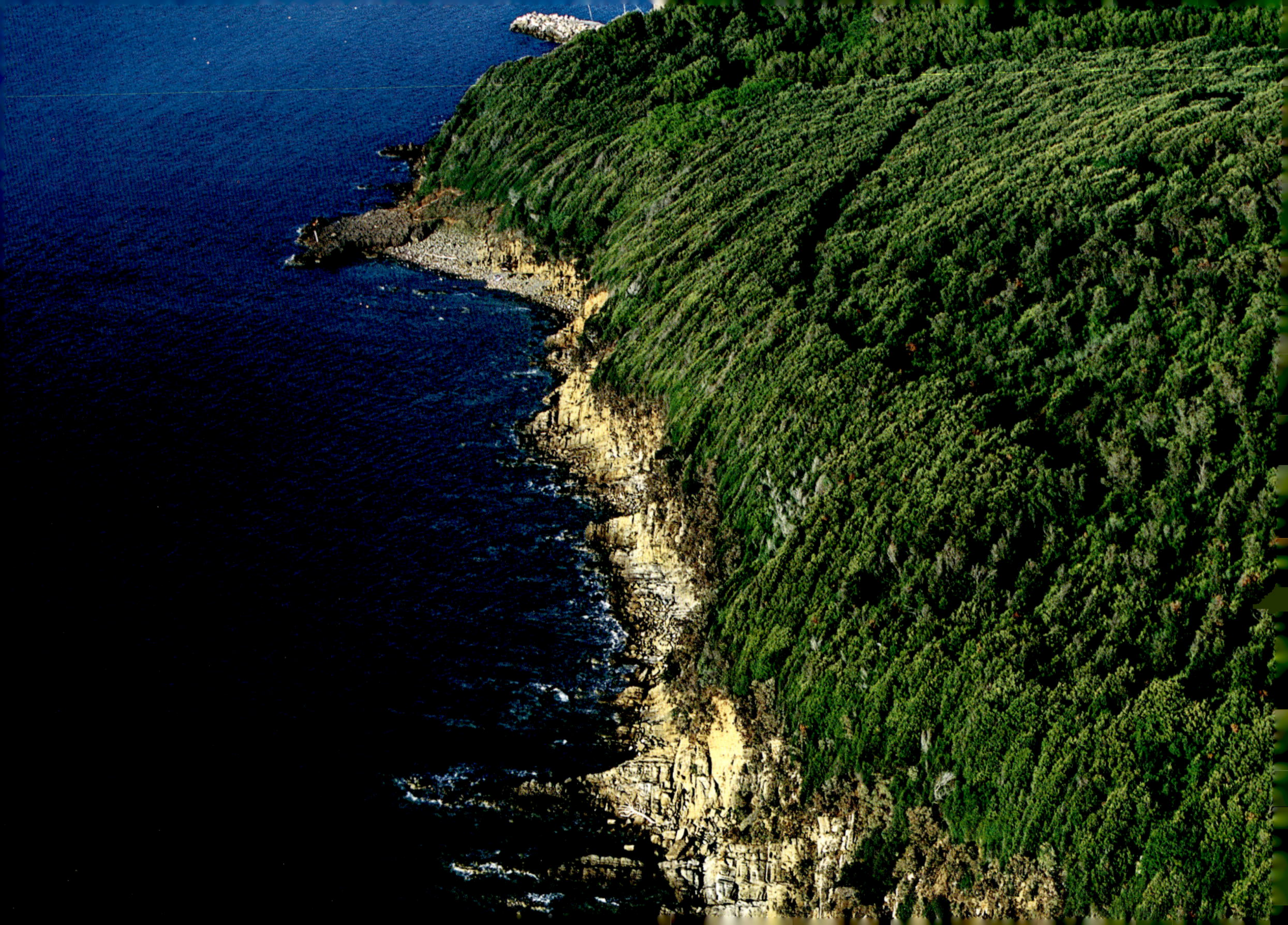

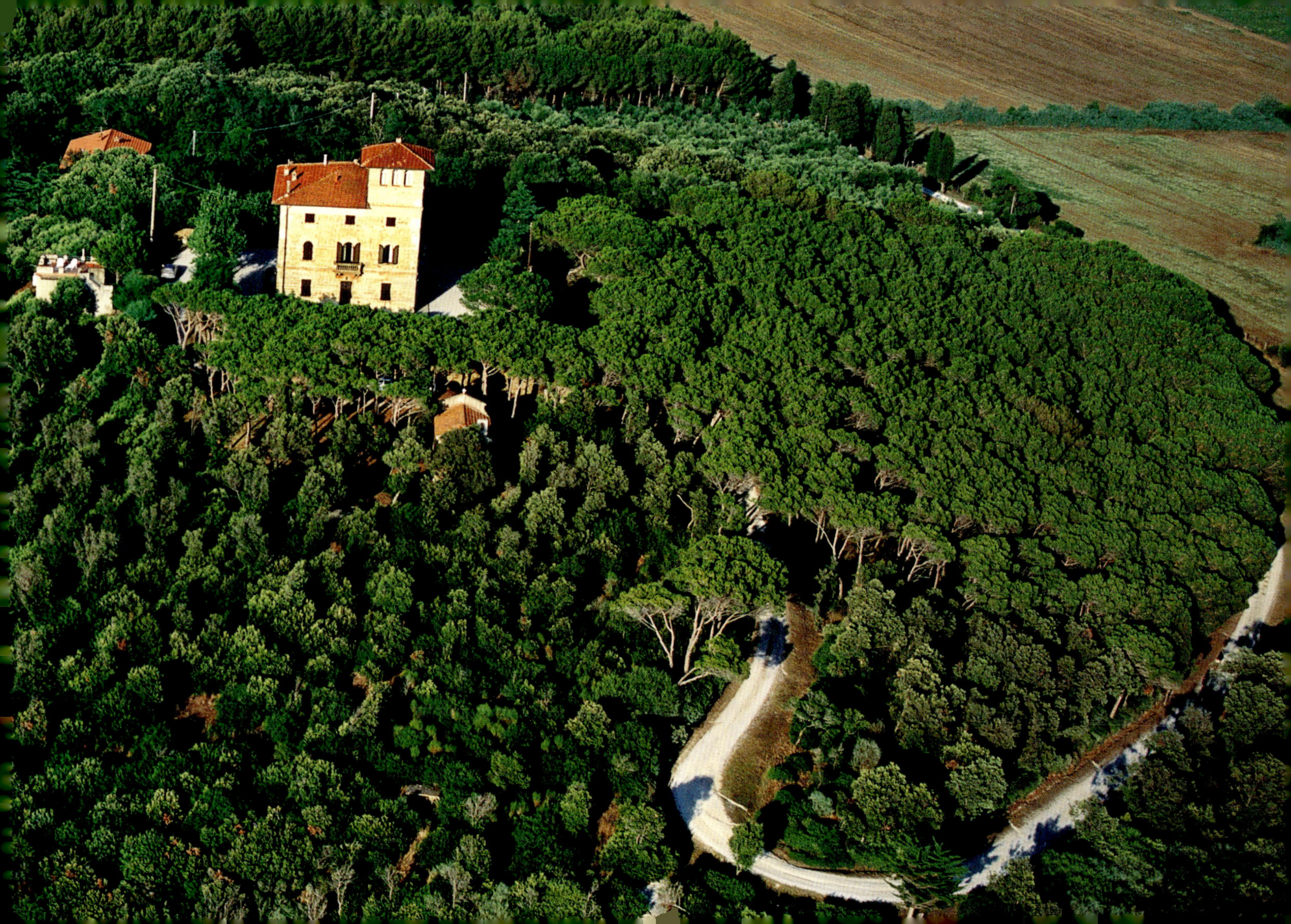

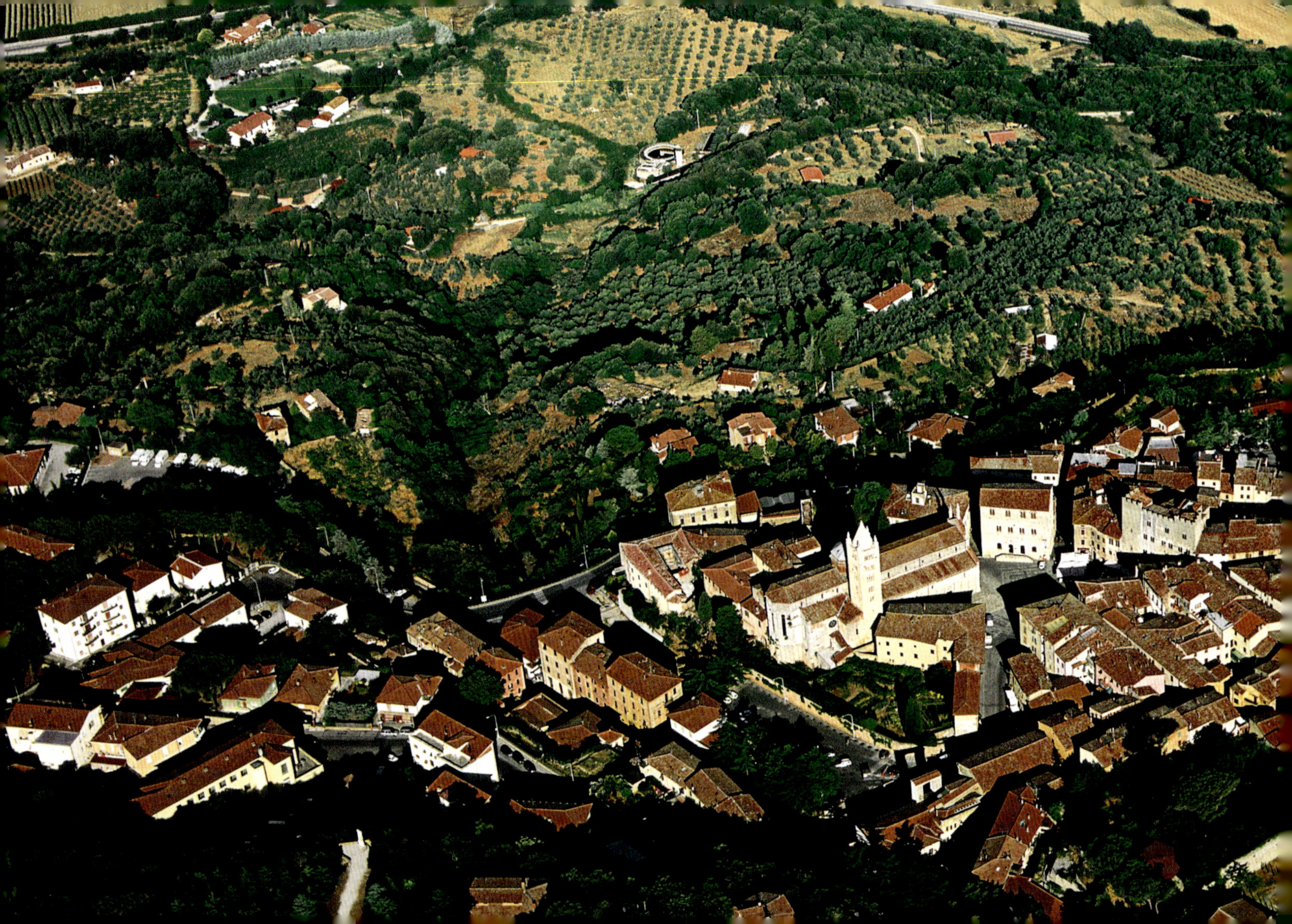

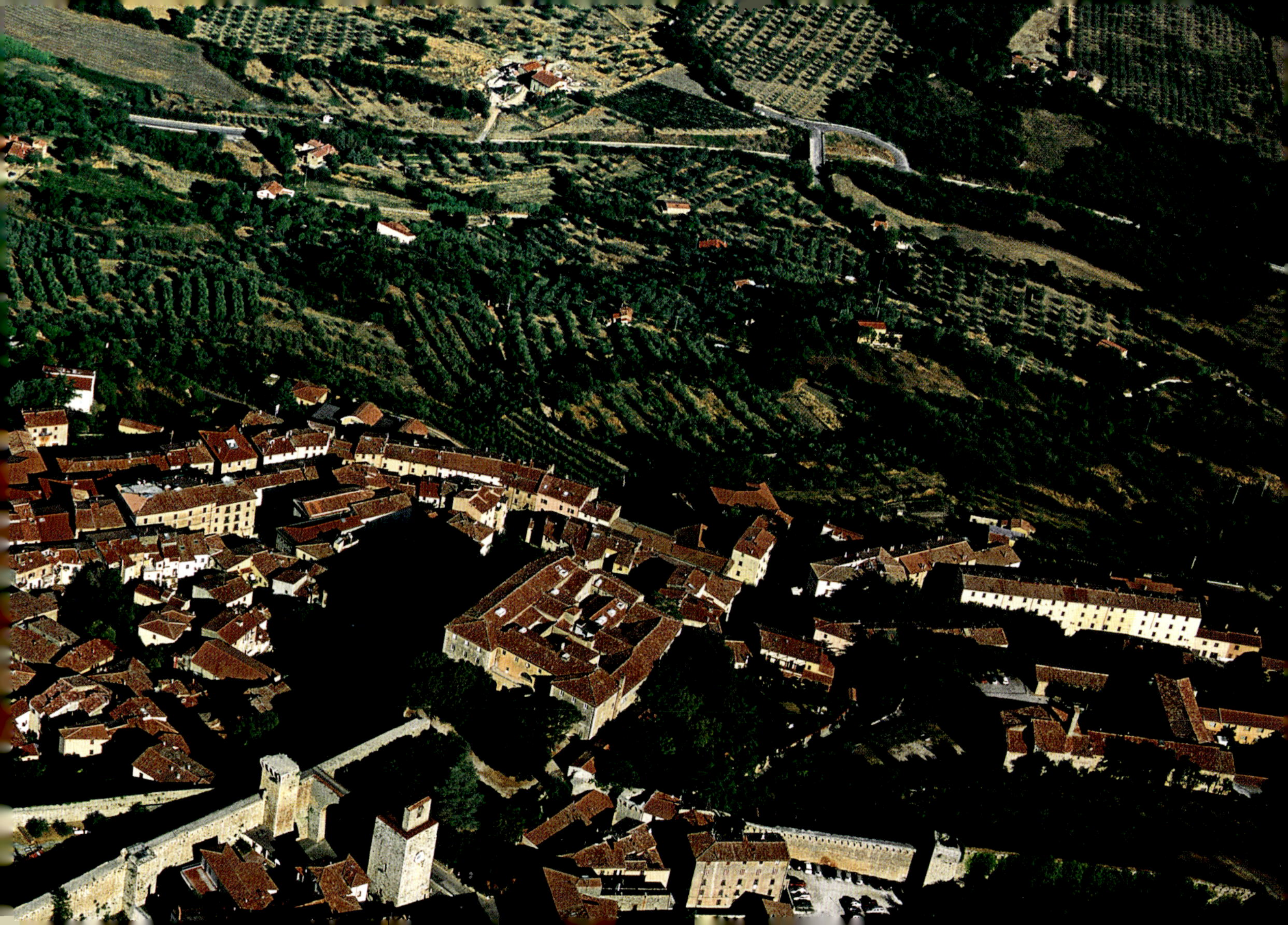

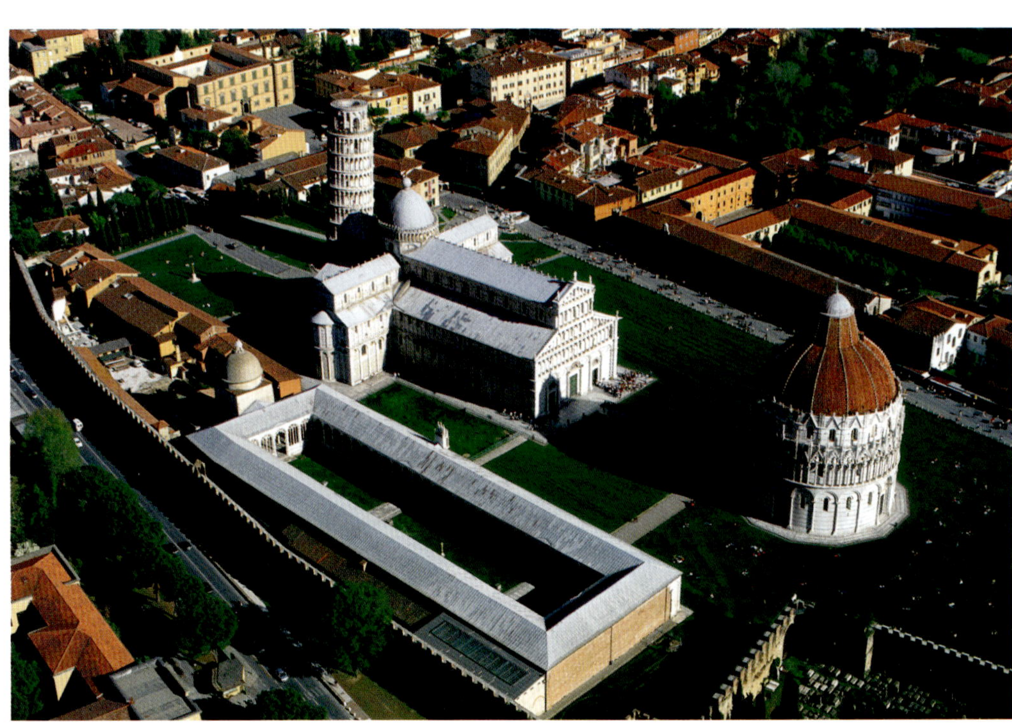

Introduction

TUSCANY WAS CREATED LIKE A WORK OF ART BY A PEOPLE WHO HAD NO OTHER PREOCCUPATION THAN WITH BEAUTY. IT IS THE RESULT OF THE SLOW AND PATIENT WORK OF THOSE WHO, GENERATION AFTER GENERATION, TRANSFORMED HILLSIDE, VALLEY AND MEADOW INTO A PERFECT AND UNIQUE COUNTRYSIDE, ACHIEVING A HARMONY THAT MIXES NATURE'S BEAUTY WITH HUMANKIND'S CREATIVE GENIUS. HERE EVERYTHING IS PLEASANT AND FIT FOR GOOD LIVING: THE PEOPLE, THE ART, THE SEASONS, THE COUNTRYSIDE, THE CELEBRATIONS, THE FLAVORS AND AROMAS; ALL CREATE A PLEASURABLE EXPERIENCE FOR THE SENSES.

THROUGHOUT THE YEAR (ALTHOUGH FALL AND WINTER ARE UNIVERSALLY QUIETER, MORE SOLITARY SEASONS), THIS REGION "DRESSES

22
Campo de' Miracoli, a jewel of medieval art, has brought international fame to the ancient coastal city of Pisa.

Introduction

UP" IN ITS MOST BEAUTIFUL ATTIRE; IT HIDES ITS WRINKLES UNDER ACCURATELY APPLIED MAKE-UP AND ADVANCES, EVEN AT THIS AGE, WITH THE ELEGANCE AND GRACE OF A DANCER: IT IS AN ELDERLY WOMAN, ATTRACTIVE AND IRONIC, WHO GAZES INTO THE MIRROR AND SEES REFLECTED FLORA FROM BOTTICELLI'S *PRIMAVERA*.

STILL, FROM THE TIME OF THE REGION'S LEGENDARY CHIEFTAIN LARS PORSENNA (5TH CENTURY B.C.) TO THE PRESENT, TUSCANY HAS ALWAYS BEEN YOUTHFUL, AND THIS MASK OF A MAJESTIC MADAME IS MERELY A TRICK TO SURPRISE US SO THAT WE DO NOT TAKE HER FOR GRANTED. A LAND THAT NEVER REPEATS ITSELF, A LAND THAT ONE MUST CHASE TO KEEP UP WITH ITS CONTINUOUS CHANGES (OF FORMS, COLORS, LIGHT, ATMOSPHERE) BUT ONE THAT IF OBSERVED FROM A DISTANCE, AS A WHOLE, UNVEILS ITSELF COMPLETELY, SURRENDERING ITSELF TO THE OBSERVER.

HOWEVER, MADAME TUSCANY LOSES HER MODESTY, HER CAPACITY OF TRANSFORMATION AND ALSO HER PRIVACY IF VIEWED FROM

Introduction

ABOVE, AS IN *TUSCANY FLYING HIGH*. FROM ABOVE THE DIVERSITY OF THIS LAND STANDS OUT AND ASSUMES EASILY RECOGNIZABLE FEATURES. FOR EXAMPLE, A FOREST OF WHITE FIRS COVERS THAT SLICE OF THE APENNINES CALLED THE CASENTINO AND REPRESENTS A LIVING METAPHOR OF THE RELIGIOUS INSPIRATION AND SPIRITUALITY THAT HAS ALWAYS CHARACTERIZED THIS AREA.

HERE, ST ROMUALDO FOUNDED THE CAMALDOLI HERMITAGE AND ST FRANCIS, WHO WAS NOT TUSCAN, RECEIVED THE STIGMATA: TIMELESS PLACES, INSPIRING THIS 'JOURNEY TOWARD GOD' THROUGHOUT THE CENTURIES AND MANIFESTED IN A DEEP RESPECT FOR THE SURROUNDING NATURAL WORLD, A PRECIOUS CREATION.

RIGHT AFTER THIS SCENERY, WITH A *COUP DE THÉATRE*, MADAME REVEALS HERSELF AS THE POPULATED VALLEY ALONG THE ARNO, A RIVER THAT SPRINGS FROM THE SILENCE OF THE CASENTINO BUT, AFTER "DISDAINFULLY TURNING AWAY" (AS WROTE PETRARCH, THE GREAT POET FROM AREZZO, A QUIET AND CULTURAL CITY), IT WINDS

Introduction

AMONG THE NOISE AND ODORS OF THE LEATHER-PROCESSING FACTORIES UNTIL IT FINALLY RETURNS TO THE SILENCE OF THE ANCIENT MEDITERRANEAN SEA.

THIS IS THE SCENERY: ENDLESS COUNTRYSIDE, CITY AFTER CITY. TO THE MUNDANE AND SCENOGRAPHIC CHIANTI, THAT ABSORBS THE VISITOR'S SIGHT AND INEBRIATES LIKE ITS STRONG WINE, IS OPPOSED THE QUIET VAL D'ORCIA, WHERE A SOLITARY TREE ON THE TOP OF A CUPOLA-SHAPED HILL AMID FIELDS OF SWAYING WHEAT, A GOLDEN CLOAK, BRINGS TO MIND THE BACKGROUND OF ONE OF LUCA SIGNORELLI'S PAINTINGS.

CONTINUING: A MANY-TOWERED VILLAGE IN THE VAL D'ELSA, AS SHARPLY DEFINED FROM ABOVE AS AN ENGRAVING, AND THEN MUGELLO'S SINUOUS, NOISY RACE-CAR CIRCUIT; THE MOST BEAUTIFUL FARMHOUSE IN THE SIENESE AREA IS A MANOR IN THE LUCCHESIA; A SMALL PORT IN MARCIANA MARINA ON THE ISLAND OF ELBA LOOKS FROM ABOVE LIKE THE ILLUSTRATION IN A CALENDAR – AND

Introduction

PIOMBINO'S INDUSTRIAL ARCHITECTURE, CHAOTIC AND OBSOLETE, BRINGS TO MIND AN ABANDONED SPACE STATION FROM SOME FILM (IT WILL EVENTUALLY BECOME A MUSEUM, IT SEEMS); SOLITARY DUNES IN THE UCCELLINA NATURE RESERVE AND THE COLORFUL, CROWDED UMBRELLAS ON THE BEACHES OF VERSILIA OR THE ETRUSCAN COAST.

AND THE CITIES, FROM ABOVE, REVEAL THEIR DESIGN AND STRUCTURE AS IF THEY WERE WOODEN MODELS. POPE PIUS II MUST HAVE SEEN HIS CITY, PIENZA, THIS WAY IN A MODEL AND WAS AS PLEASED AS WE ARE WITH OUR BIRD'S-EYE VIEW; LUCCA IS PERFECT, CLOSED LIKE A PEARL IN ITS WALLS, AND SIENA'S CAMPO SQUARE REALLY IS IN THE FORM OF A SHELL.

ABOVE FLORENCE, STRUCK INCREDULOUS WE ADMIRE BRUNELLESCHI'S DOME: FROM BELOW IT'S SO HIGH AND BEAUTIFUL BUT IMPOSSIBLE TO EMBRACE VISUALLY, BUT FROM ABOVE WE SEE A HUGE ROSE, THE COLOR OF TERRACOTTA WITH WHITE MARBLE RIBS THAT

29
The false acacia trees form a dark green wave that laps against houses and farmland near Montepulciano.

30-31
The Maremma uplands are Tuscany's greenest area, rich with vineyards and olive groves.

SEEM TO SPILL ONTO THE ENTIRE CITY: FINALLY WE COMPREHEND THAT IT IS A MIRACLE OF ENGINEERING, HARMONY AND LOVE.
APART FROM ALL WE CAN ACTUALLY SEE FROM ABOVE IS ALSO ALL THAT WE CAN IMAGINE. IF THE MAREMMA IS NOW BELOW, THEN THE BROWN SPOTS THAT SLOWLY MOVE AMONG THE YELLOWED GRASS ARE THE SAME LONG-HORNED OXEN THAT GIOVANNI FATTORI PAINTED. THAT TINY DOT THAT CROSSES CARMINE SQUARE IN FLORENCE IS AN OLD WOMAN, BECKONED TO MASS BY THE CHURCH BELLS, GOING TO VISIT MASACCIO. THE REFLECTION THAT PLAYS AMONG THE WAVES ON THE COAST OF CAPRAIA CAN ONLY BE THE BOAT OF A FISHERMAN SEARCHING FOR A LOST TREASURE HIDDEN ON THE ISLE OF MONTECRISTO. THE SKY ABOVE, AND TUSCANY BELOW:
MANY WOULD CONSIDER THEMSELVES ALMOST IN PARADISE.

32-33
The Apuan Alps are known for the beauty of their marble and the deep abysses in their karstic rock.

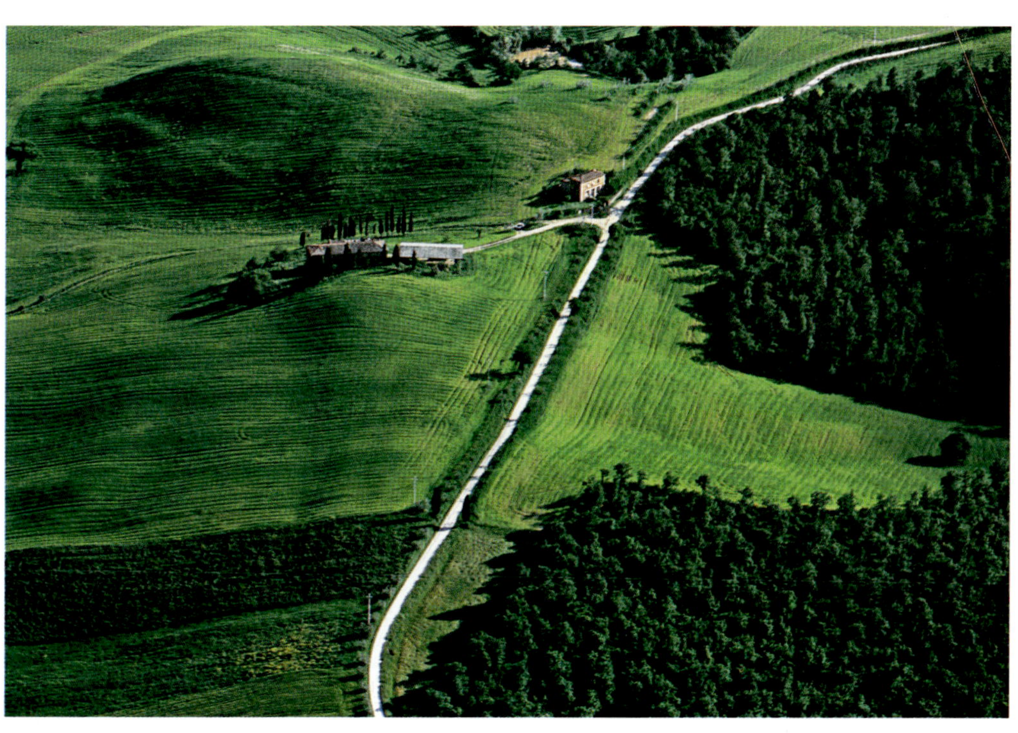

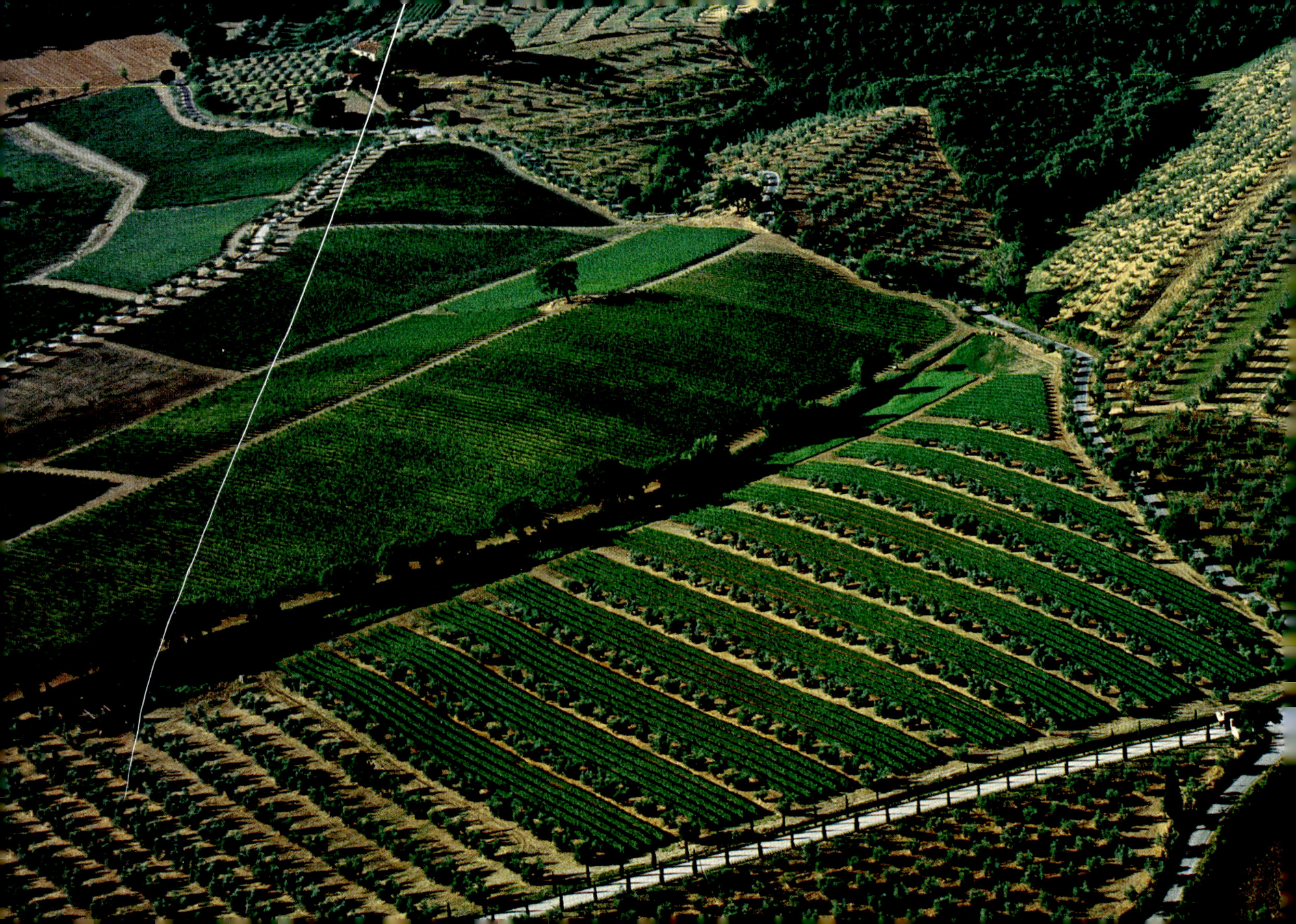

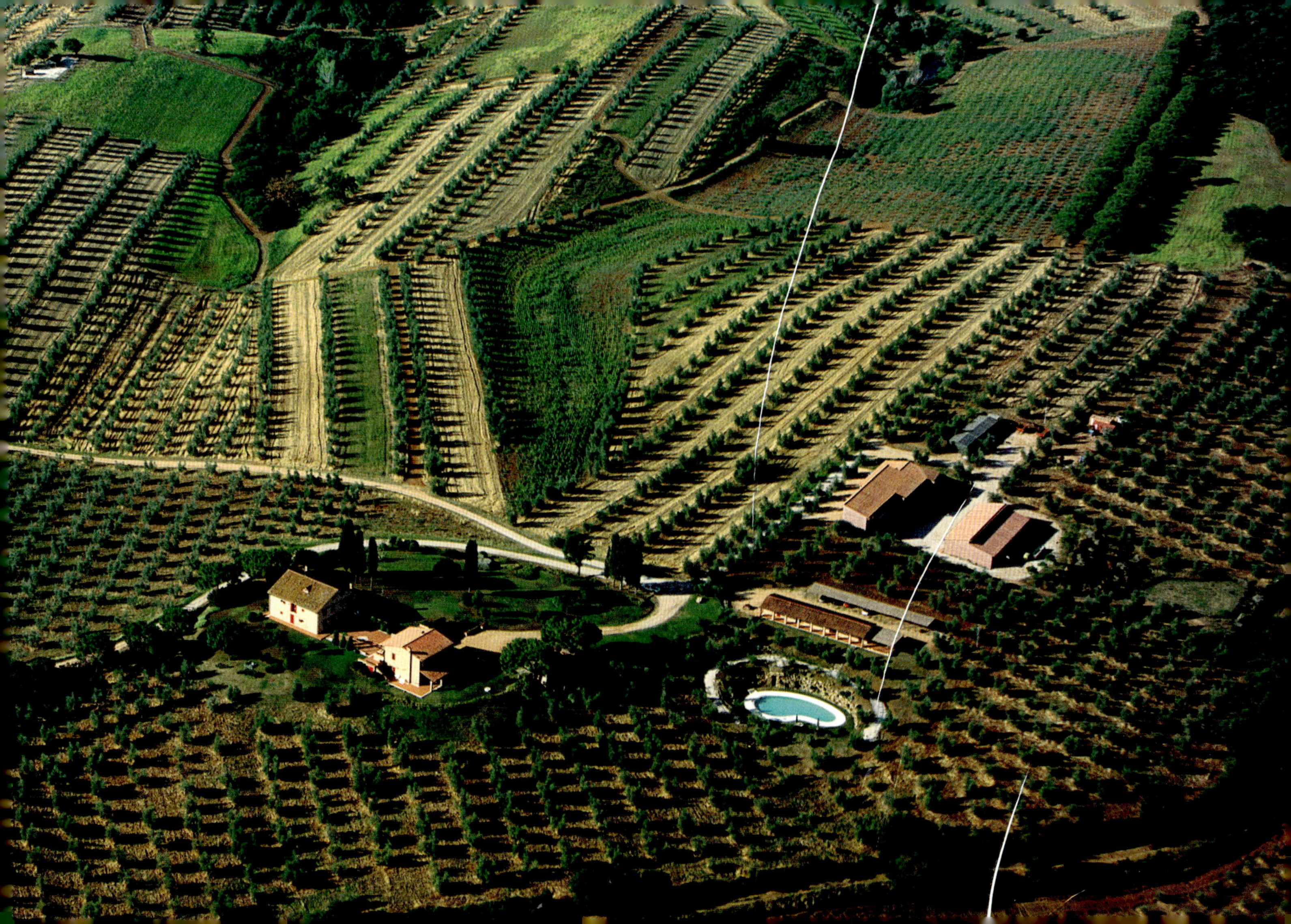

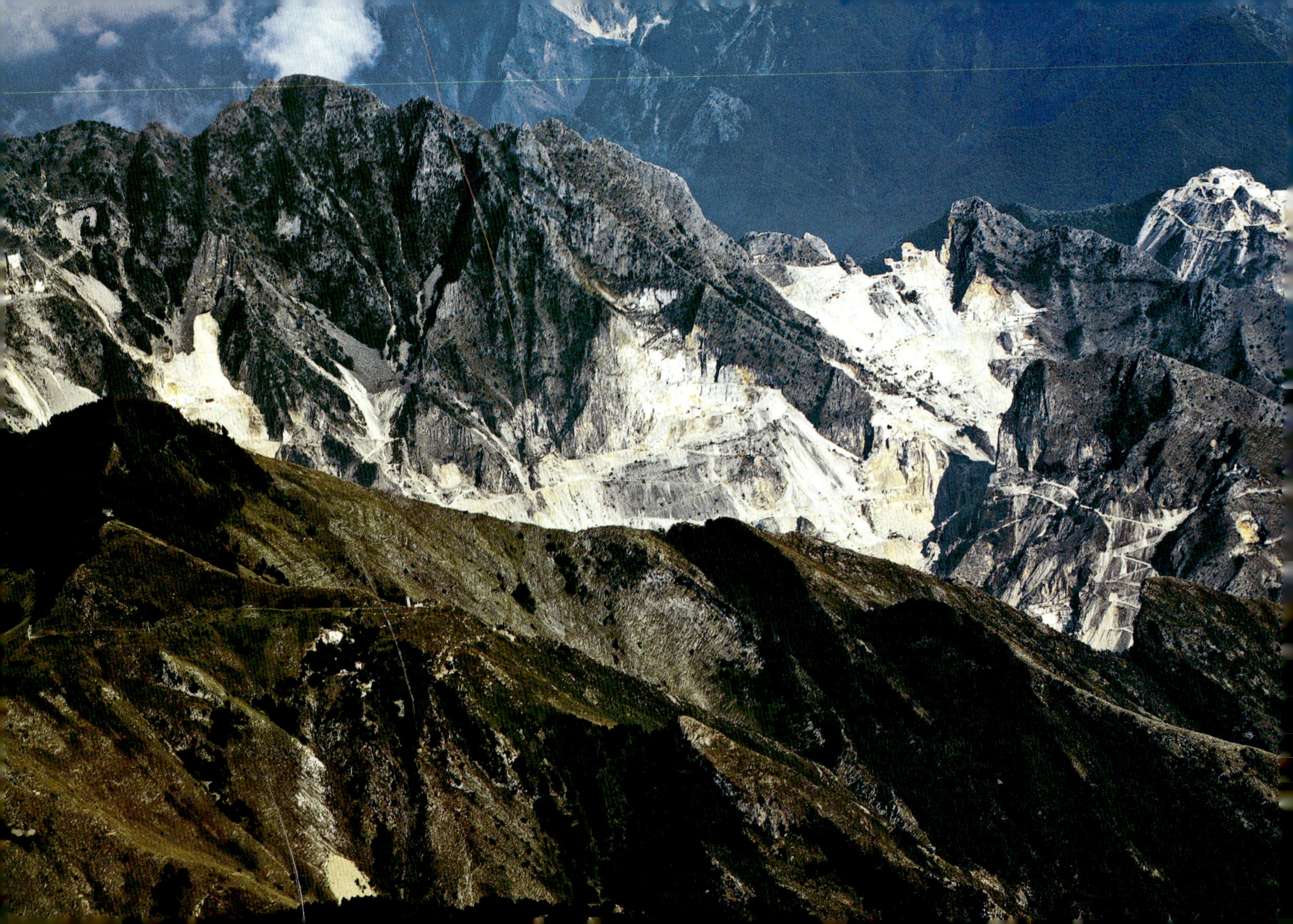

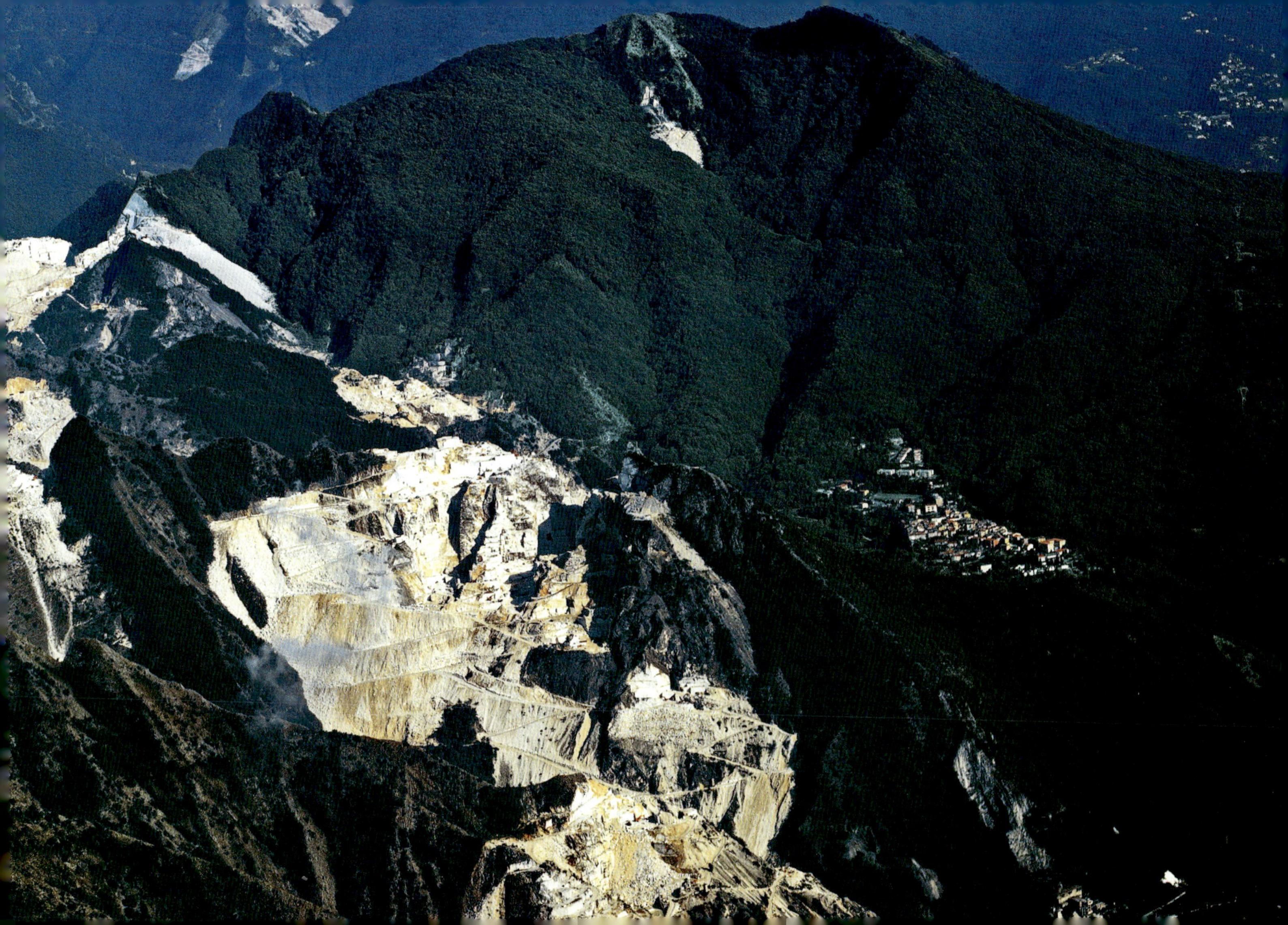

A NATURAL FRESCO

FLYING HIGH

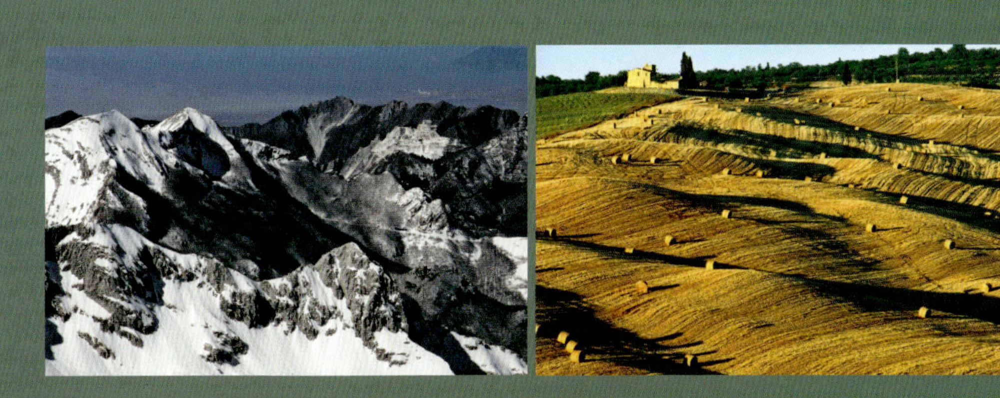

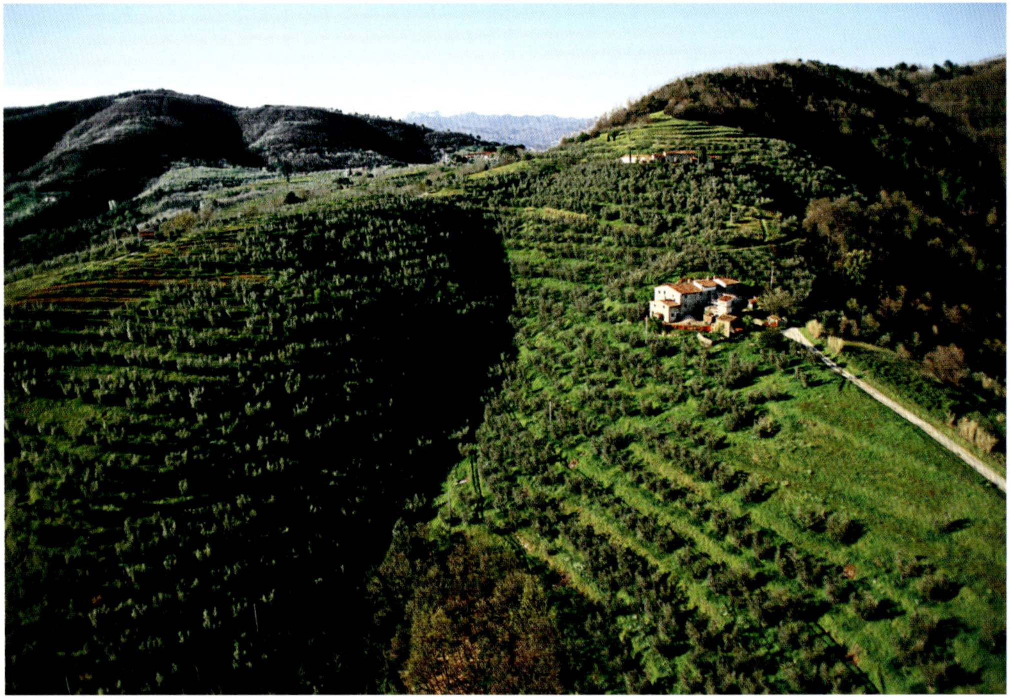

35 left

Fractured white marble, looking like snow, covers the peaks of the Apuan Alps.

35 right

Orange-yellow waves of grain flow down this slope in the heart of the Metalliferous Hills.

At first sight, the Apennine Mountains that frame northern Tuscany seem like a rather monotonous succession of summits in parallel chains. Beautiful mountains, 5900-6560 ft (1800-2000 m) in height, raise their rocky backs just above the limit of trees and shrubs, but when the Apuane Alps suddenly appear, brilliantly reflecting their marble veins in the green sea below on the coast of Versilia, the view becomes breathtaking: naked, abrupt peaks, walls carved with steep channels, pointed crests, huge spurs amid the white debris of the immense quarry, white enough to be mistaken, from a distance, for snow.

The Apuane are titanic mountains that have no equals in Tuscany or in Italy, if we exclude the harsh Prealps and the narrow peaks of the Dolomites. To encounter another true mountain we must go south of the Arno. Here rises the solitary Amiata, a peak that that has forgotten its volcanic origins and ancient turbulence to become a gentle giant guarding the Sienese valleys and the fields of the Maremma. From its summit, when the north wind blows, we can see the islands of Corsica and Sardinia. The rest of the Tuscan territory appears as a vertical unfolding of hills that separate the fertile basins of the Mugello, Arno, Elsa, Era, Chiana rivers, etc....

This infinite series of hills and valleys renders this landscape unique and inimitable. Unique in the true sense of the word, without equal,

36

Hills formed by Ice-Age moraines are now dappled with olive trees, and surround the alluvial plain where the city of Prato is located, to the northwest of Florence.

A Natural Fresco

because the natural characteristics of Tuscany are diverse, yet create a harmonious whole.
The view from above exalts this harmony. From above the landscape is recomposed, its woven design is revealed. There are no longer the Garfagnana, the Mugello, Chianti, Valdarno or other regional zones, each with its own, peculiar characteristics, but one beautiful and good land, created by God on the sixth day when, satisfied, He rested.

Actually God only left a sketch, letting the people of Tuscany finish the picture. Humankind has always intervened and continues to intervene on the countryside with an expert hand. For this reason, while flying over Tuscany, we are reminded of Ambrogio Lorenzetti's *Good Government*, in Siena's Town Hall, in which, with a bird's-eye view (the aerial photography of that era) the artist guides the observer's attention across the gentle folds of the countryside, the cultivated fields, isolated farmhouses, villages completely integrated into the surrounding territory.

Flying low, it is easy to understand that Tuscany has something for everyone's taste (we are obviously not referring to the regional cooking which must be enjoyed comfortably on the ground, either in a country trattoria or a well-known restaurant).

If you want the solitude of the countryside, open spaces with no obstacles as far as the eye can see, with rare farm houses that can only be reached along small sinuous roads, then the Val d'Orcia or Volterra are for you. Where the first is almost feminine in its gentleness, with warm intimate colors, the second is masculine and surly in its monochrome landscape, almost treeless and tormented by crags and gullies. Attention: here more than anywhere else, the presence of the Etruscans is felt.

A Natural Fresco

For more demanding palates, the Val d'Elsa proposes breathtaking views. The practice of sharecropping has preserved this countryside since the second half of the 1300s; the identity of interests – at least in theory – between landowner and farmer has permitted the Val d'Elsa to keep its physiognomy and personality intact. The cultivation, threshing, cutting and burning of the stubble, the plowing, harvesting, field rotation continues with rhythms that seem programmed to enhance the iconographical expressivity of the landscape rather than to rationalize its agricultural production. Let us not forget the villages, rich in history and culture, jewels of art and scrolls of tradition: in fact, below are the towers of San Gimignano, not far from the crown-like wall encircling Monteriggioni, which deeply impressed Dante (*Inferno* XXXI, 40-42).

According to many, the ultimate remains Chianti, recently baptized "Chiantishire," as if it were a part of the British Commonwealth. Chianti (the area, not the wine) was ruined by the cinema, says a feisty native Chianti resident, who wishes to be protected by the World Wildlife Fund as an endangered species. This is not really true (this land is still very Tuscan, especially in spirit) even though films like *The English Patient* (1996; directed by Antony Minghella), or *Stealing Beauty* (1996, directed by Bernardo Bertolucci) have lent an overly polished representation of this countryside and environment. However, to own a "farmhouse" in Chianti has become, in certain international circles, a status symbol.

The English began, followed by the Germans and Swiss up to the recently rich Russians and Arabs with their petro-dollars.

Today, the natives recognize that these wealthy immigrants saved Chianti from downfall and abandon, infecting the distracted former landowners with their enthusiasm. Together, they restored the beautiful old stone houses and gave back form and design to a poly-

41
A fertile crescent peeks out of the forest. Farther away, uncultivated land gives way to plowed fields in this part of the Arezzo region.

chrome landscape, characterized by rows of grape vines perfectly aligned along the hillsides. Here is the "garden of grapes" where there are no other plants, only vines and olive trees, with the fruit that they bear. Rendering the area even more precious are the villages, castles, churches and monasteries, like Passignano Badia whose charm is the product of the harmony between an intense spirituality and artistic fervor, inspired by the embracing beauty of its surrounding landscape. Finally the Maremma, totally different from the way it was in the 1800s. Were there once were malaria-ridden marshes with untilled pasture land and an intricate Mediterranean vegetation, now there is vital farm land with the typical low stone walls separating the properties or wooden fences confining the typical local wild horses and oxen.

One can still feel something wild here, an Italian Wild West, where the cowboys are called *butteri* (a noble term, derived from the Greek *butoros* which means "he who goads the oxen"). Towards the sea the natural landscape is even more transformed, with the introduction of vast pine forests whose dark umbrellas cover more than 1480 acres (600 hectares) of territory. Naturally, there is still much more to say about the Tuscan countryside. We could have said much about the Garfagnana, a noteworthy land; it would be best though, to express our admiration in eight-line stanzas, like the poet Ariosto who, in 1525, was governor of the Garfagnana under the Duke of Este.

We have also omitted the Mugello basin, the Metalliferous Hills, a suggestive, singular and less-trodden corner among the locations listed in visitors' guides, as well as other places that merit our attention. But let's now abandon words and descriptions and enjoy our flight over Tuscany; it's just like bringing an album of beautiful photographs to life.

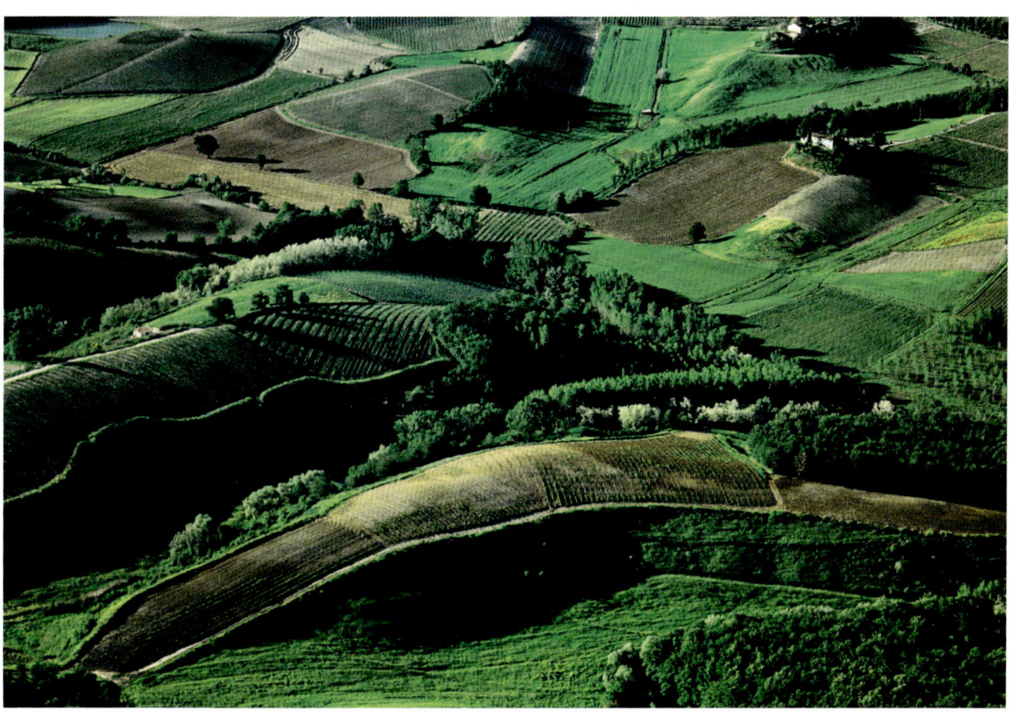

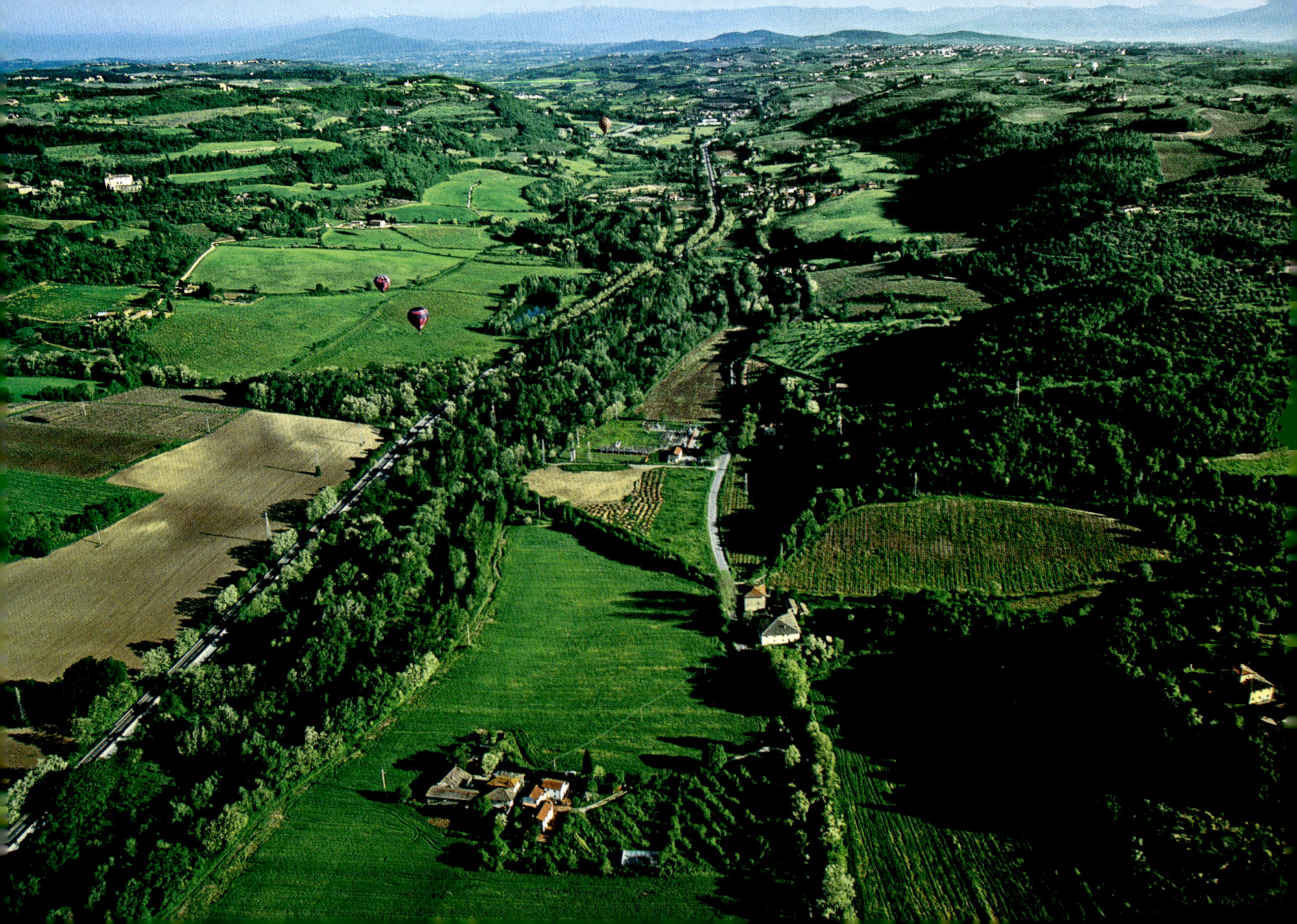

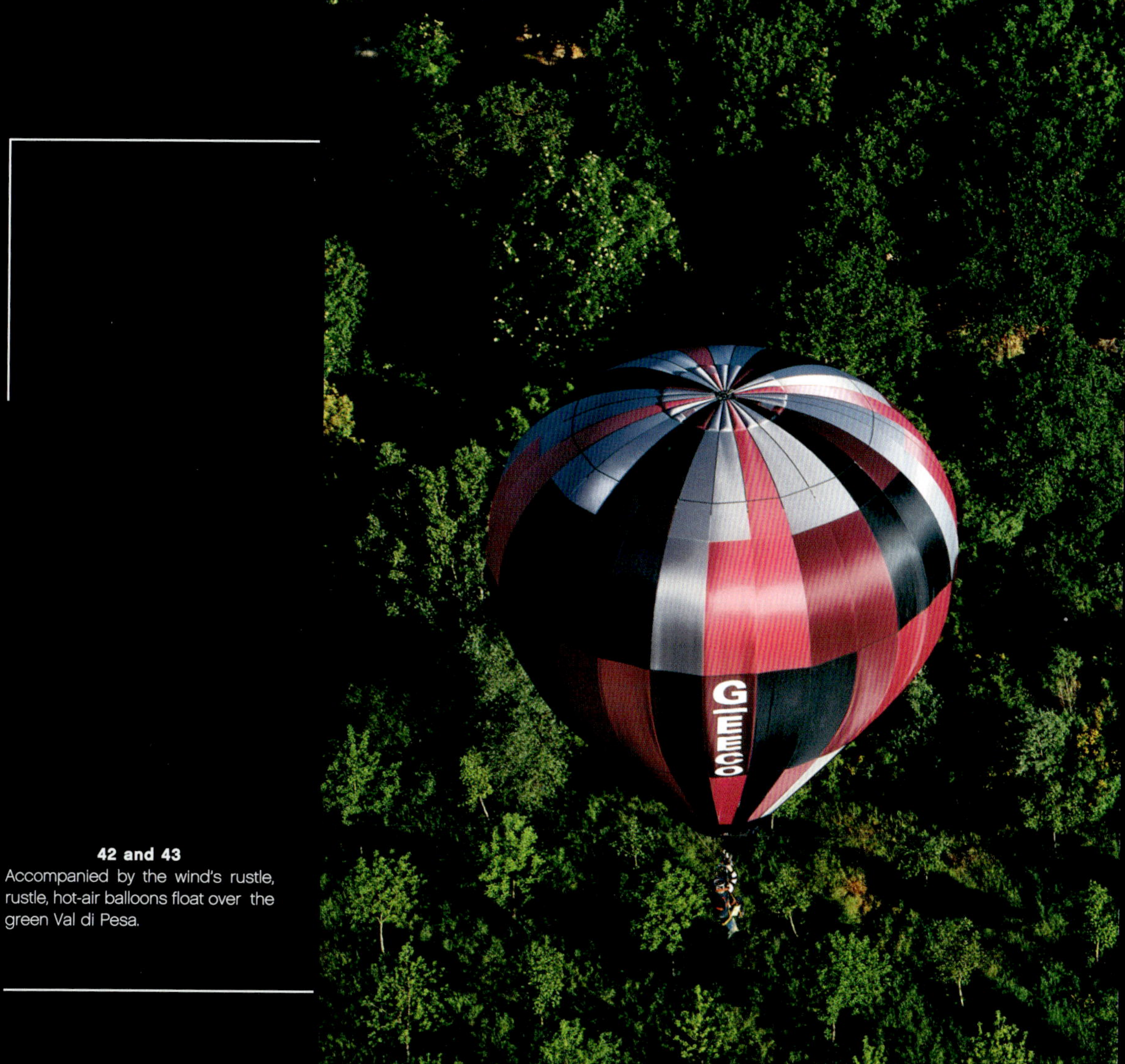

42 and 43
Accompanied by the wind's rustle, rustle, hot-air balloons float over the green Val di Pesa.

45
The balloon's shadow slips over the vineyards of Tavernelle, in Val di Pesa, in the Chianti Classico region.

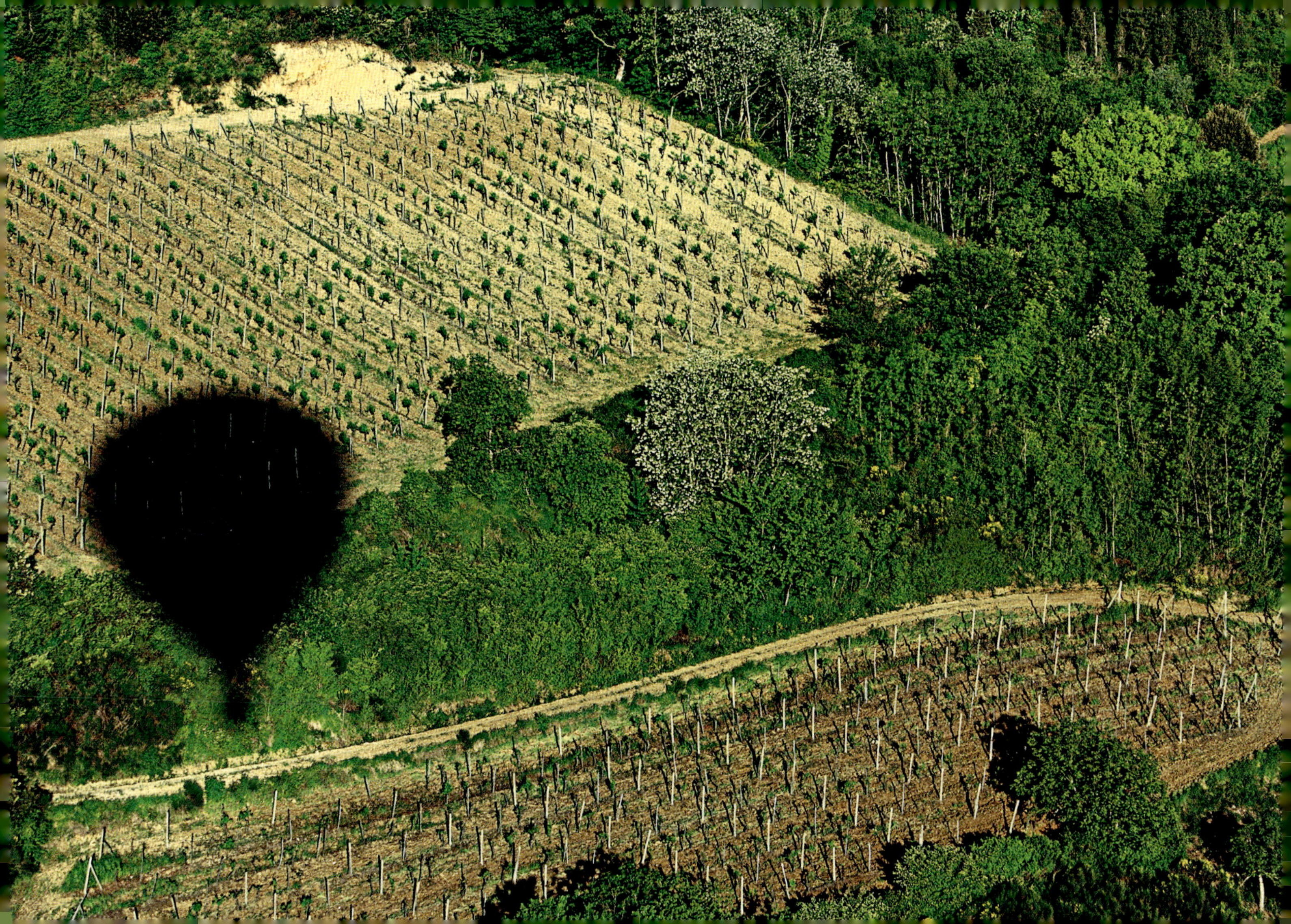

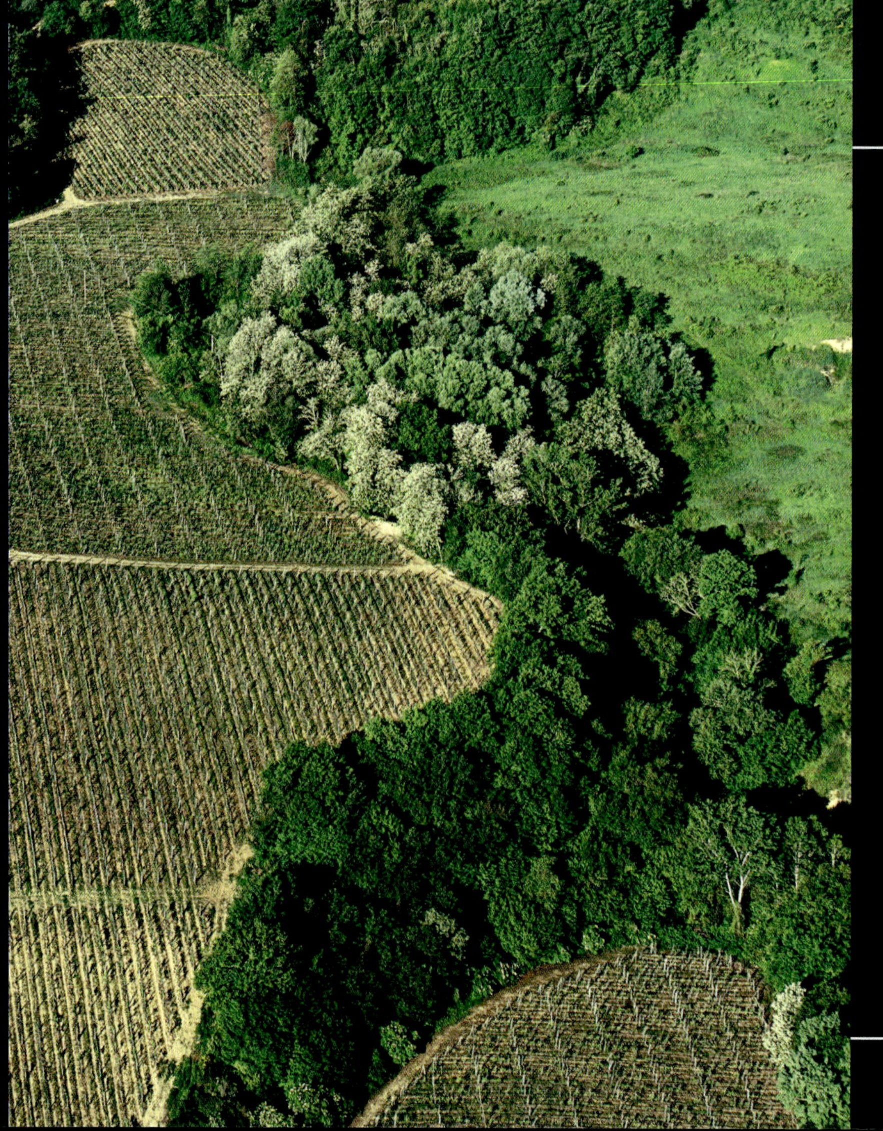

46

The Tuscan hills' complex morphology results in a patchwork of irregularly shaped fields. Not all are suitable for the traditional vineyards and olive groves.

47

Here in the Tuscan countryside, a small tree-lined canal borders a large green field; its green surface is marked by parallel tractor tracks.

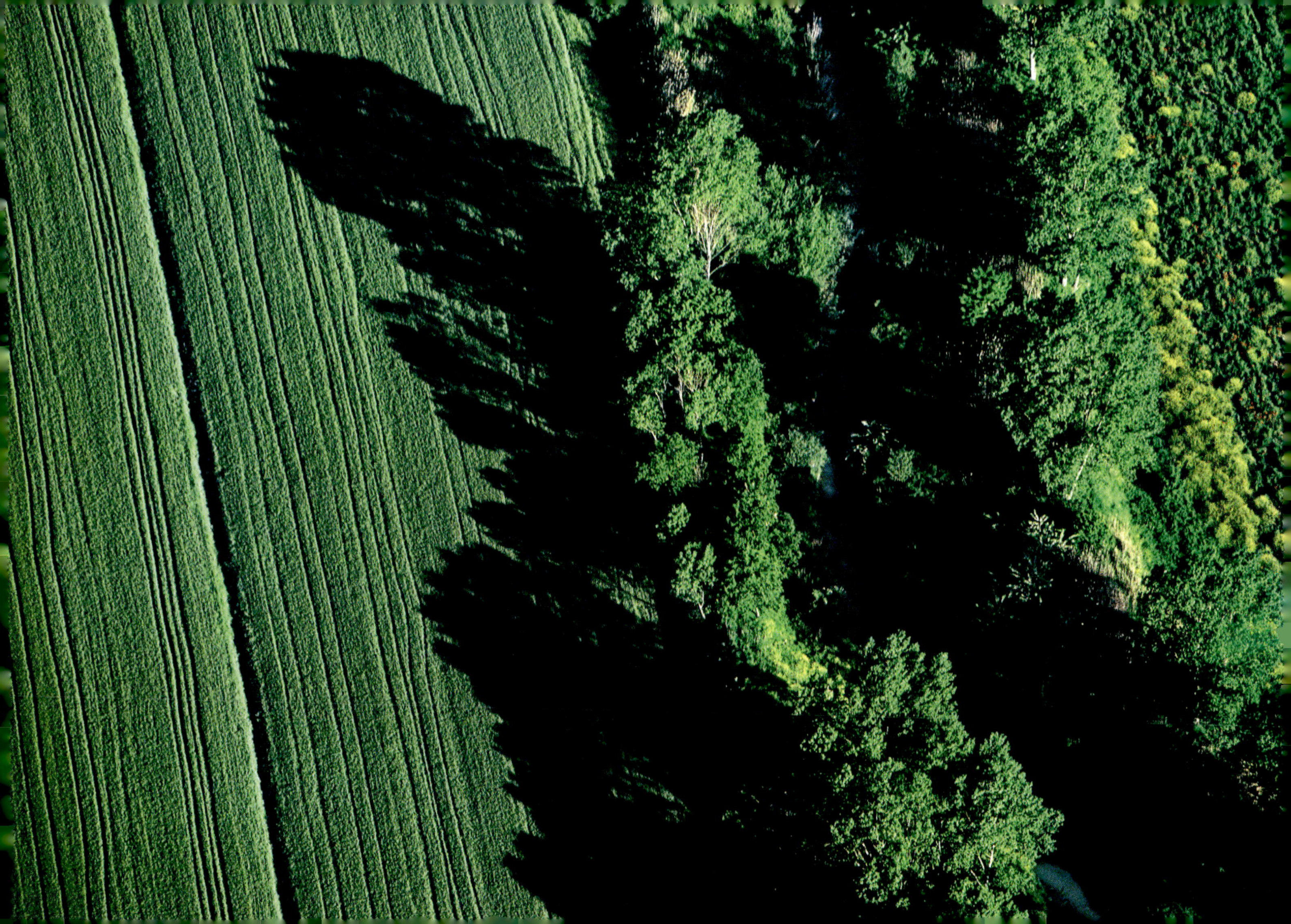

49
This extensive property, with a watchtower that reveals its noble heritage, has been transformed into a farm resort, as have many old farm properties in the Val di Pesa.

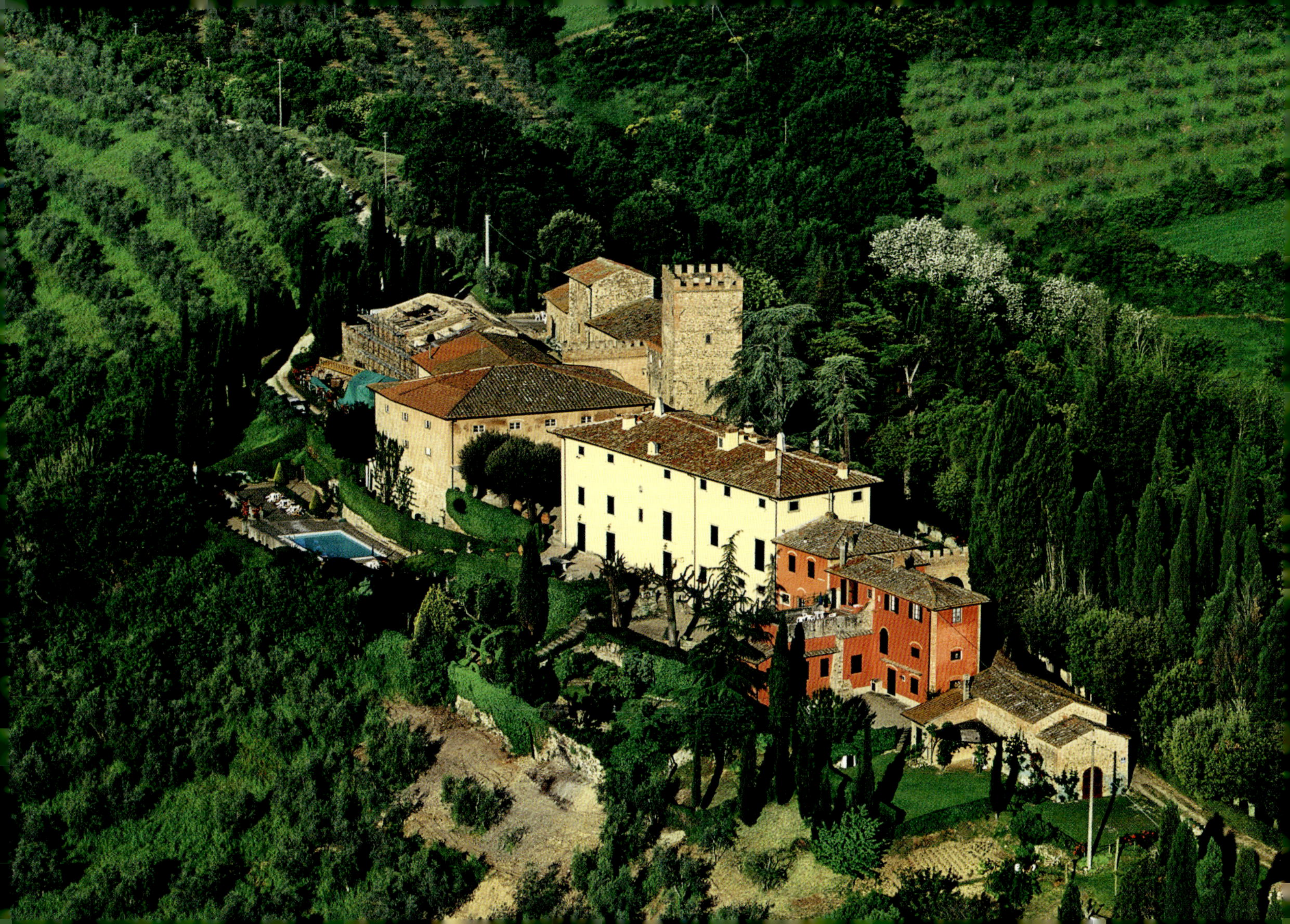

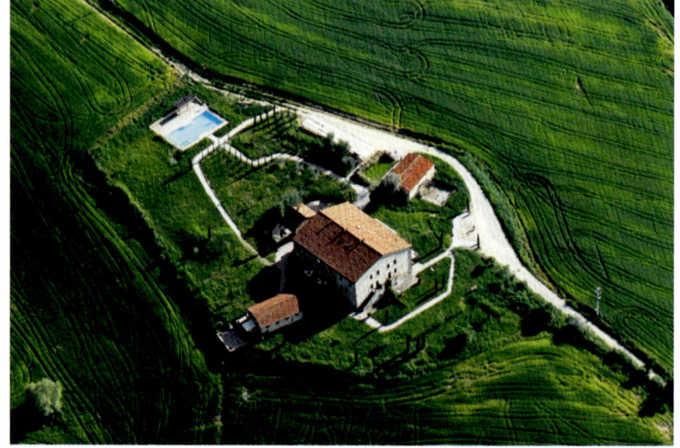

50
Transformed into a farm resort, this property near Montepulciano has a lovely new pool.

51
A dirt road leads to this rural paradise in the Val di Pesa. The parallel tracks around the house were left by a tractor and reflect farming activity.

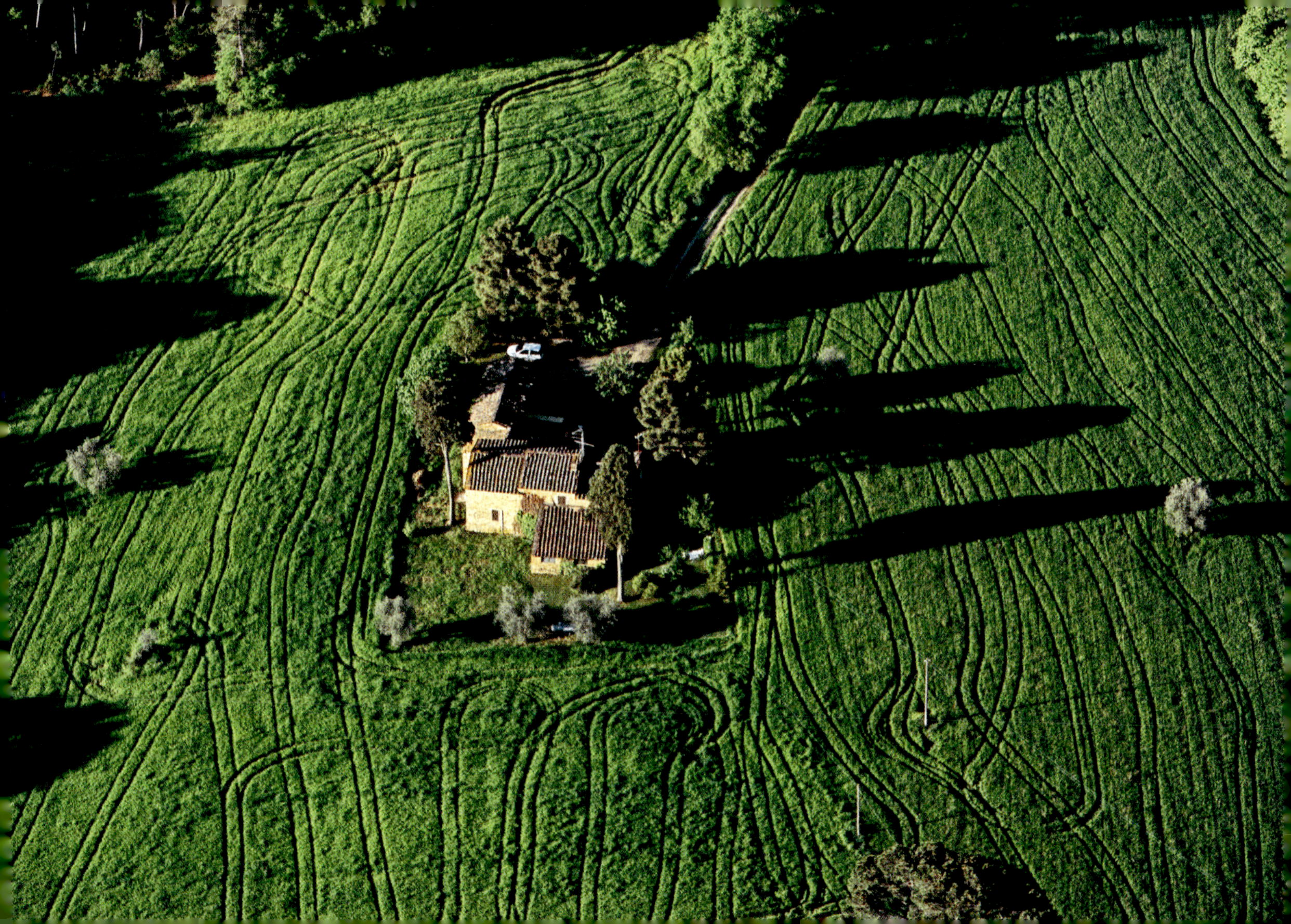

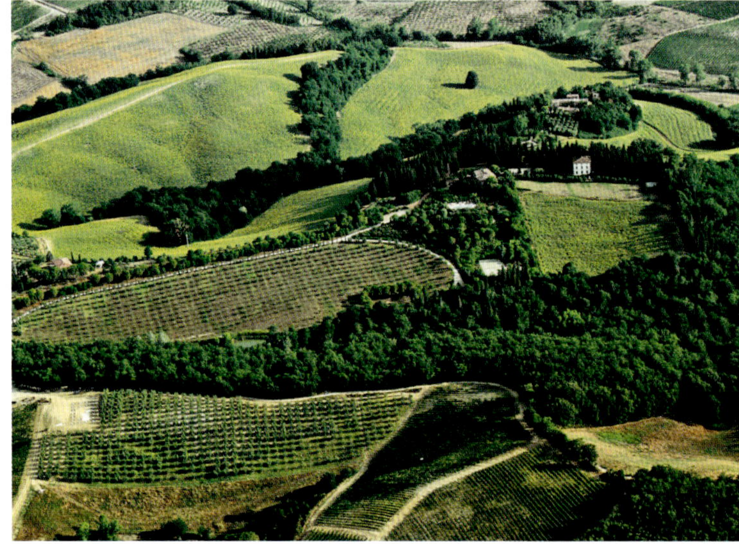

52 and 53

Certaldo, extending over a hillside near San Gimignano, has a long history, reflected in its forested countryside.

54-55

Plowed land alternates with green fields and small forests: the hills of Chianti are a rural paradise just a short distance from Florence.

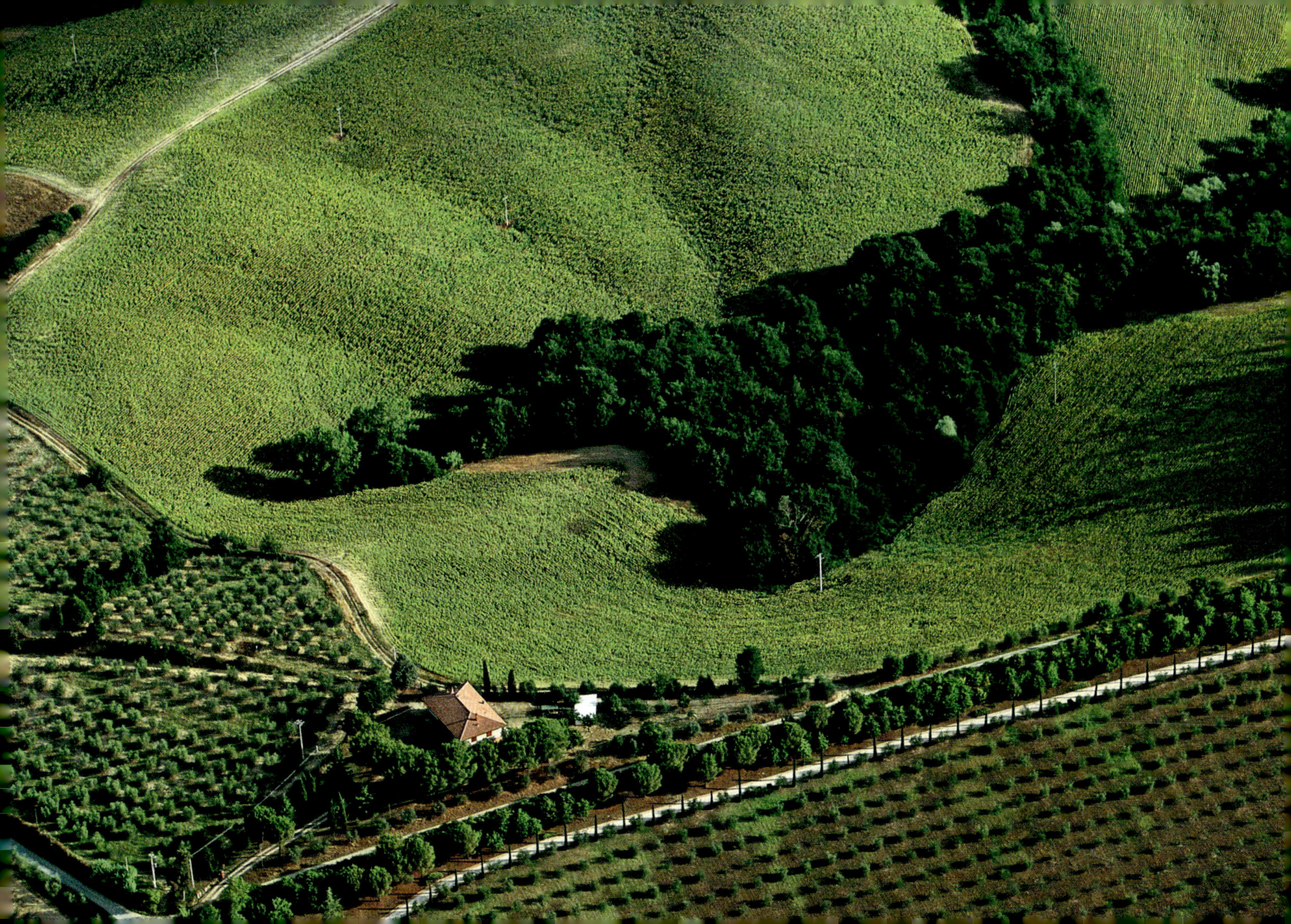

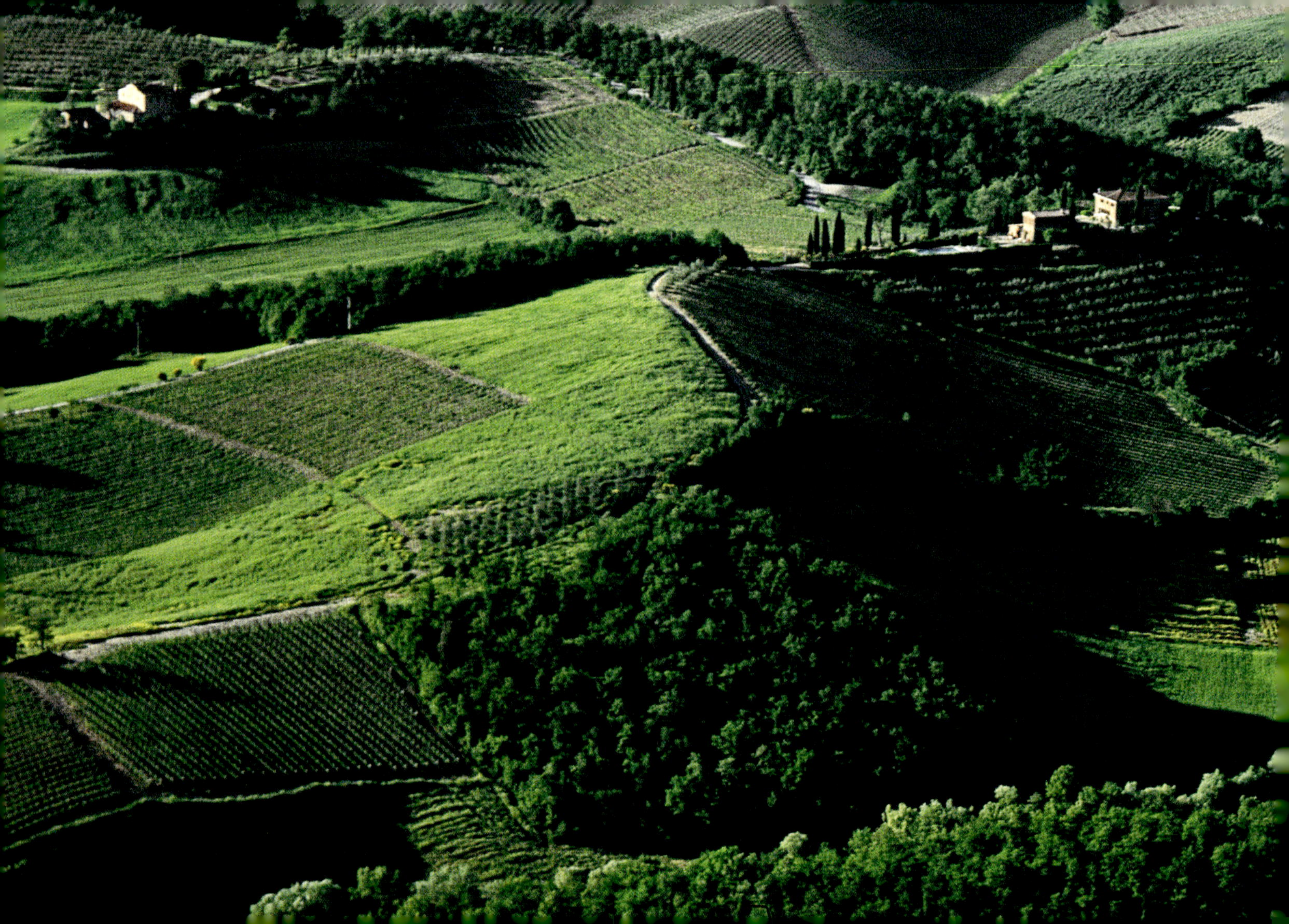

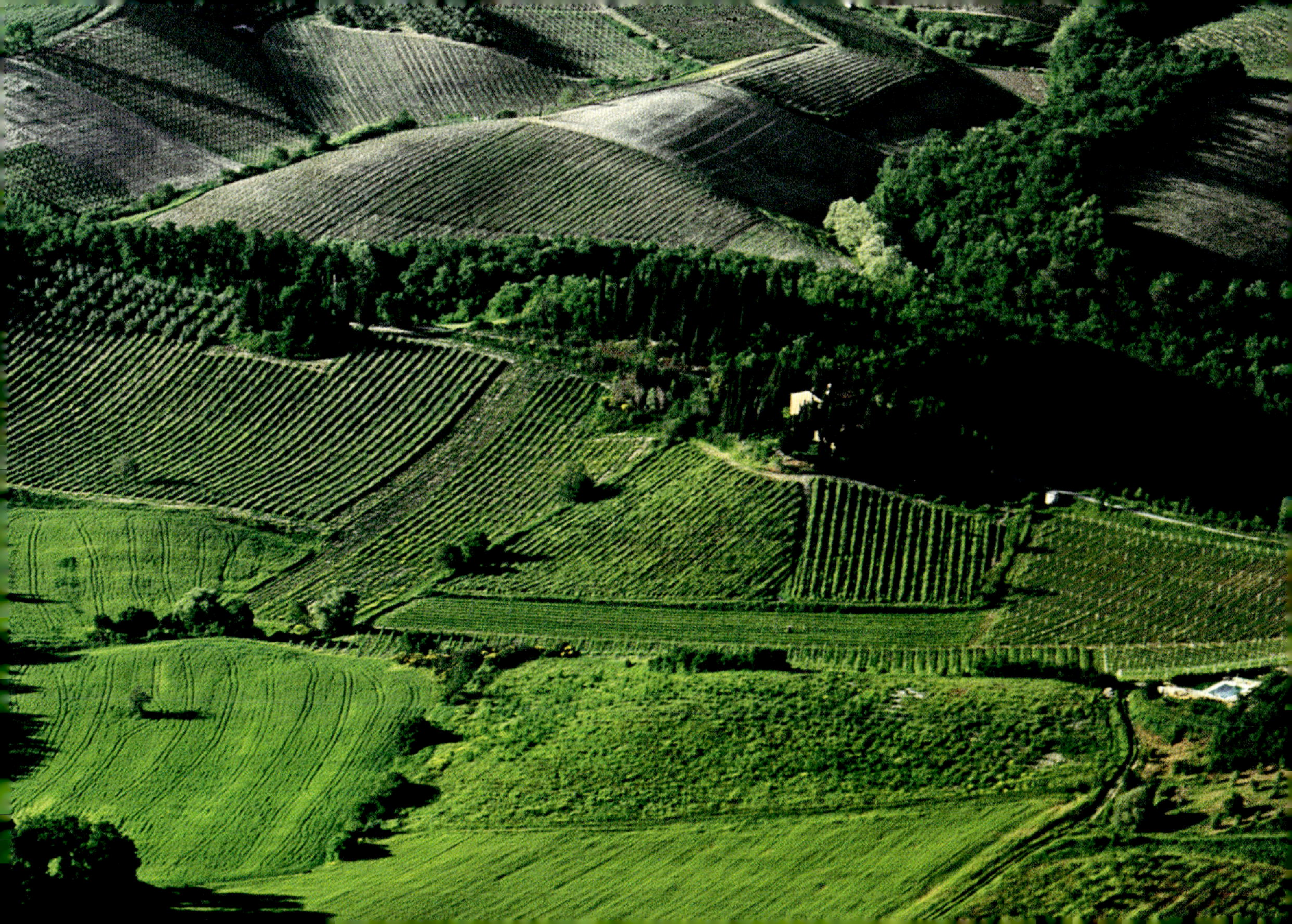

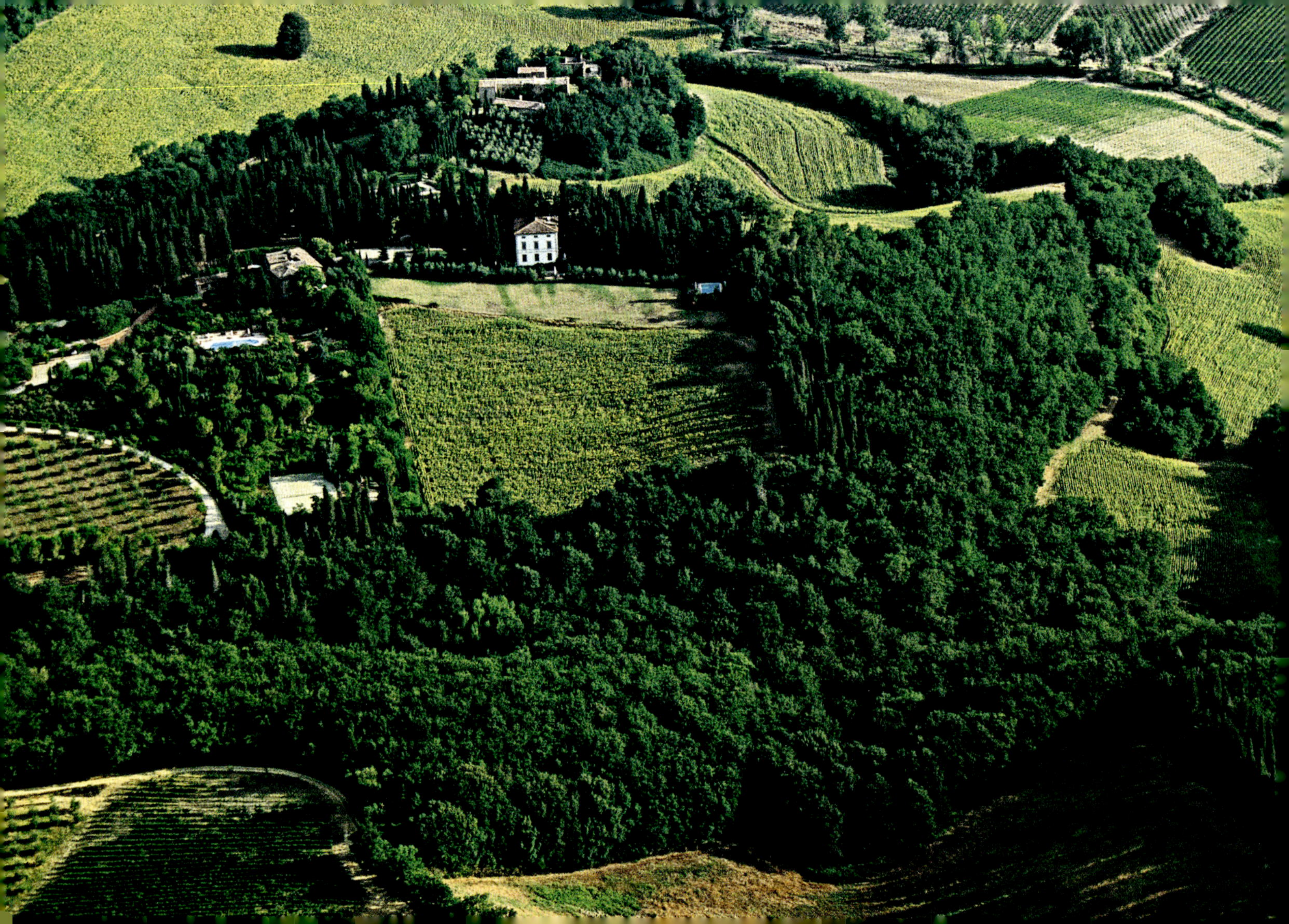

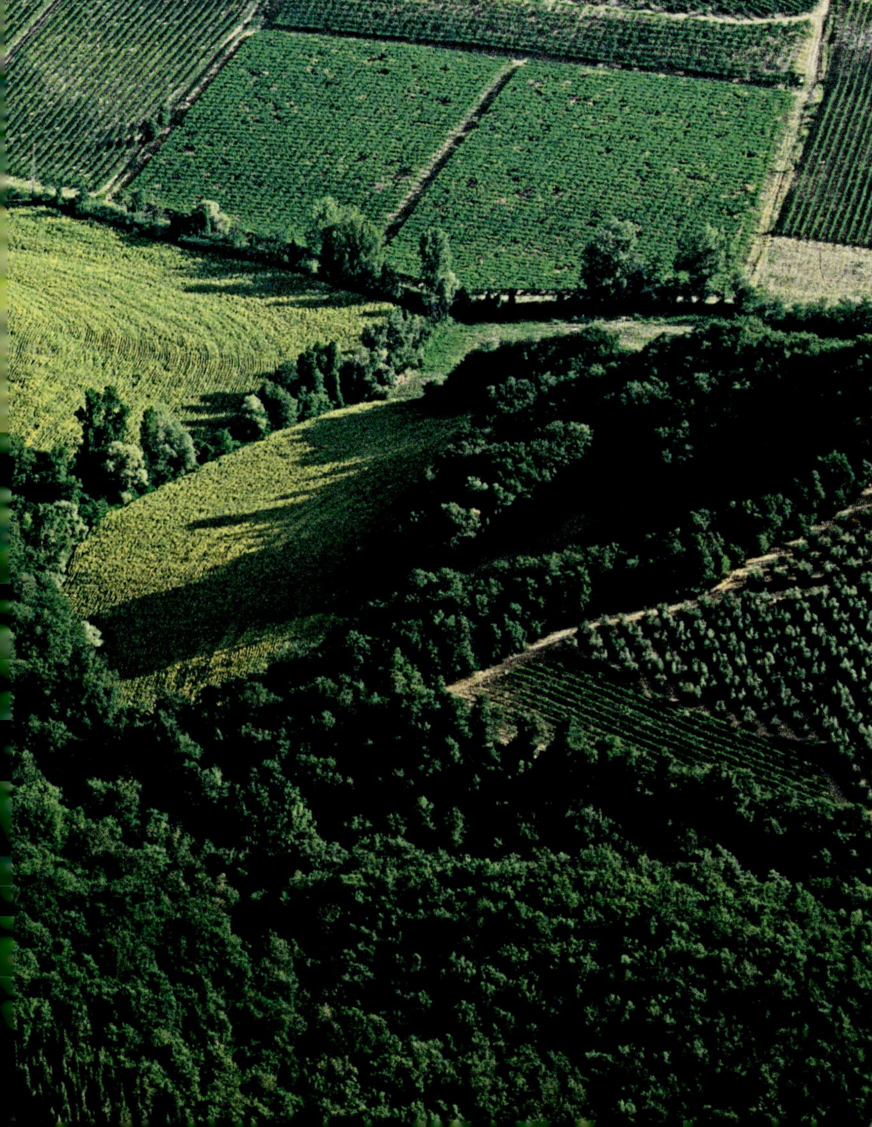

56-57
This lovely property, close to Certaldo's center, includes a rather large forest and some priceless Chianti vineyards.

58-59
The hills between Florence and Siena form the extensive Chianti region, known for its high-quality vineyards, the source of excellent red wines.

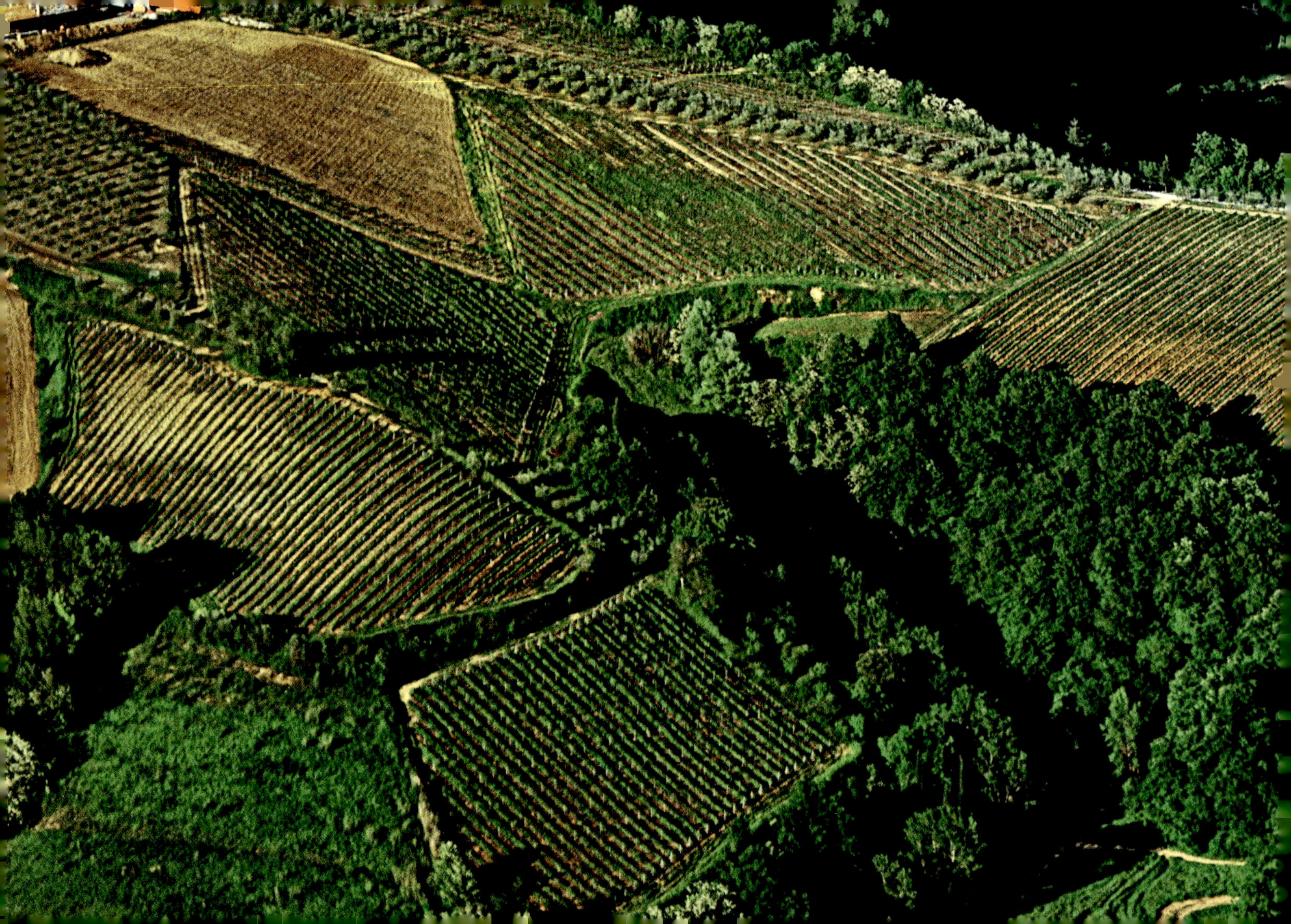

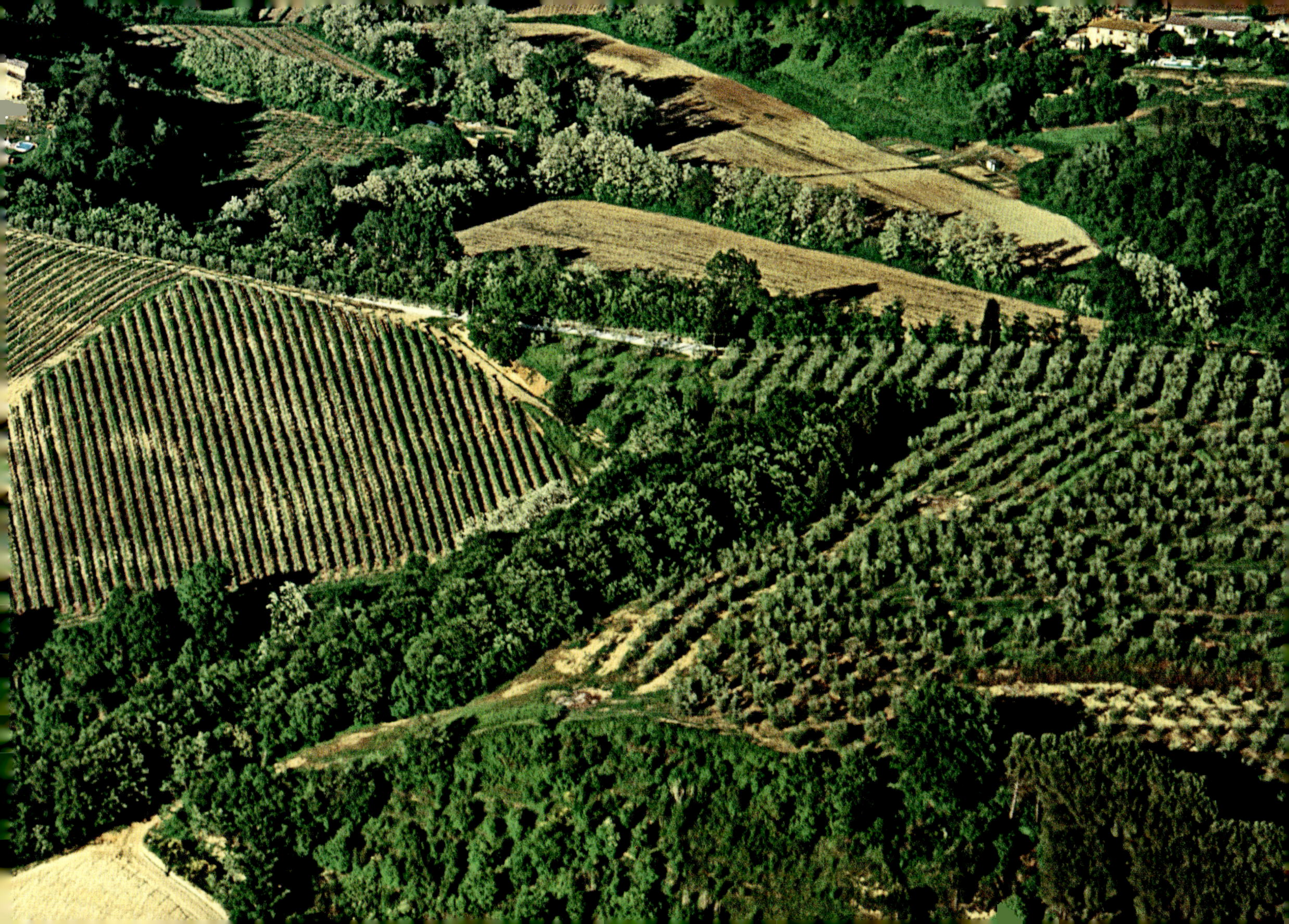

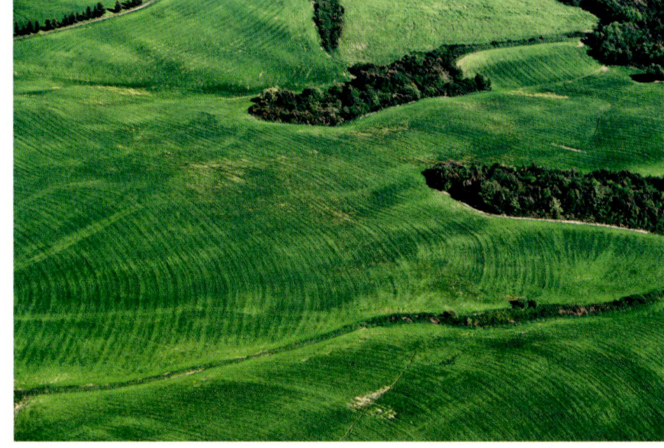

60 and 61
Around the hill town of San Gimignano, on the lower slopes, the fields are larger and those of grain take on different shade of green in the spring.

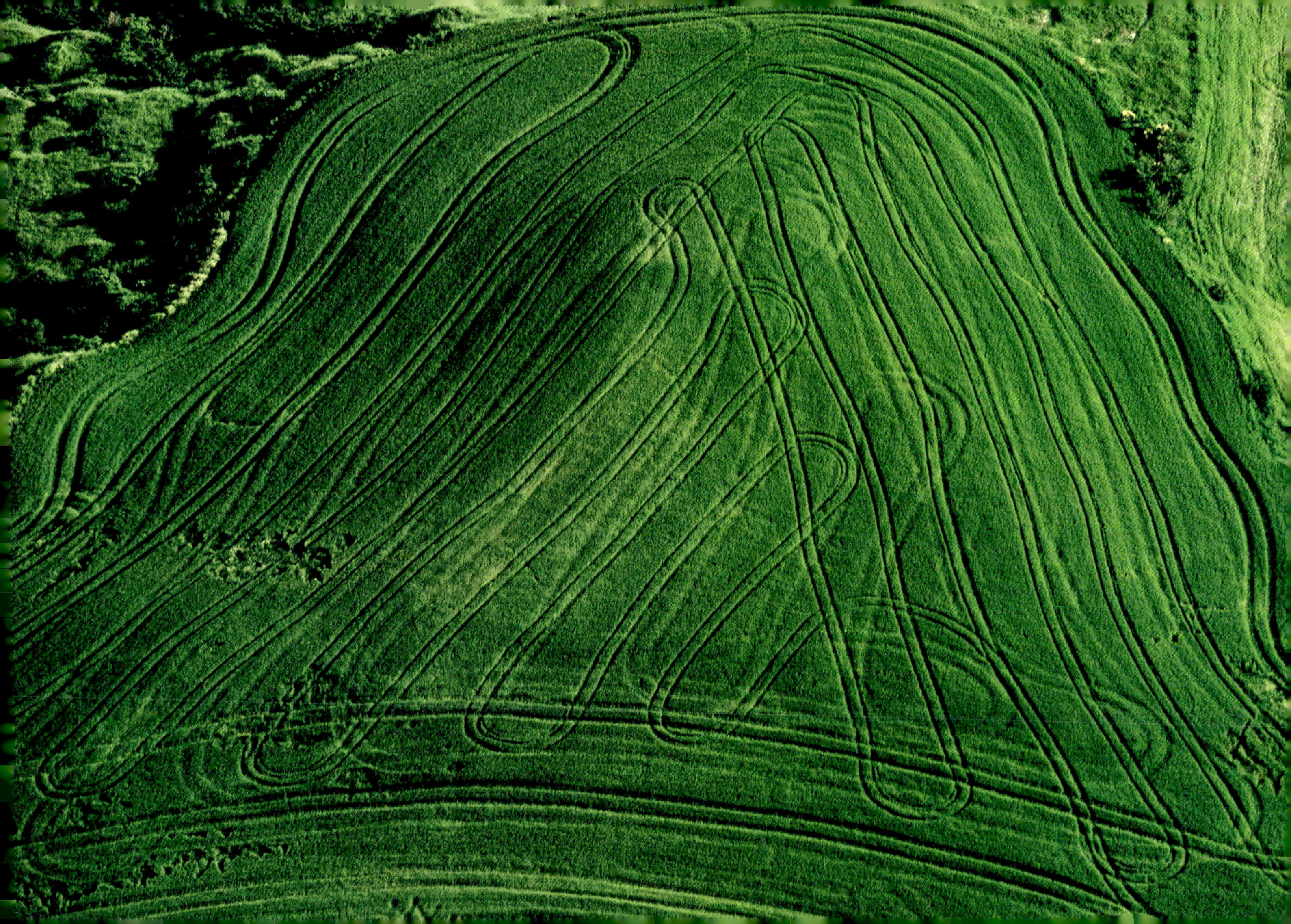

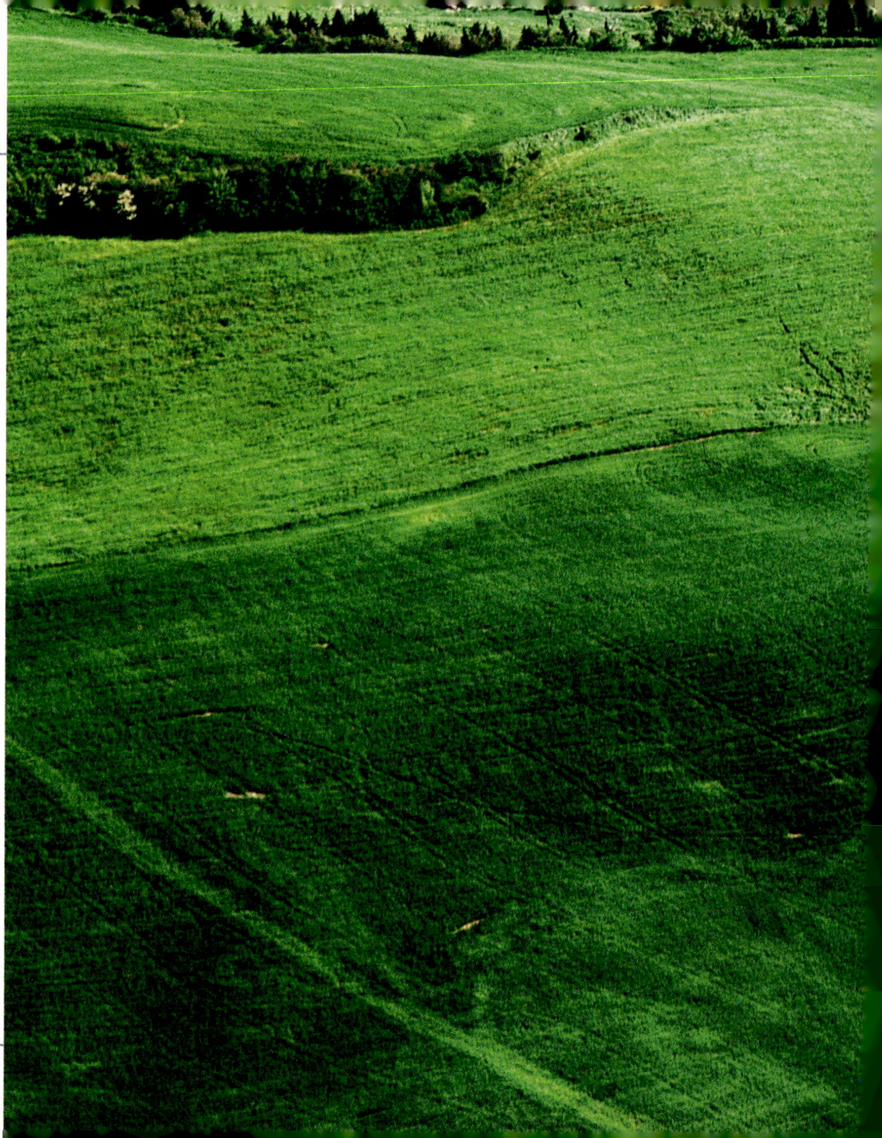

62-63

A winding country road, lined by cypress trees on either side, leads to San Gimignano; a few country homes and small ponds are scattered in the wheat fields.

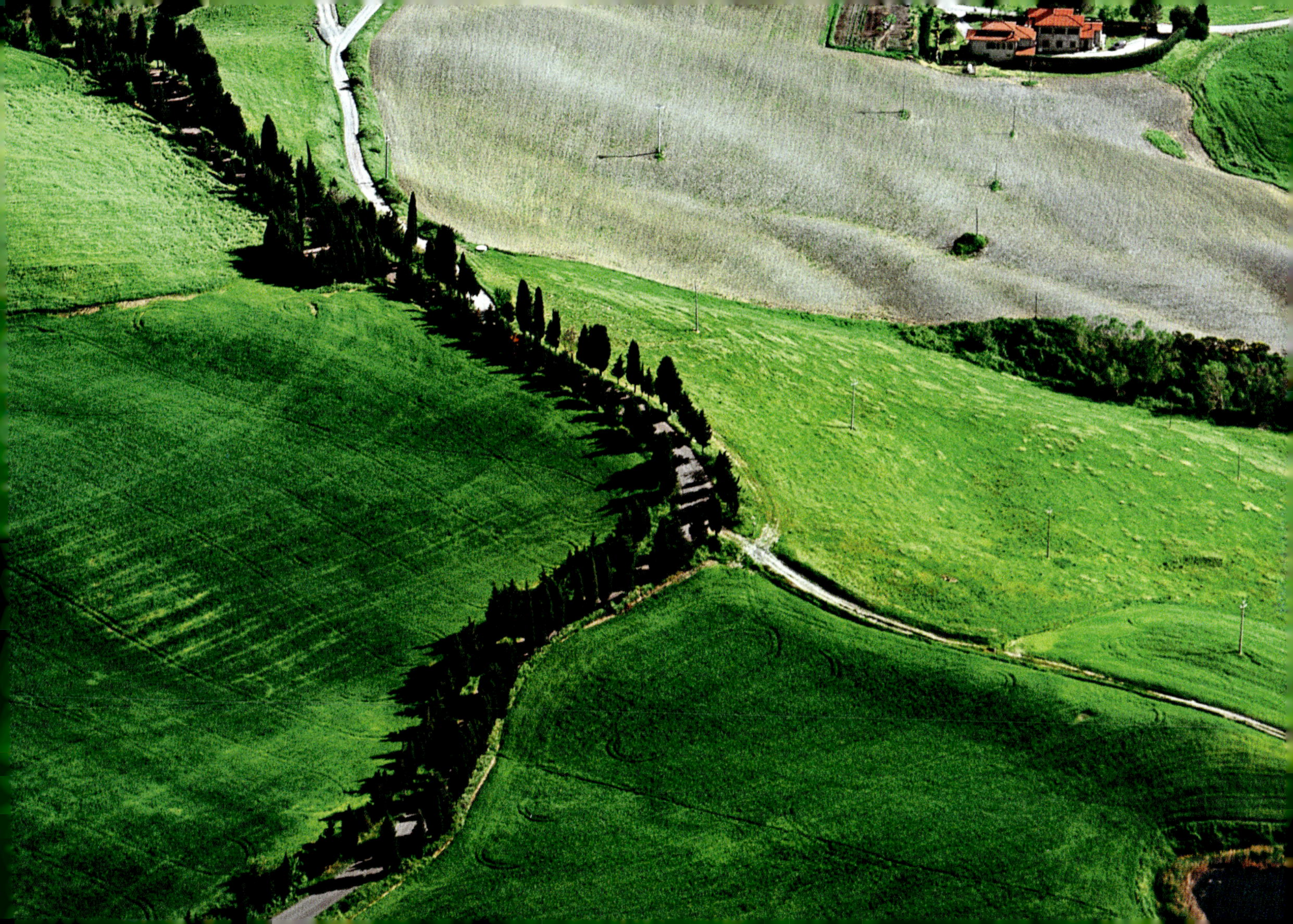

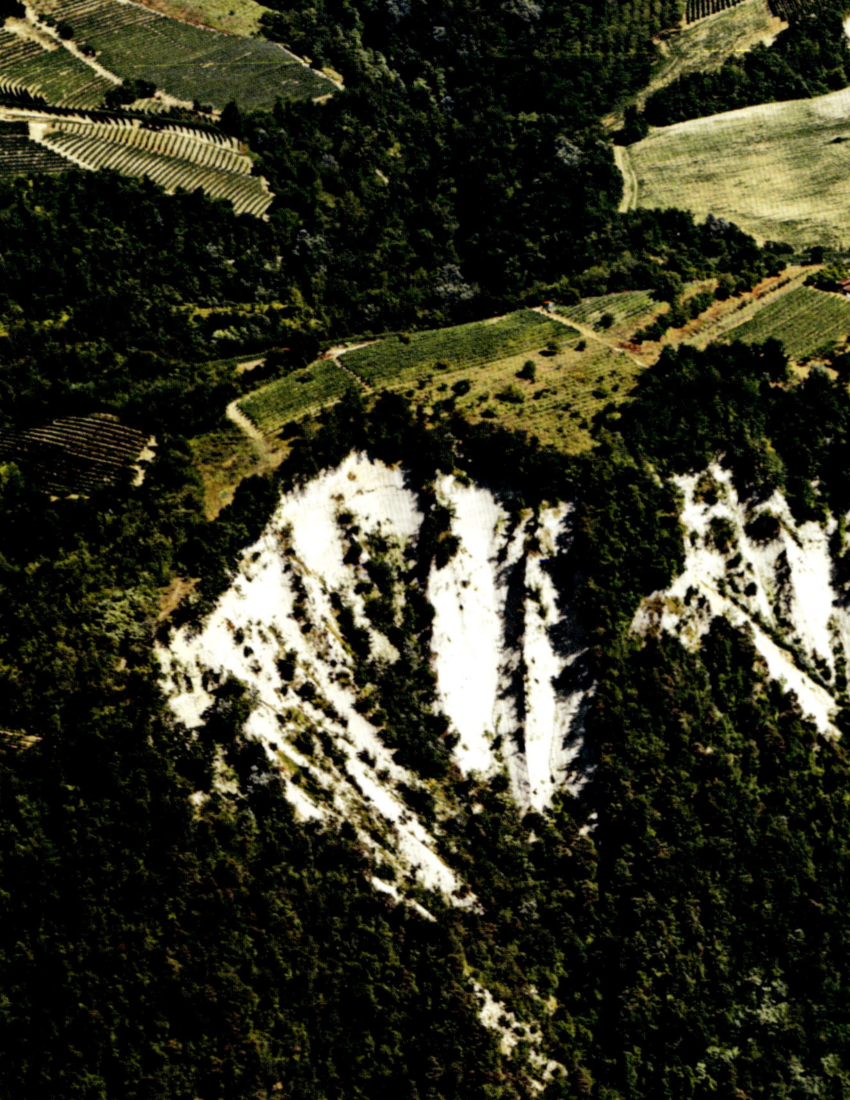

64-65
Great cliffs of clay dominate the Volterra region, often close to sandy deposits. The erosion of the two materials has produced the majestic Crags seen here.

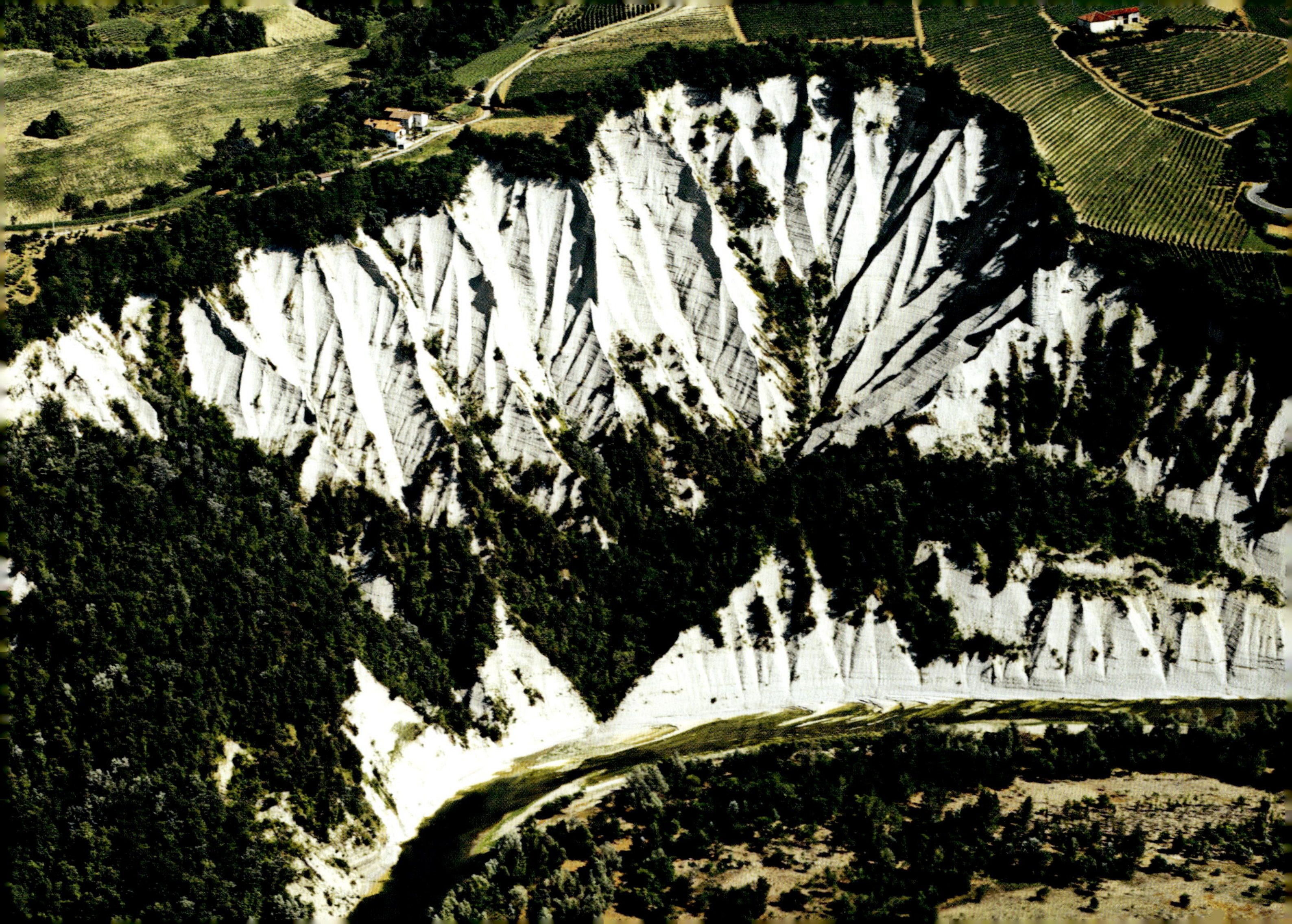

67

In spring, the gentle Sienese hills, here photographed at dawn, seem to be clothed with a tender yellow and green down.

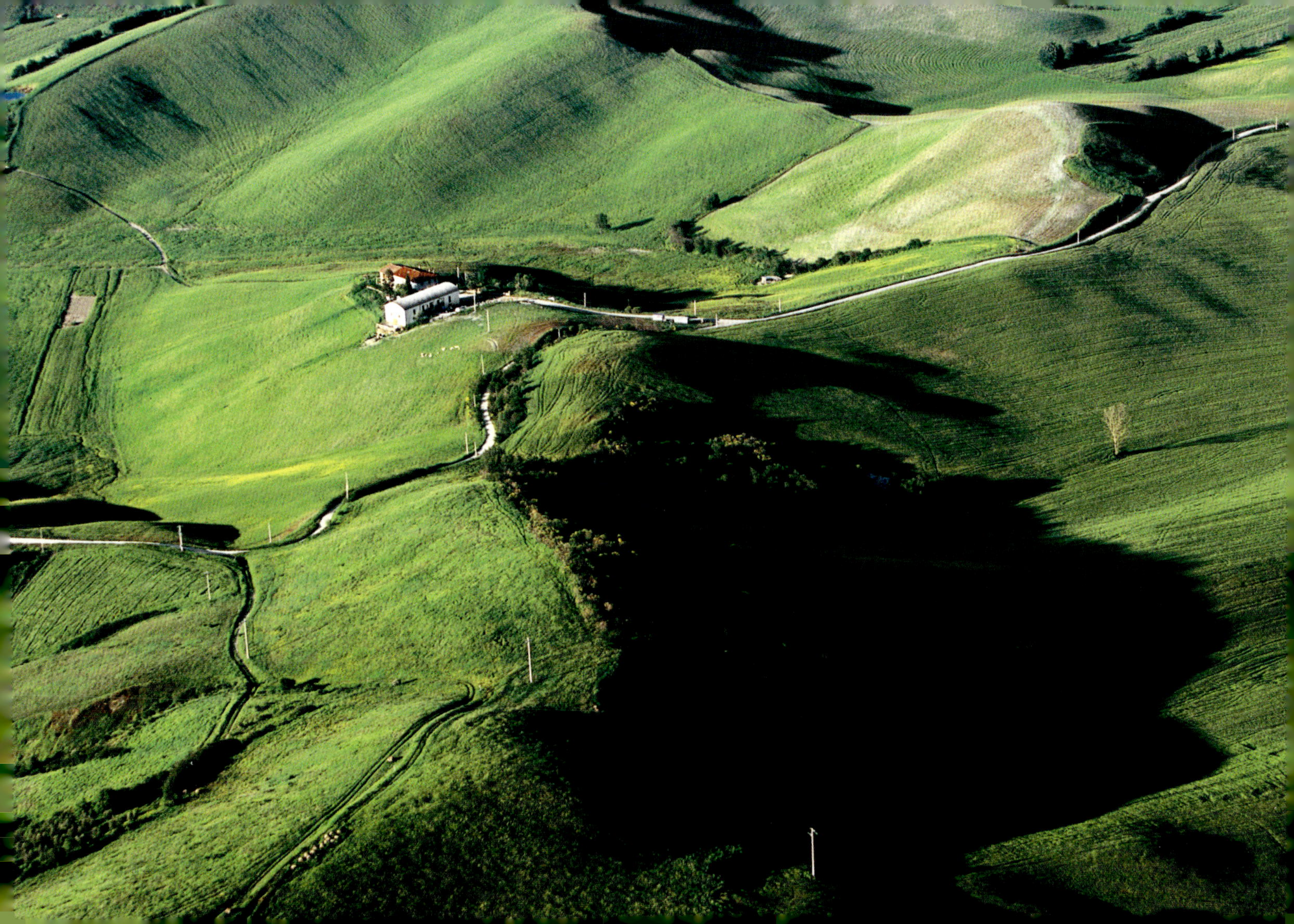

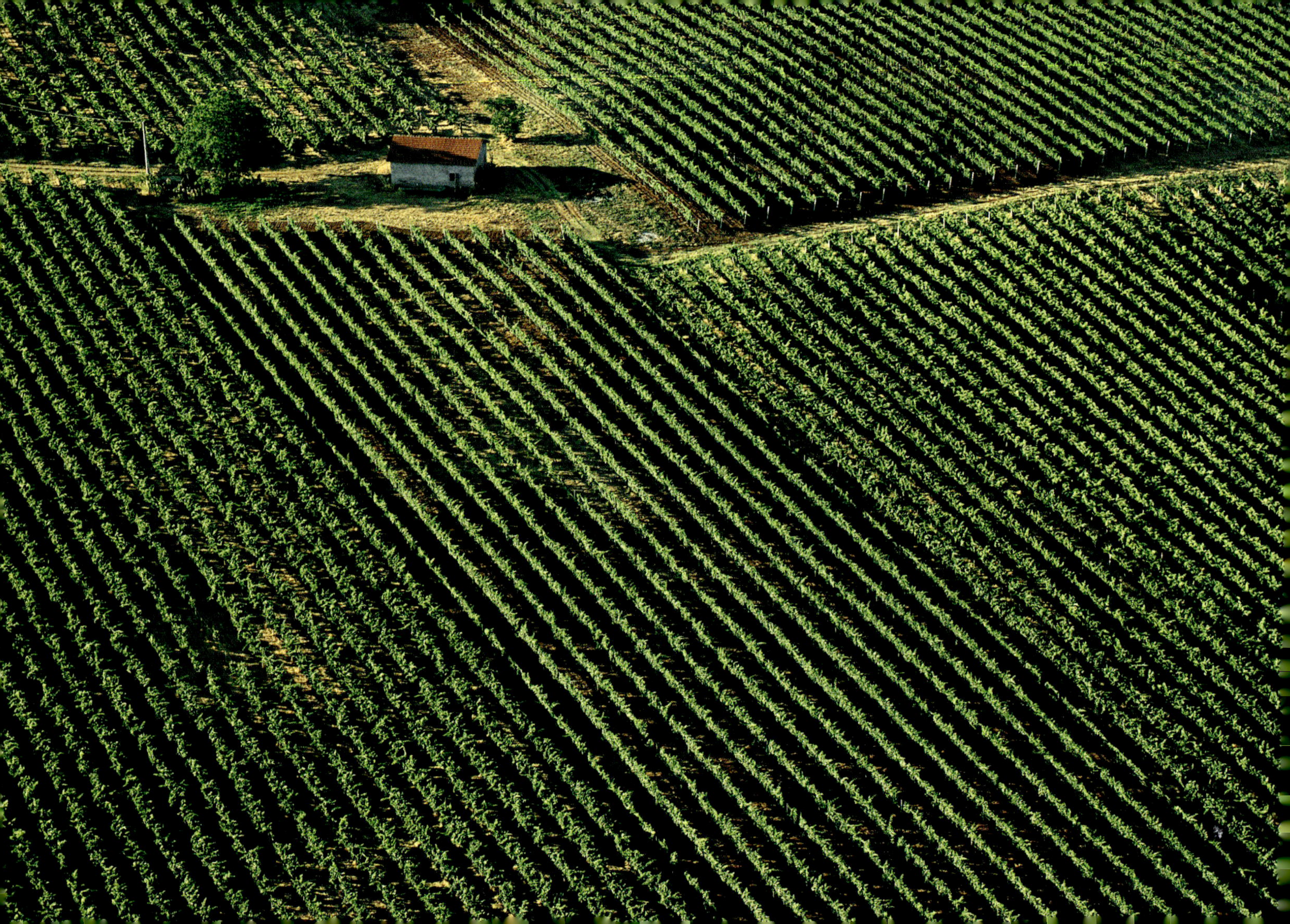

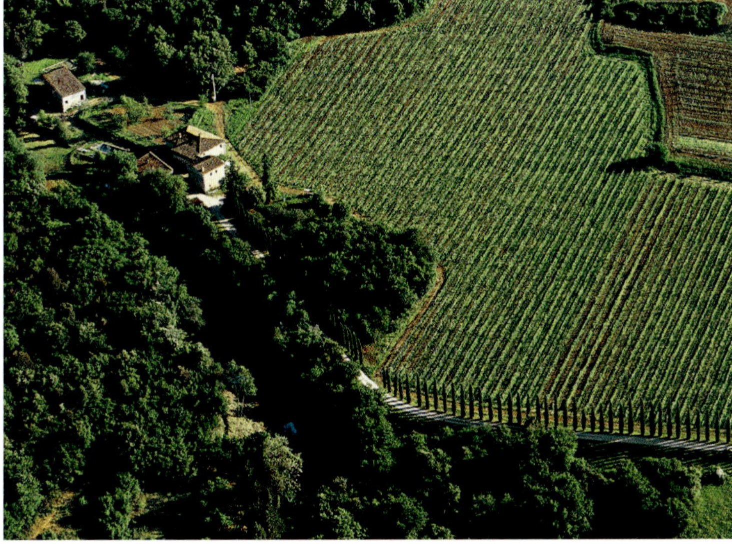

68
Long uninterrupted rows of vines wind around the slopes of a hill near Saturnia, a city famous for its hot springs.

69
Land of olives and grape vines, Tuscany offers numerous landscapes like this one, photographed at Monteriggioni, showing a farm and its well-defined property.

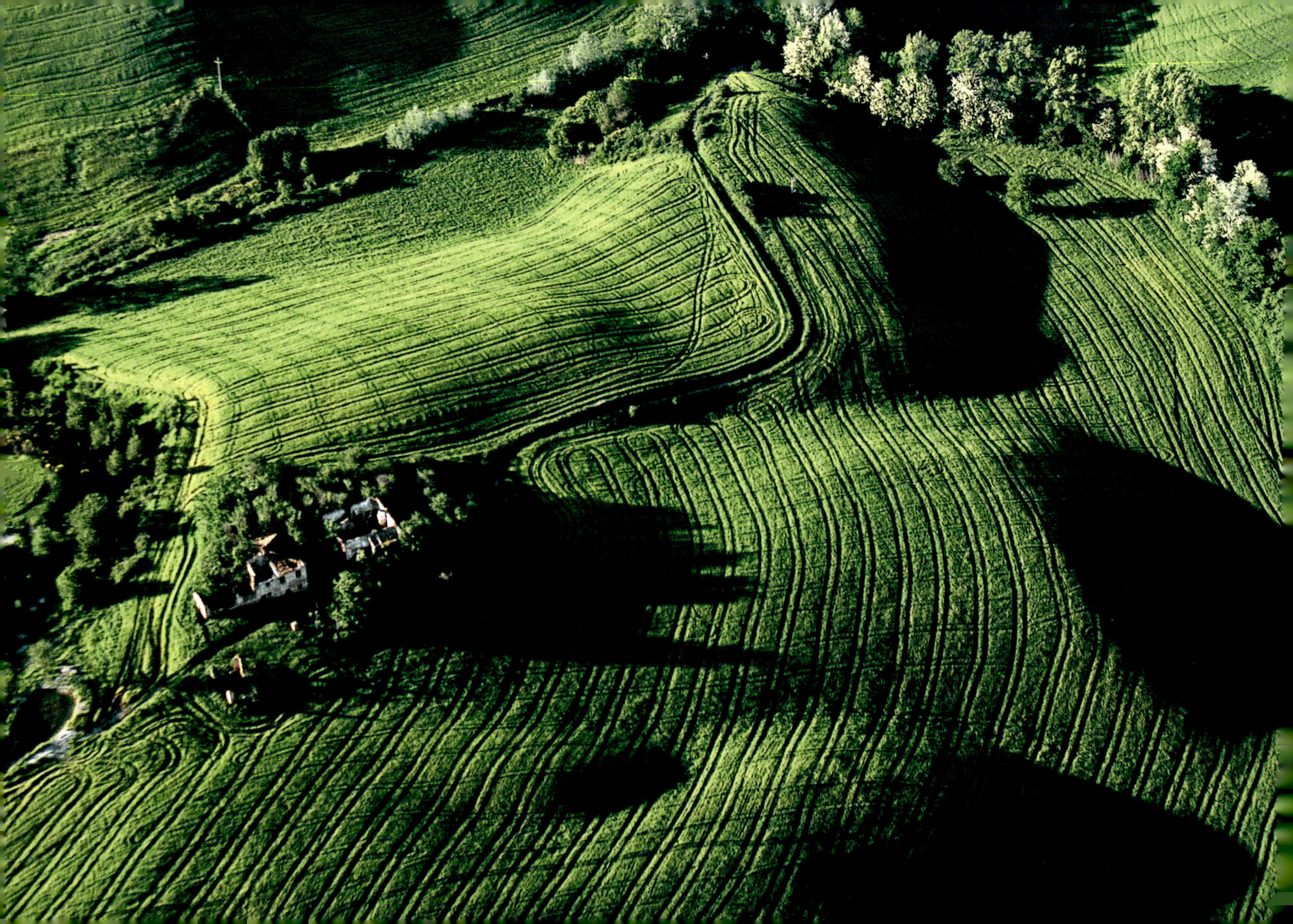

70
Traditionally, inner Tuscan land has not been used for large-scale one-crop farming; instead there is a patchwork of grain fields, hay fields, olive groves and vineyards.

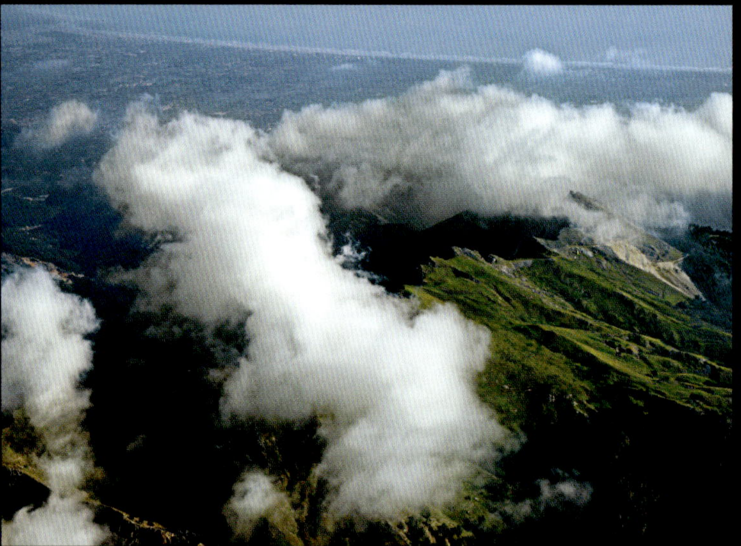

72

The northernmost crests of the Apuan Alps peak out from behind the clouds. This is a particularly fascinating zone of the Tuscan Apennines, both for its landscape and geology.

73

Mount Altissimo, despite its name, is barely over 4920 ft (1500 m) high. But it is impressive because of its sharp, craggy peaks.

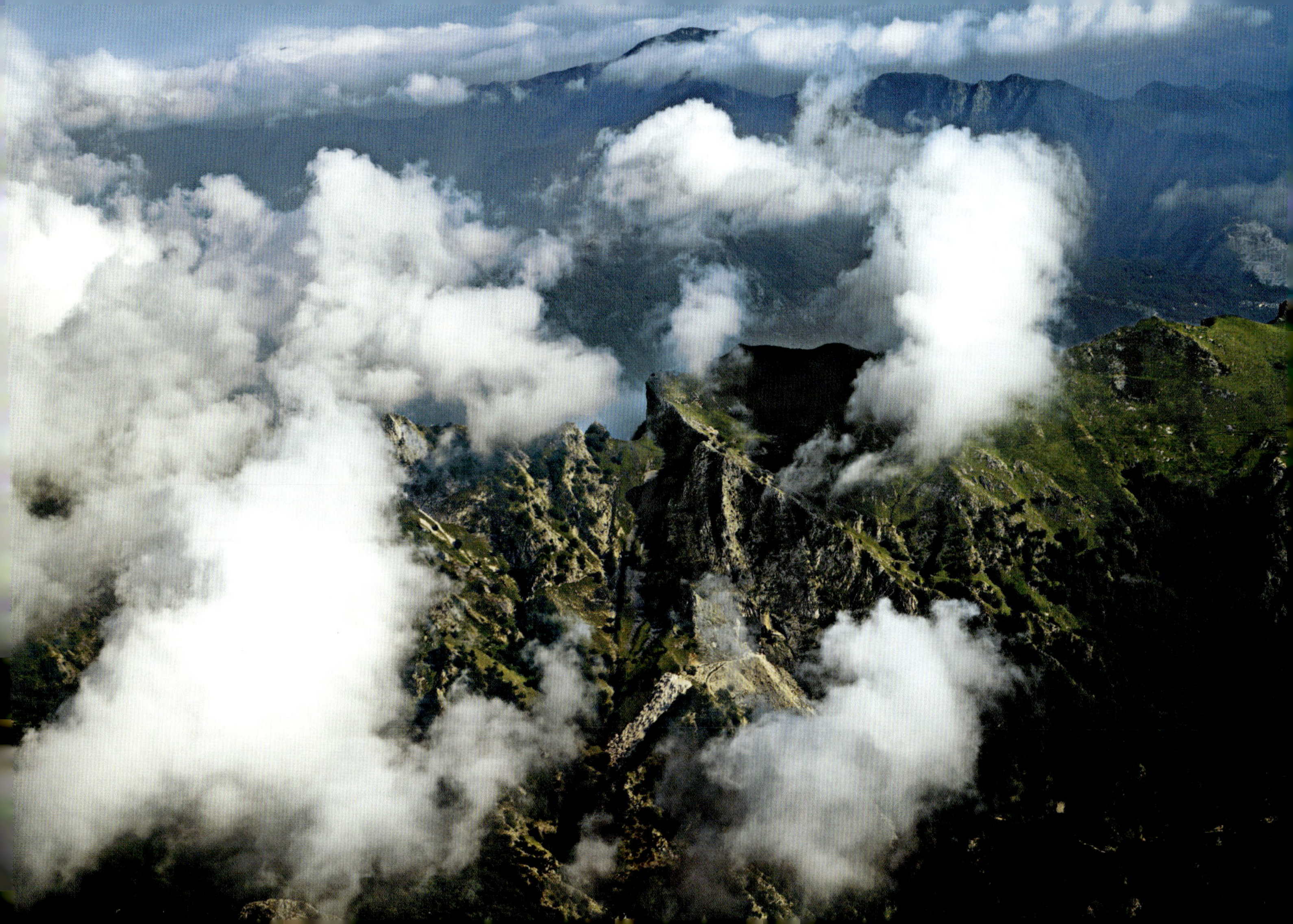

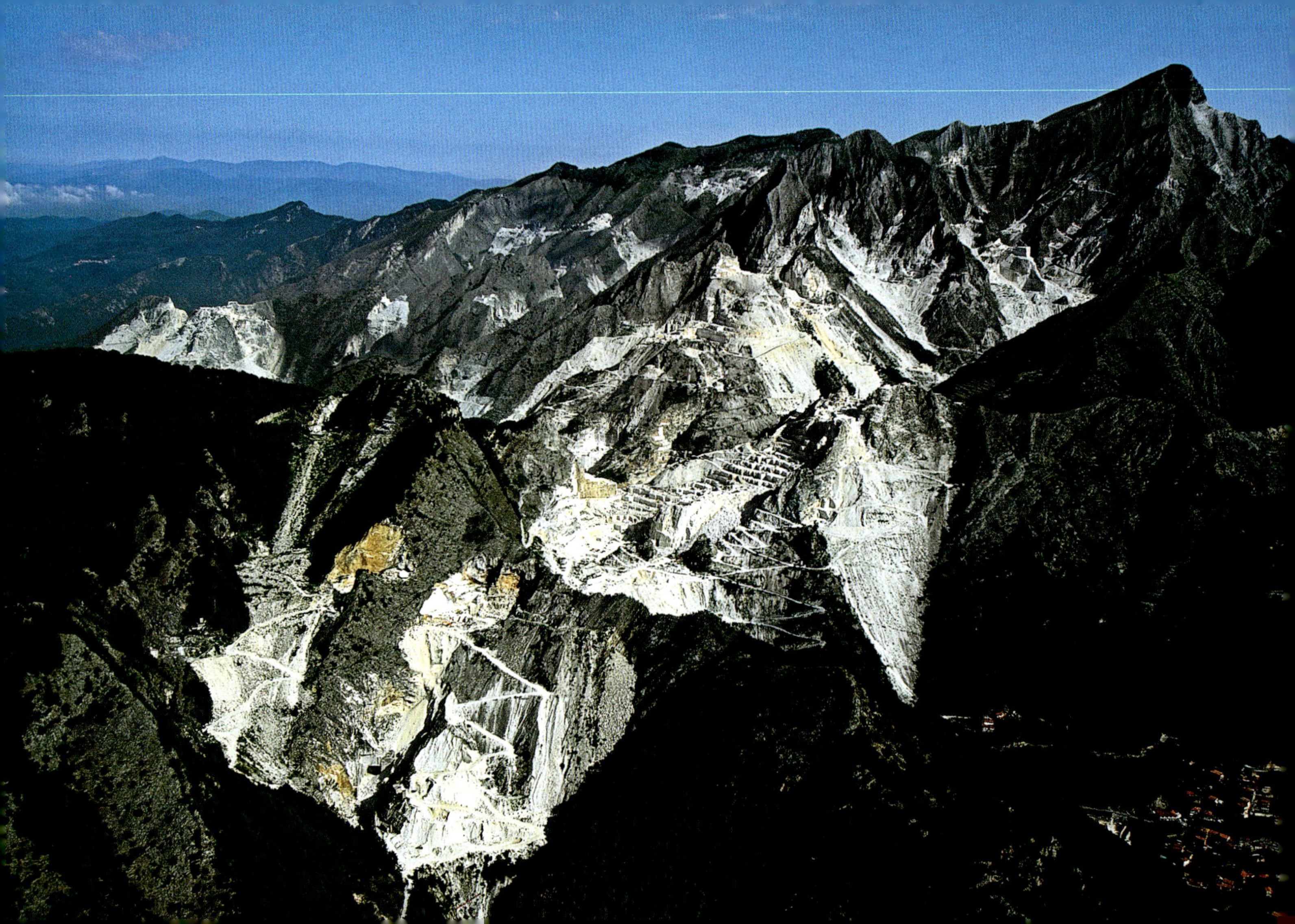

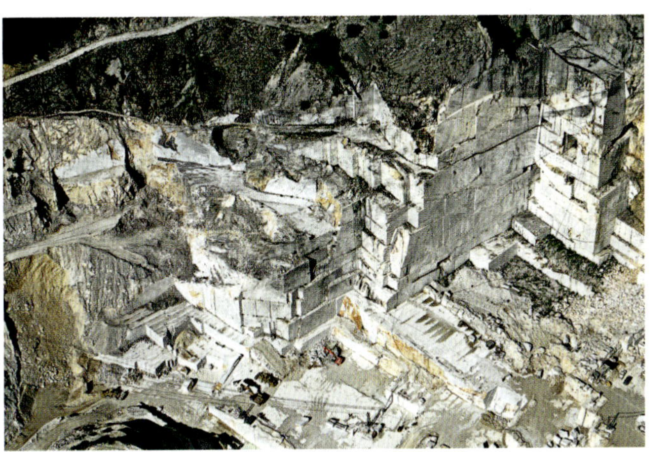

74
The Apuan Alps owe their name to Boccaccio, who made reference to the Ligurian Apuans, the area's ancient inhabitants. However, the Romans were first to extract marble, establishing the open-air quarries that still line the mountainsides.

75
More than 300 marble quarries, spread over more than 30 miles (50 km) mark the Apuan Alps.

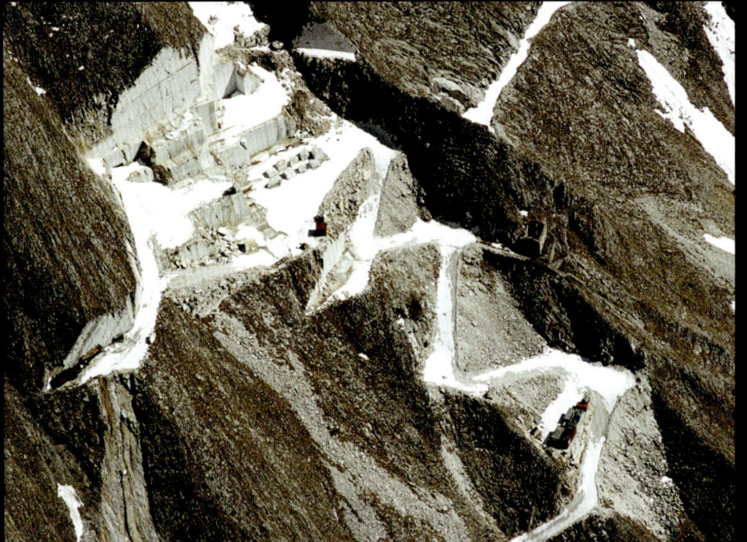

76 and 77

Apuan marble is renowned for its high calcium carbonate content. In the case of the famous, Ravaccione quarries, the marble is close to 100% pure calcium carbonate.

78-79

The presence of calcareous and dolomitic rock gives the Apuan Alps their characteristic barren, sculptural landscapes.

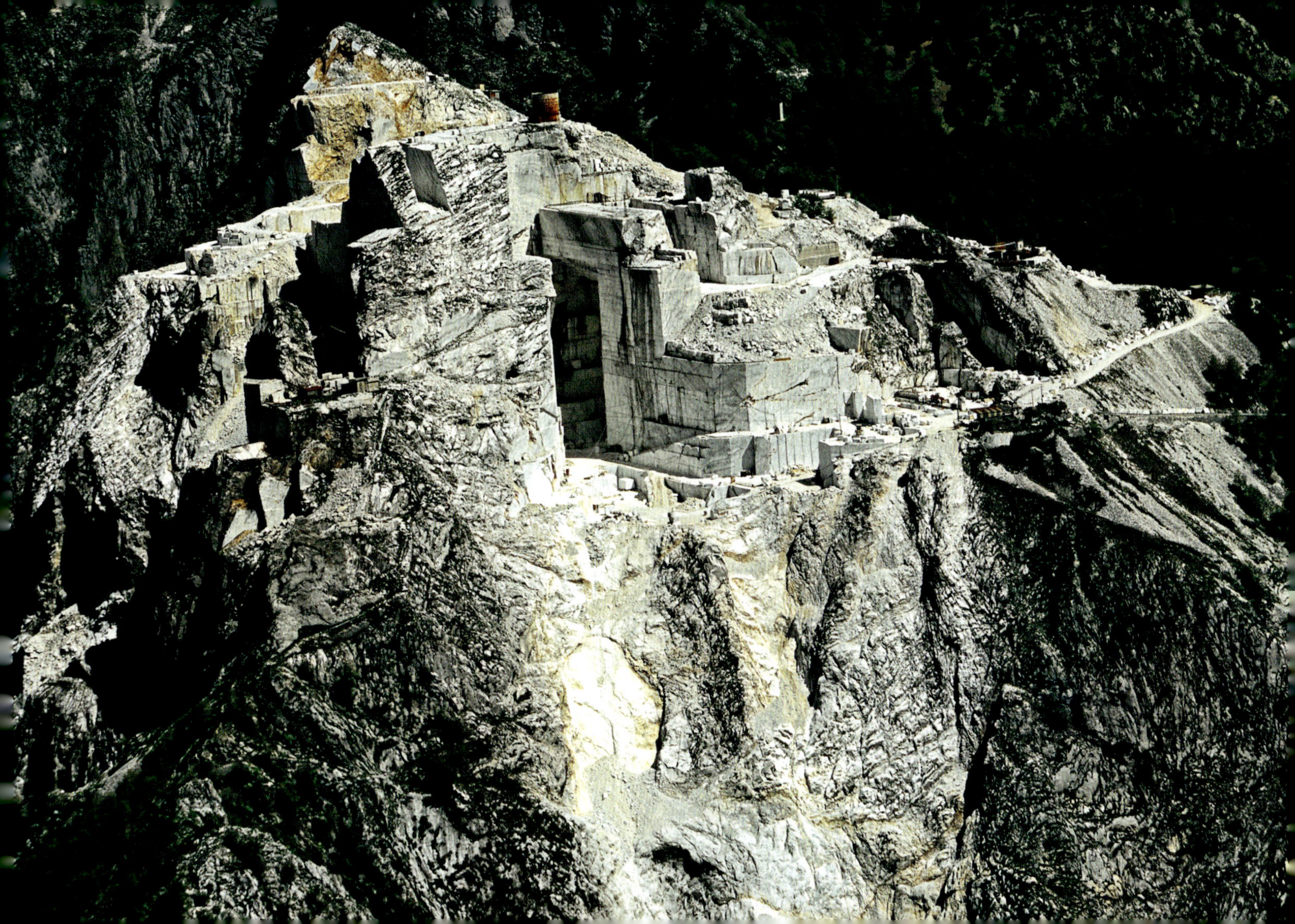

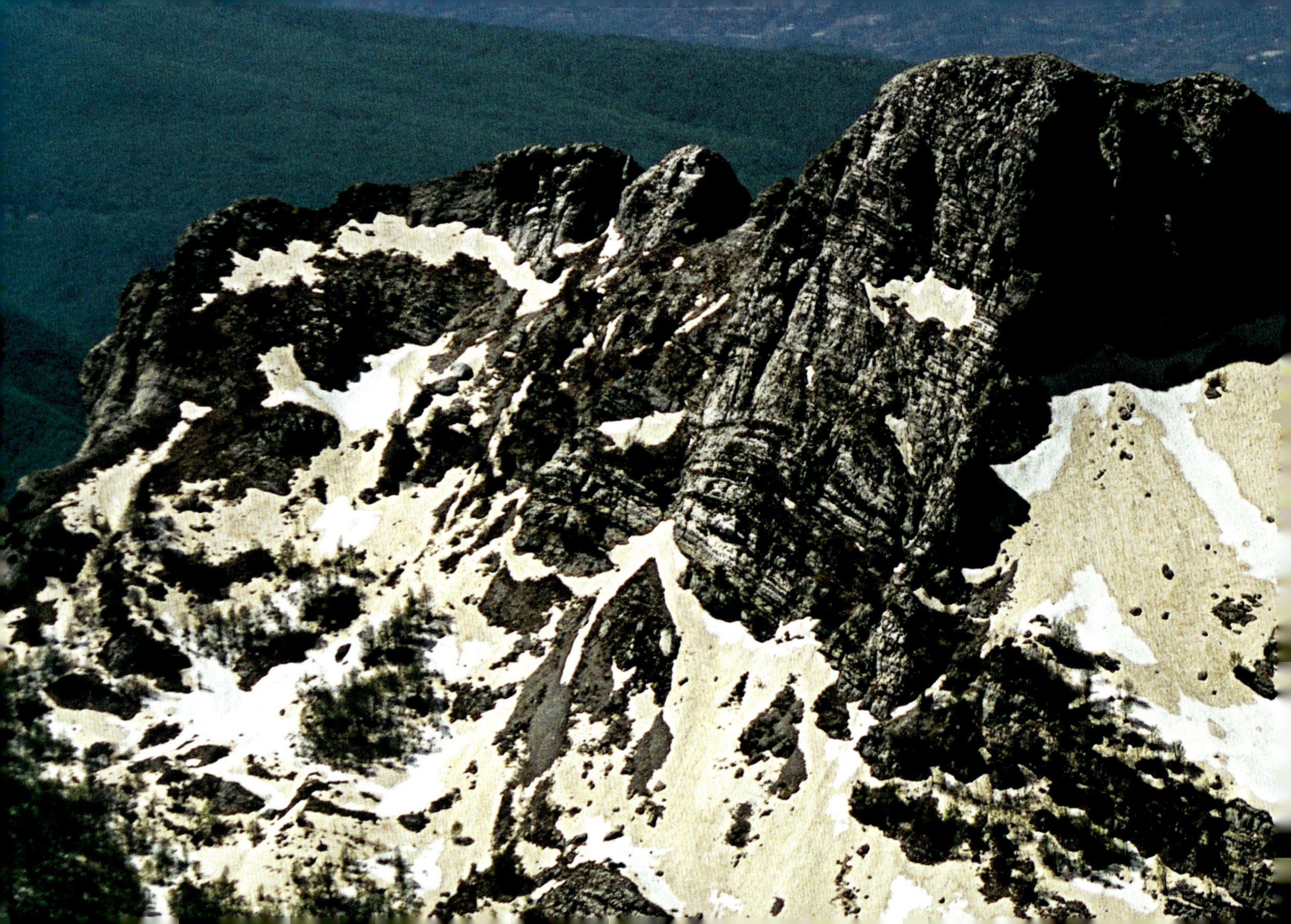

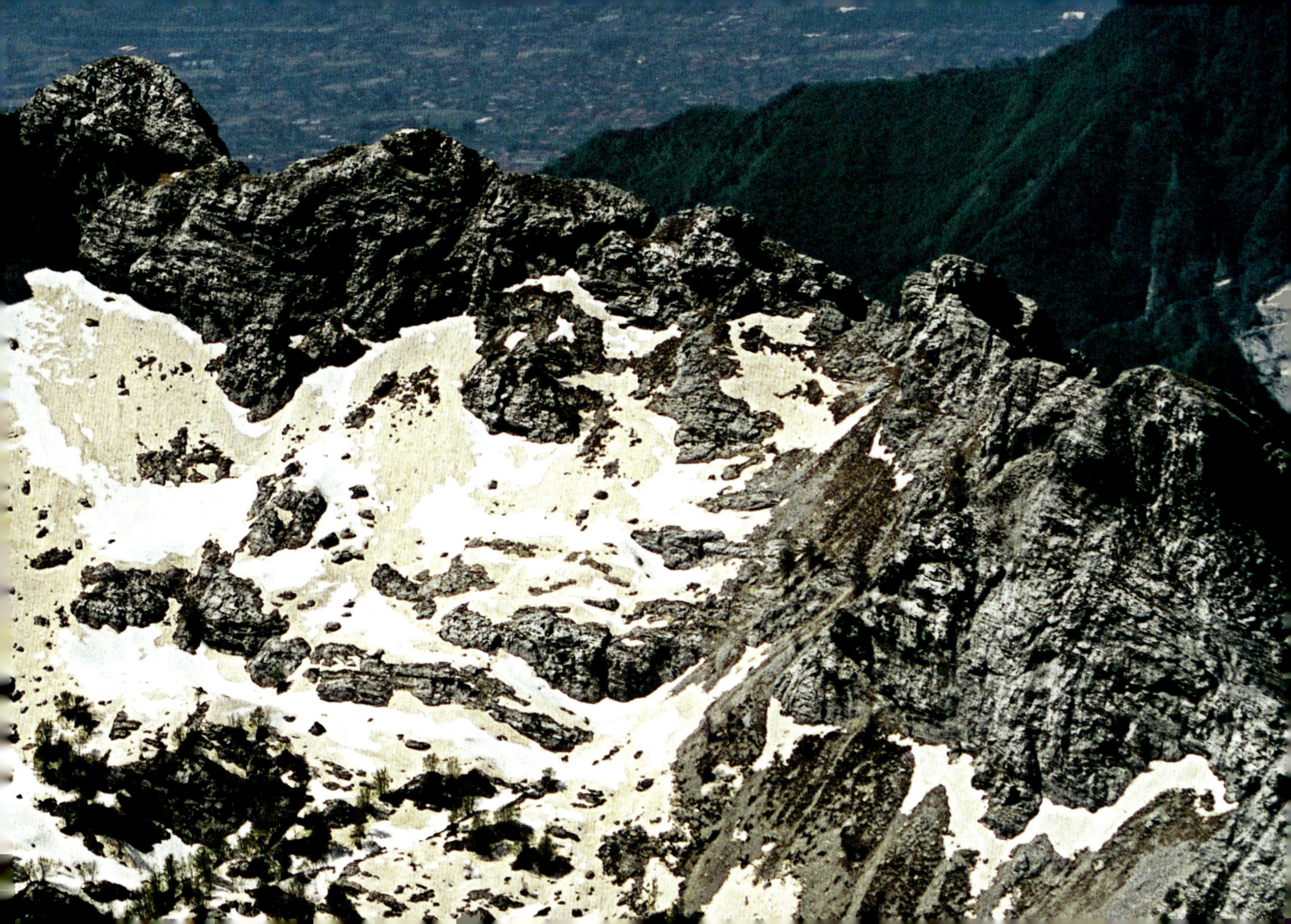

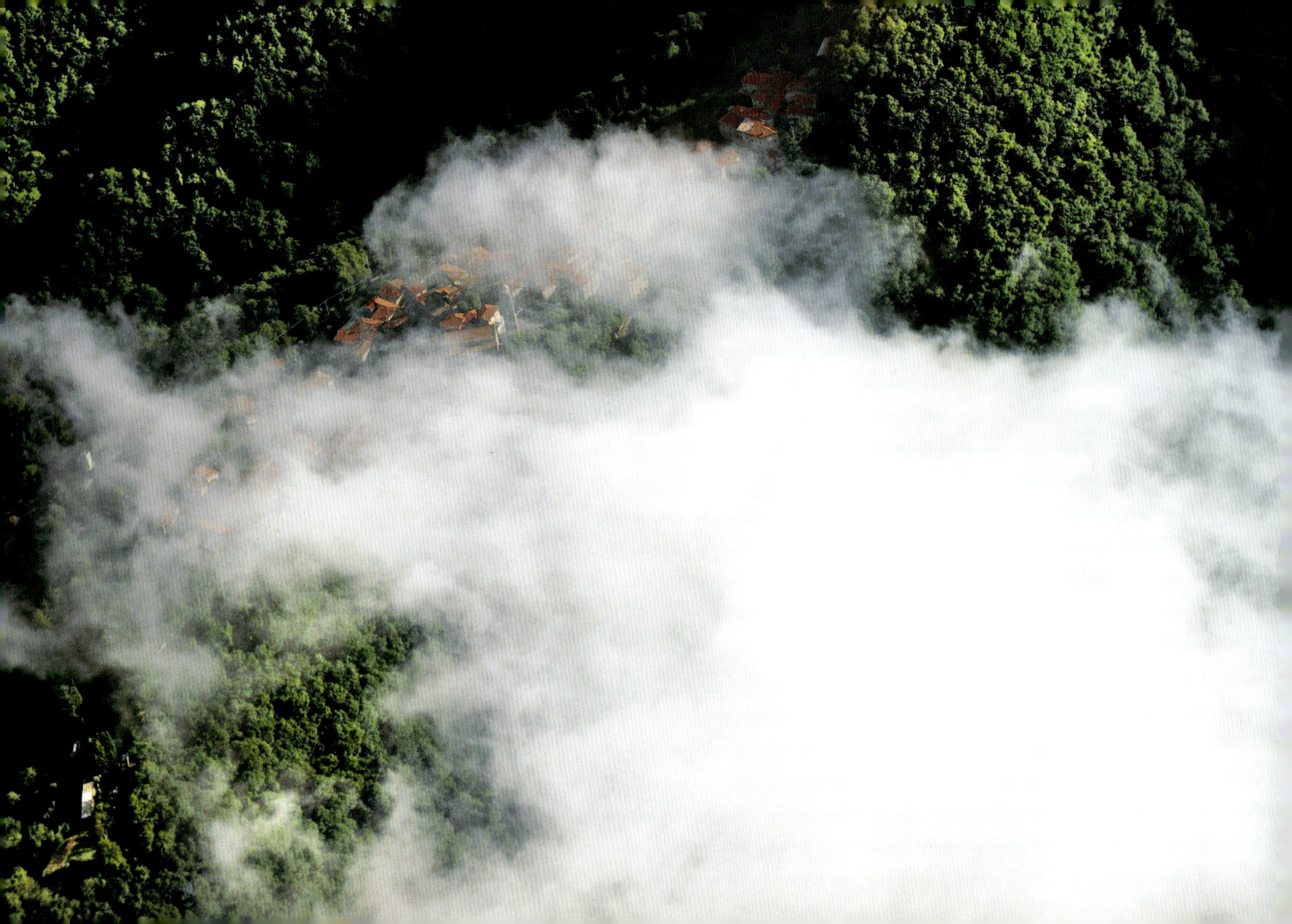

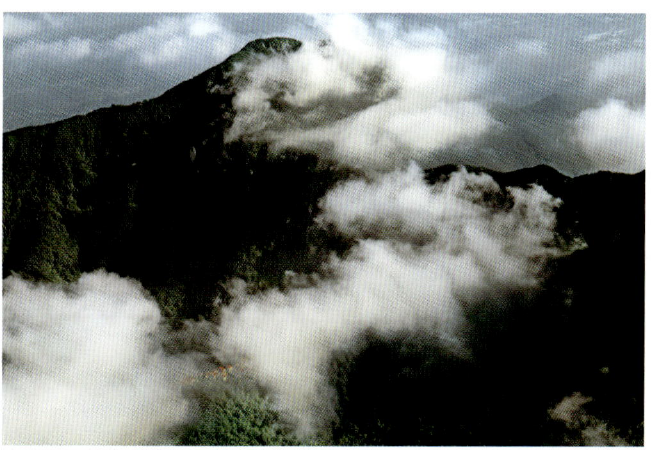

80
A small village peaks out from the clouds that cover the Garfagnana forest.

81
Mount Altissimo seems particularly majestic on the Tyrrhenian side. Its silhouette impressed Michelangelo, who scaled its peak in search of valuable marble for his statues.

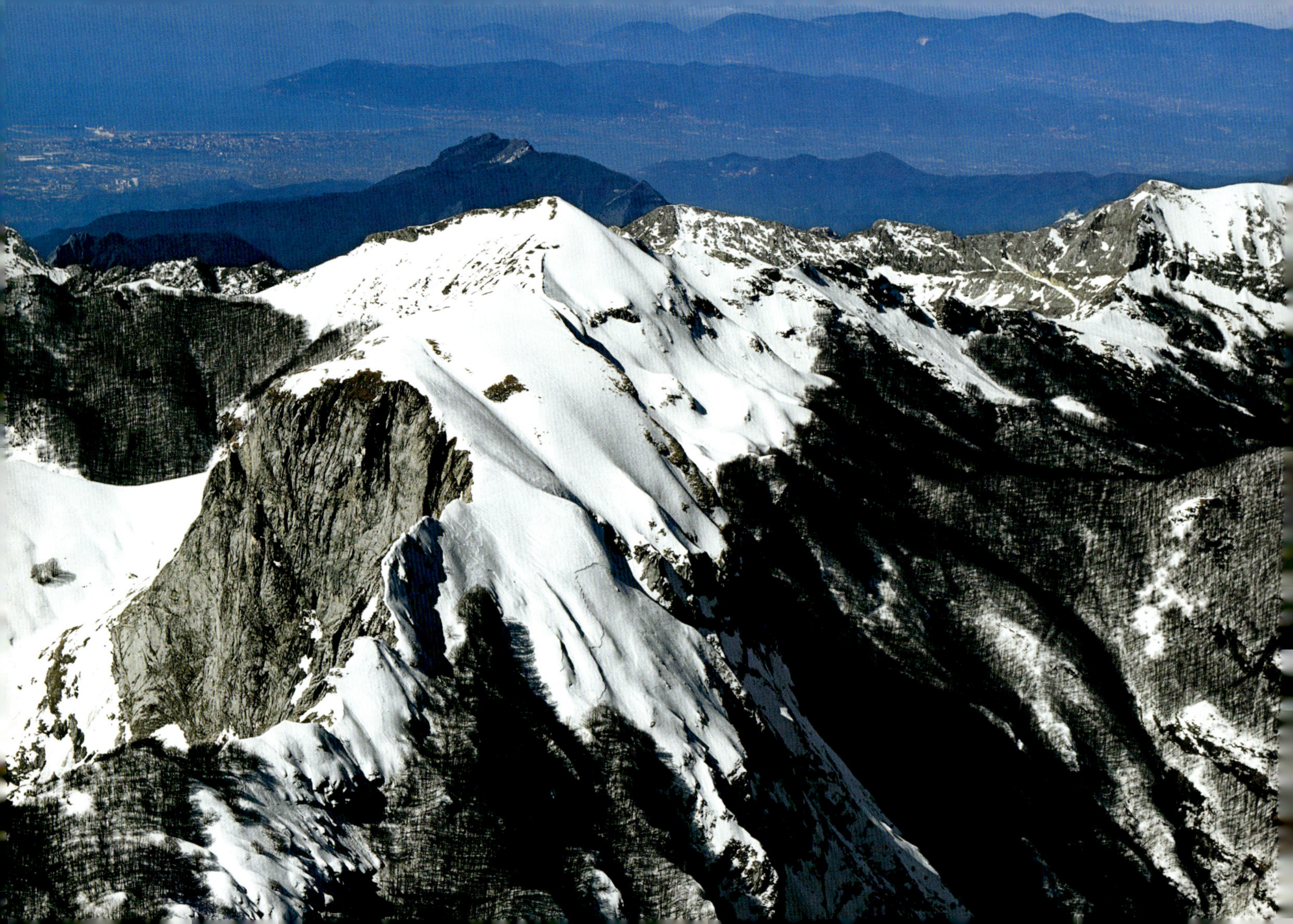

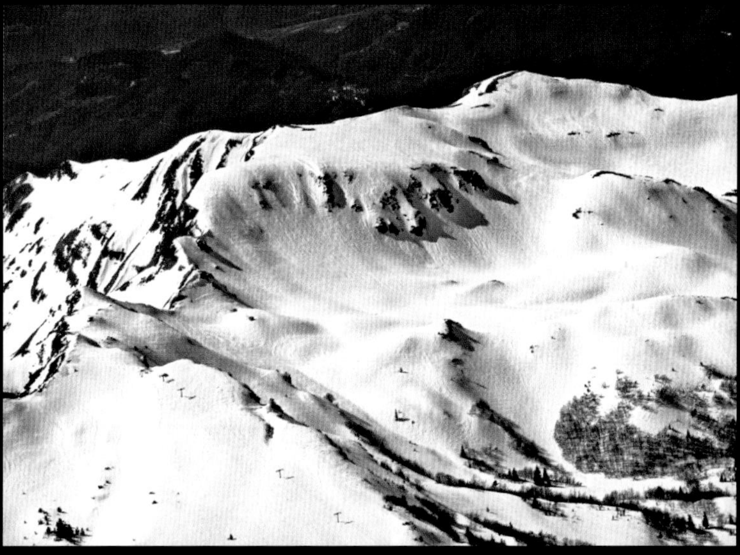

82 and 83
The highest peaks of the Tuscan-Emilian Apennines are on the border with Emilia- Romagna. Abundant snows make Abetone, at 6560 ft (2000 m), a popular ski resort.

85
At high altitudes, the Tuscan-Emilian Apennine peaks are exposed to atmospheric elements that sculpt interesting forms and comb the snow drifts into small manes.

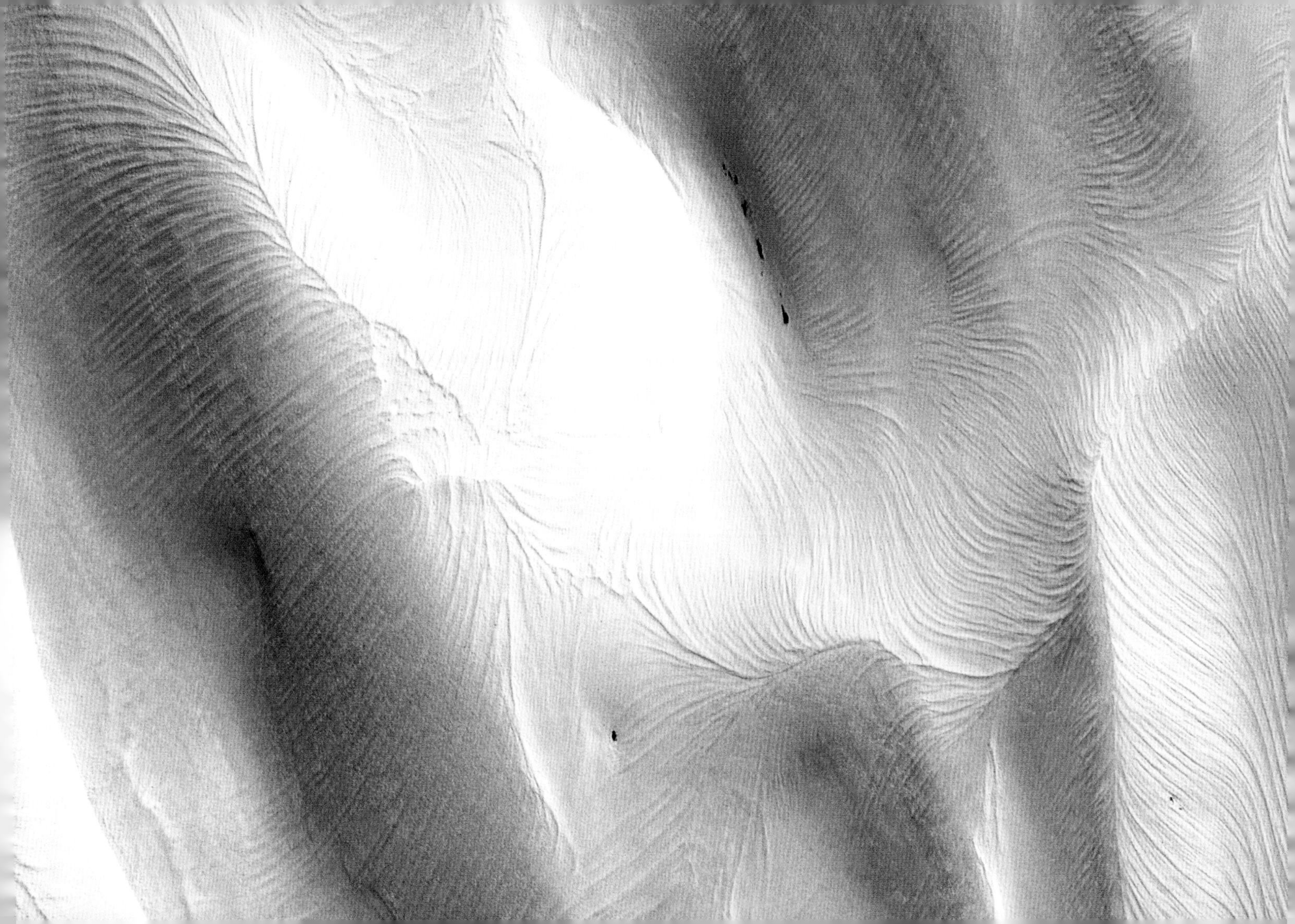

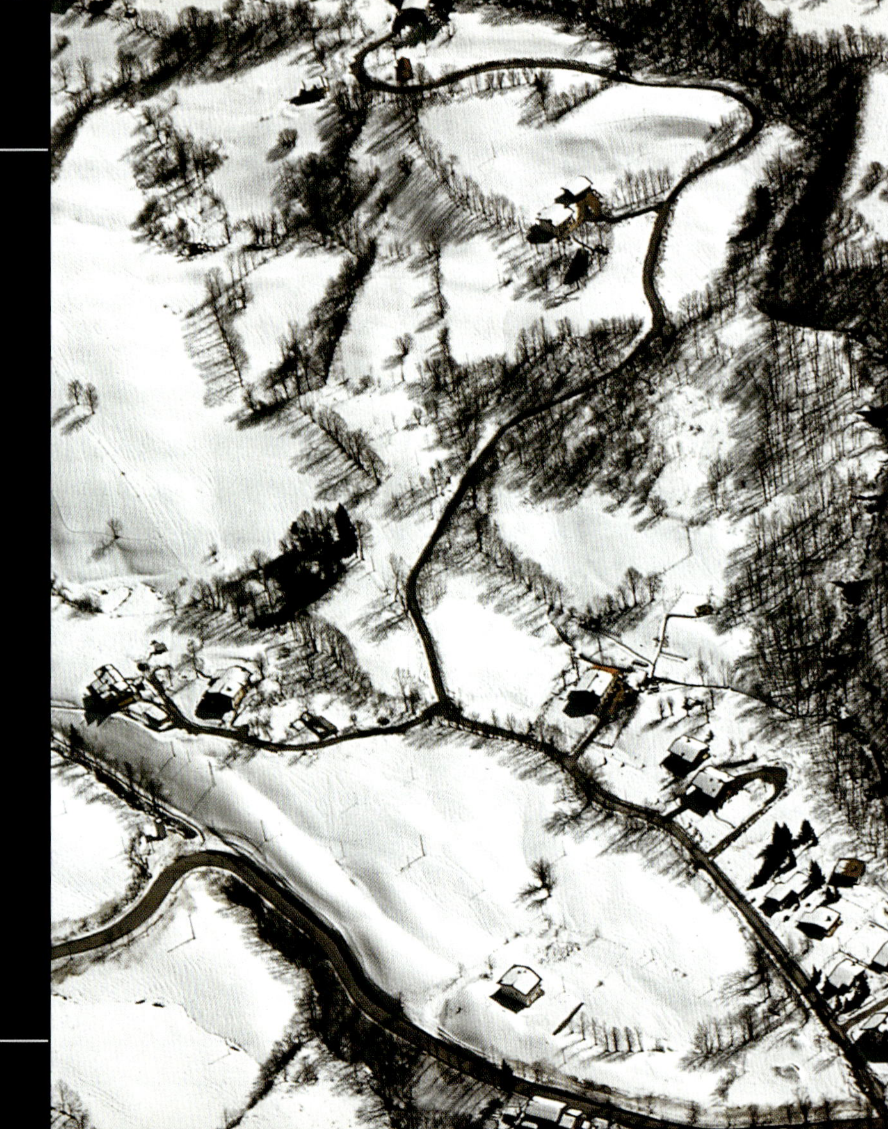

86-87
Like galleries in an ant colony, the cleared roads of this small village at the foot of Abetone form a network that leads to the pristine mountainside.

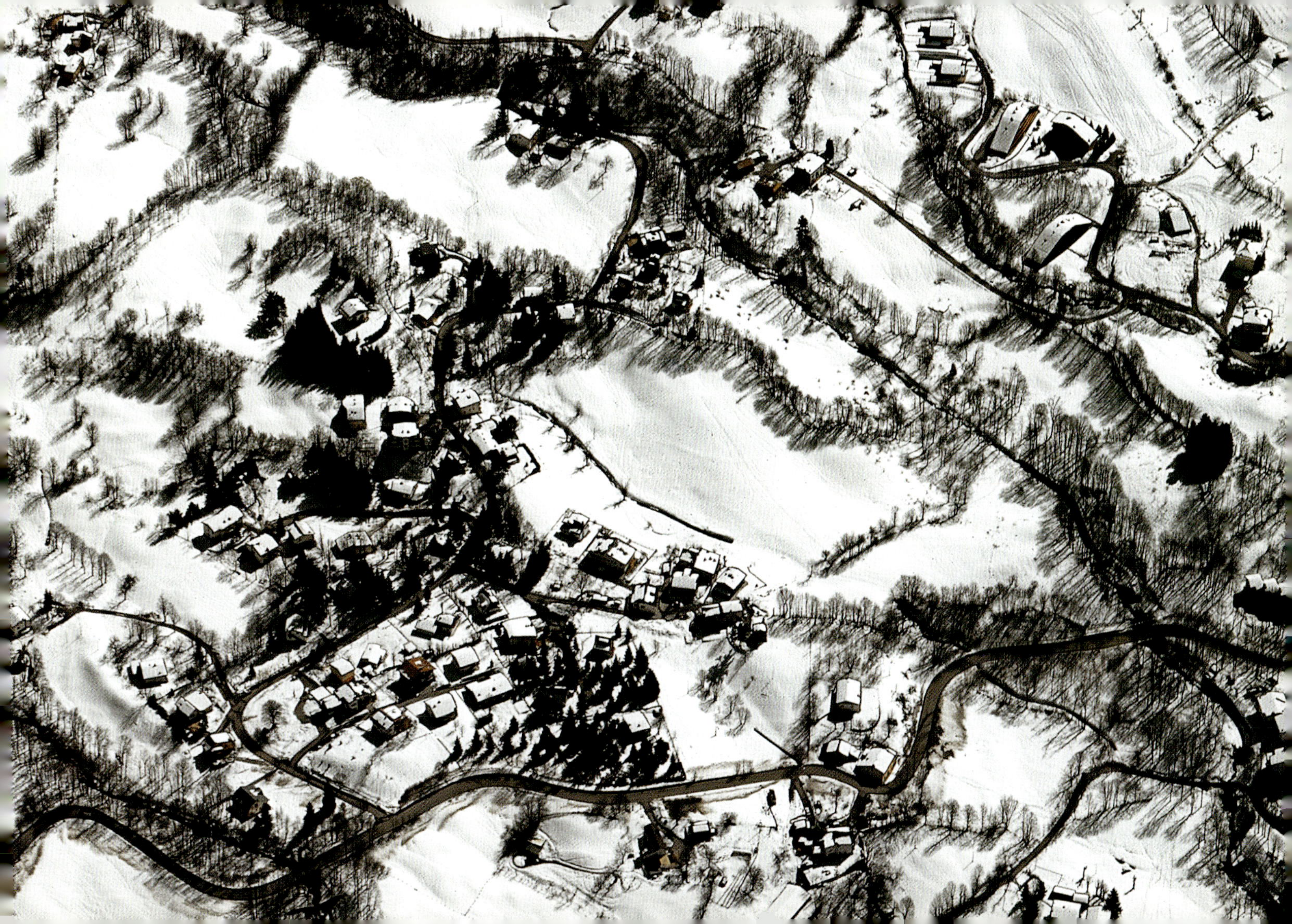

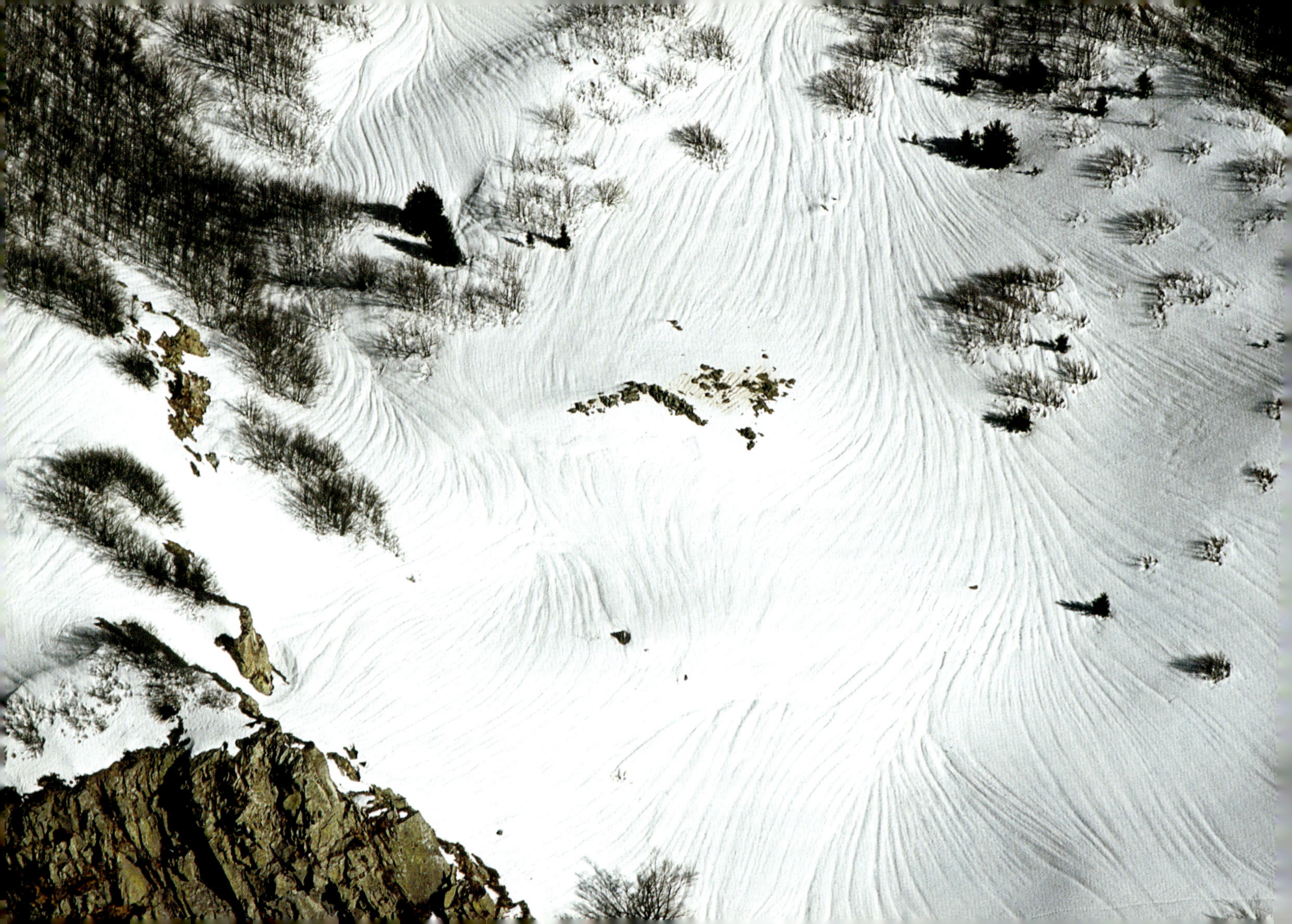

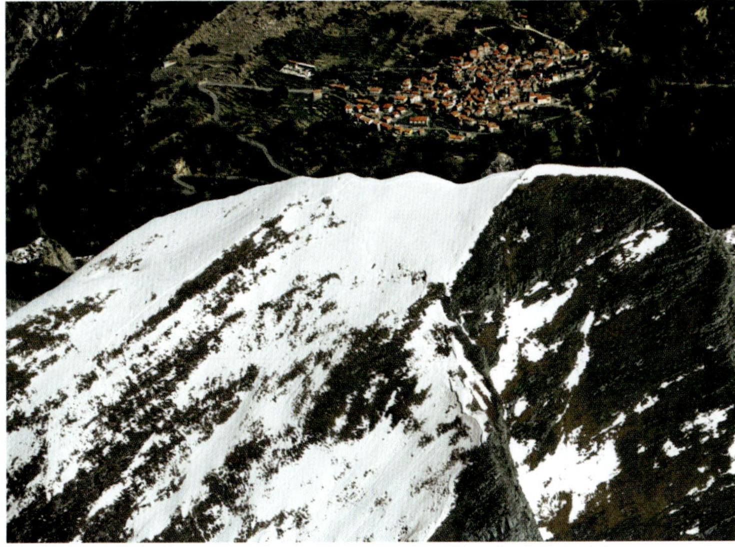

88
These wind-carved channels in the white expanses of the heart of the Tuscan-Emilian Apennines follow altimetrical lines, as if designed by man.

89
The Garfagnana mountains offer very evocative panoramas, especially in Apuan Alps Regional Park.

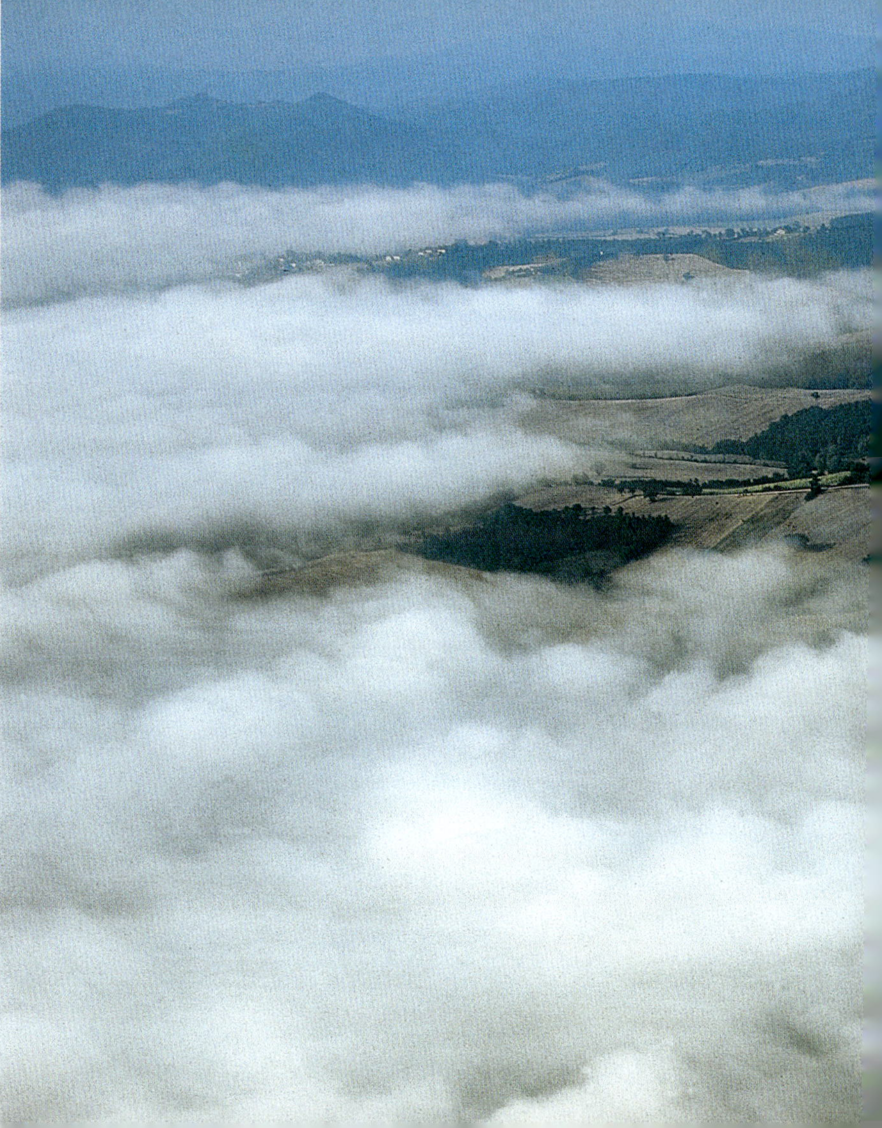

90-91
The Metalliferous Hills – the upland spine of ancient Etruria – offer fascinating sights. In this image, the darker splashes of color below the cloud cover are patches of the Chiusdino countryside.

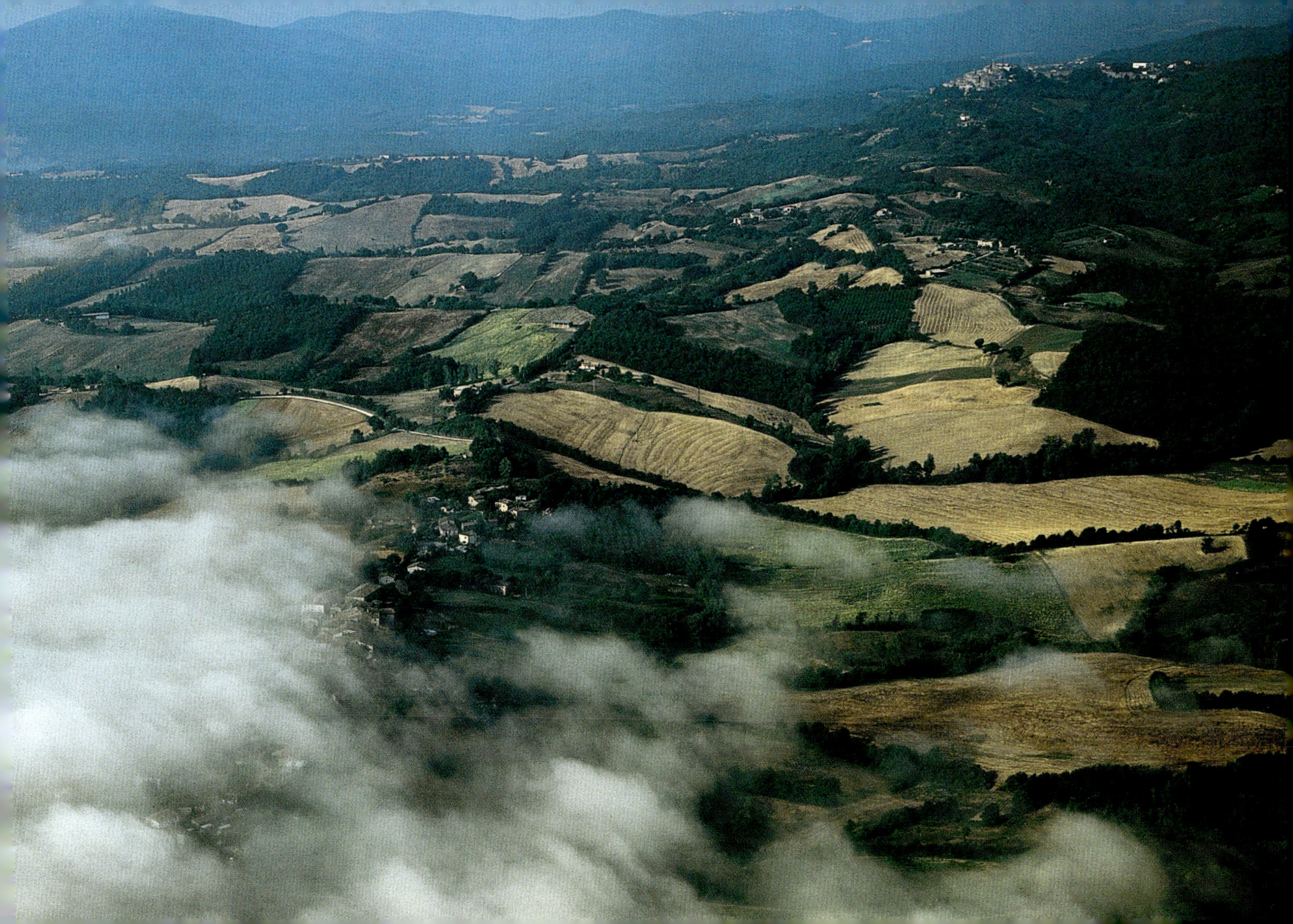

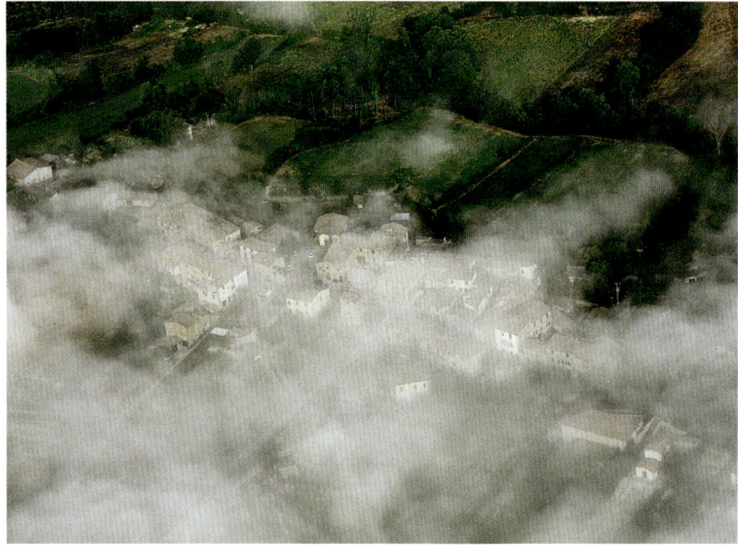

92
Chiusdino rises atop a hill, in an area of the Sienese province considered strategic since the 11th century.

93
The Metalliferous Hills wind between Volterra and Massa Marittima. Their name refers to the many colorations of the mineral-rich region, where, in the past, minerals were the principal source of income.

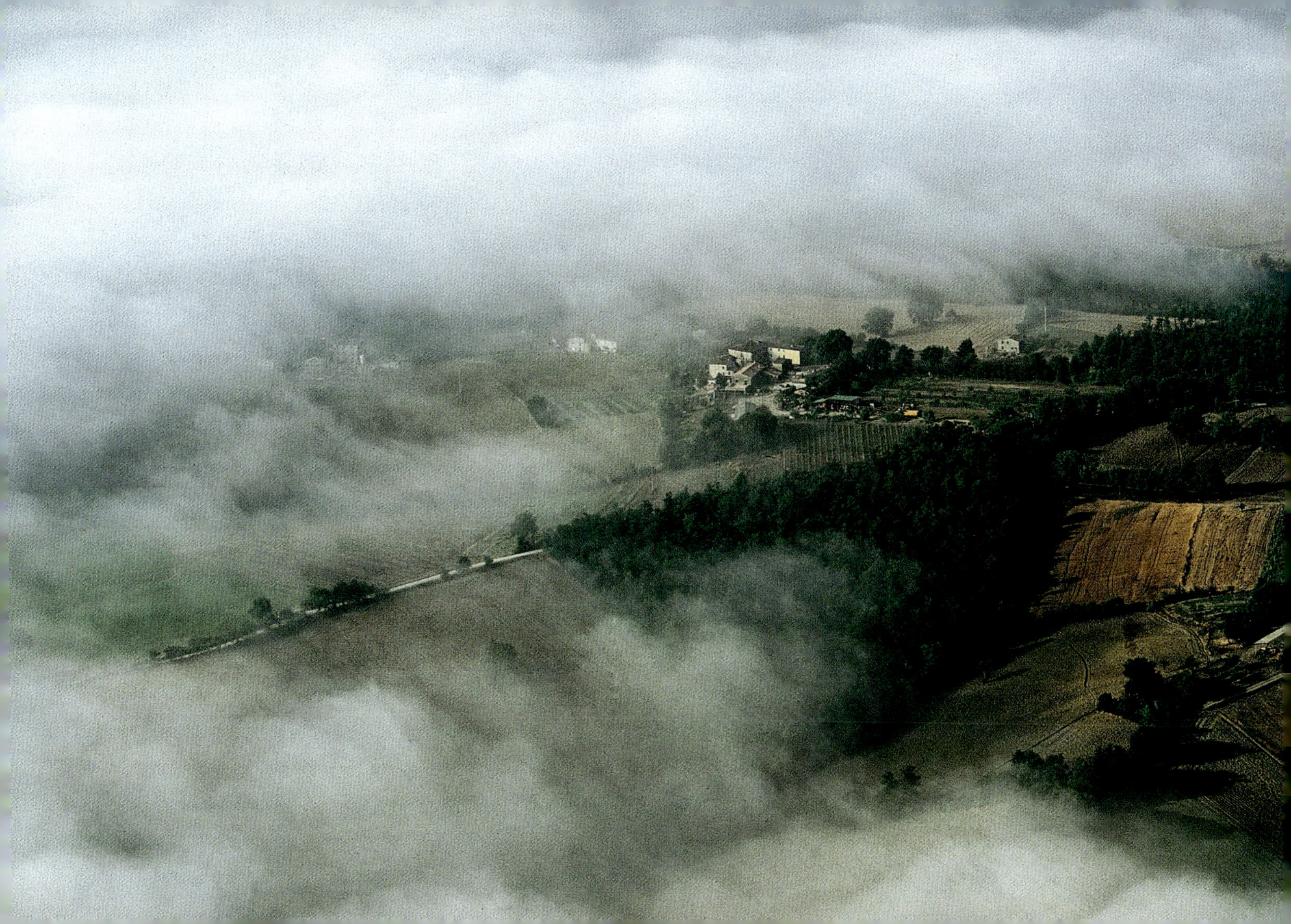

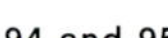

94 and 95

The woodland areas that border cultivated land in the Metalliferous Hills are the remnants of the forest that once covered the entire region. Much was felled for fuel; the remaining areas are now protected by rigid environmental laws.

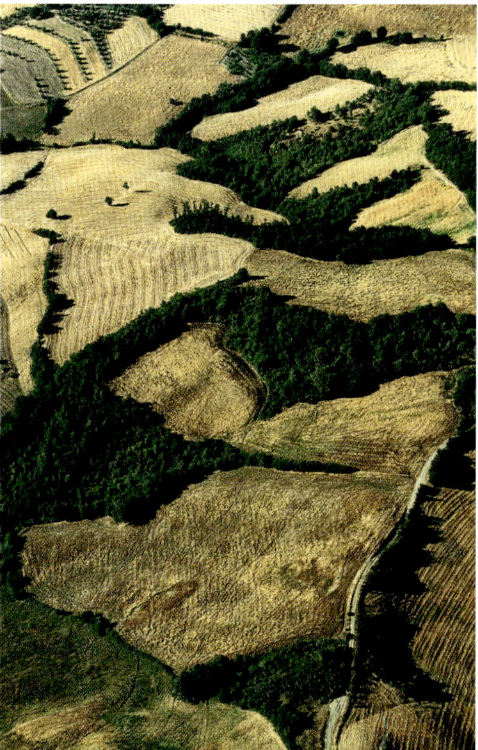

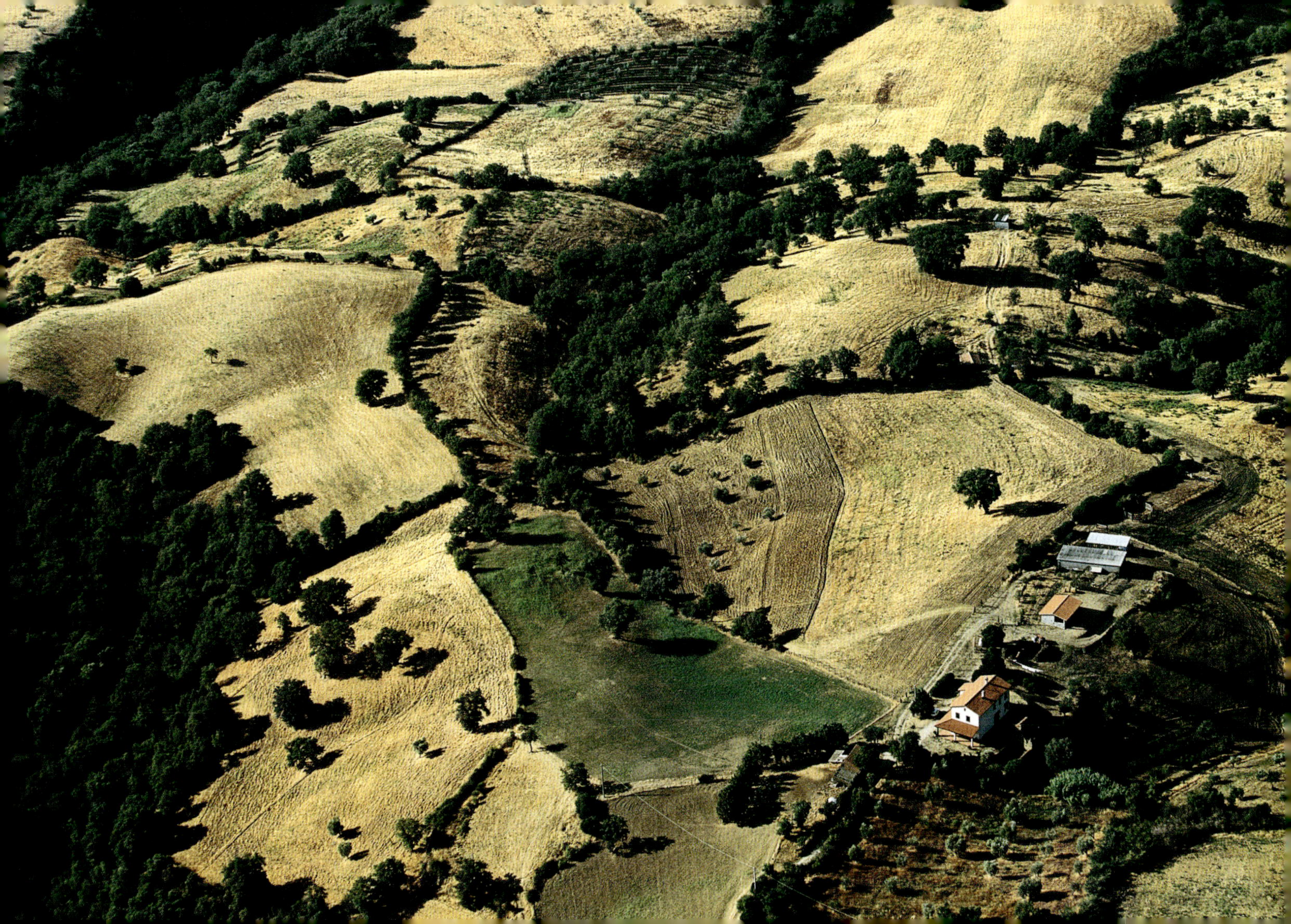

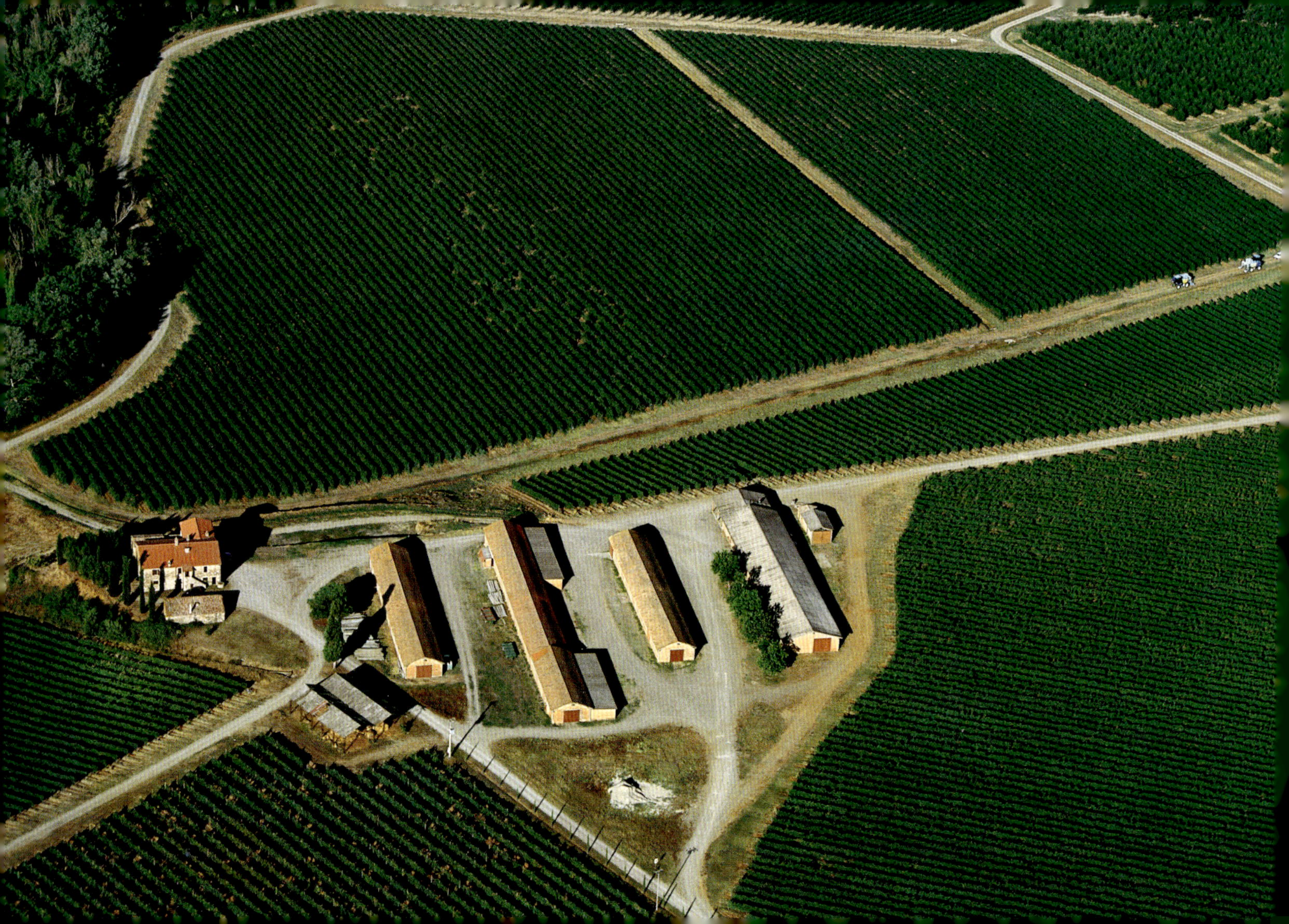

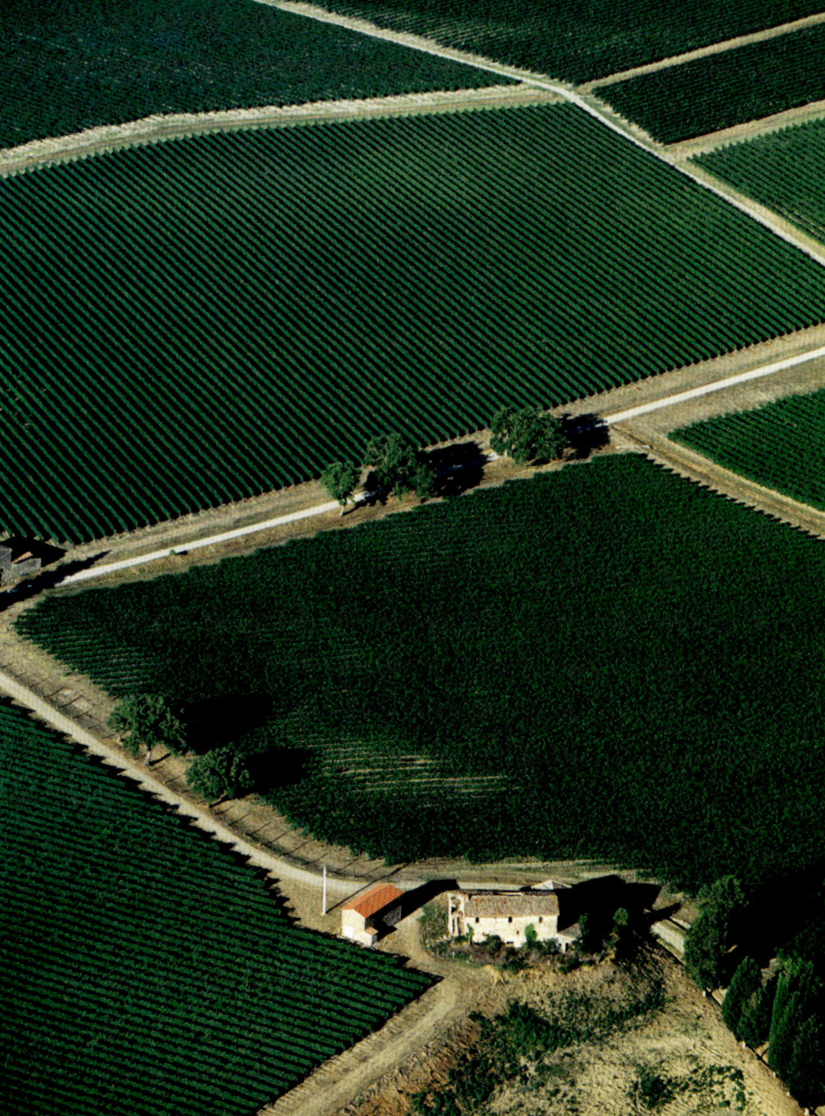

96 and 97
Vast rows of grape vines characterize the southern part of the Metalliferous Hills. No longer dependent on the extraction of pyrites, copper, zinc and lead sulfurs, the inhabitants of this part of Tuscany can still count on the land's fertility, its geothermic riches, and the beautiful landscape.

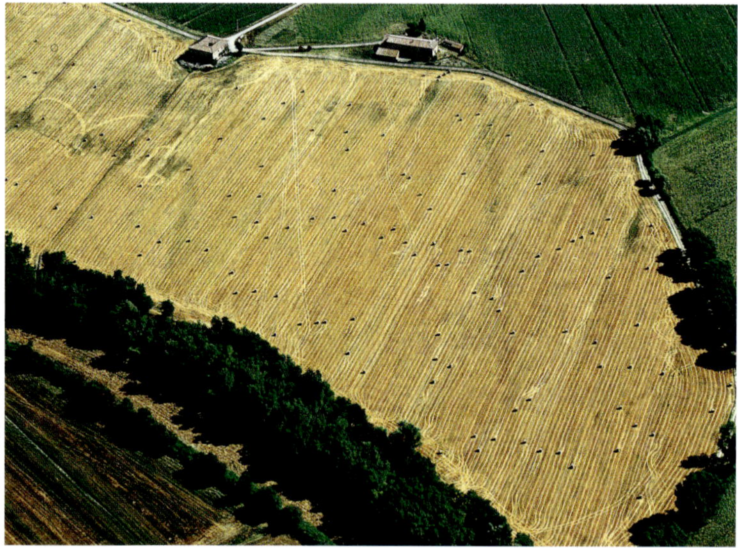

98 and 99

Once the harvest is over, the panorama of the Metalliferous Hills region offers a contrast between the green of the forests and the yellow of the harvested fields, dappled with bales.

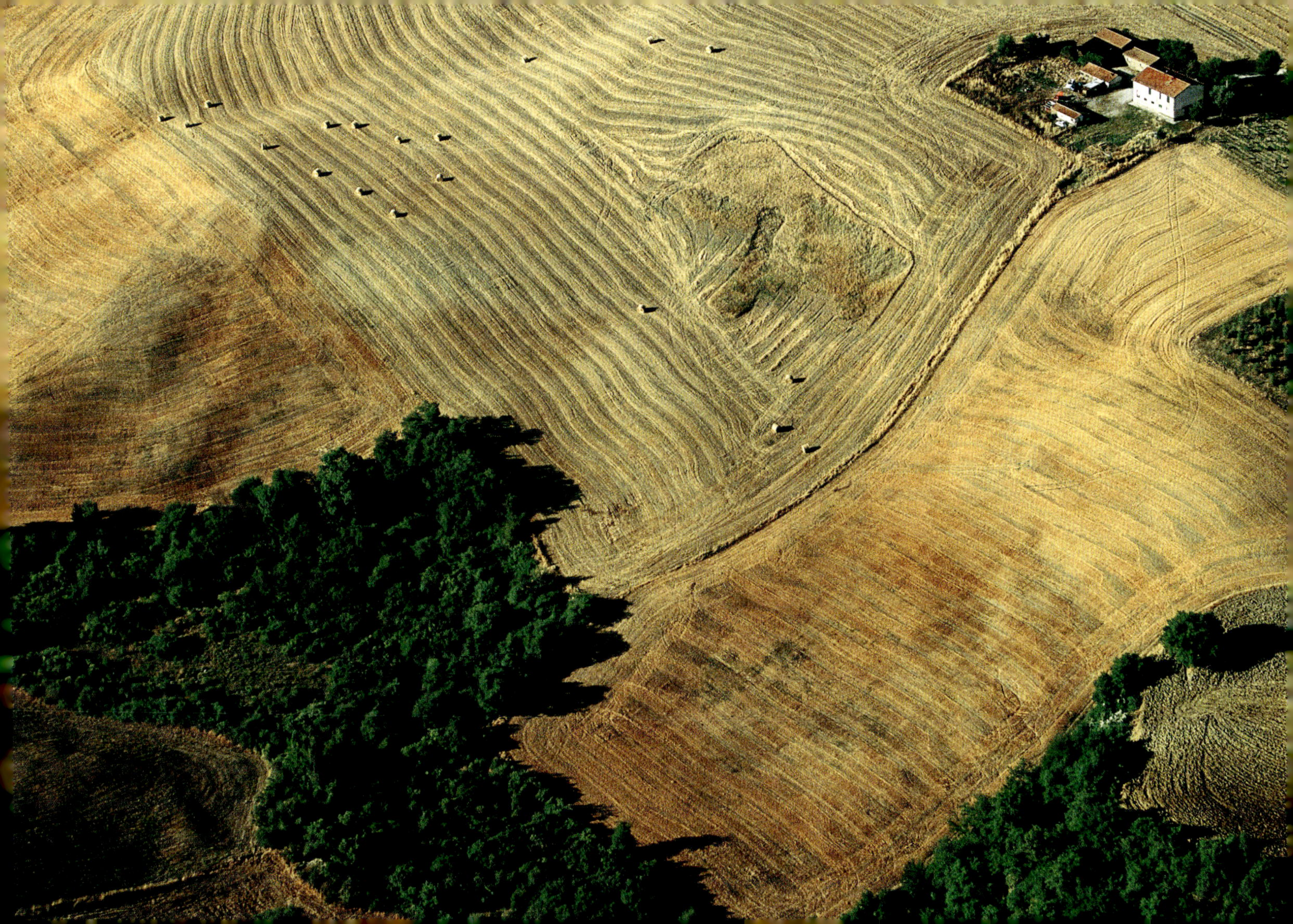

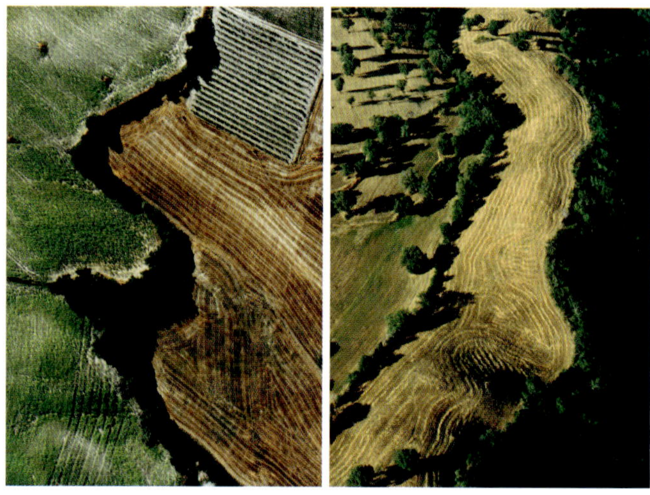

100 and 101

In this area of the Metalliferous Hills, copses of chestnuts and cork trees alternate with fields of grain, creating a pathwork of various textures and colors, bound together by the green trees that line the paths.

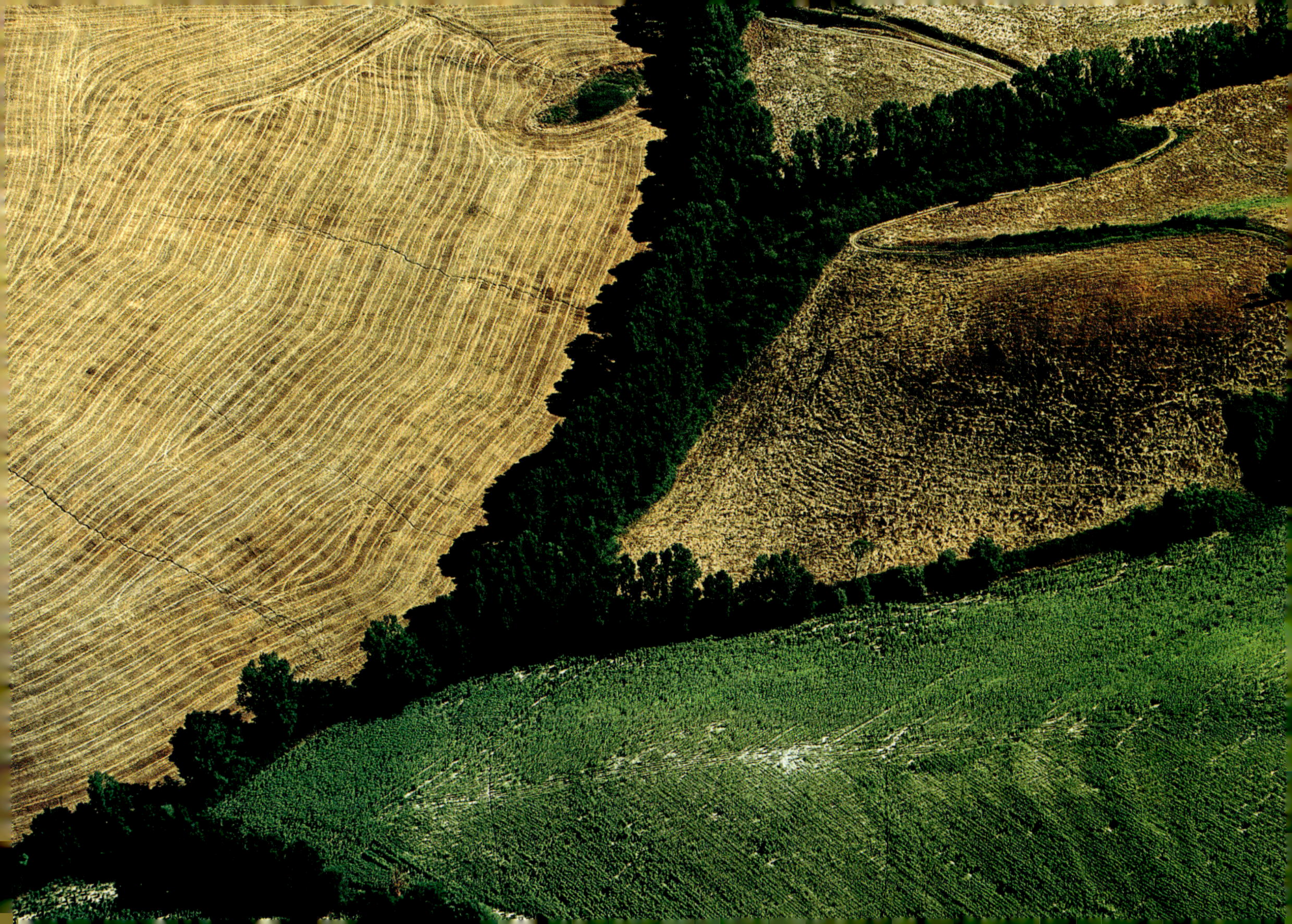

103

This estate dominates one of the hills in the Metalliferous Hill region. The copses around the estate testify to the rapidity with which nature takes back land not constantly cultivated or reclaimed.

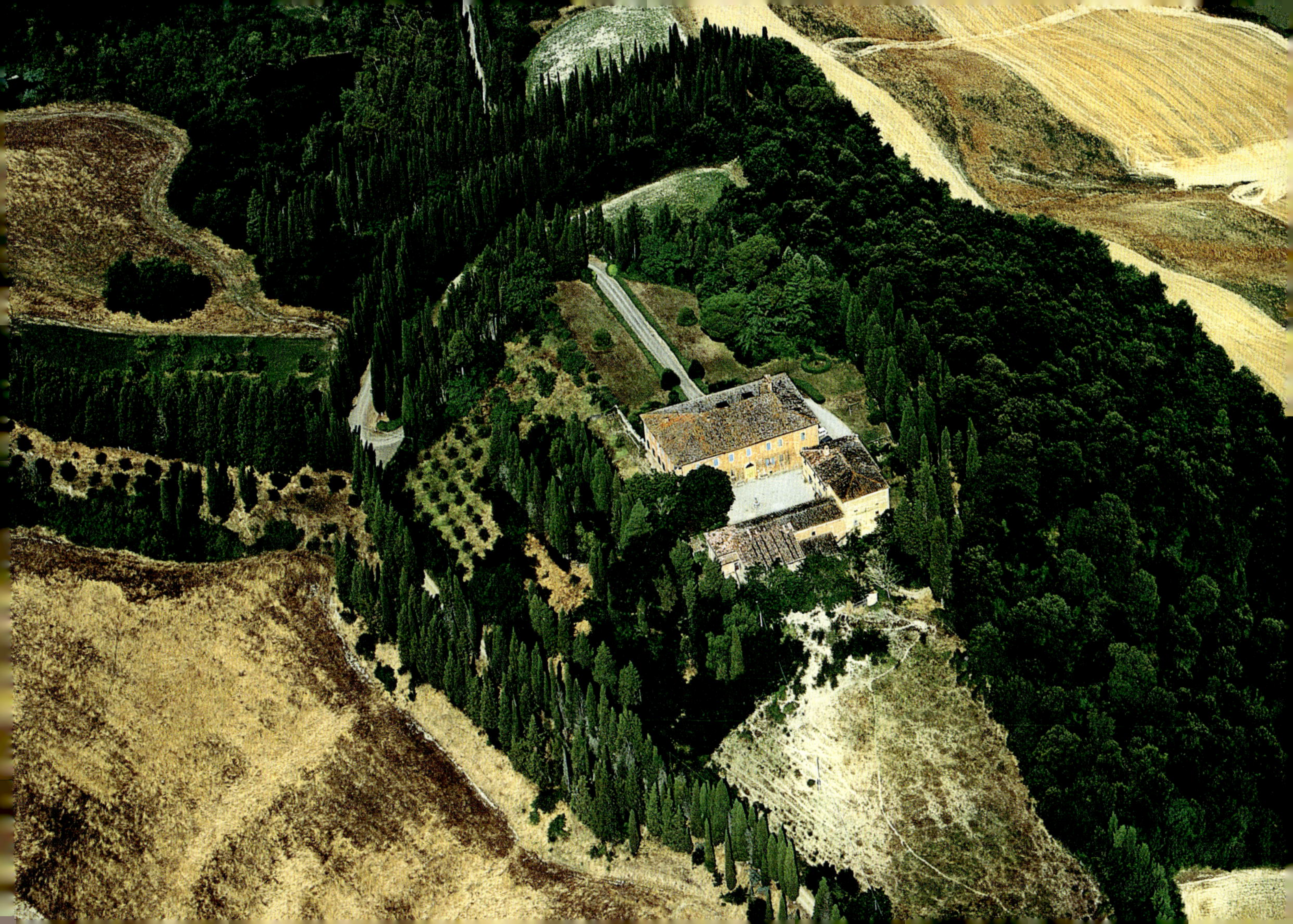

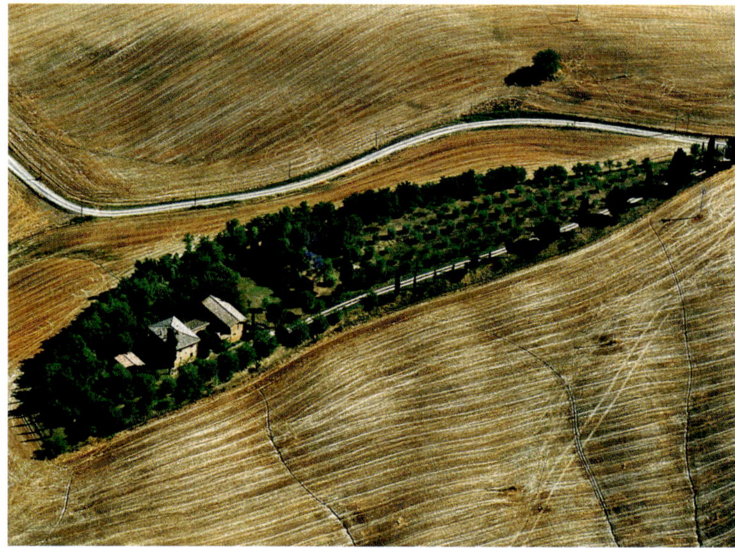

104
A swathe of green stands out in the Sienese countryside, a island in a sea of sun-bleached grass.

105
The seemingly random concentric tracks left by the tractors collecting bales of hay overlap the long, straight tracks of the combine harvester.

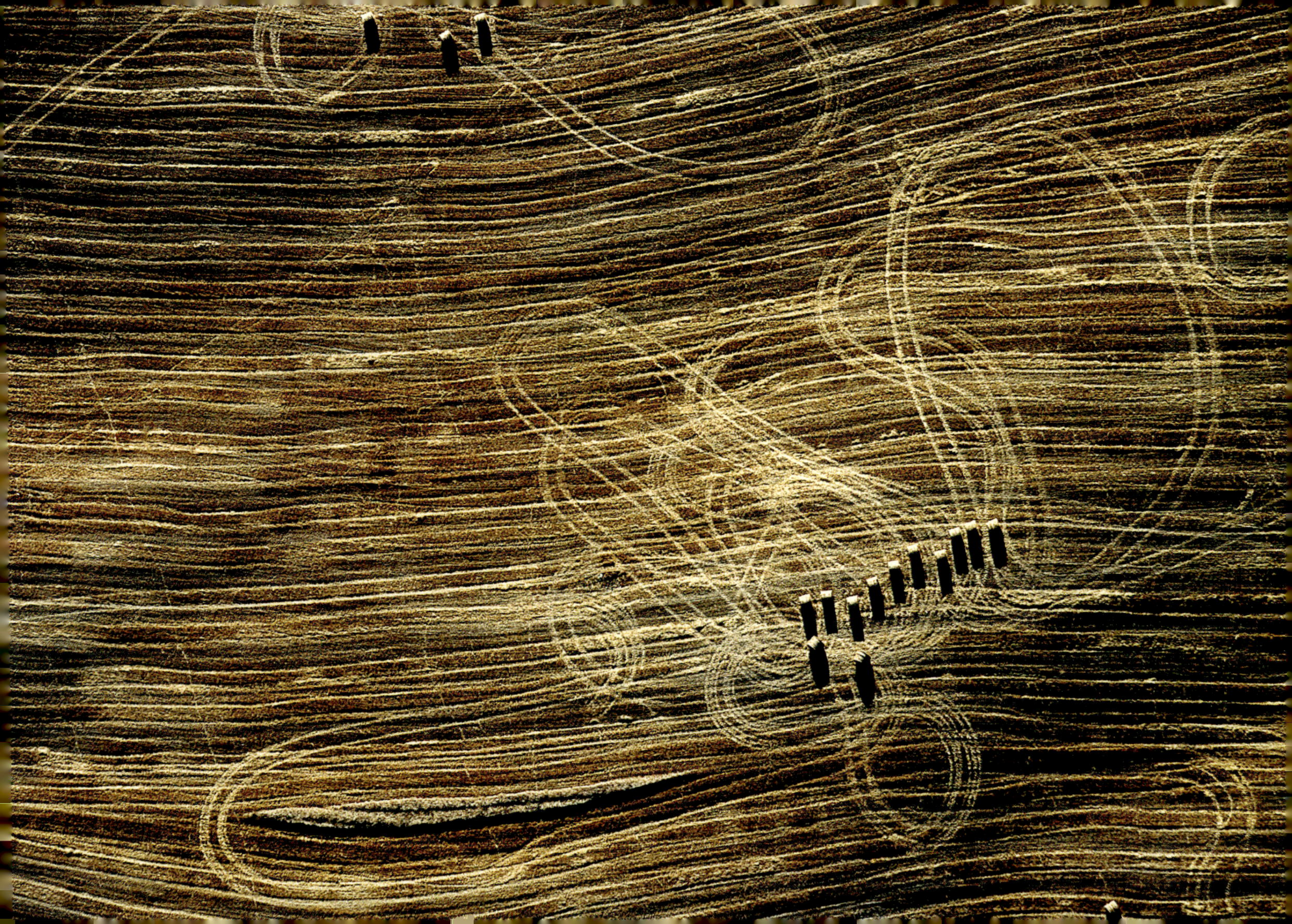

107

A herd of aproximately 200 sheep grazing in a field near Chiusdino, rendering white the typically ocher-colored land of the Siena-region Metalliferous Hills.

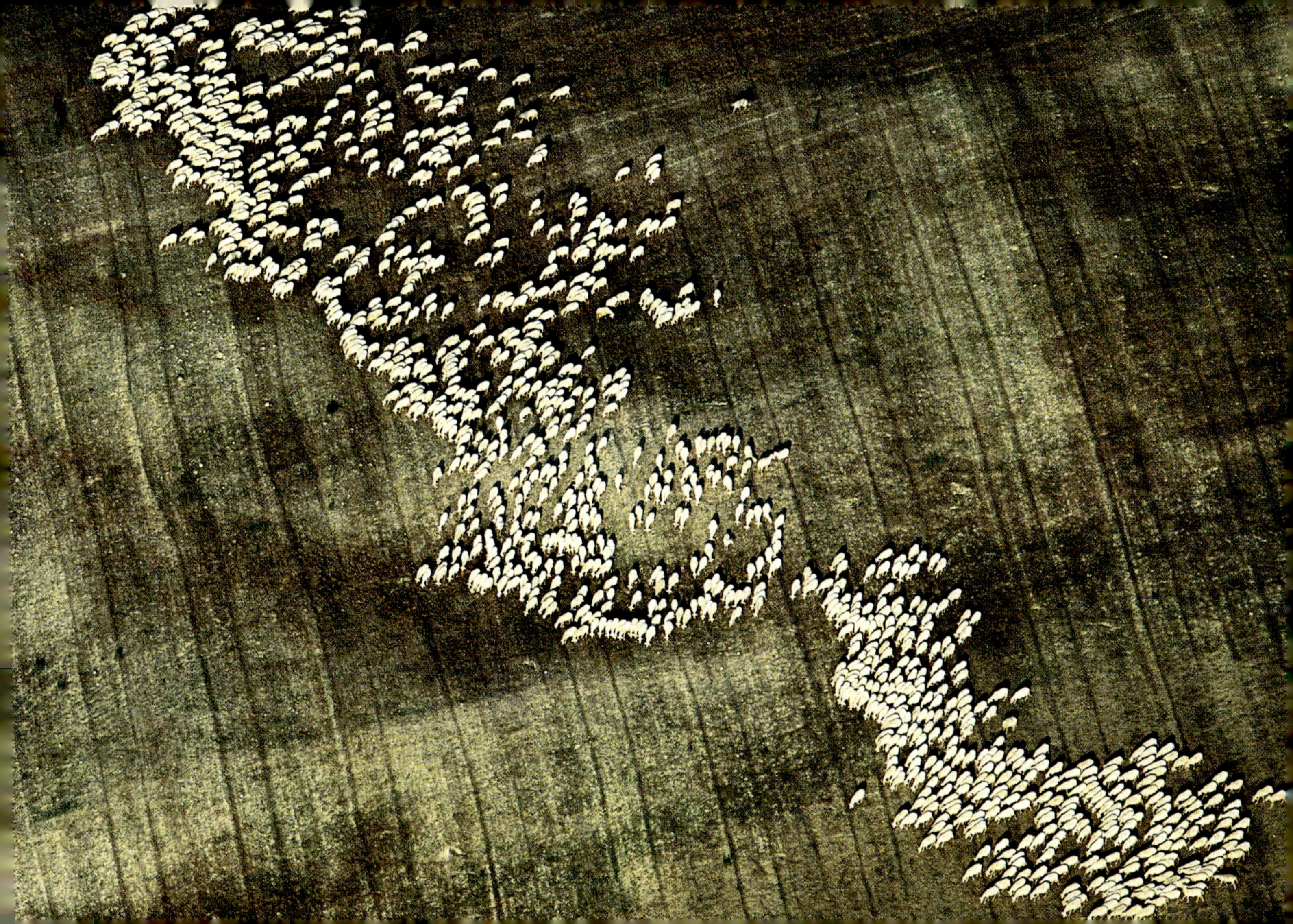

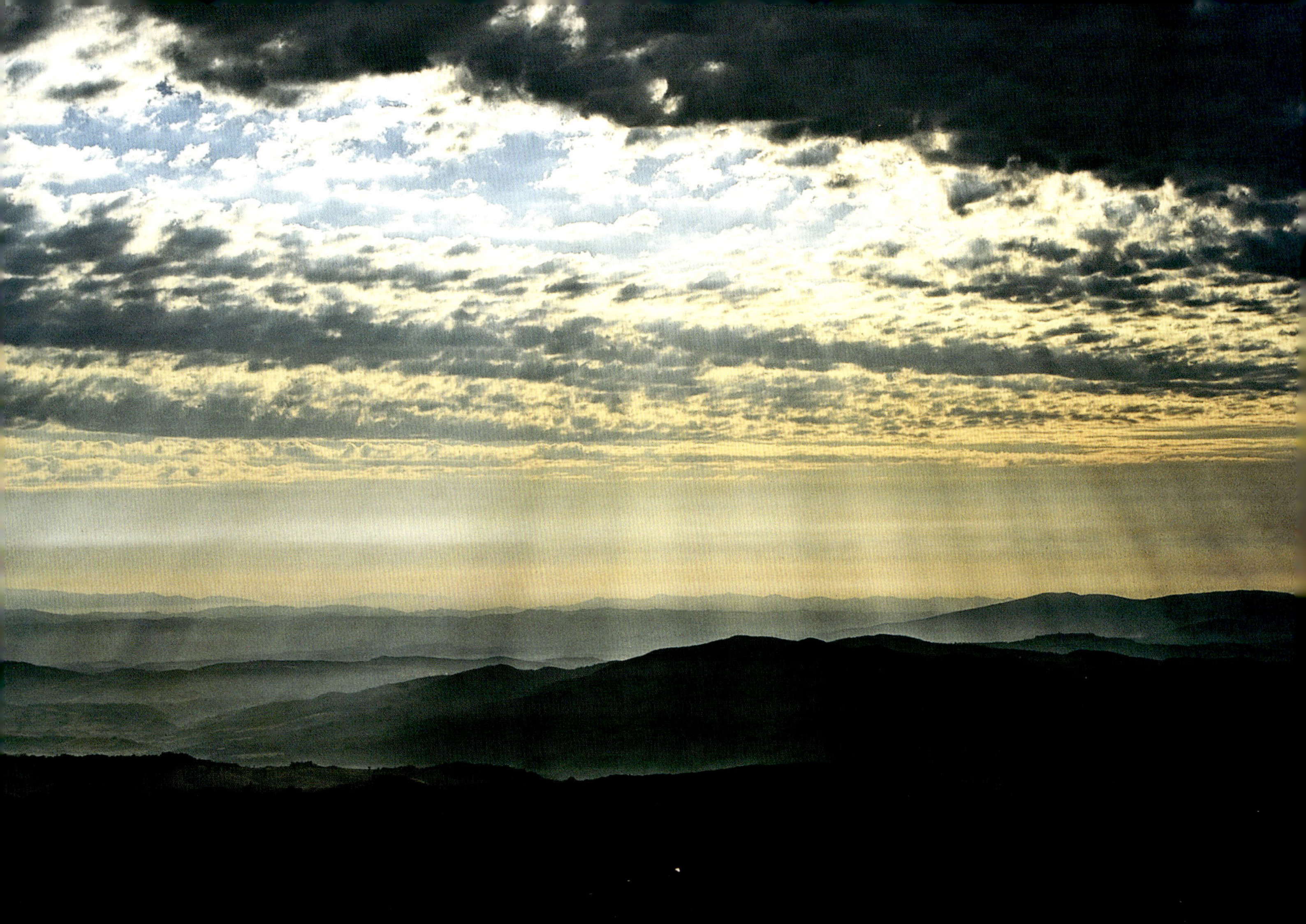

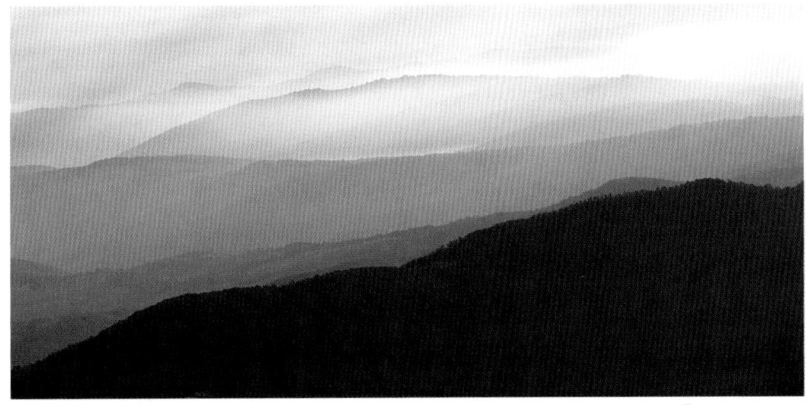

108 and 109

A flight over the region that extends from Volterra to Massa Marittima offers the splendid sight of the southern Metalliferous Hills, which descend toward the plains of the Maremma.

110

This bizarre abstract design at Manciano is a sort of rural bas-relief created by the green of the forest and the ocher of the cultivated land.

111

This hilltop estate, a few miles from Capannoli, is bounded by an unpaved road. The presence of the copse, grape vines, olive groves, grain fields and pasture land suggests its medieval, mixed-use origins.

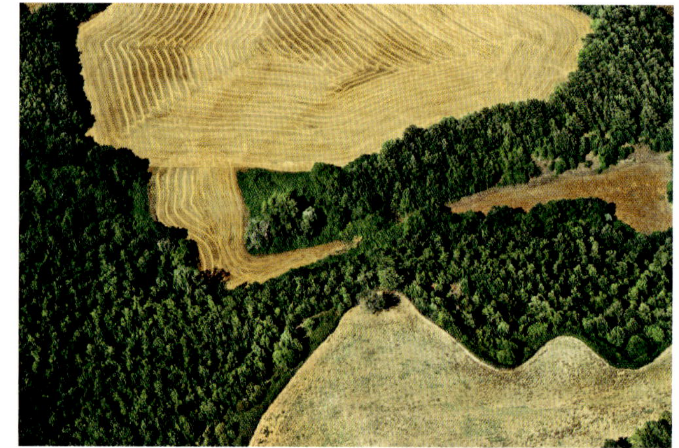

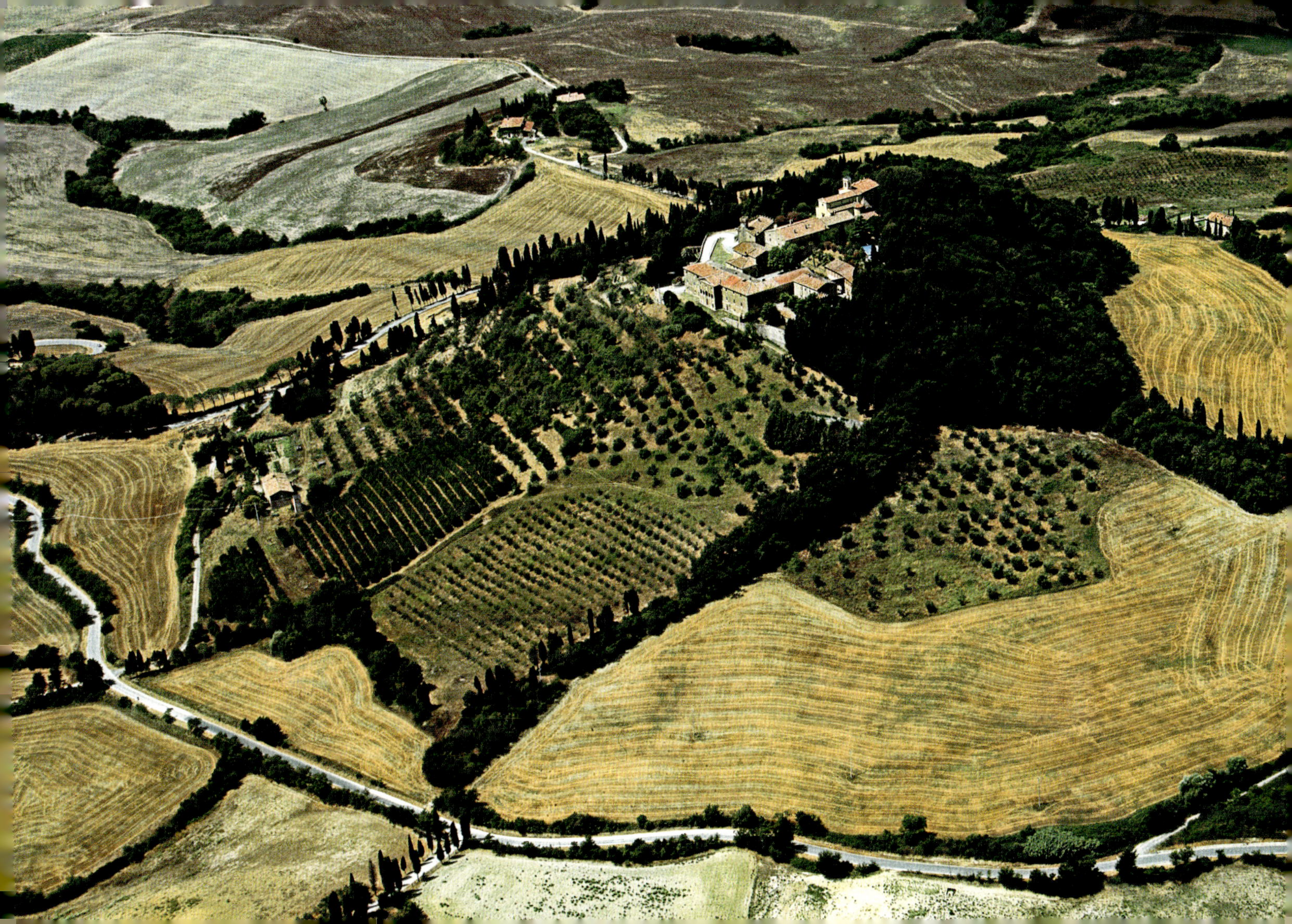

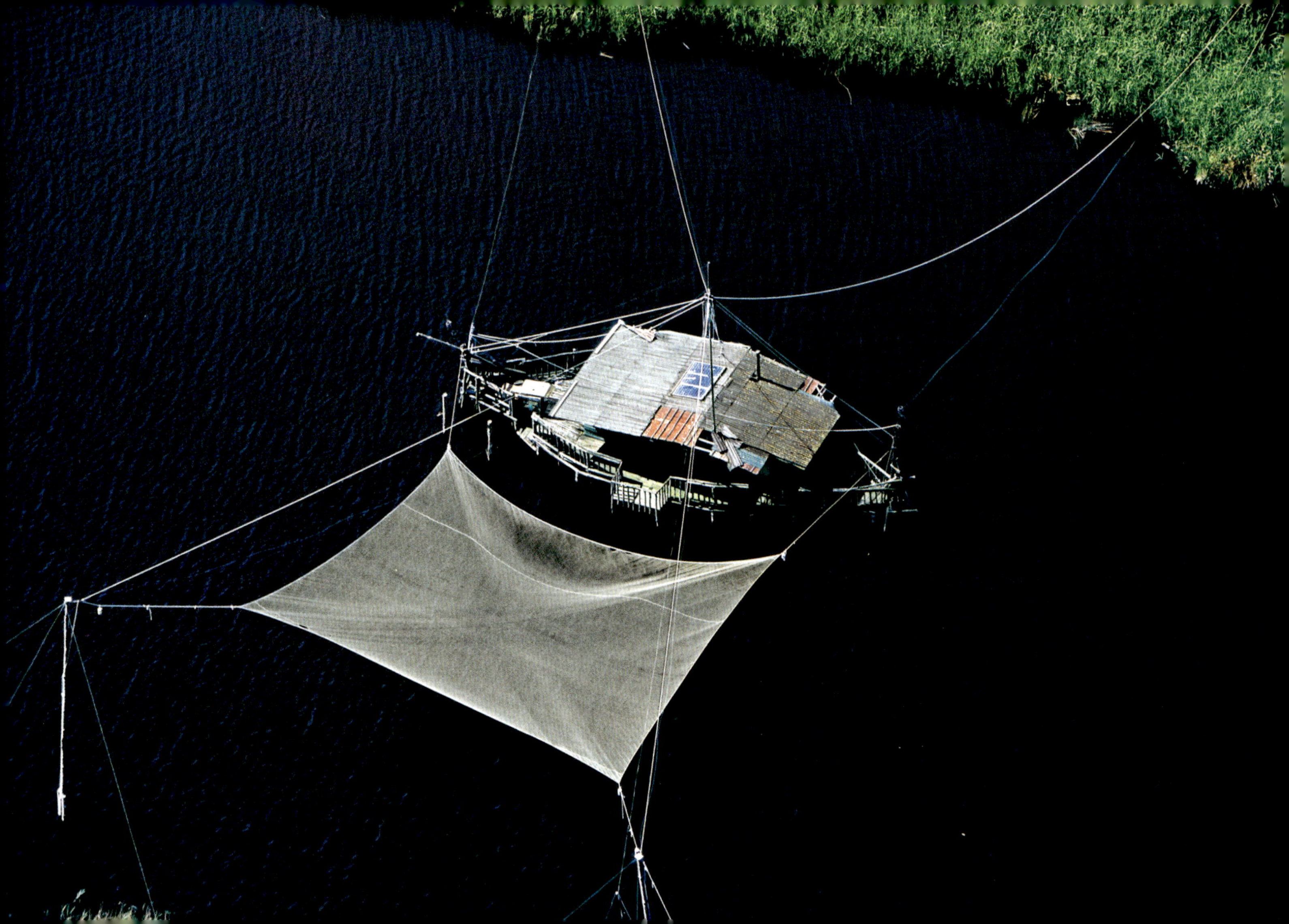

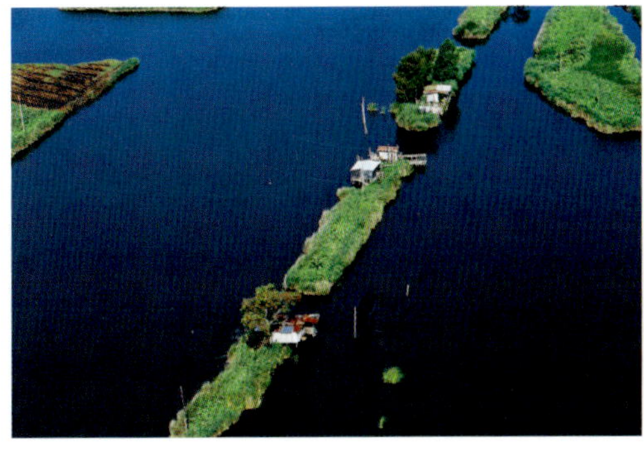

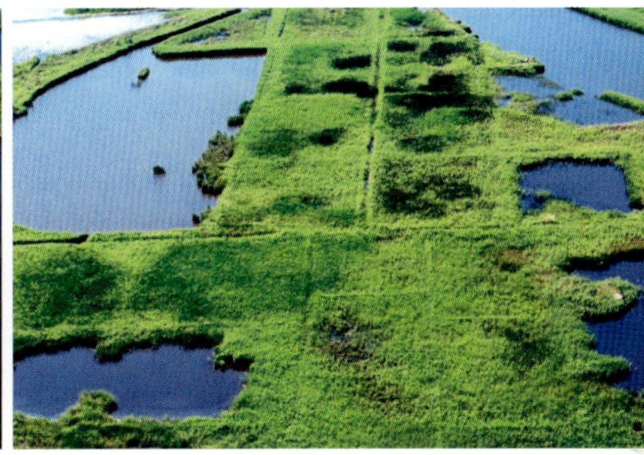

112 and 113
Lake Massaciuccoli, not far from Viareggio and Pisa opens onto land reclaimed only in the 18th century. The lake, where fishing and hunting are practiced, is the only marshland left in this part of Tuscany.

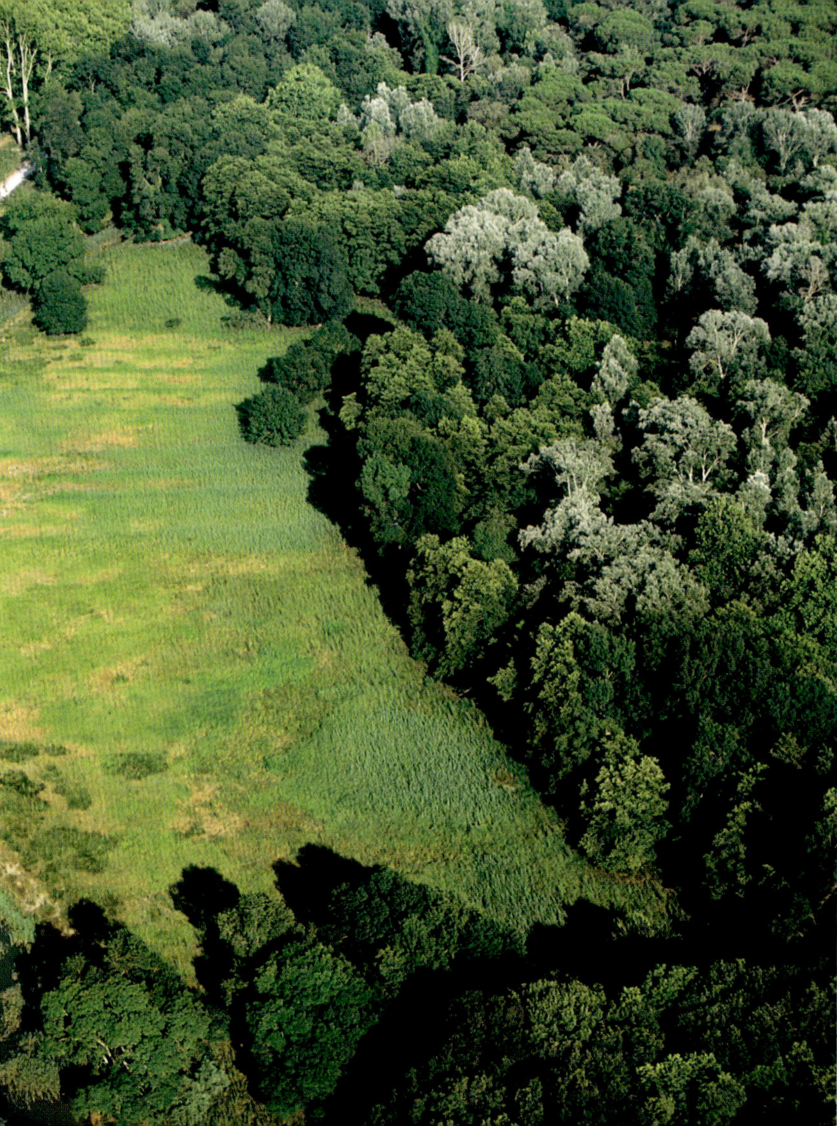

114 and 115
Migliarino Natural Park covers over 70 sq. miles (14,000 hectares) along the coast near Pisa. It contains extraordinary forests and marshes in the heart of its vast pine woods.

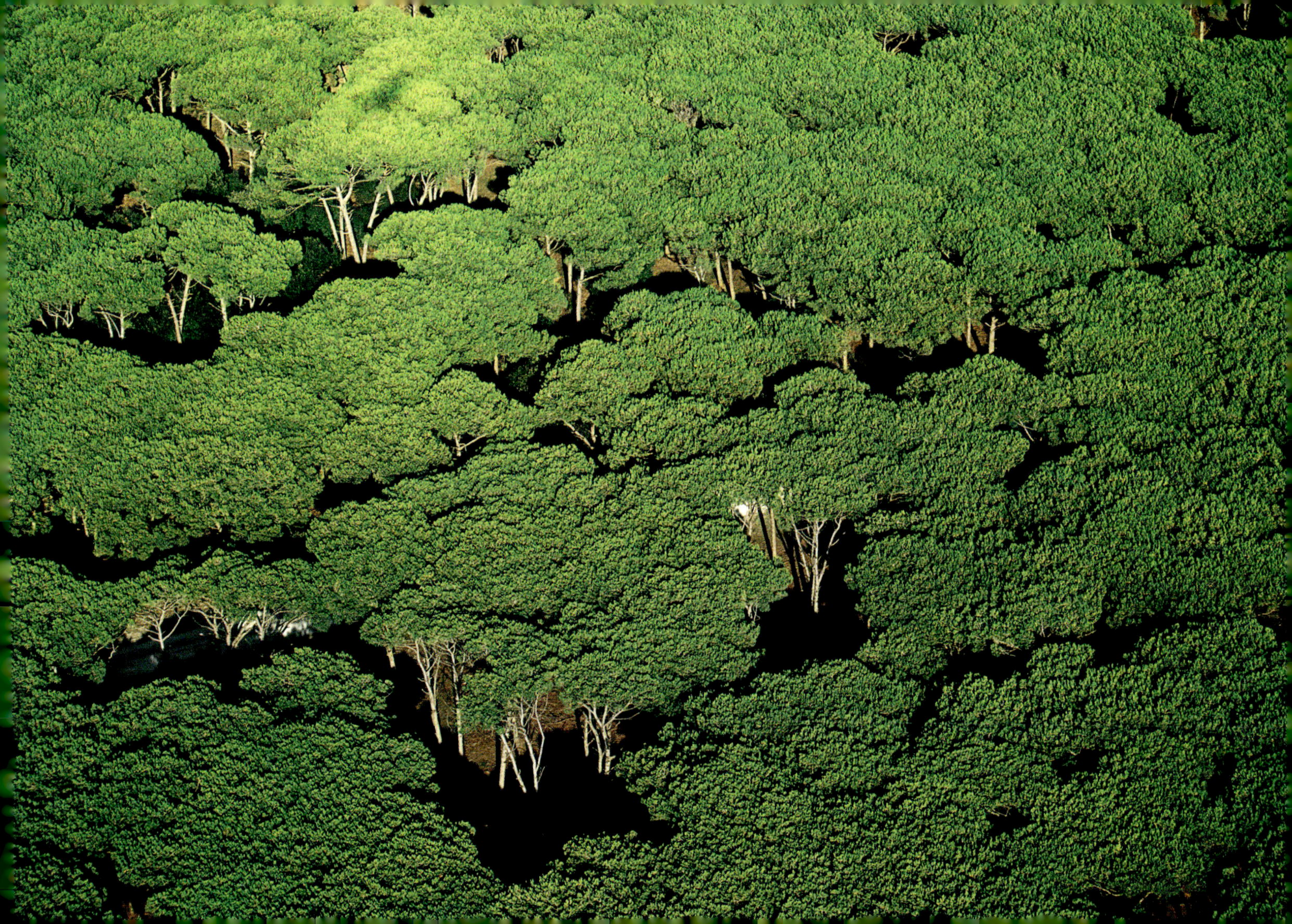

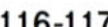

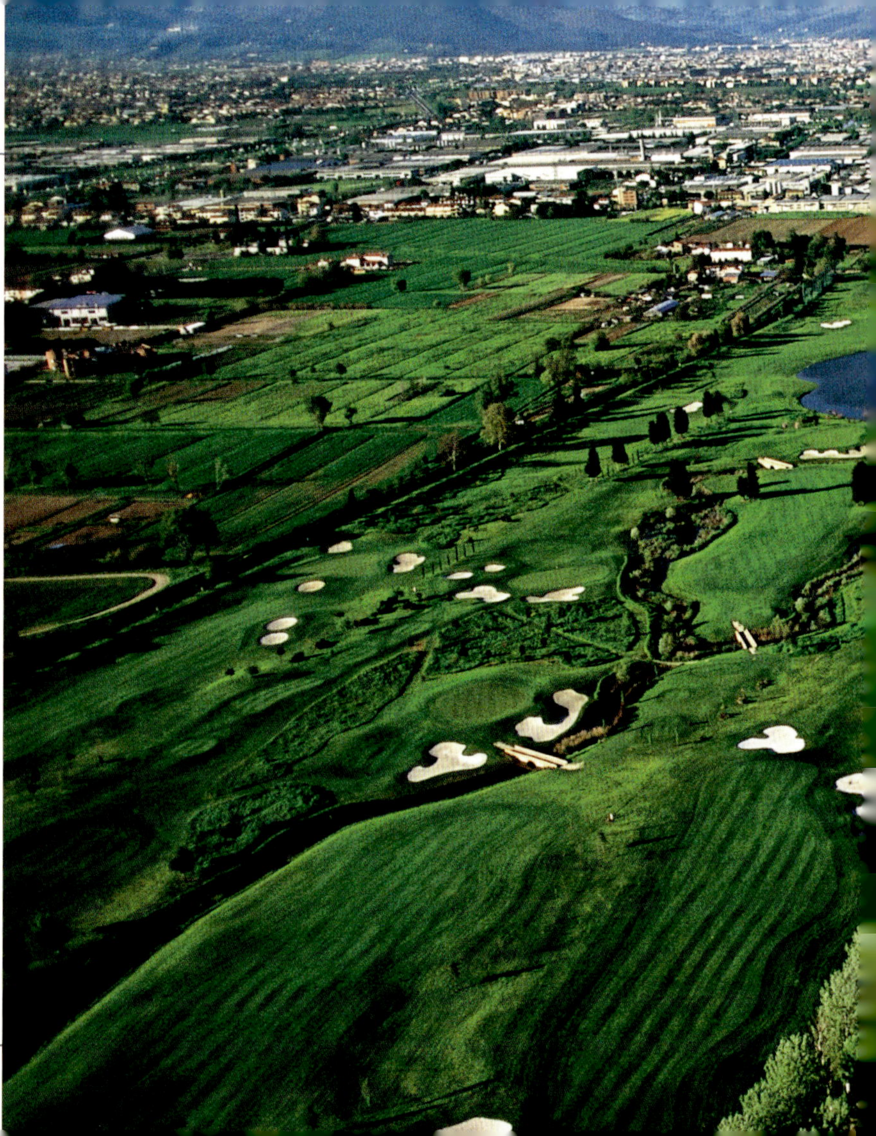

116-117

Prato extends over an alluvial plain bounded by the Tuscan-Emilian Mountains. The immense green area is the Le Pavoniere Golf Club.

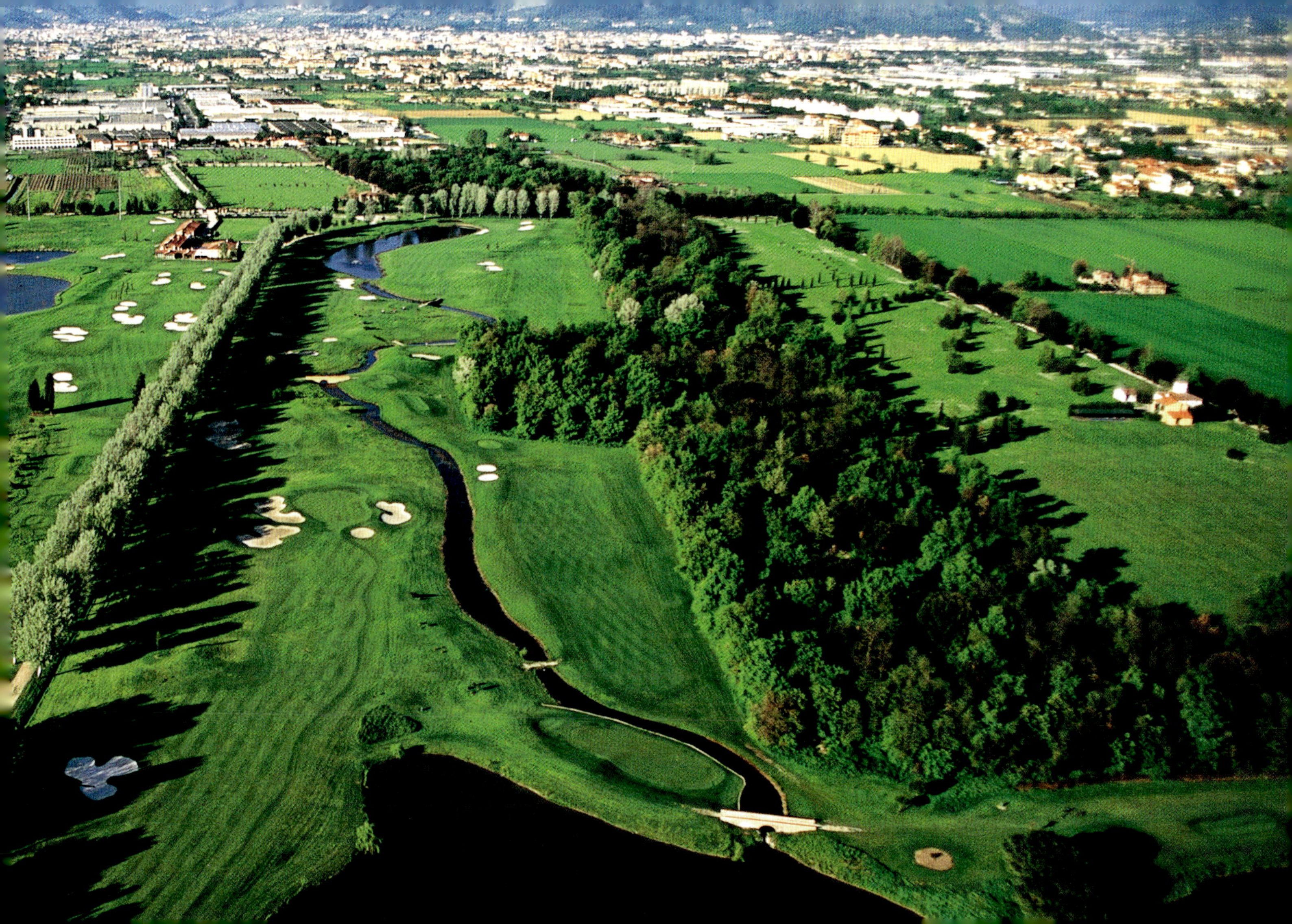

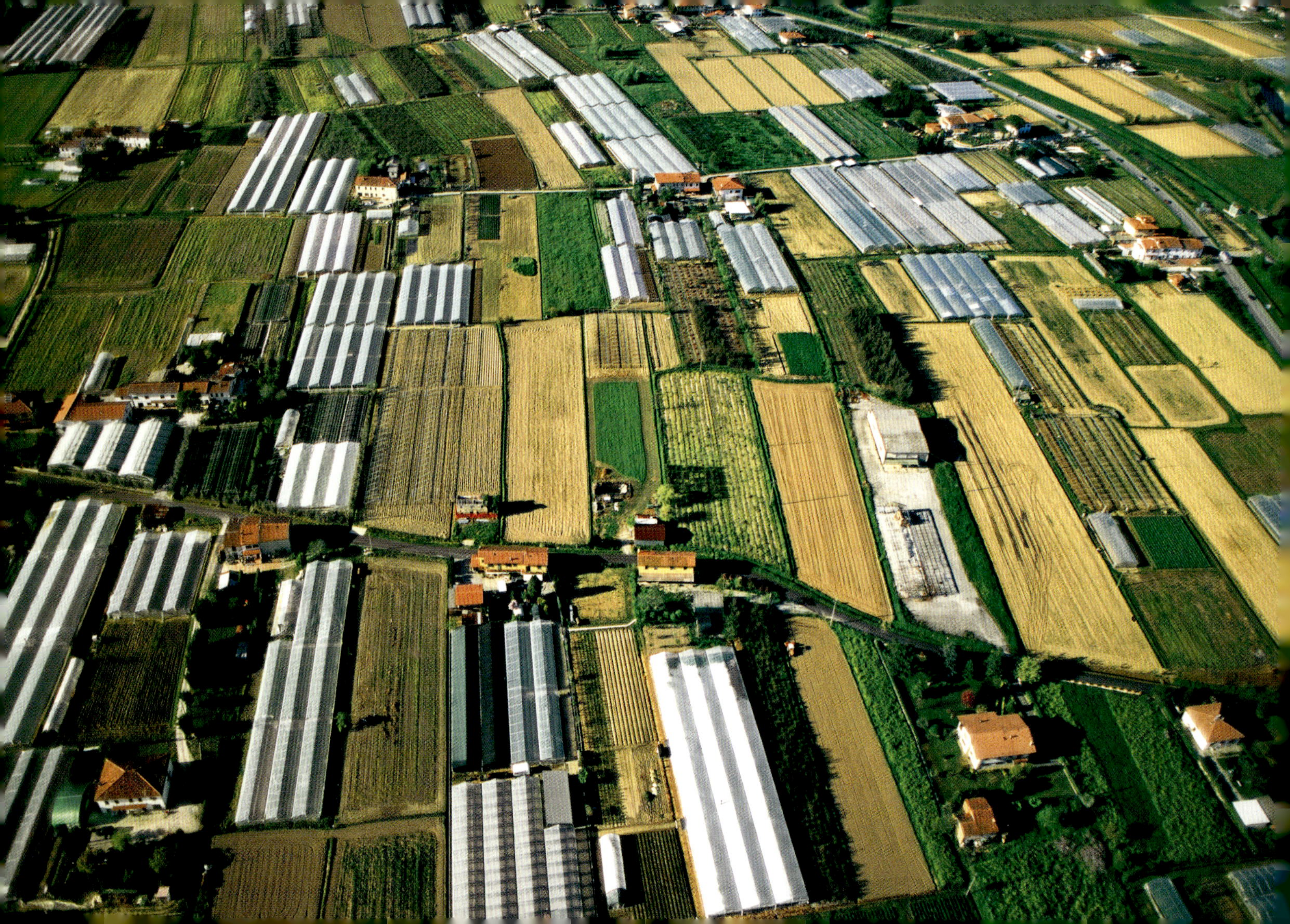

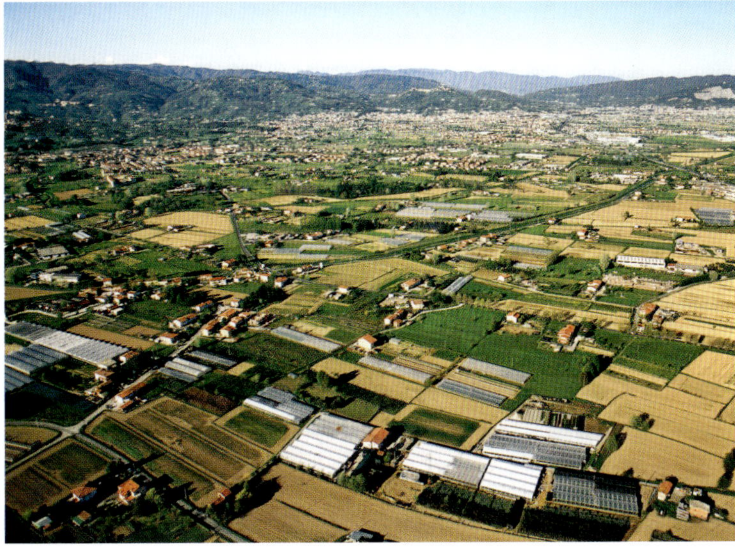

118
The fruit and vegetable farming and nursery gardening are Prato's traditional activities and fill the territory with hothouses like those in the image, a few miles from the city's outskirts.

119
When approaching Pisa from the north, the visitor sees the crown of hills that surrounds the city's outskirts and also the cultivated land along the Arno.

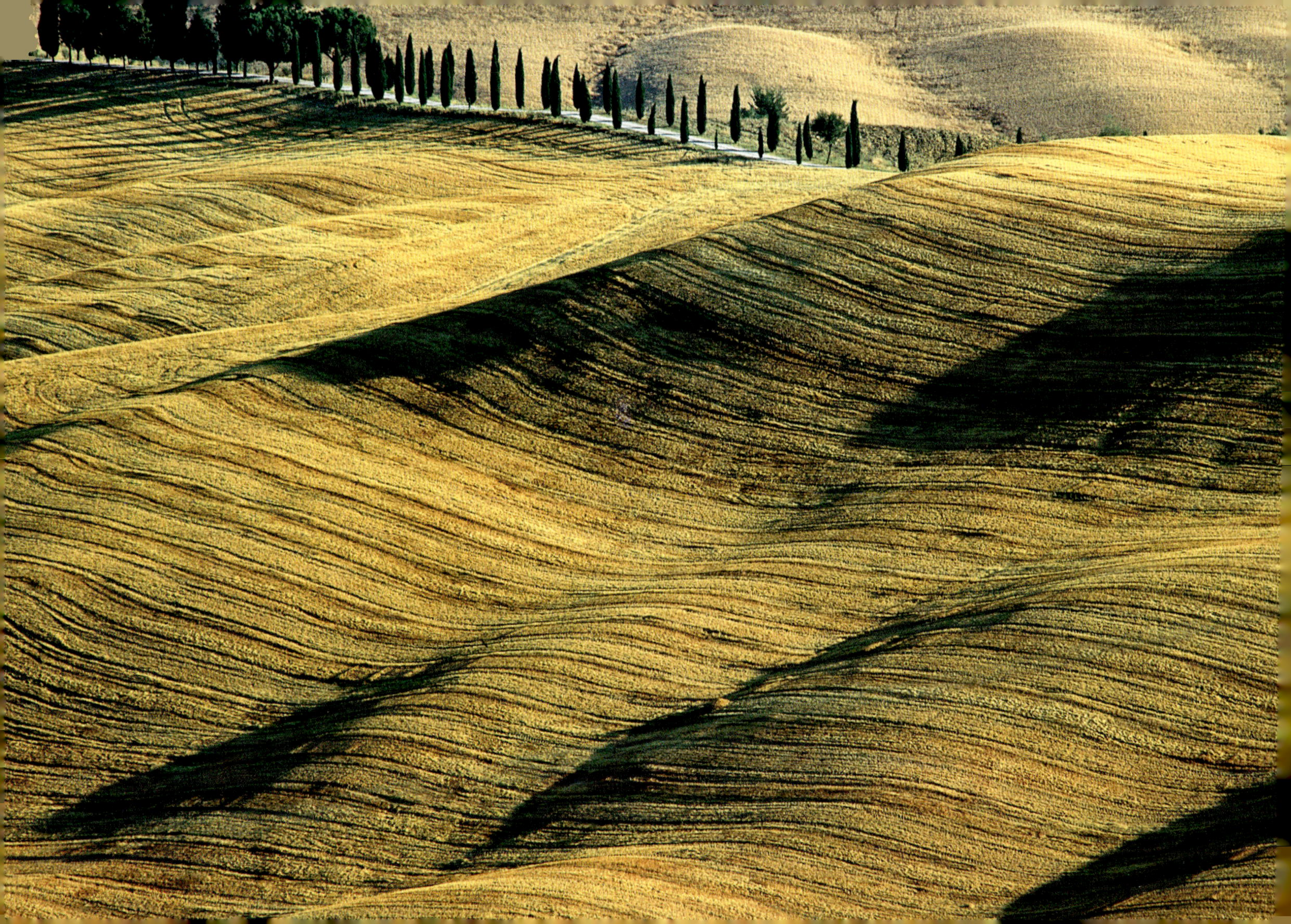

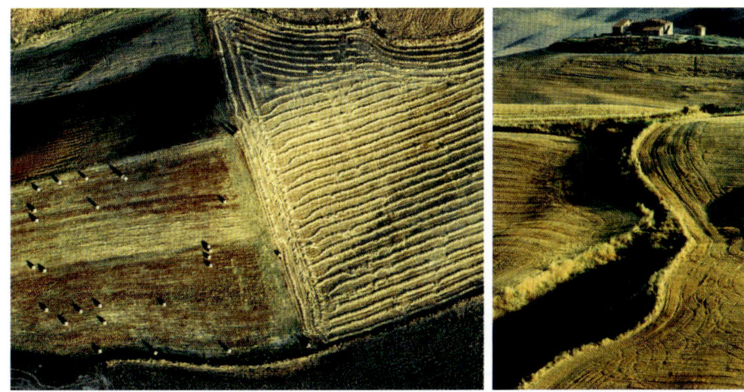

120
The Sienese Cretes, between Siena and Montalcino, create a lunar landscape, fascinating and magical.

121 left
A giant comb seems to have produced this singular mane, rendering this land near Saturnia particularly interesting.

121 right
The Sienese Cretes is argillaceous land, almost completely void of tall vegetation, dominated by the color grey, whose shades change according to the time of day and the season.

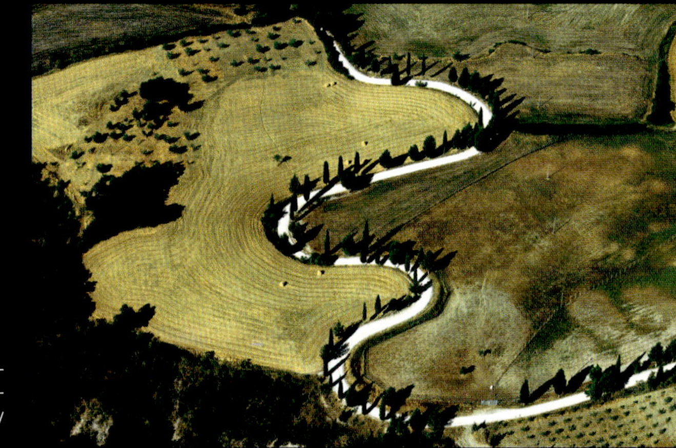

122 and 123
The hills near Siena are indescribably beautiful. Here, a white country road, flanked on either side by cypresses, winds along a hill.

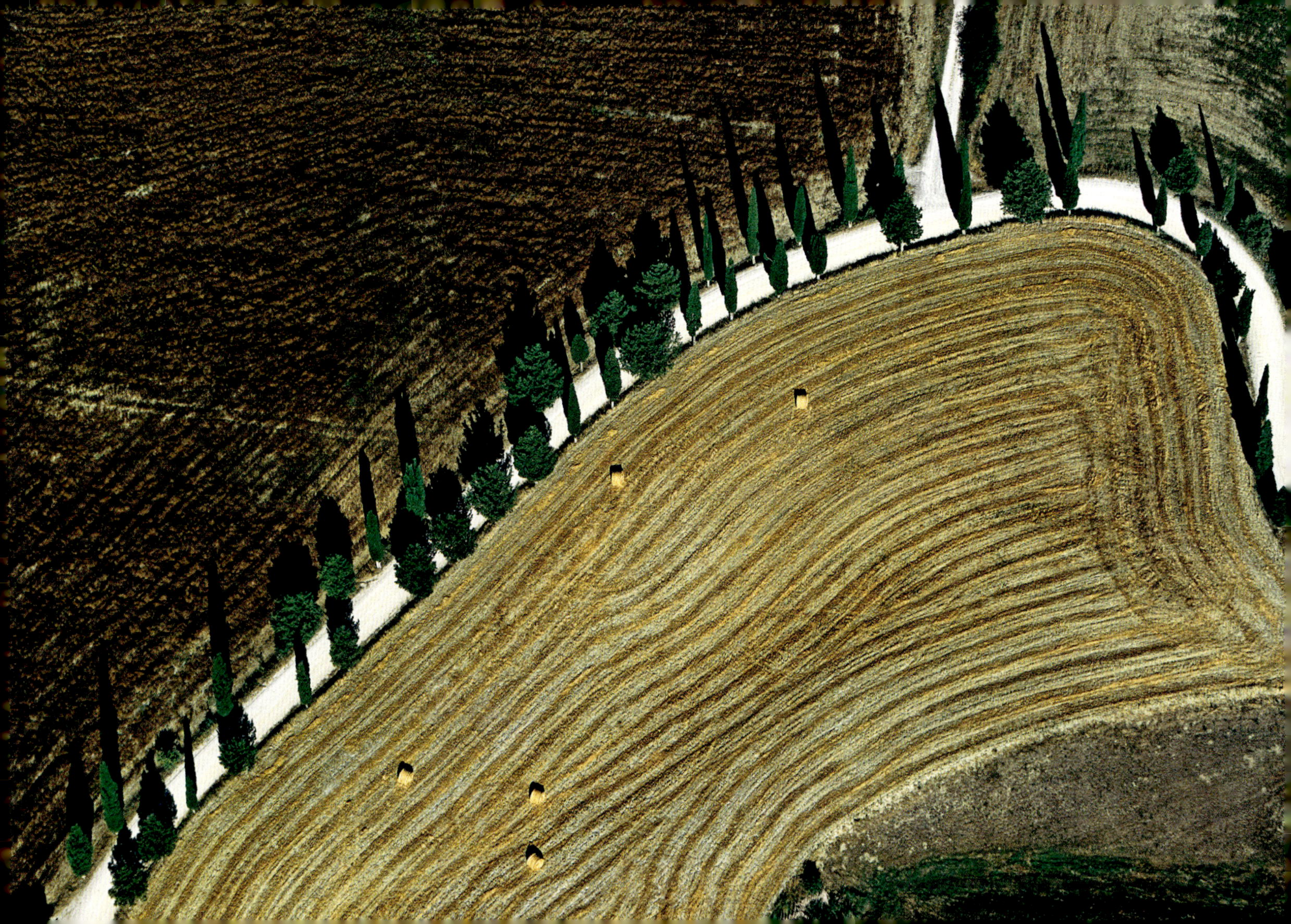

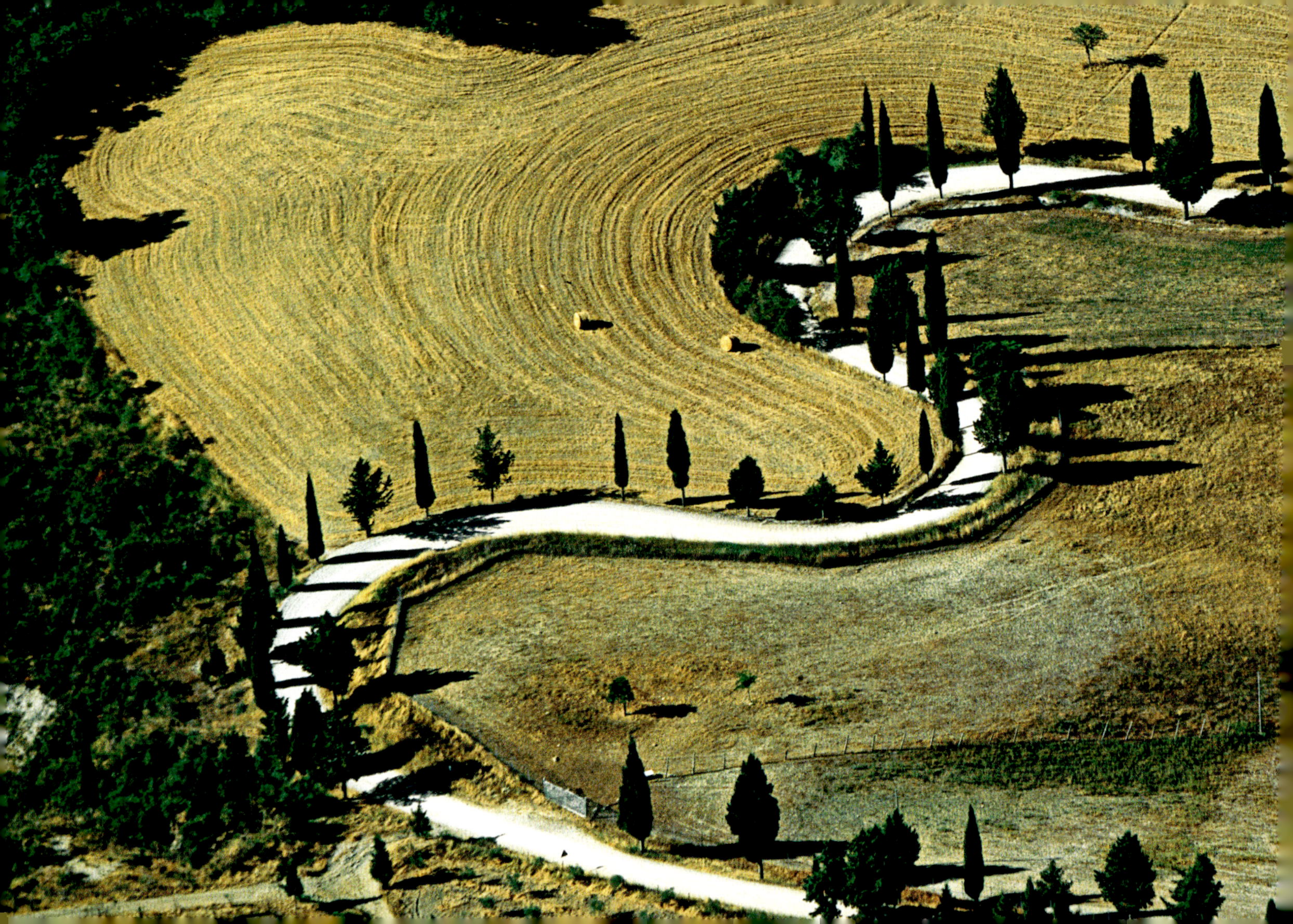

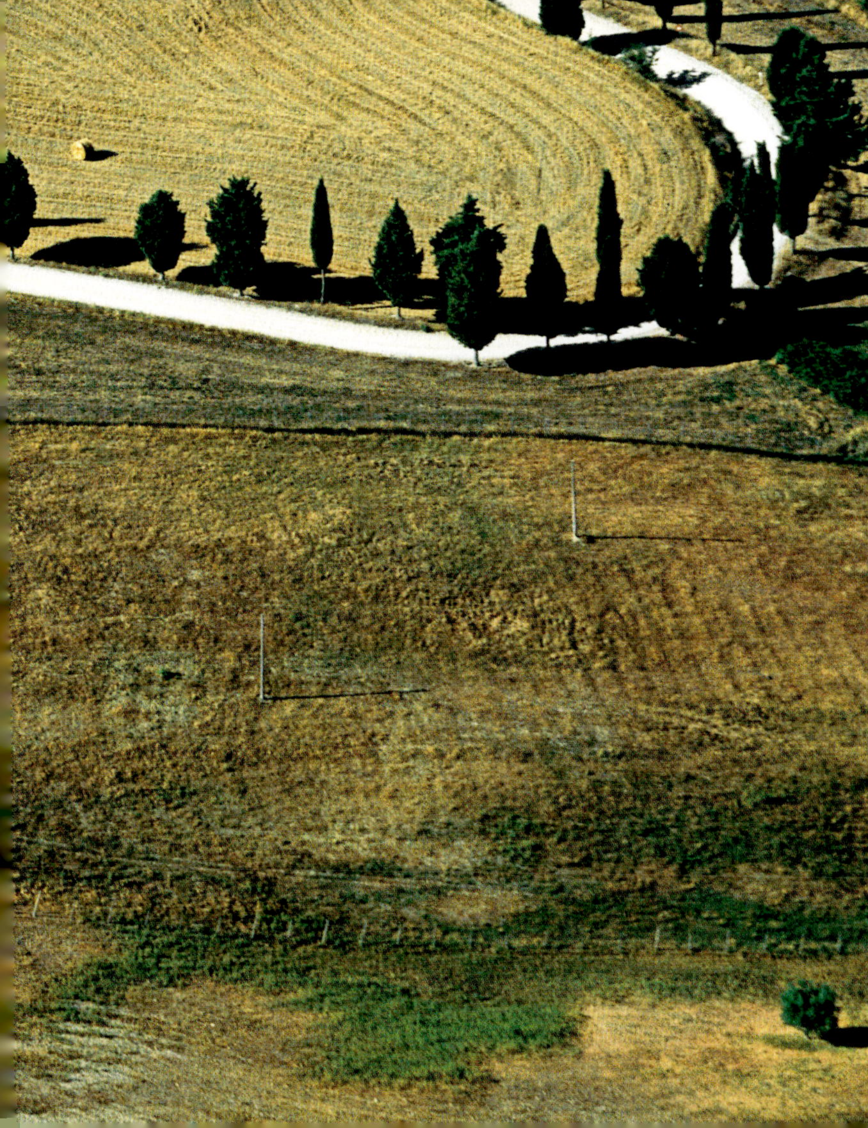

124-125

The cypresses that characterize the Tuscan countryside have long inspired artists and enchanted tourists. They render this Sienese country road uinique and spectacular. Unfortunately, these trees risk extinction due to a disease similar to cancer and to infestation by a very aggressive parasite.

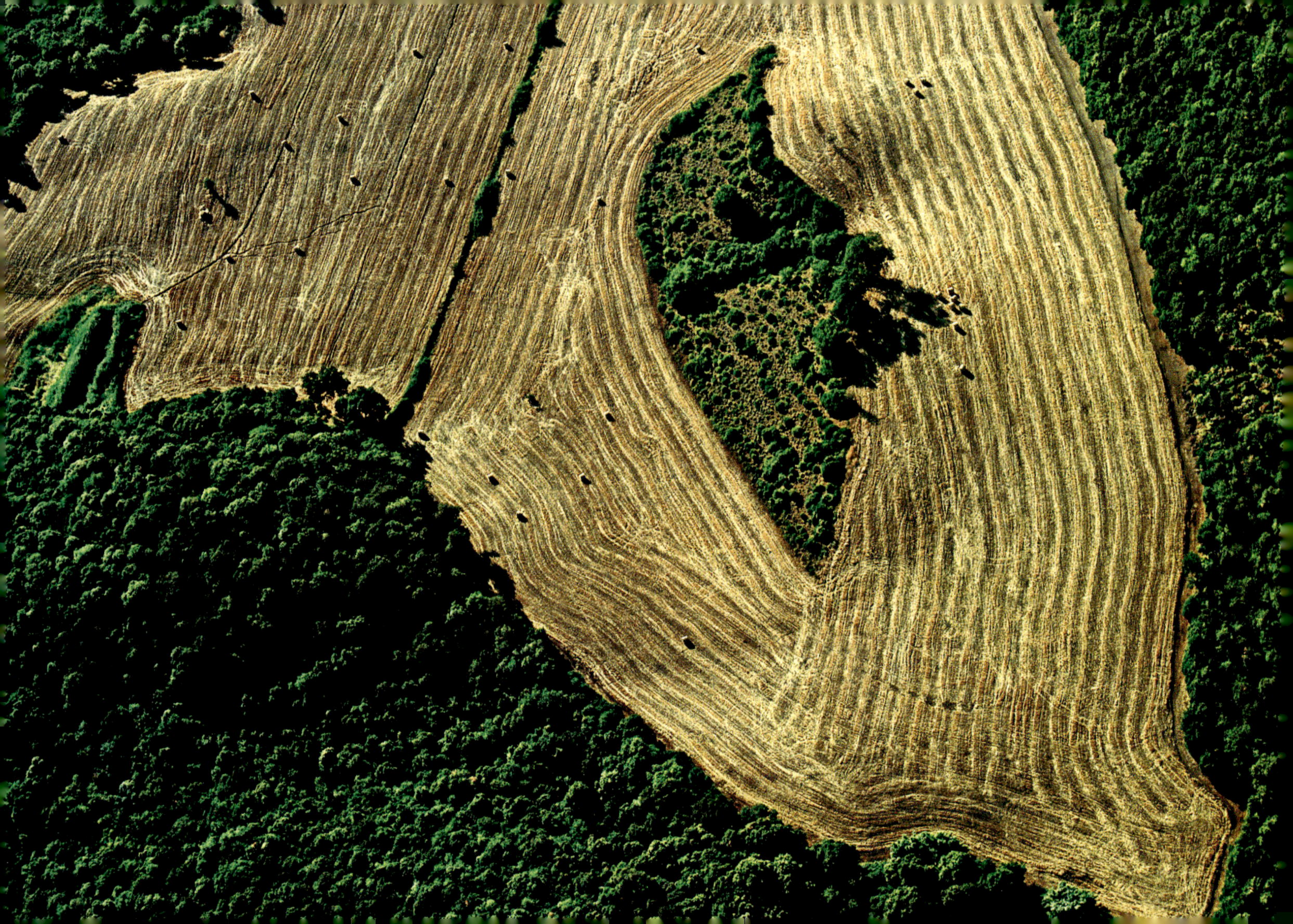

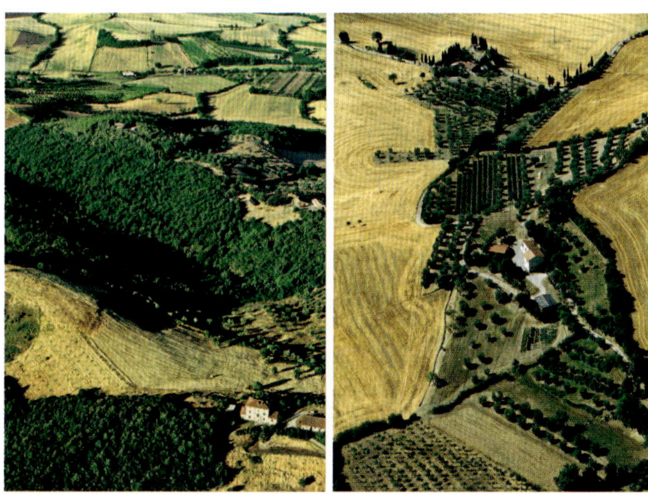

126 and 127 left

The presence of forests on the Metalliferous Hills has made man's efforts at recovering cultivatible land even more arduous.

127 right

Rows of grape vines, olive trees, fruit trees, planted in seemingly random patches, surround this Sienese farm: a green strip amid a yellow expanse of grain fields.

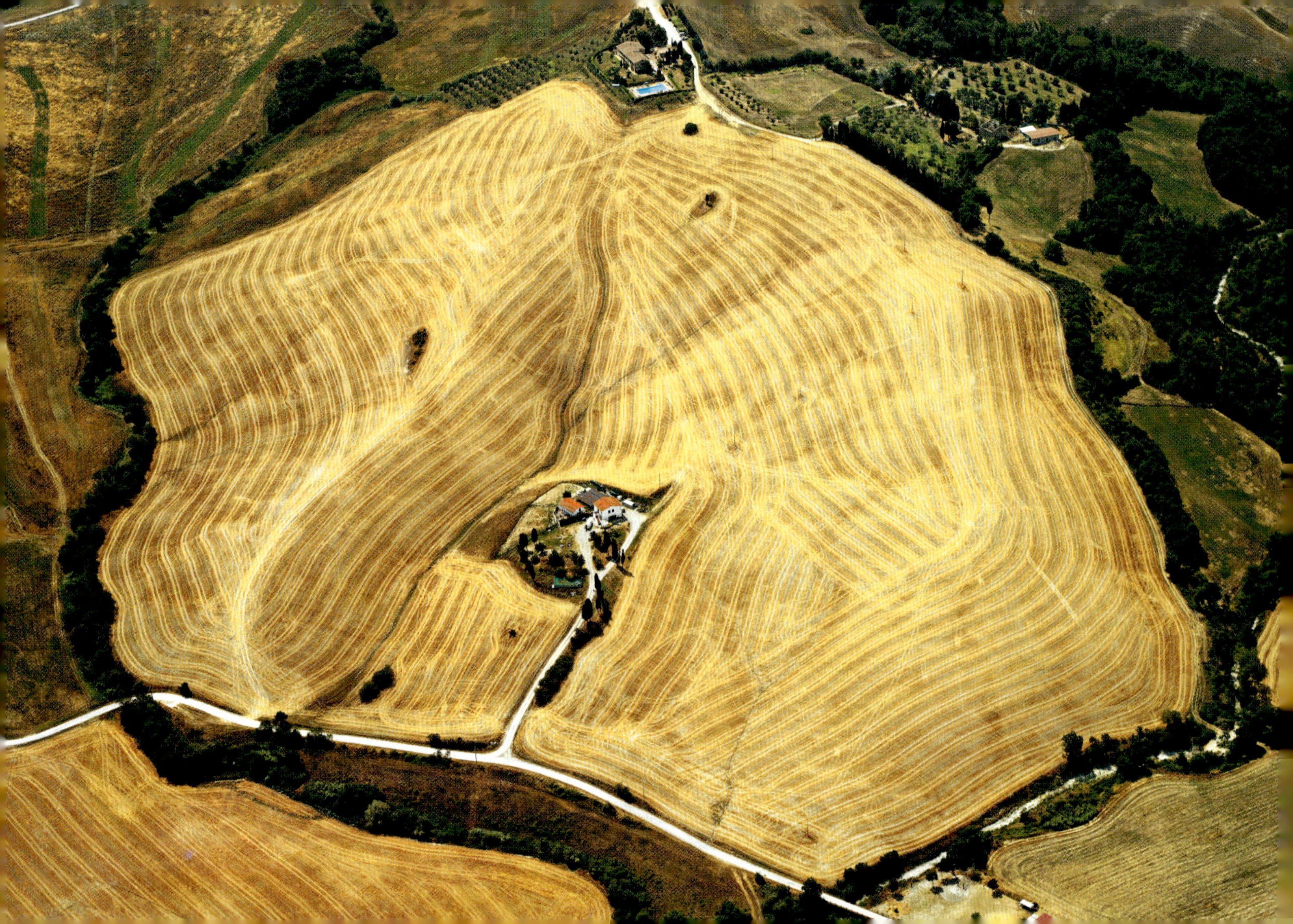

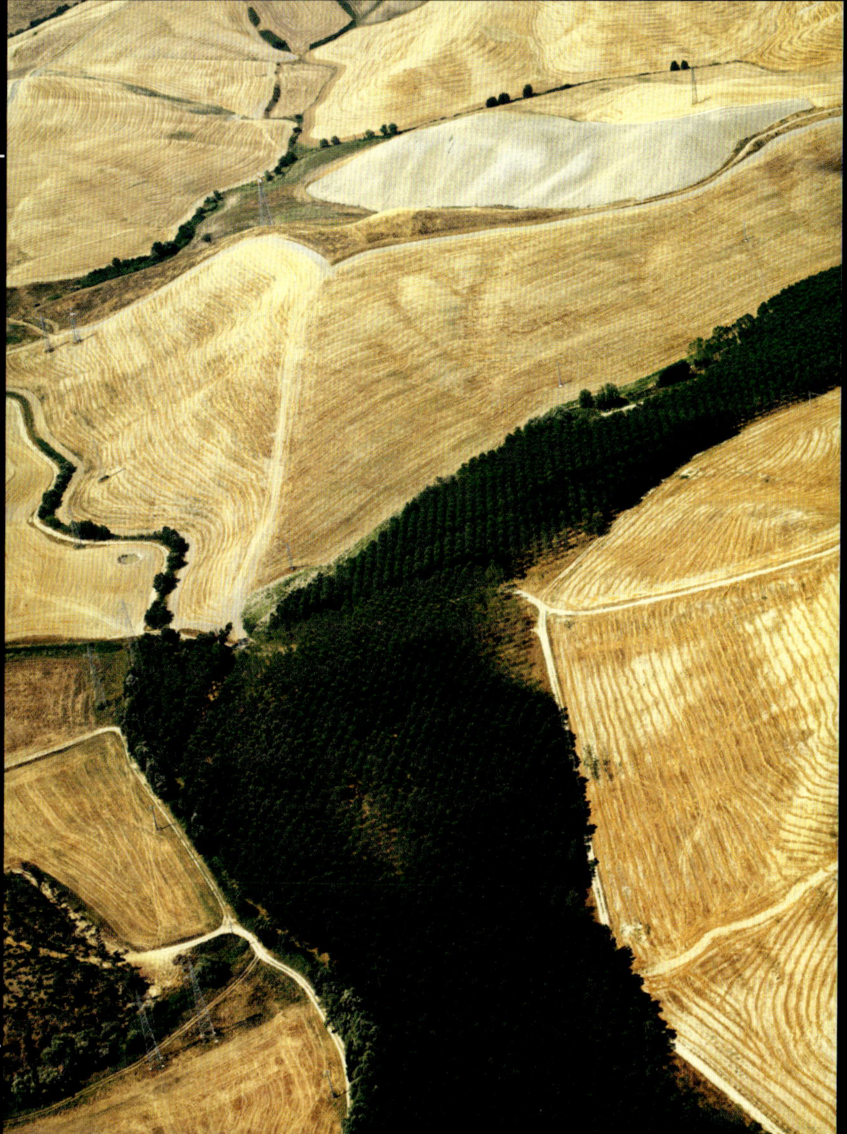

128

Two farms: two ways of integration into Siena's rural flanks: above, one farm with a swimming pool, probably installed for tourists; below, the other, with a haystack and traditional farm equipment, left in the field.

129

Orderly and in precise rows, the olive trees form a large green swathe among the ocher expanse of freshly harvested fields.

130-131

At Tuscany's extreme southern tip, at the border with the Maremma, fertile fields abound, where the yellow of wheat and the ocher of plowed earth dominate.

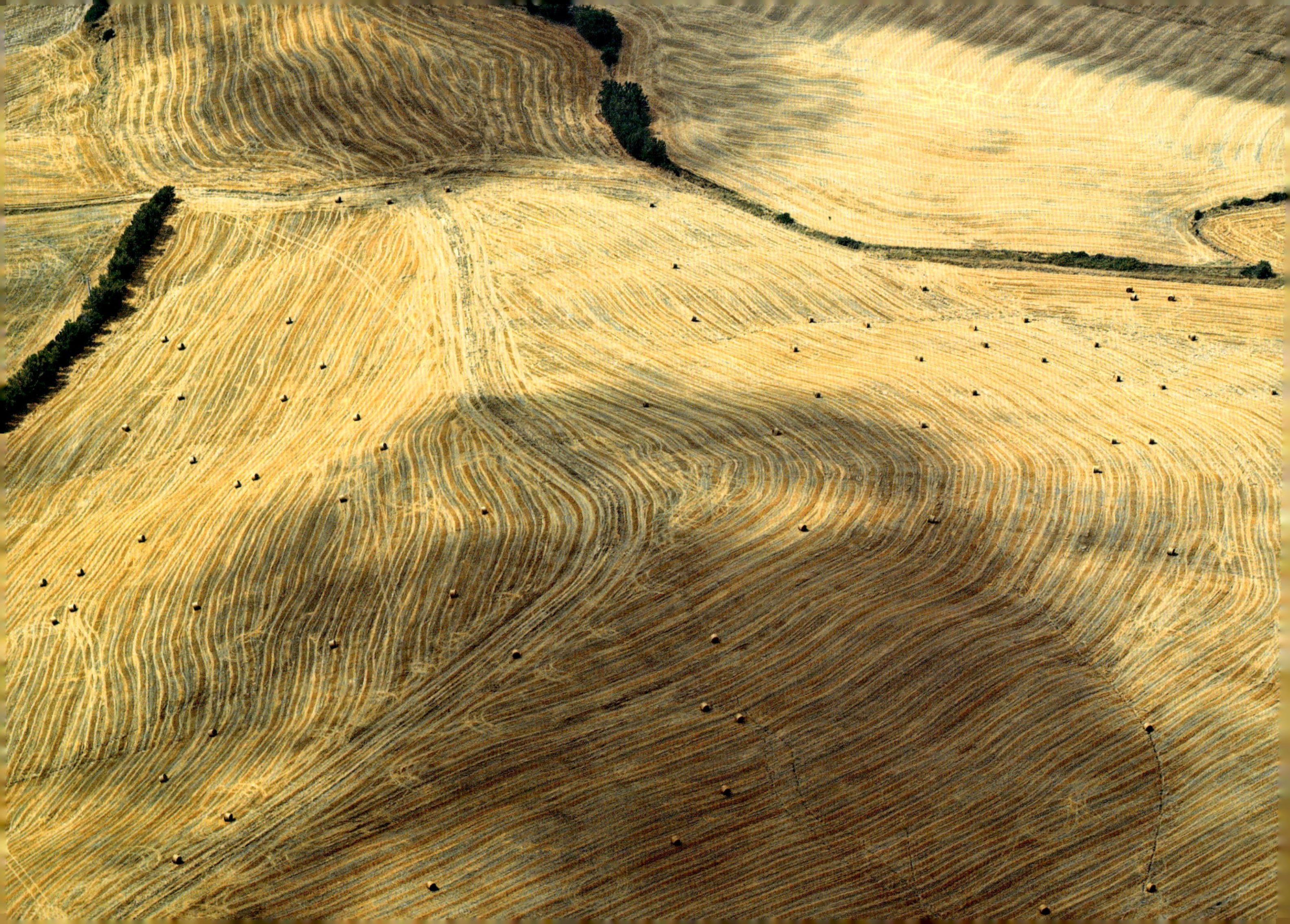

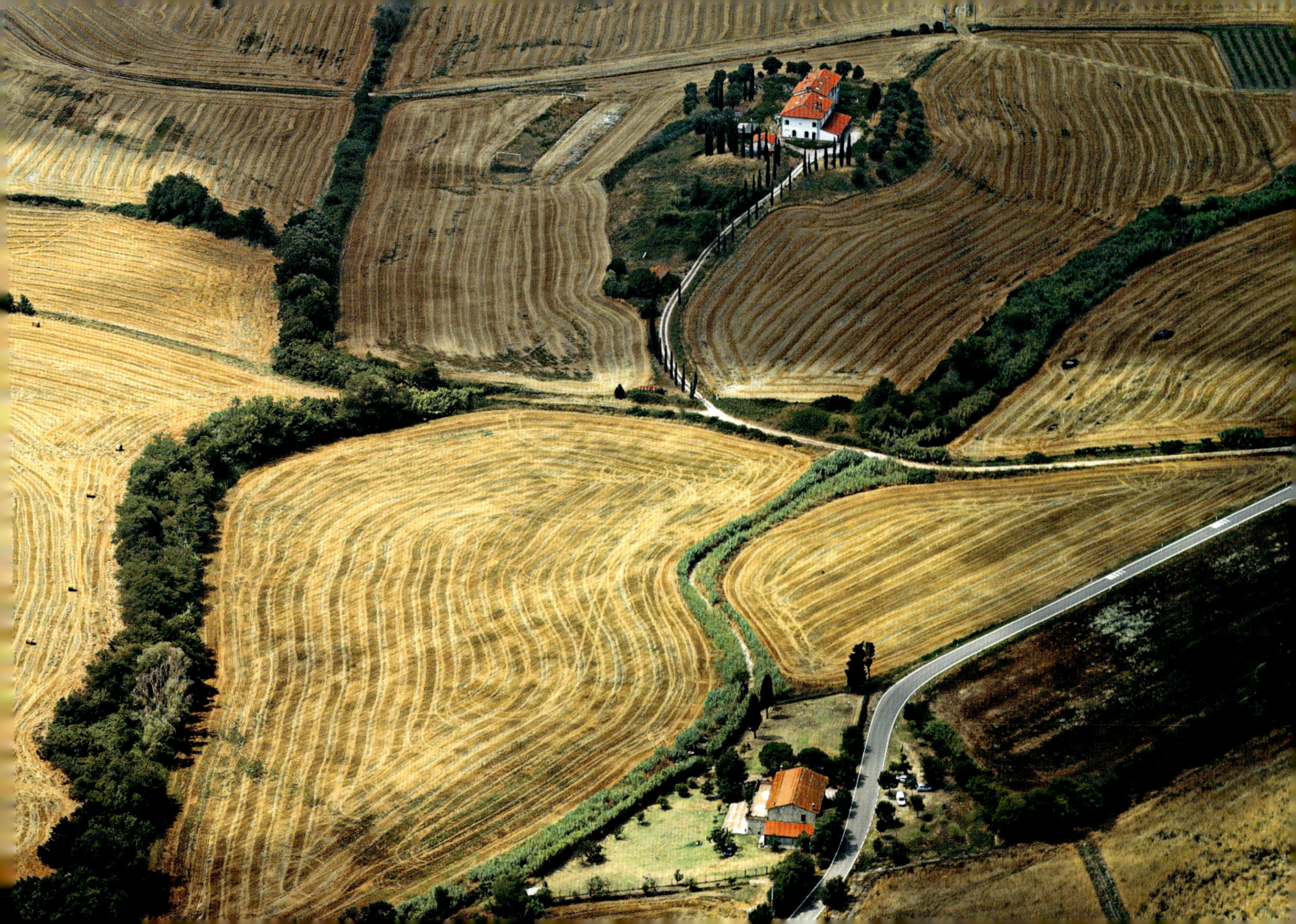

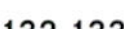

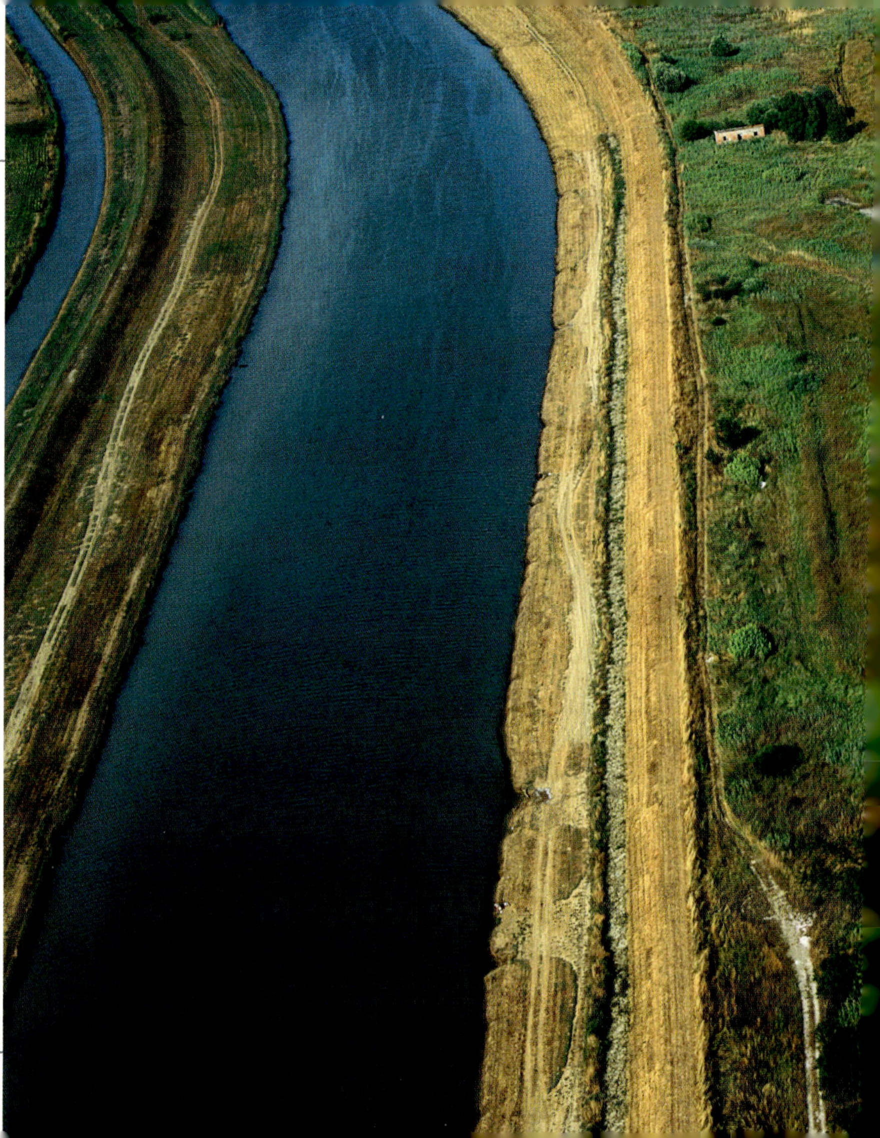

132-133

For centuries the Maremma was swamp land, due to the sandbars and dunes that blocked the flow of the rivers. After the reclamation projects of the 1900s, the marshy areas, like this one, photographed near Castiglione della Pescaia, became scarce.

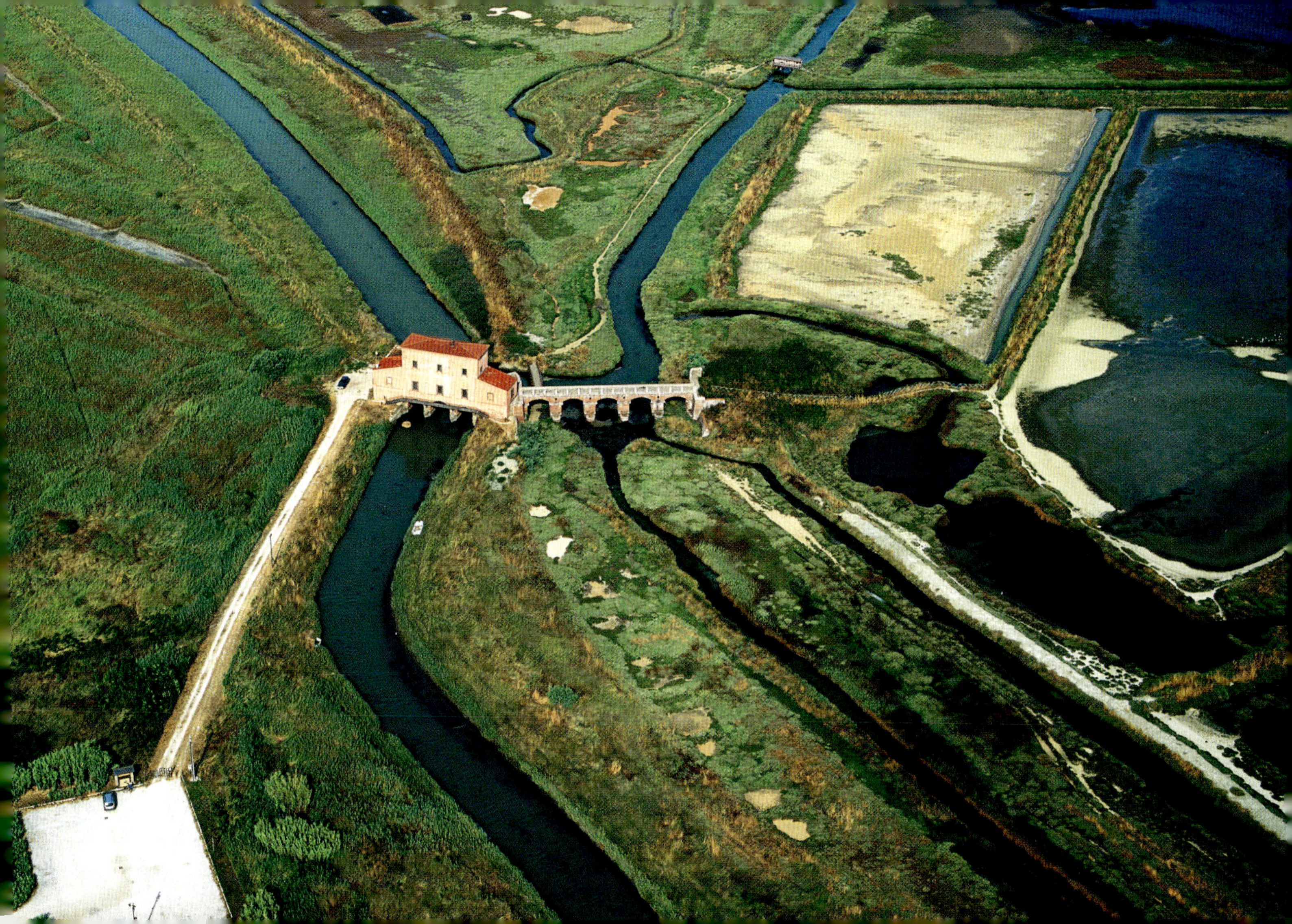

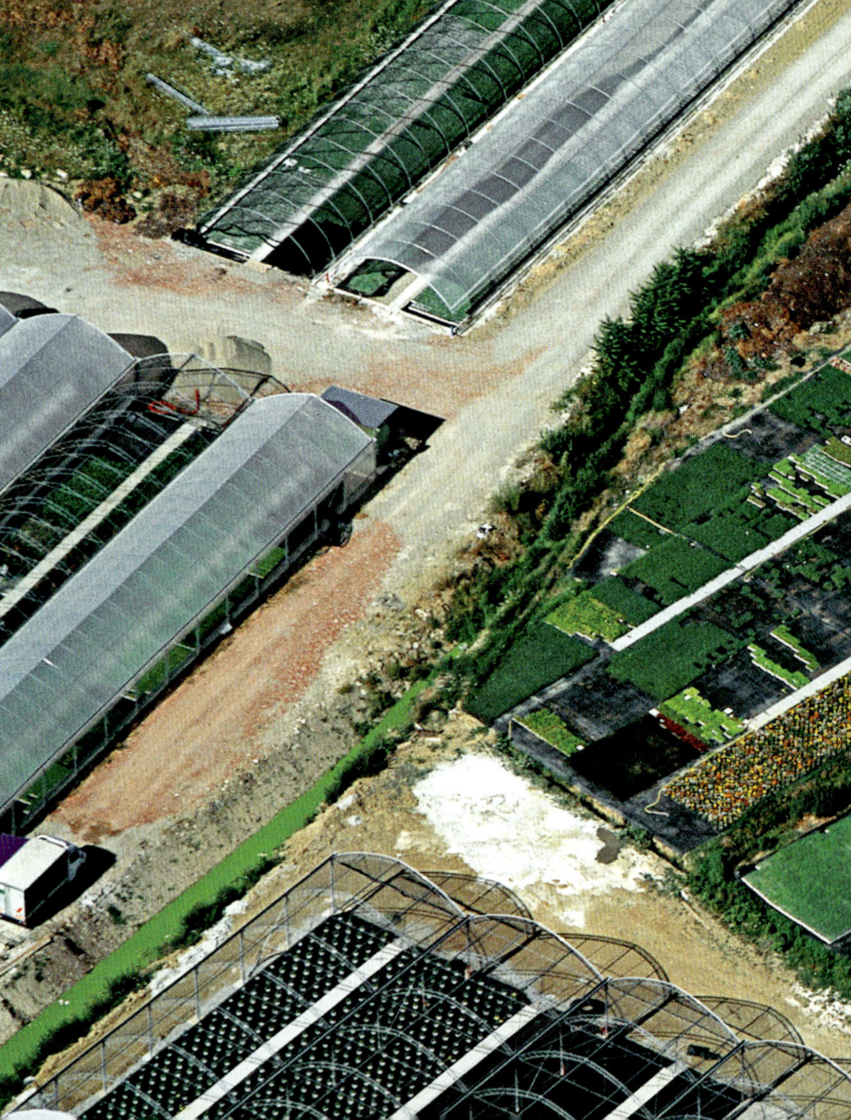

134-135
The nurseries of Castiglion Fiorentino are palettes of color that bloom each spring.

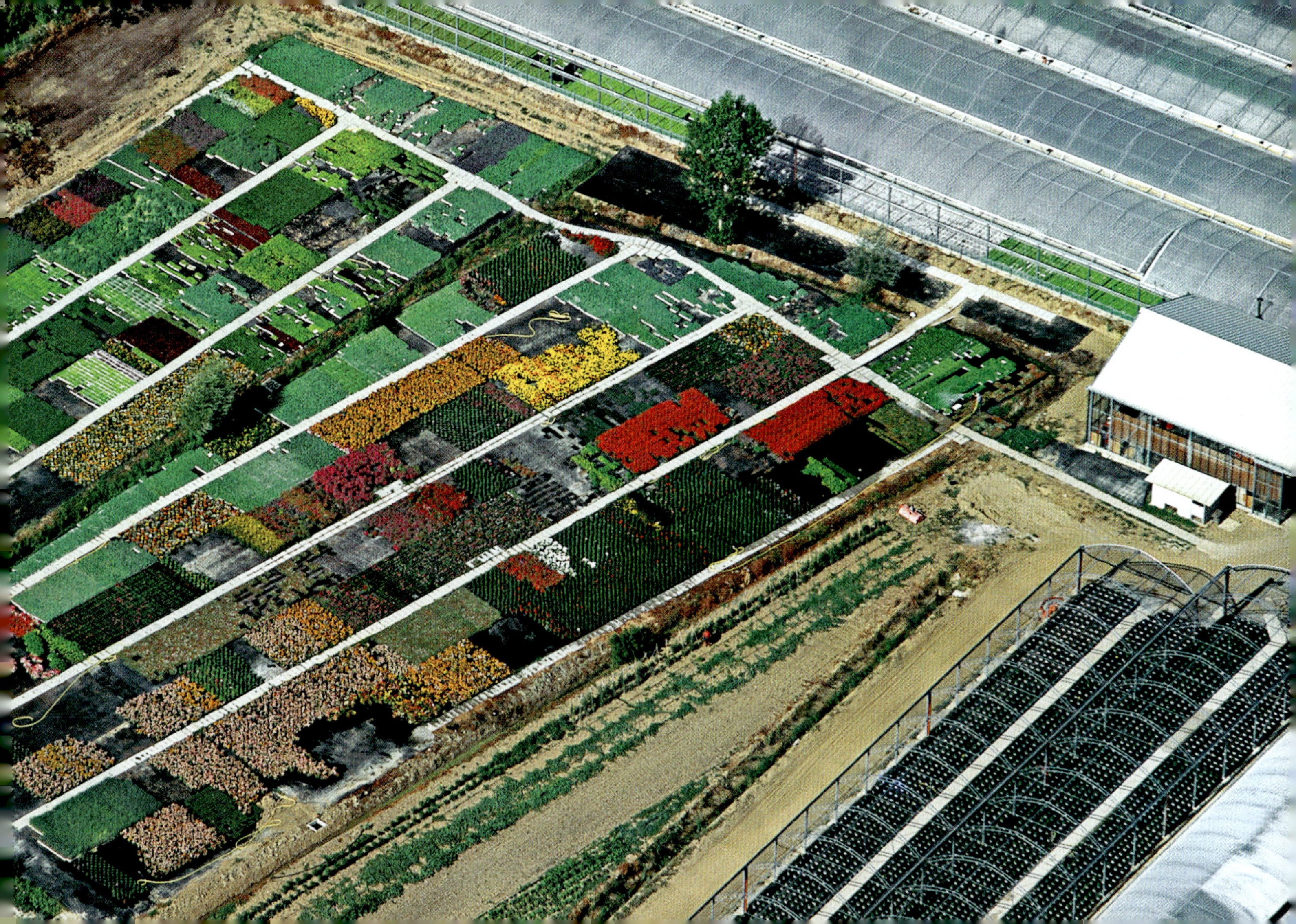

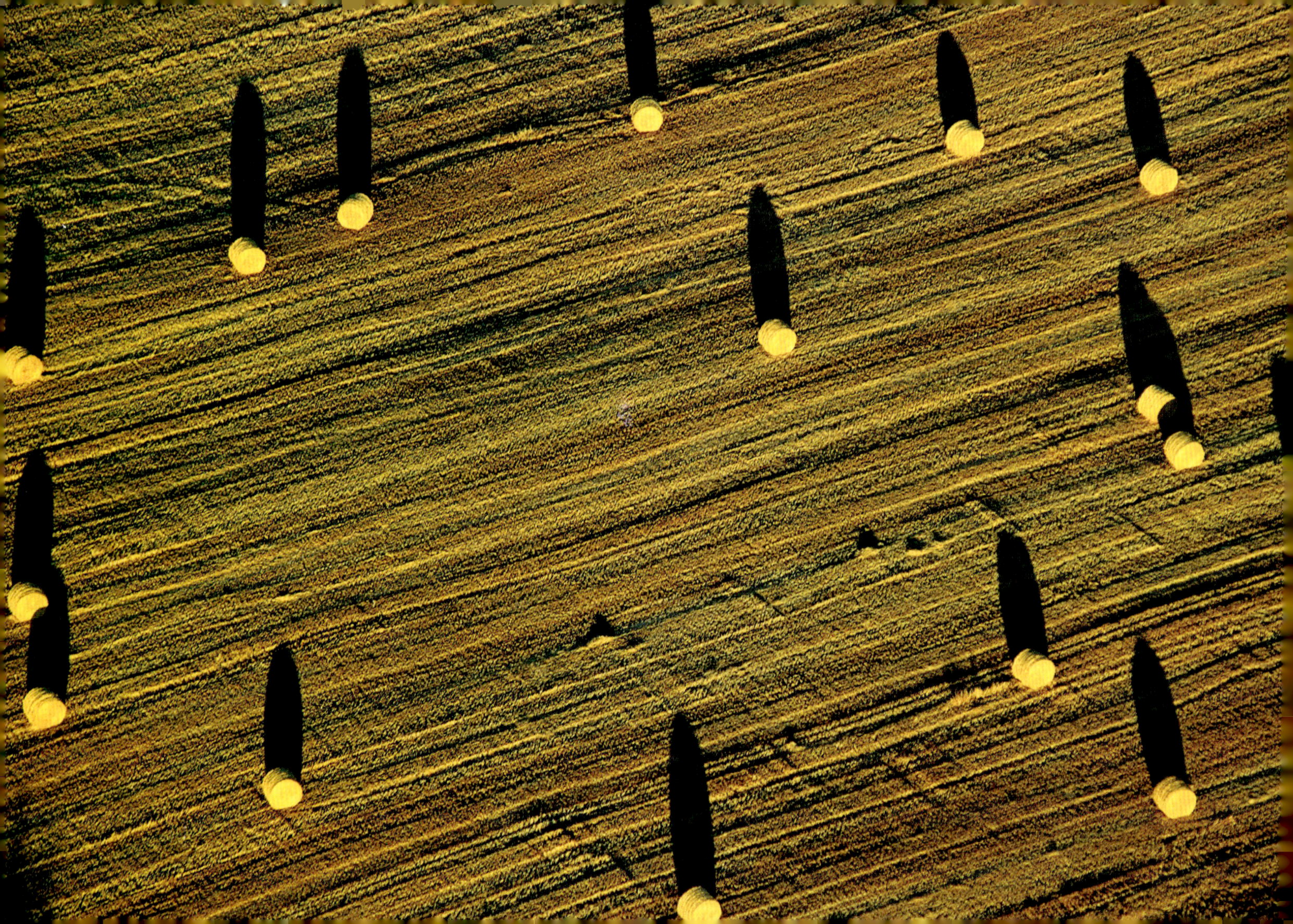

136
Circular bales of hay await transport from the farms of Saturnia: the shadows projected by the setting sun play on the tracks left by the tractors.

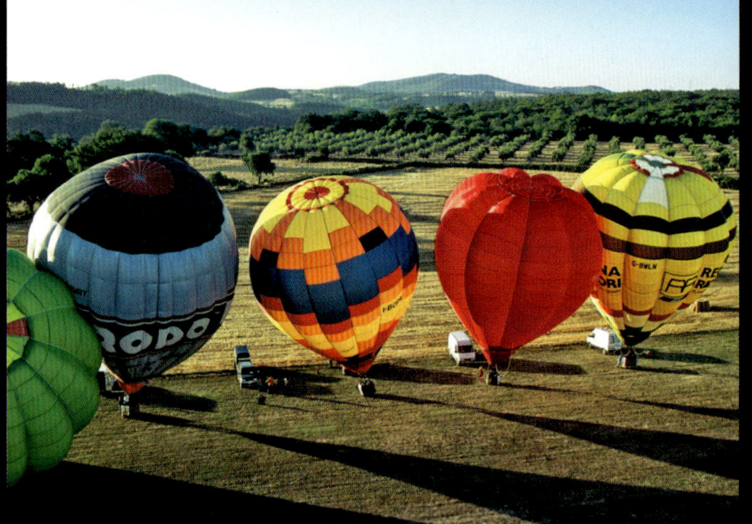

138 and 139

Hot-air balloons let us glide silently over the marvelous panorama of this part of Tuscany. The countryside around Saturnia, in the heart of the Maremma, offers numerous opportunities for lovers of this sport.

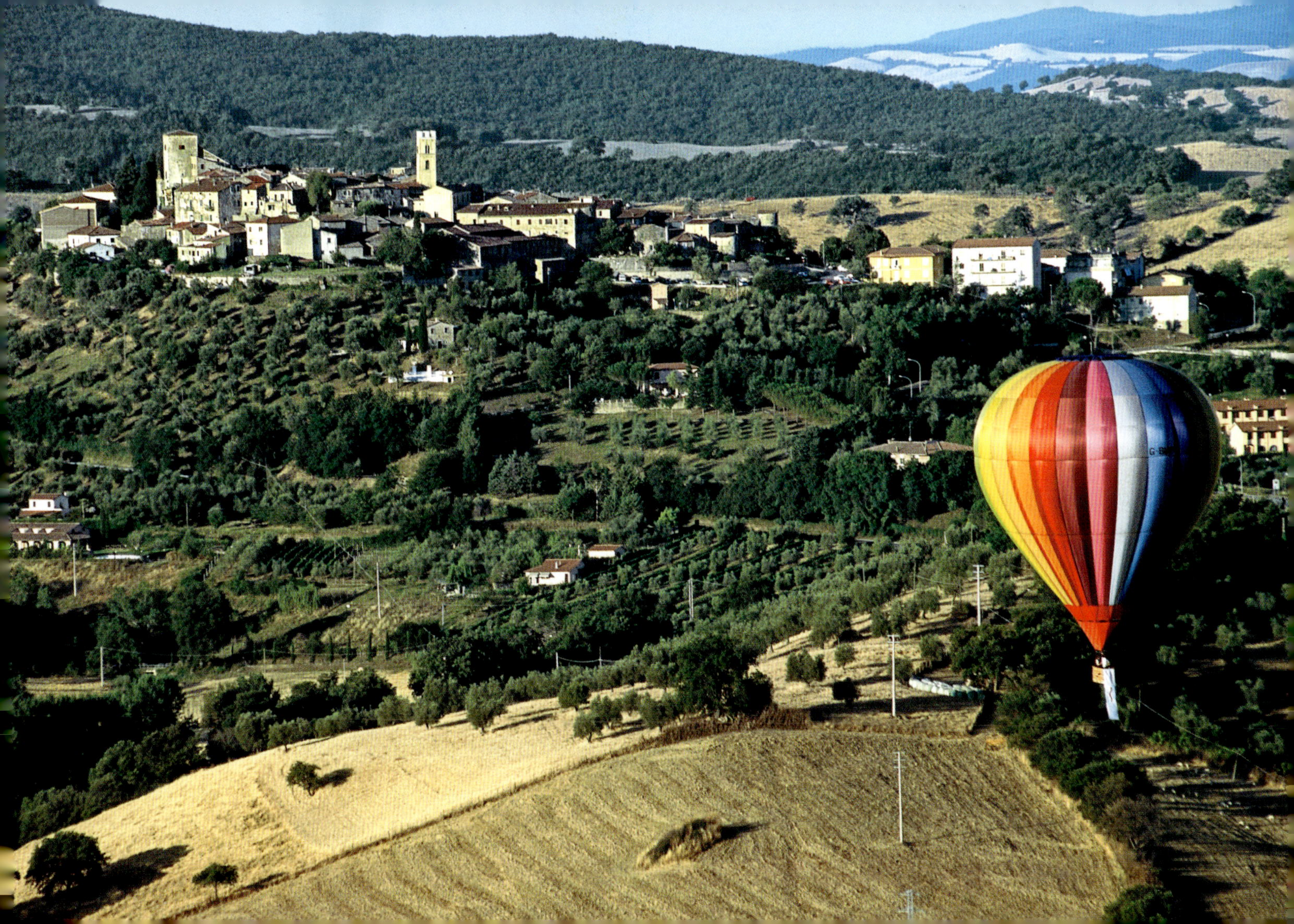

140
Among the irregular fields, the geometric forms of these near Scansano stand out.

141
A road winds through the forest and cultivated fields that surround Manciano, an agricultural center near Lazio.

142-143
All imaginable shades of green are visible in this pine forest near Pitigliano.

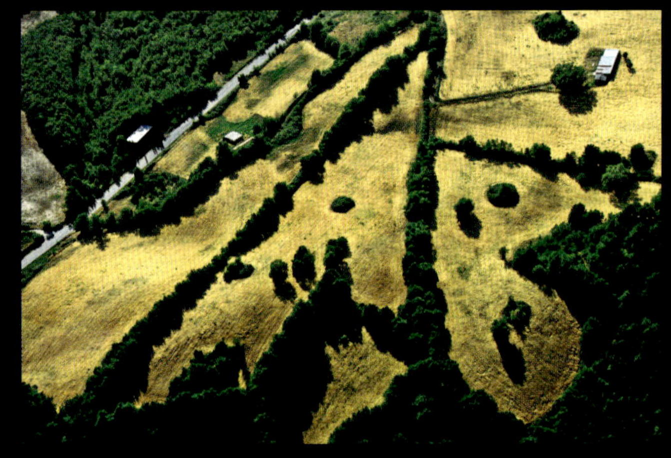

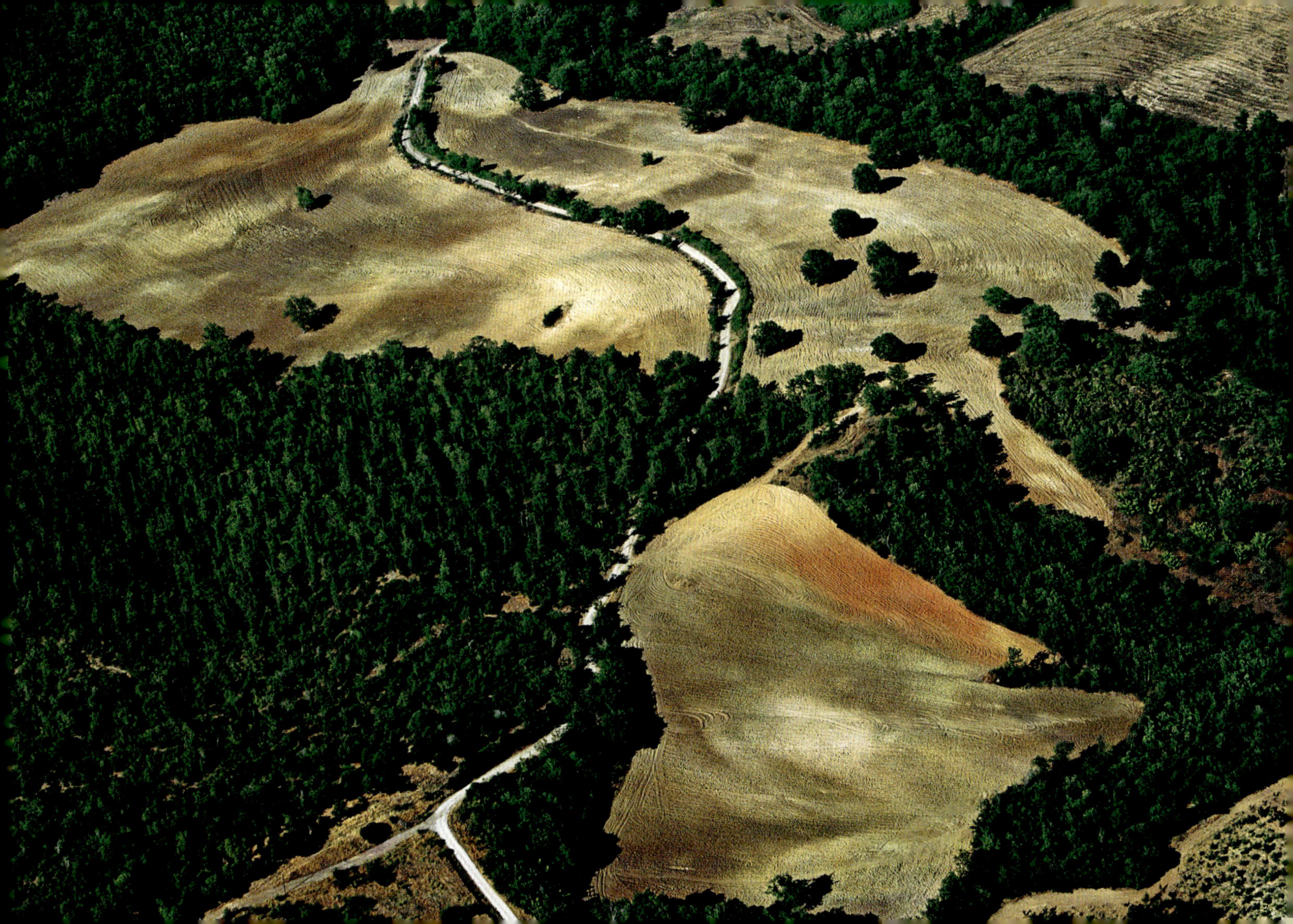

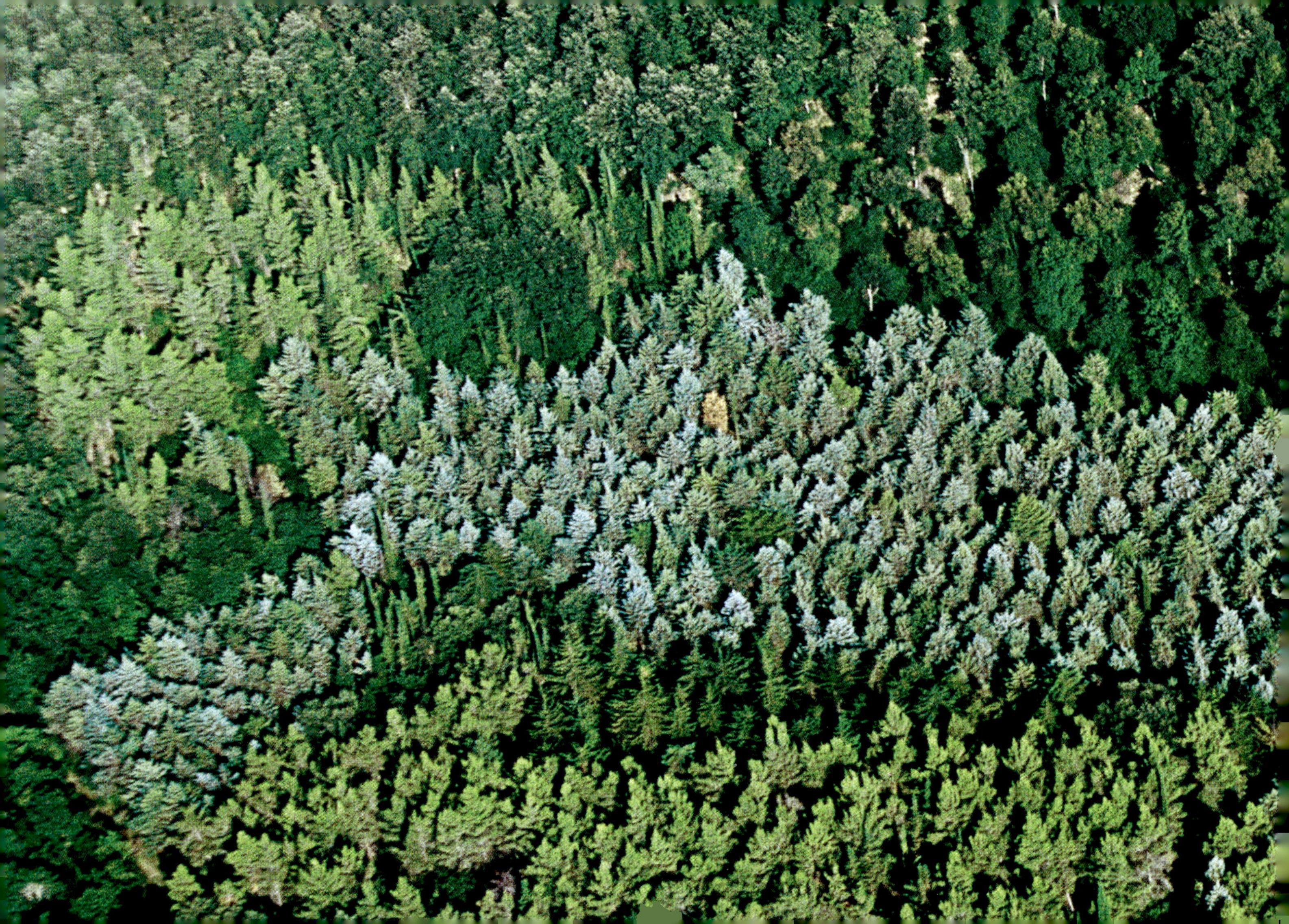

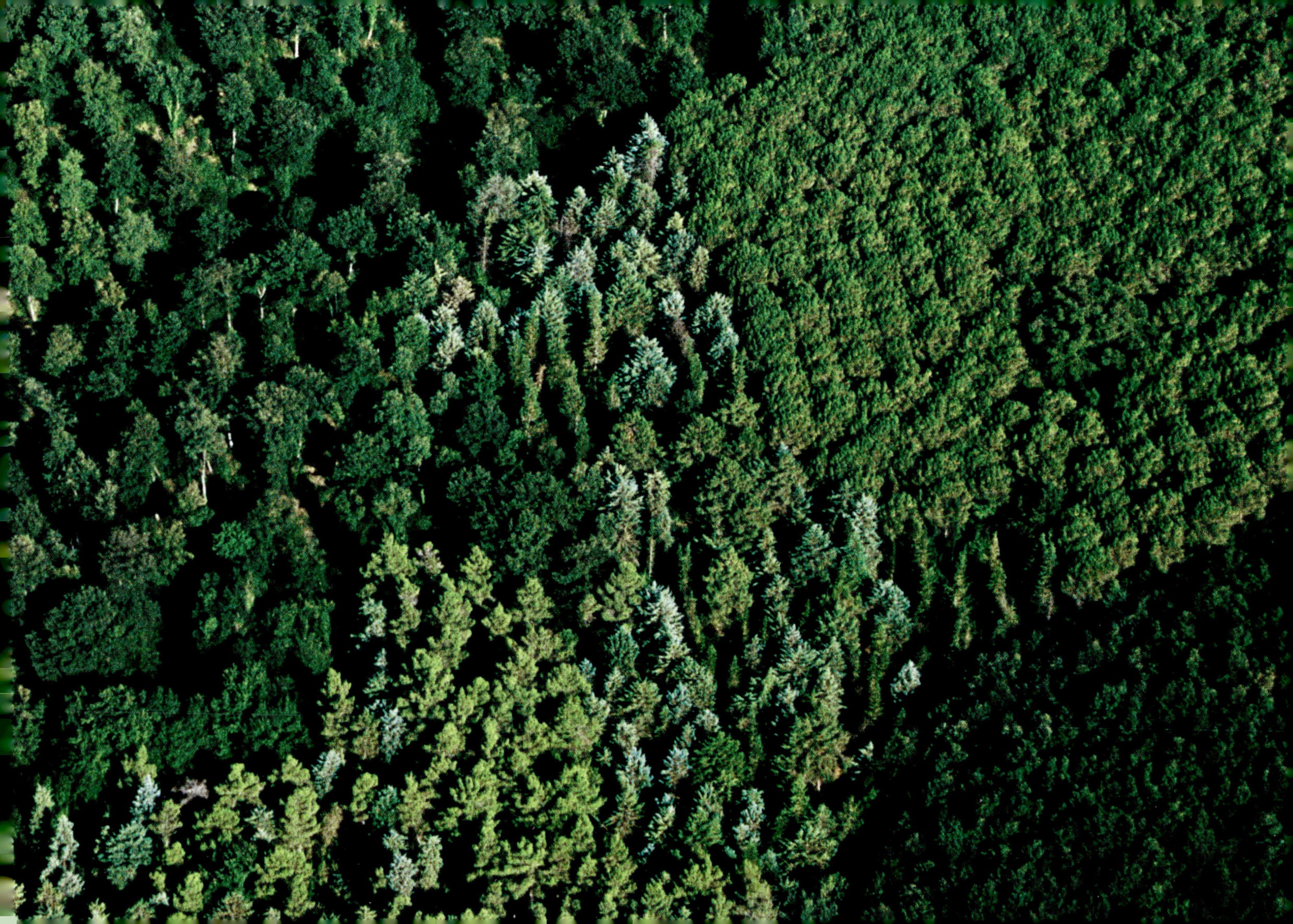

THE CITIES REVEAL THEMSELVES

FLYING HIGH

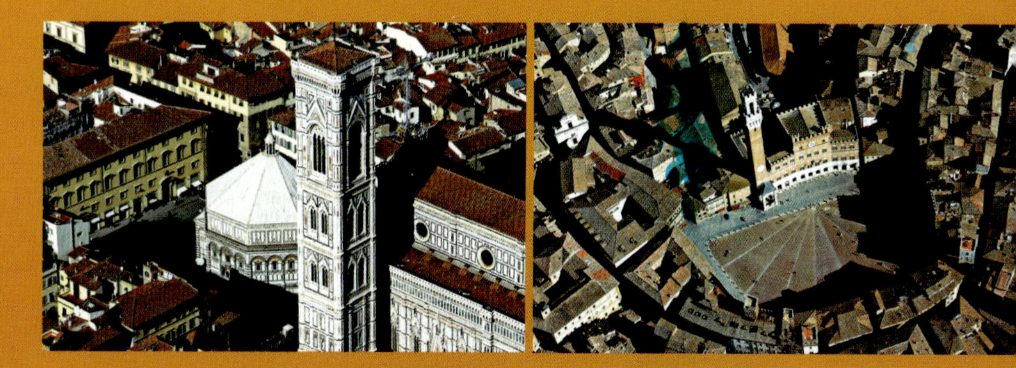

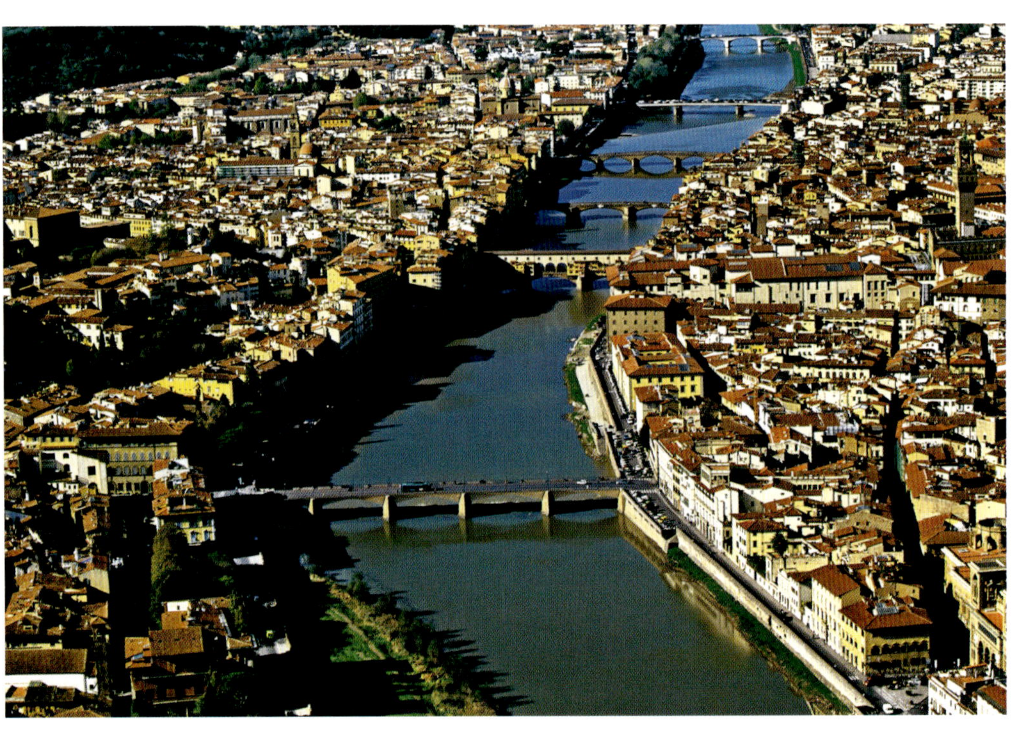

145 left
Giotto's Campanile, with the Cathedral, guards the center of Florence.

145 right
From above, the shell shape of Siena's Piazza del Campo is evident.

To fly over a city signifies not only embracing its monuments from an unusual perspective, perceiving its structure, reading its urban texture, but also paging through its history which, over the centuries, has left tracks not always evident to those who walk its streets or piazzas. Florence, Lucca, Pisa, Siena, and Pistoia were not only the main protagonists of Tuscan's medieval history, they were also important Roman colonies, developed in the 2nd and 1st centuries B.C., where one can still perceive a structure based on the *decumanus* (main west-east axis) gate although, especially in Florence, the historic center has undergone the devastating effects of reconstruction during the 1800s. The phantom of *Florentia* (since we are now right over Florence) still hovers over the ancient ford that is now the Ponte Vecchio, the most photographed bridge in the world, and Piazza del Duomo, the section of the city included within the original walls erected in 30 B.C. Two elements of Florence's landscape, one natural and the other a manifestation of architectural talent, instantly stand out: the River Arno and the Duomo. The Arno, which divides the city in half, is crossed by many bridges in the historic center of town, reflected with perfect symmetry in water once described as "silver." It's a serene river, the Florentines say: in the summertime it almost dries up but the winter rains cause it to swell and become nasty.

The cupola, Brunelleschi's masterpiece, rises higher than all the city's roofs, higher than the towers and church steeples; it steals the scene like a pri-

146
More or less in mid-course in the heart of Florence, the Arno passes under the arches of Ponte Vecchio, at the center of the image.

The Cities Reveal Themselves

madonna and dominates our "air space." It is impossibile to ignore, imposing, powerful and perfect. If Brunelleschi had ever been able to leave the ground (maybe on one of Leonardo's crazy flying machines) and could have seen his creation from above as we do now, not to confirm the architectural result (of which he was certain) but to feel the emotion it lends, he would have studied his cupola from every angle and declared: "Nothing more can be done...." and he would have laid down his tools. After the cupola, the Piazza del Duomo, with the Baptistry and Giotto's bell tower, is the city's most famous offering: here a group of artists created a new art form that overcame the confines of their city and Italy to conquer all of western Europe.

But Florence is not just the Renaissance. The Palazzo della Signoria, from above, resembles a massive cube-shaped fortress, whose tower rises above all others in Florence because it represents the municipal authority. Also powerful is the Franciscan Santa Croce basilica, dating to the 1200s, that closes the rectangular Piazza where, each June, during the week dedicated to St John, the city's protector, that comical massacre called "soccer in costume" is held. Whoever believes that this is an historical re-enactment put on for tourists is mistaken: this is a bloody fight and at the end of the 'game' there are a dozen of dislocated shoulders, broken ribs, noses and teeth; a few years ago one player's ear was bitten off, but he still held his defense position!

After our vertical vision of dozens of perfect cloisters, private courtyards, a web of streets that wind and intertwine and seem to lead nowhere, we appreciate the geometric order of Palazzo Pitti, across the Arno, that opens onto the splendid Boboli Gardens, with fountains and statues, amphitheater and stone stairways, sculpted topiary shrubs, dominated by the perfect star-shaped fortress of the Belvedere, erected against the arrogance of the Holy Roman Emperor Charles V, with

The Cities Reveal Themselves

the collaboration of the republican Michelangelo. When we get to the Cascine, Florence's biggest park, we are already on the way to Lucca-Pisa-Livorno, indicated by the Arno's flow, the sites of other wonders. But first we must fly over the Emperor's Castle in Prato, which resembles the Swabian castles of Puglia and Sicily, and over Pistoia with its intimate medieval atmosphere.

Lucca jealously conserves the character of every walled in city. The white circle of 12 fortified panels from the 1500s, binds eleven bastions with eight entrances, embracing the entire city but never needed as defense. Inside the walls, our birdseye view affords a clear vision of the Roman *decumanal* structure (i.e., a layout based on a main west-east axis) but the urban architecture, numerous houses, towers and churches are confusedly packed within a myriad of narrow winding roads. Barely visible is the Romanesque cathedral of San Martino with a triple-layered façade of polychrome loggias that of San Michele in Foro, a rich Pisan-Luccan-style structure from whose summit rises the Archangel Michael. Very evident in the eastern part of the city is the planimetry of the Roman amphitheater on whose periphery arises a ring of houses; the arena, framed by four arches, is enlivened by a colorful open-air market.

From Lucca, the trip to Pisa is a matter of minutes. Again, the Arno divides the city, but the river is now very close to the sea and flows toward the delta between high parapets of *pietra serena*, saluted by the spires and cusps of the gothic Spina Chapel, the last great monument to be seen on the river's journey to the sea. A little farther away are the sumptuous monuments that have made Pisa famous worldwide. It is easy to comprehend why the carpet of green grass on which they stand has been defined as the Field of Miracles; our vision from above supports this because one glance is enough to embrace the Duomo, the Leaning Tower, the circular Baptistry and the huge Cemetery, framed by the ancient city walls: an incomparable

151
Breaking the line of its neighboring buildings, Santa Maria della Spina church adorns the Lungarno Gambacorti, in Pisa.

architectonic gem that testifies to cultural influx and exchange re-elaborated with great originality.
It is well known that the inhabitants of Pisa pretend that Livorno doesn't exist (and if you mention Pisans to the Livornese, they look at you as if you've mentioned Martians), so we sneak off toward the Labro – the modern name is Livorno (often Leghorn in English). The damage done to this city during World War II has given rise to modern neighborhoods around the historic center, which consist of the Medicean area dating to the 1600s, built along the canals. Livorno is dominated by its Fortezza Vecchia, all in brick, surrounded by the massive fortress from the 1300s. After circumnavigating the busy port, we can't miss two of the city's symbols: the nearby monument of the four chained Moors and the Naval Academy where, if not at sea manned by cadets in training, one can see the famous sailing ship *Amerigo Vespucci*.
Now, to Siena, a city characterized by the Gothic. We are met by the superb cathedral, exuberantly decorated, with its black and white striped bell tower (these are colors of the city's flag). The Palazzo Pubblico is one of the most elegant examples of Tuscan Gothic, from which rises the Mangia Tower, in *terracotta*, crowned by its white bell chamber, overlooking the Piazza del Campo (where twice yearly the Sienese go wild over the Palio) atop the three hills on which the city was constructed. In fact, the center is a tortuous knot of steep winding roads, framed by solid aristocratic buildings. Arezzo, a city of art, is dominated by Piazza Grande, surrounded by buildings that represent the historic phases of this city with the piazza and St Francis church, erected in the austere Franciscan Gothic style.
We have also flown over the hexagonal walls surrounding the historic center of Grosseto (16th century), while over Massa we were struck by the medieval nucleus dominated by the Fortress with the Malaspina renaissance castle, with the 15th century city spread at its feet.

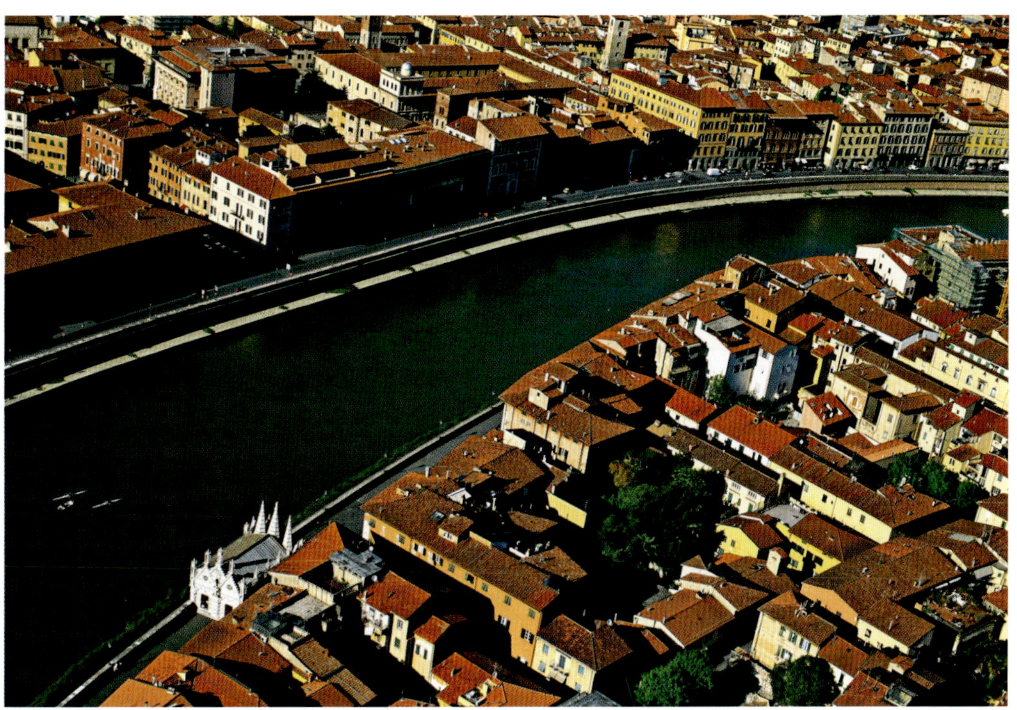

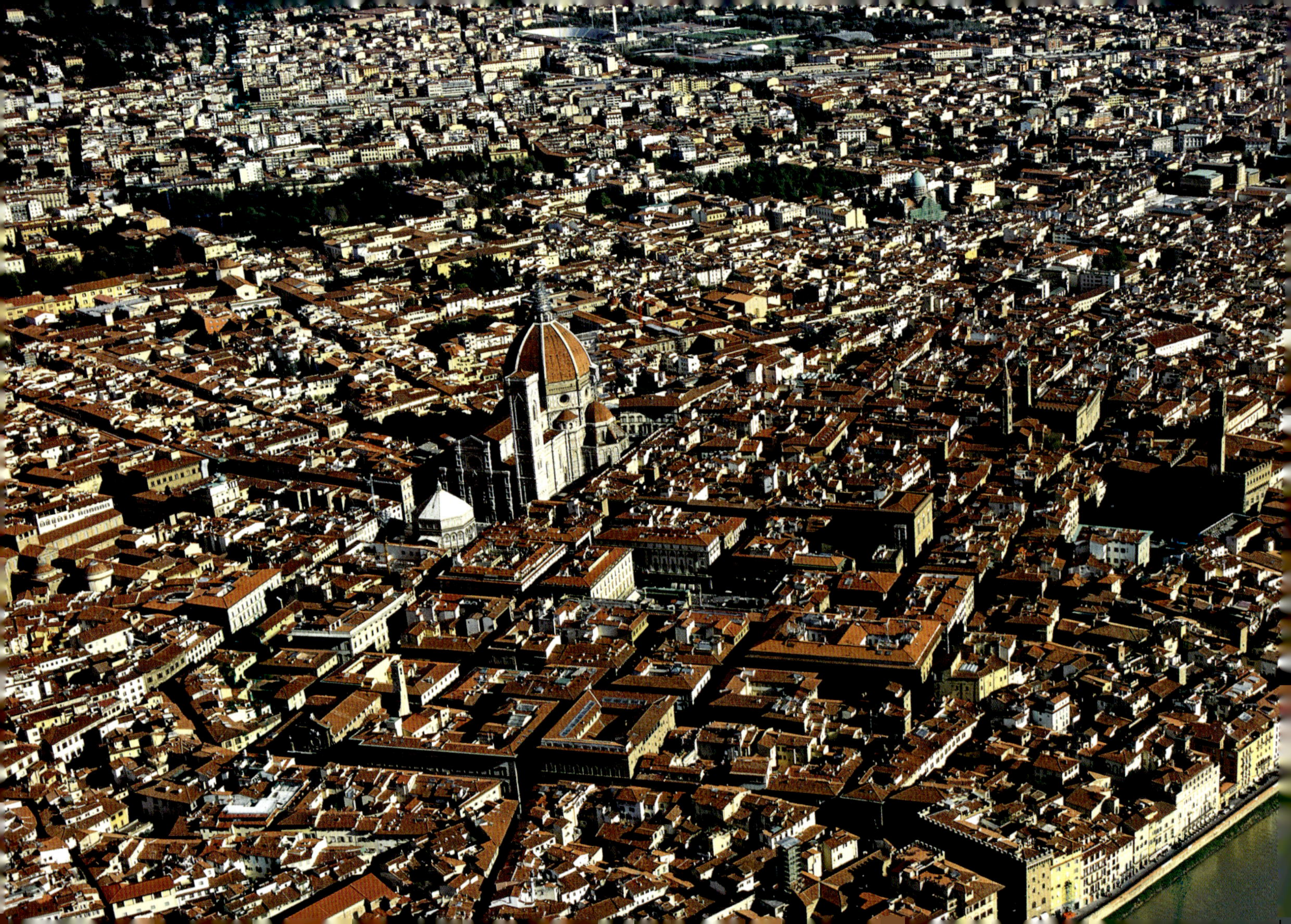

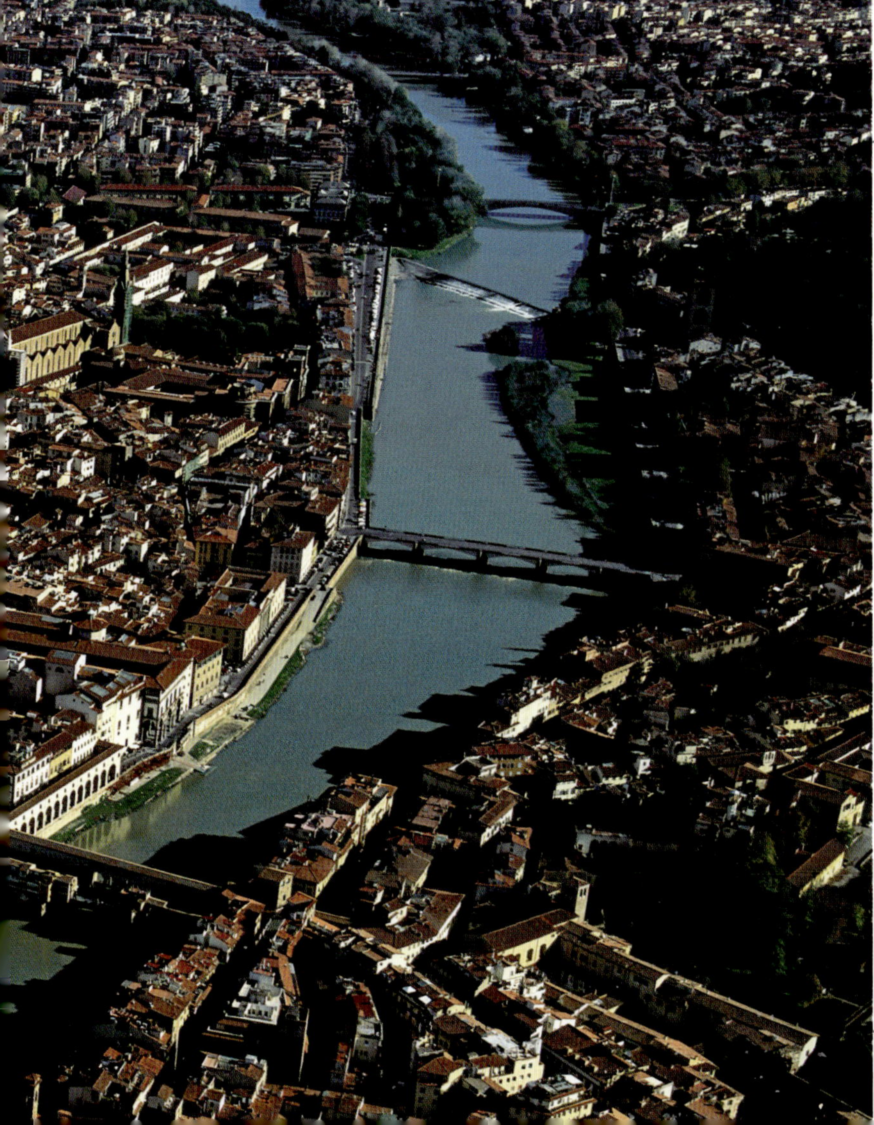

Florence

152-153
In one of Europe's most famous urban vistas, the cupola of Santa Maria del Fiore (the Duomo), the Baptistery and, to the right, Giotto's Campanile, form the heart of Florence.

155

Symbol of a great Renaissance achievement, the Duomo's octagon-shaped cupola is higher than all other nearby buildings. Although architecturally complex, the building is a miracle of sobriety and balance.

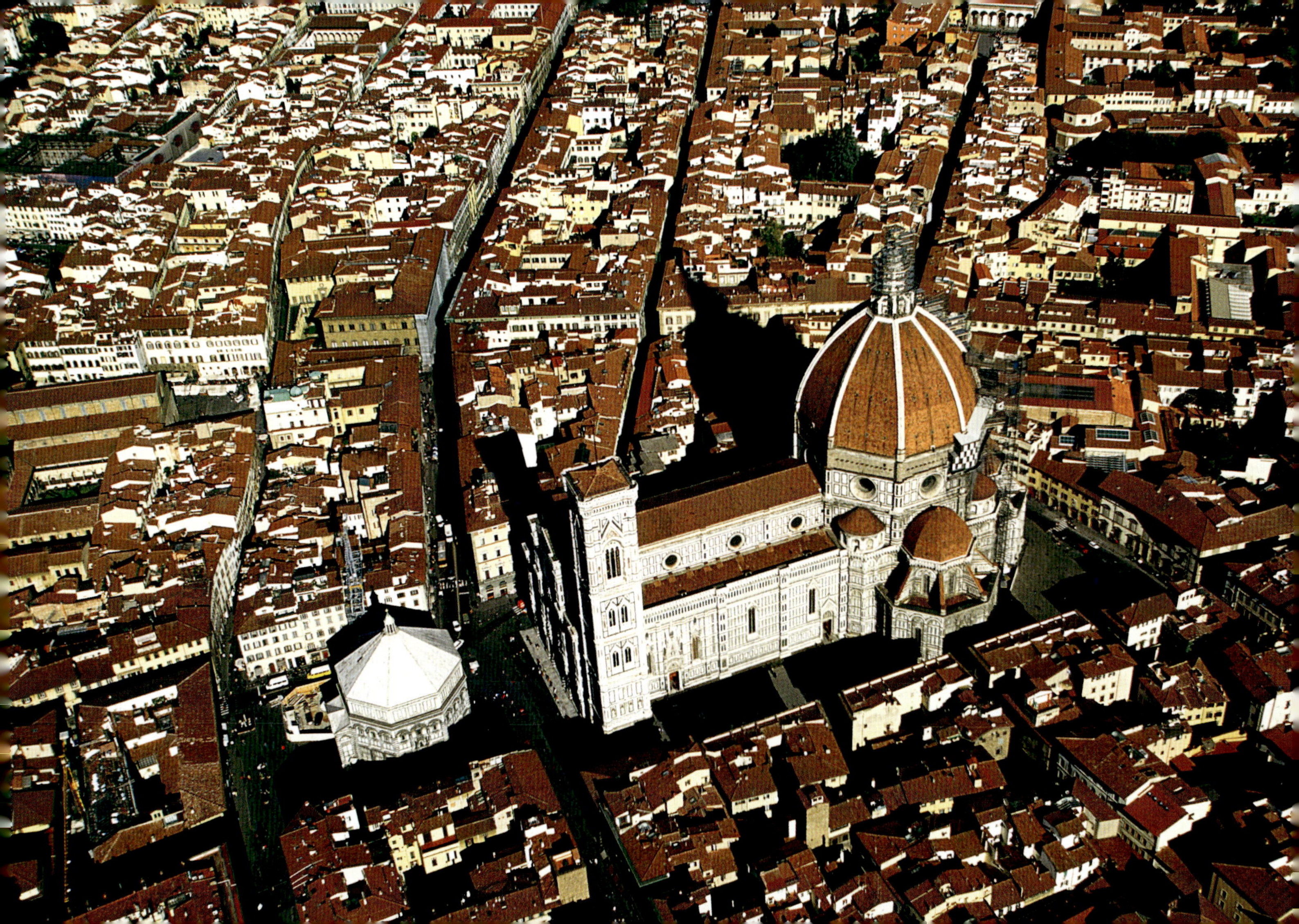

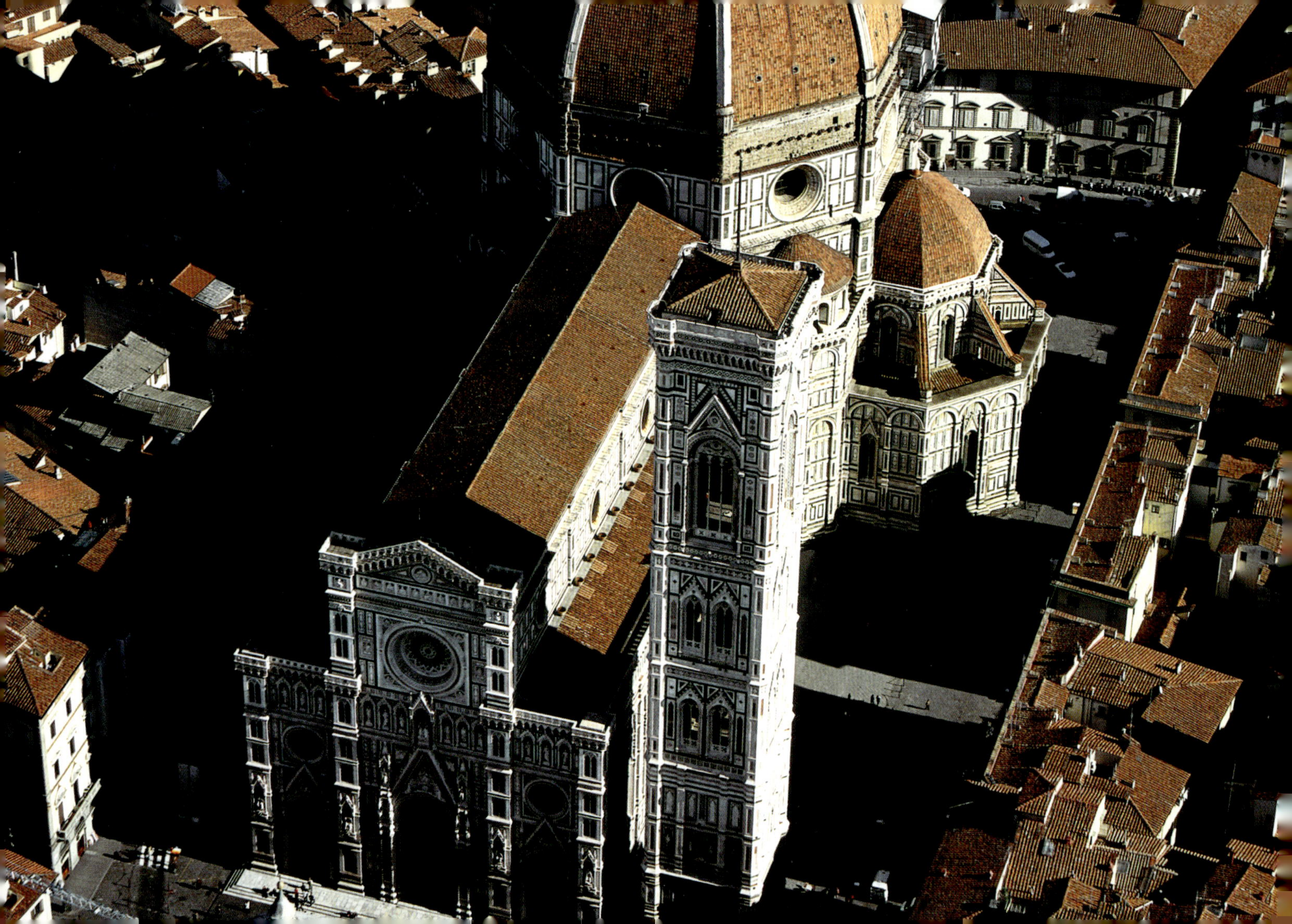

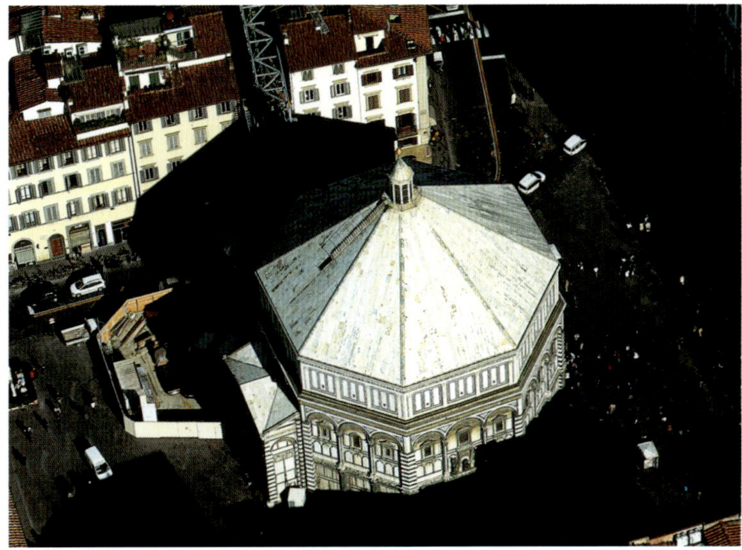

156

Both the Duomo and the Campanile as well as the Baptistery (not visible here), are decorated with a geometric motif made of valuable marble, one of Tuscany's riches.

157

A pyramid-shaped cover hides the true cupola of the San Giovanni Baptistery, whose origin dates back to the 11th century. On the left, the octagonal- shaped building has an adjoining n apse added in 1202, the so-called "purse."

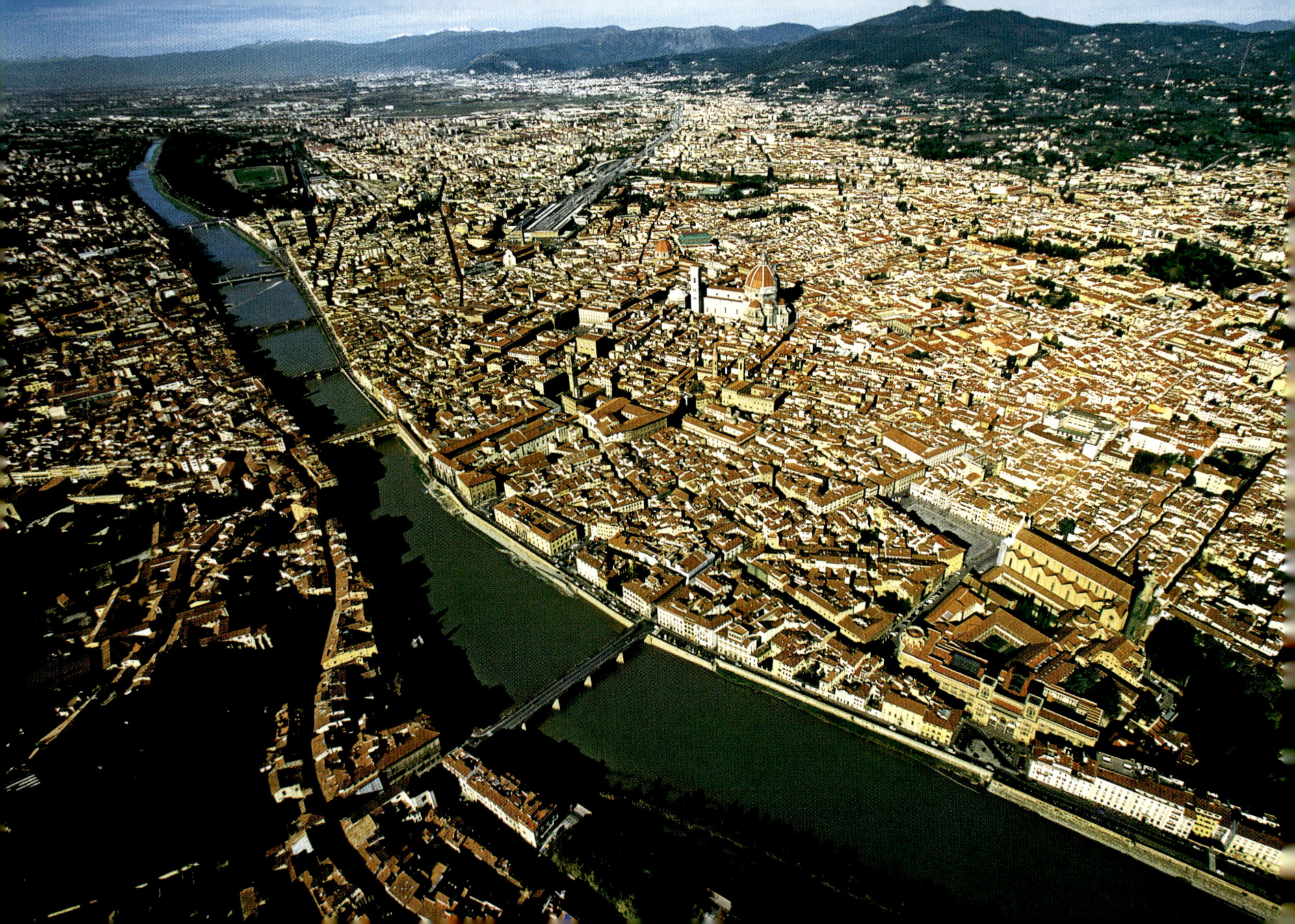

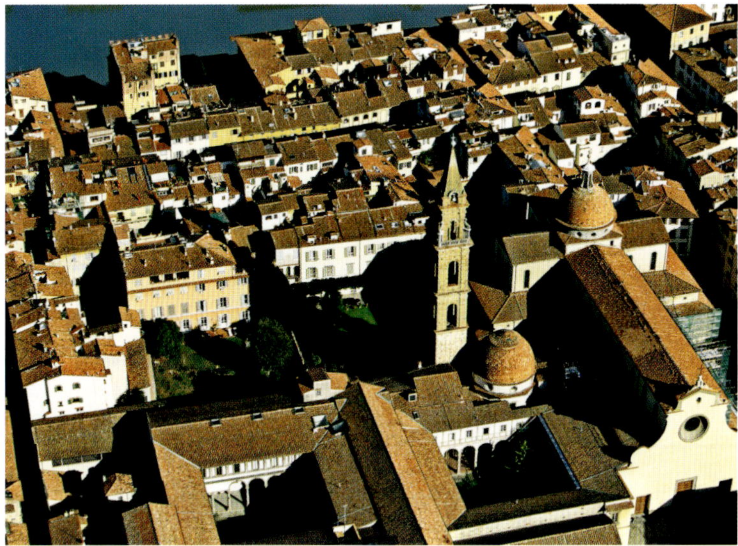

158
An extensive panorama of the center of Florence, focusing on Brunelleschi's dome. At the bottom, to the right, beyond the Arno, the long, dark, and splendid Santa Croce church is next to the National Library.

159
The Santo Spirito church, to the right, one of Brunelleschi's masterpieces, is at the epicenter of the urban section of Oltrarno – "Across the Arno."

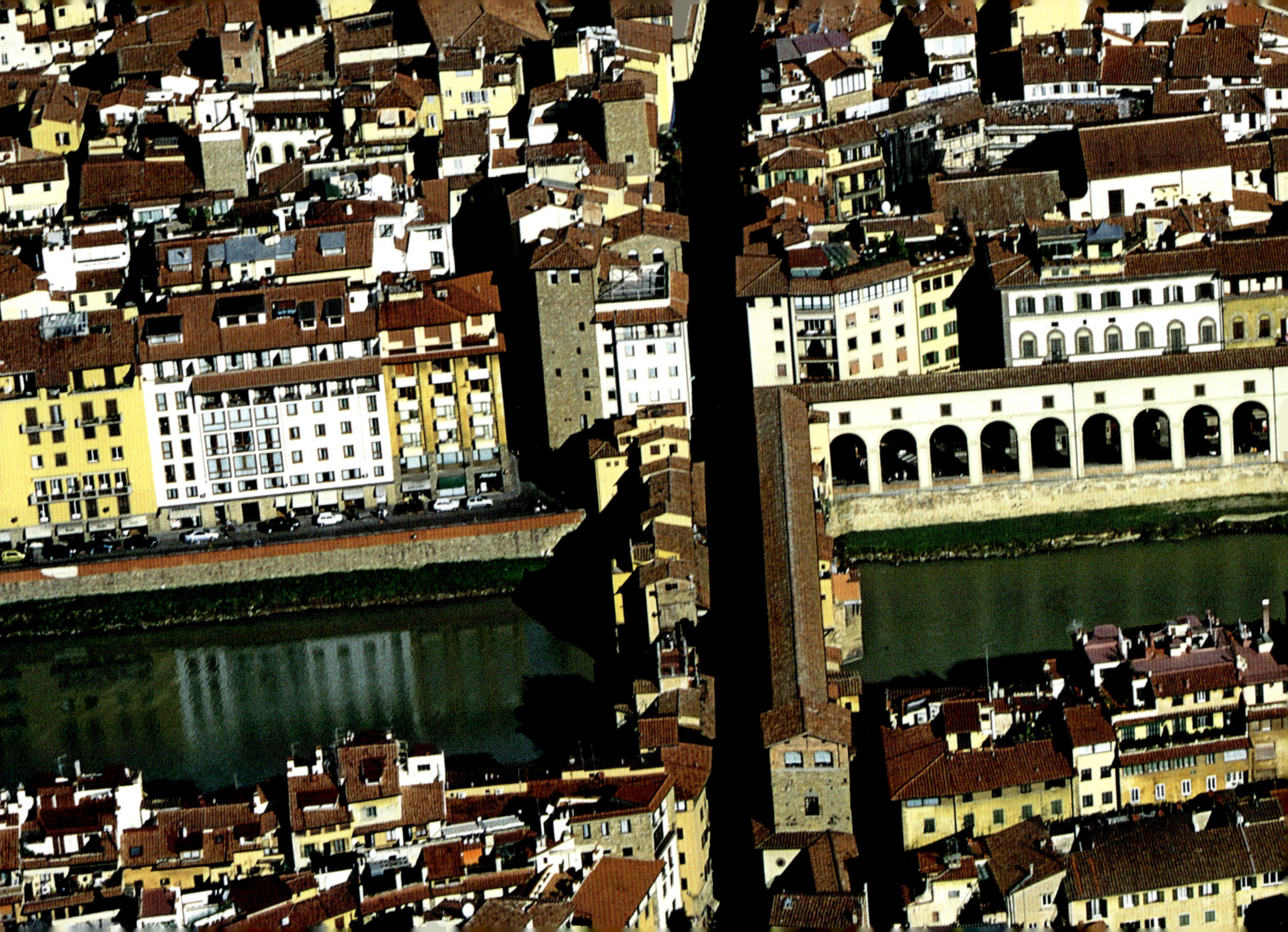

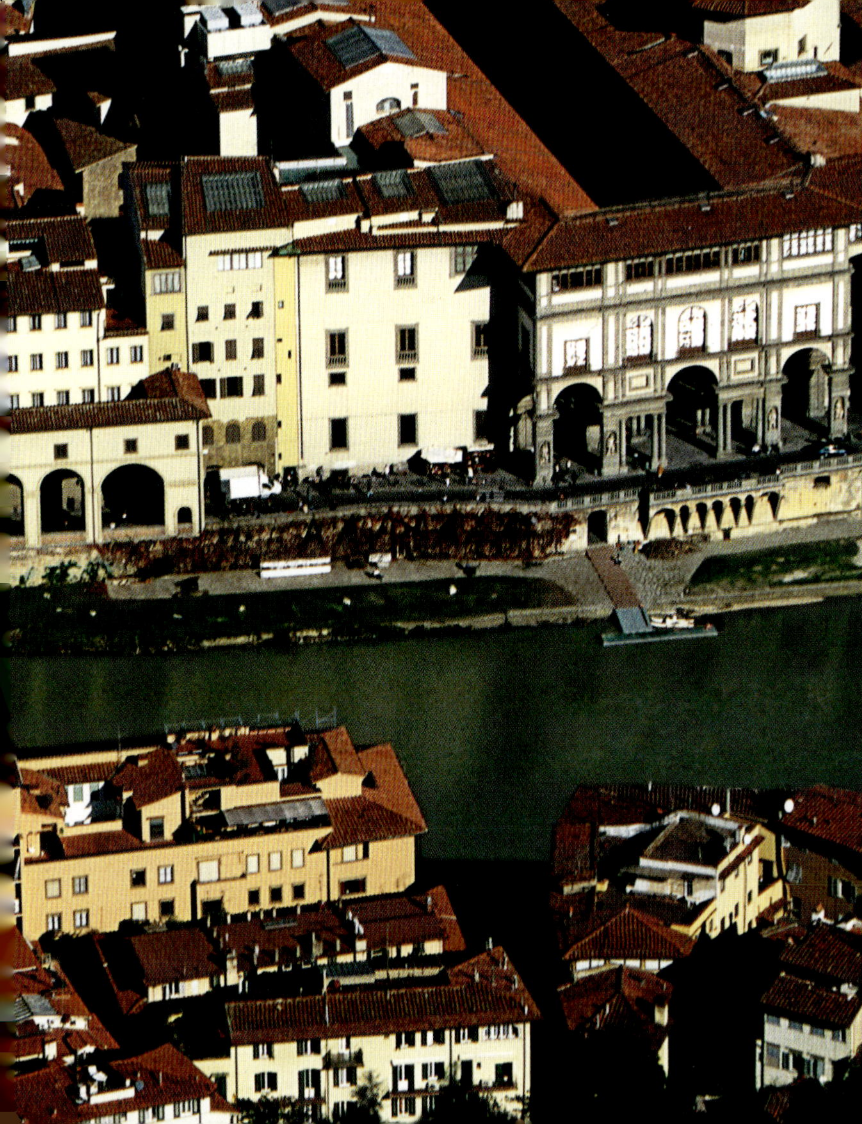

160-161
The Arno is the great artery around which Florence developed. Along its banks, ancient buildings accompany its flow and monumental bridges, like the Ponte Vecchio, cross its waters.

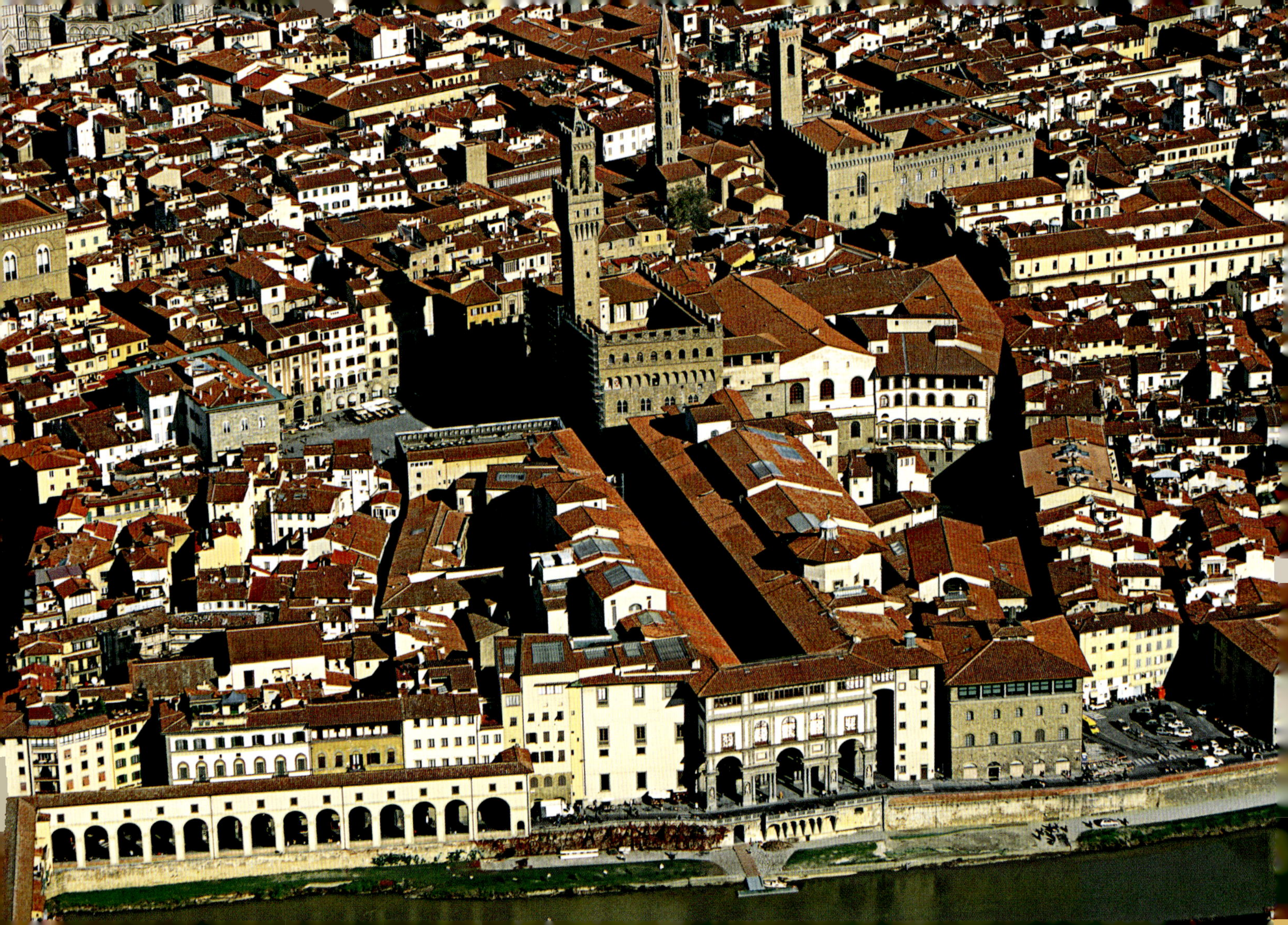

162
The group of buildings from Piazza della Signoria and Palazzo Vecchio (middle) to the 14th-century Palazzo del Bargello (top right) and toward the Arno, to the Uffizi Gallery, together form the heart of Medicean Florence.

163
Piazza della Santissima Annunciata, here taken from different angles, forms an "enlarged Renaissance courtyard," according to Brunelleschi's design.

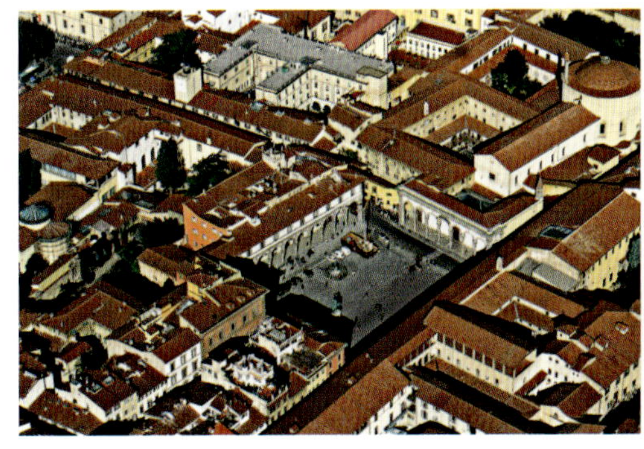

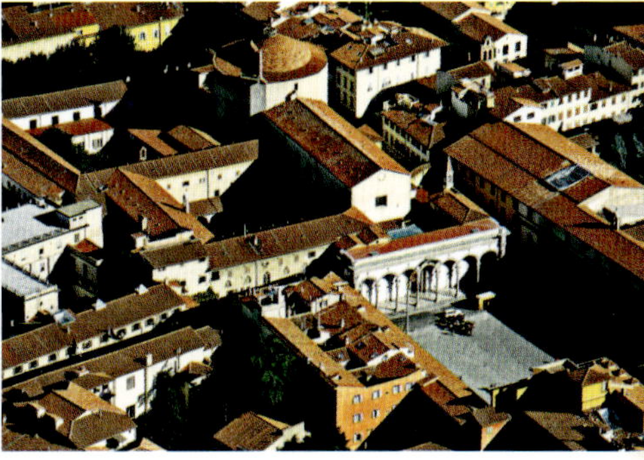

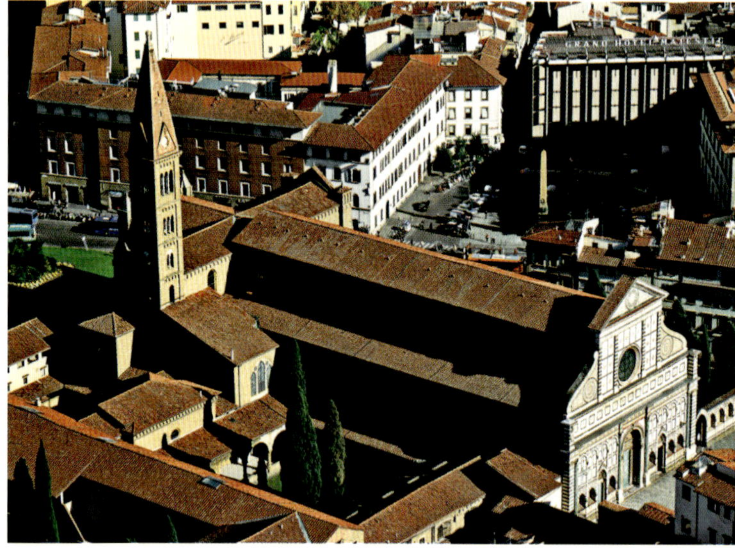

164

If Santa Croce was the Franciscans' headquarters in Renaissance Florence, Santa Maria Novella was Dominicans' bastion. Built between 1278 and 1458, this church is a harmonious integration of Gothic and Renaissance elements.

165

Santa Maria Novella, with the train station at its back, faces the piazza that bears its name, commissioned by the Rucellai family.

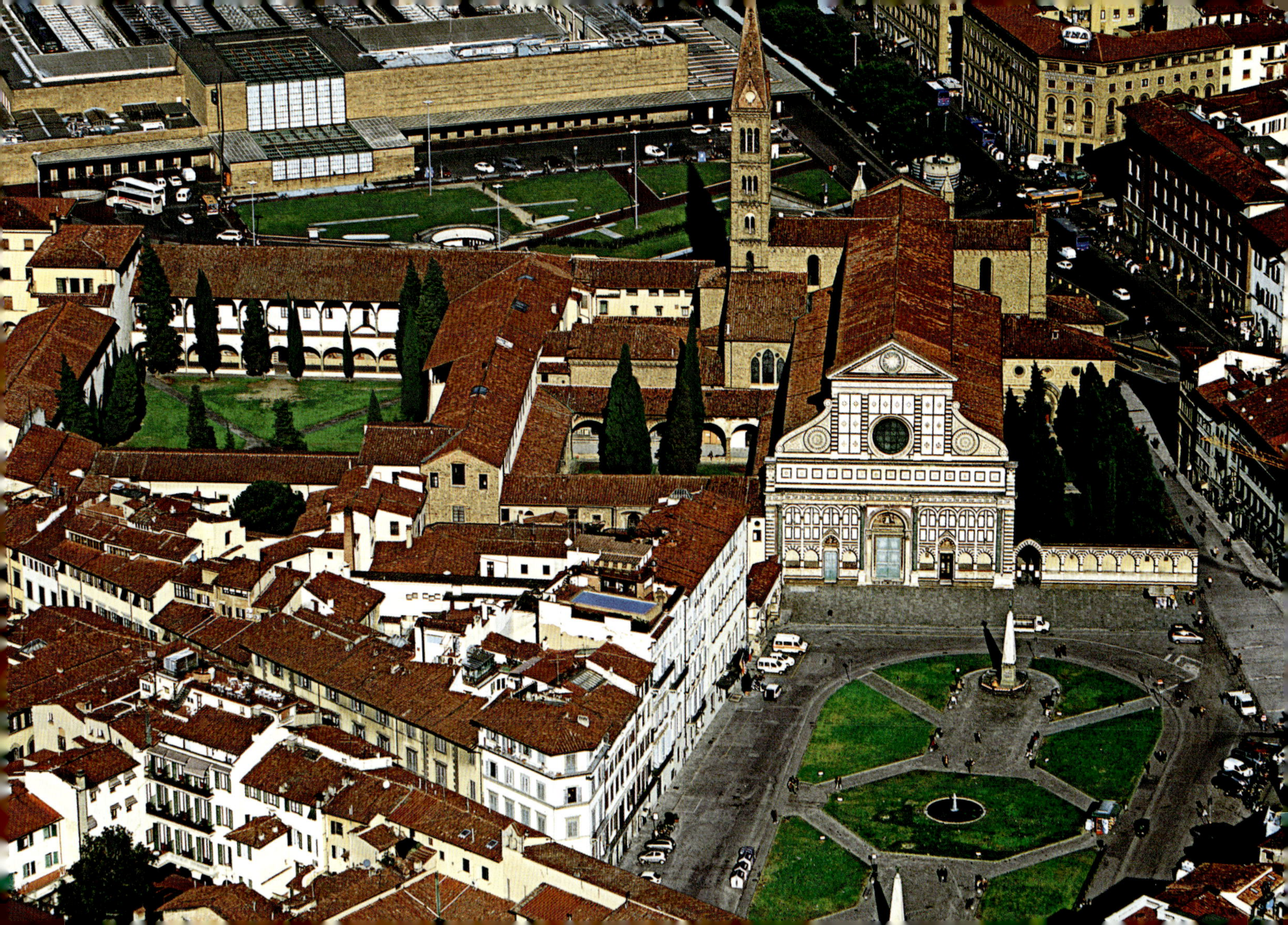

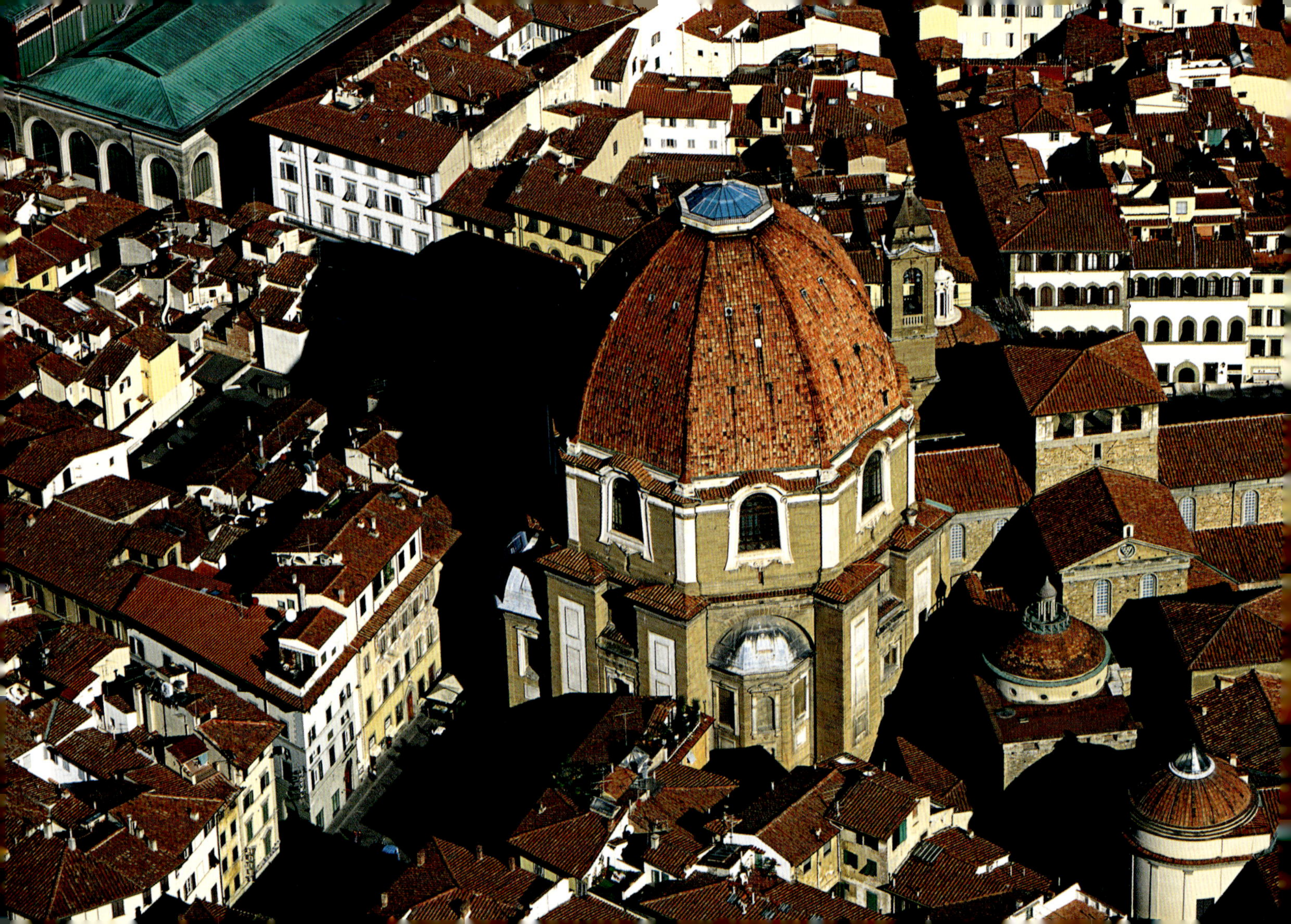

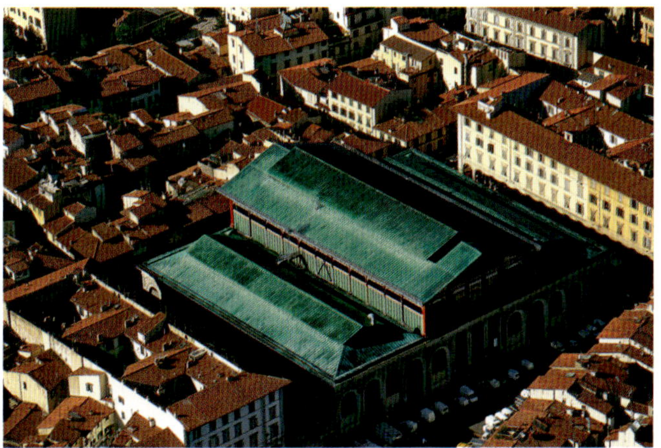

166
The Medicean Chapels, which include the Cappella dei Principi (foreground) and the Sagrestia Nuova (right) host the elaborate self-celebratory mausoleum commissioned by the Medicis in the 16th century.

167
Not far from San Lorenzo is the Central Market, a characteristic 19th-century iron-and-glass building.

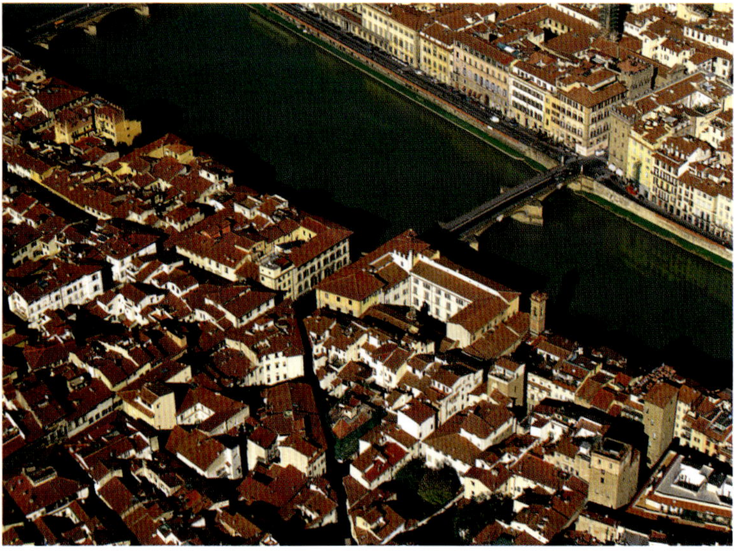

168

Over the centuries the capricious Arno has flooded Florence more than sixty times, the last time, in 1966. For more than a month the 1966 flood burdened residents with substantial problems.

169

The Ponte Vecchio, constructed in 1345, was home to butchers' and greengrocers' shops before becoming a major location for jewelry shops.

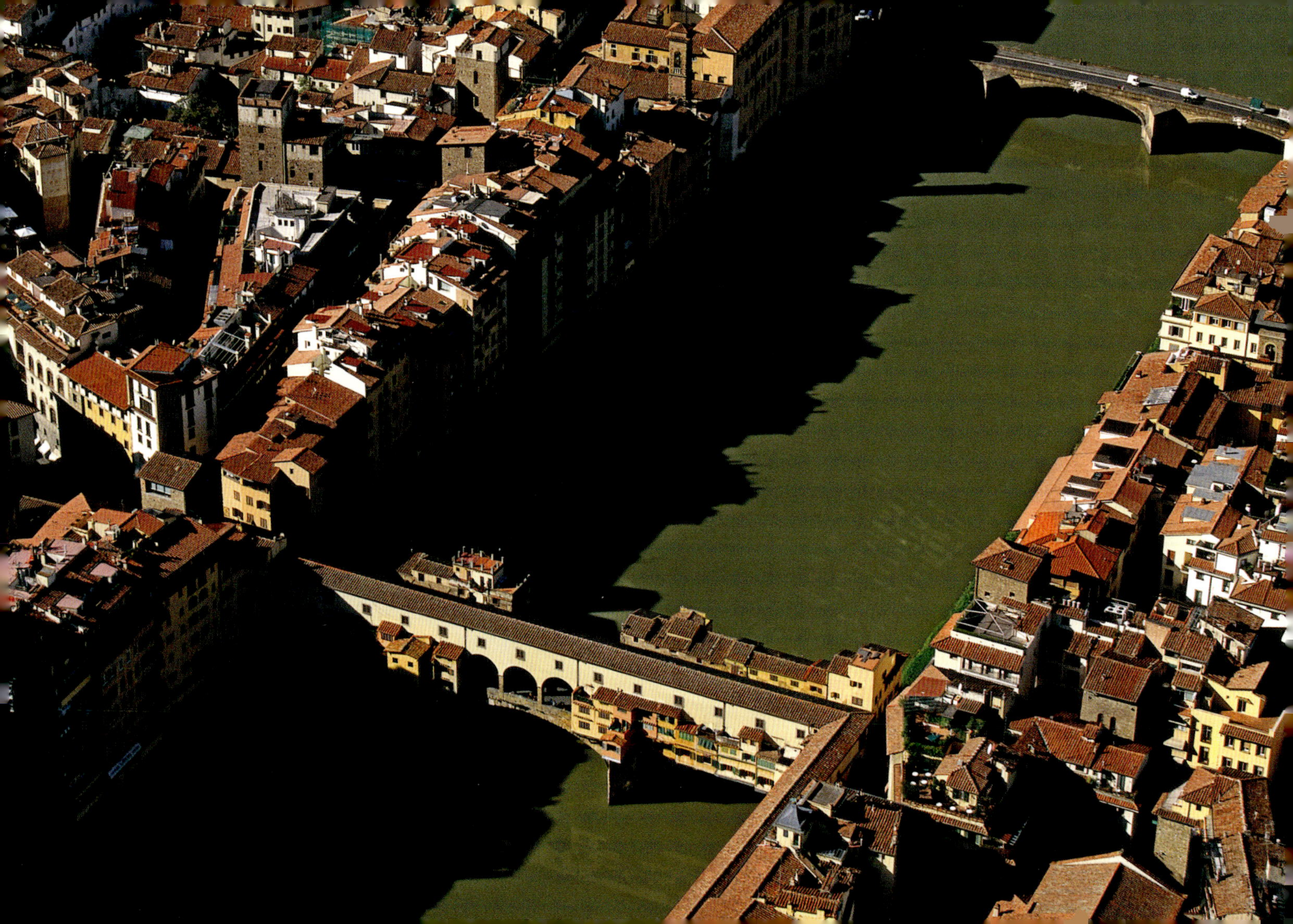

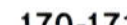

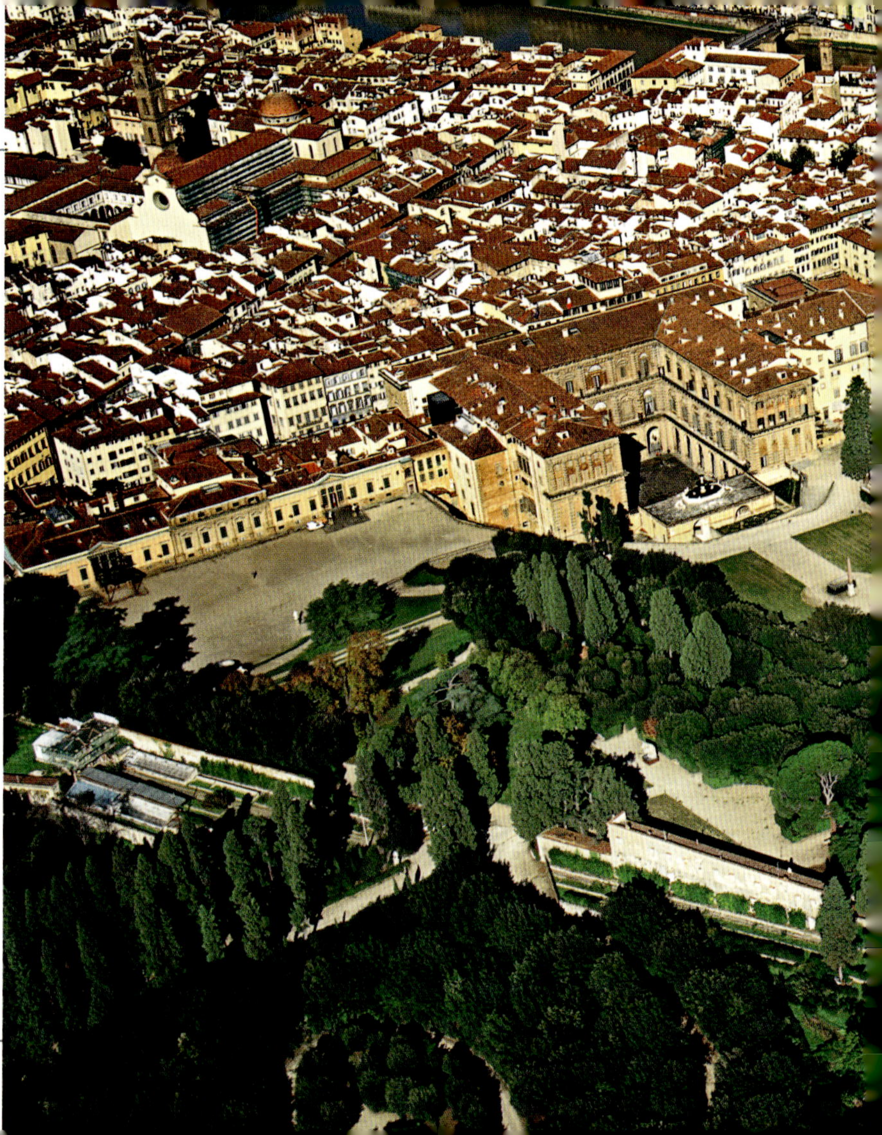

170-171
The Boboli Garden, a huge green area in Oltrarno, extends south from Palazzo Pitti, covering some 11 acres (4.5 hectares).

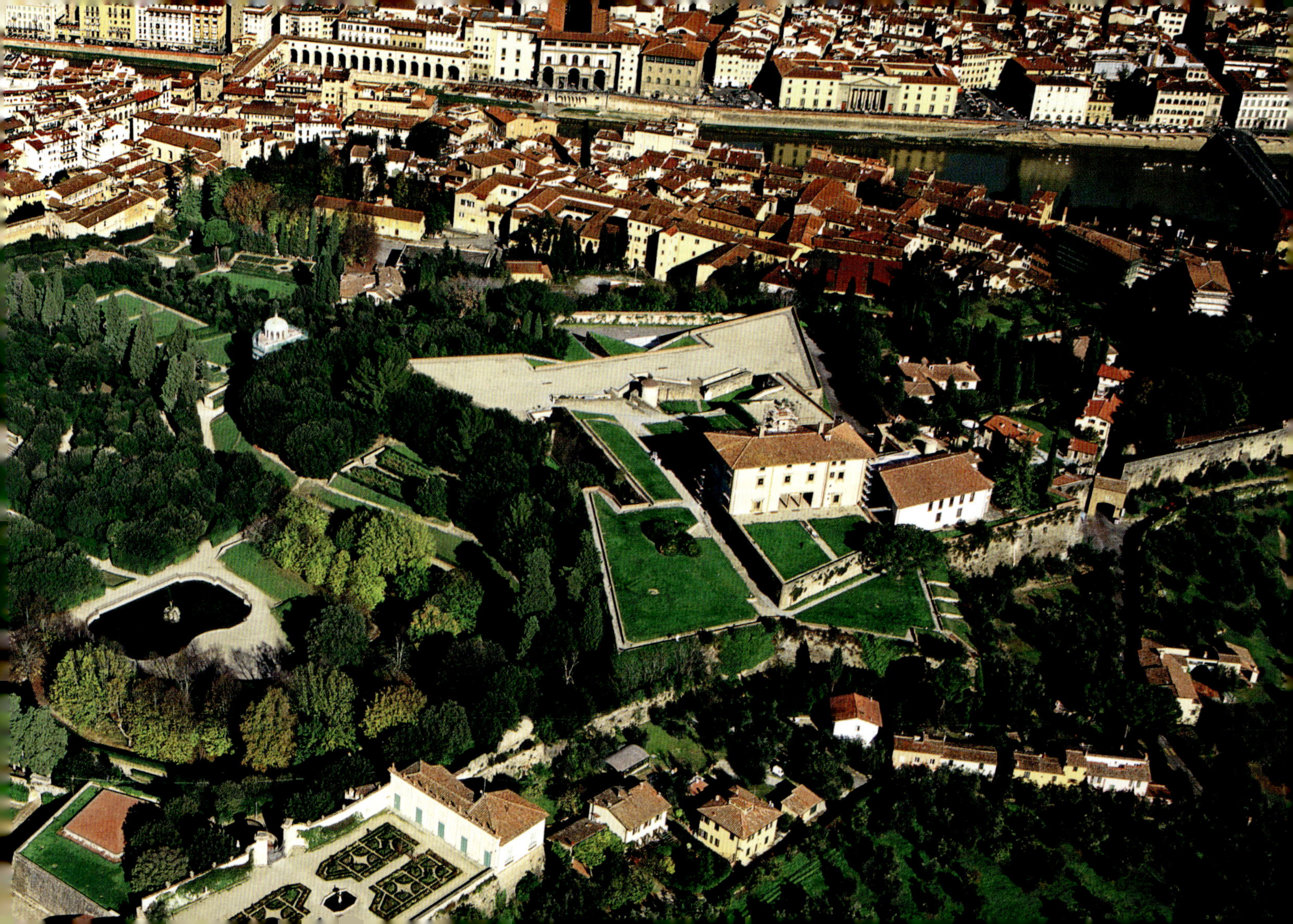

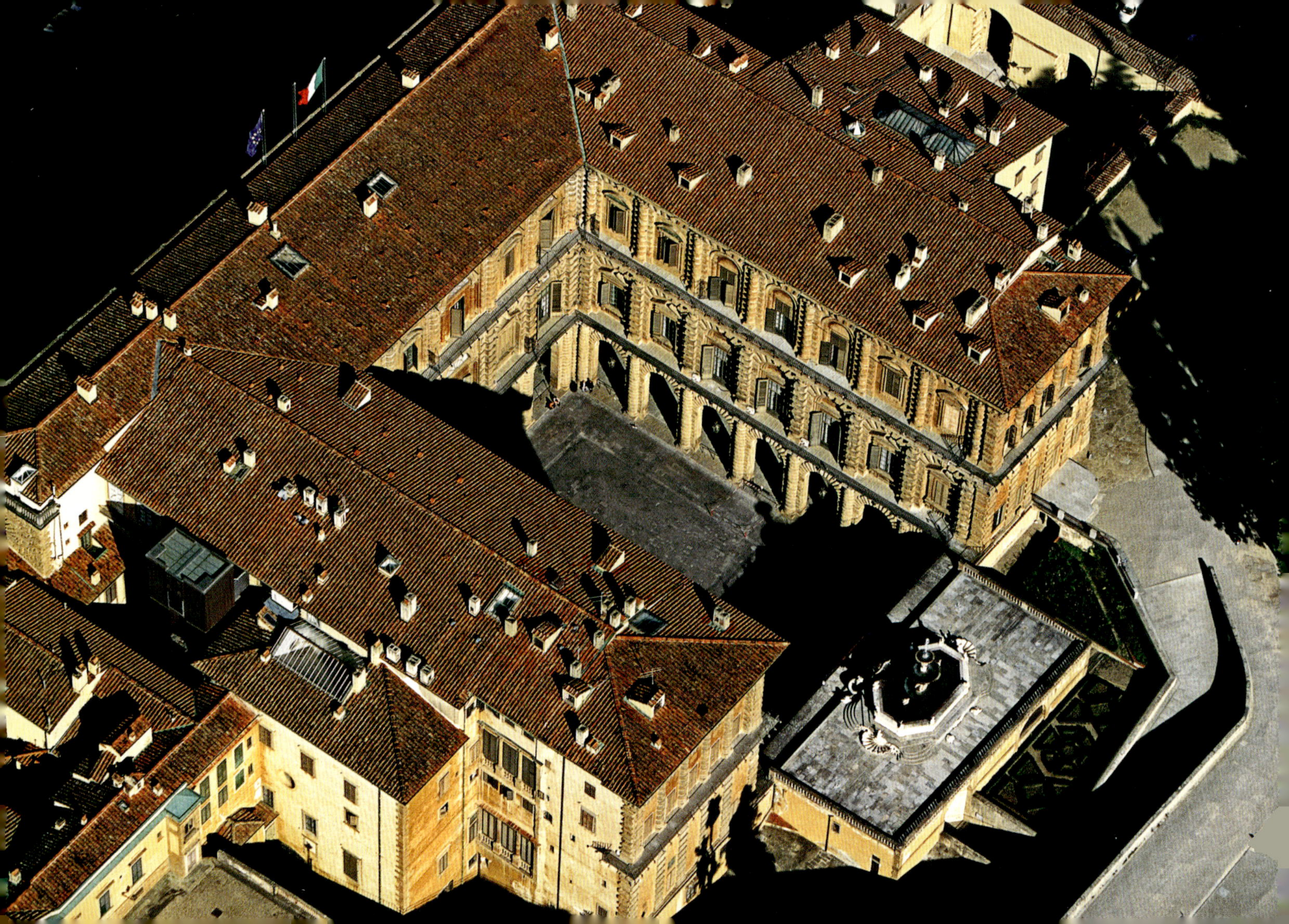

172
Palazzo Pitti, built in the 15th century, is one of Brunelleschi's many masterpieces. Today it houses the Palatina Gallery.

173 left
The large Piazza Isolotto dominates the highest section of Boboli. On the island in the center of the basin is the Ocean Fountain, designed by Giambologna (Jean de Boulogne of Douai).

173 right
The Belvedere Fortress was built in the late 1500s on the hill above Boboli, and was designed to defend the city.

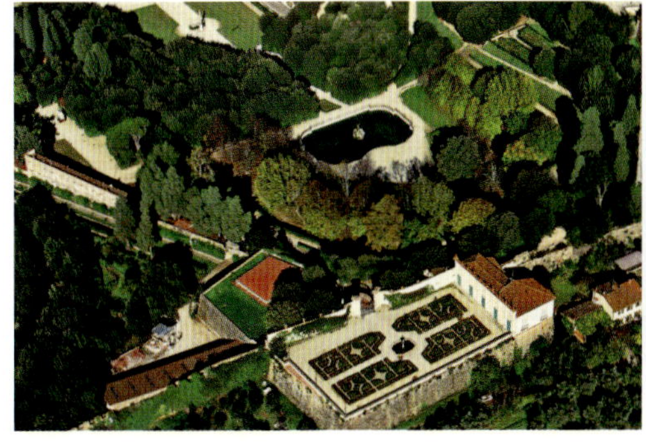

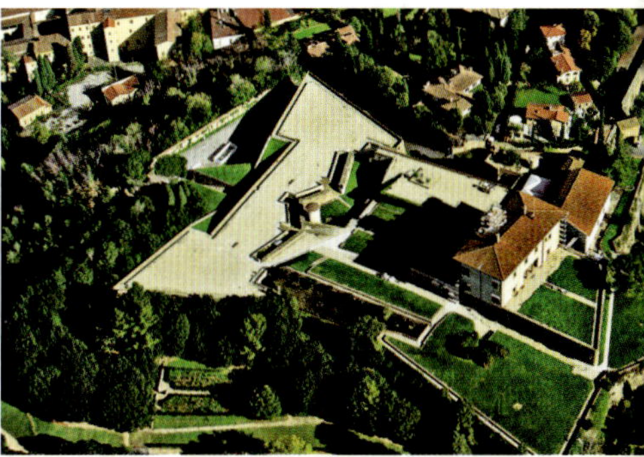

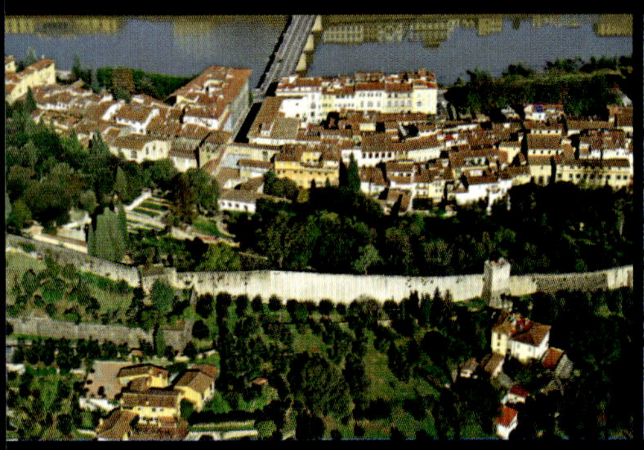

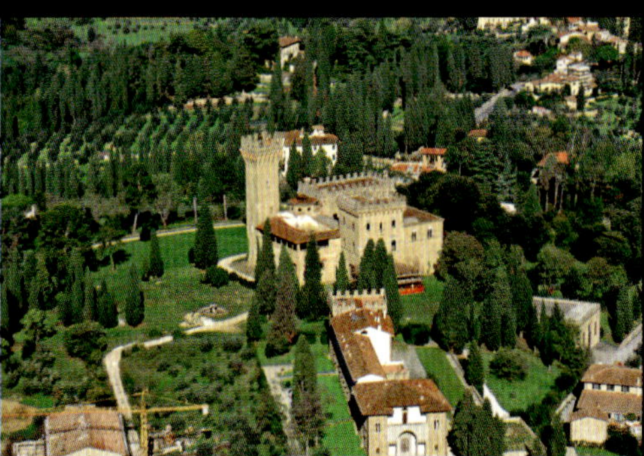

174 left
Via del Belvedere, along the ancient walls of the Oltrarno, connect Porta San Giorgio with Piazzale Michelangelo and Porta San Nicolò.

174 right
Medieval Vincigliata Castle dominates the hills in Fiesole, a few miles from Florence.

175
Luxurious homes have been built on the hills of Fiesole; several can be seen amid the trees of this green area.

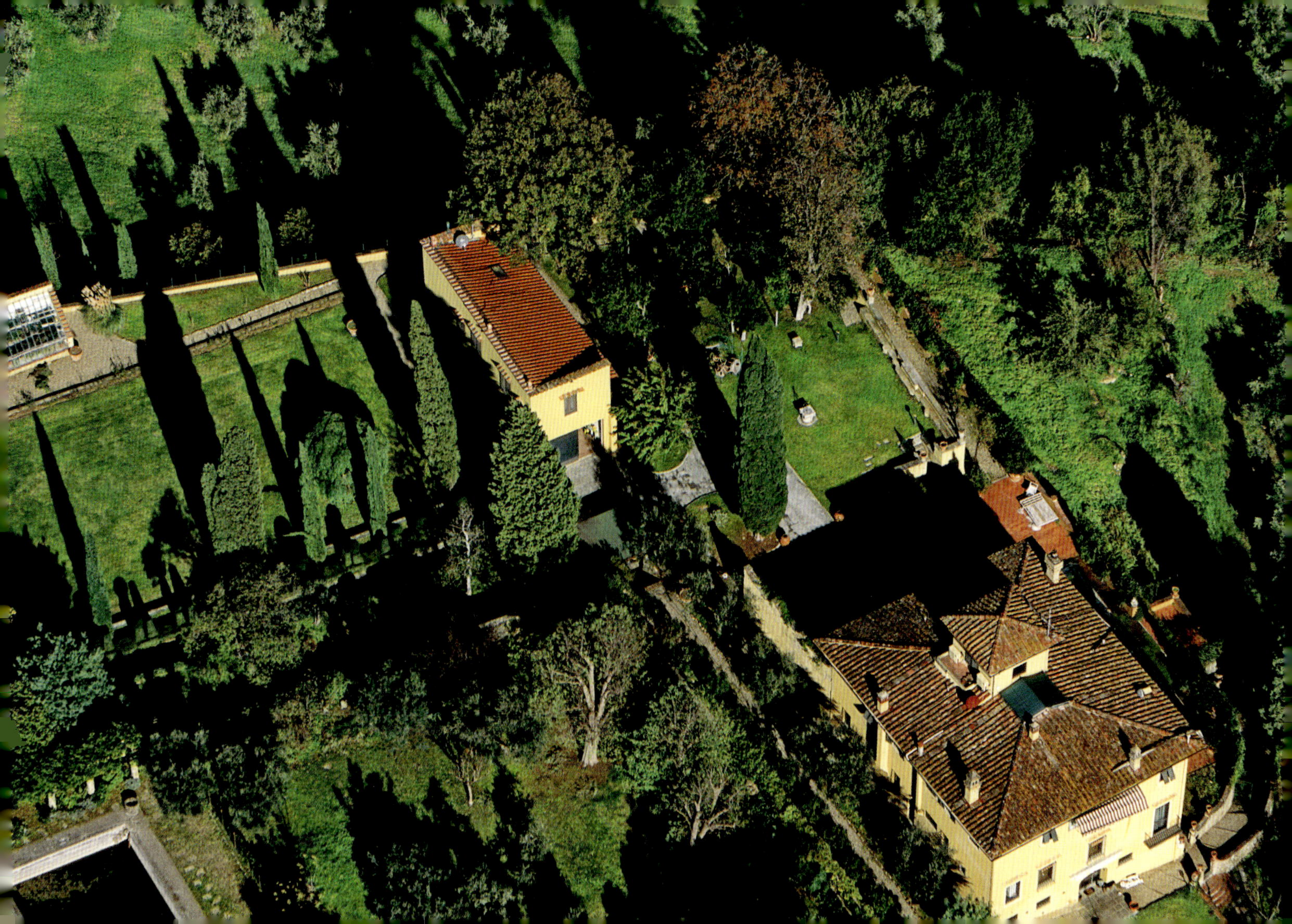

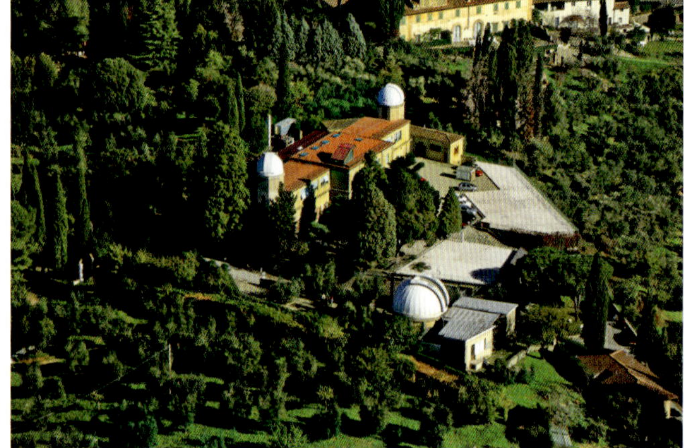

176 and 177
On Arcetri hill, not far from Florence, stands the historic Arcetri Observatory, built in 1872 near Galileo Galilei's last residence. The observatory, which also has a sun tower, remains one of Italy's key centers for astronomic research.

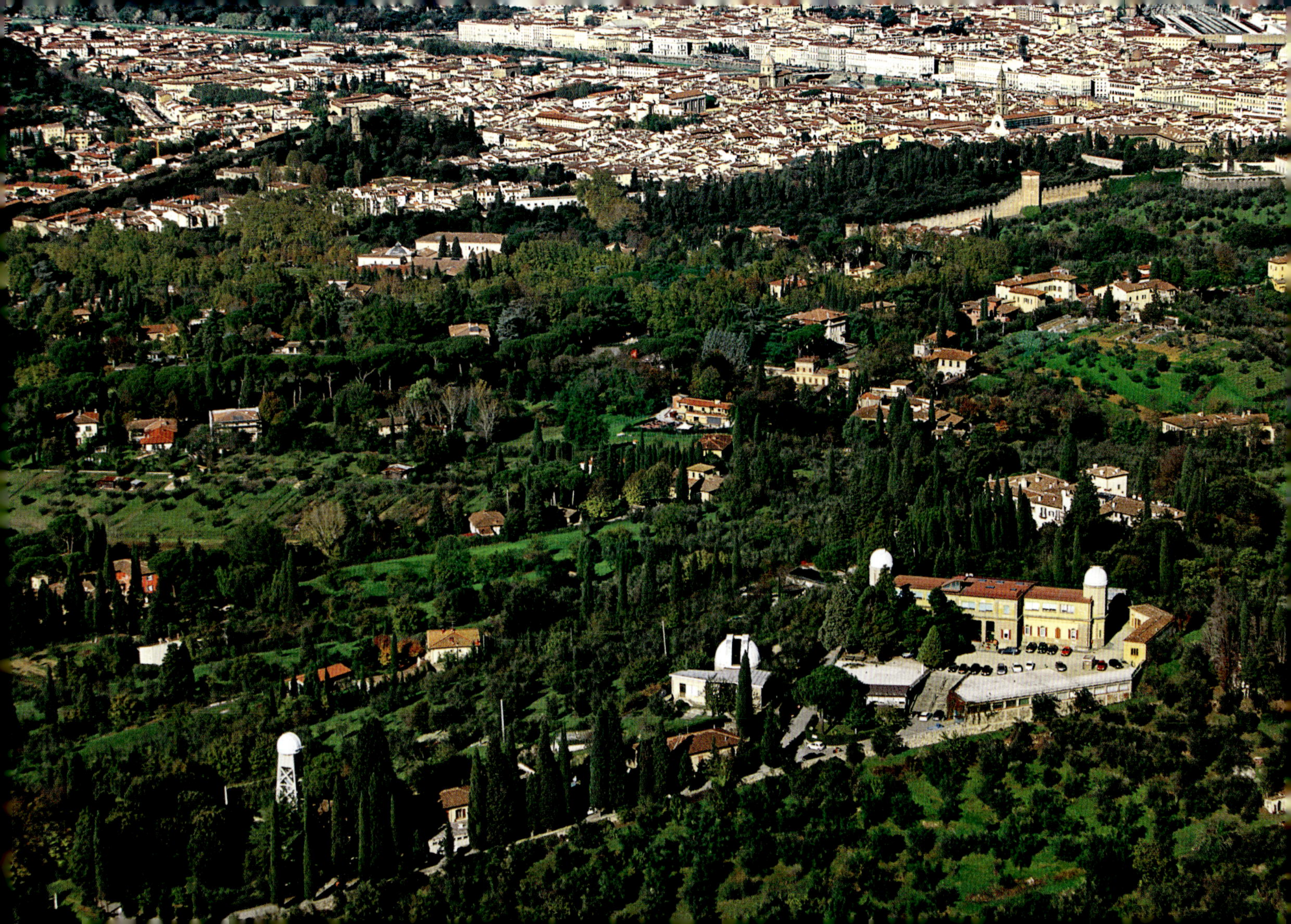

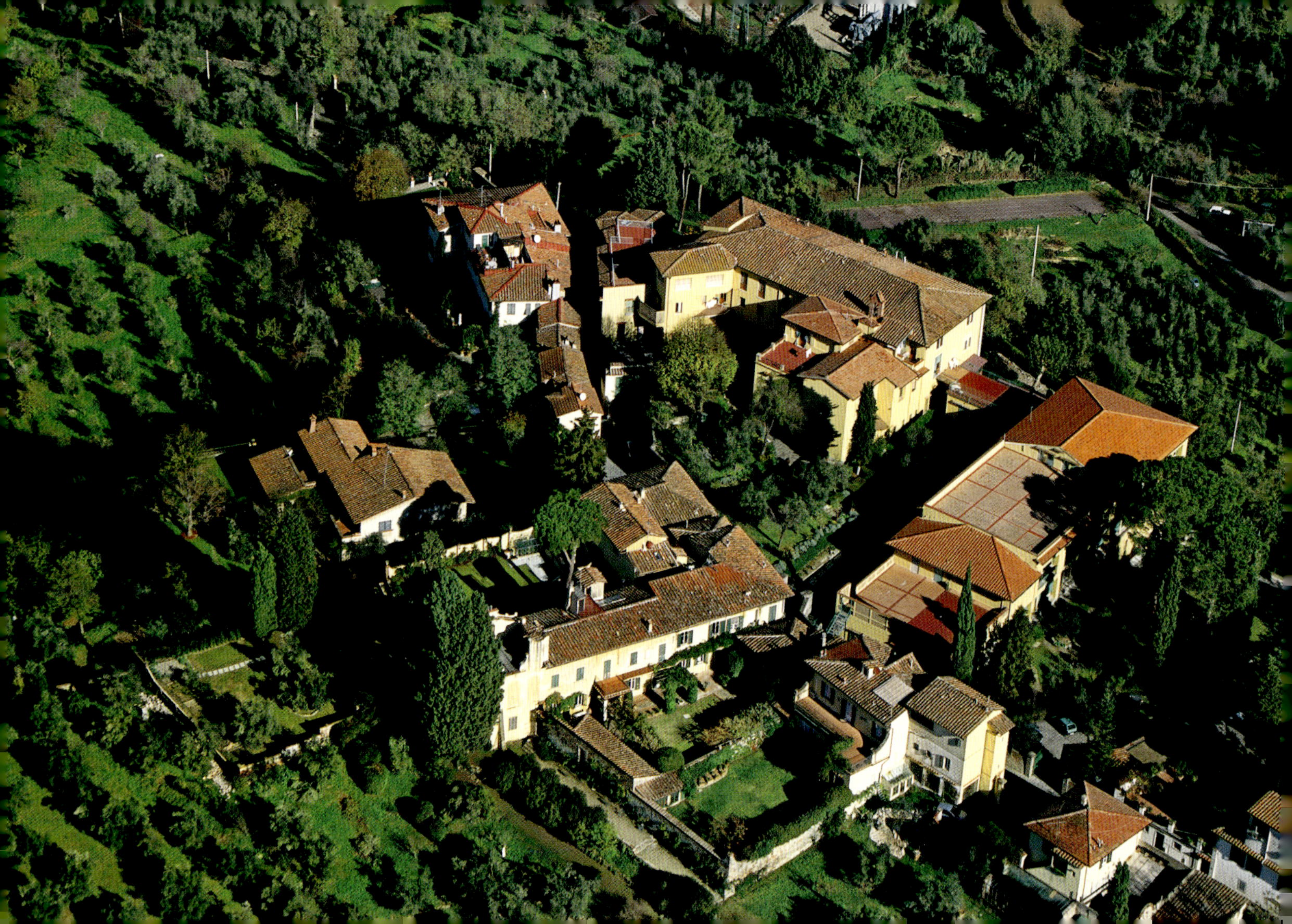

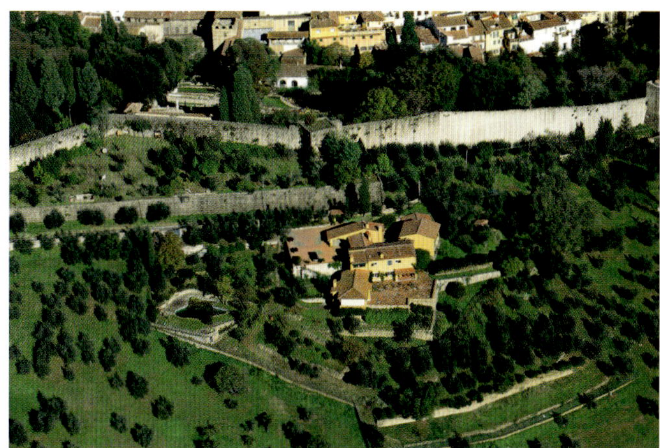

178 and 179
Beyond the city walls and the Boboli Gardens in southeastern Florence, a large park extends. Once full of fruit trees, it now known for its old houses and olive groves.

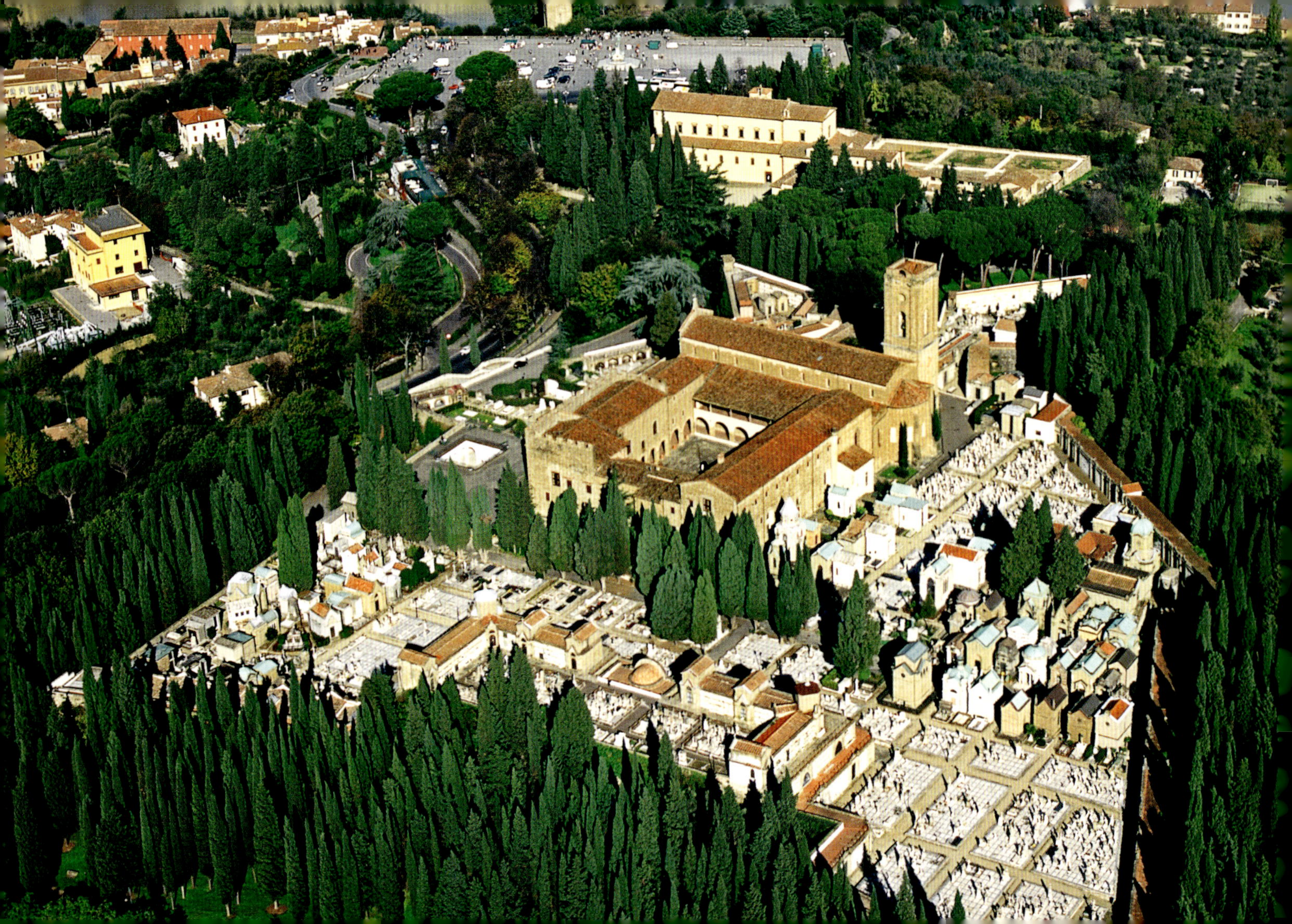

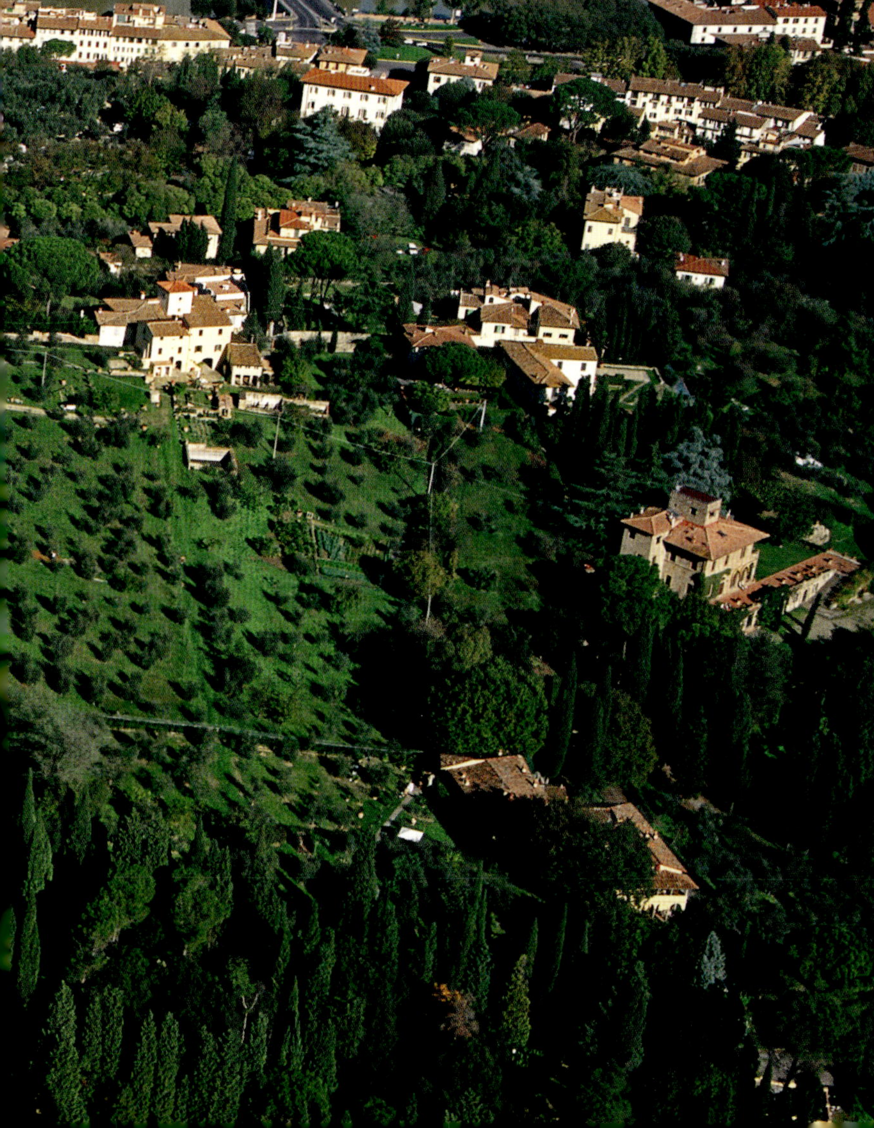

180-181
The Galluzzo Cemetery (foreground), surrounded by cypresses and green parks, faces the numerous houses that, beyond the Arno, make up one of the world's most beautiful cities.

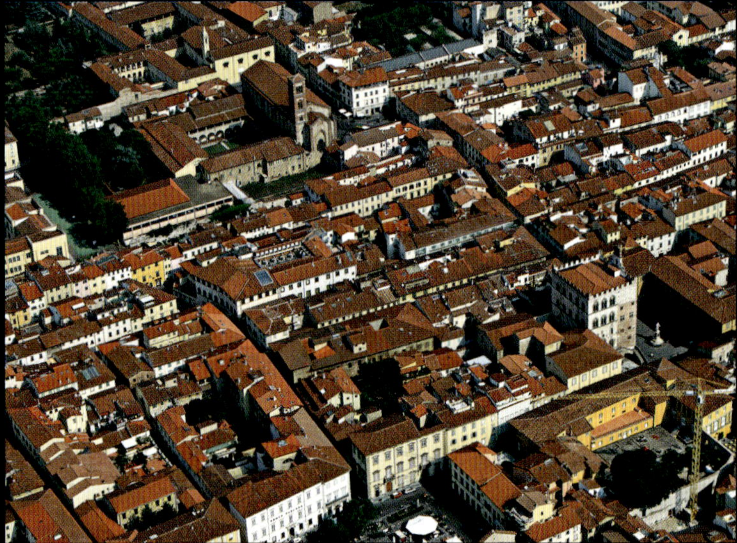

182 and 183
For centuries Prato, Tuscany's second city, has lived in Florence's shadow. Its historic medieval center (left) and the impressive Emperor's Castle testify the nobility and wealth of this still economically strong city.

Prato

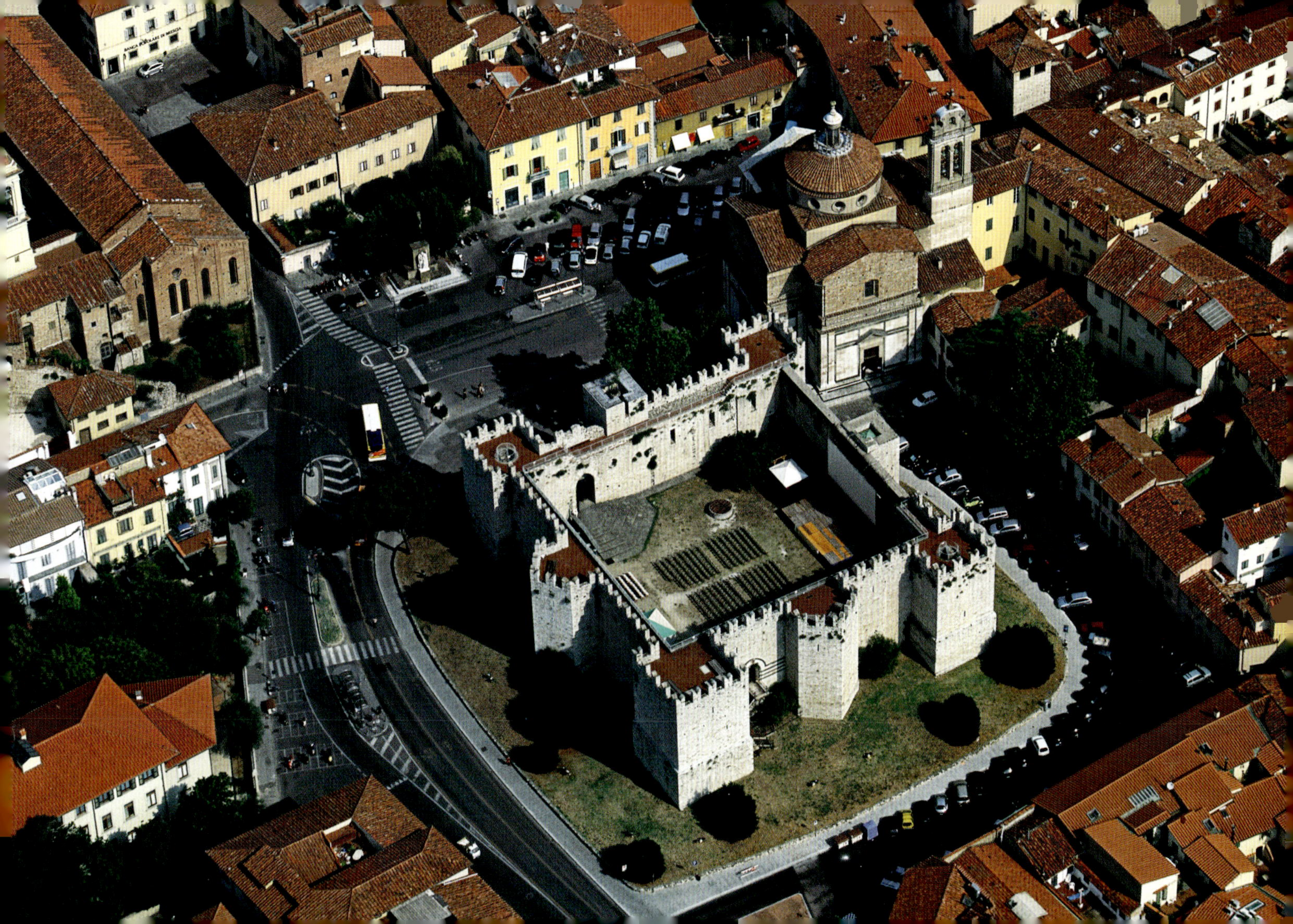

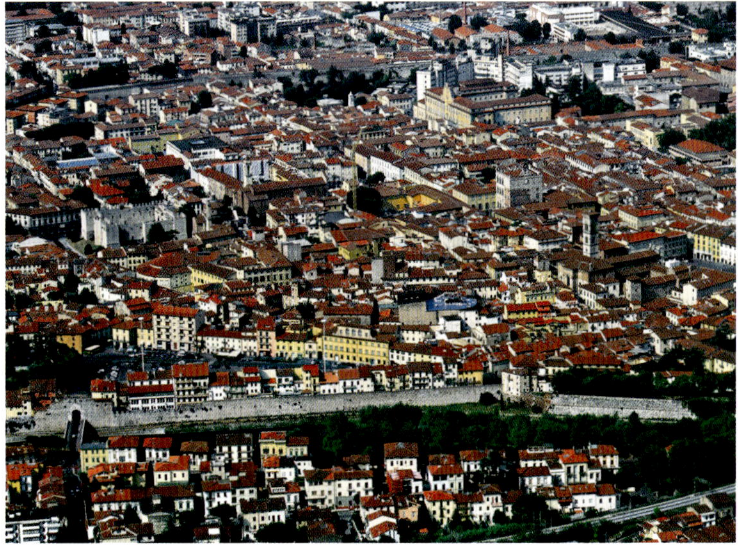

184 and 185
Empoli developed in a territory crossed by four waterways. The city has Roman origins and, in the Roman era, was an important agricultural center.

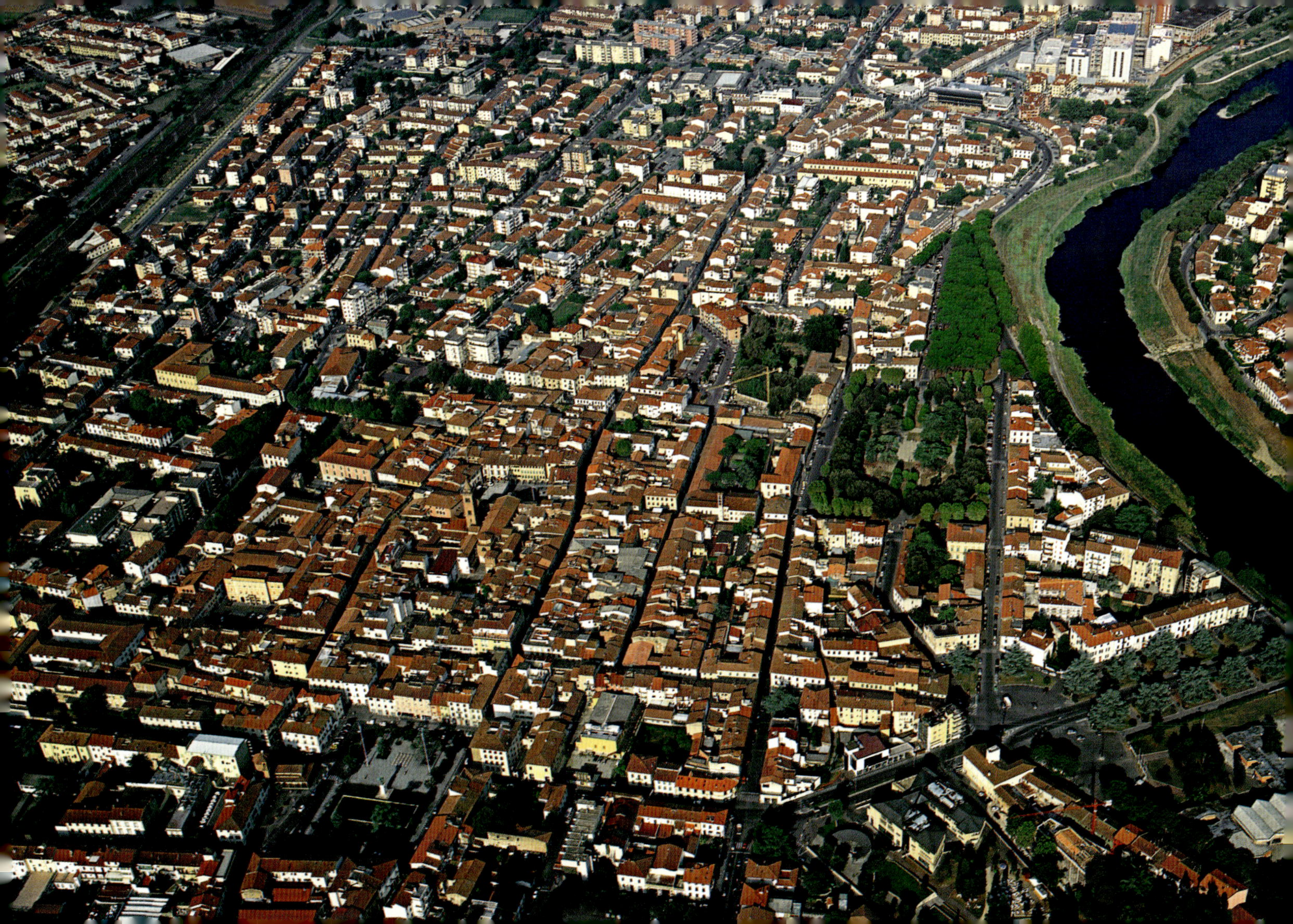

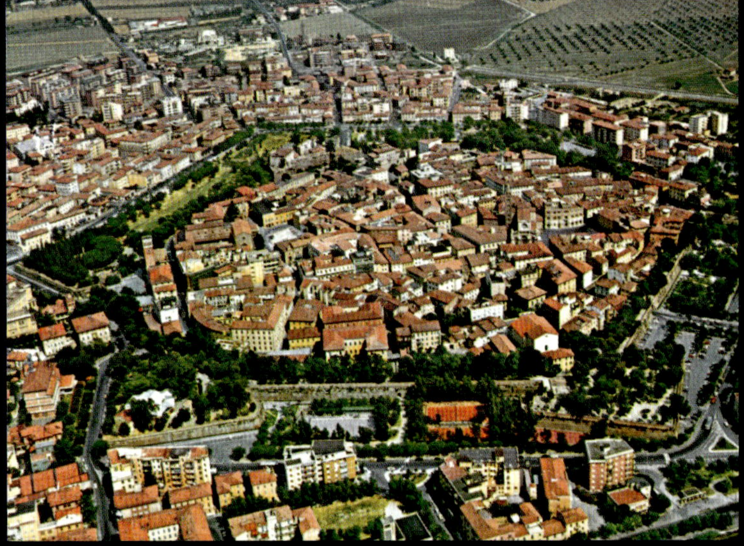

186
Compact within its Medicean walls, Grosseto is a medieval city, with winding, narrow streets.

187
Piazza Dante, with the Cathedral and the Municipal Building, is the center of this city in the Maremma.

Grosseto

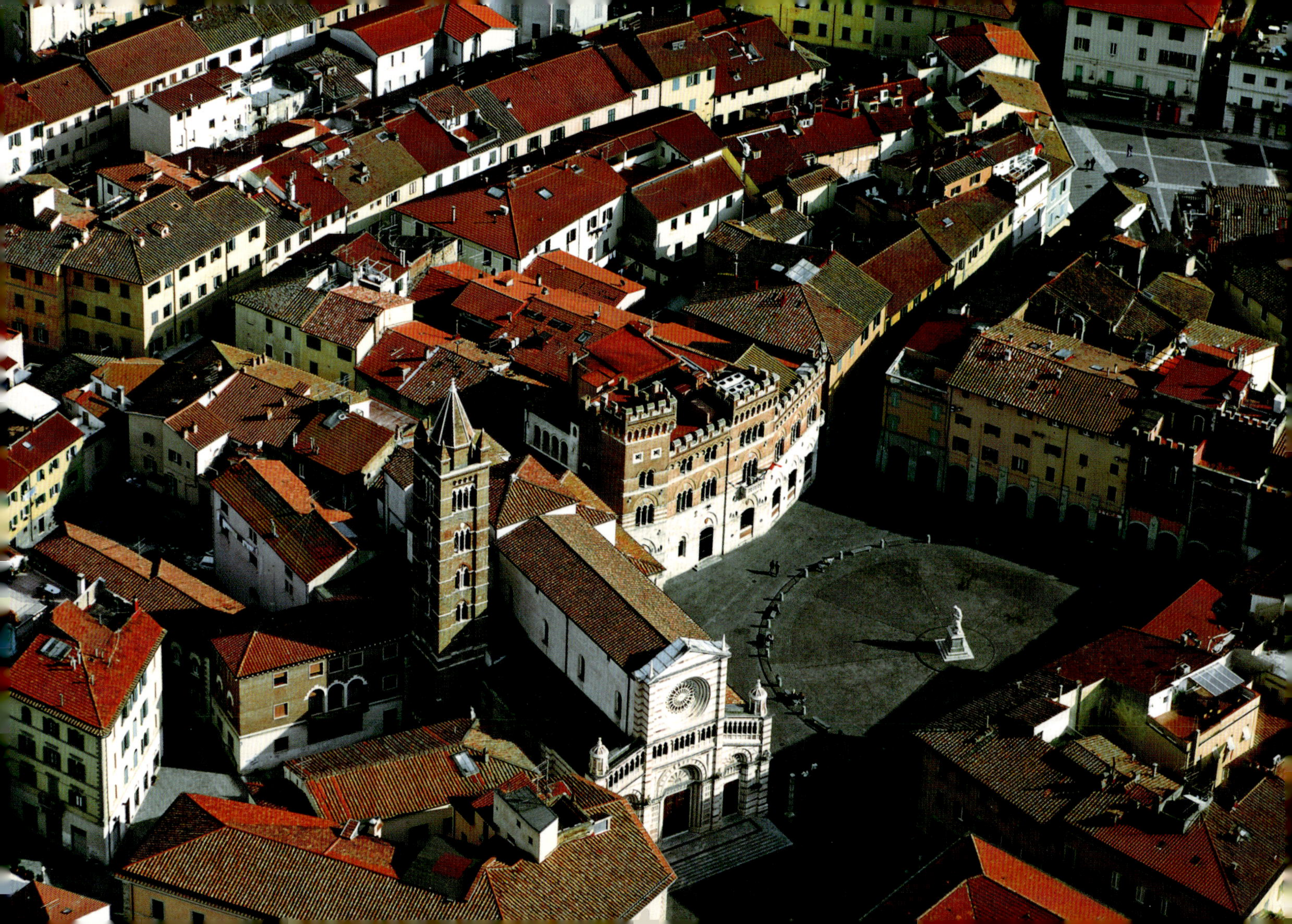

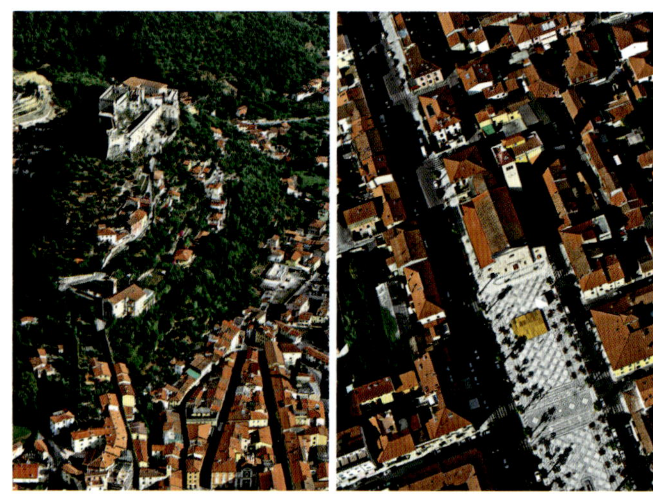

188 left
A paved road leads to the 14th-century Fortress of Massa.

188 right
Carrara is the marble capital, as made evident by its historic center.

189
Piazza degli Aranci and Palazzo Cybo Malaspina are the nucleus of Massa, founded by Alberico Cybo Malaspina in the 16th century as the capital of his principality.

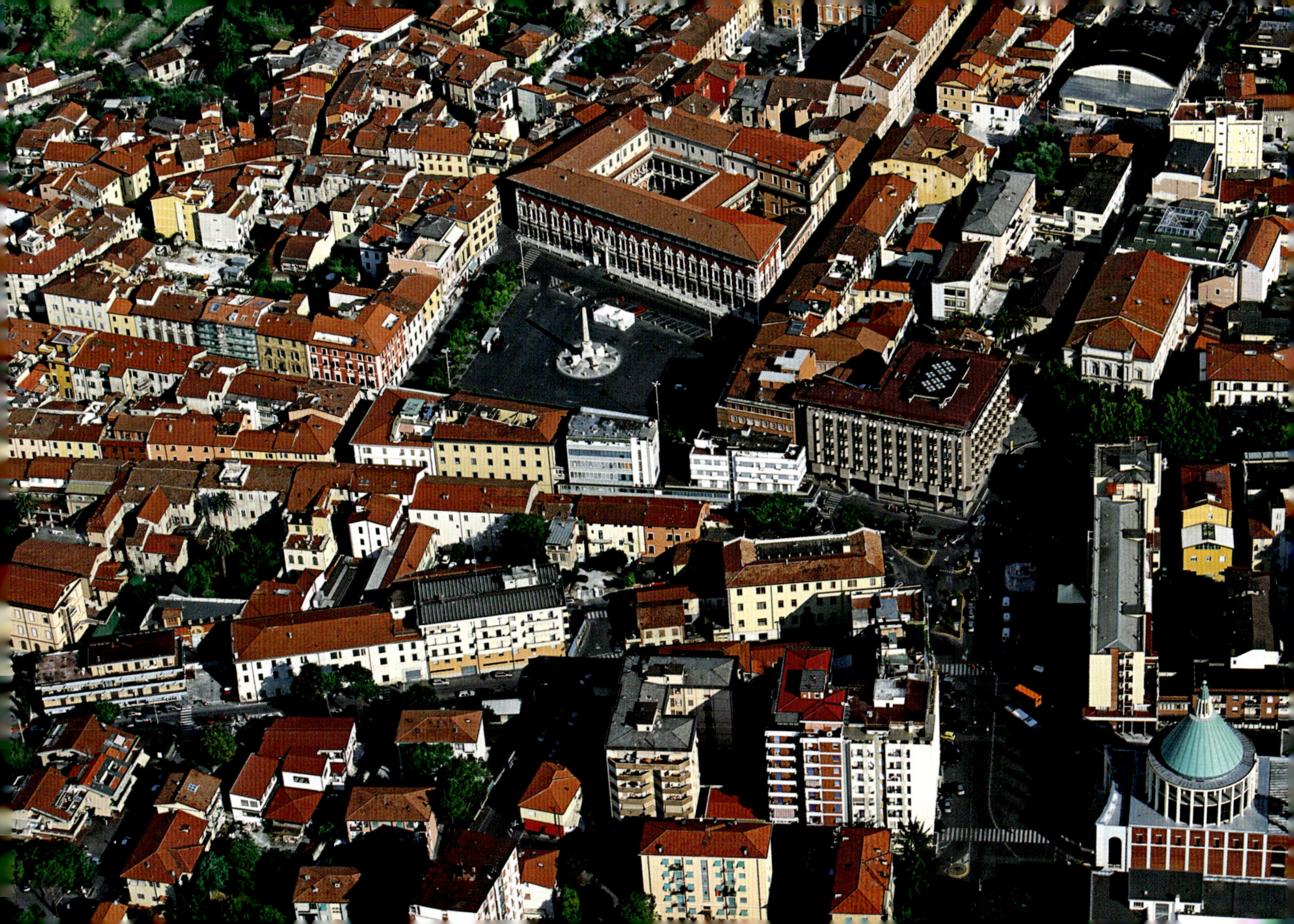

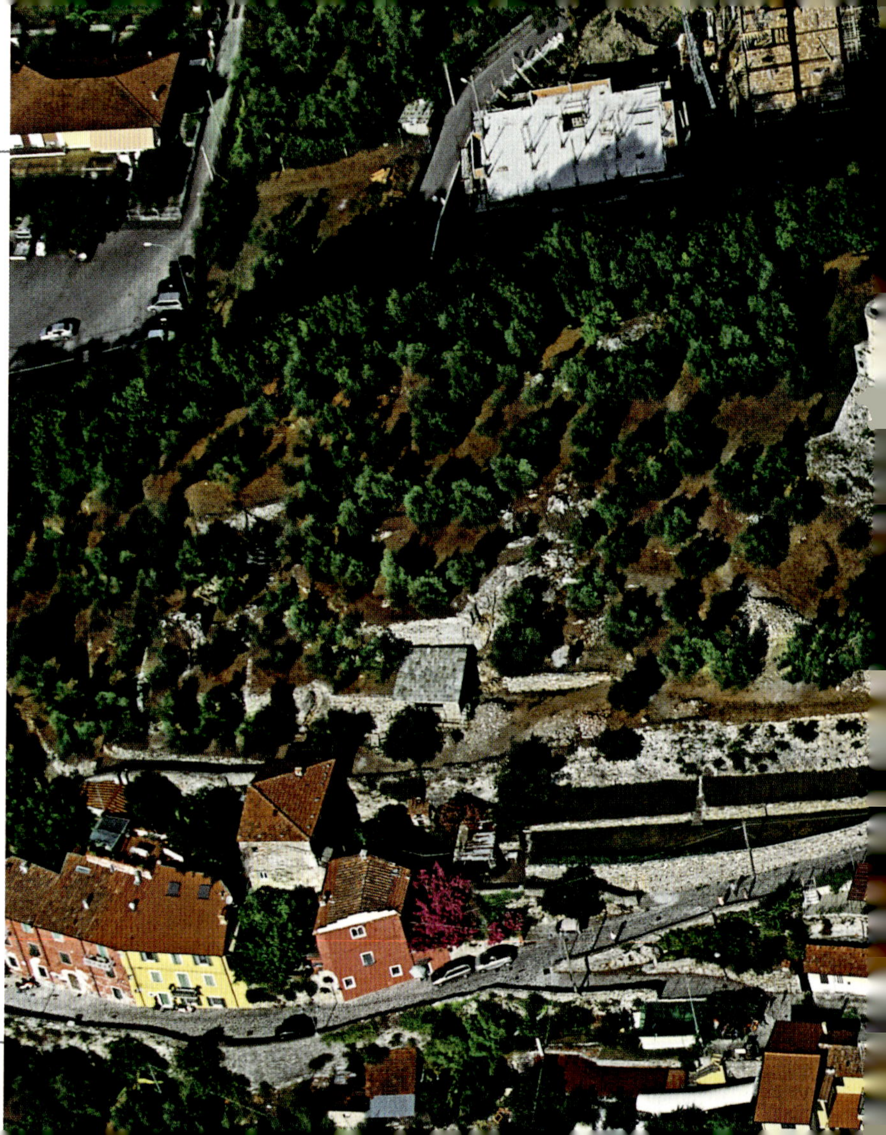

190-191
The fortress, built on the medieval city's highest point, dominates Massa and its beautiful plains that descend down to the sea.

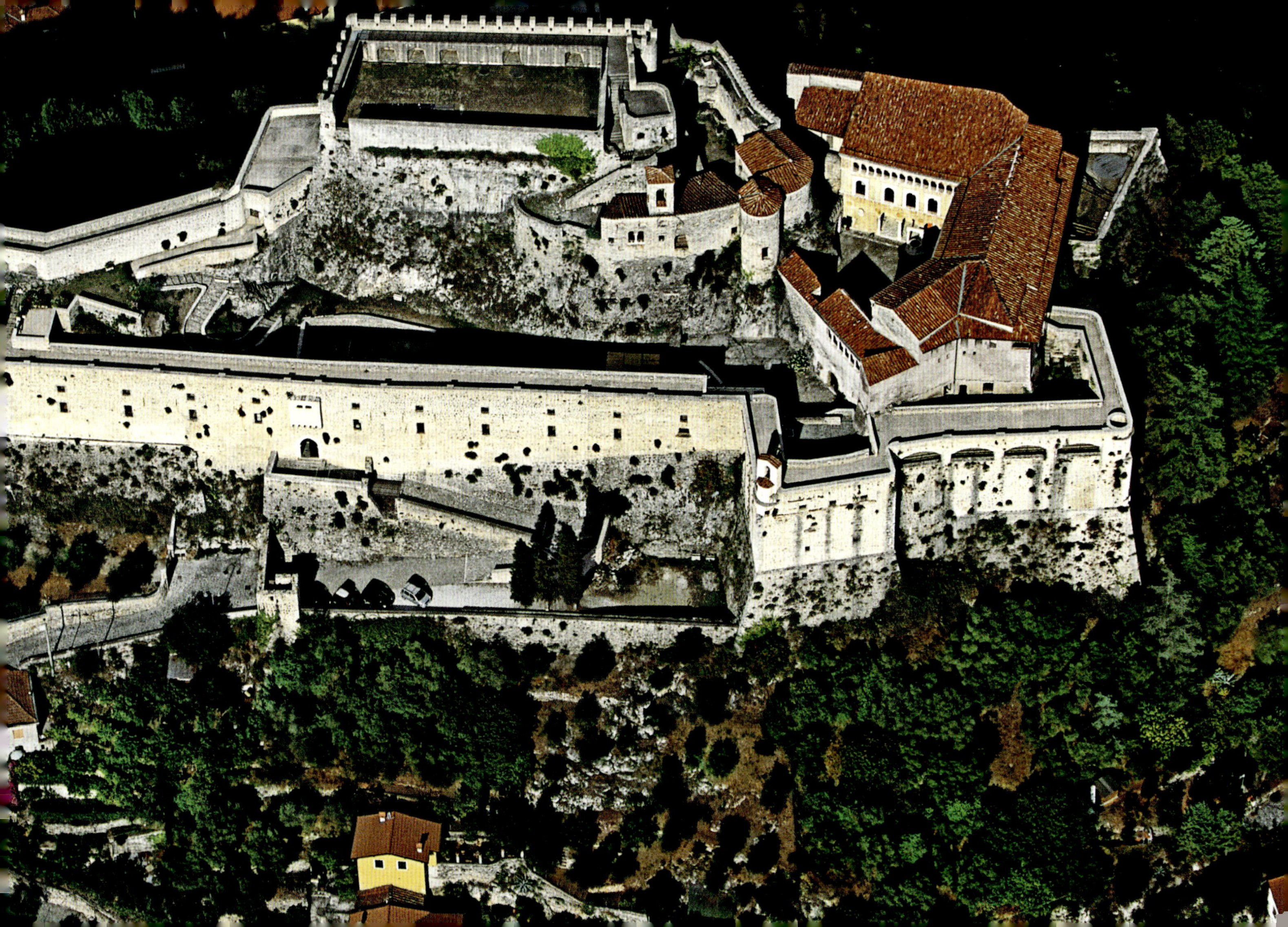

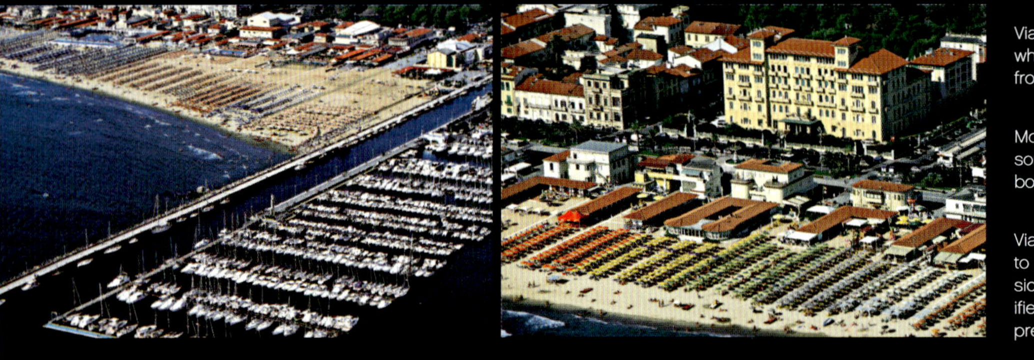

192 left
Viale Manin ends at the Burlamacca canal, which separates Viareggio's residential areas from the shipyard and the port.

192 right
Monumental buildings and historic "bathing resorts" line viale Giosuè Carducci, Viareggio's boardwalk.

193
Viareggio was one of the first European cities to take advantage of the phenomenon of seaside vacations. This enthusiasm radically modified the town's structure, and gave rise its present airy and modern layout.

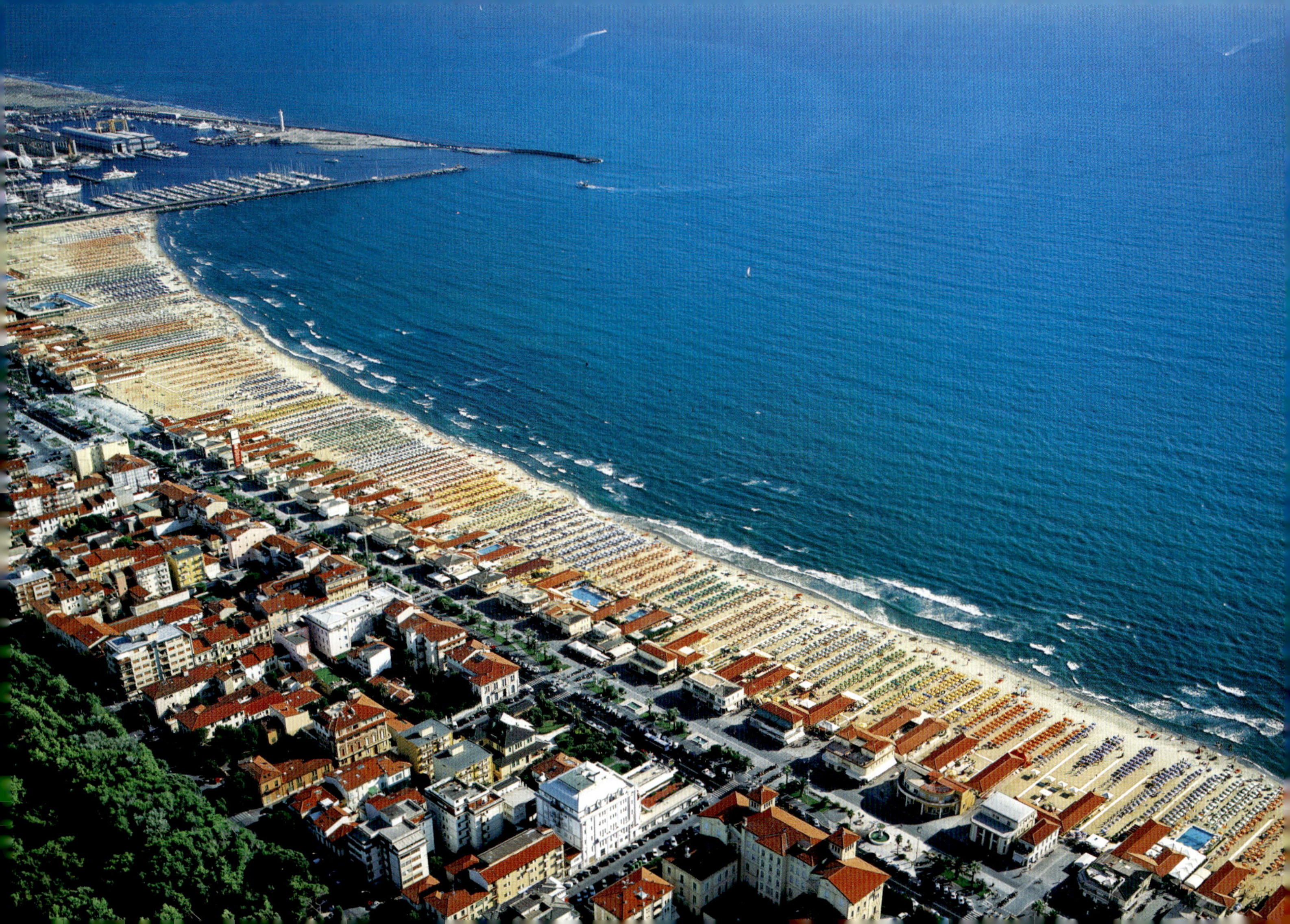

Lucca

194-195
This panorama of Lucca offers a view of the mostly medieval inner city center, and clearly shows the ancient encircling wall, now a tree-lined road.

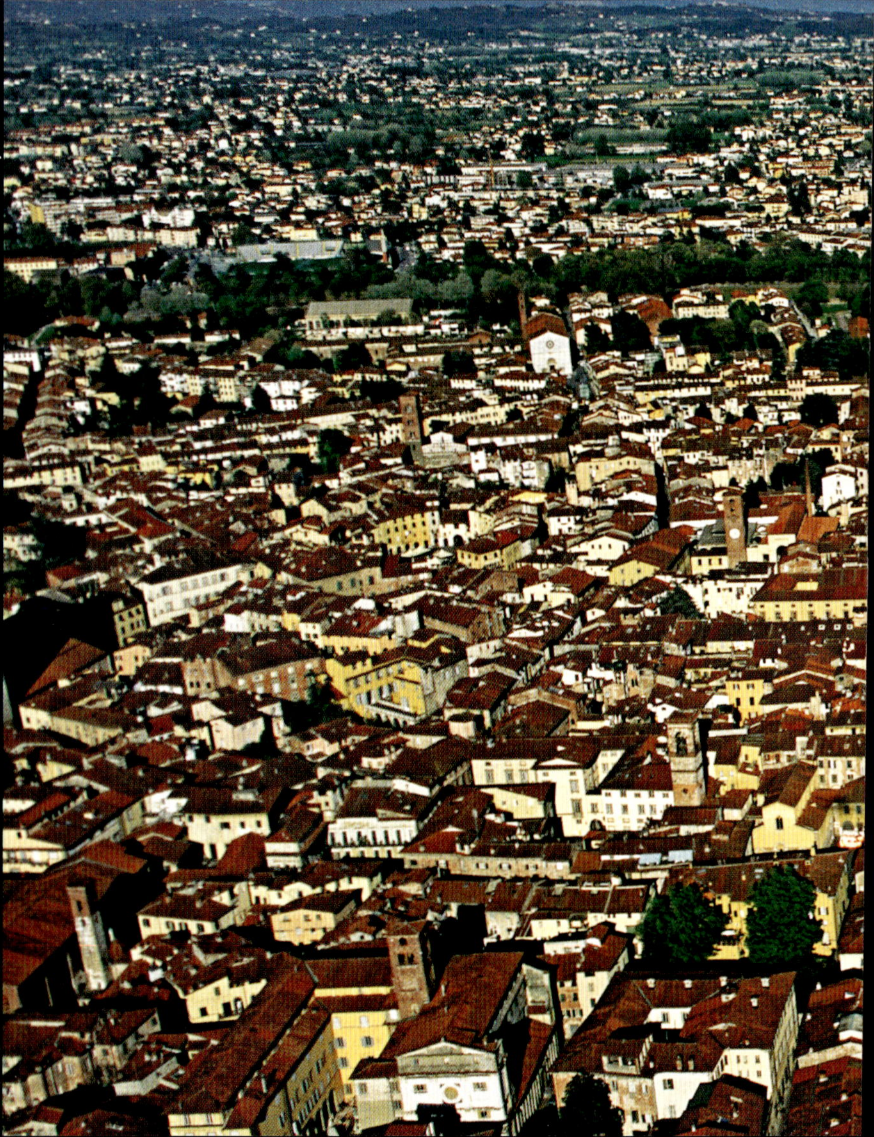

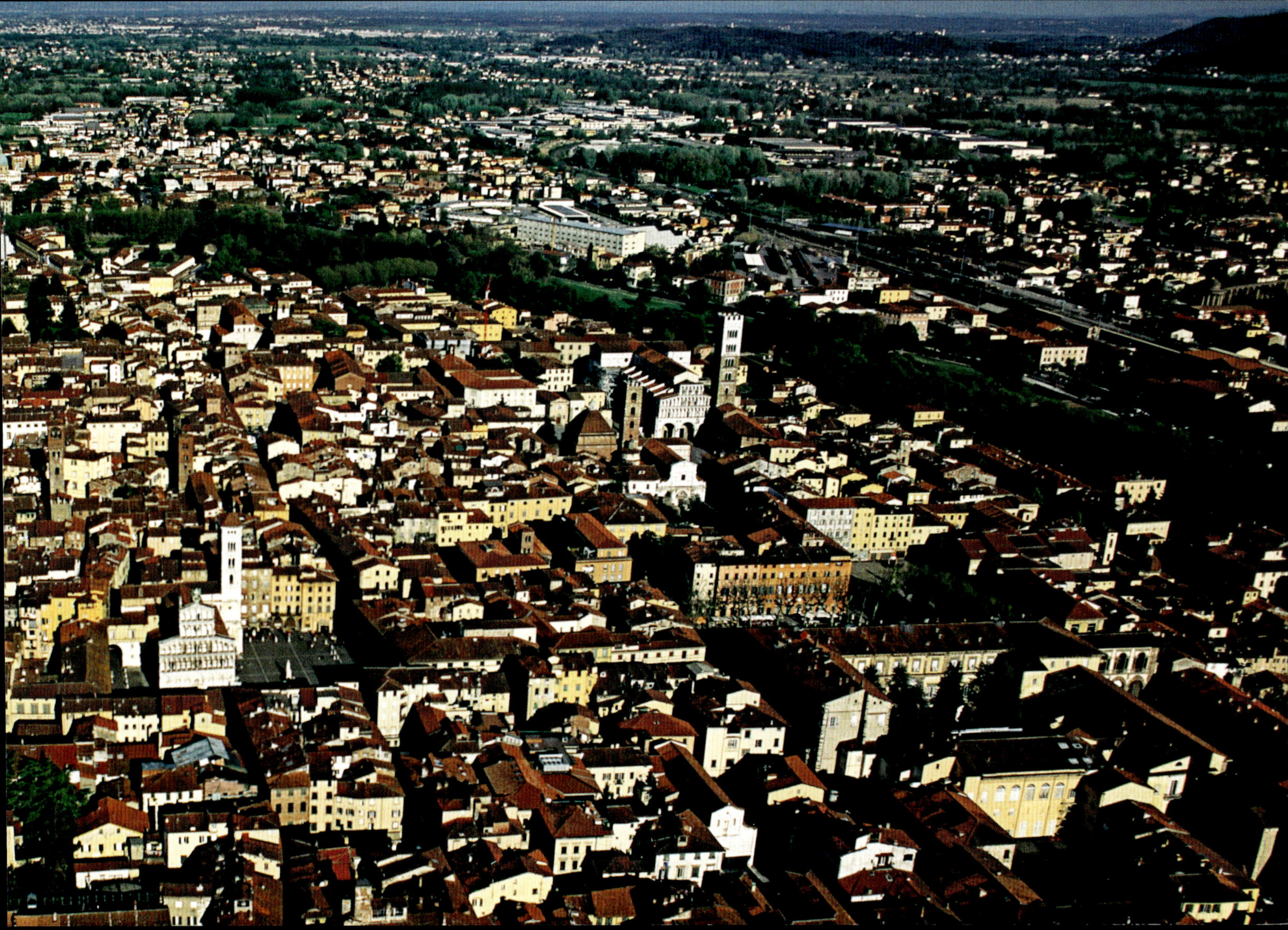

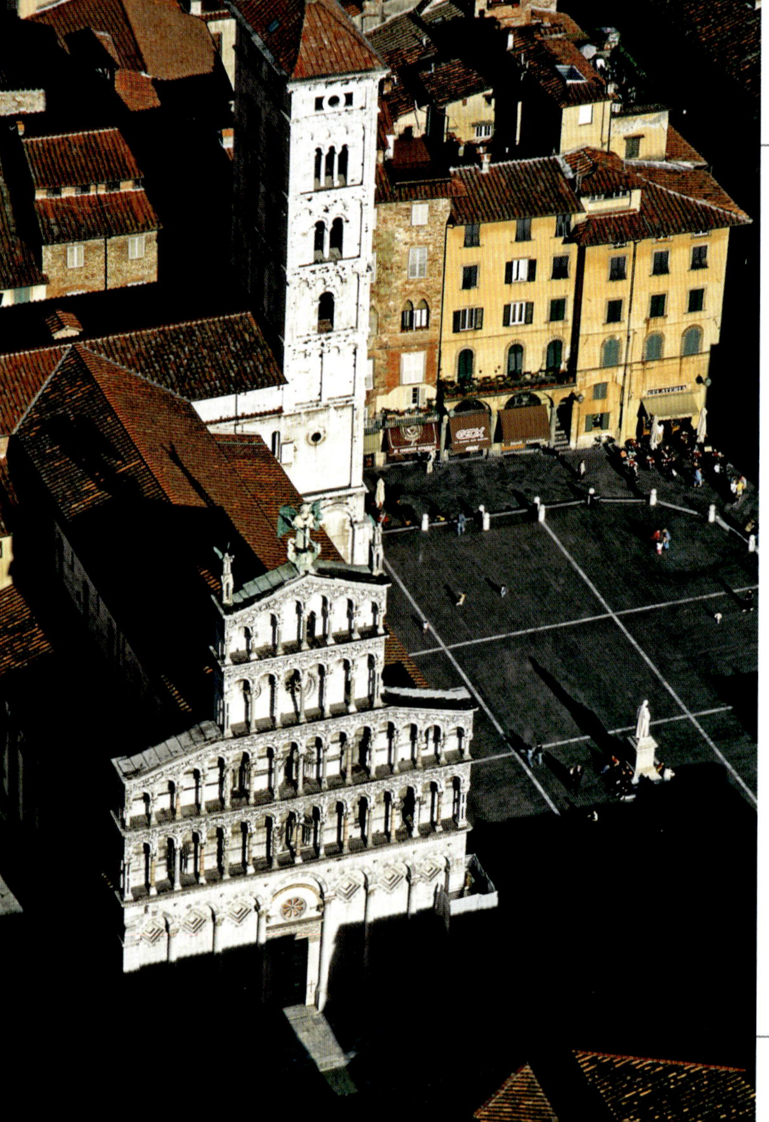

196
Piazza San Michele is considered Lucca's meeting place. The church, begun in the 11th century is light and elegant and forms, with the other medieval buildings, an extraordinary backdrop to the city.

197
The Cathedral, with its piazza and the nearby Piazza Antelminelli, mixes Classical style and decorative exuberance, integrated perfectly into this section of Lucca, which dates from the 1200s.

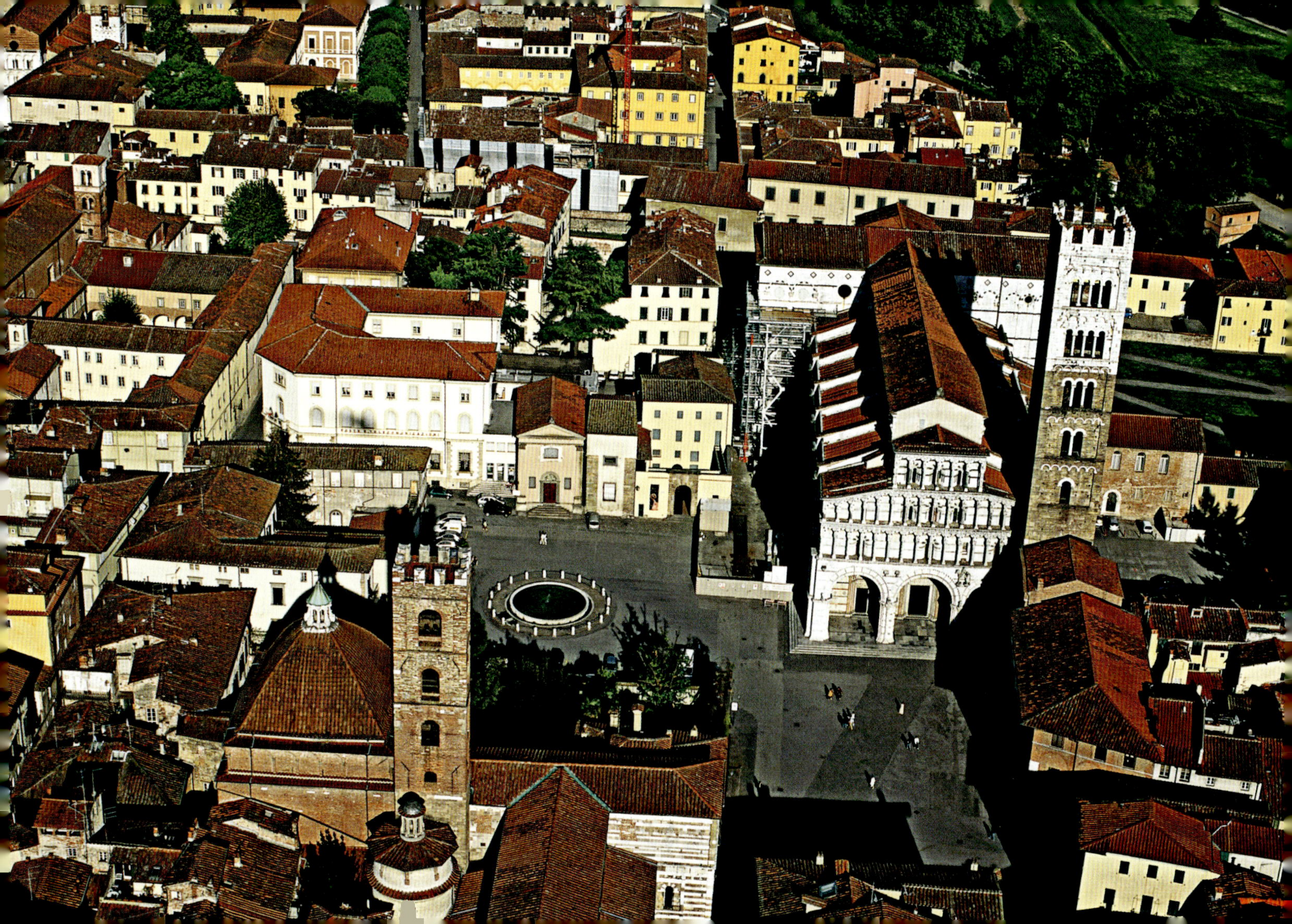

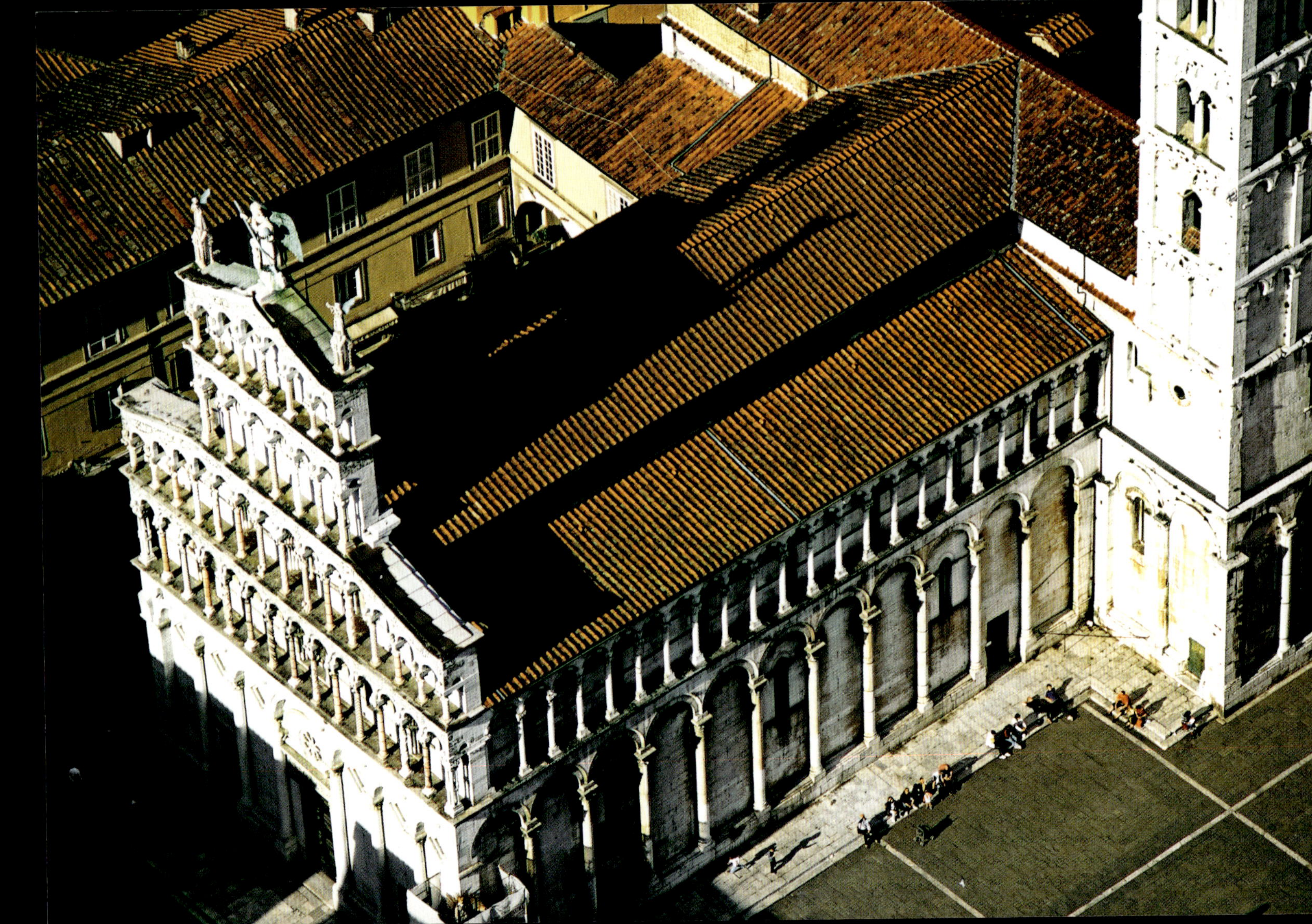

198
At San Michele in Foro, the Romanesque and Gothic intertwine, giving life to a modest basilica, in which verticality is emphasized to enhance a bottom-heavy structure.

199
San Freudiano, which dates to the 12th century, has a rectangular shape and battlemented tower of medieval origin.

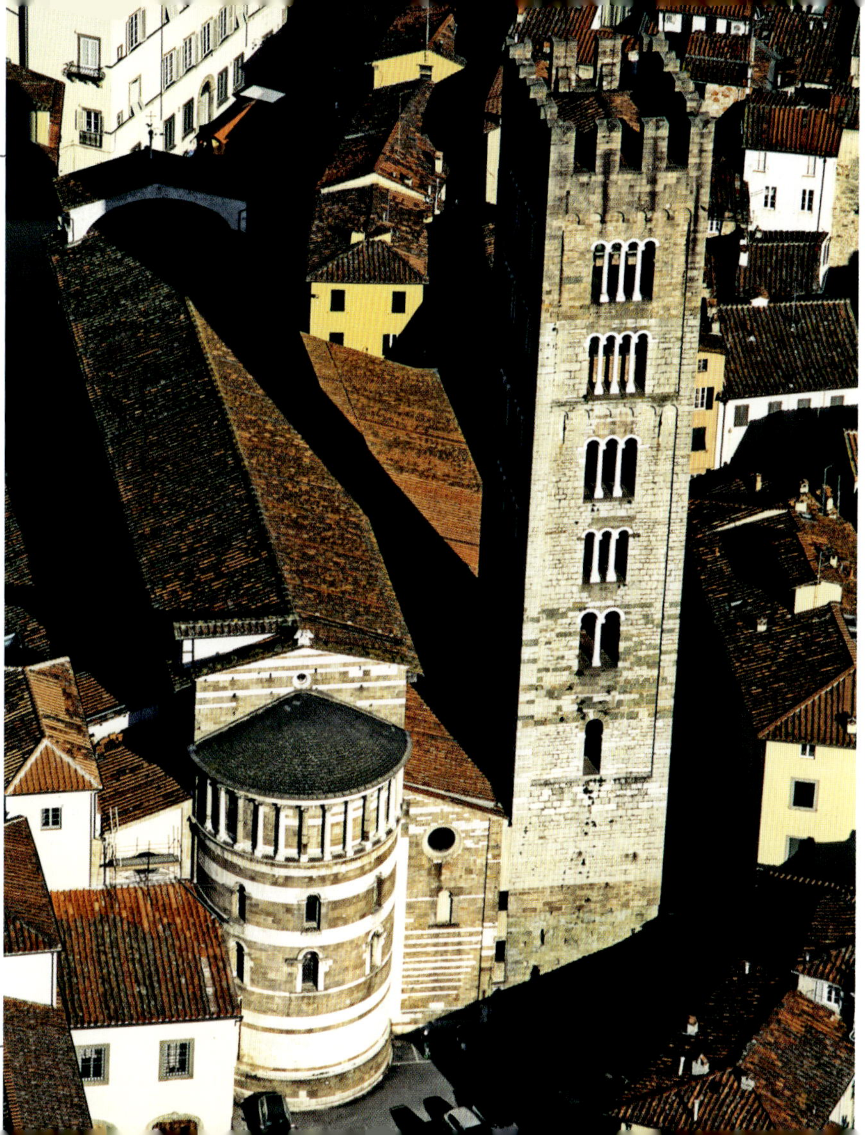

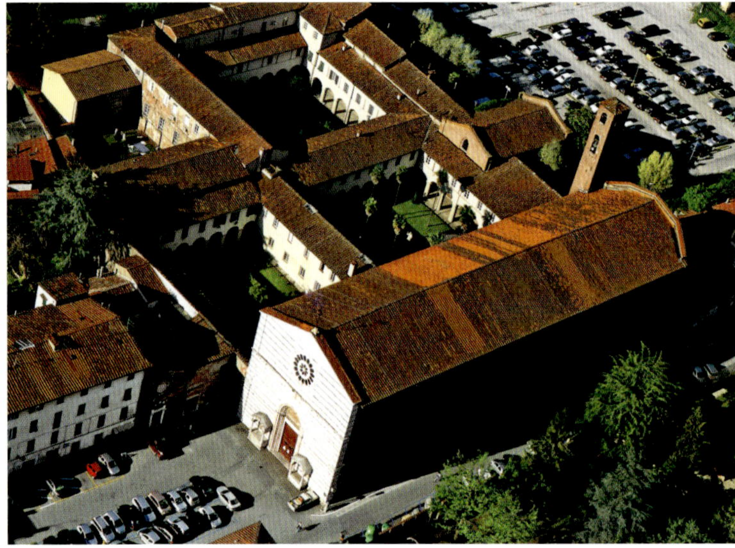

200
The San Francesco complex, which unites a simple Romanesque church and related monastery, rises near the eastern section of Lucca's outer walls.

201
The name Piazza Anfiteatro (also called the Market Square) clearly derives from a 2nd- century A.D. Roman design, of typical elliptical shape.

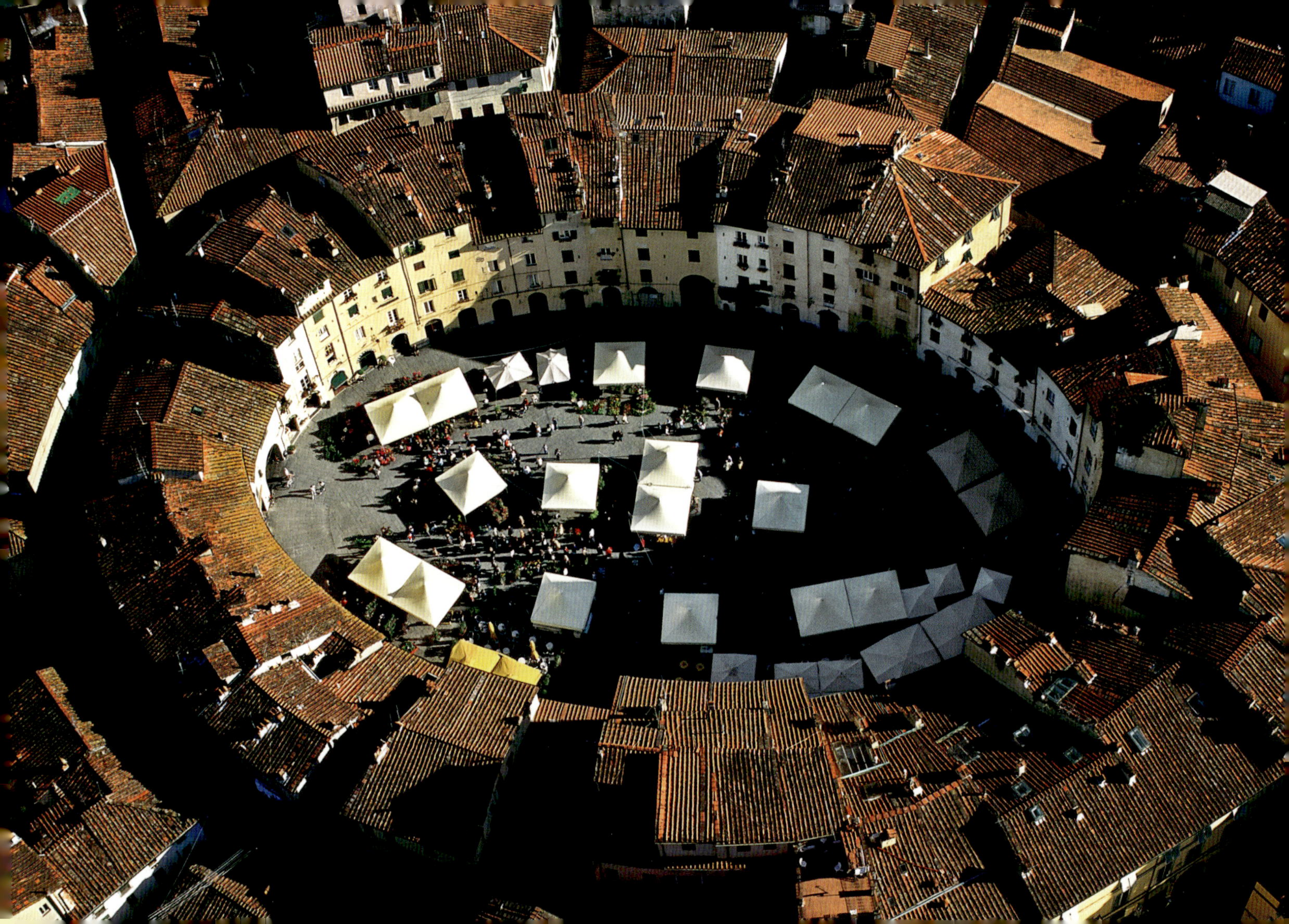

Pistoia

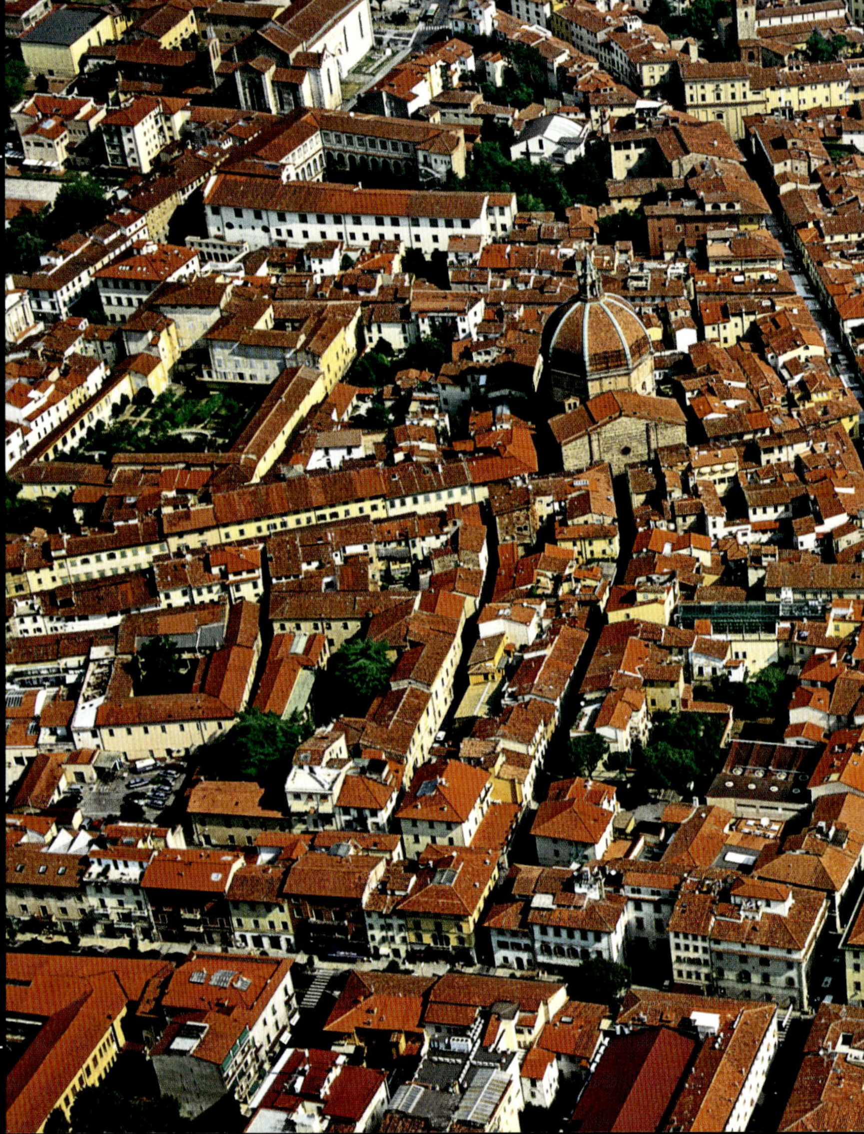

202-203
Pistoia's civil and religious monuments decorate the city's medieval center. From the dense network of streets and buildings, Piazza del Duomo stands out with its basilica (center) and the cupola of the Madonna dell'Umiltà.

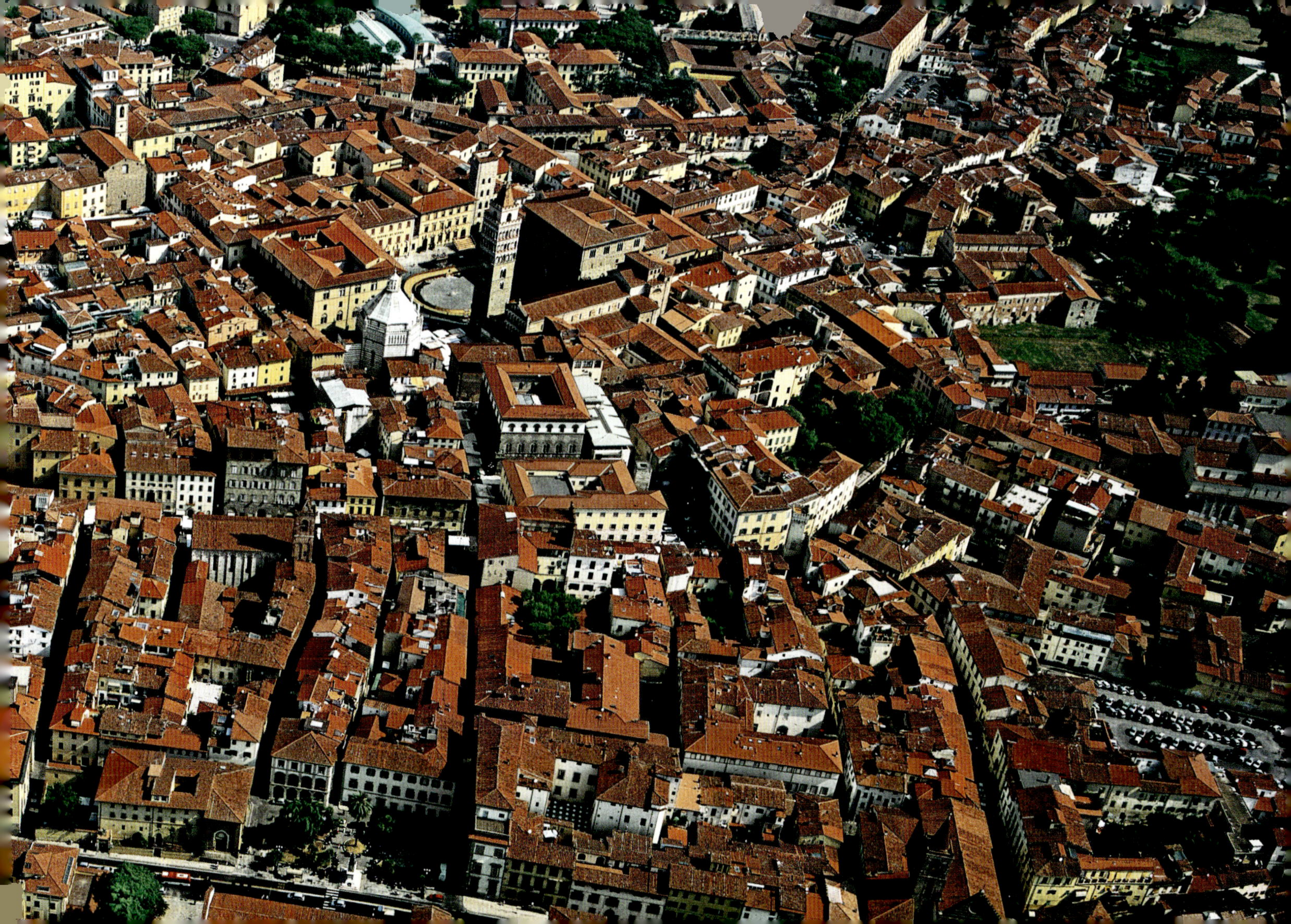

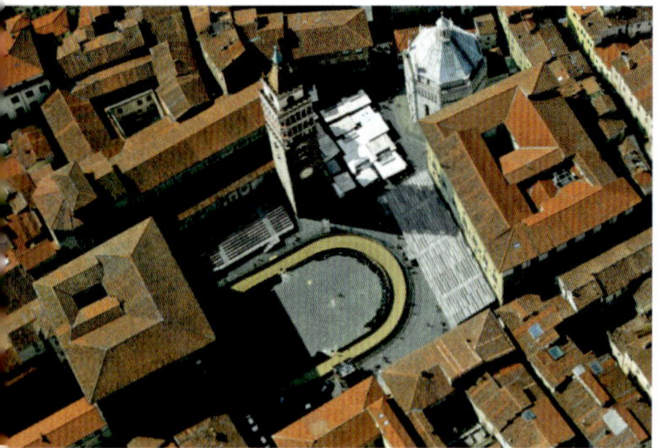

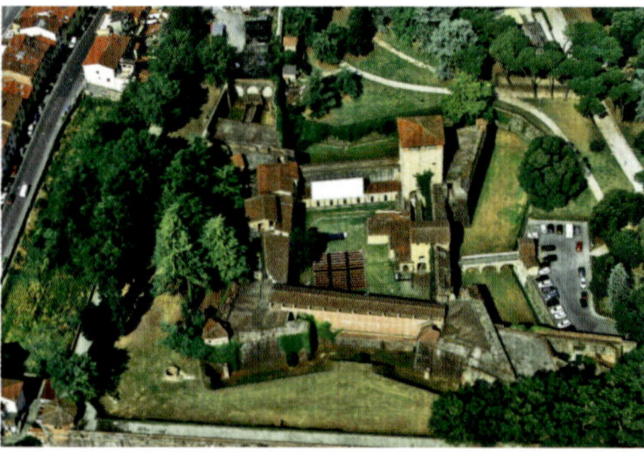

204 left

Piazza del Duomo unites the most important monuments in Pistoia: the Cathedral, the Baptistery, Palazzo Vescovile, Palazzo della Podestà (the Municipal Building).

204 right

The Medicean fortress of Santa Barbara, from the 1500s, occupies the city walls' southeastern high point.

205

Palazzo dello Spirito Santo, dedicated to the Romanesque church next to it, is one of Pistoia's most ancient sites.

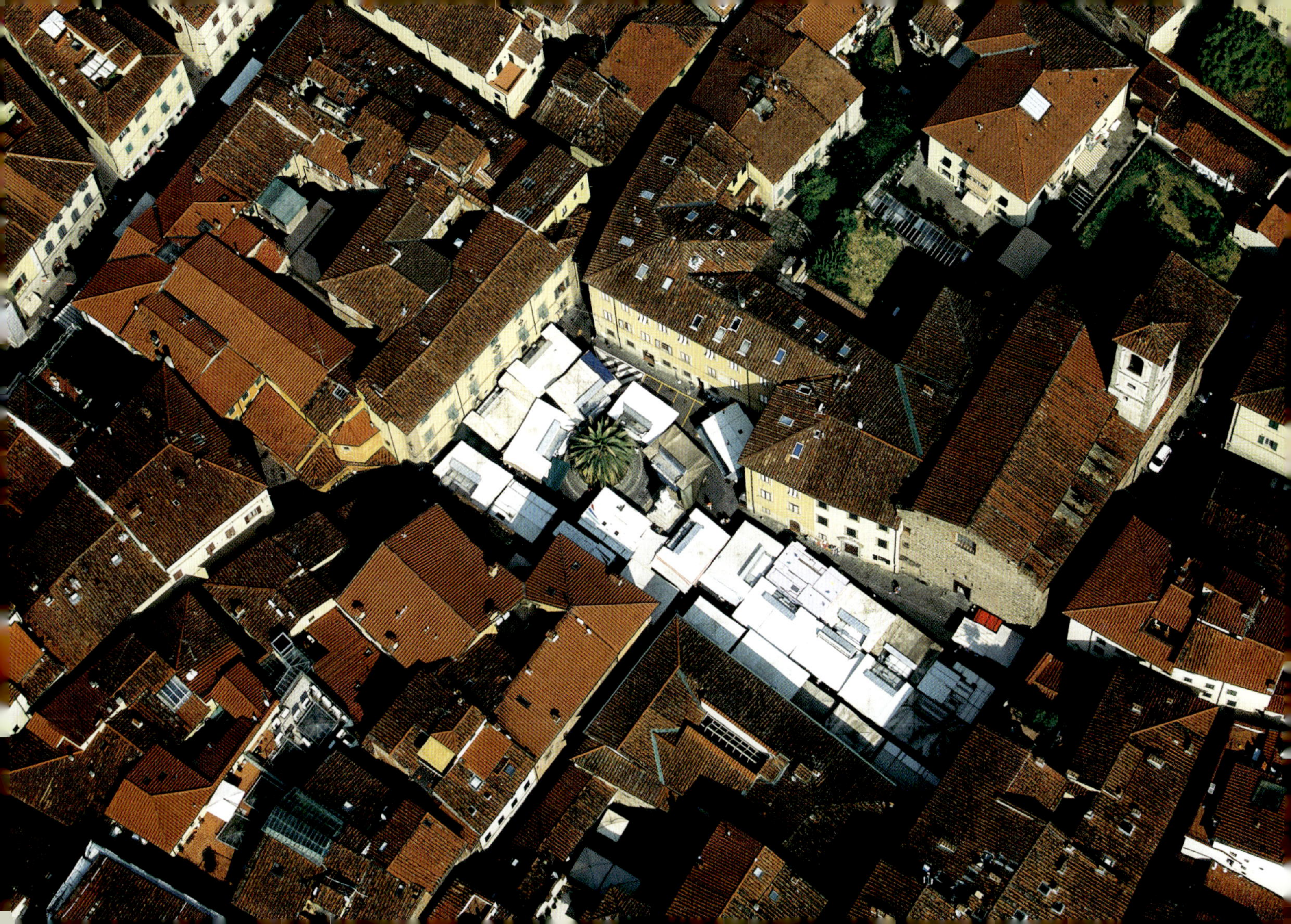

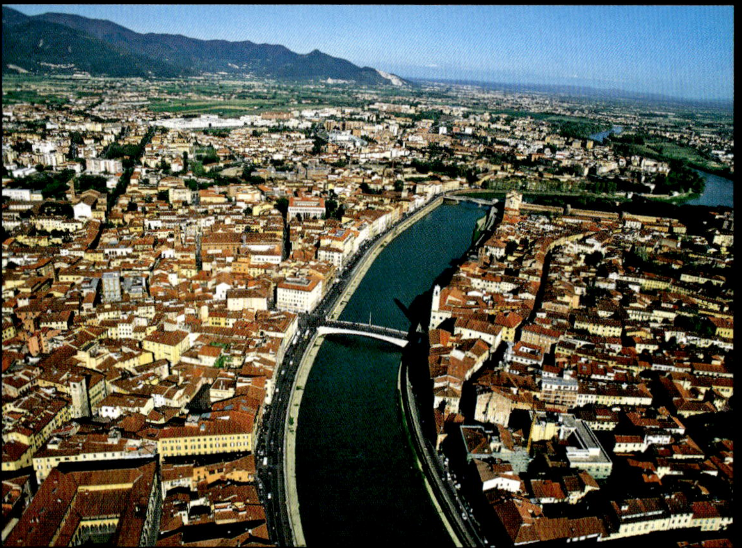

206

Pisa, an important seaport on the Arno valley, is today also a beautiful, elegant city.

207

Campo de' Miracoli harmoniously unites some of the most famous buildings in Italy's architectural history. Pisa's medieval section extends along the banks of the Arno, while around it extends the modern city.

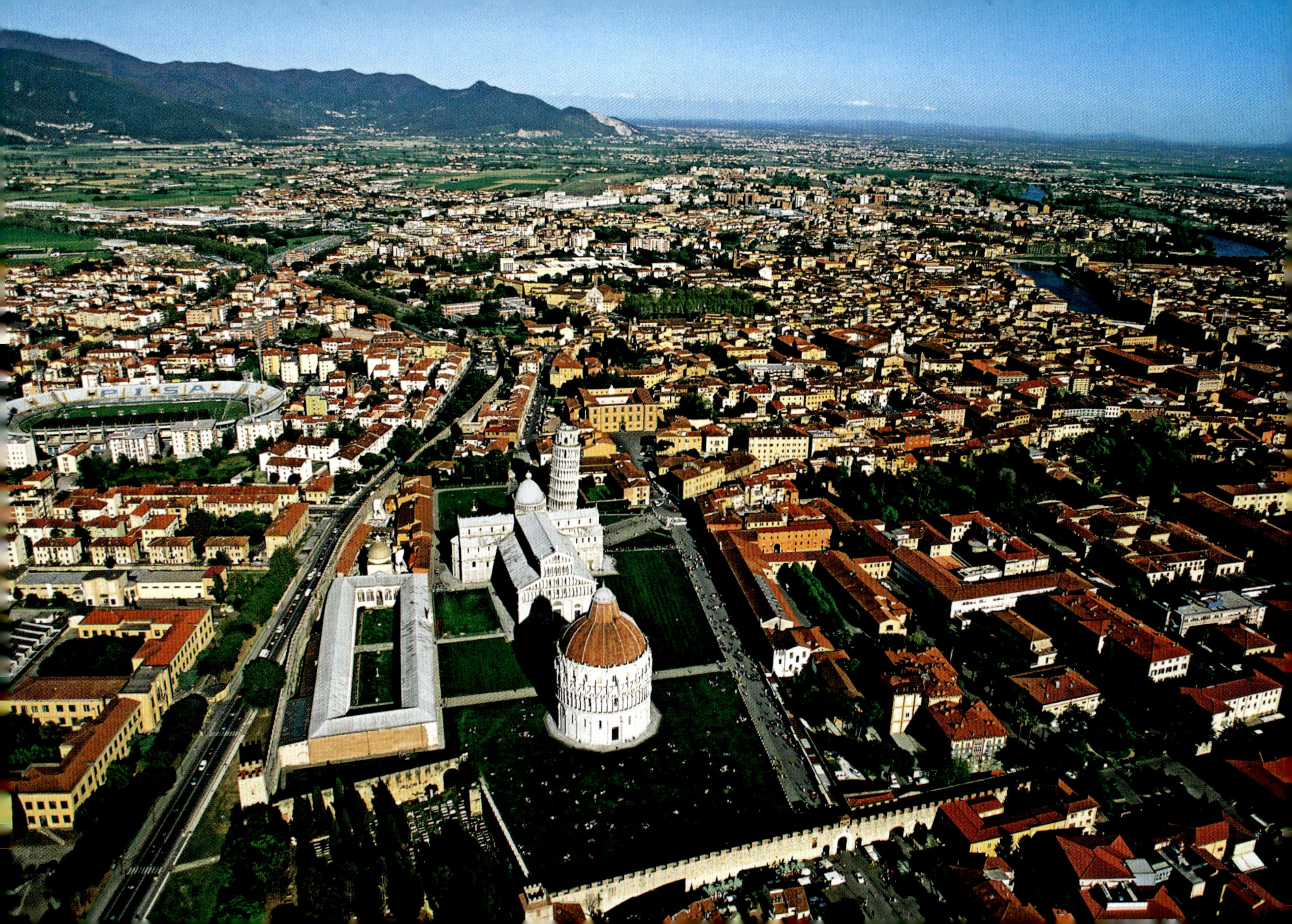
PISA

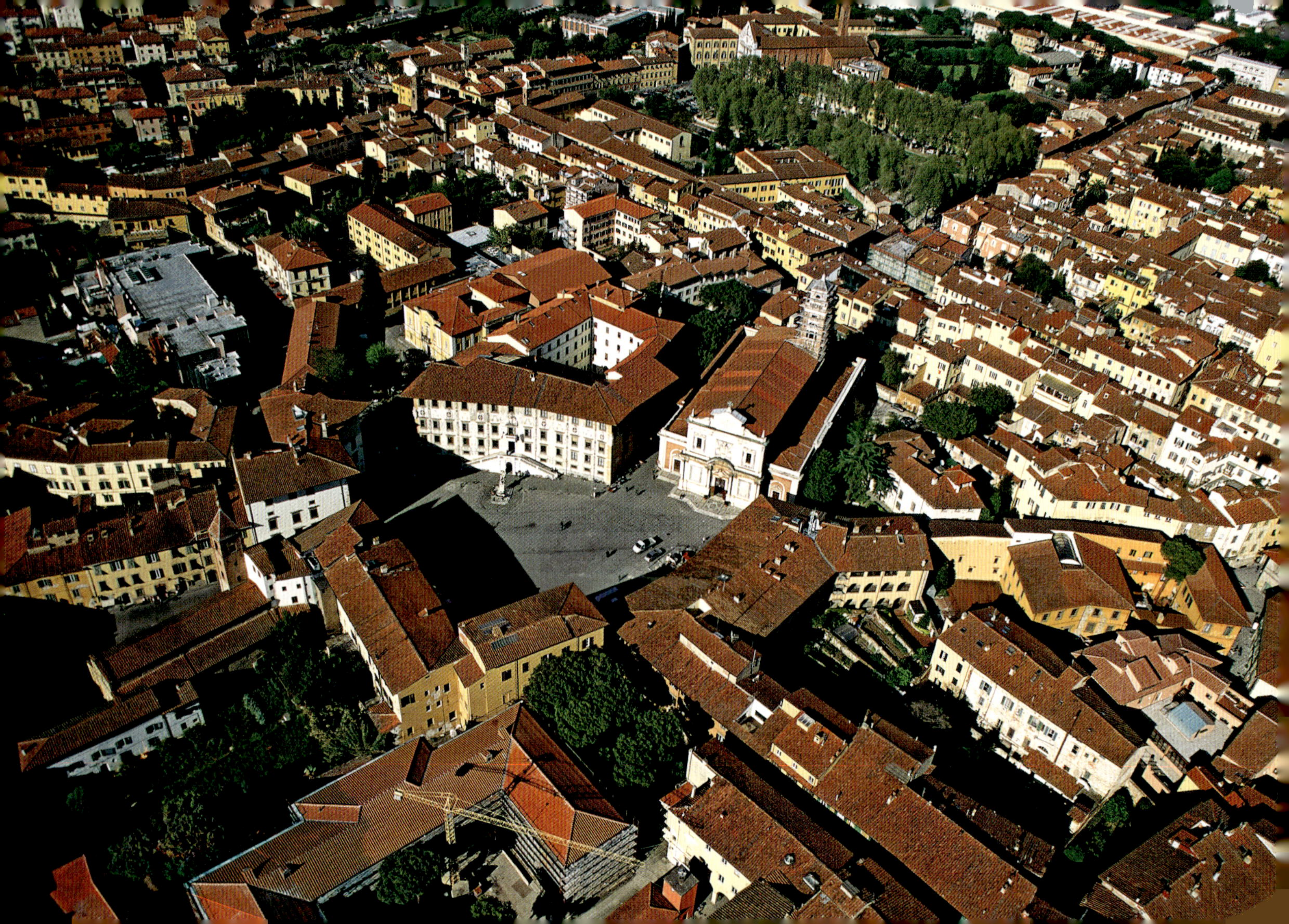

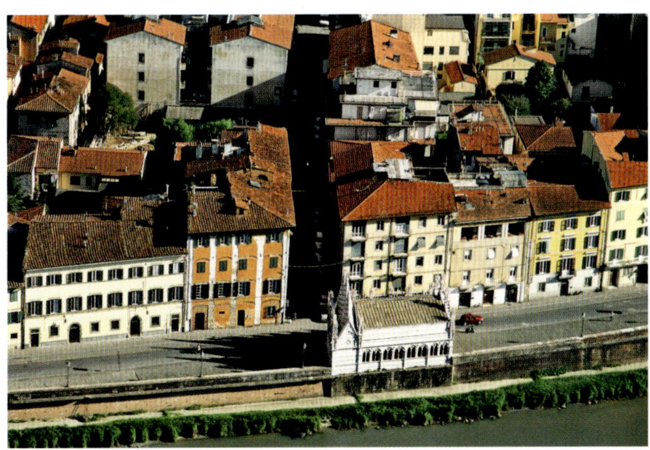

208
Piazza del Cavalieri occupies the heart of medieval Pisa and is decorated by the splendid façades of the Palazzo dei Cavalieri and of Santo Stefano.

209
The massive Santa Maria della Spina dating from the 1300s, on the banks of the Arno, is characterized by spires, cusps, pinnacles and niches.

211
The Cathedral, consecrated in 1118, is a triumph of marble, loggias, intarsia and sculpture. Latin-cross in style, it unites the Classical tradition with diverse elements, inherited from the Lombards, Arabs, Byzantines and Normans.

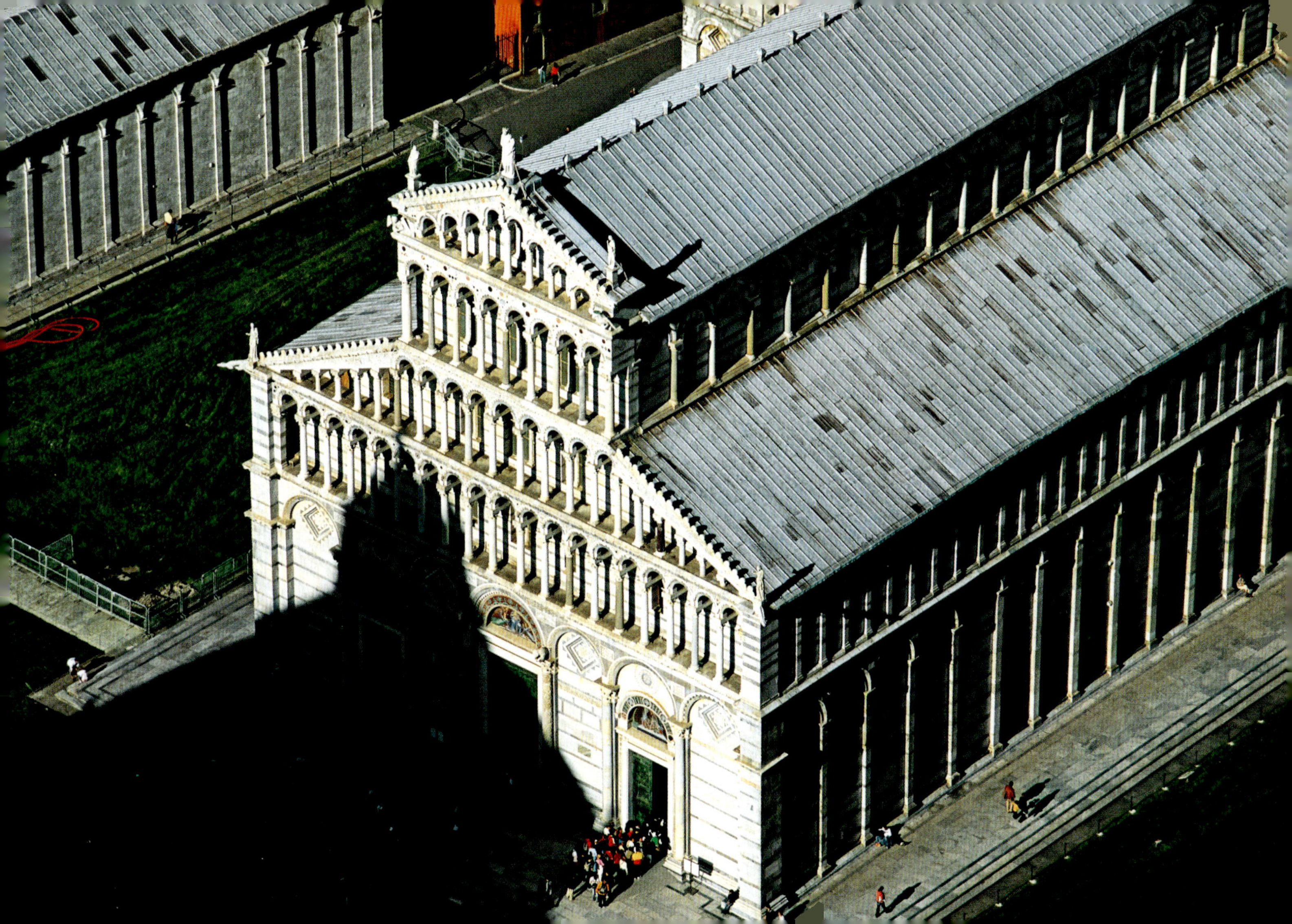

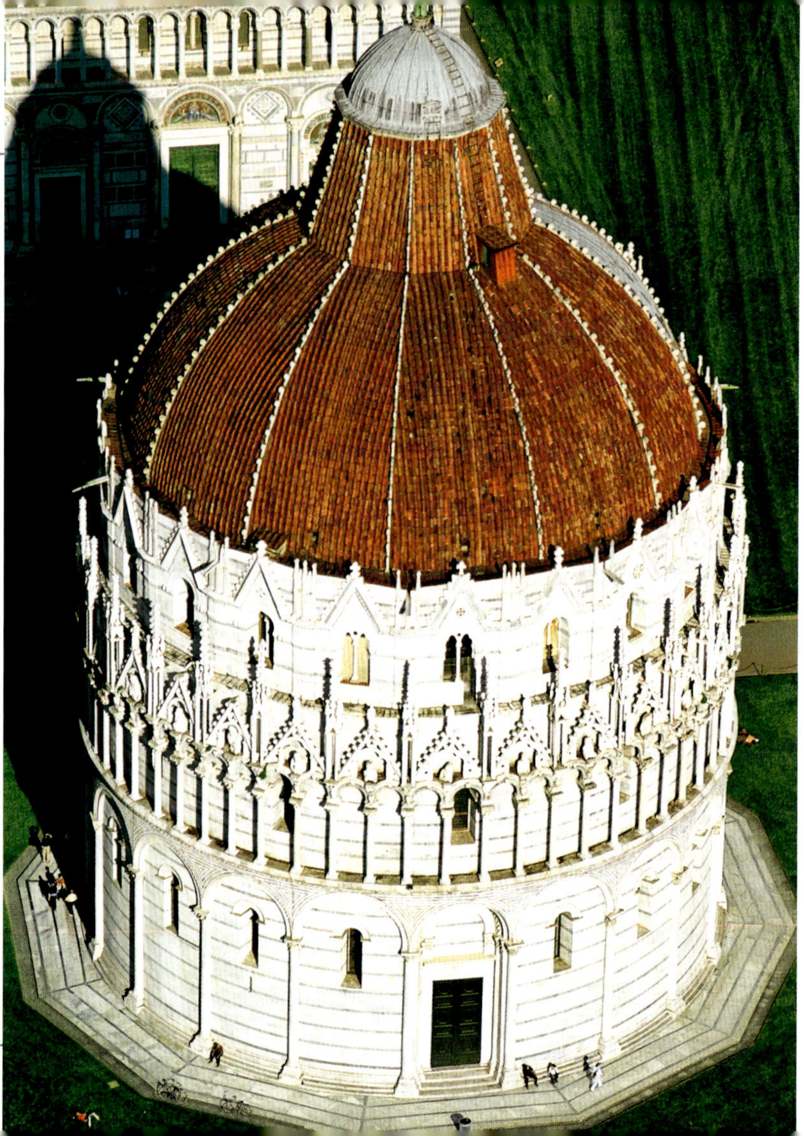

212

The Baptistery is a grandiose Romanesque temple, erected in 1152. It is the first step of man's idealized journey, represented in the Campo de' Miracoli, that extends beyond other buildings to end at the Monumental Cemetery.

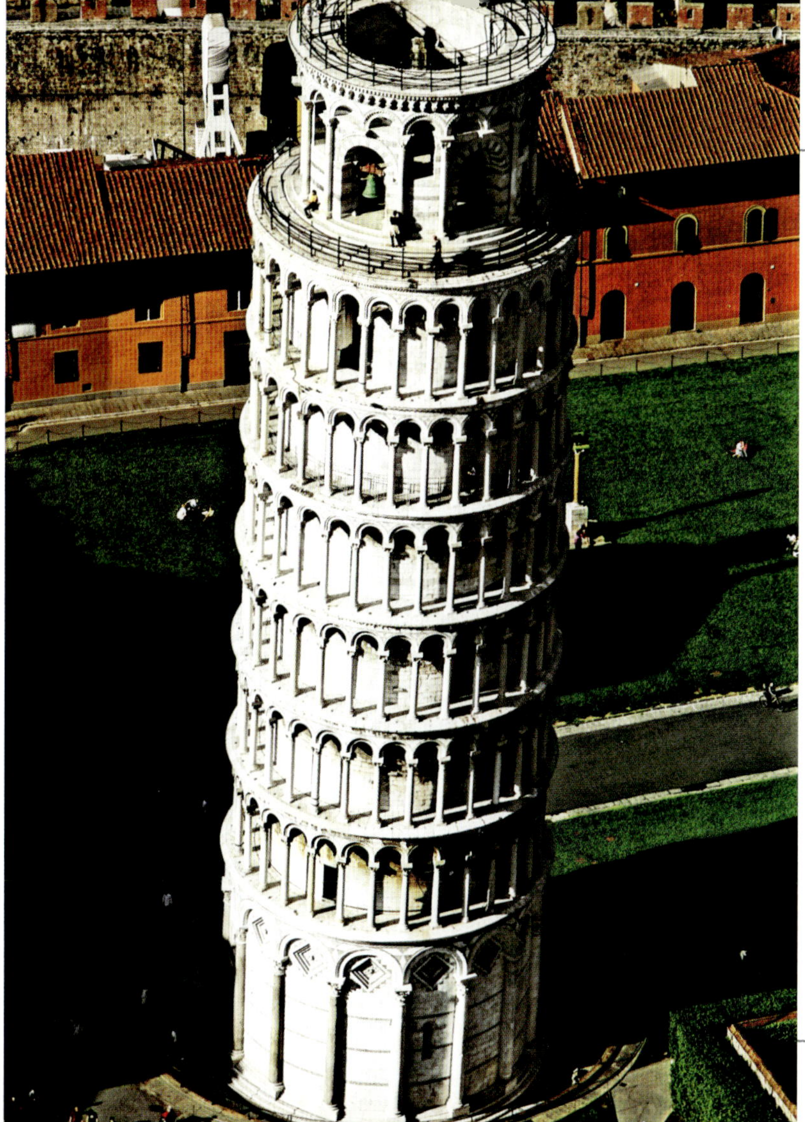

213

The Campanile is one of the most famous monuments of Italy's late-Medieval period. Begun in 1173, the so-called Leaning Tower began to tilt almost instantly, giving it this unmistakable appearance.

Livorno

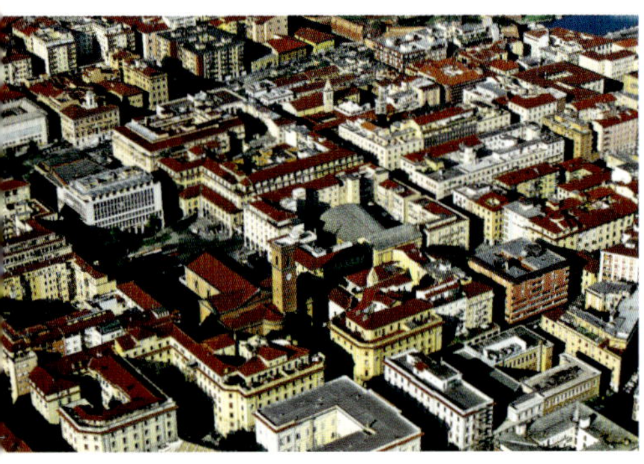

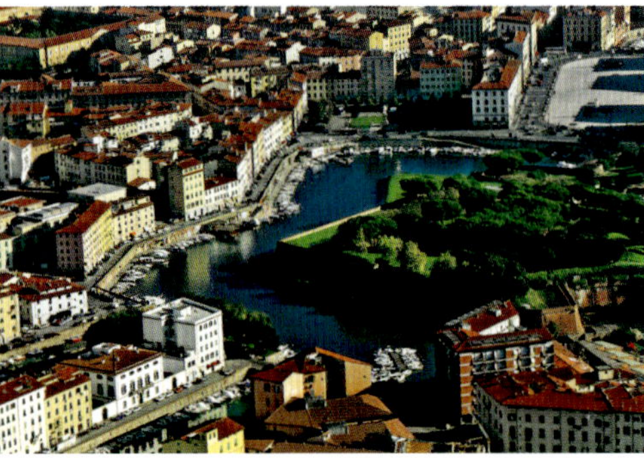

214 left
Livorno was founded in the 16th century by Cosimo I Medici, who wished to transform an ancient military settlement into an "ideal city."

214 right
The great complex of Livorno's Fortezza Nuova (New Fortress), dating from the 1500s, arose inn New Venice, named for the presence of many canals and waterways.

215
The New Fortress, the Fosso Reale that surrounds it, and the nearby elliptical Piazza della Reppublica are the heart of Livorno.

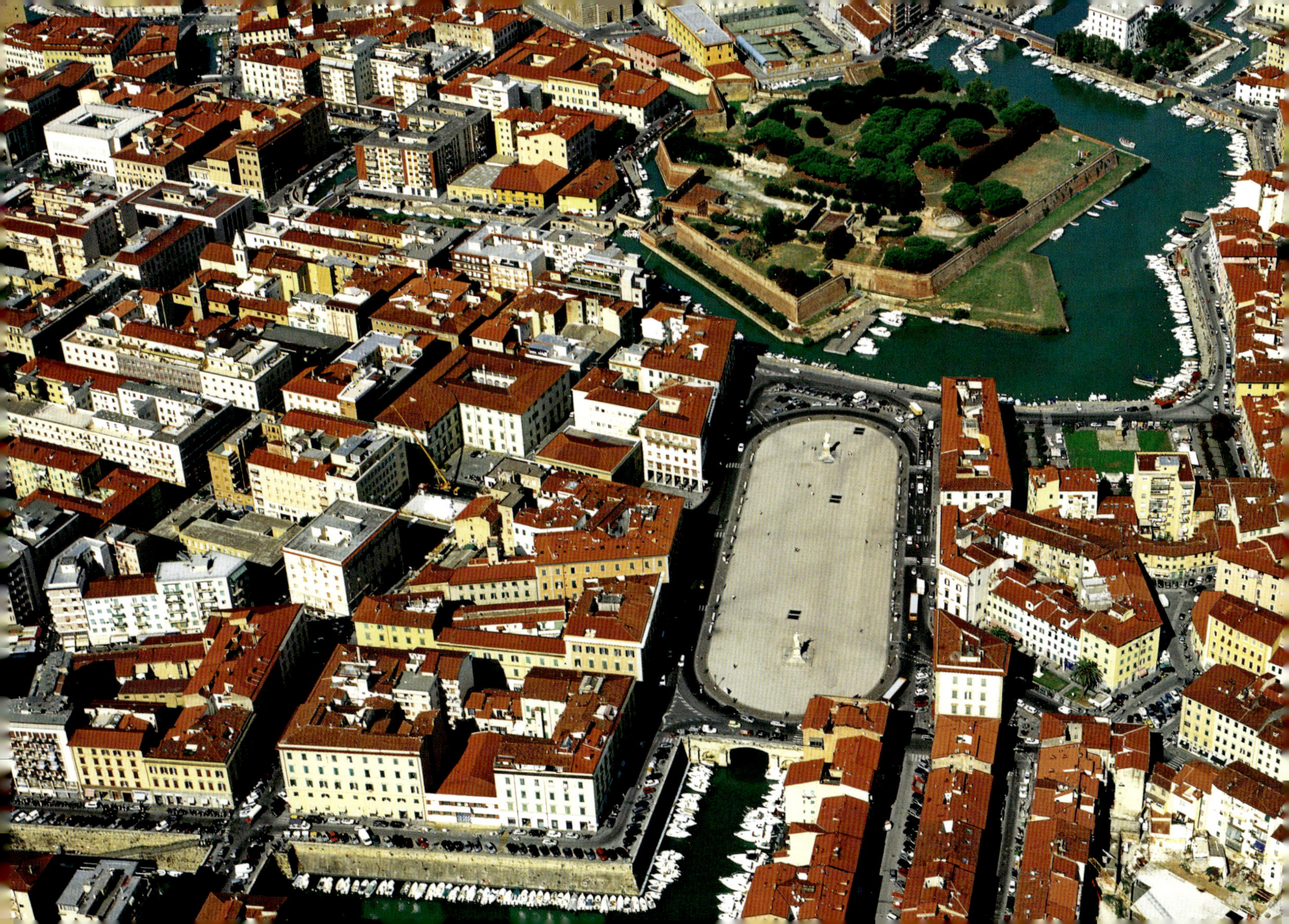

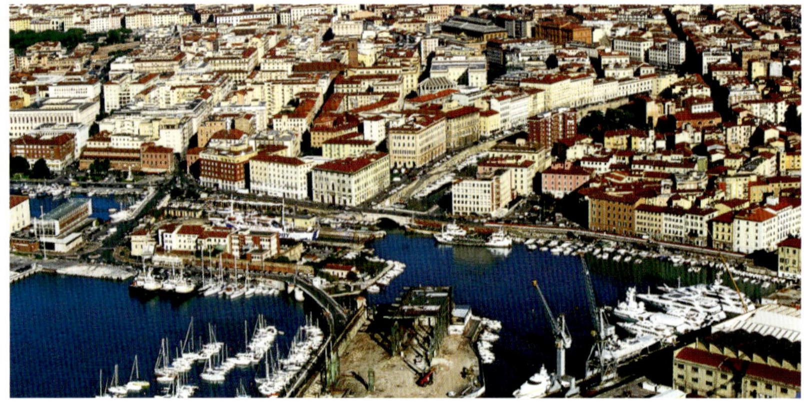

216
The port of Livorno, which handles both commercial activity and transportation to the Tuscan Archipelago, reached its peak of activity at the end of the 17th century, when the city was under the rule of the House of Lorraine.

217
Livorno's economic and industrial growth continued until the end of the Second World War; the bombs that struck its center and port put an end to its development. Today Livorno has a new identity of modern city that does not forget its past history.

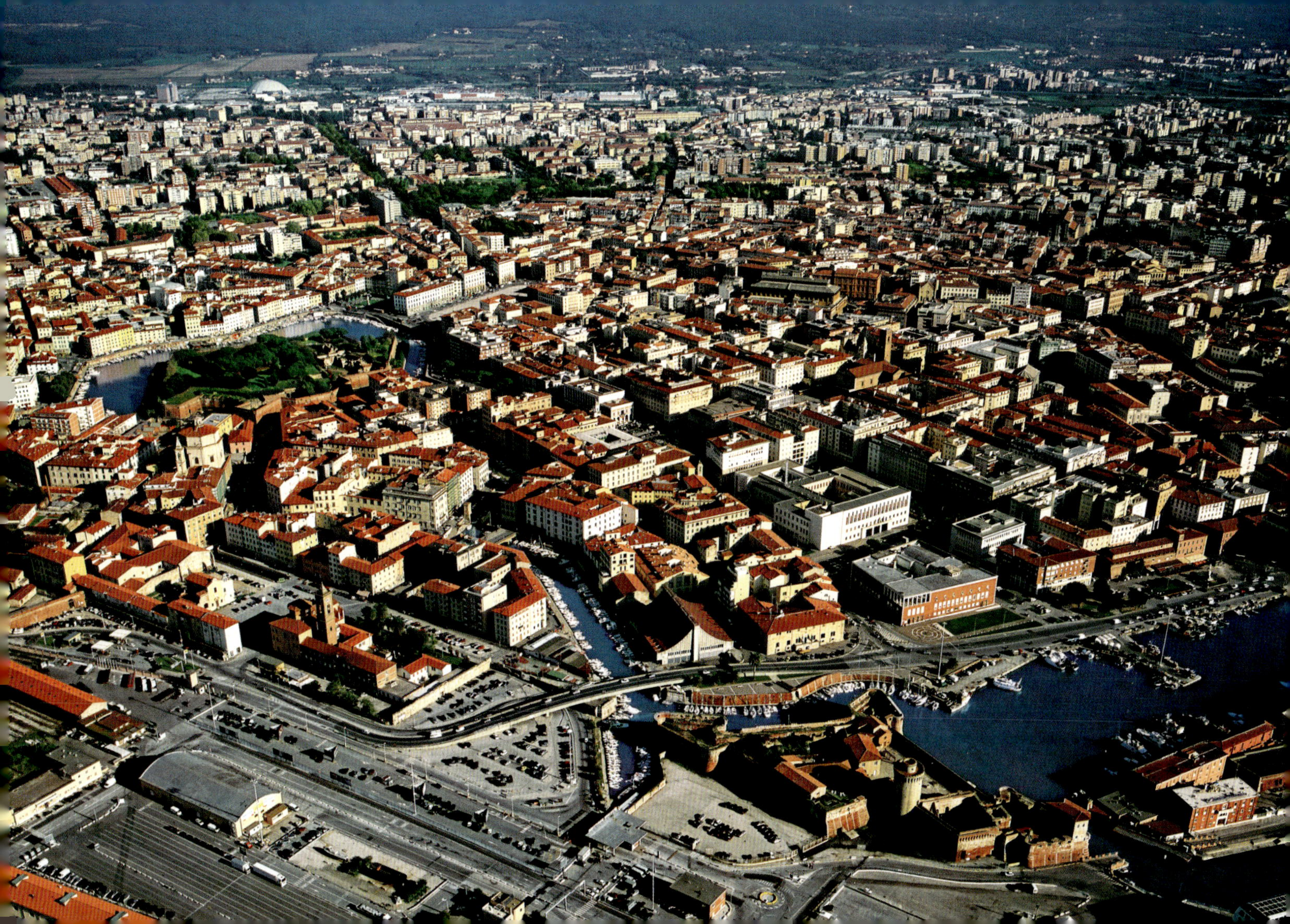

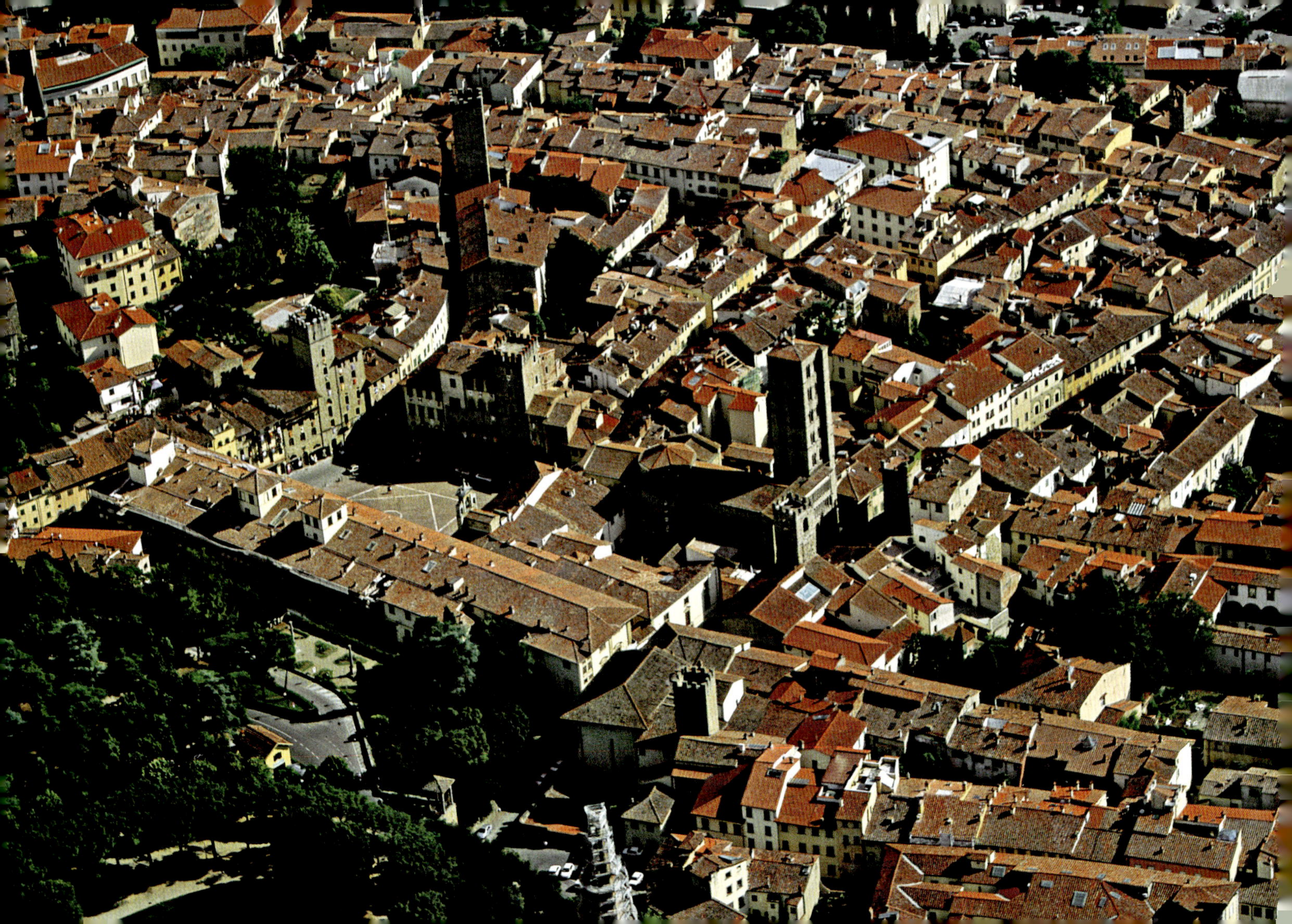

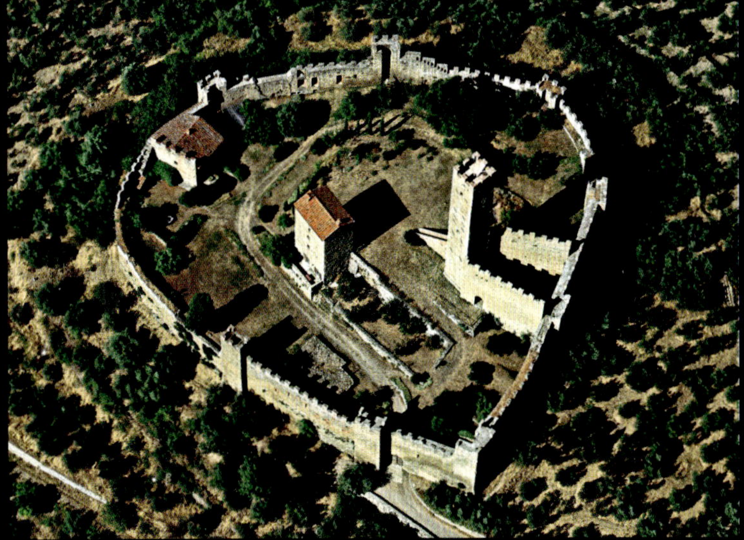

218
Piazza Grande, constructed in the 13th century, is the monumental center of Arezzo's medieval section, and reflects the wealth and growth the city had achieved.

219
The castle of Montecchio Vesponi, with its battlemented, heart-shaped wall, was built in the 11th century. It is located between Arezzo and Cortona.

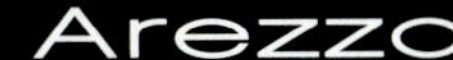

Siena

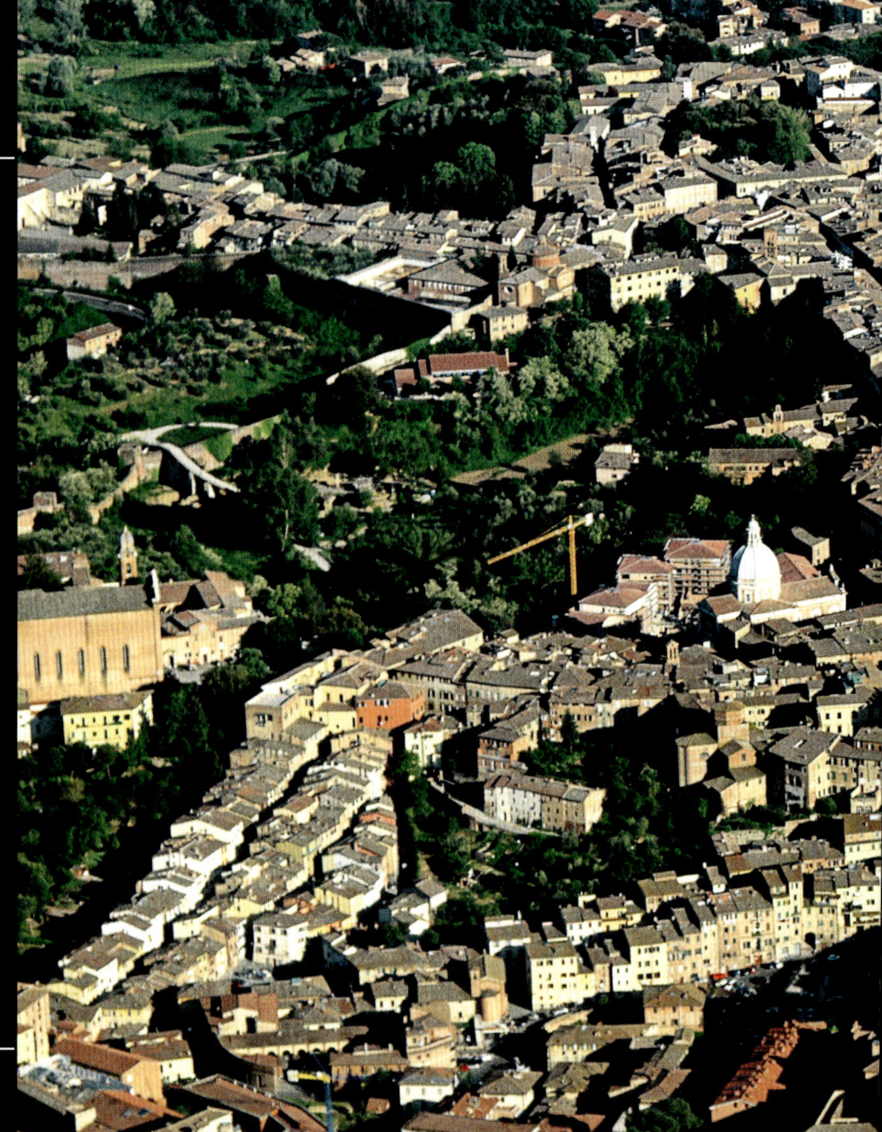

220-221
The rival of Florence in the Dark Ages and at the beginning of the Renaissance, Siena rivals it also in beauty and artistic wealth. This image shows the two main monuments: the Cathedral (right) and the Municipal Building (center).

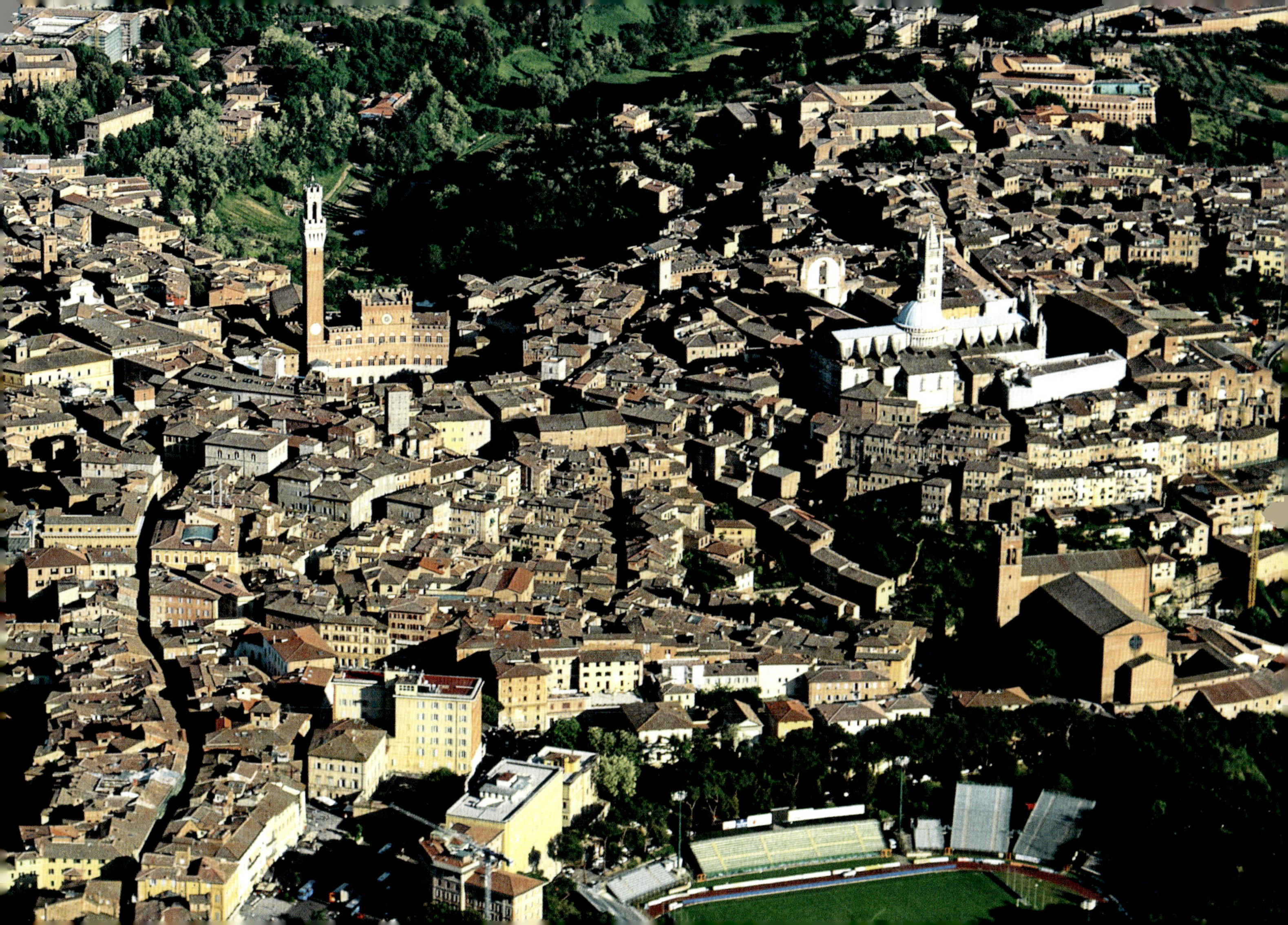

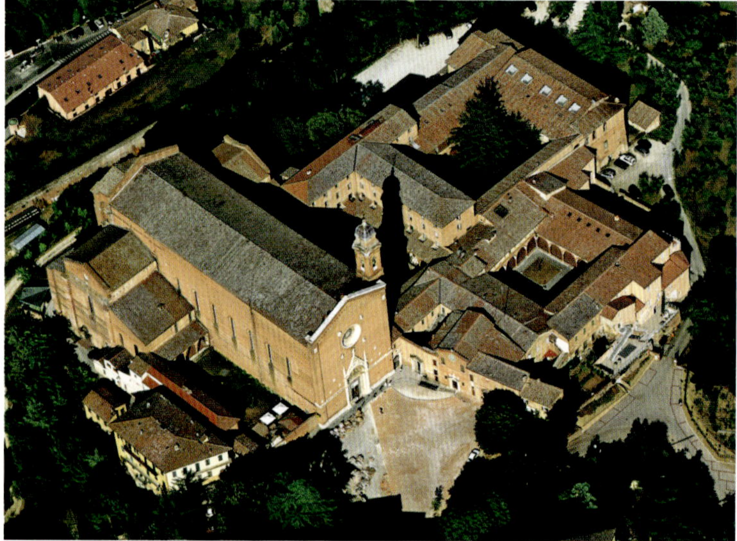

222
San Francesco, built between the late 14th and early 15th centuries, with its convent attached, is another of Siena's monuments.

223
The city's life rotates around two monumento: Piazza del Campo, with the Mangia Tower, and the Cathedral, dedicated to the Assumption.

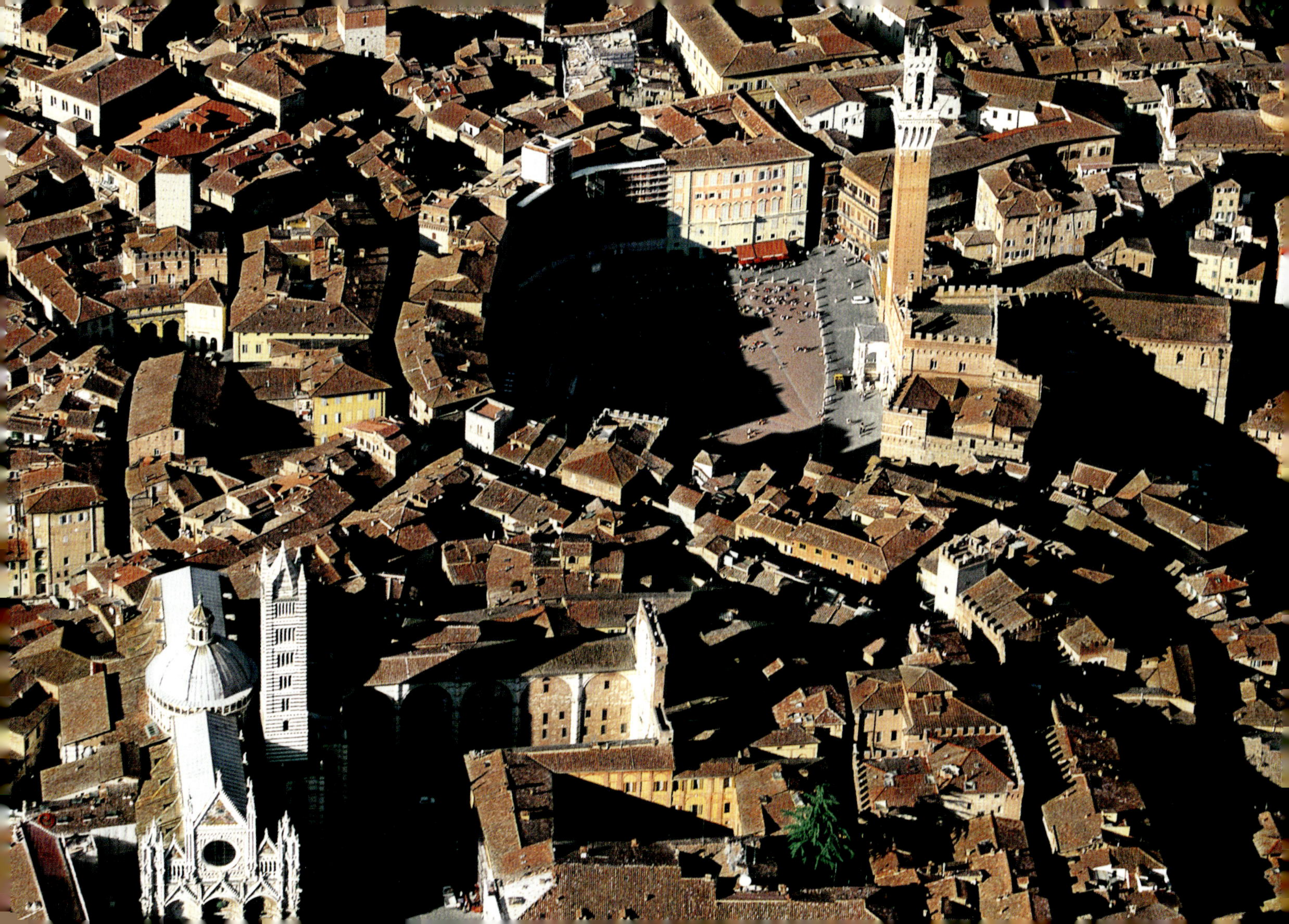

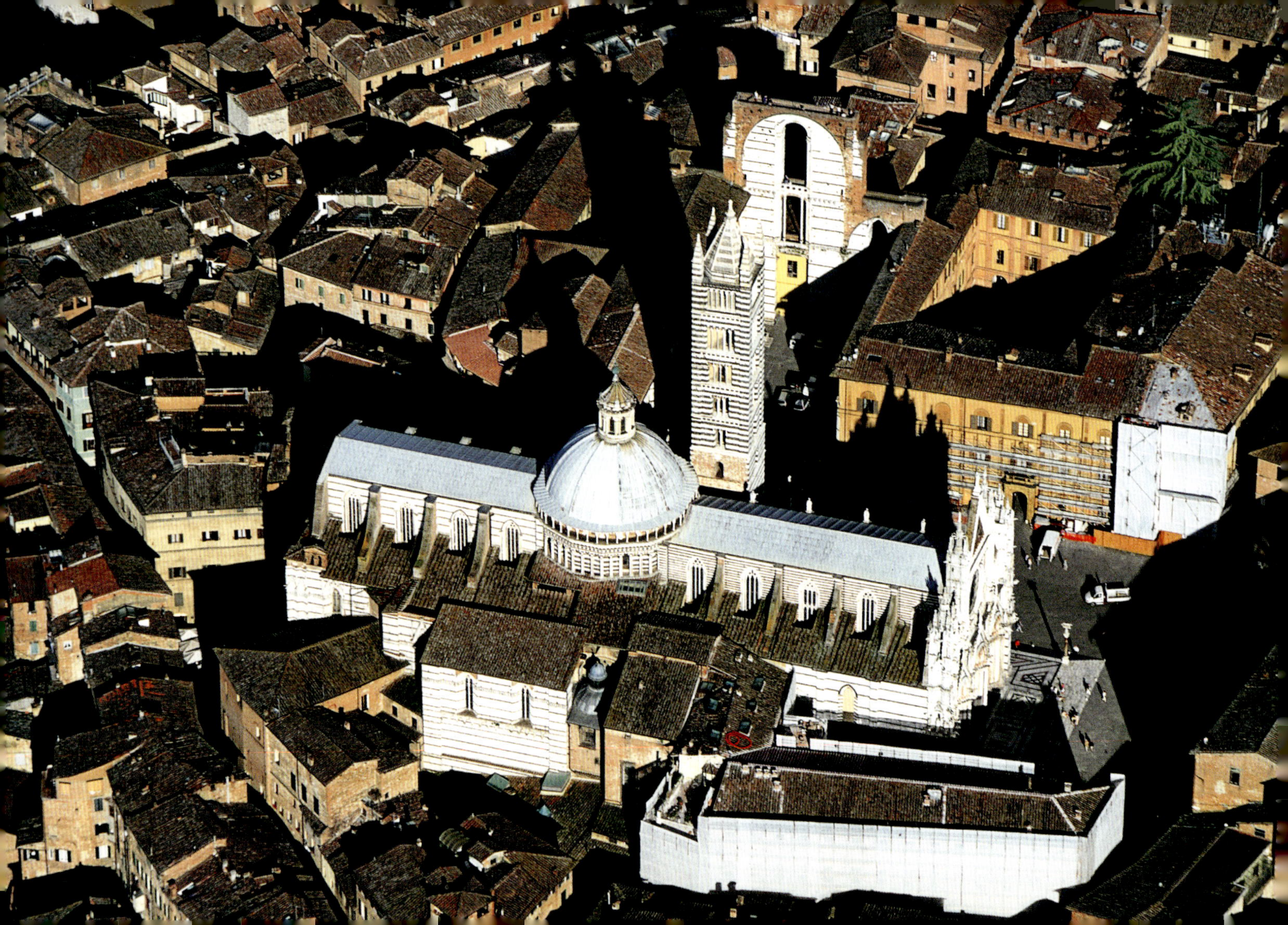

224

This image hints at the original ambitious project that called for the transformation of the existing Cathedral into a majestic, gigantic one.

225

Consecrated in 1215, Siena's Cathedral has a Latin-cross structure, a richly decorated façade and Romanesque campanile, with black and white stripes.

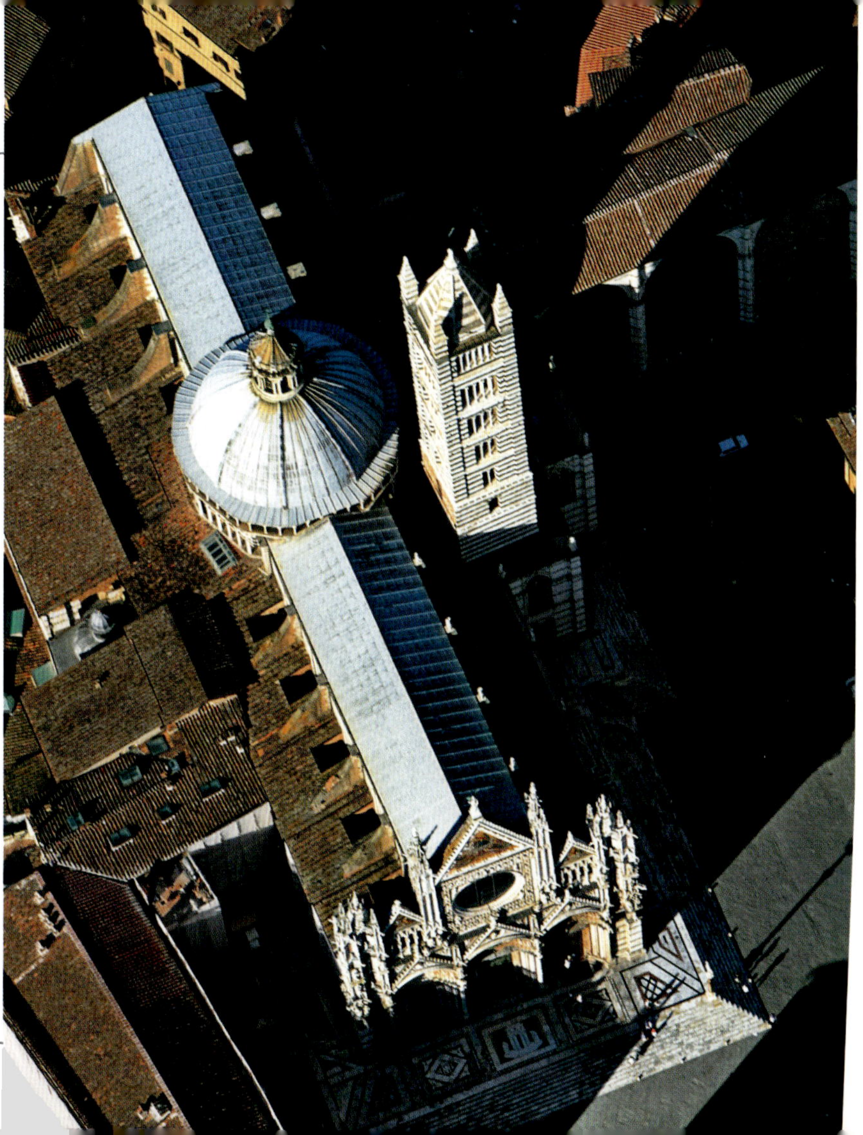

226

TREASURES AMONG THE WAVES

Flying High

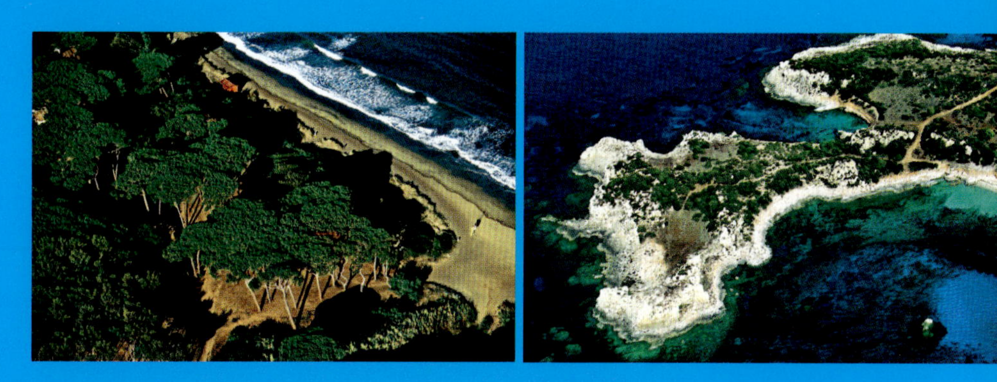

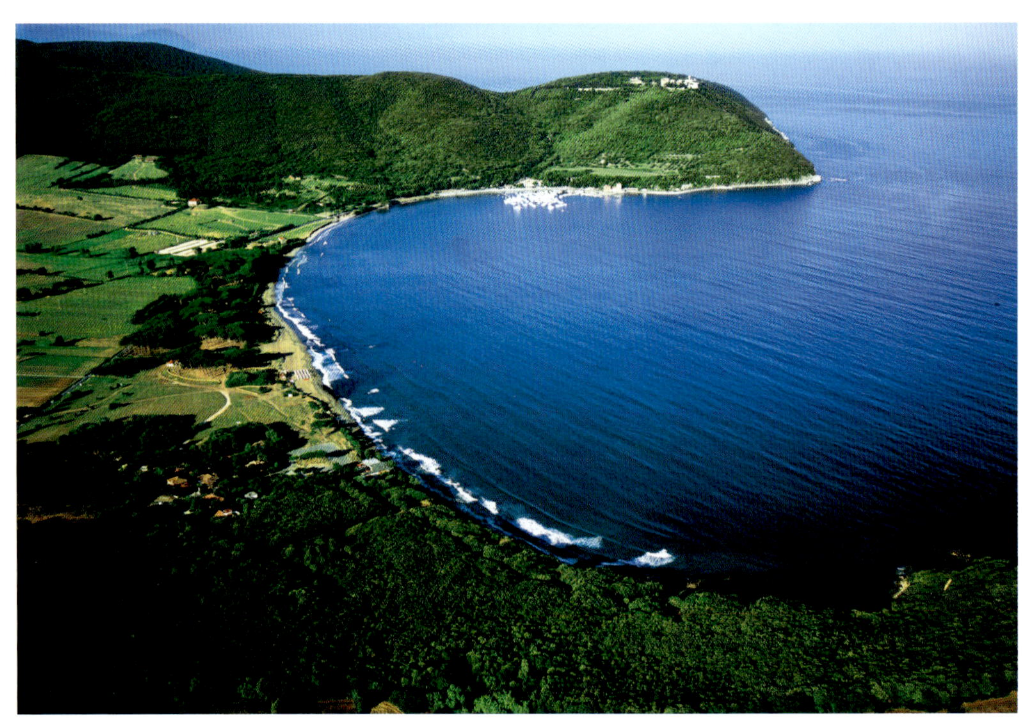

227
The Etruscan Riviera (left) enjoys a fortunate environment; Giannutri Island (right) is calcareous and flat.

Tuscany possesses 205 miles (329 km) of mostly sandy coast along the Italian mainland and, off-shore, seven islands and 40 islets positioned in a semicircle in the Tyrrhenian Sea between Livorno and Argentario, approximately 115 sq. miles (300 sq. km) of land and 96 sq. miles (249 sq. km) of coastal land. This is the Tuscan Archipelago, varied in its geologic history, nature and landscape. Seen from above it seems composed of precious gems, taken from the necklace of a lovely woman. The sea is calm, with sirocco winds that promise to turn into southwesterlies; visibility is perfect. Here are the seven superb islands with their storm-beaten cliffs, carved by the waves of each high tide that, like crowns of foamy fragments, decorates them.

The first stop during our flight is Gorgona, the northernmost and smallest of the archipelago's islands: 0.9 sq. miles (2.23 sq. km) of harsh cliffs, isolated in the middle of the sea and exposed to winds that ravish it with the force of small tornadoes. Livorno is 18 miles (29 km) away, Capraia, the closest island, is 19.5 miles (31 km) distant. From a distance, Gorgona appears as an emerald set in a deep blue sea but as you get closer, you realize that it is a fragment of eroded rock, geological wreckage that millions of years ago broke off of Corsica and slid, solitary, into the middle of the Tyrrhenian sea: an authentic, dangerous hiding place fit for legendary pirates. On certain days here the waves break at force eight and for three or four months it is impossible to land.

228
A transparent, crystalline sea, bordered by a dense pine forest and typical Mediterranean vegetation, bathes San Vincenzo, whose splendid fine golden sand beach extends for miles.

Treasures Among the Waves

But today Gorgona offers her best side: the twisted pattern of her cliffs, the splendid seabed of Cala Scirocco, the cove at Cala di Pancia, the Pisan rock at the Torre Vecchio, this natural amphitheater, frequented by infinite flights of Corsican seagulls (among the most rare in the Mediterranean) and pilgrim hawks from Cala Maestra. The green color, that makes this island resemble an emerald, is due to the Mediterranean scrub, the pine forests of Aleppo oak, rosemary bushes, arbutus berry, pomegranates and carob. It's a pity that tourists are not admitted: Gorgonia is a penal-colony that hosts approximately 100 prisoners and 10 guards.

Now, off to Capraia, once the island of wild goats but now goatless. Closer to Corsica than to the Tuscan coast, Capraia is the most "foreign" island in the archipelago, also for its geological origins, evident in the scarlet rocks of Cala Rossa, the fire-colored wall of a volcano that, nine million years ago, forced Capraia to emerge from the depths of the seabed. The contrast with the vegetation, dominated by huge yellow bouquets of euphorbia euphorbia produces an extraordinary, lush effect. The glittering reflection off of the waters of the Stagnone indicates the only lake in the entire archipelago, although little more than 3 feet (1 m) deep and about 1076 sq. ft (100 sq. m) in size. Coastal corners with incomparable cliffs and a seabed to discover with mask and flippers, make of this island a timeless place, indescribably beautiful.

Elba is the biggest and most varied of the archipelago's islands. Seen from above (from very high) it seems like a crudely carved Paleozoic fish that has struggled to rise from the depths of the sea to check out the ongoing evolution above. Flying lower, one comes to understand that here evolution was at its best, that nothing could be improved, especially the coast. There are bays with silky sand at Punta del Cotoncello or at the Enfola isthmus, a beach with a small pine forest

Treasures Among the Waves

at Fetovaia or at the trendy Bay of Cavoli; also the large, organized family beach at Marina di Campo, or Capoliveri, favored by the young because of its resemblance to Versilia. More typically "Elban" are the slices of granite, modeled by the sea at Cape Sant'Andrea, the steep stone pit in the gulf of Lacuna, the white pebbles of Portoferraio. At the center of the island, rises the stately granite massif of Monte Capanne, 3343 ft (1019 m) covered with chestnut forests, domestic pine and oak, arbutus berry, broom, and mimosa. In this exuberant vegetation there are a few, scattered houses, small villages and ten bigger towns like Capoliveri, Rio nell'Elba, Porto Azzurro, Marciana, Marina di Campo. Impressive, from above, is the design of Elba's Medici-period fortress at Porto ferraiao, "Elba's main port," with the Forte della Stella guarding the shipyard and lighthouse.

Close to Elba is Pianosa, a flat island, a clay "raft" suspended 65 ft (20 m) above the Tyrrhenian sea. If it weren't for a play of lights on the ocher cliffs of Punta Libeccio, we could miss it altogether. The landscape is empty, apparently abandoned. Up until about ten years ago it was a penal colony, inaccessibile, and even today is difficult to visit. The Roman port is a beautiful bay protected by winds and rough sea. Unreliable witnesses attest to the return of the nun seals to the Gulf of Botte: let's take their word for it even though the last sure sighting dates back to 1909.

To the southeast we can make out the massive profile of a treasure island, the inaccessible Montecristo, where today, not even Edmond Dantès, Alexandre Dumas' ineffable Count, could set foot. Declared a Nature Reserve in 1917, it is in fact the most priceless and protected island in Europe: nobody may navigate, anchor or fish within 3280 ft (1000 m) from the shore. Only 4.9 sq. miles (10 sq. km) of rock and Mediterranean vegetation in steep hills, up to the peak of Fortress mountain, 2116 ft (645 m) high, Montecristo knows no footfalls other than those of Consiglio Nazionale delle

233
According to legend, Elba and the other islands of the Tuscan Archipelago were the pearls on Venus' necklace.

234-235
Every summer, the beach at Marina di Massa is colorfully patterned by umbrellas and beach chairs.

Ricerche (CNR) staff, who analyze its fauna, flora and ecological characteristics. The islet's treasure remains a secret dream.

On Giglio, half the island's territory is off limits to the army of tourists that crowd Giglio Porto, the renowned main center where ferry boats anchor from Argentario, or who visit Castello Giglio, situated 1300 ft (400 m) up, atop a hill, as well as the long Campese beach. This island has inaccessible coastline, interrupted by beautiful inlets with some of the most enchanting seabeds in the Tyrrhenian. The last gem of the archipelago (last according to our route and because it is the southernmost island) is Giannutri, between Giglio and the continent, possessing extraordinarily beautiful coves and inlets together with the well-conserved ruins of a Roman villa from the 1st to 2nd century A.D. At that time, the villa at Cala Maestra (and the whole island) was the property of one family, the Domitii Ahenobarbi, to which Nero belonged. Today, Giannutri is a deluxe condominium owned by under two hundred inhabitants of whom only twenty are year-round residents. After years of vacationing there, these persons fell in love with the island and decided to acquire and manage it. Here, one can only visit for the day because there are no towns, hotels or camping sites.

After just a few minutes of flight we are again on the mainland, flying up the Tuscan coast from Argentario to the Apuan Mountains. The coast is scalloped with long stretches of sandy beach and dunes, interrupted by promontories, once islands but now attached to the mainland. Unique is Argentario, a mountain connected to the coast by sandy beaches (sand-bars) that embrace the Orbettello lagoon. It's worth flying low over the dunes of Uccellina Reserve and Talamone; the long stretch of Mediterranean scrub along the Etruscan Riviera between Piombino and Cecina; the seaside resorts at Castiglioncello and Viareggio and the worldly Versilia, a flight that brings us back to the foothills of the Apuan mountains.

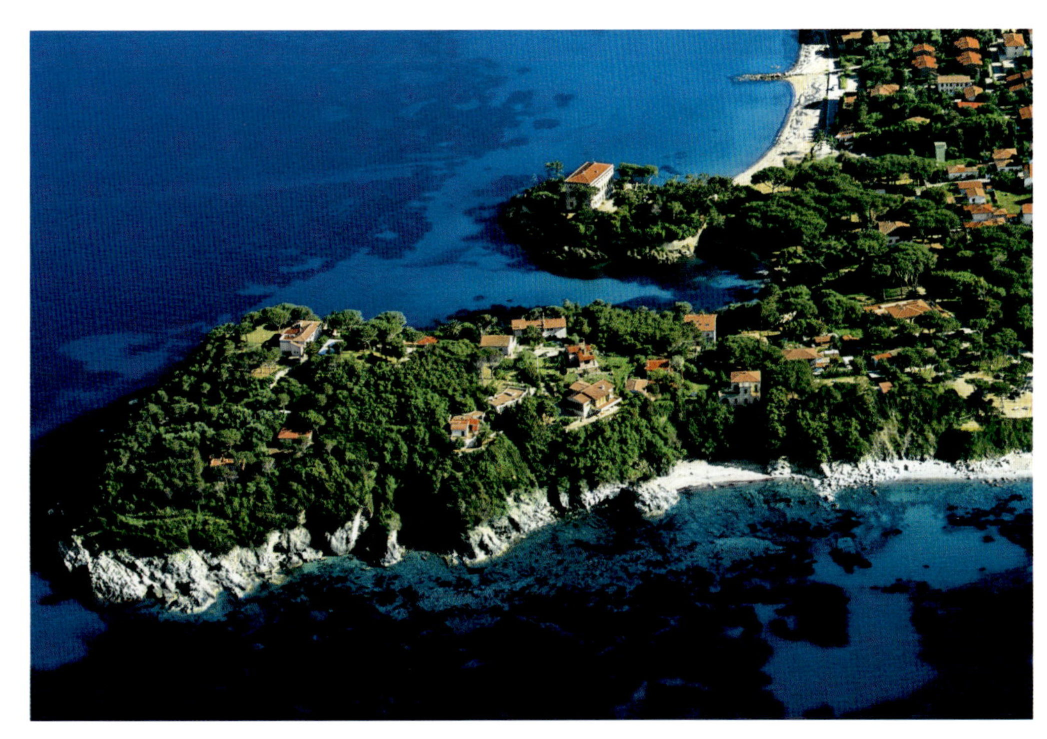

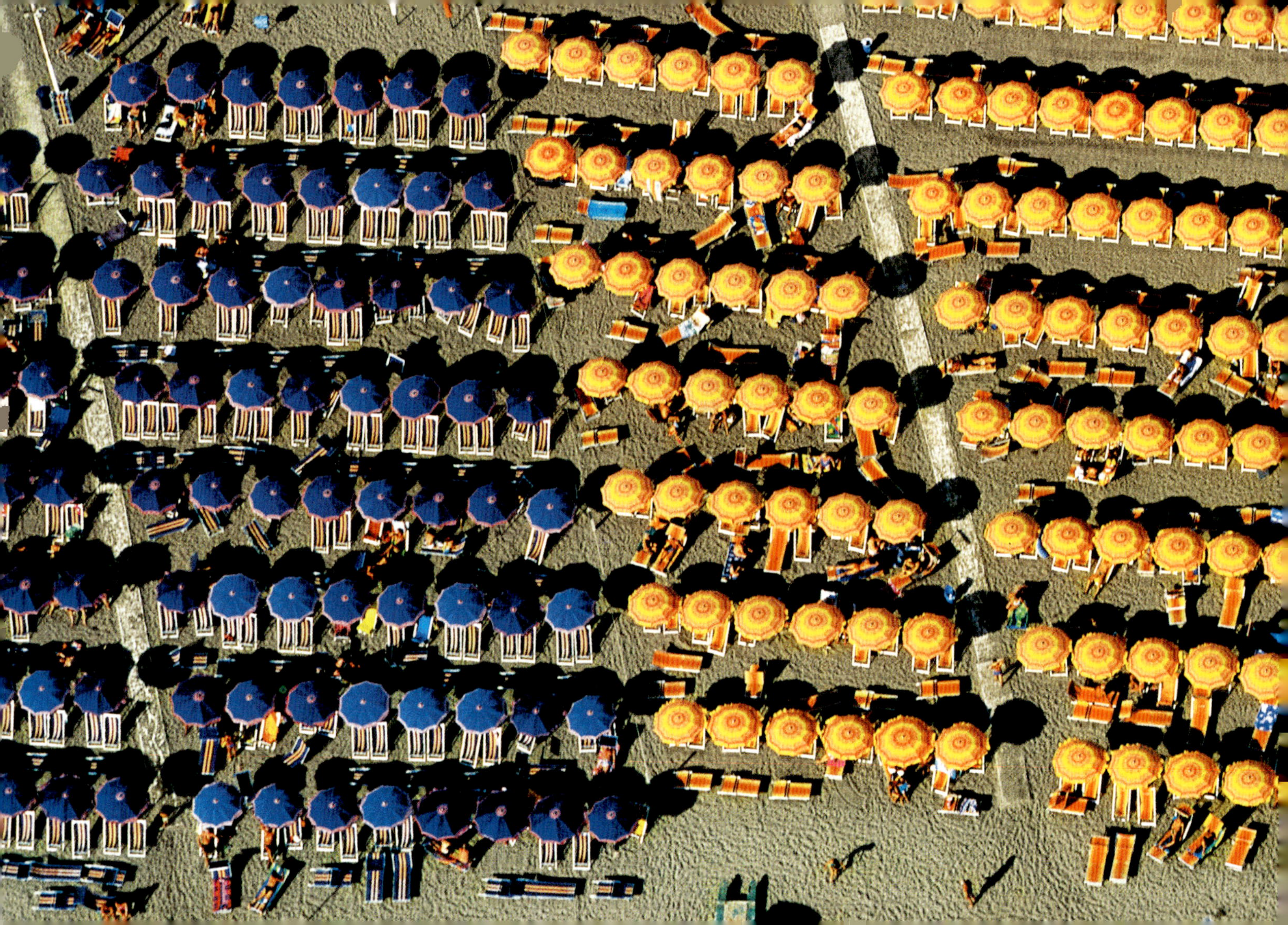

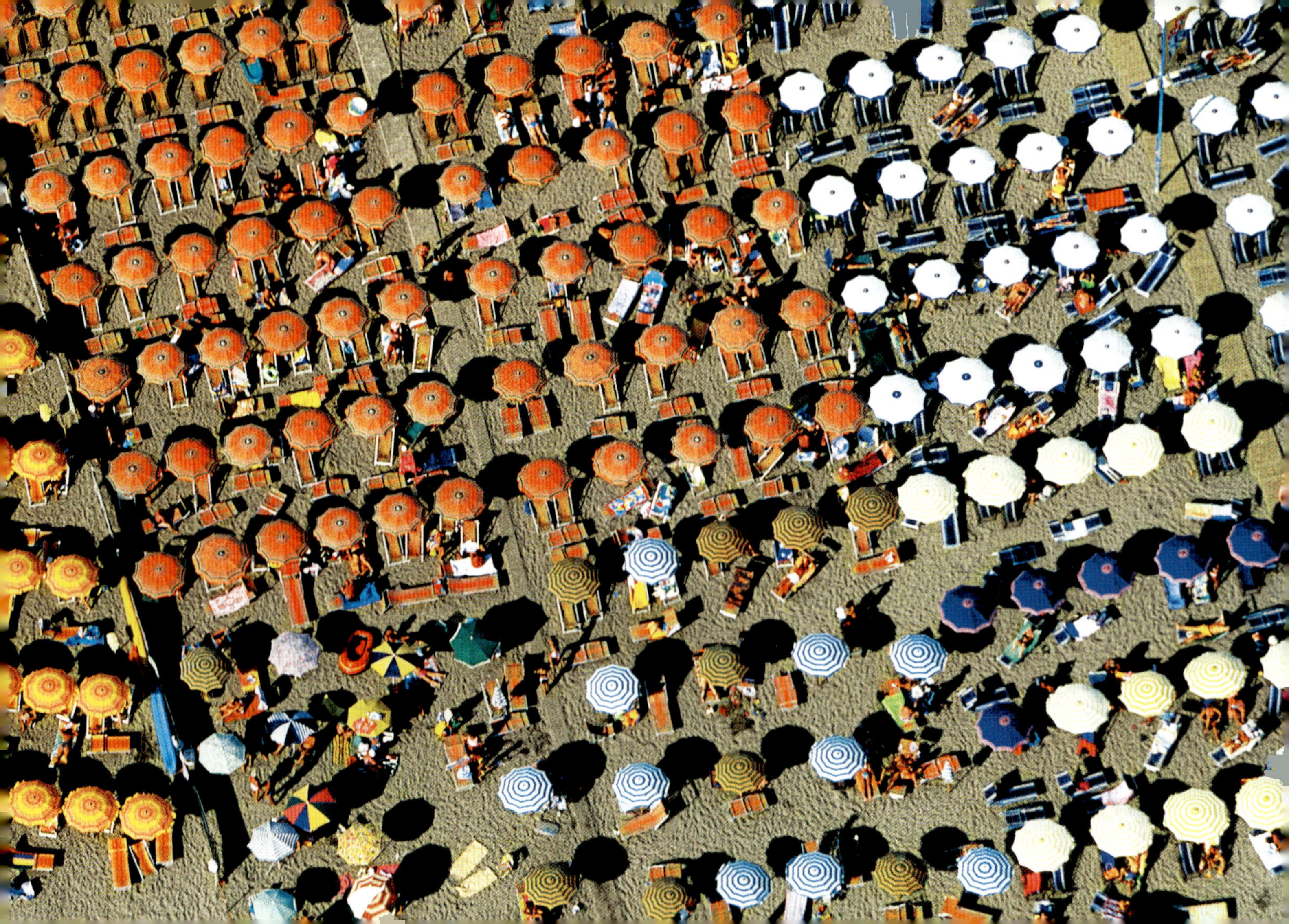

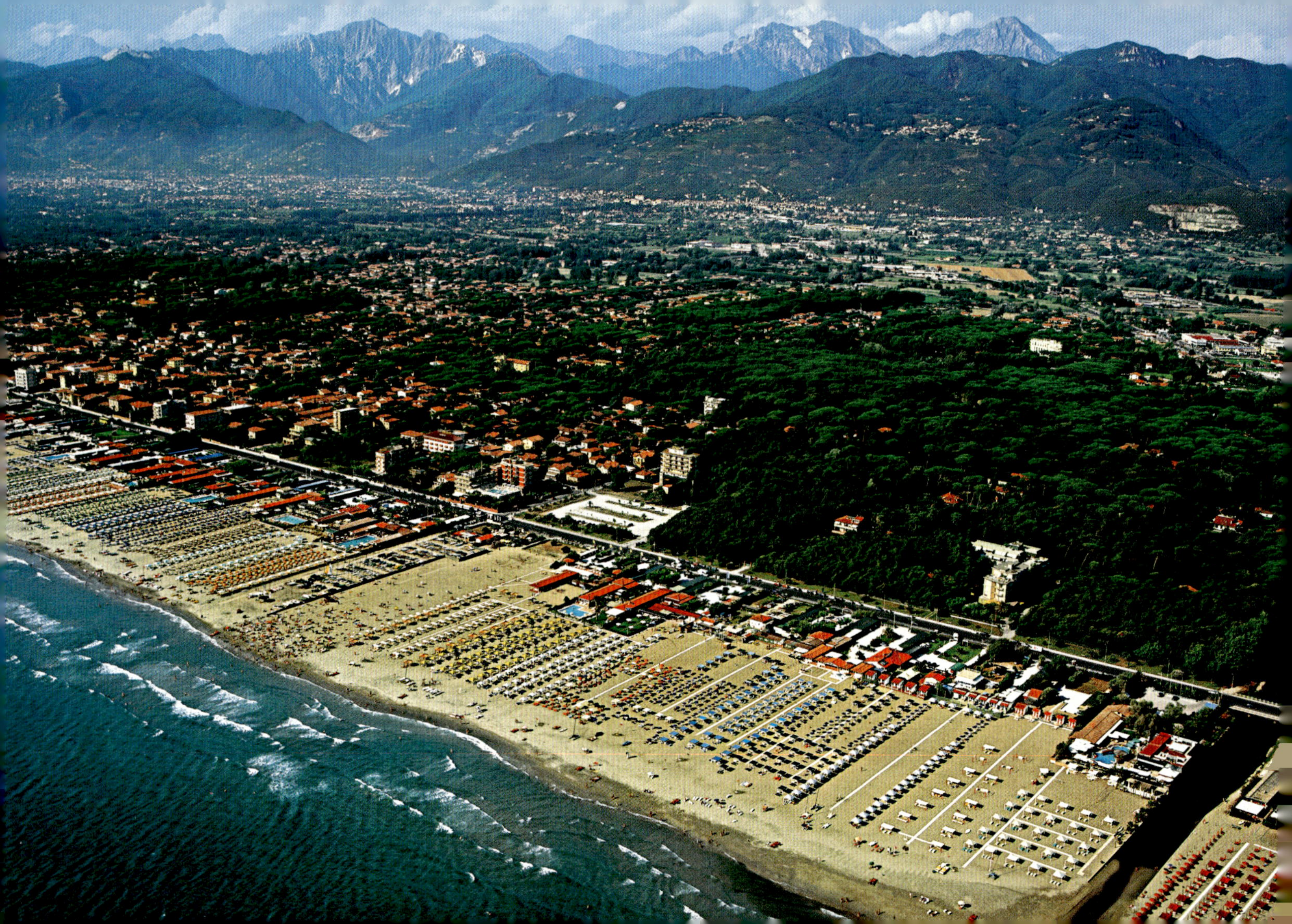

236
The green of the hills and pine forests mixes with the blue of the sea, rendering Viareggio unique.

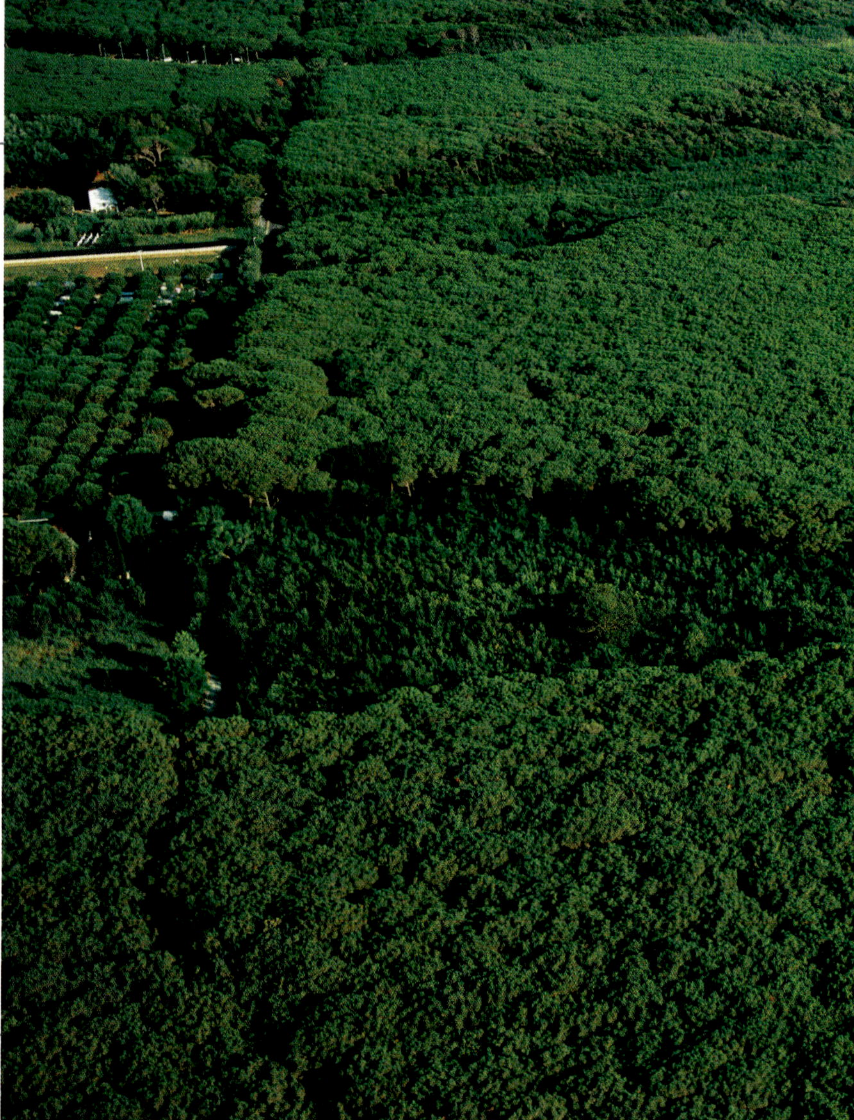

238-239
Along the coast at Cecina a dense pine forest leads to the sea. The wide sandy beach is equipped for bathers.

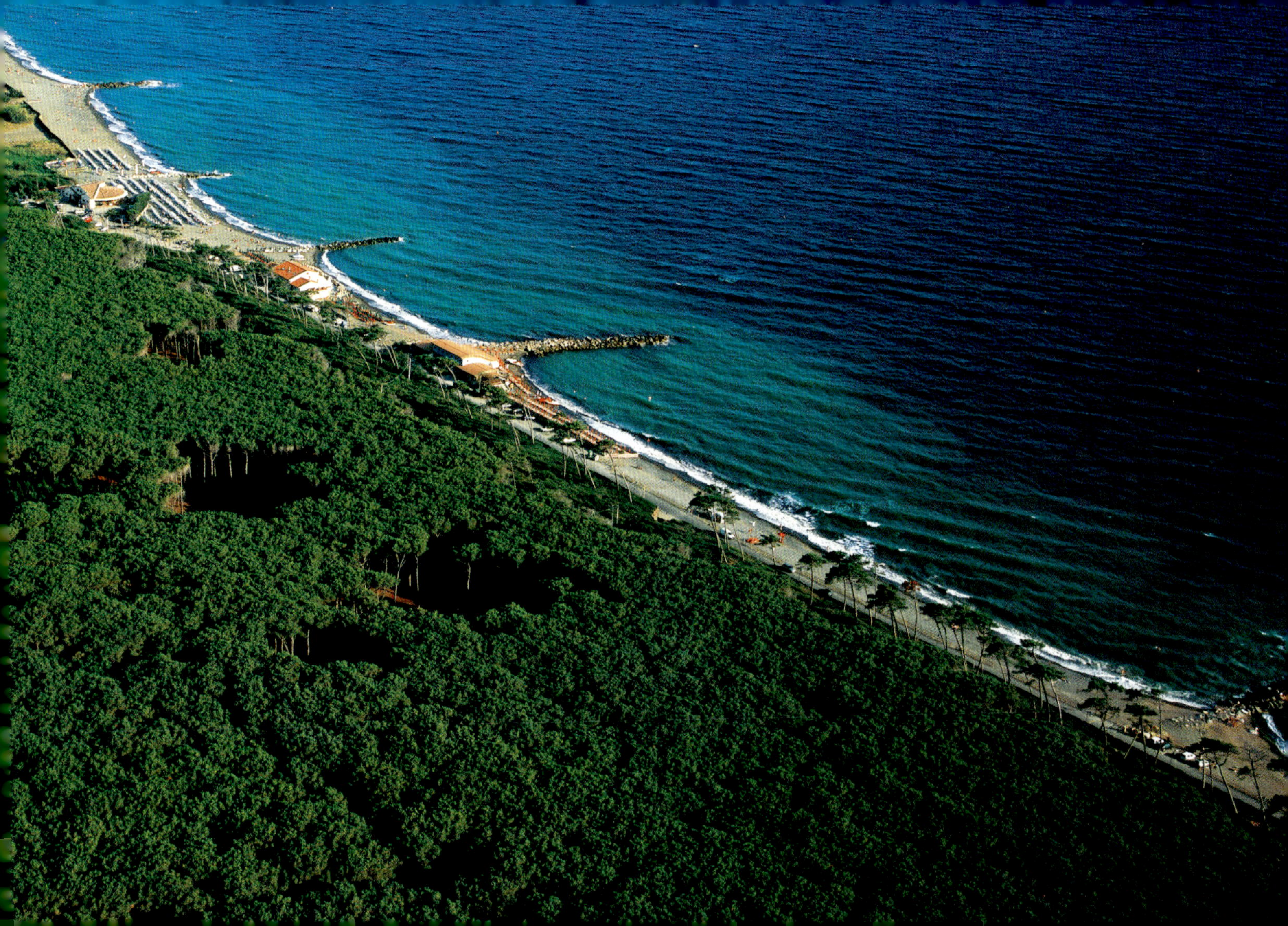

241

Cecina's beach, aproximately 65 ft (20 m) wide, winds along the city's edge. To protect farmland from the salty sea air, Duke Leopold of Tuscany had a pine forest planted along 9 miles (15 km) of coast.

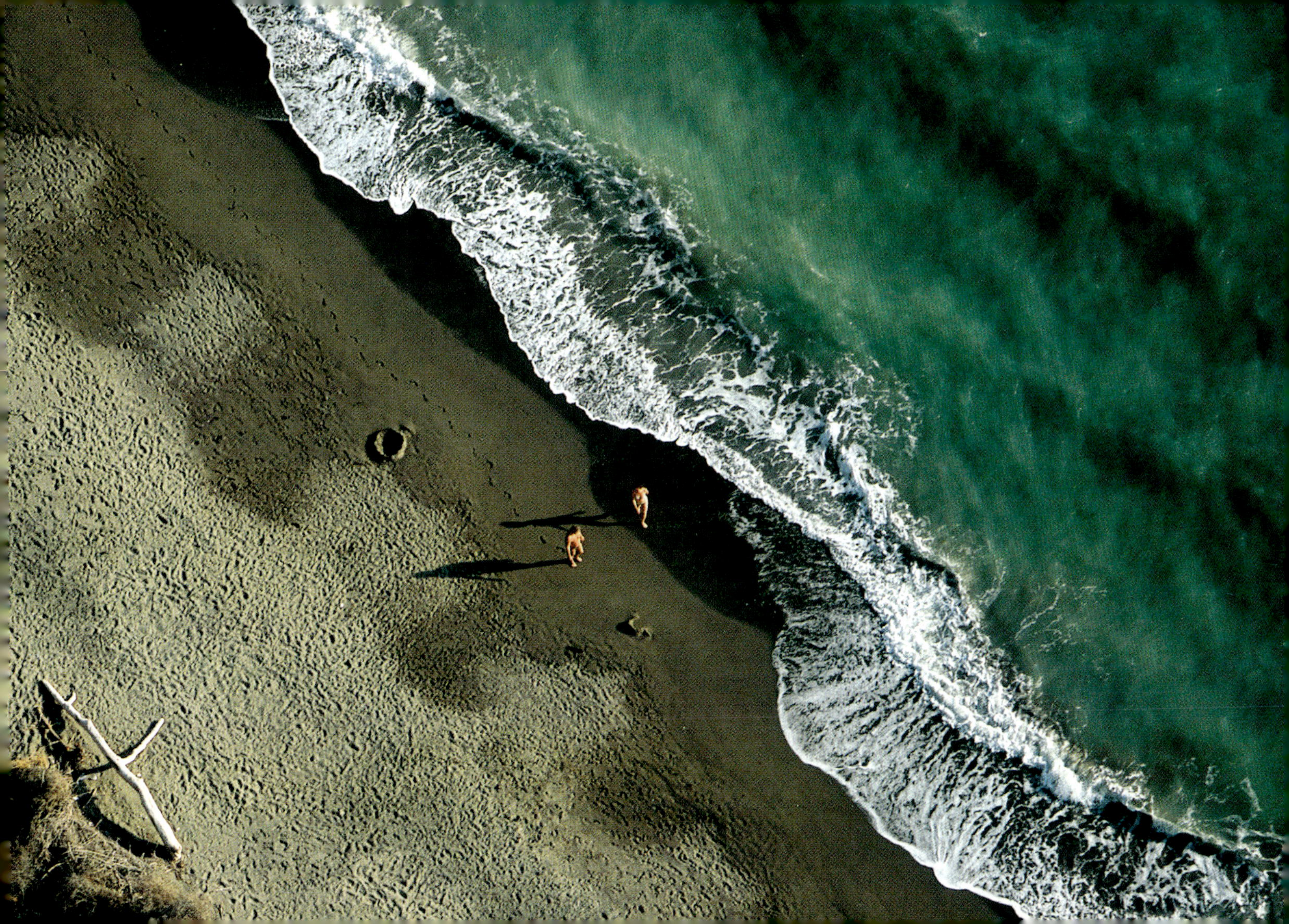

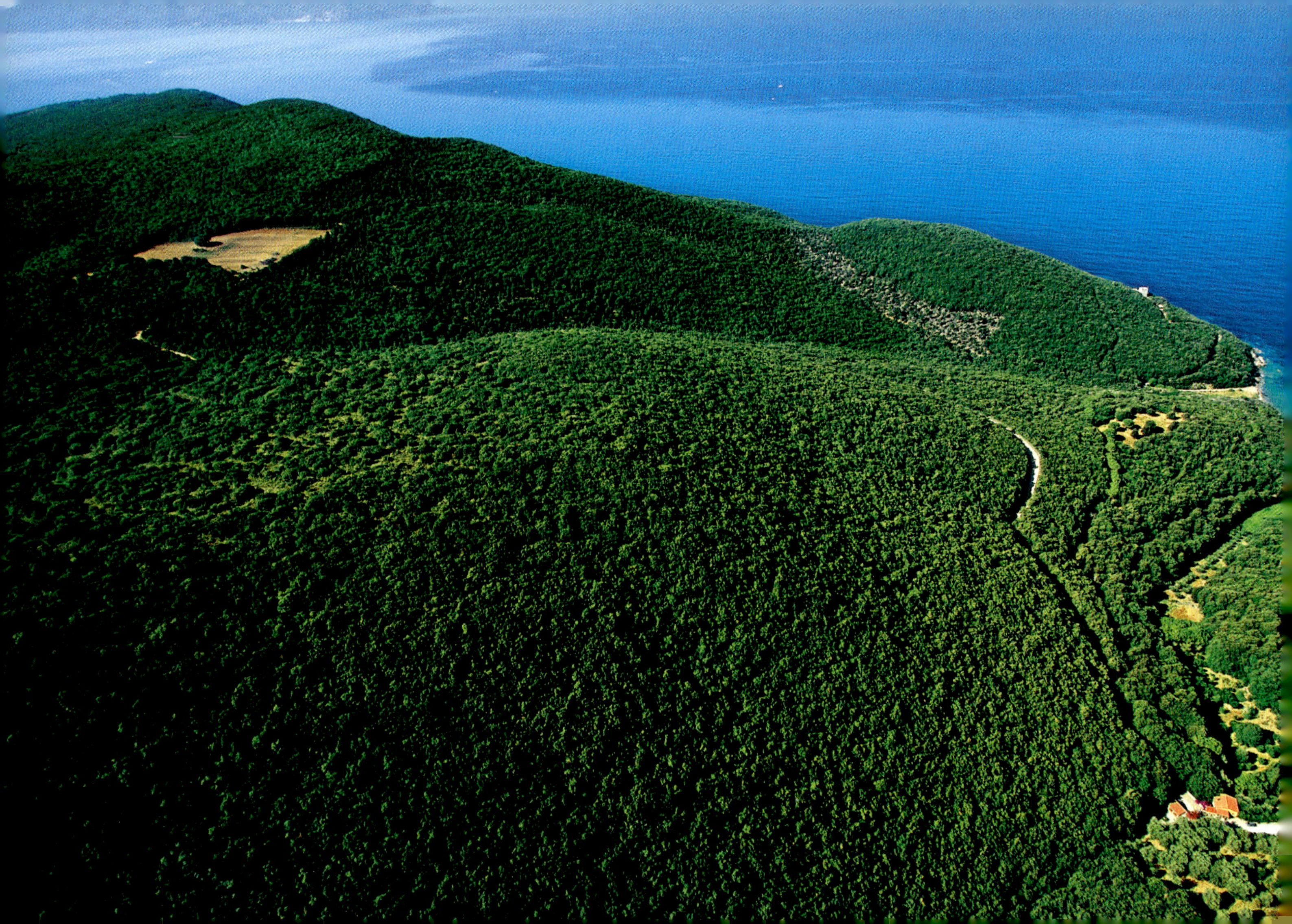

242

The Uccellino Mountains occupy the central and southern section of the Uccellina Natural Park and reach their highest point at Poggio dei Lecci, from where one can see the whole Tyrrhenian coast.

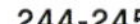

244-245

The section of shoreline that includes San Vincenzo is called the Etruscan Coast: sea, nature, art and history coexist here in perfect harmony.

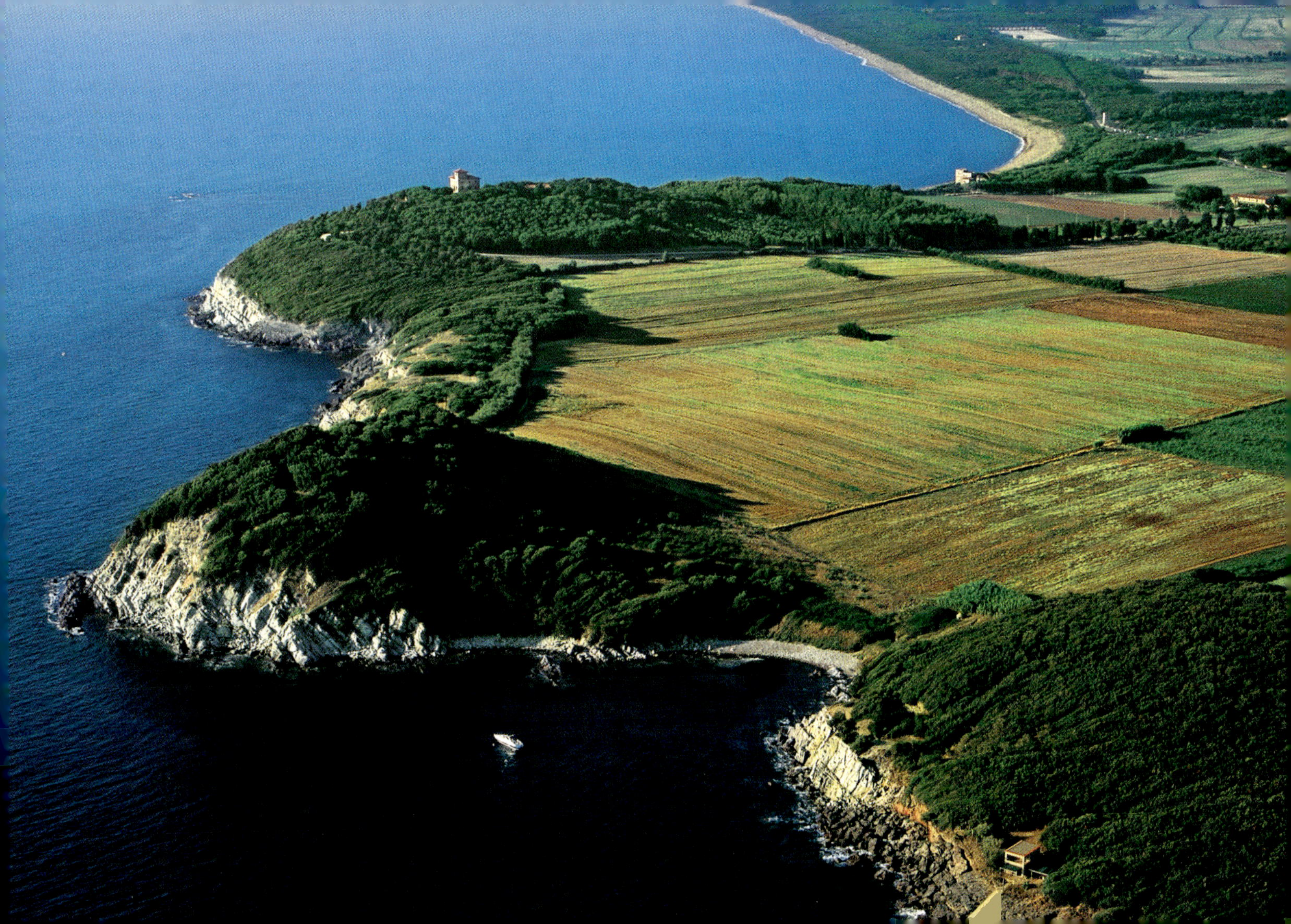

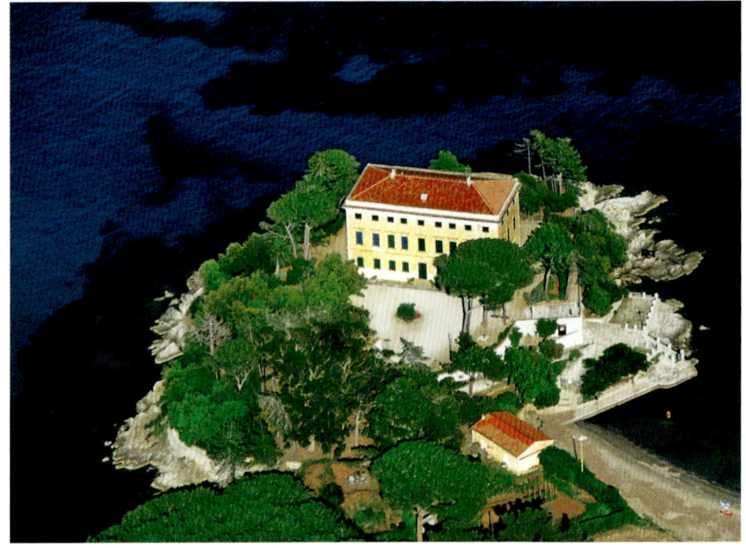

246 and 247
Splendid vintage villas face the cobalt sea that bathes the coast of San Vincenzo.

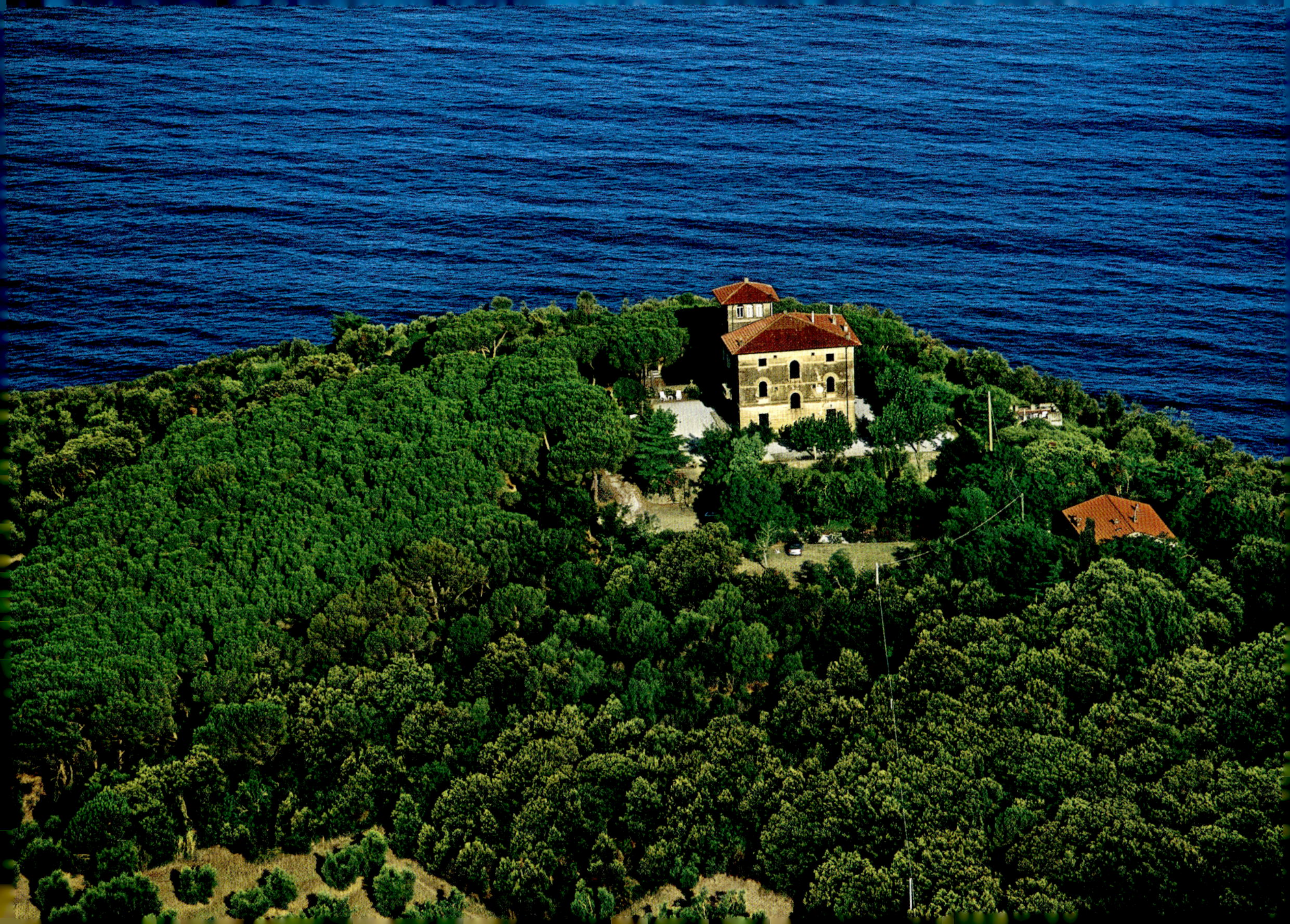

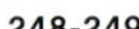

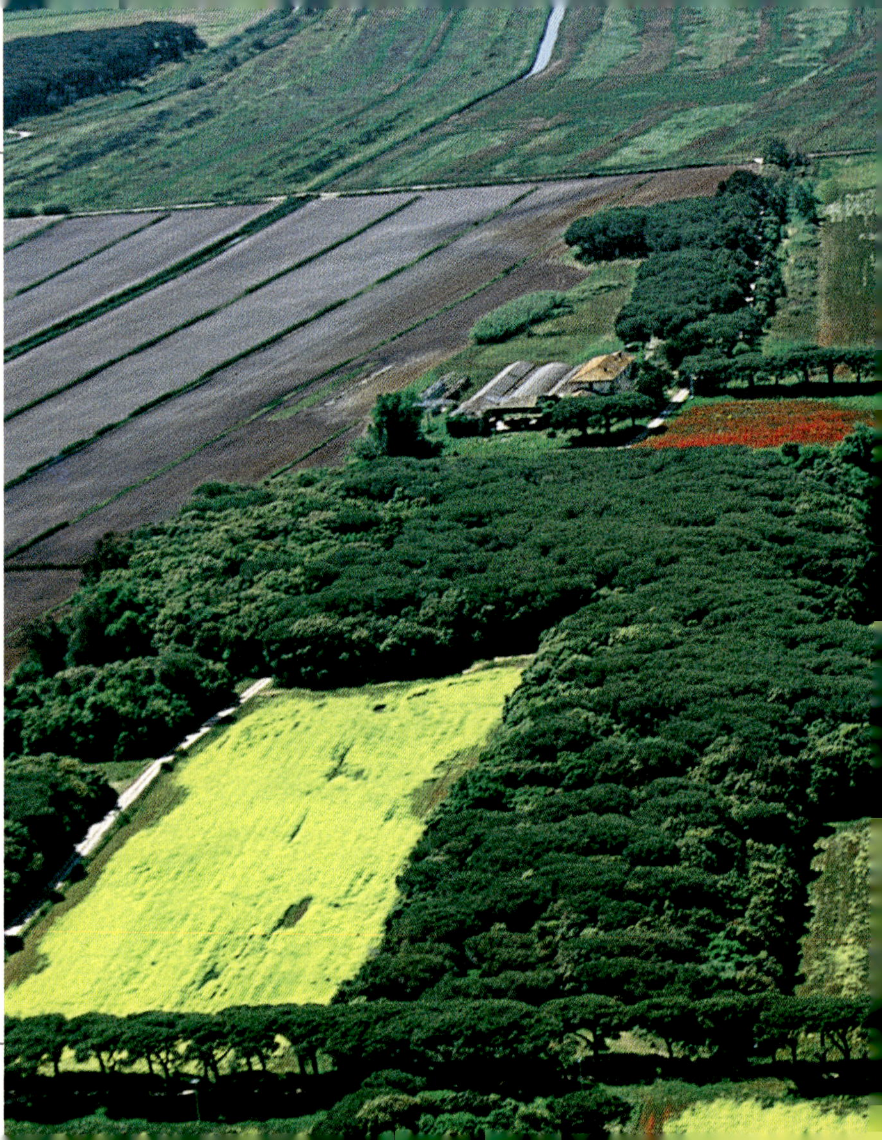

248-249

Fields of colza, poppy flowers and plowed, seeded earth are separated from the coast of Castiglion della Pescaia by what remains of the ancient pine forest.

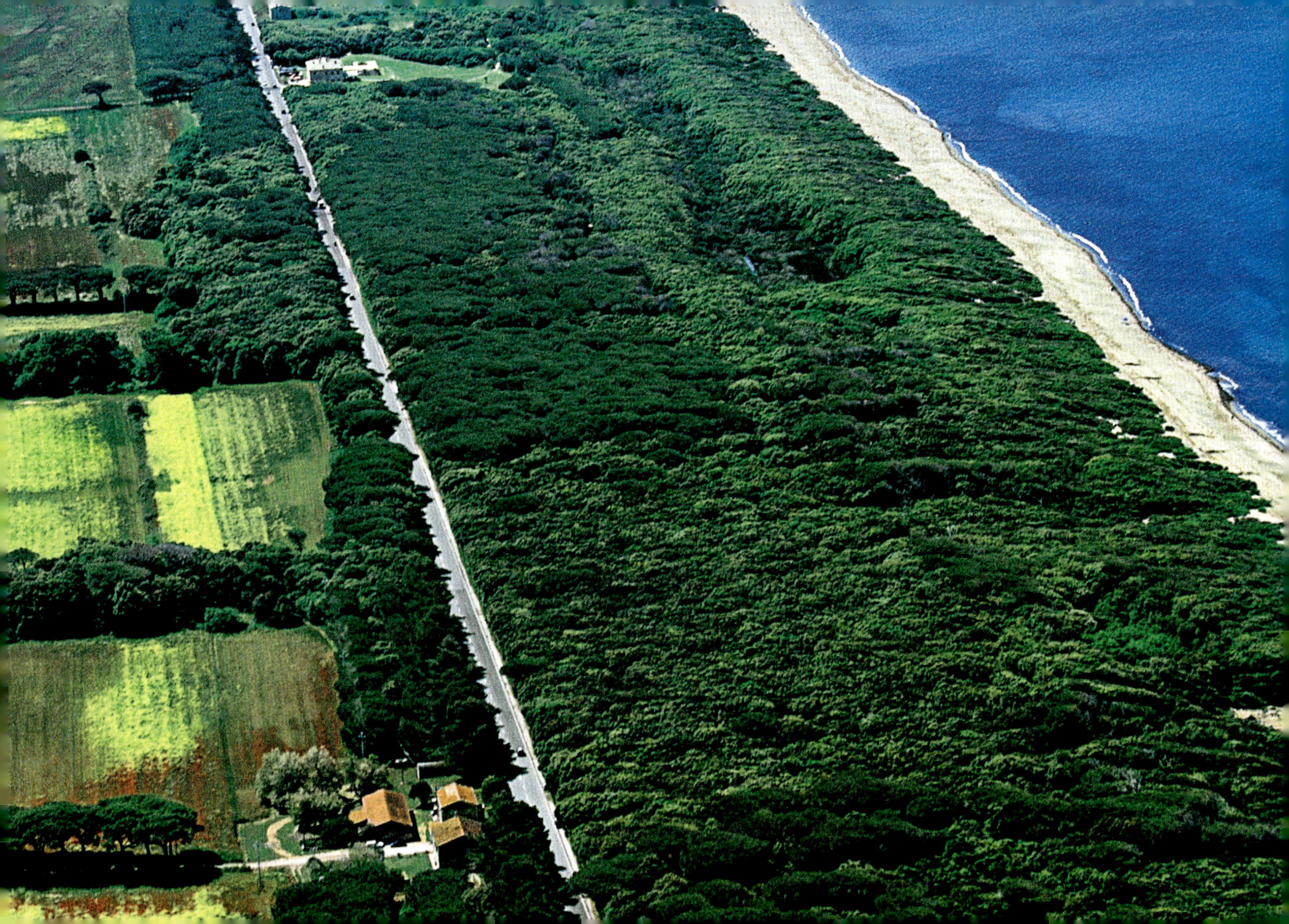

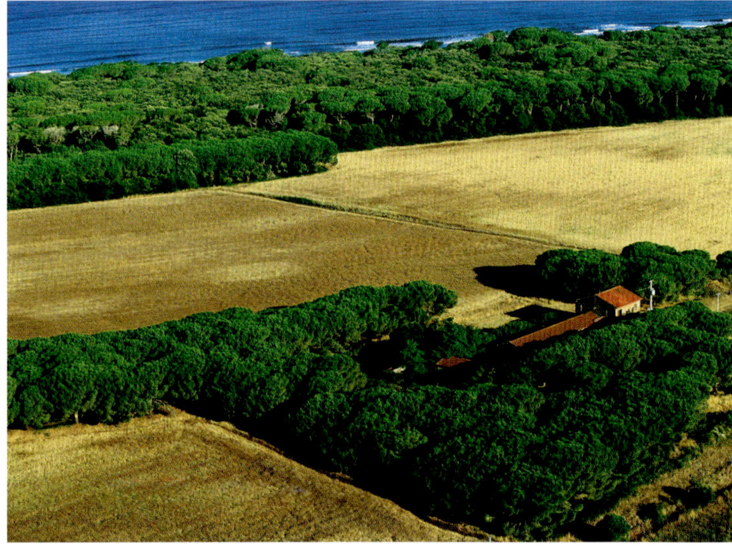

250, 251 and 252-253

Evergreen trees dominate the horizon of the San Vincenzo coastline that extends from the sea to the plains and up to hills as high as 820 ft (250 m).

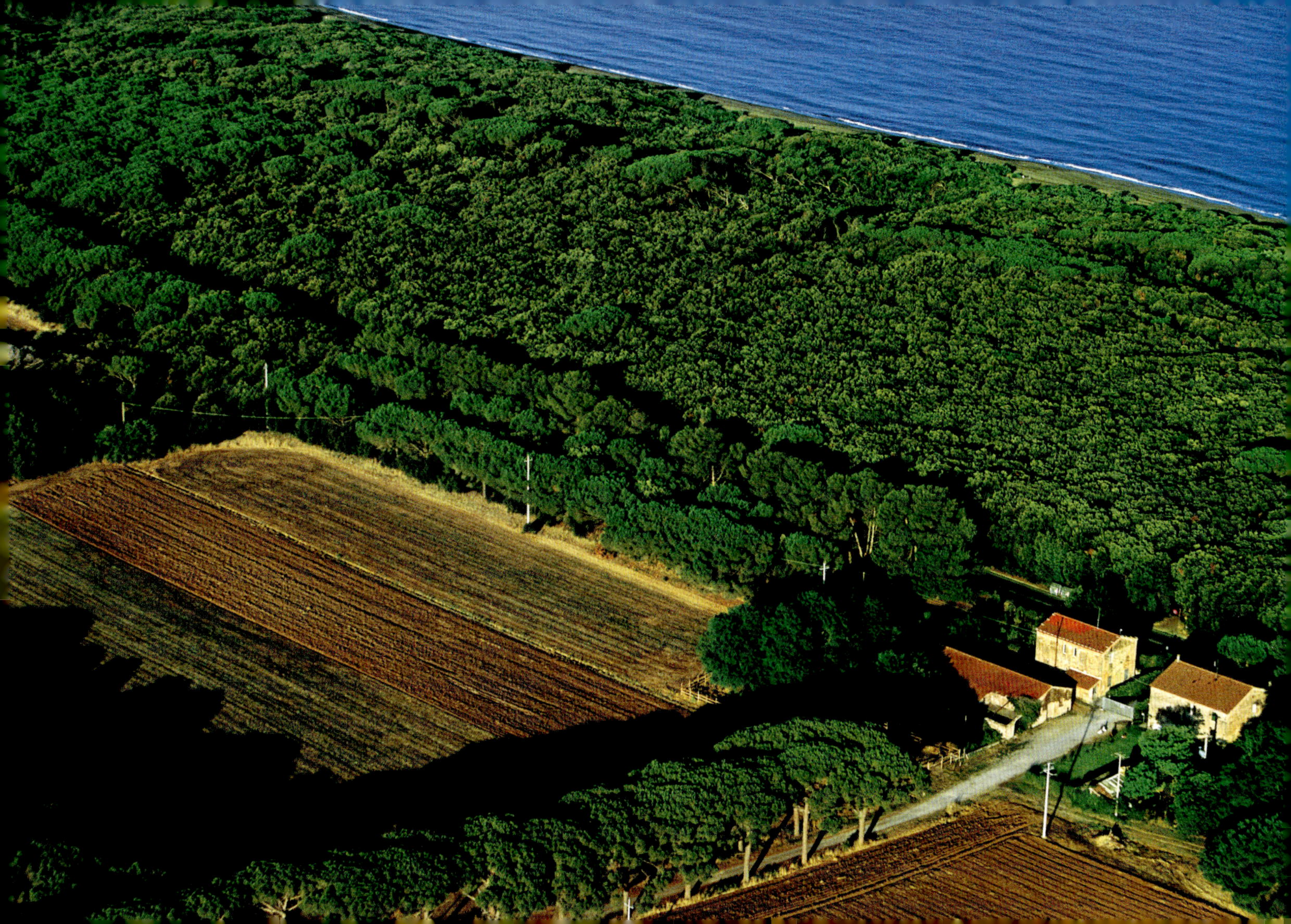

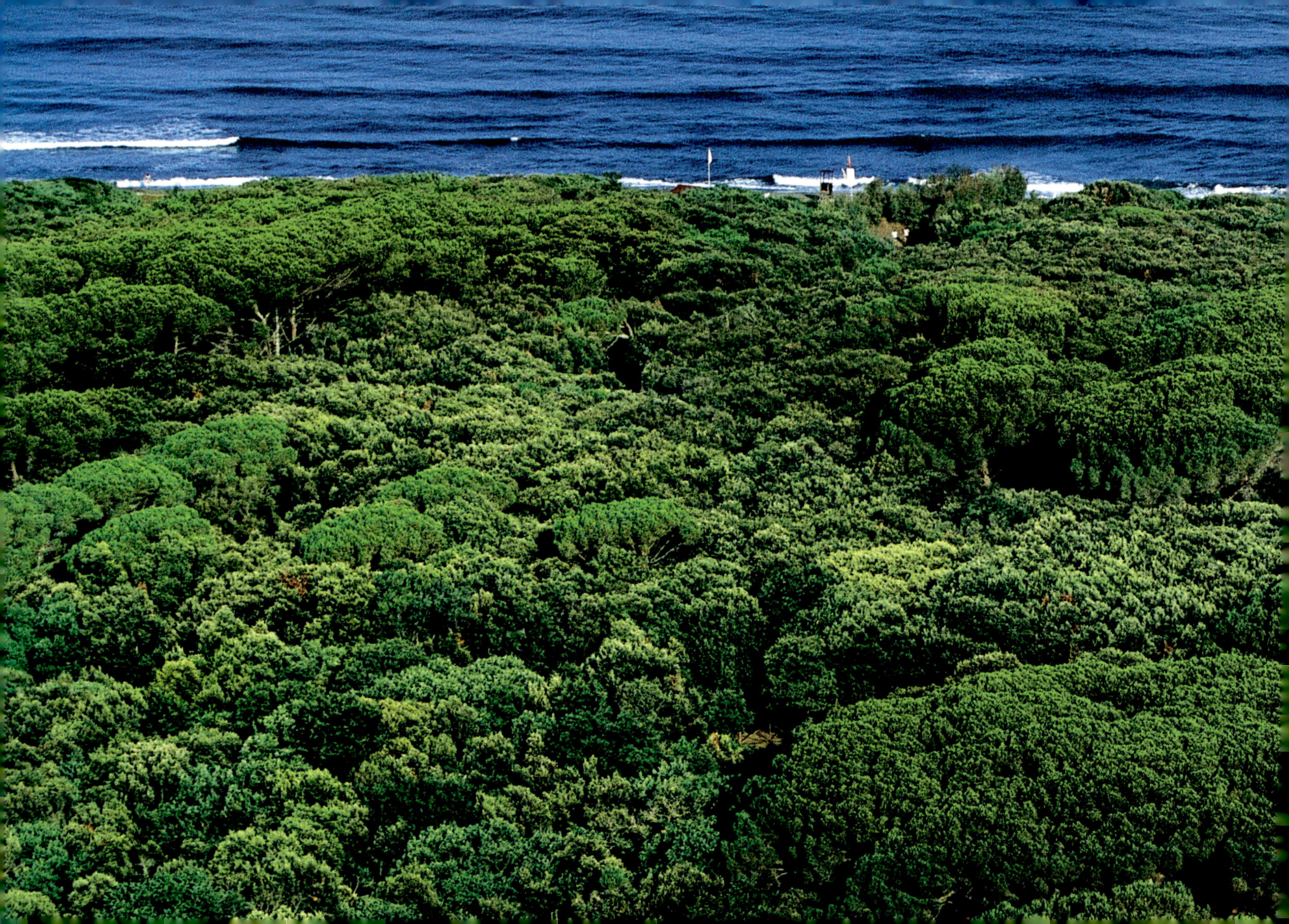

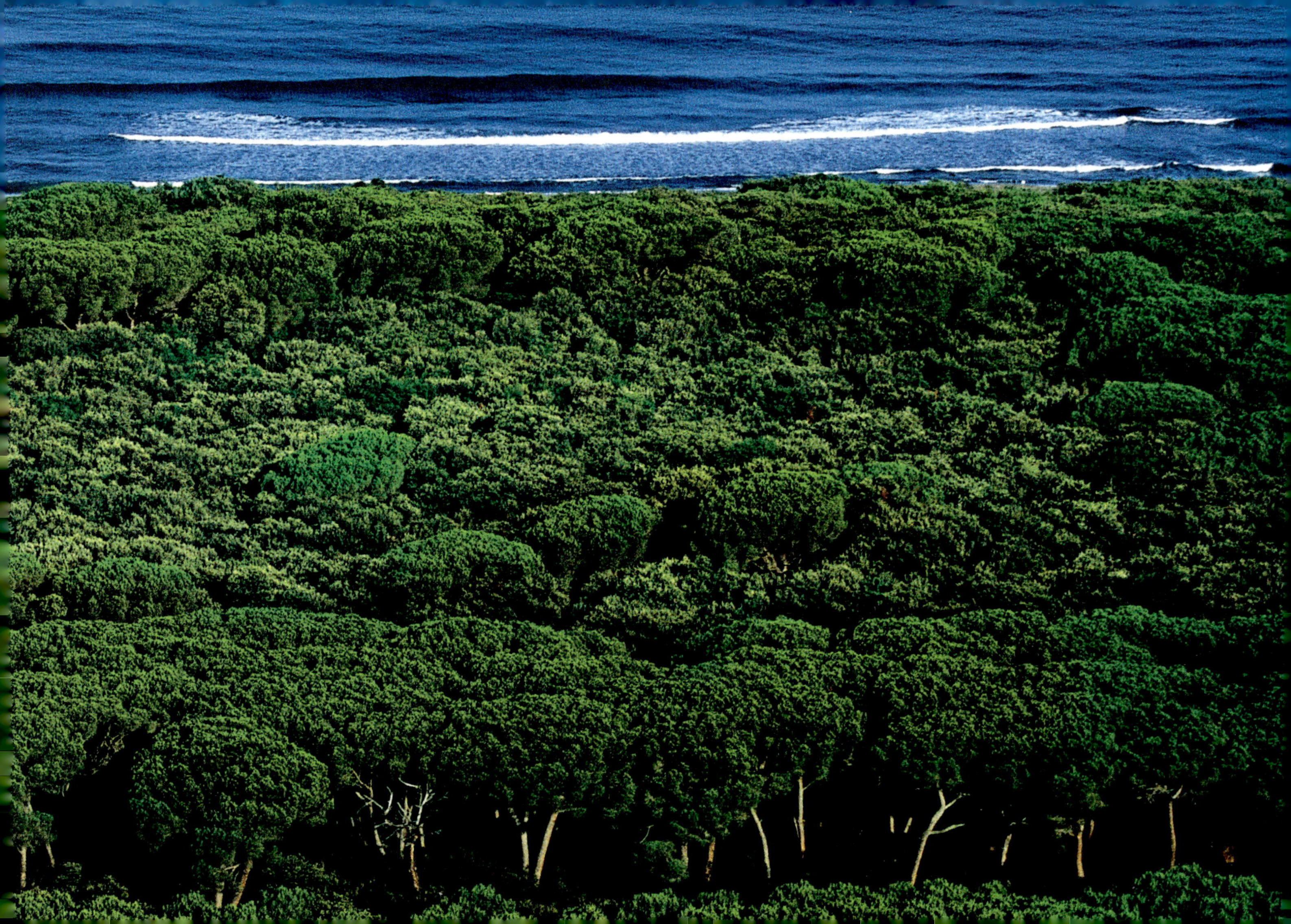

254-255
A splendid inlet, beaches with fine sand and a clear blue sea make the Etruscan Riviera a great vacation destination.

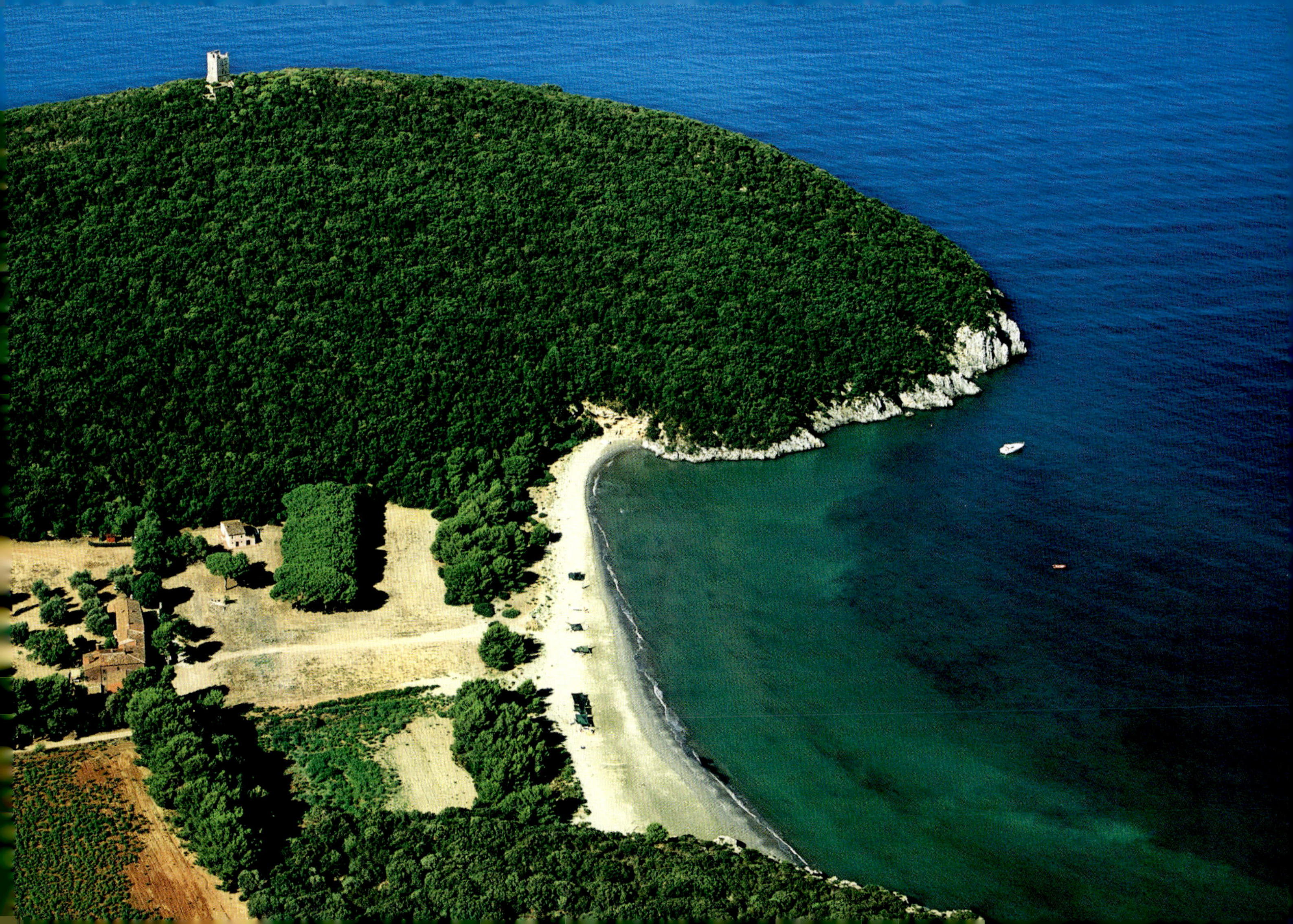

257

At Populonia, the yellow-orange of the countryside creates a wonderful contrast with the green Mediterranean vegetation and crystalline blue sea.

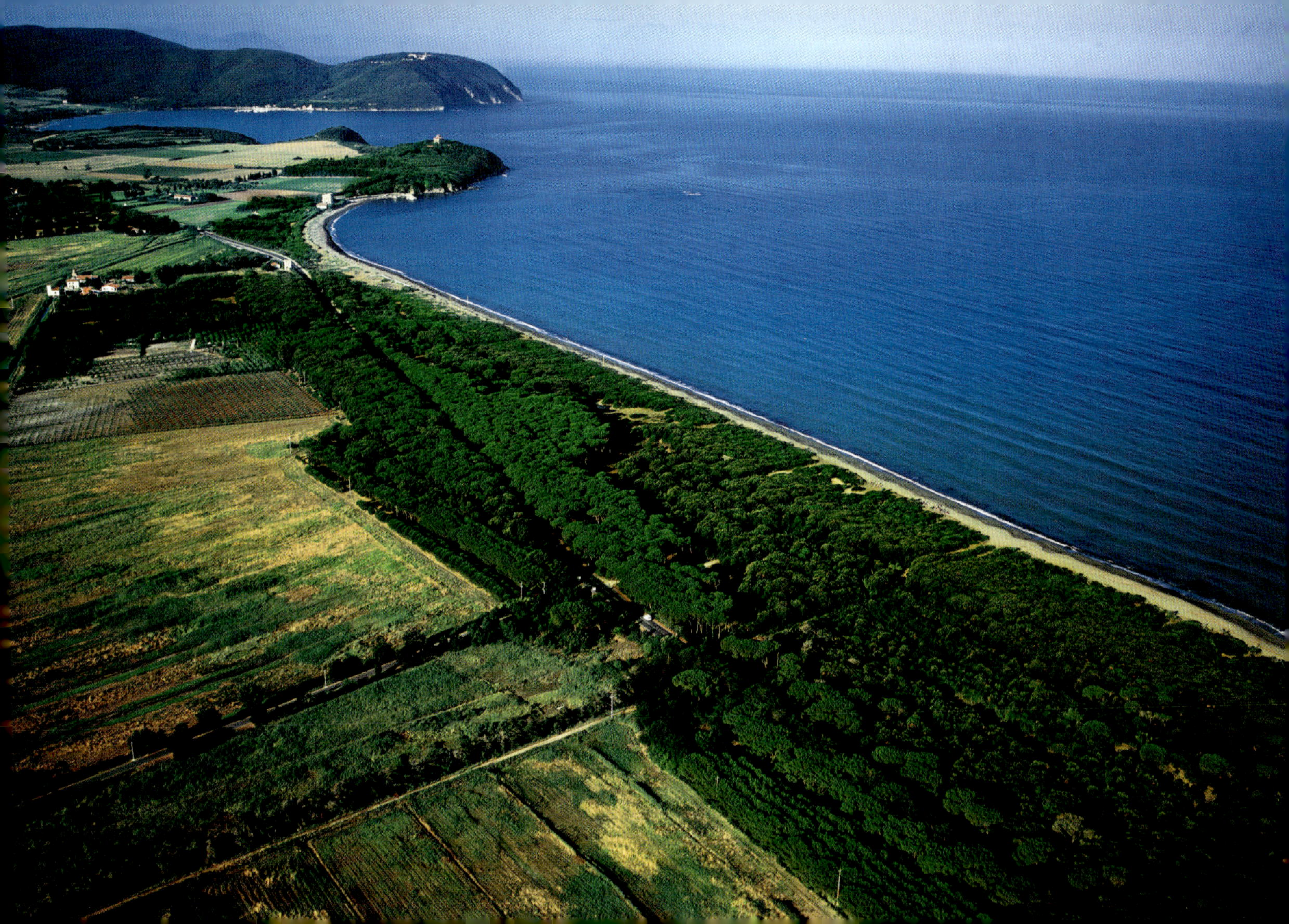

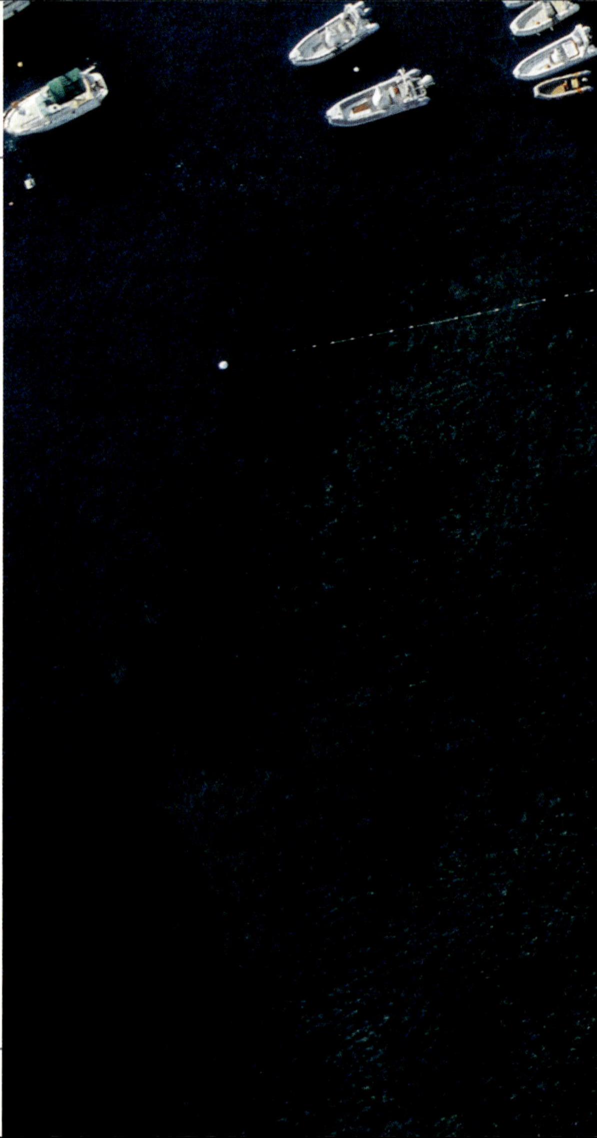

258-259
The Gulf of Baratti is known for the beauty of its beach and sea. Yachtsmen and sail- boat aficionados greatly appreciate this part of the Tyrrhenian coast.

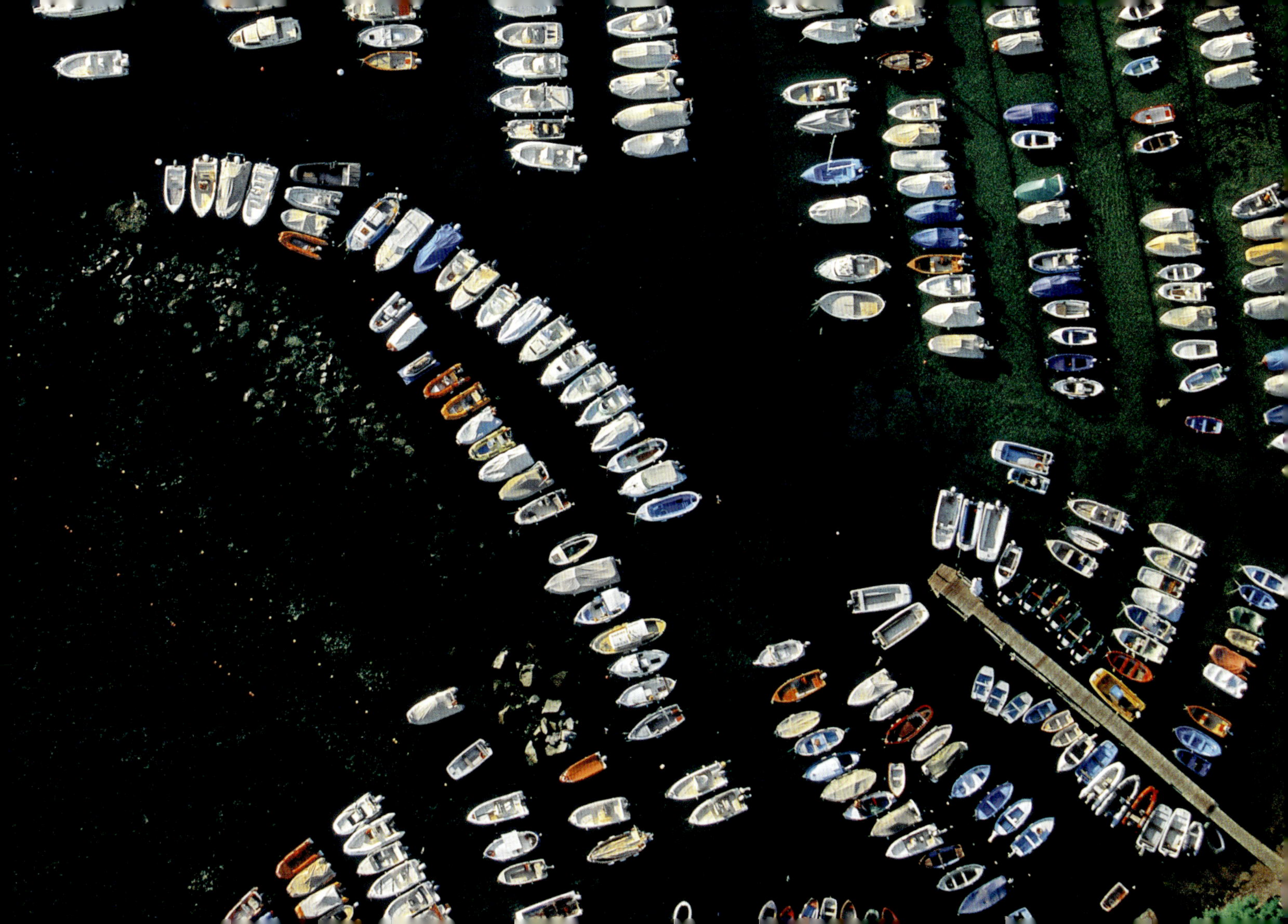

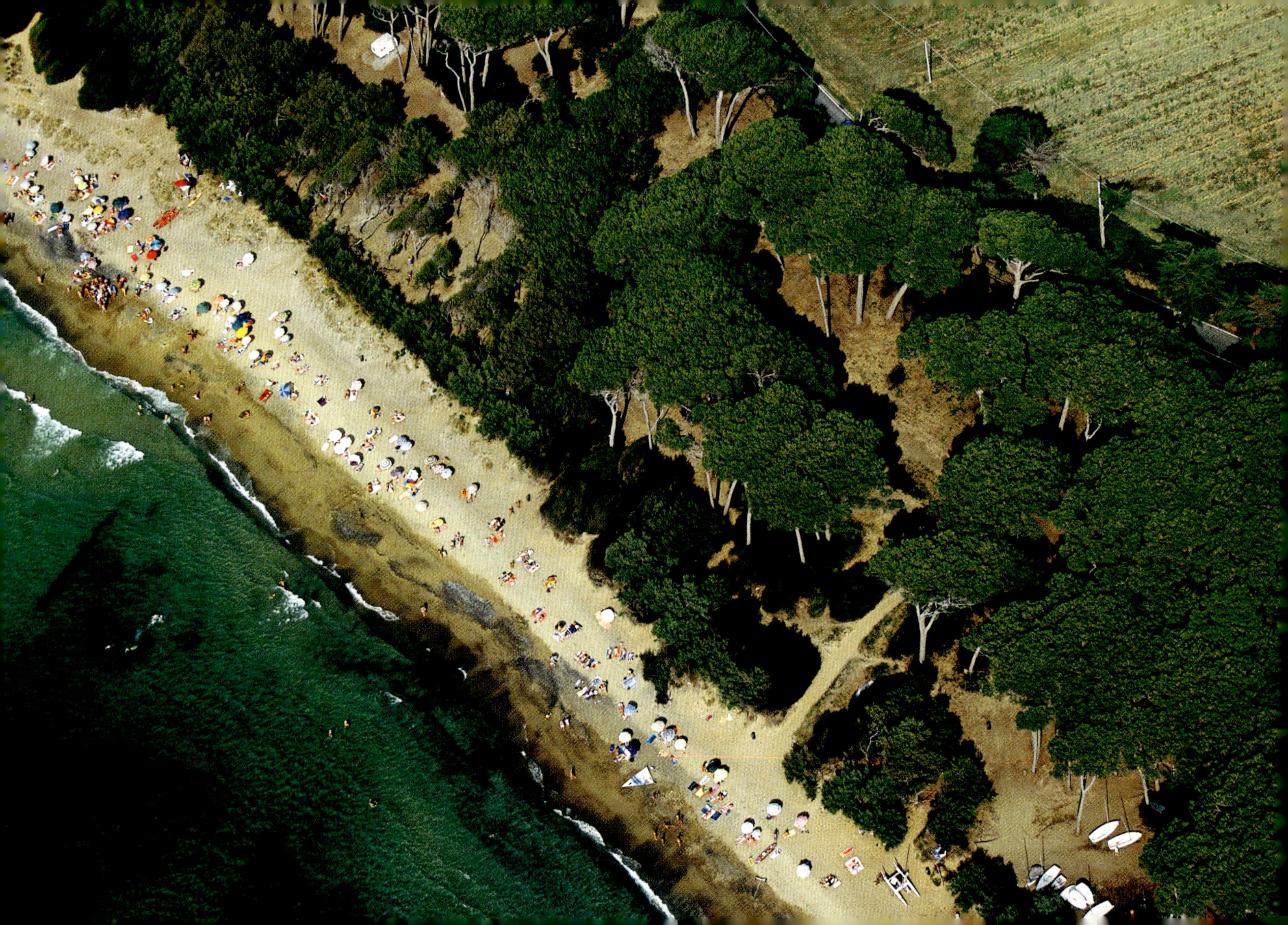

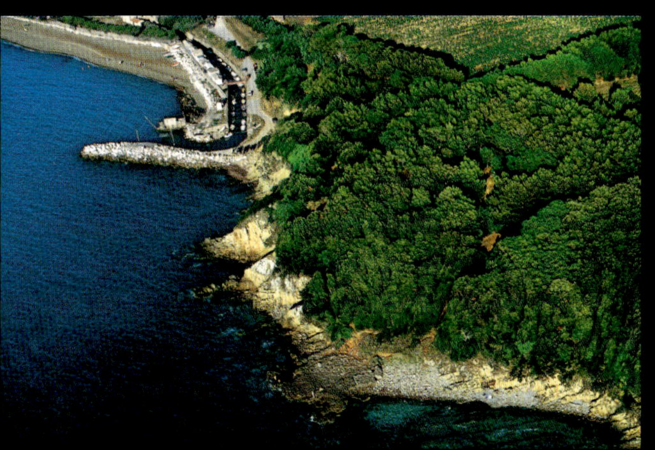

260
The coast around Populonia offers many accesses to the sea; mostly small sandy beaches surrounded by pine trees.

261
The rocky massif that ends with Mt. Massoncello creates a high, rugged coastline that begins at Port Baratti and ends at the port of Piombino.

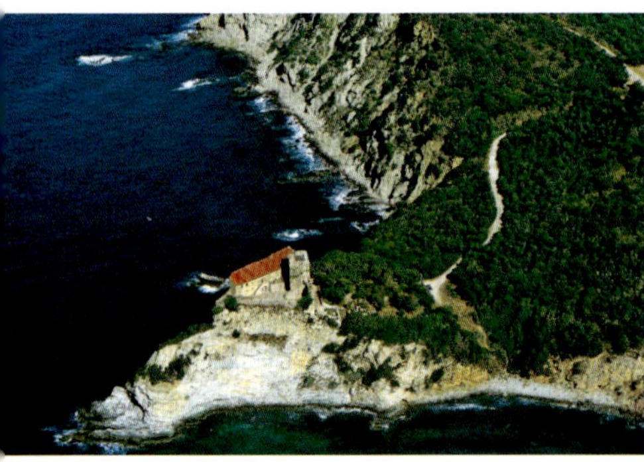

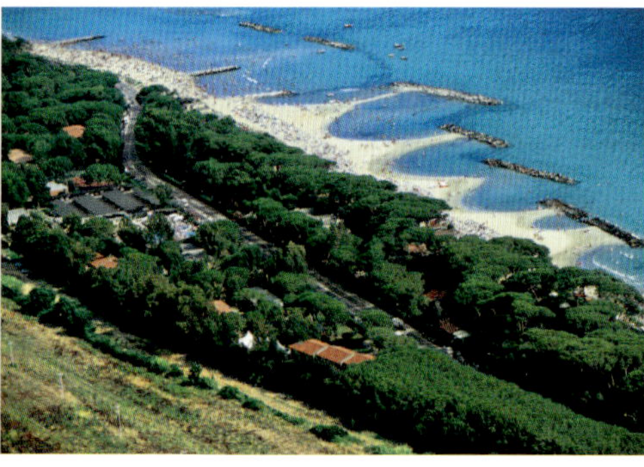

262
Along the coast at Follonica, cliffs give way to beaches bordered by pine forests.

263
The splendid and uncontaminated Gulf of Follonica extends from Piombino to Punta Ala. The coast, appreciated for the beauty of its countryside, is dappled with lovely vintage villas, like this one in the photograph.

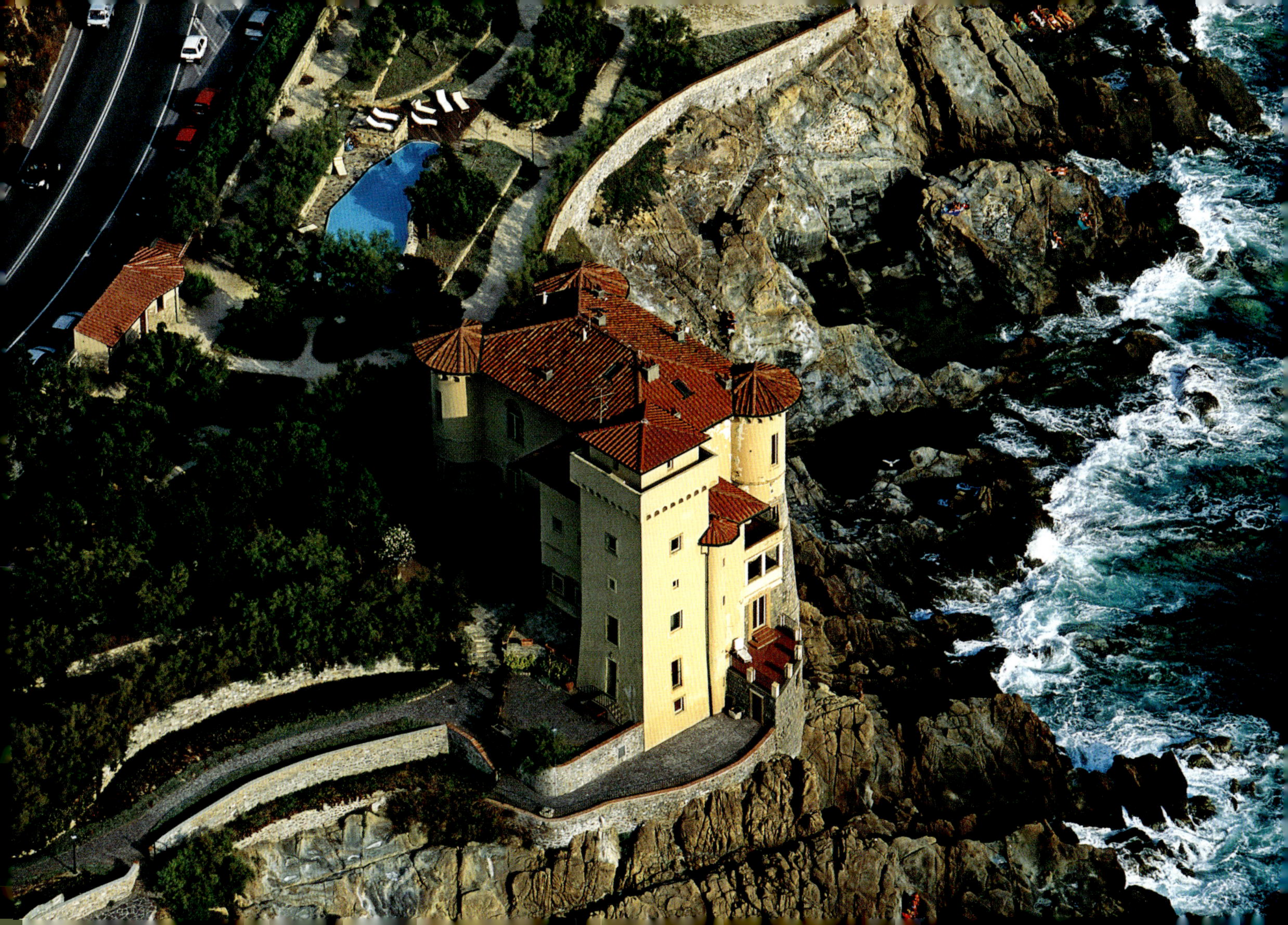

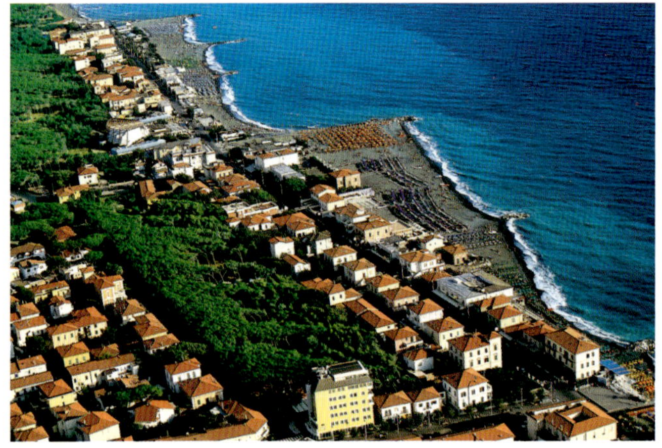

264
Cecina, of Etruscan origin, has had many periods of prosperity deriving from commerce. But in the 20th century, this seaside town established its identity as a beach resort.

265
Follonica, facing the Gulf of Follonica, is a lovely beach resort attracting many visitors.

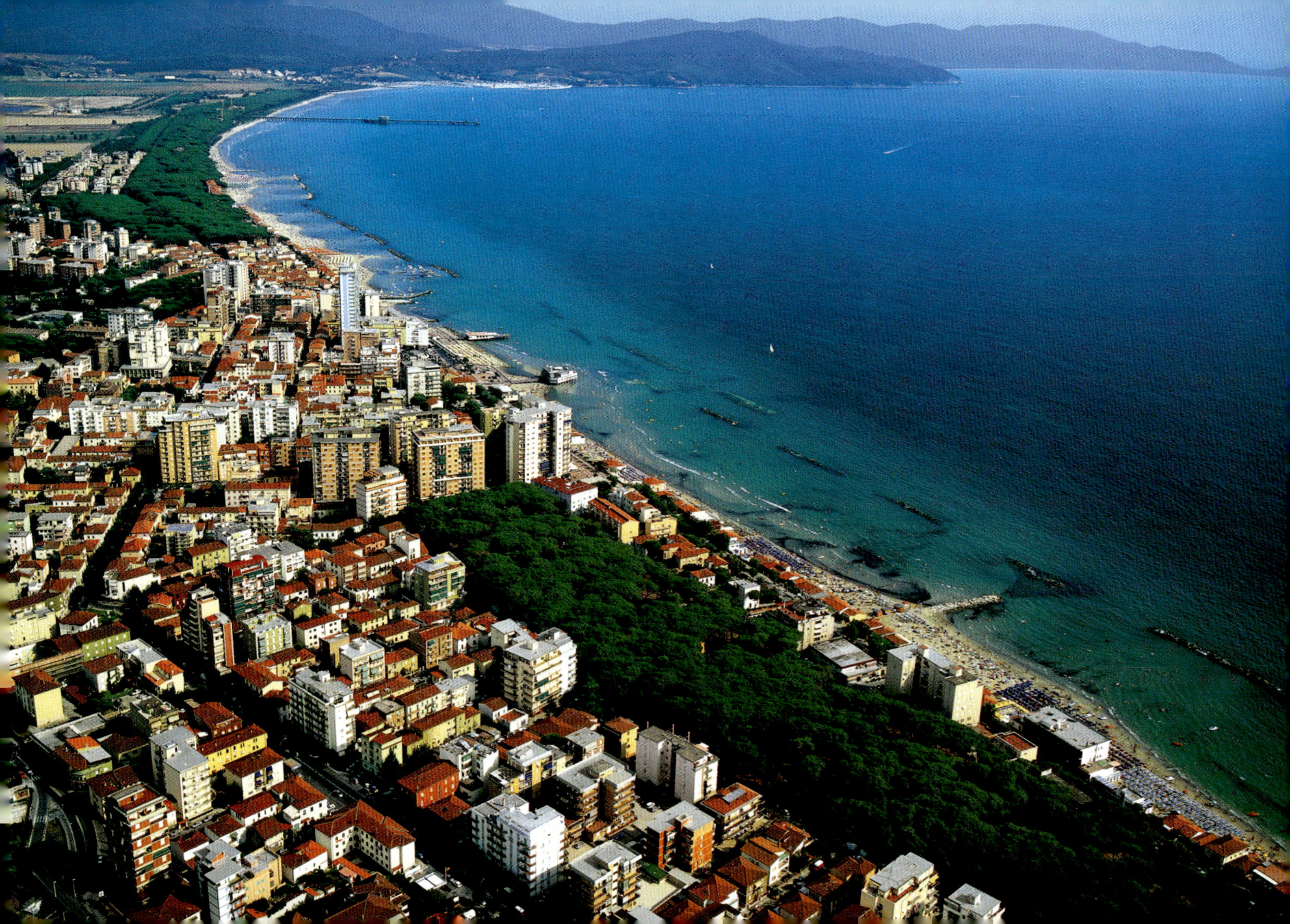

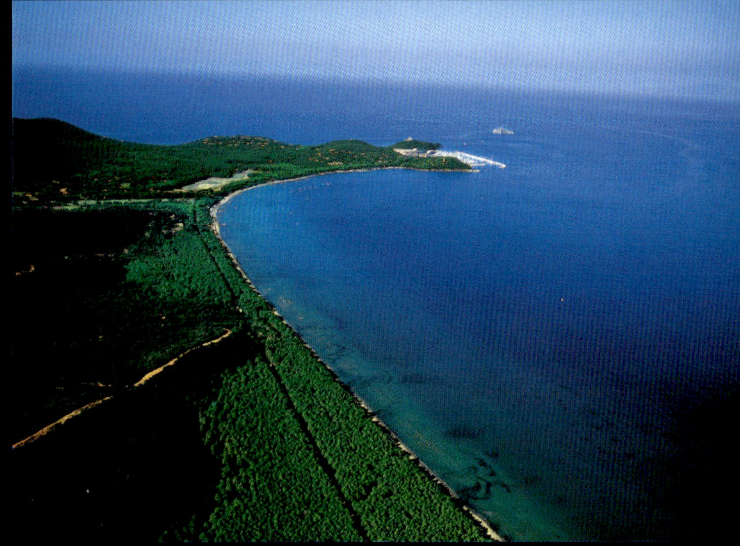

266 and 267
Punta Ala is a splendid promontory, covered by dense pine forests and lush Mediterranean vegetation, sloping down to the breathtaking sea.

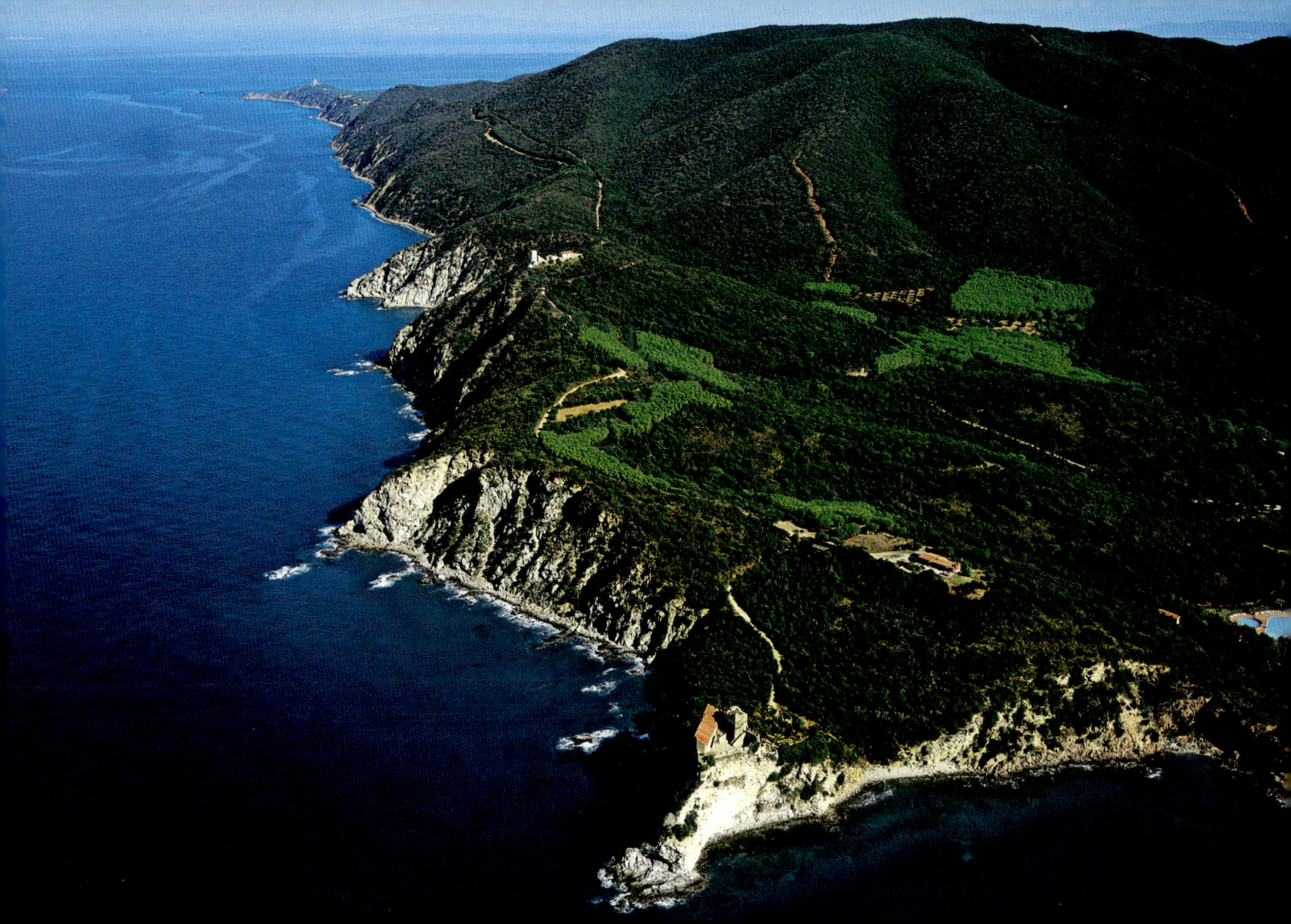

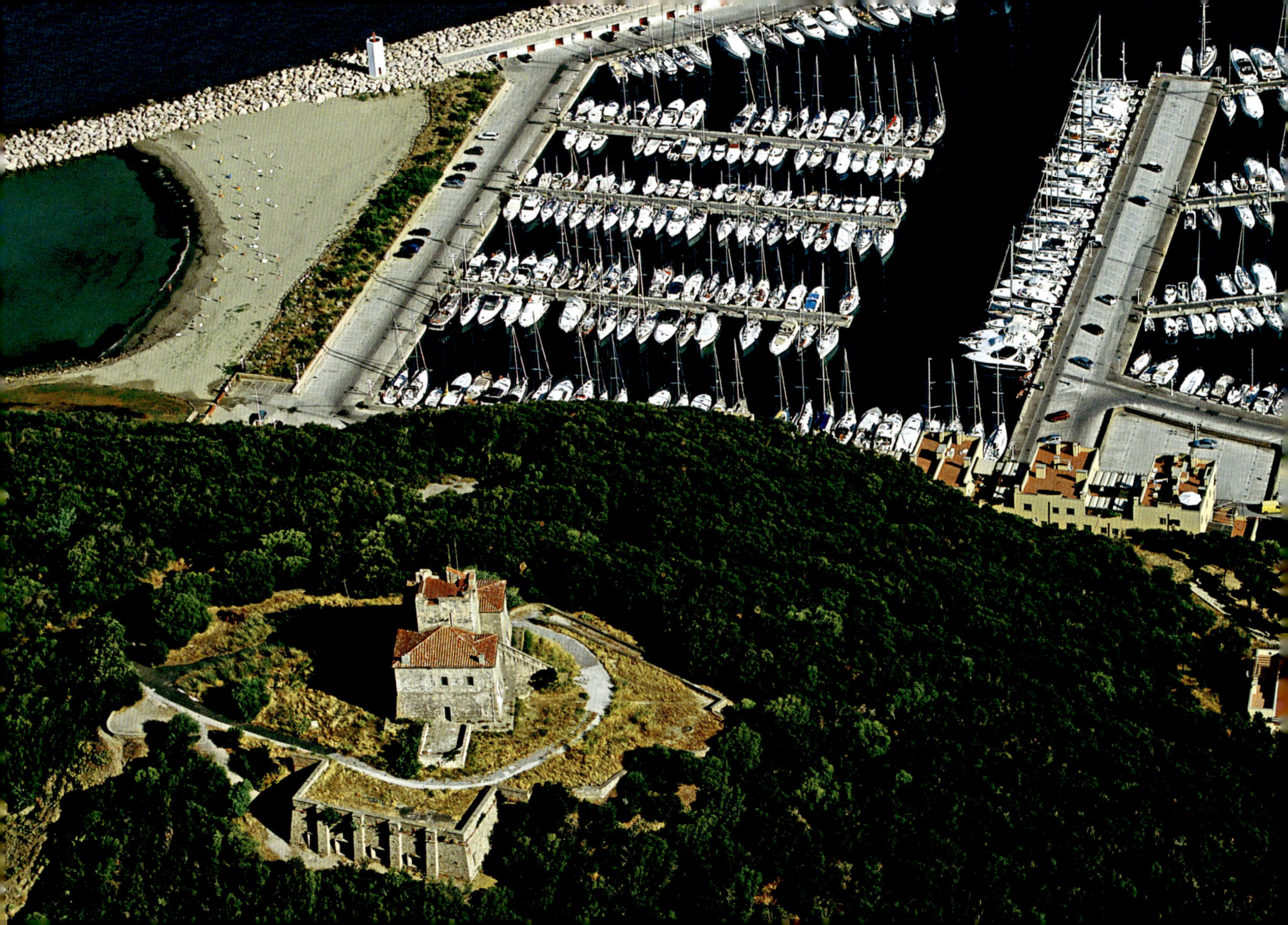

268
The exclusive Punta Ala Marina was constructed with strict environmental protection standards.

269 left
Though known mostly for its port, Punta Ala is also famous for its marina and sail boats.

269 right
Punta Ala (Point Wing) was so named by the Italian air ace Italo Balbo, who often flew over the Tyrrhenian coast and decided to purchase more than 2470 acres (1000 hectares) of forested land.

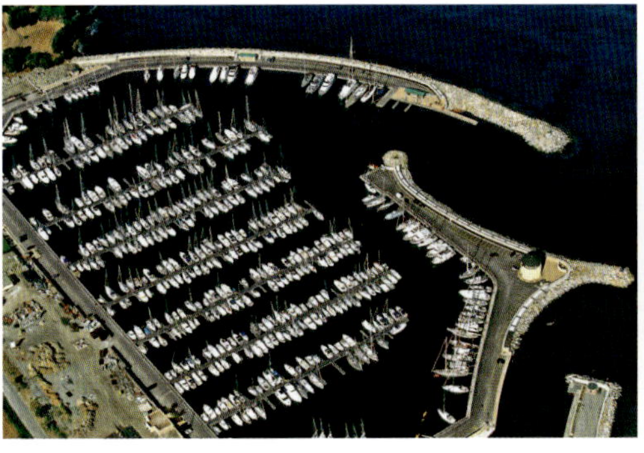

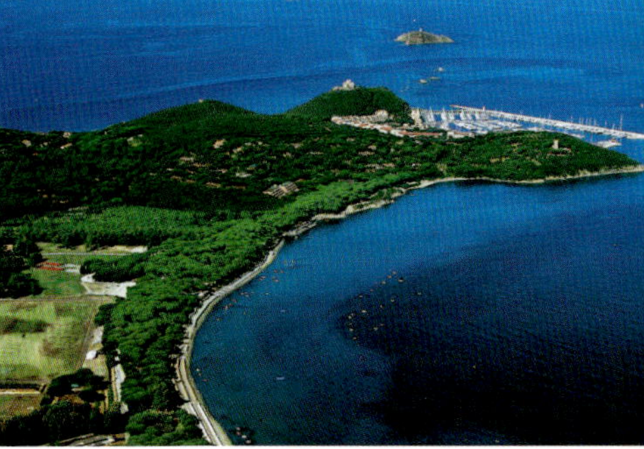

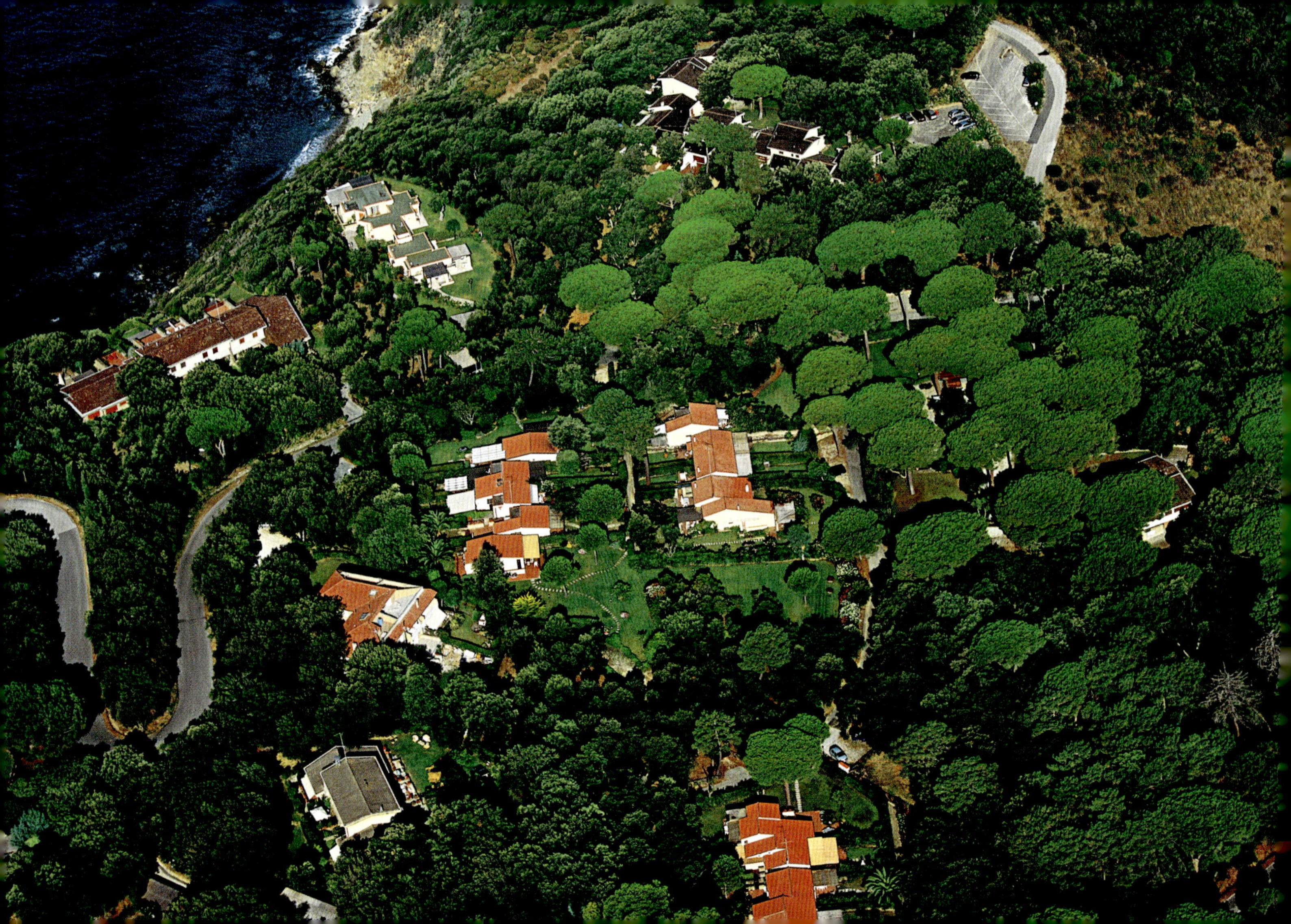

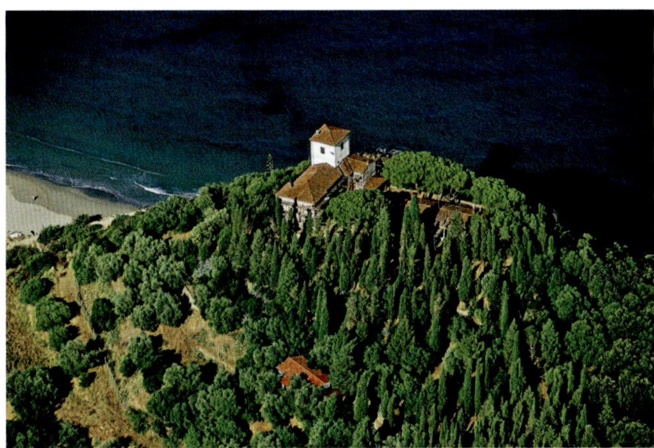

270 and 271
On this wooded rocky spur on the coast near Calafuria, many private homes have been constructed, but with standards that protect the environment.

272-273

Covered in lush and unspoiled Mediterranean vegetation, the beaches of Punta Ala are among the most beautiful on the Tyrrhenian coast.

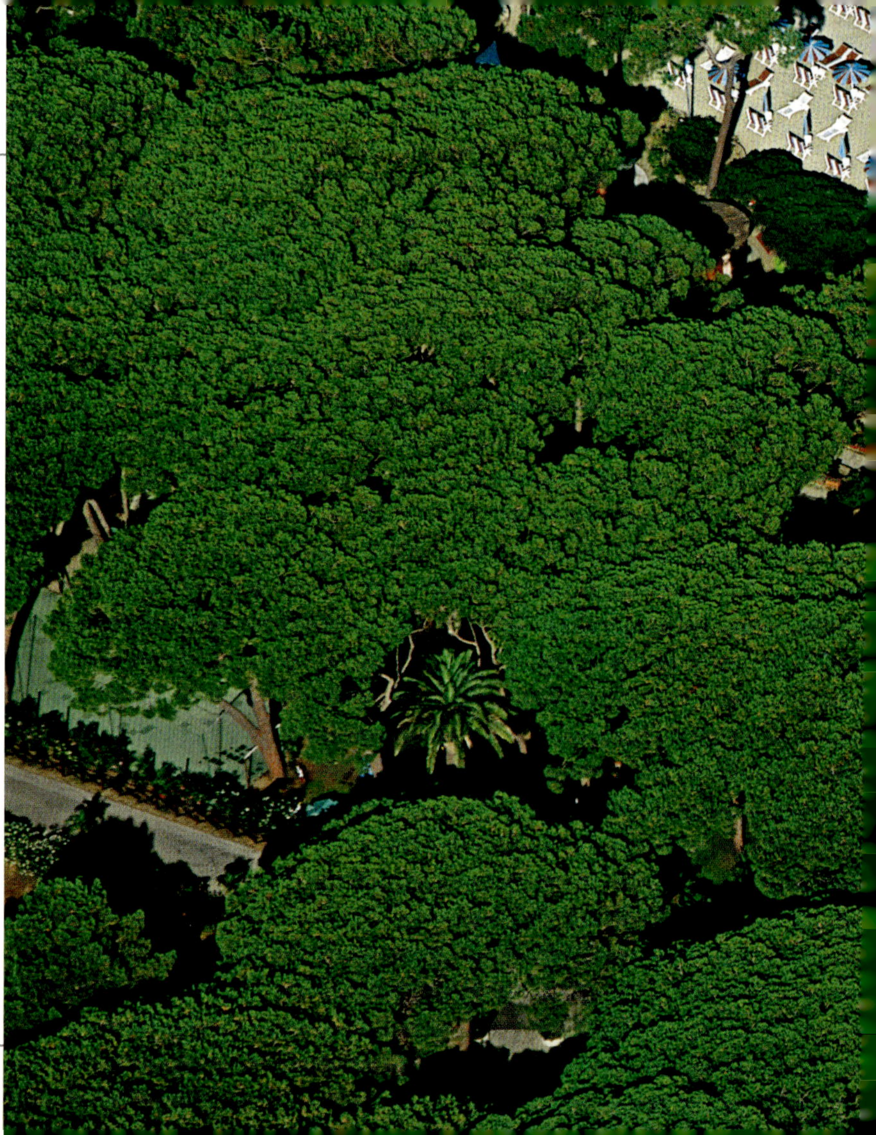

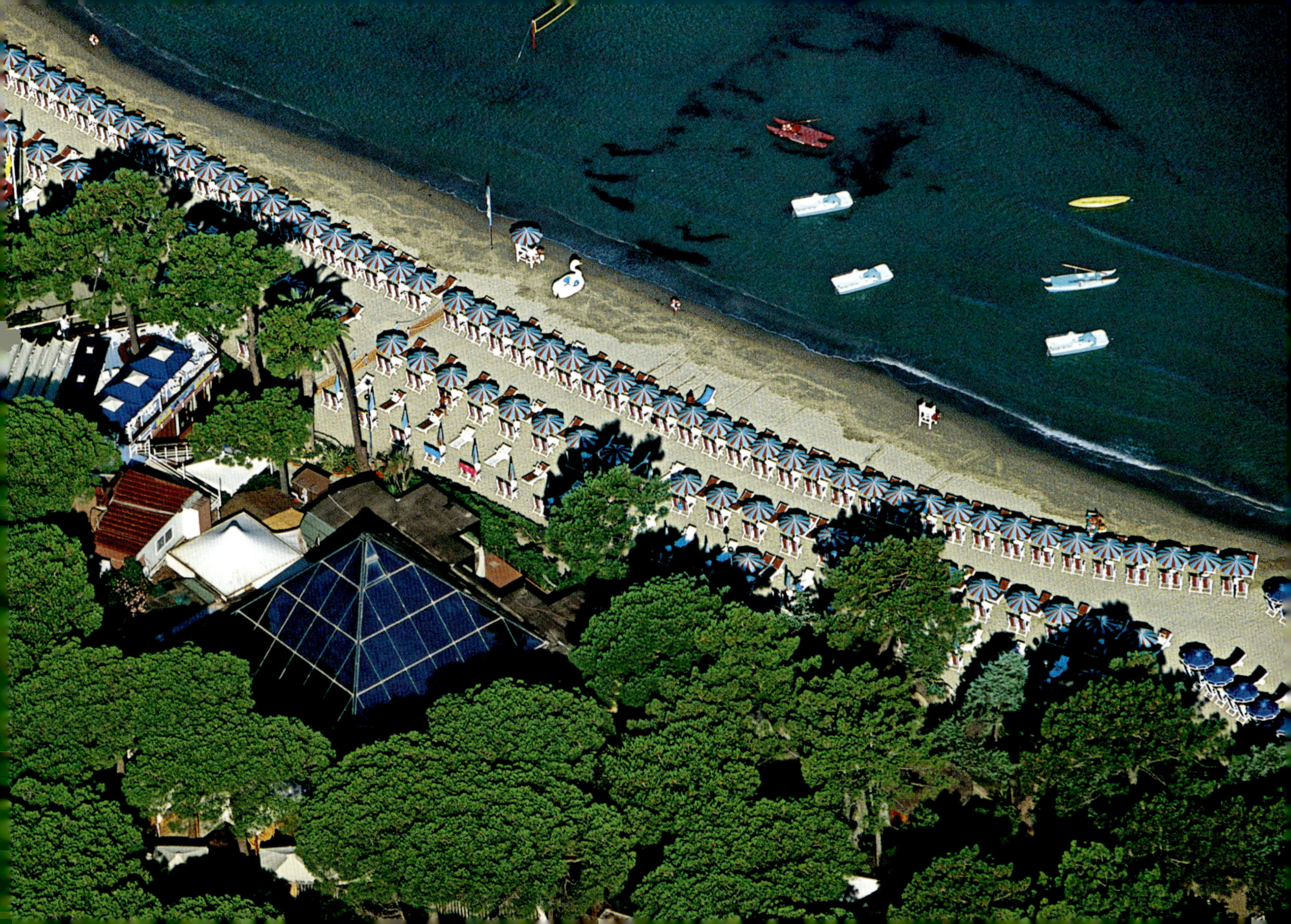

274-275
Talamone, on a promontory above the sea at the end of the Uccellina Mountains, enjoys a unique natural environment.

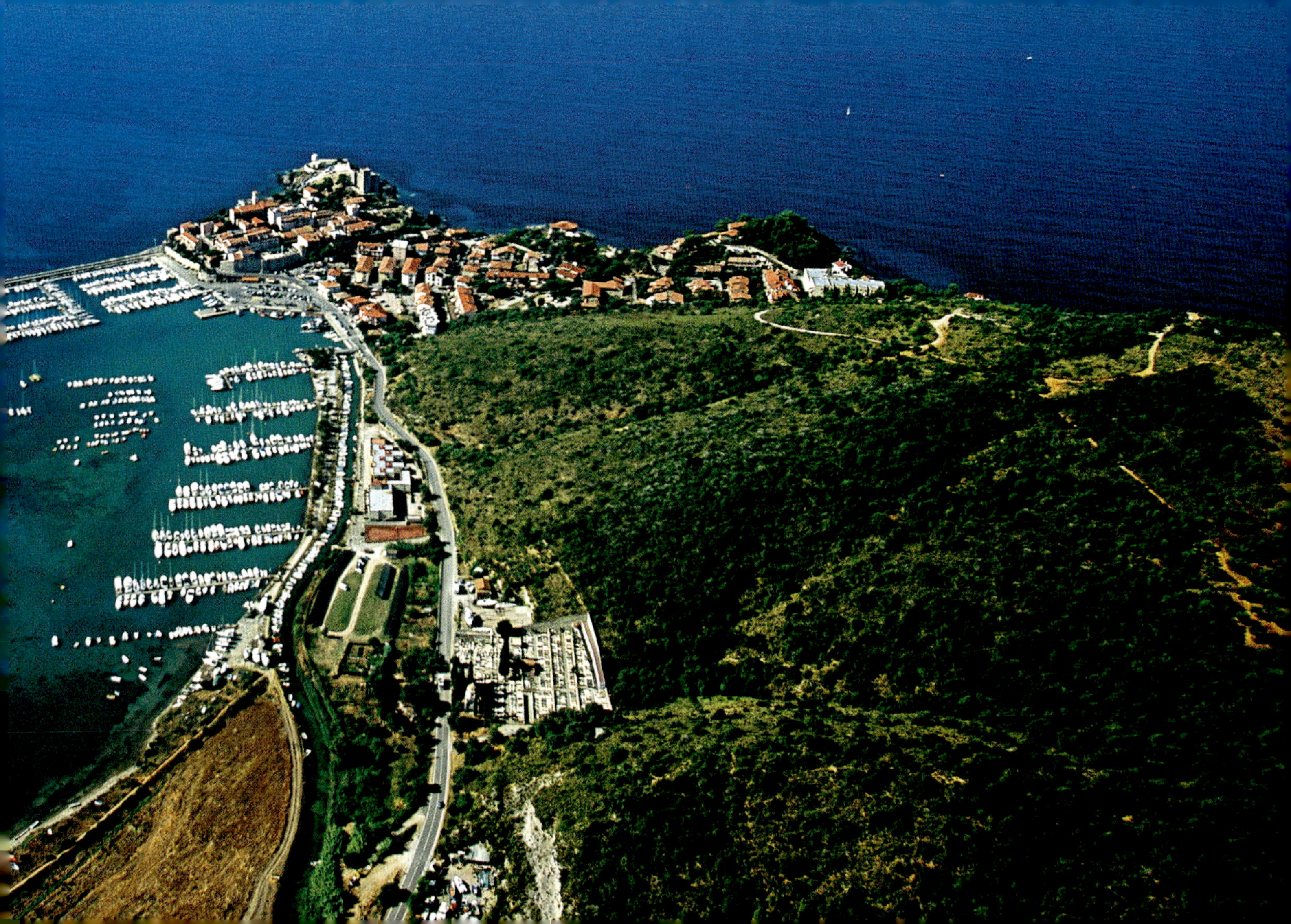

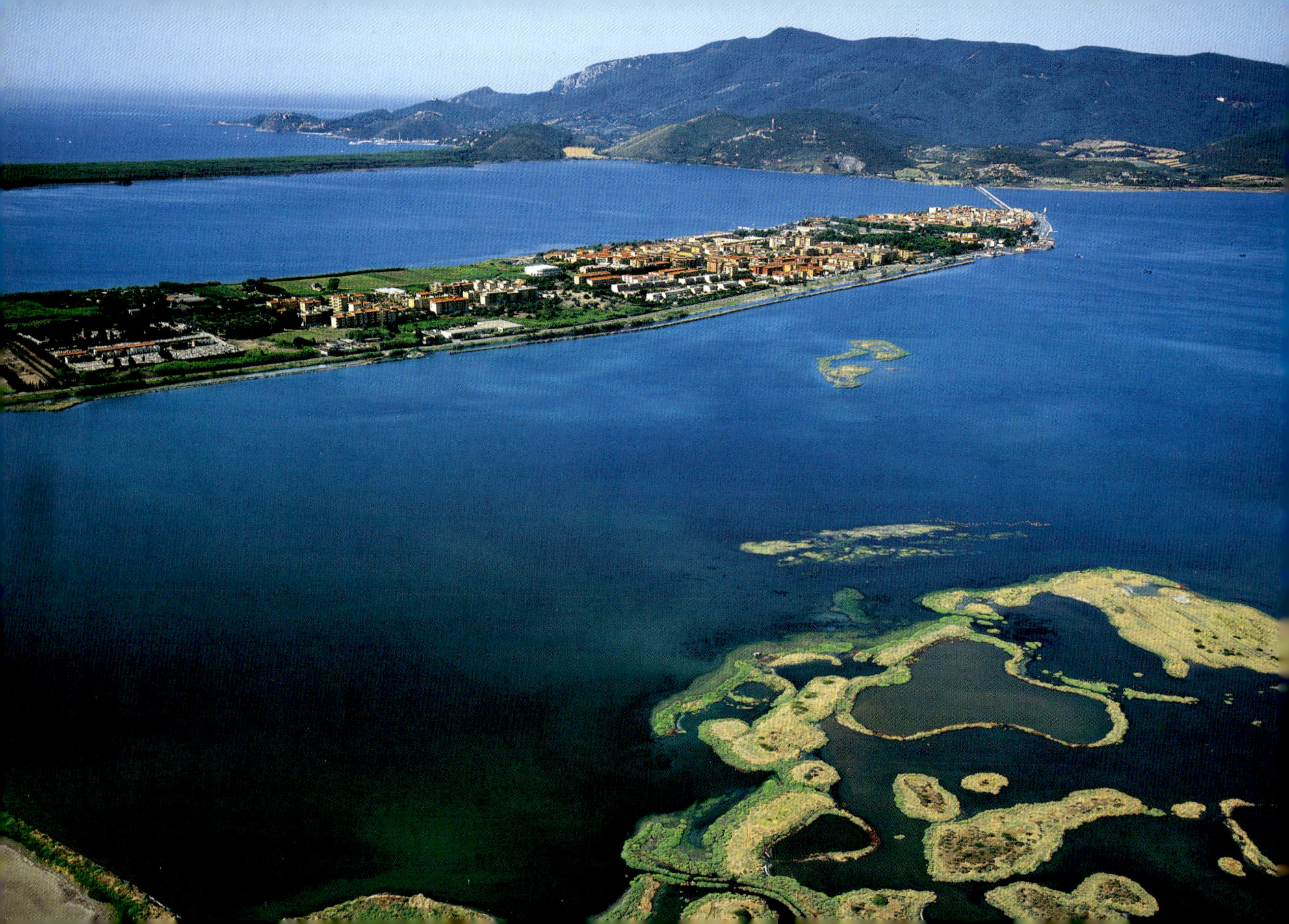

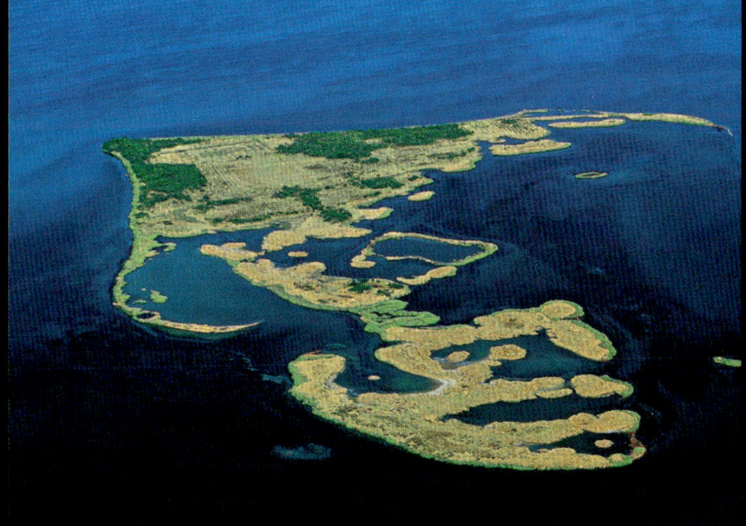

276
The city of Orbetello is at the center of a laguna, in front of Argentario, on a thin strip of land that connects it to the peninsula.

277
Orbetello's lagoon is a nature reserve that occupies 6 sq. miles (1553 hectares).

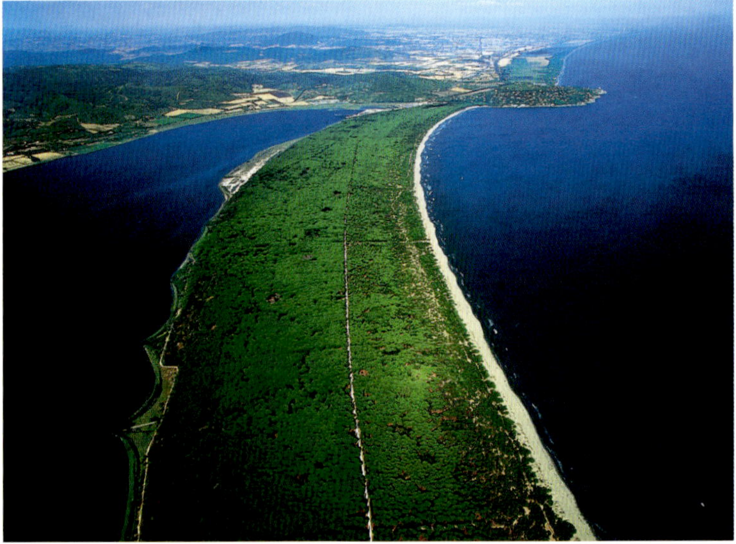

278
Numerous varieties of Mediterranean plants and animal species thrive in and around the Orbetello lagoon.

279
Porto Ercole, situated at the northern tip of the Argentario promontory, has maintained its ancient charm.

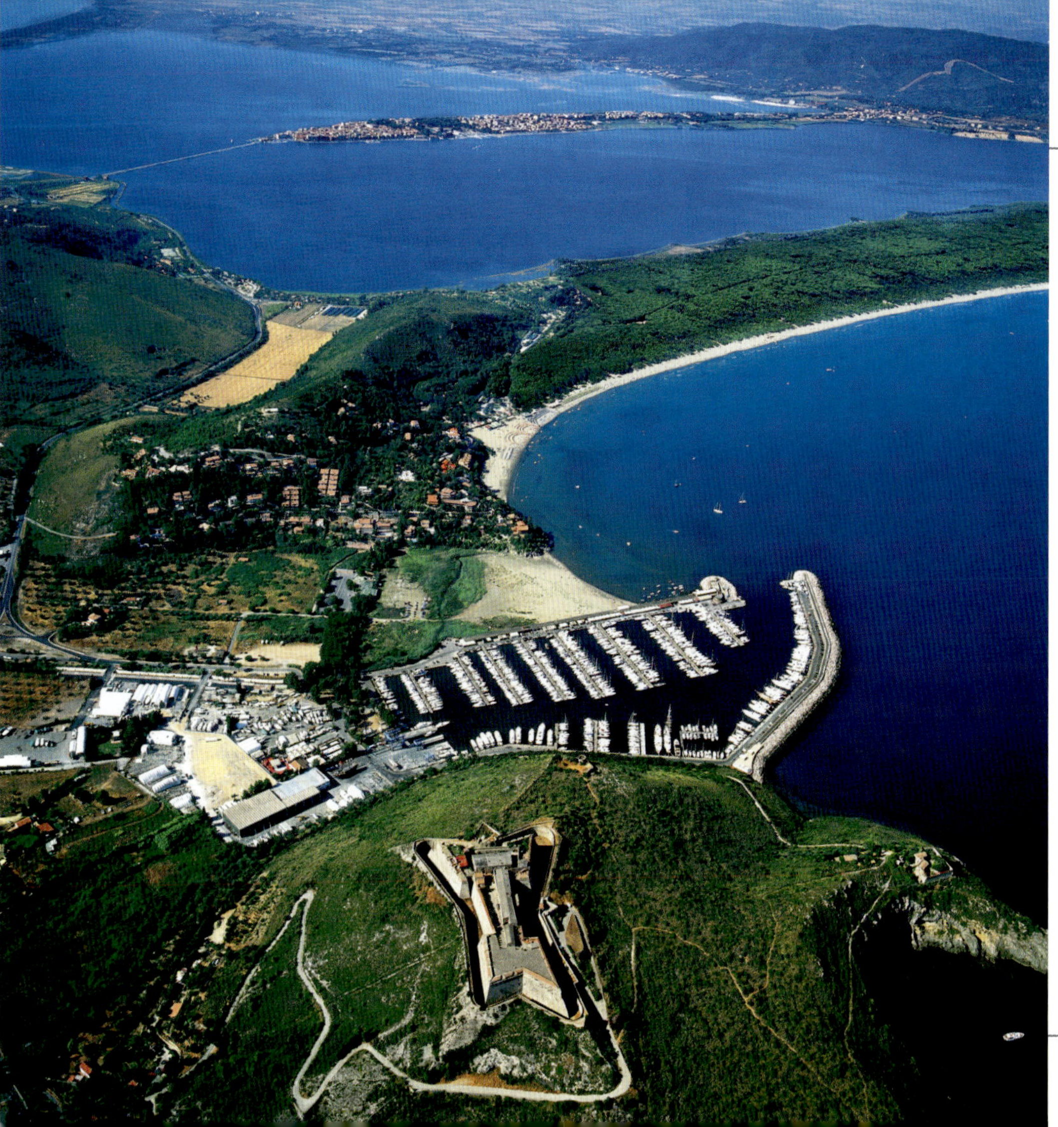

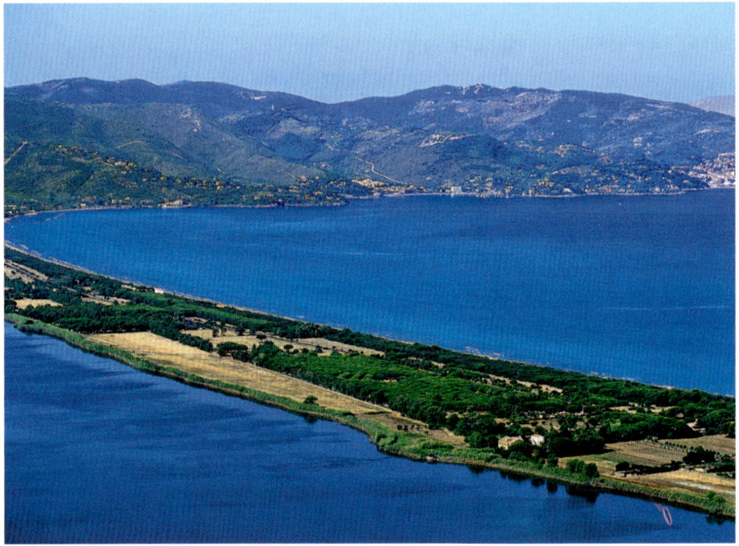

280 and 281
From above, Orbetello and its lagoon offer a unique and spectacular sight.

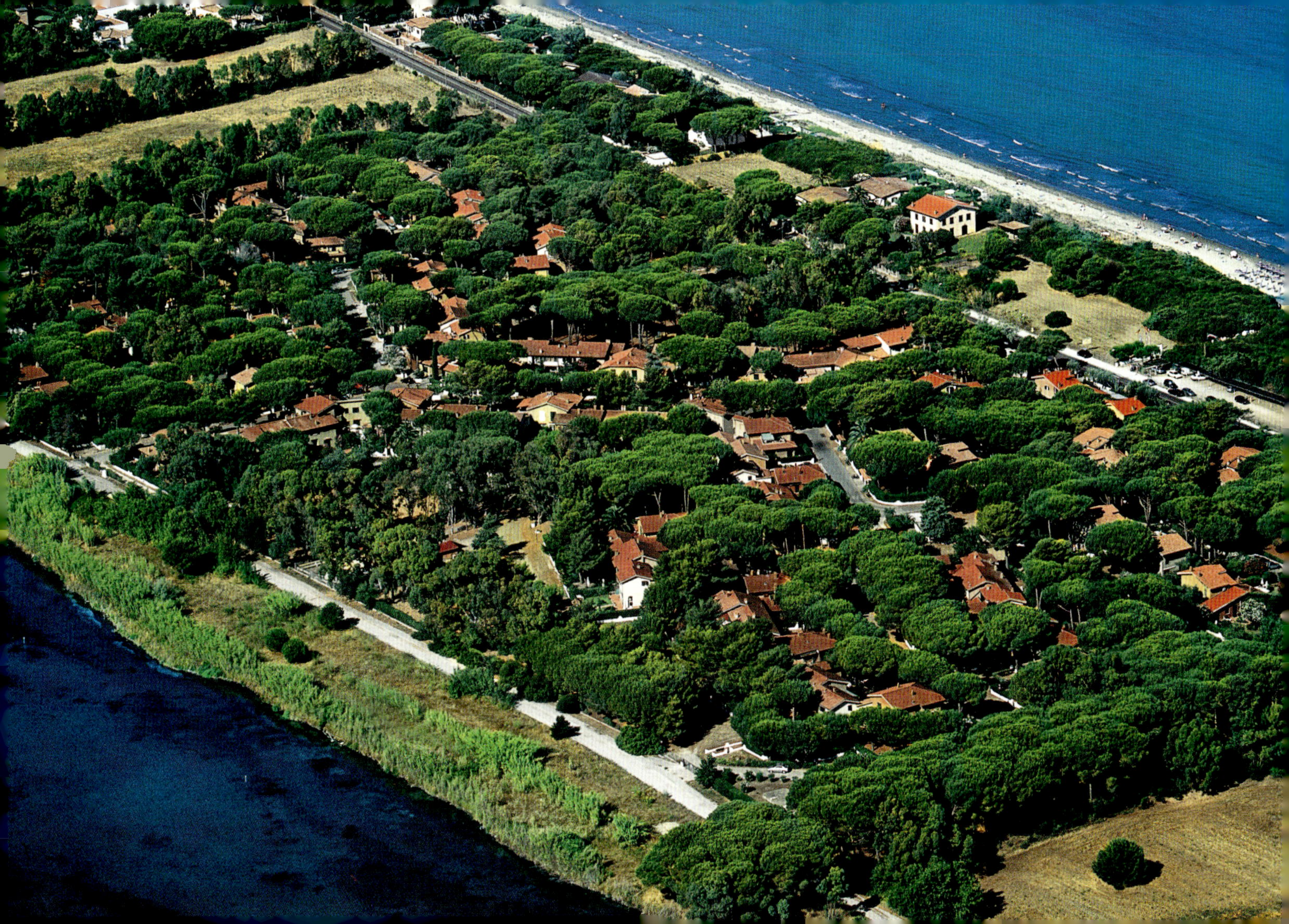

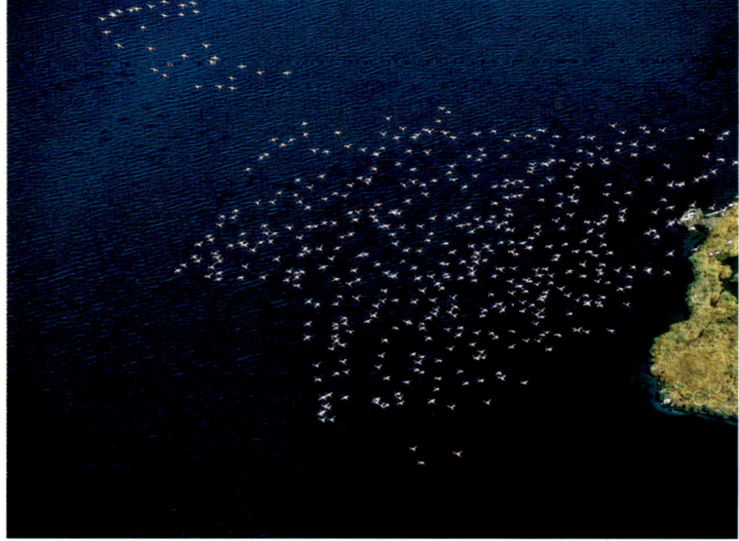

282 and 283
The Orbetello lagoon is a primary destination for migratory birds flying along the Tyrrhenian route.

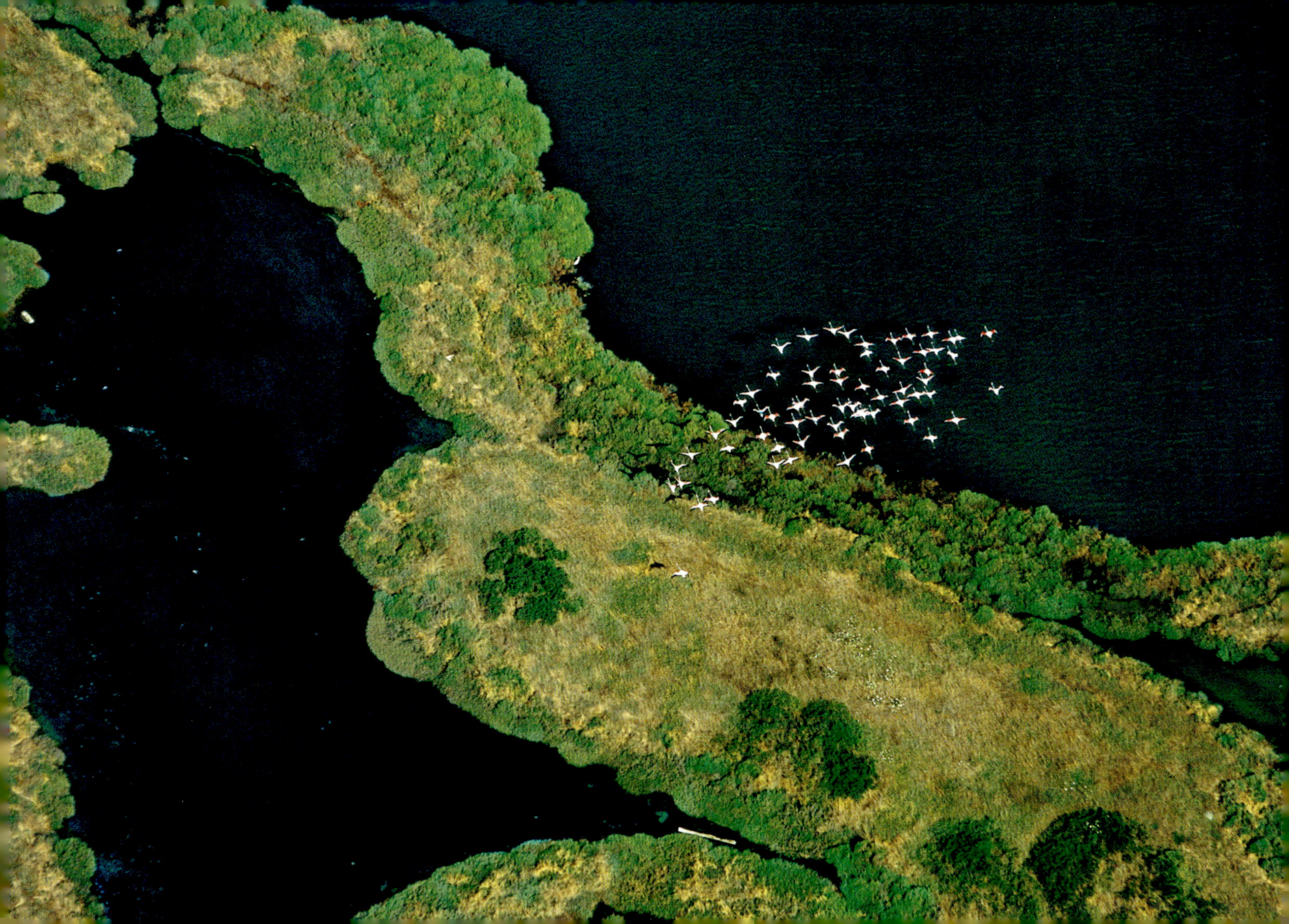

Treasures Among the Waves

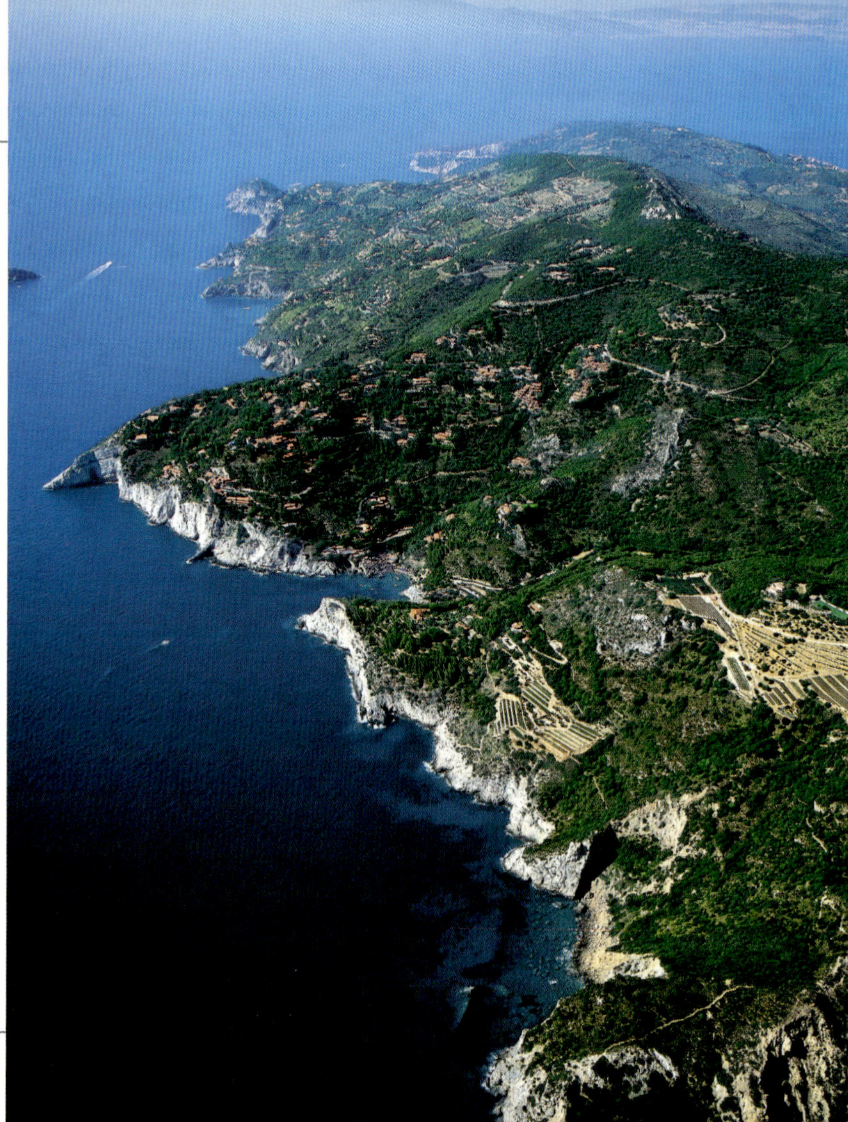

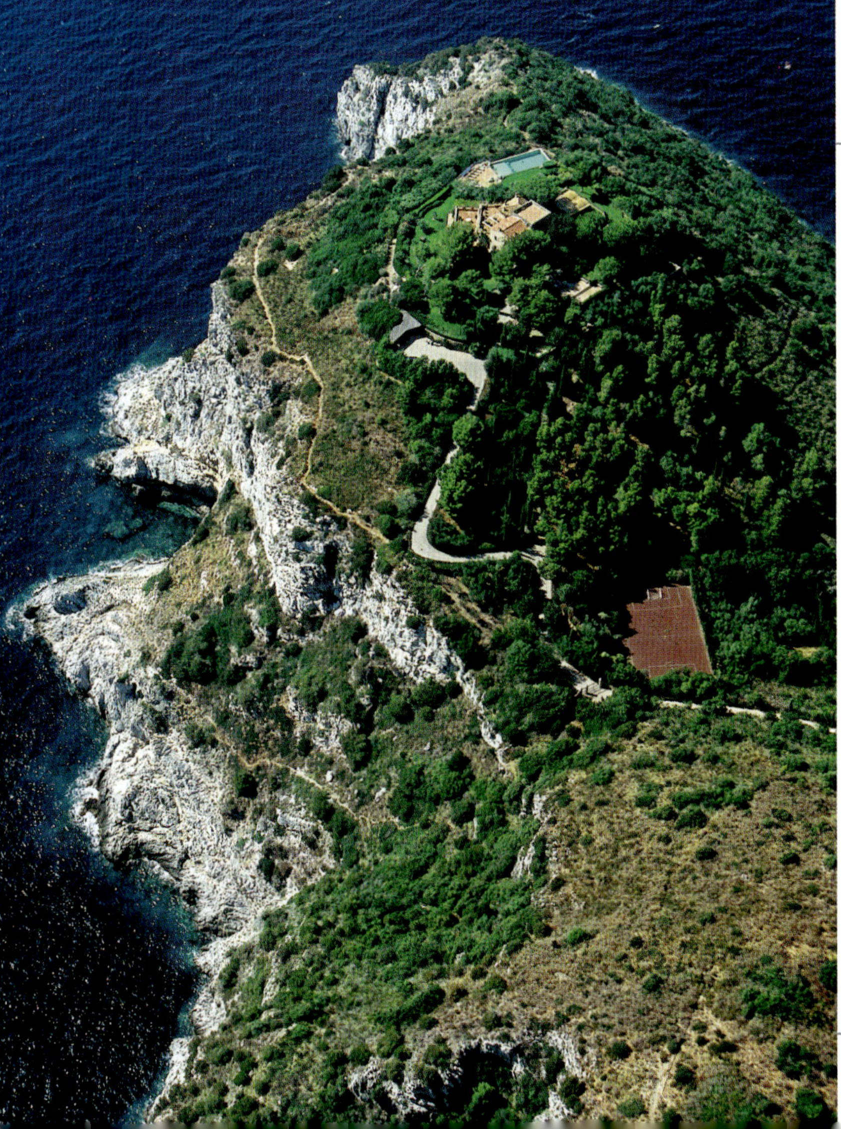

284 and 285
Argentario, now a rocky promontory dominated by Mount Telegraph, was once an island, but over the centuries became anchored to the mainland.

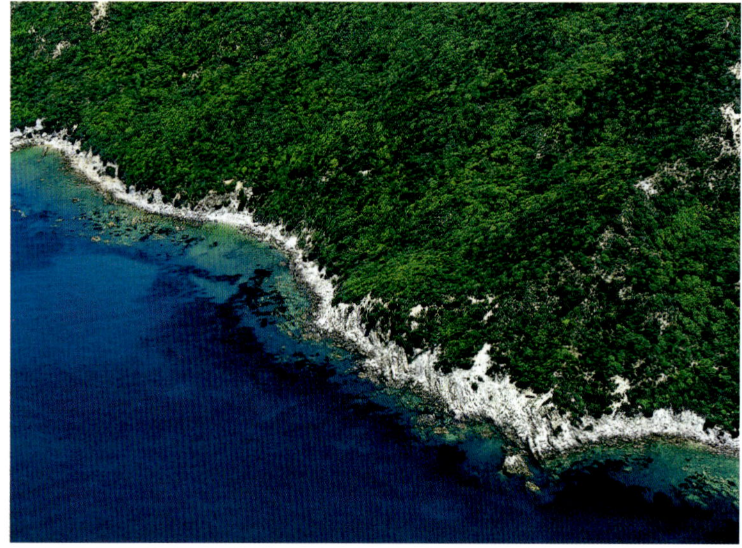

286 and 287
Characterized by a gulf, tiny islands and suggestive bays, Argentario dominates the Maremma coast.

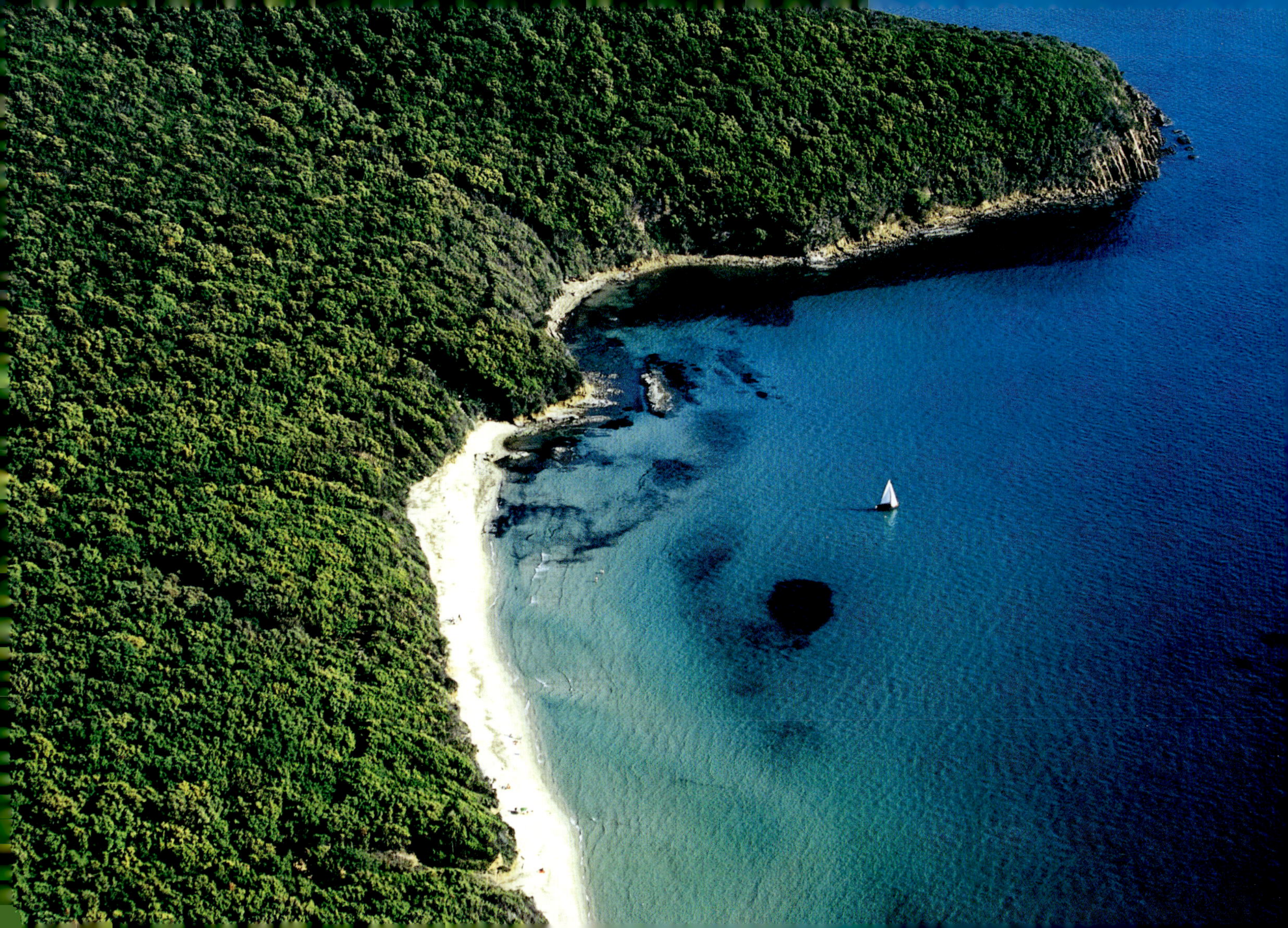

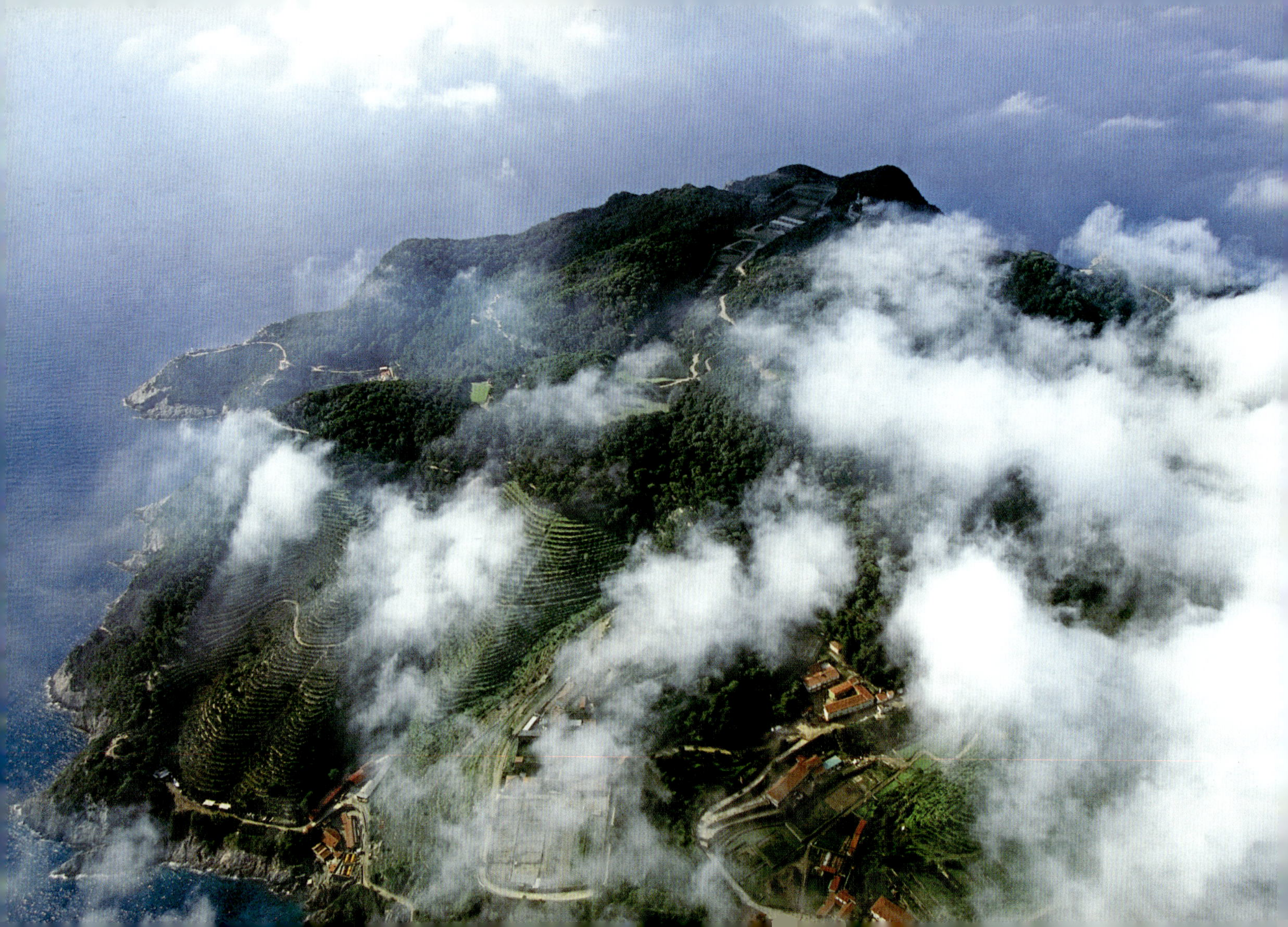

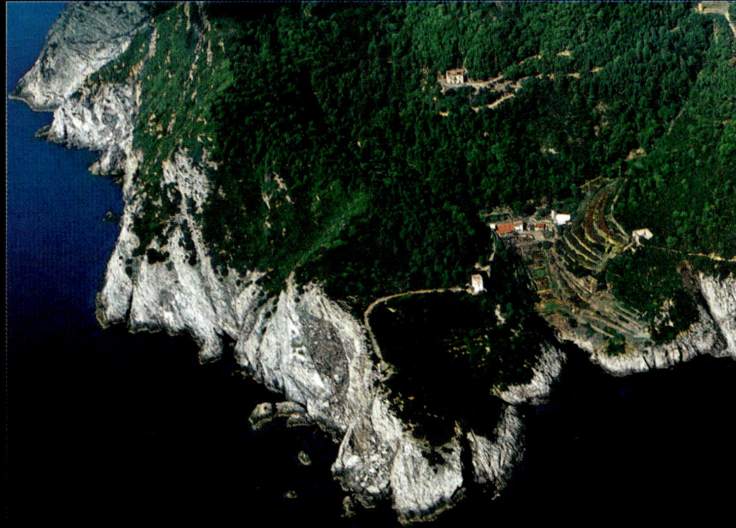

288 and 289
Gorgona, which is the northermost and smallest island in the Tuscan Archipelago, extends over 0.85 sq. miles (220 hectares). Although very rocky, it is 90% covered by Mediterranean vegetation. It is nearly 25 miles (40 km) from Livorno.

Gorgona Island

291
Gorgona, the ancient Urgon perhaps inhabited by the Etruscans and certainly by the Romans, is today one of the Mediterranean's pearls, appreciated by tourists and underwater divers for its dense forests and clear waters.

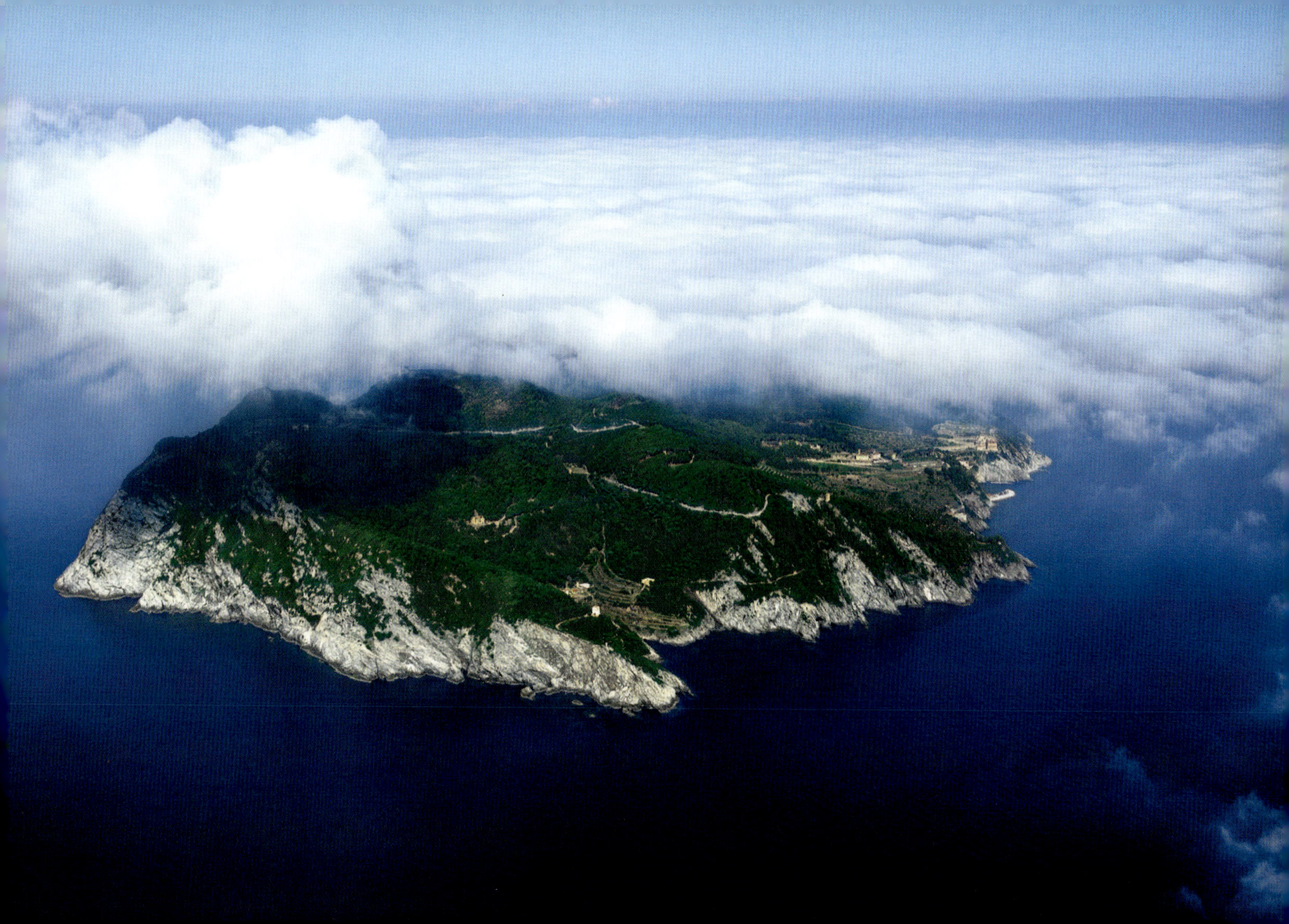

Capraia Island

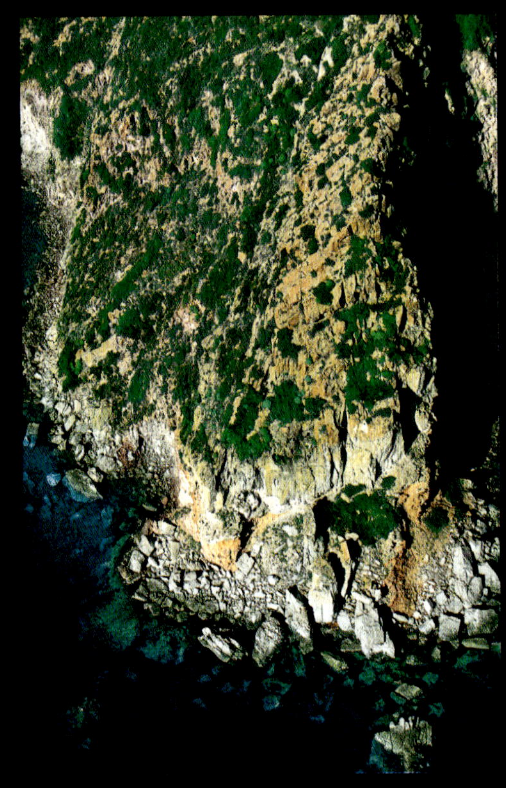

292 and 293
Capraia, one of the Tuscan Archipelago's seven islands, is a favorite with geologists because of its rocky volcanic origins, with divers because of its fascinating seabed, and with tourists because of the unforgettable panorama of its colorful coasts.

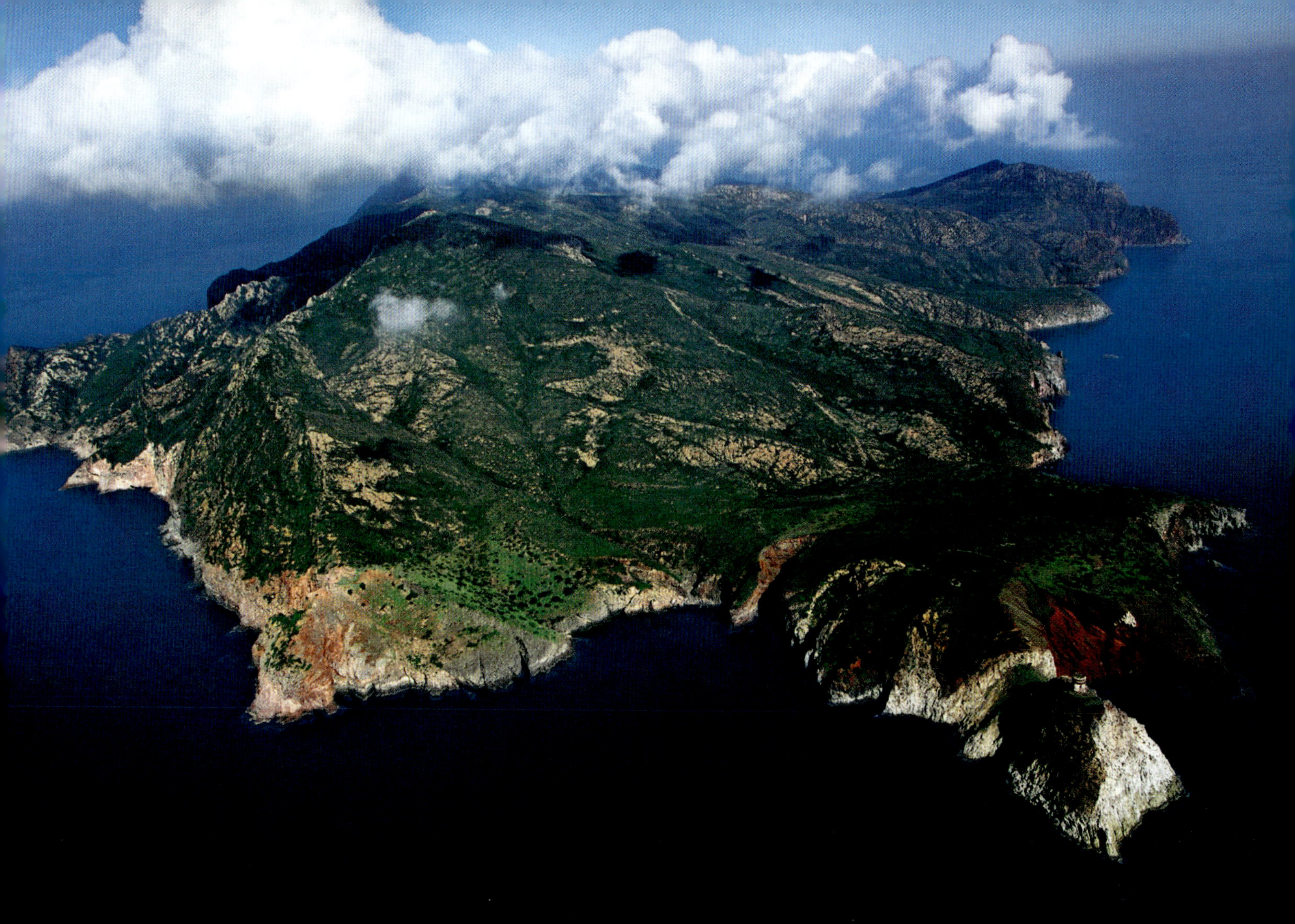

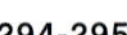

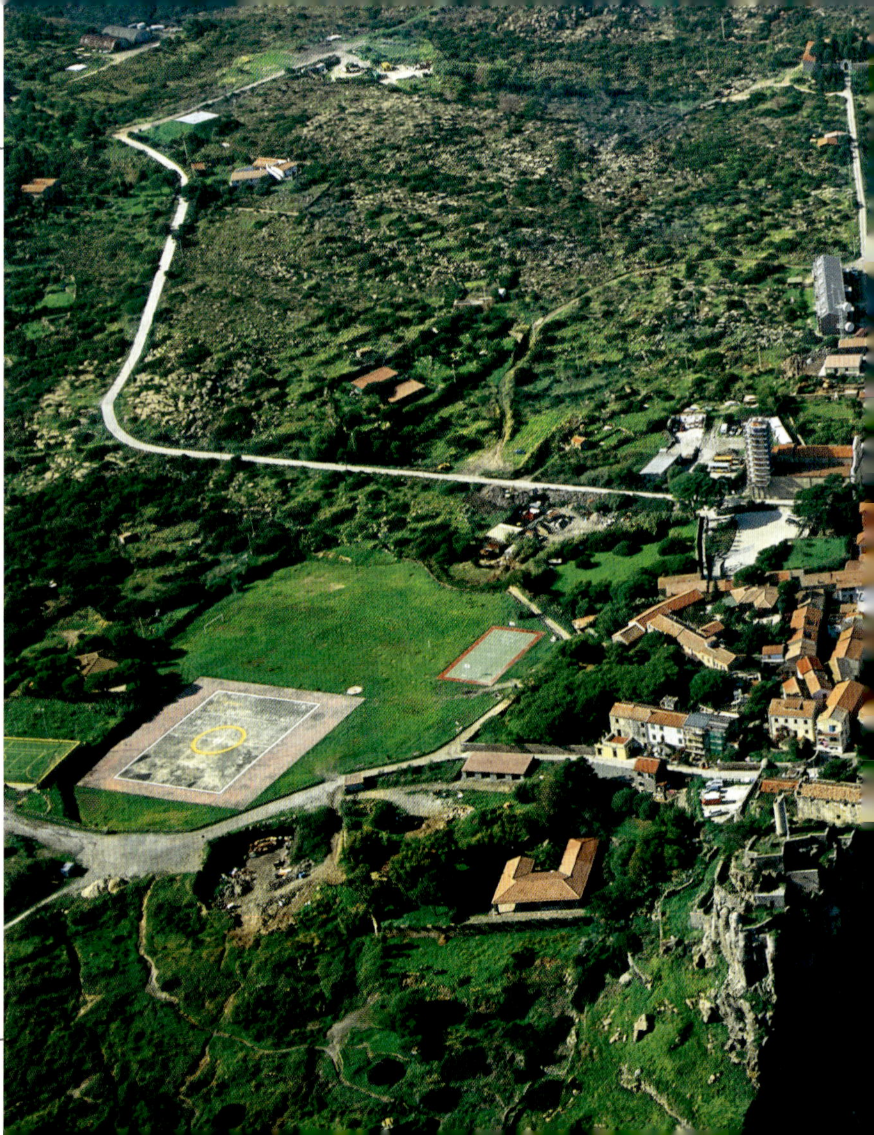

294-295

This upland village, with the San Giorgio fortress, dominates Capraia. Below, the port is the entry point for the many visitors drawn to the island in every season by its extraordinary natural beauty.

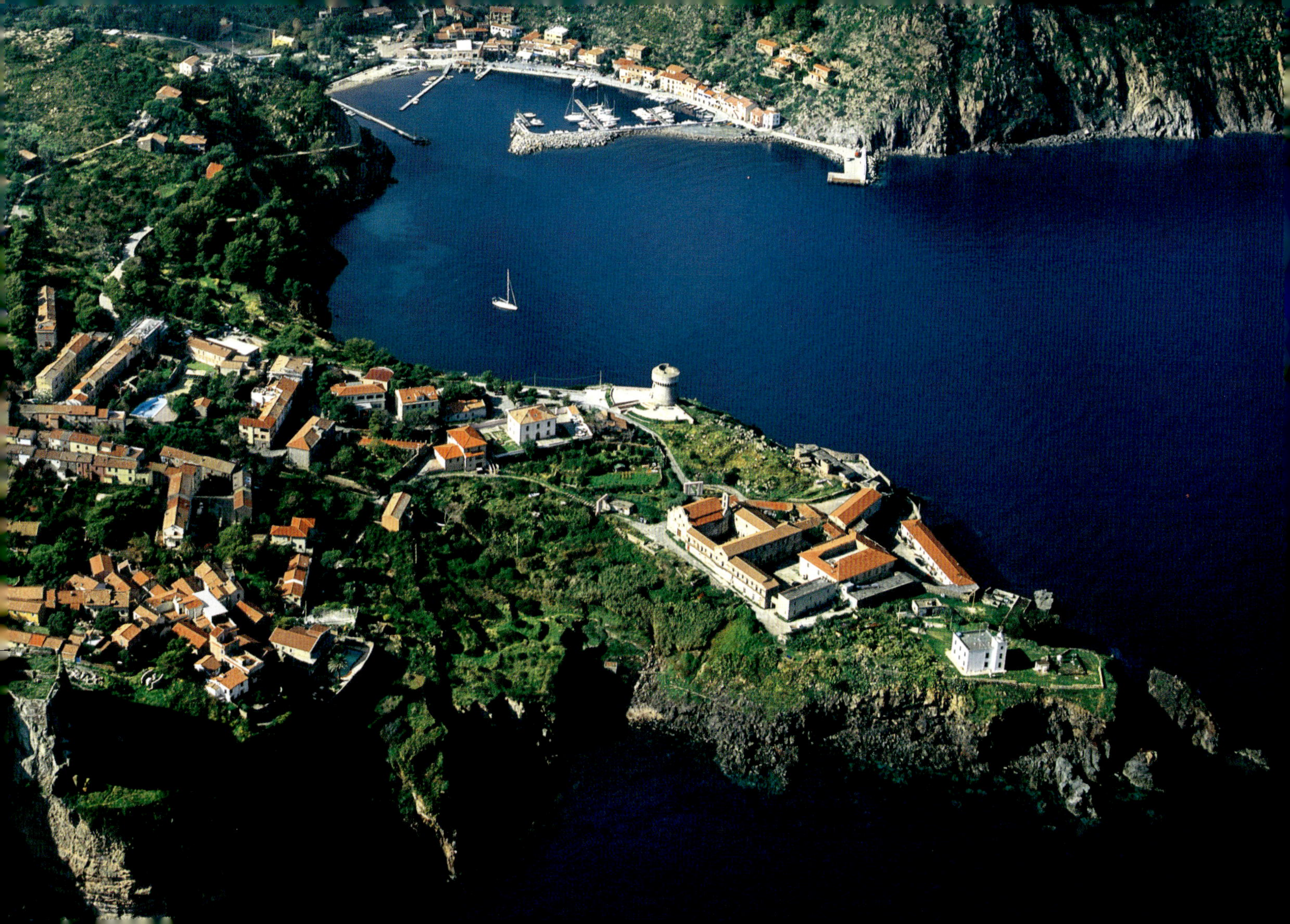

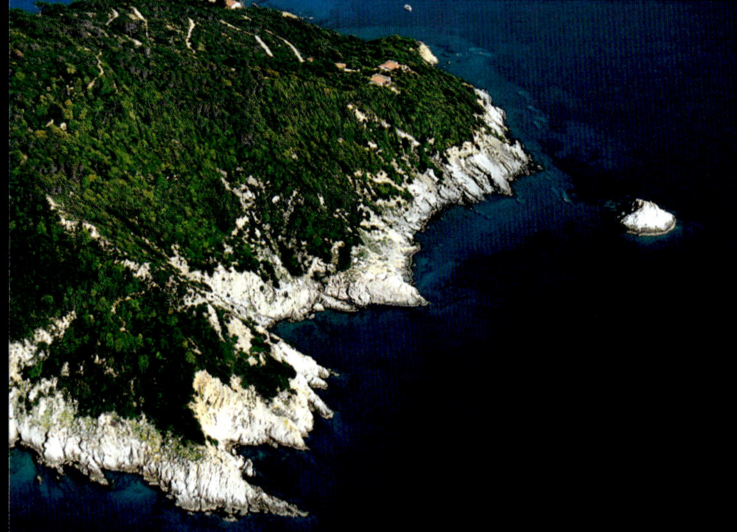

296 and 297
The island of Elba's coasts, wide beaches, cliffs, bays and tiny indentations have always attracted tourists.

Elba Island

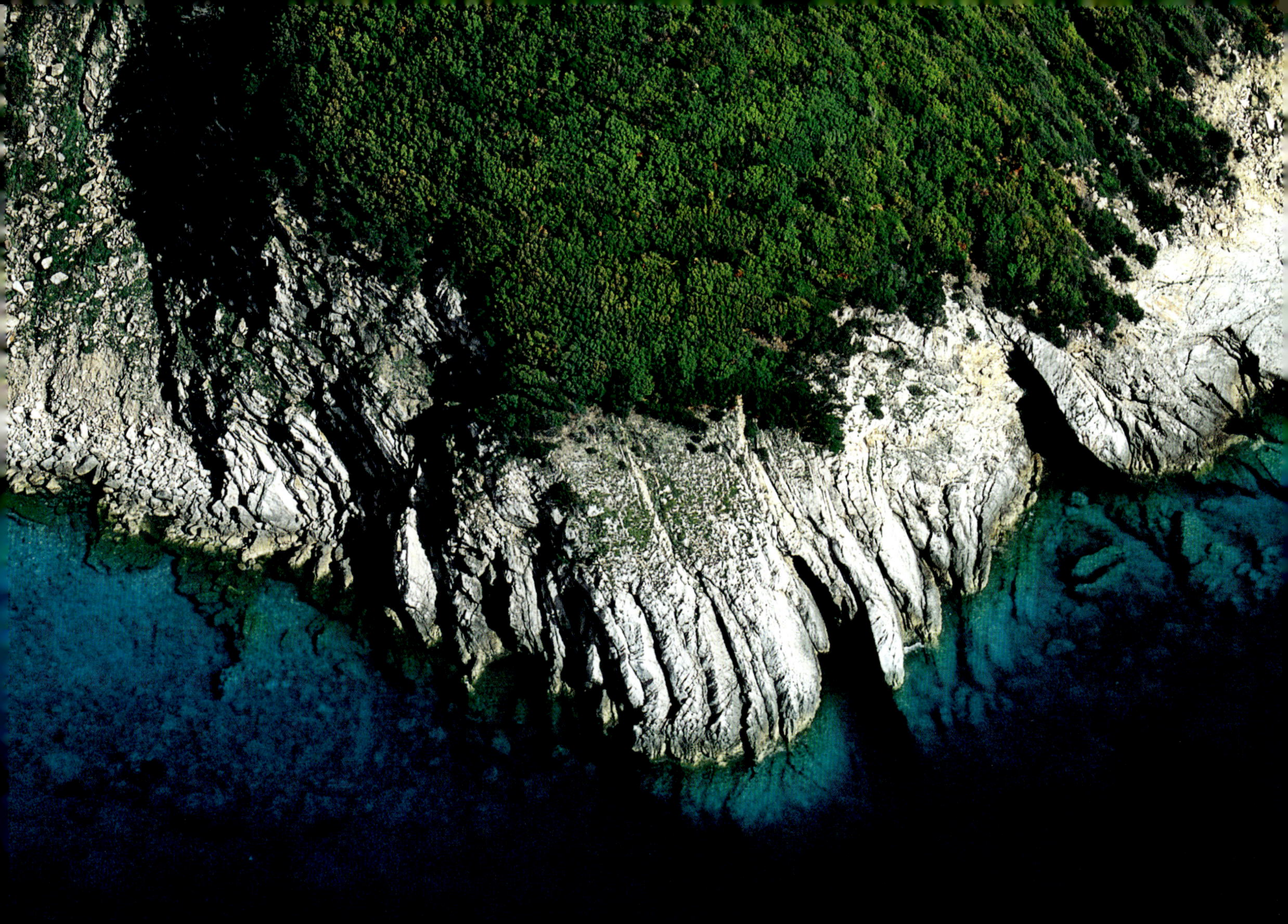

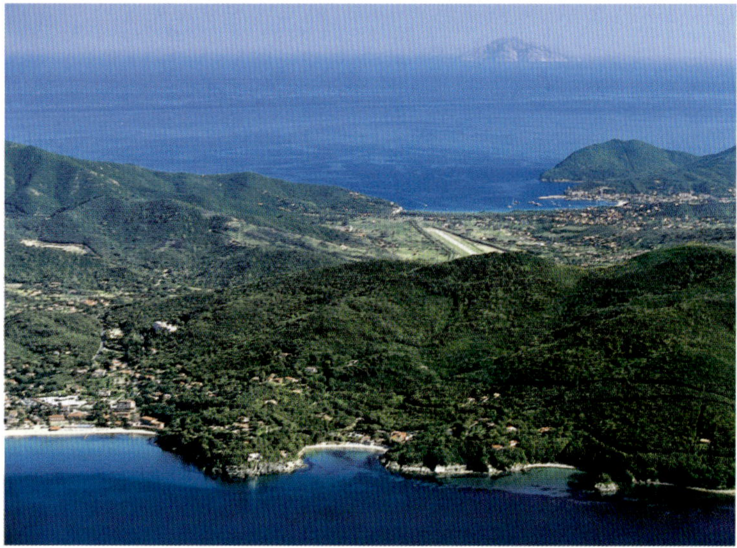

298
Elba's mines and minerals have been appreciated since ancient times, but today the island is most appreciated by visitors and deep-sea divers worldwide.

299
Marina di Campo is one of Elba's most important tourist spots.

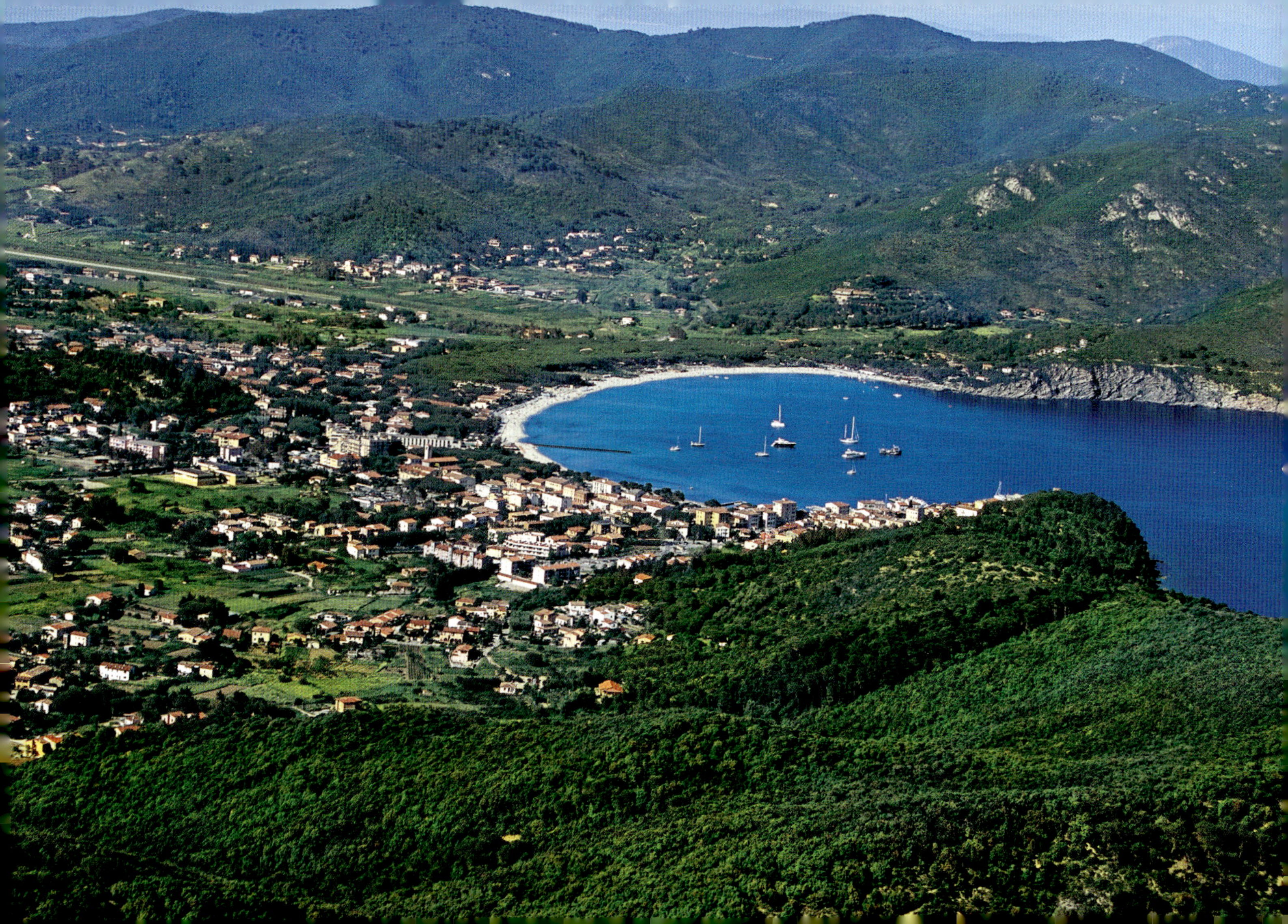

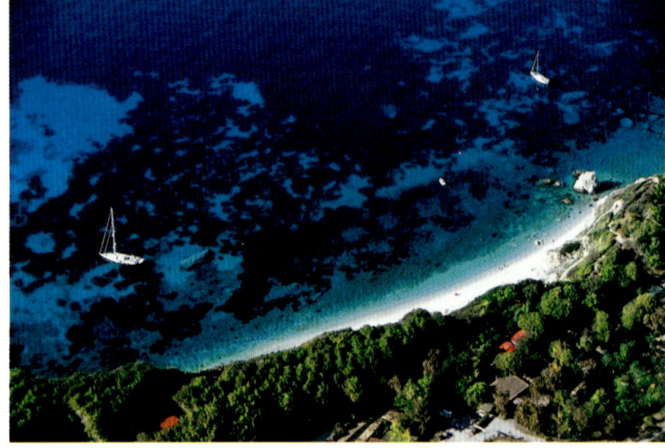

300 and 301
Hiking along paths through the Mediterranean vegetation, the visitor comes across panoramic vistas like Fetovaia Bay (right).

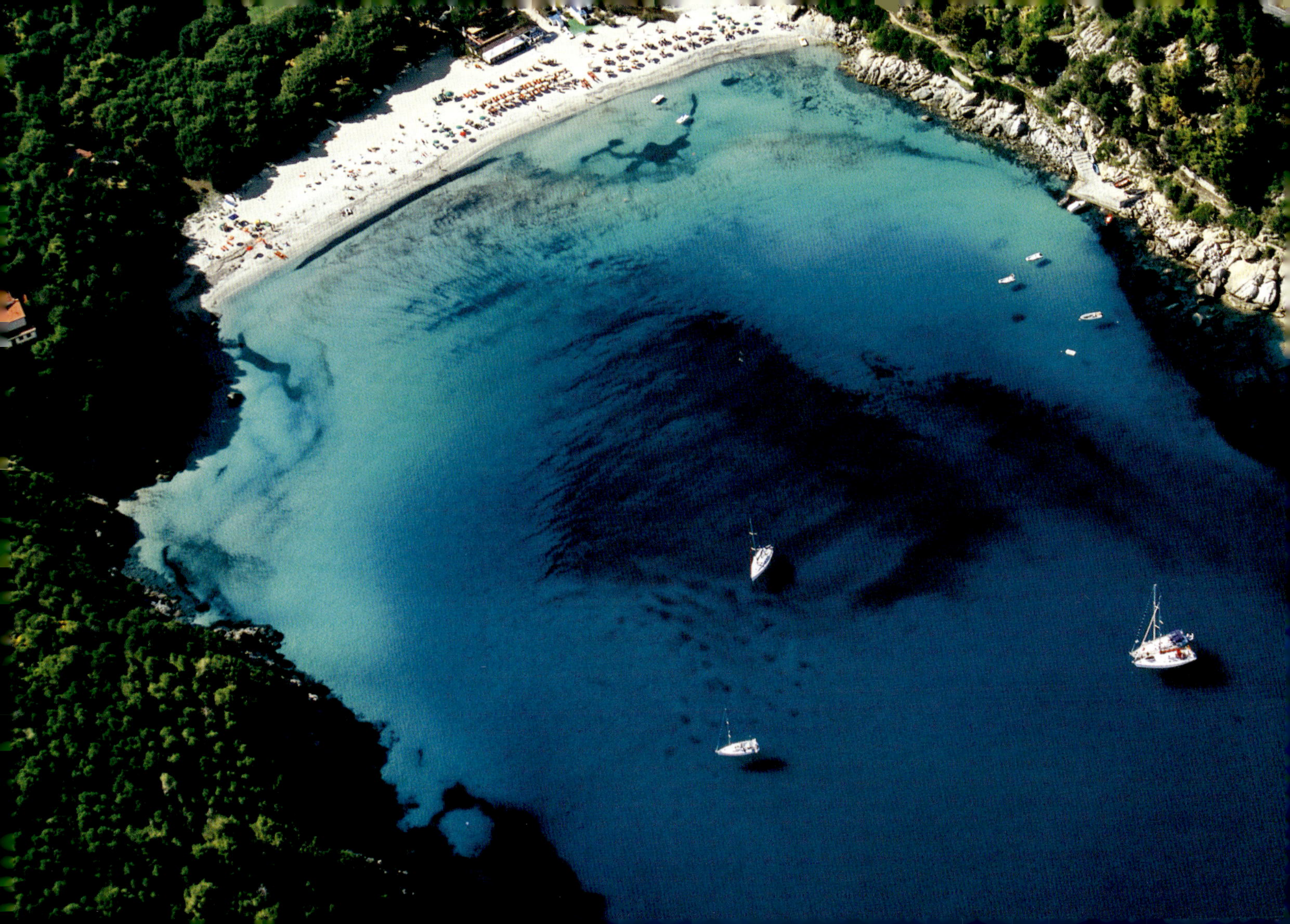

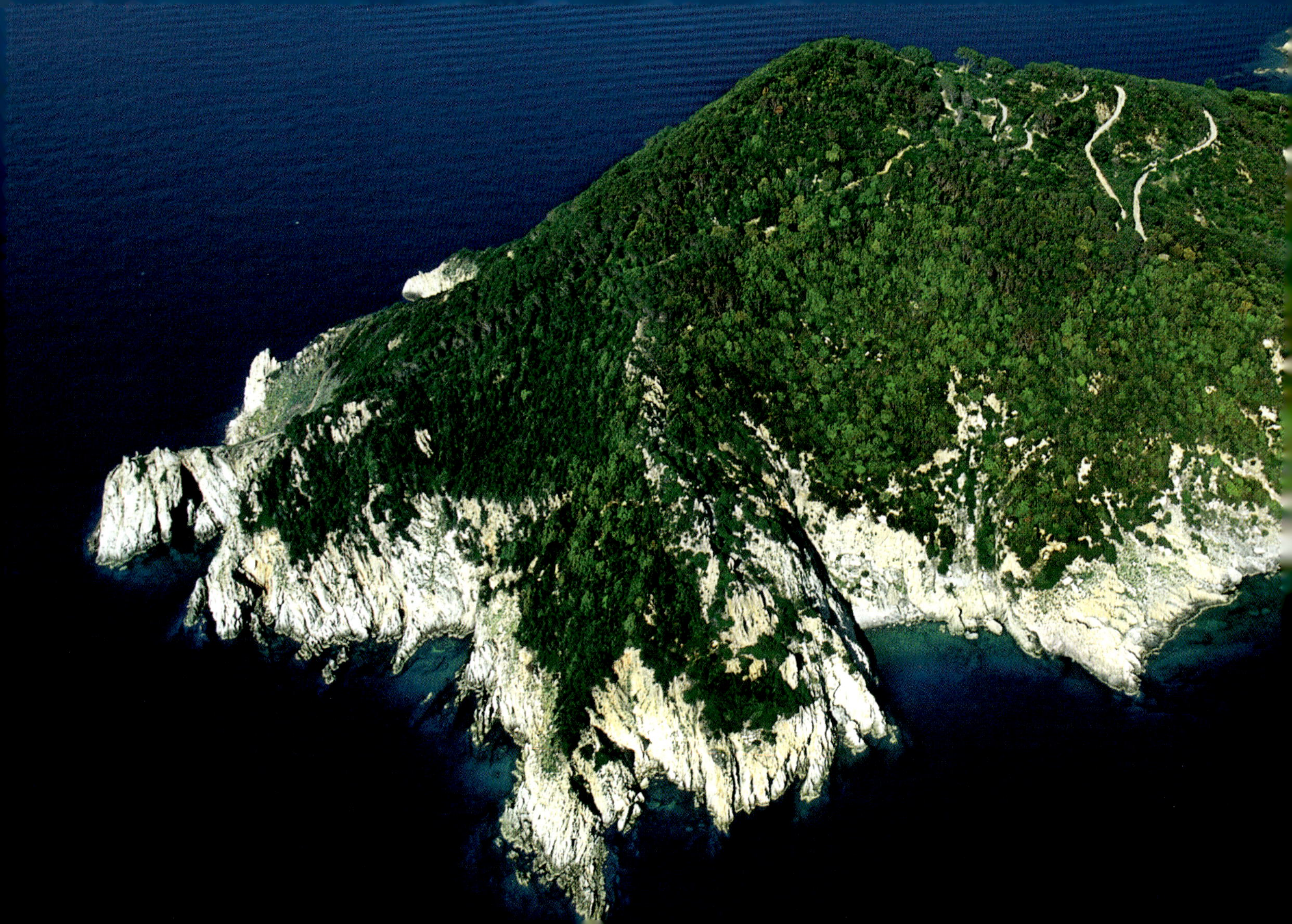

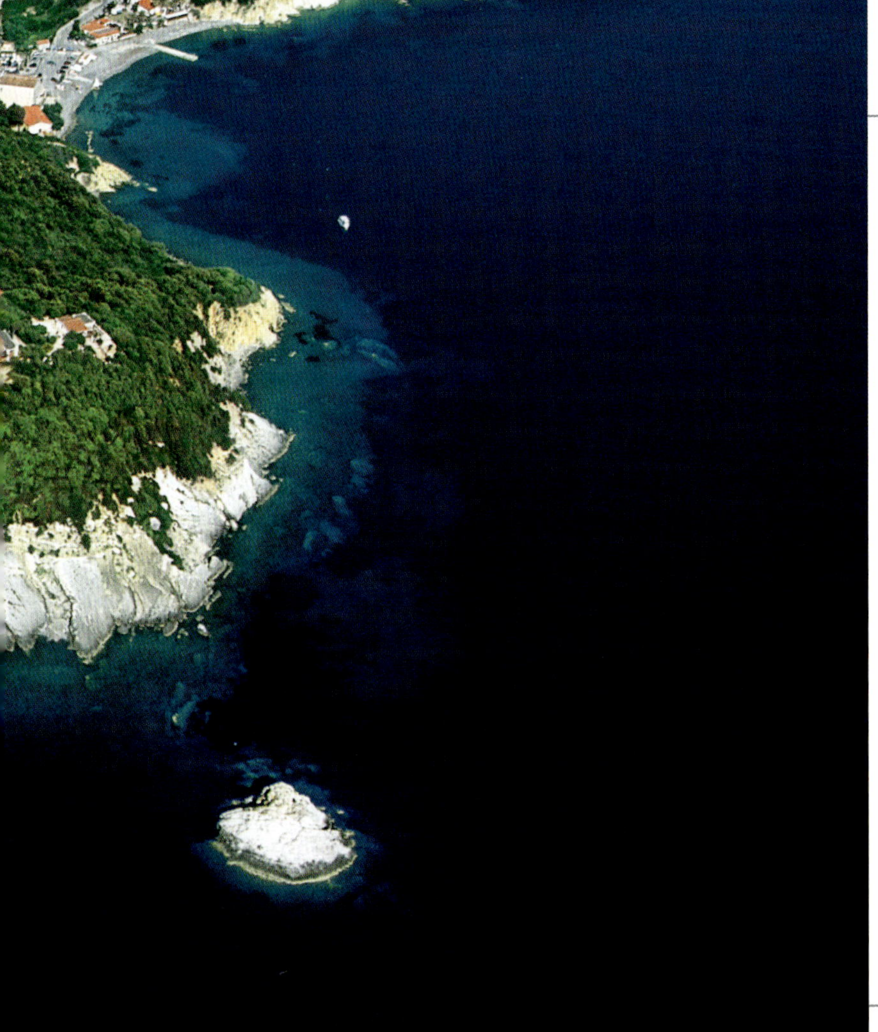

302-303
The Enfola promontory is connected to Elba by a narrow strip of land that until the 1950s was the location of a now-abandoned tuna-processing plant.

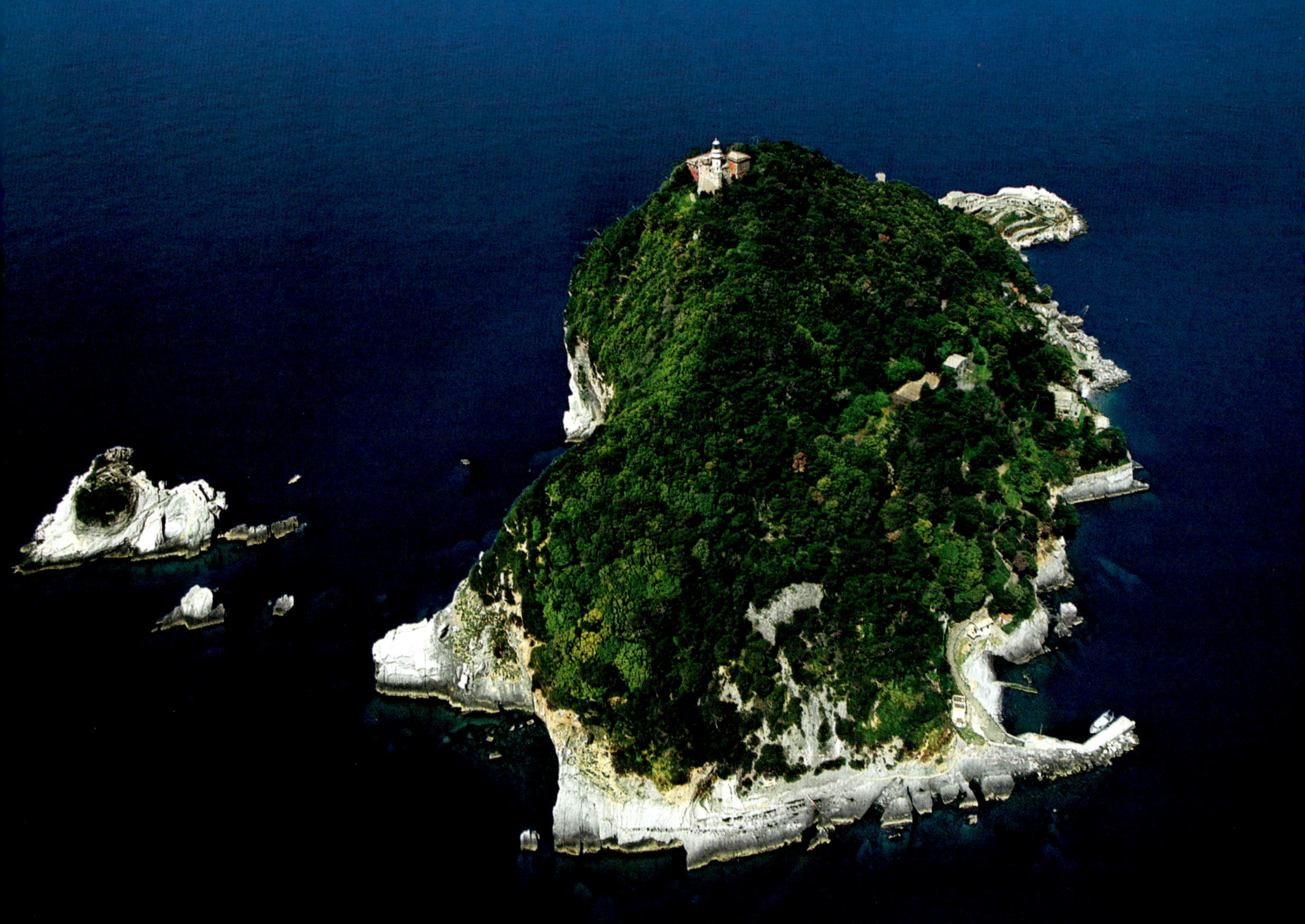

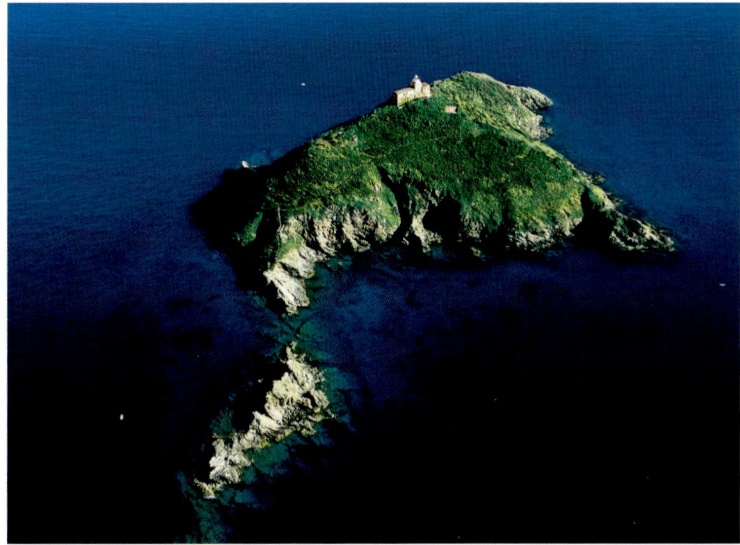

304 and 305

The uninhabited island of Palmaiola, in the Piombino Channel, is an important nesting ground for marine birds. It is characterized by inaccessible cliffs and stunted plant growth.

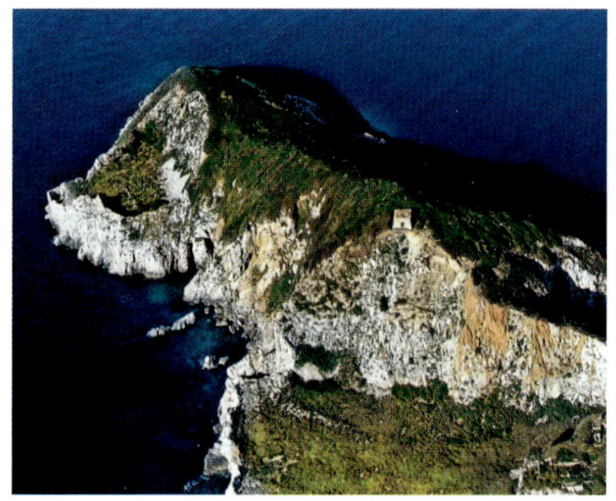

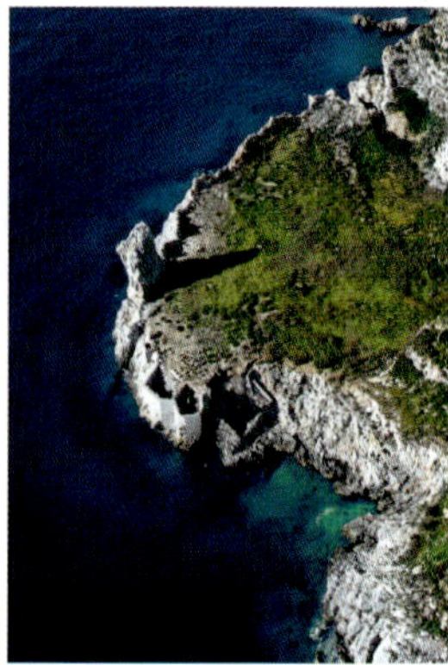

306 and 307
Cerboli, a calcareous island in the middle of the Piombino Channel, is completely covered by marine rock rose, garrigue and lentisk.

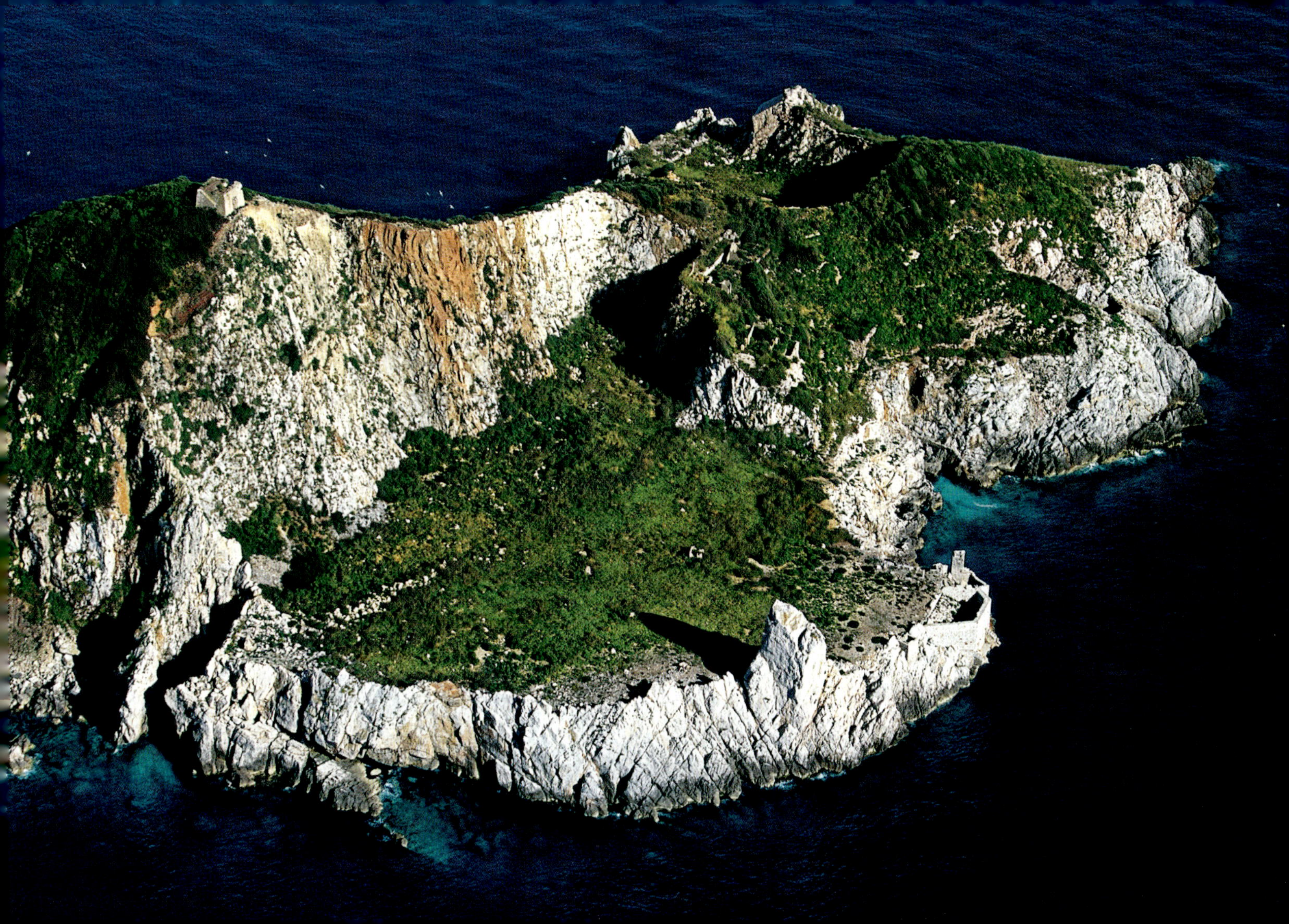

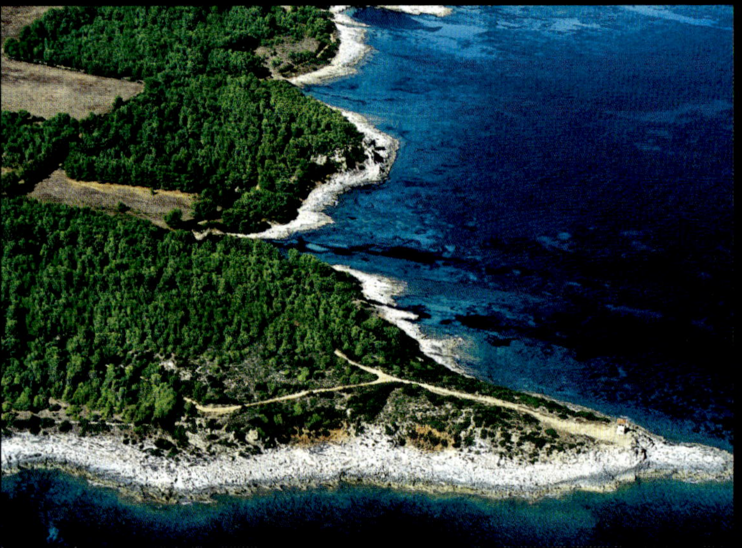

308
Pianosa Island is part of the Tuscan Archipelago National Park and is the only island composed entirely of sedimentary rock.

309
Pianosa, called "Planaria" in the distant past, owes its name to its almost complete flatness, broken only by slight rises.

Pianosa Island

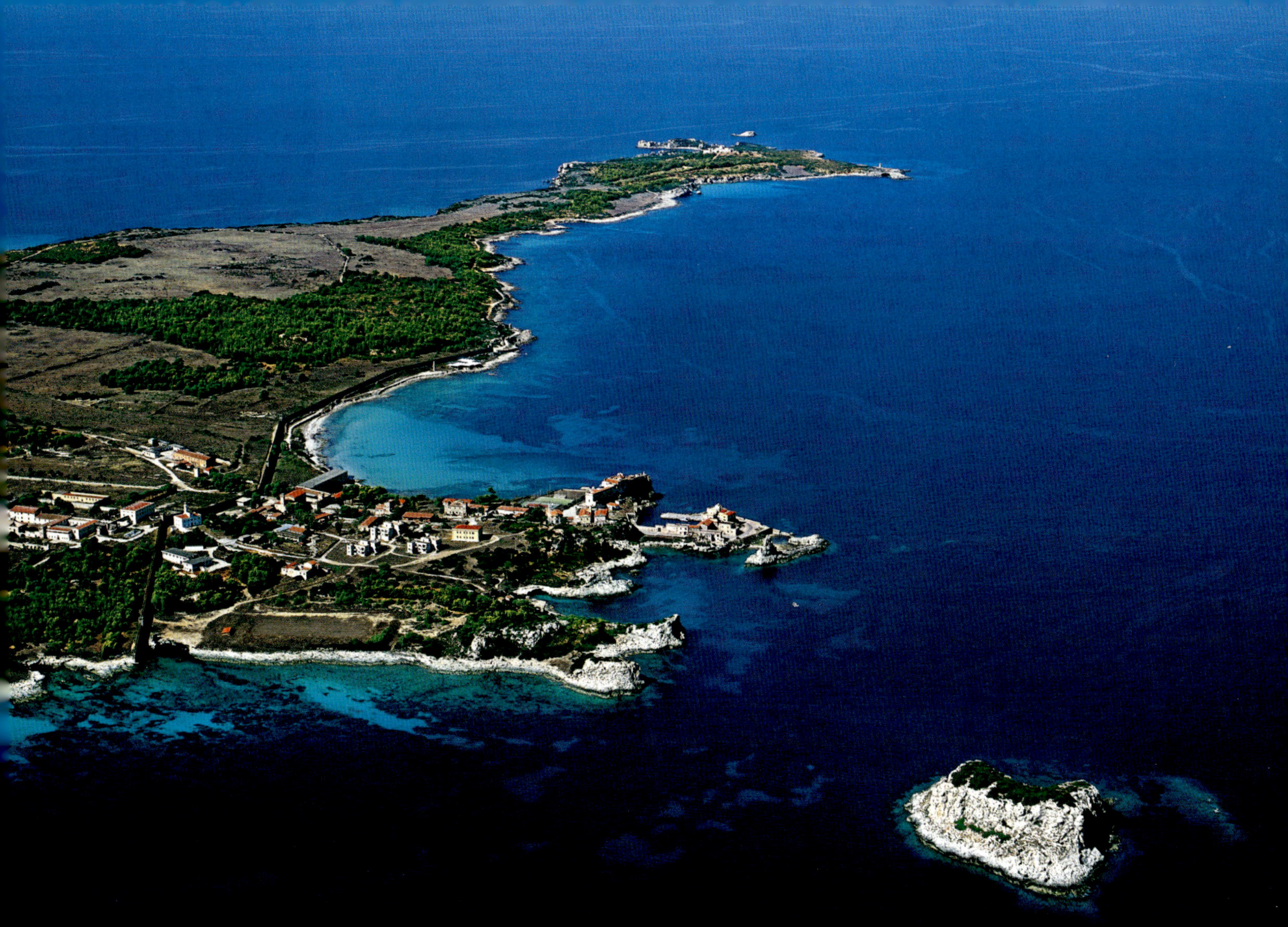

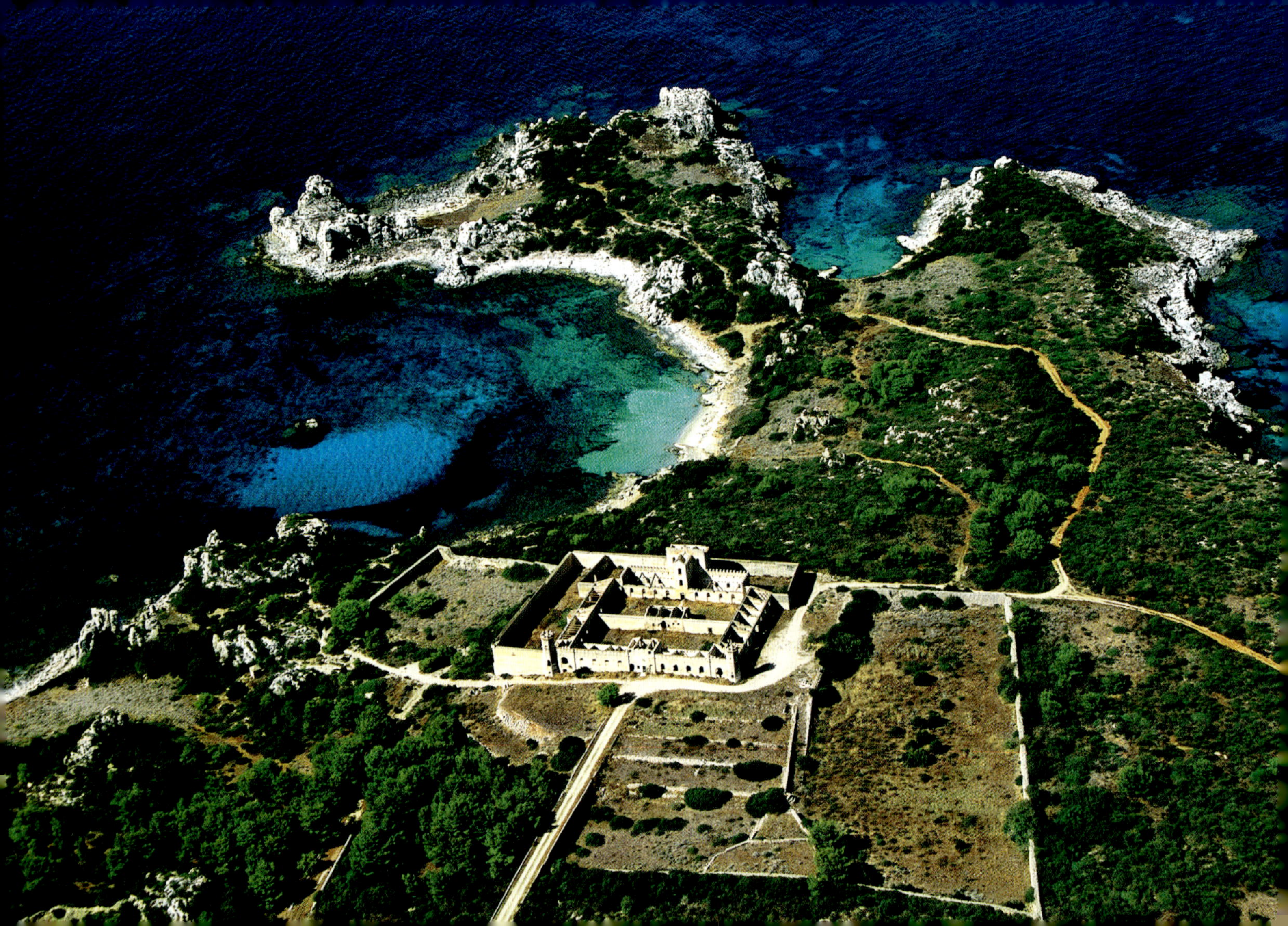

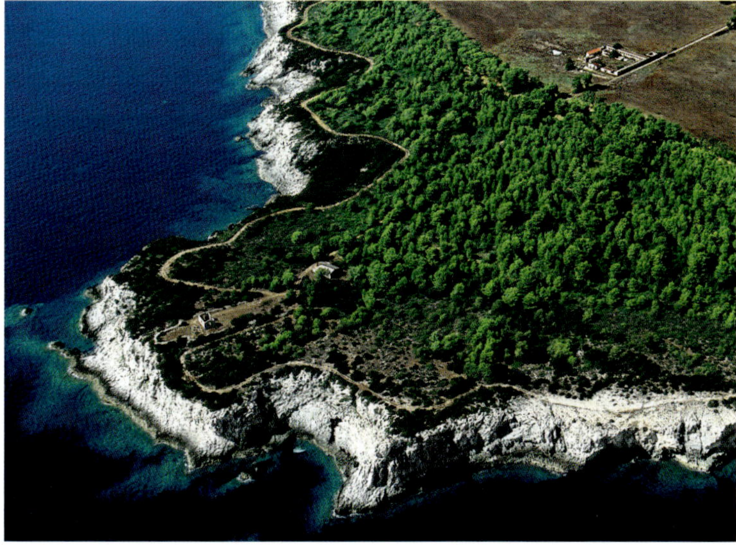

310 and 311
Pianosa, which for over a century and a half was used as a penal colony, has remained practically uncontaminated. Most of the island is cultivated; the land was cleared in ancient times and used for agriculture because of its flatness and favorable climate. Of the original forest that covered the island, only small patches remain today.

Island of Giglio

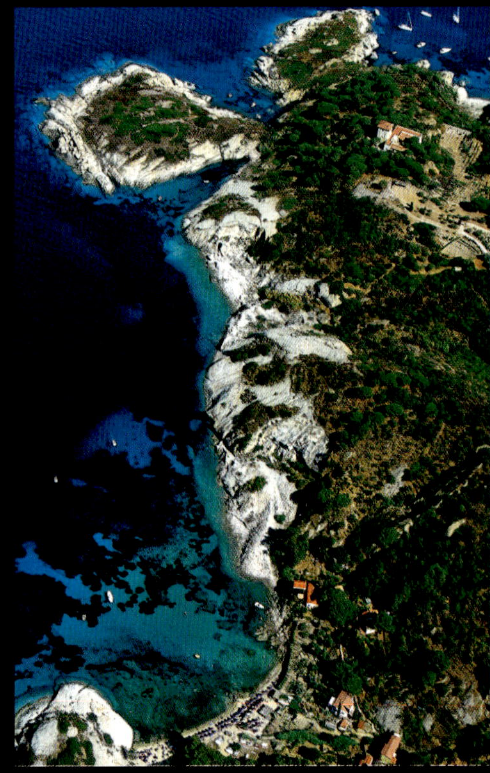

312
The island of Giglio has a rocky profile that slopes gently to the sea.

313
Composed mostly of granite, Giglio offers extraordinary landscapes.

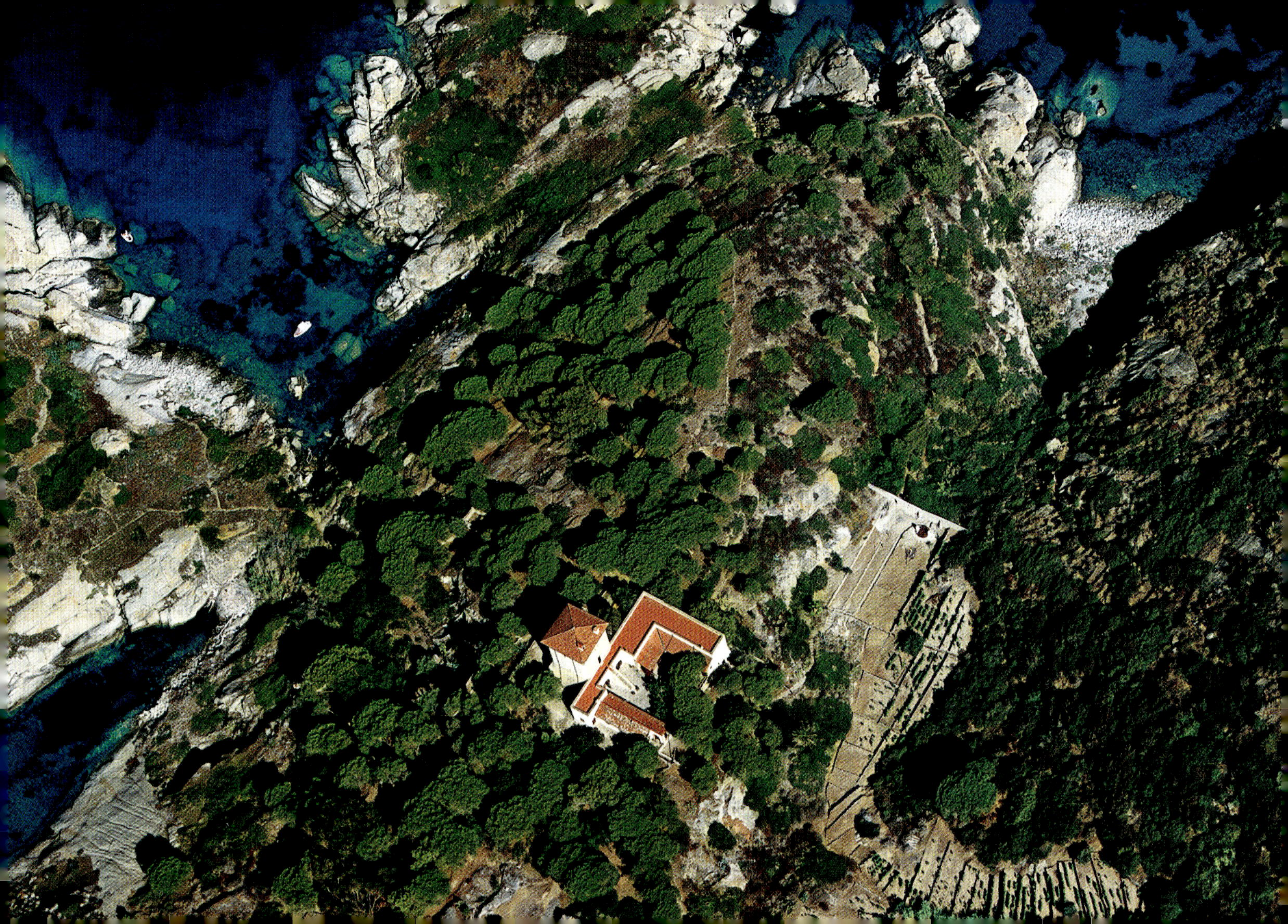

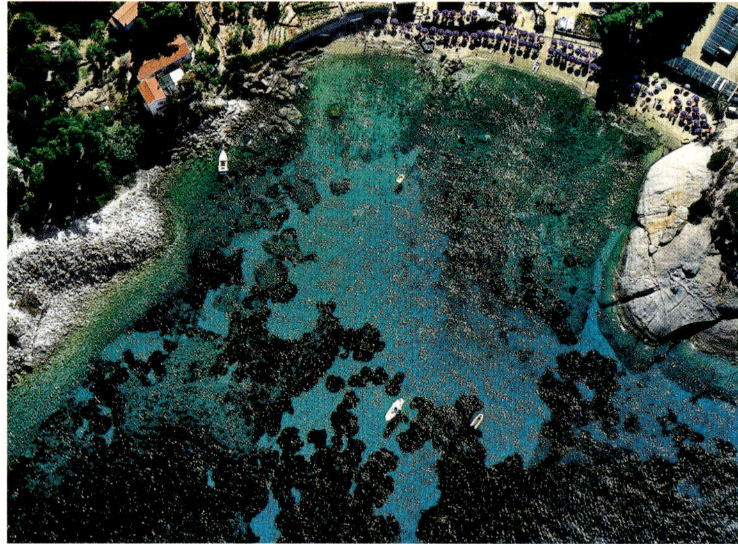

314

From Giglio's sandy surrounding seabed emerge impressive granitic formations that render it extraordinary and unique.

315

The tower that dominates Giglio's Campese Bay was erected by the Medici dukes between 1670 and 1705 to defend the inhabitants from pirates.

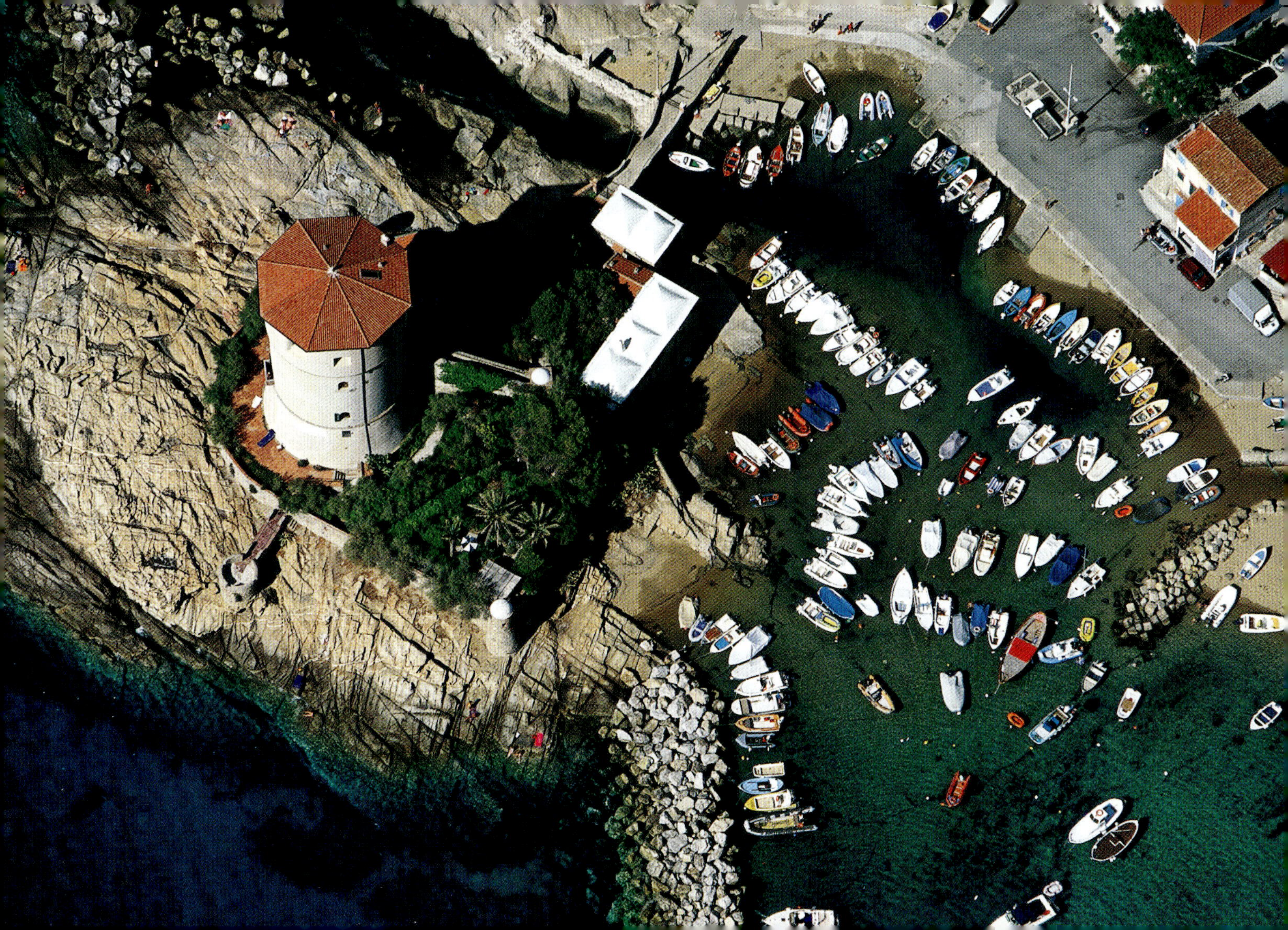

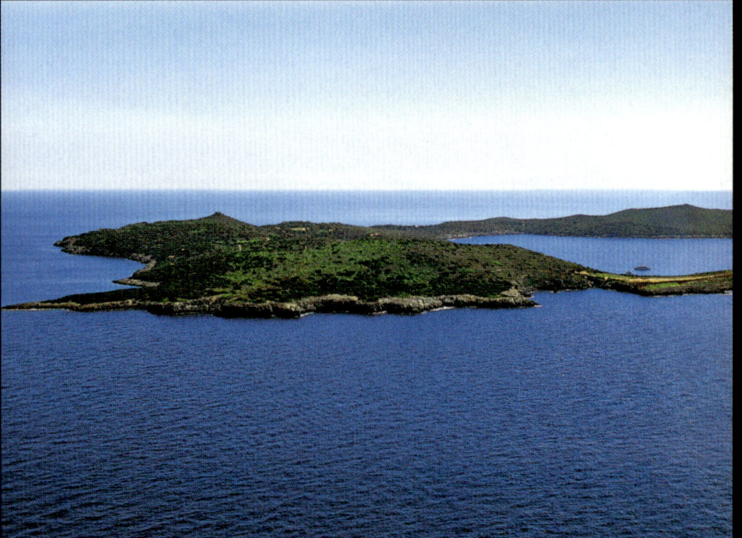

315 and **316**
Narrow and no longer than 3 miles (5 km), Giannutri is a natural paradise in the Tuscan Archipelago. Its turquoise waters are particularly appreciated, and have yielded precious relics from the Roman era.

Giannutri Island

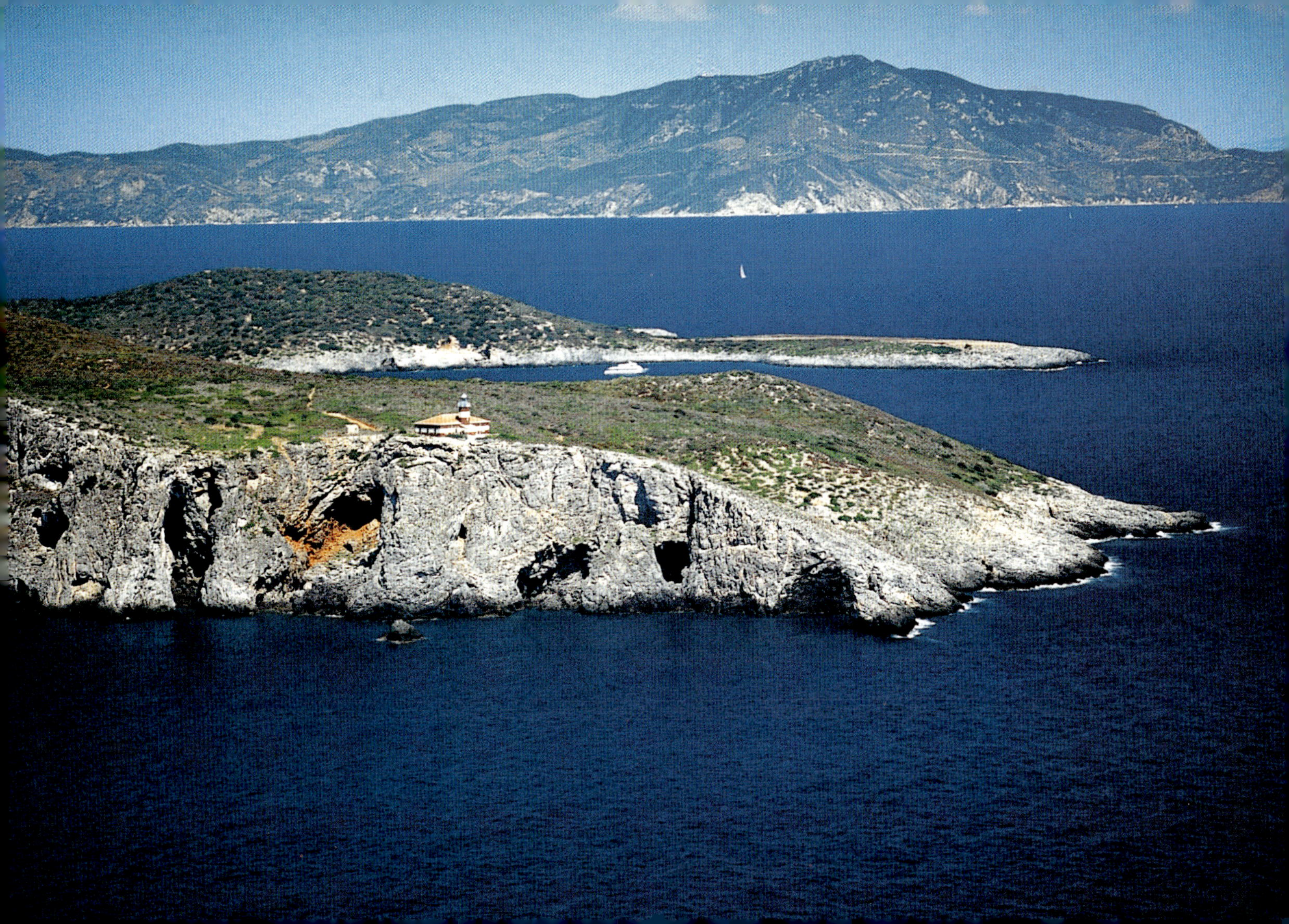

318

THE BEAUTY OF ORDER AND MEASURE

FLYING HIGH

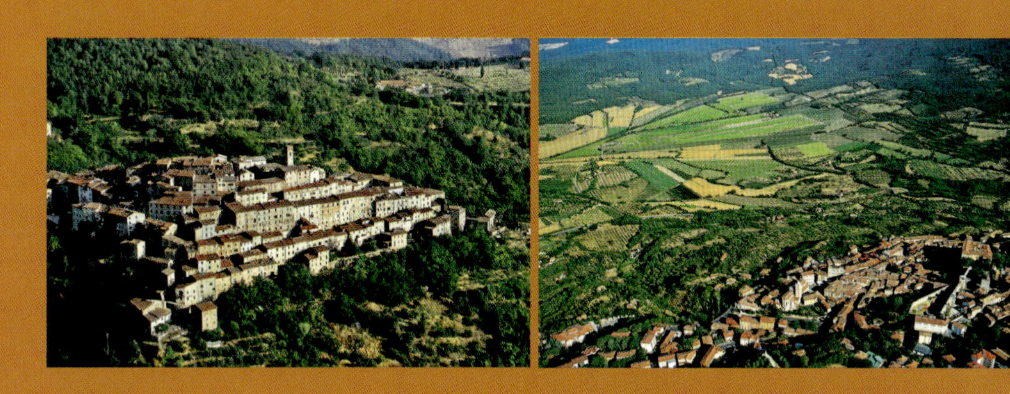

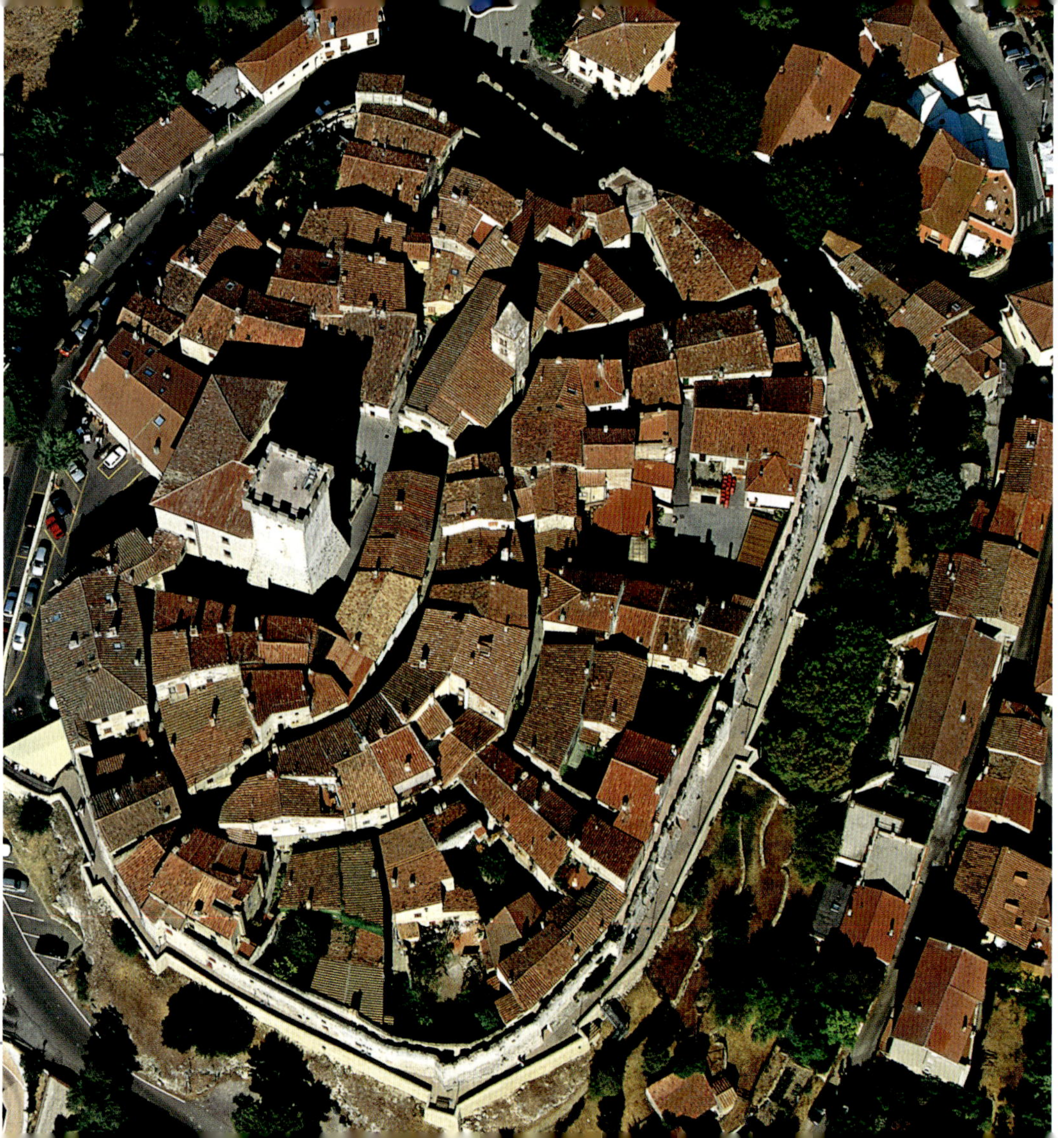

319 left
Chiusdino is built on top of one of the Metalliferous Hills of the Sienese countryside.

319 right
The Massa Marittima, a town of Etruscan origin, dominates the hills that slope from Siena.

Tuscany is characterized by its ancient urban civilization. Even at the time of the Etruscans, centers like Populonia, Volterra, Chiusi, Cortona or Fiesole gave this area a distinct urban nature and a highly civil atmosphere that finds its equal only in Magna Graecia.

The relationship still remains a mystery between that ancient Etruscan splendor and that which emerged through the centuries along with feudal and communal development, especially during the Renaissance, when the singularity of the Etruscan civilization was completely cancelled out, giving rise to that regional homogenous political entity called the Tuscan Granducato.

In the villages and towns of Tuscany (more so than in the cities where changes are more rapid and drastic) the remote past is present in everyday life: you think you are in a cellar, instead you are in an Etruscan tomb; you walk up the main street and you are actually on the *decumanus* of a *castrum*; you seek refuge in a small chapel outside of the town walls and smell the odor of barley, toasted to offer to an unknown rural divinity, on an ancient altar. But all of this, at the moment, we can neither see nor perceive, because we are flying over a small urban center that our route crosses. That which is evident, flying over ancient Tuscan towns is, usually, that which is above and inside the city walls pertains to the past and that which is underneath and outside pertains to the present.

The lovely village on the hilltop, encircled by

320
Capalbio Castle dates from the 12th century. The powerful Aldobrandeschi and Orsini families held in the early period, but the Sienese captured it in 1416.

The Beauty of Order and Measure

what remains of the walls, or precariously balanced on a cliff edge, appears as a labyrinth of narrow, tortuous roads, with sudden openings where the devoted inhabitants erected a tabernacle or cross.

The stone or brick houses seem piled one on top of another, with clay roofs which now have taken on the color of honey.

Visible from the air but also from the ground are the bell towers and public palaces, almost always with a tower. These two institutions once represented the contending poles of political and religious power; today they are merely the church and the town hall, and often face onto the same piazza, but do not oppose each other. Silence is broken only by the bells.

Under the village or beyond the walls, where until fifty years ago there were only fields for pasture, an alien landscape has now developed with highrise condominiums, small factories, sport complexes, train stations (when they exist), bordered by a river (if there is one) and highways. So, in all of their diversity, appear Volterra, among the hills of the high Cecina and Era valleys; Colle and Certaldo in the Val d'Elsa; Poppi in the Casentino; San Miniato in the Lower Valdarno; Cortona near the eastern borders of the Val di Chiana, with a view of Lake Trasimeno and many other places that we promise to visit calmly, on foot.

All of the towns that the tourist guides and local offices define as "jewels" are just that. However, we must limit ourselves to few examples, certain to regret our omissions.

When we arrive over Monteriggioni, in Siena's Val d'Elsa, we see a perfect circle of wall in which are set 14 quadrilateral towers, that once must have seemed much higher when they inspired Dante to describe them as giants.

The effect is increased by the town's isolated position atop a hill, although it is bordered on the east by the horrible highway connecting

The Beauty of Order and Measure

Florence and Siena and to the west by an ancient tract of the Francigena, recognizable only from above. Next is the famous San Gimignano, also in Val d'Elsa, with its extraordinary skyline of famous towers that numbered 72 in the 1200s (today there are only 12). The town unrolls itself on an almost rectilinear axis that leads from Porta San Giovanni to the monumental center.

This consists of the Piazza della Cisterna, which is visibly triangular from above, and the adjacent Piazza del Duomo dominated by the Podestà palace with the Rognosa tower and the Duomo reached by a high stairway.

The church is striking: its bare Romanesque-style façade conceals three naves within that are rich with frescoes by Benozzo Gozzoli and Ghirlandaio, as well as statues by Jacopo della Quercia. San Gimignano is not on any main route, but this doesn't discourage tourists, to judge by the many buses and cars parked outside the city walls. It has no factories or highrise developments to ruin its flanking countryside. The town's main commercial activity is the production of wine (Vernaccia) cultivated in the splendid vineyards that surround this gem. Naturally, we must visit Pienza, an ideal city. There are few cities, like Pienza, that have been constructed *ex novo* on commission and left entirely to the work of one artist as if it were a painting for an altar or the statue of a saint. "Make me a city." Really!

But we are talking about the 1400s when man's creative capacity was exalted and the customer in question was Enea Silvio Piccolomini, better known as Pope Pius II. Bernardo Rossellino, the architect he engaged, must have responded to this request with: "Immediately, Your Holiness!"

Actually, this is not really the way it went. Pius II wished to ennoble his birthplace, Corsignano in the Val d'Orcia, which was successively

325
Casole d'Elsa, which was originally an Etruscan settlement, is situated on hills where grapes, olives and grain crops are cultivated.

324

transformed, based on Rosellino's project and rebaptized Pienza. The entire town was demolished and reconstructed, giving life to a new plan based on perspective. The project included the Duomo, the parsonage, the ancient Prior's Palace, used as headquarters for the bishop and the Piccolomini Palace. The view from above reveals the scenographic value of this town placed around a trapezoidal piazza whose pavement, in *terracotta*, is geometrically divided by travertine strips, according to a plan that regulates the spatial relationship of the buildings around the piazza.

The architectural forms of the structures are clearly of Albertian derivation: the exterior of the Piccolomini palace masterfully recalls the Rucellai palace in Florence, constructed by the same Rosellino based on a project by Leon Battista Alberti, and the Duomo's façade is inspired by the Malatesta Temple of Forlì.

If Pienza is the result of a whimsical yet potent man (Pius II never set foot there), then let us welcome similar whims.

Another thing that flying over these small Tuscan centers confirms is that they are all (except in marginal zones) close to one another – in eyesight of each other at ground level.

In the distant past, when transport was slow and tiring, this permitted greater ease in communication and exchange (not only merchandise) and a confrontation that was often translated into local pride and competition, which in Tuscany has never subsided. This sentiment influenced not only the inhabitants of nearby villages and relatives, but also local customs and protective saints.

Colle and Poggibonsi, although only 4.4 miles (7 km) apart are unwilling even to divide their dust; in fact on April 28th, celebration of San Lucchese protector of Poggibonsi and June 30th, celebration for San Marziale, patron of Colle, it always rains!

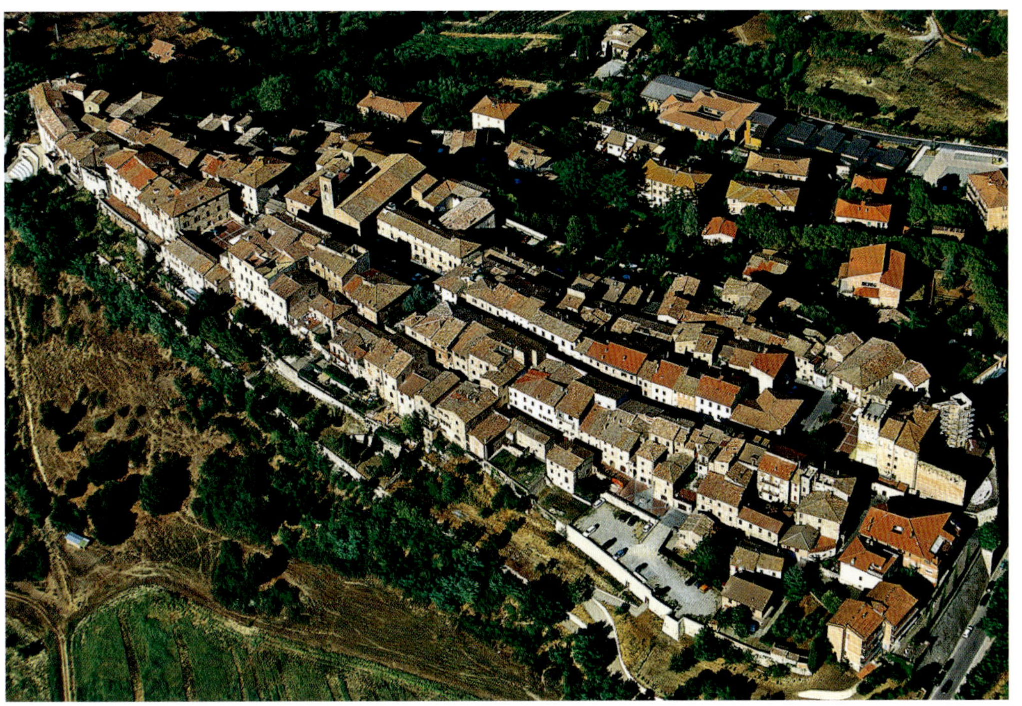

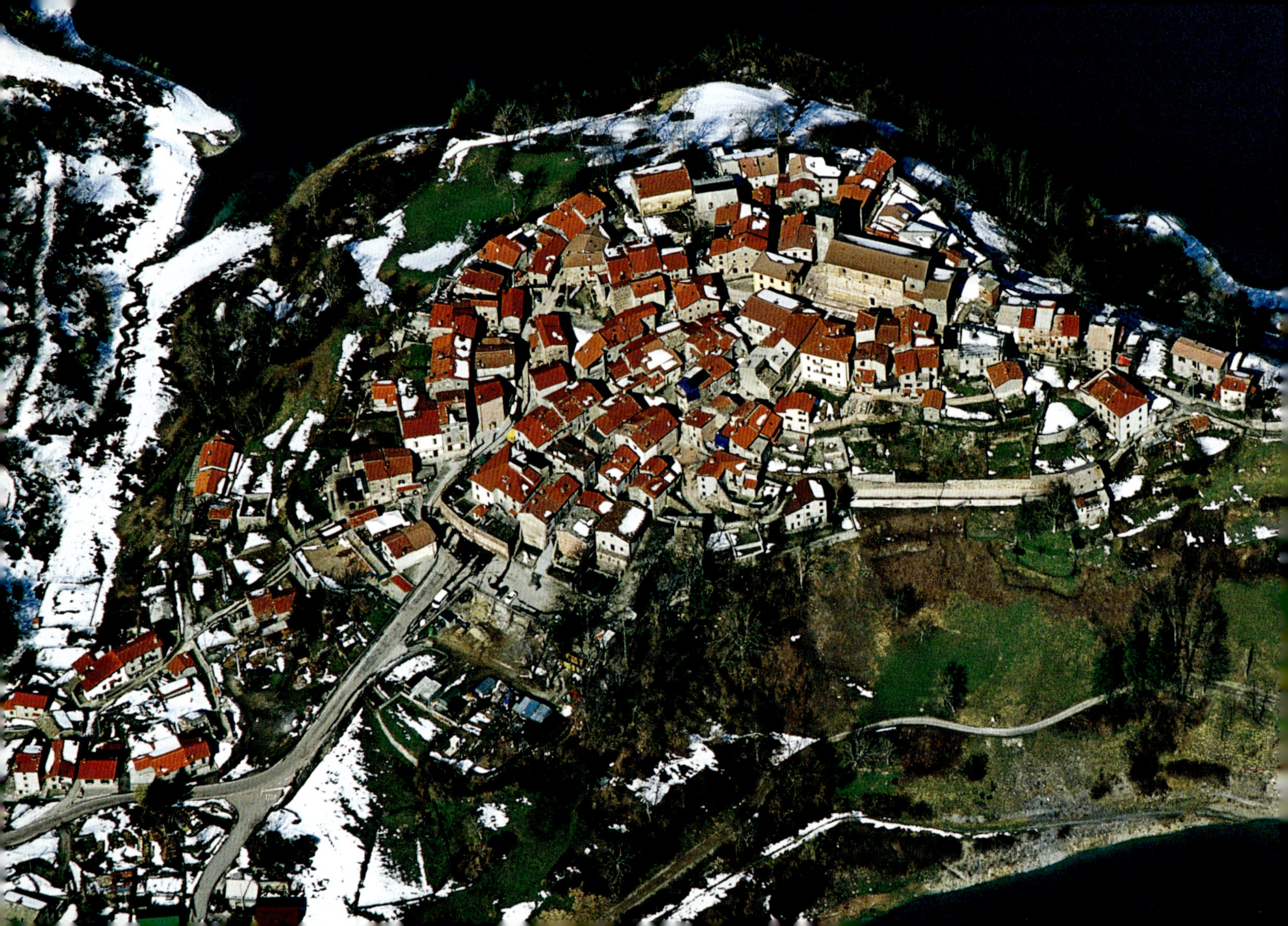

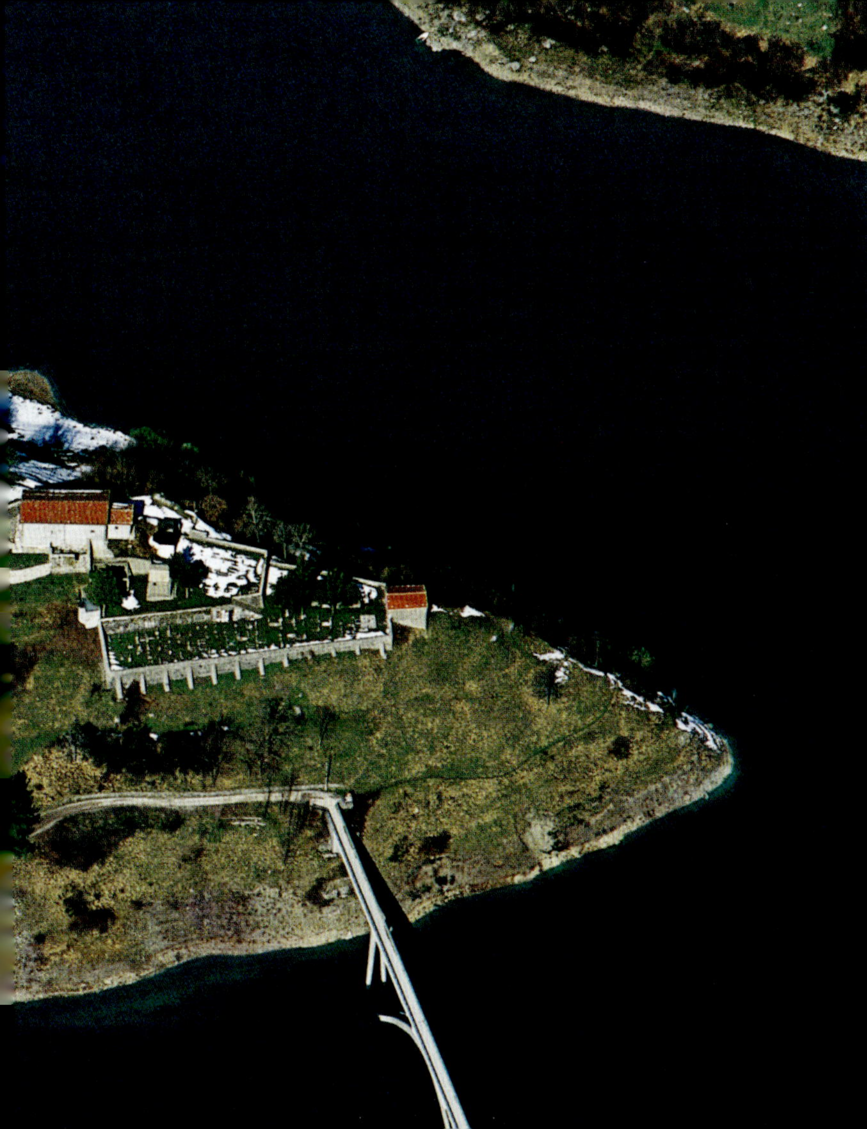

326-327
The Apuan Alps, composed mostly of calcareous rock, are characterized by varied microclimates.

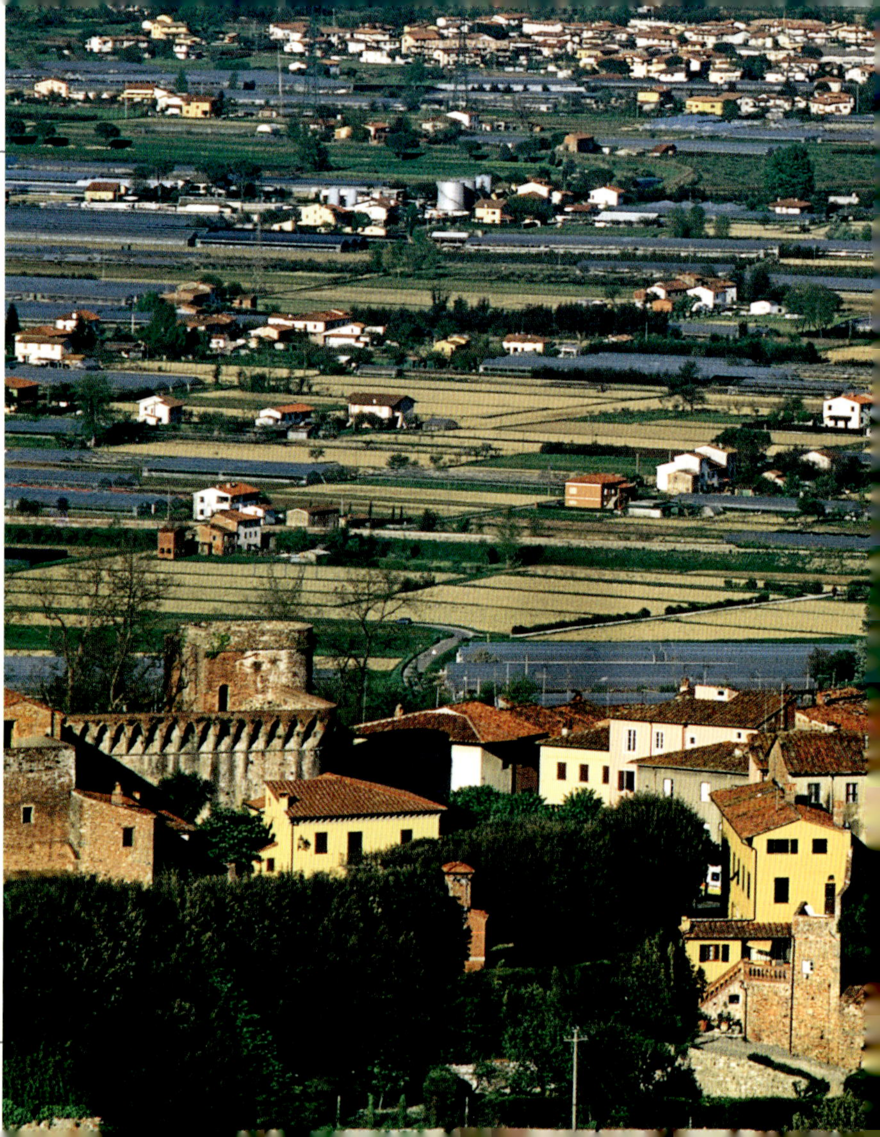

328-329
The ancient town of Montecarlo, located between Valdinievole and Lucca, is known for its DOC-Chianti wines.

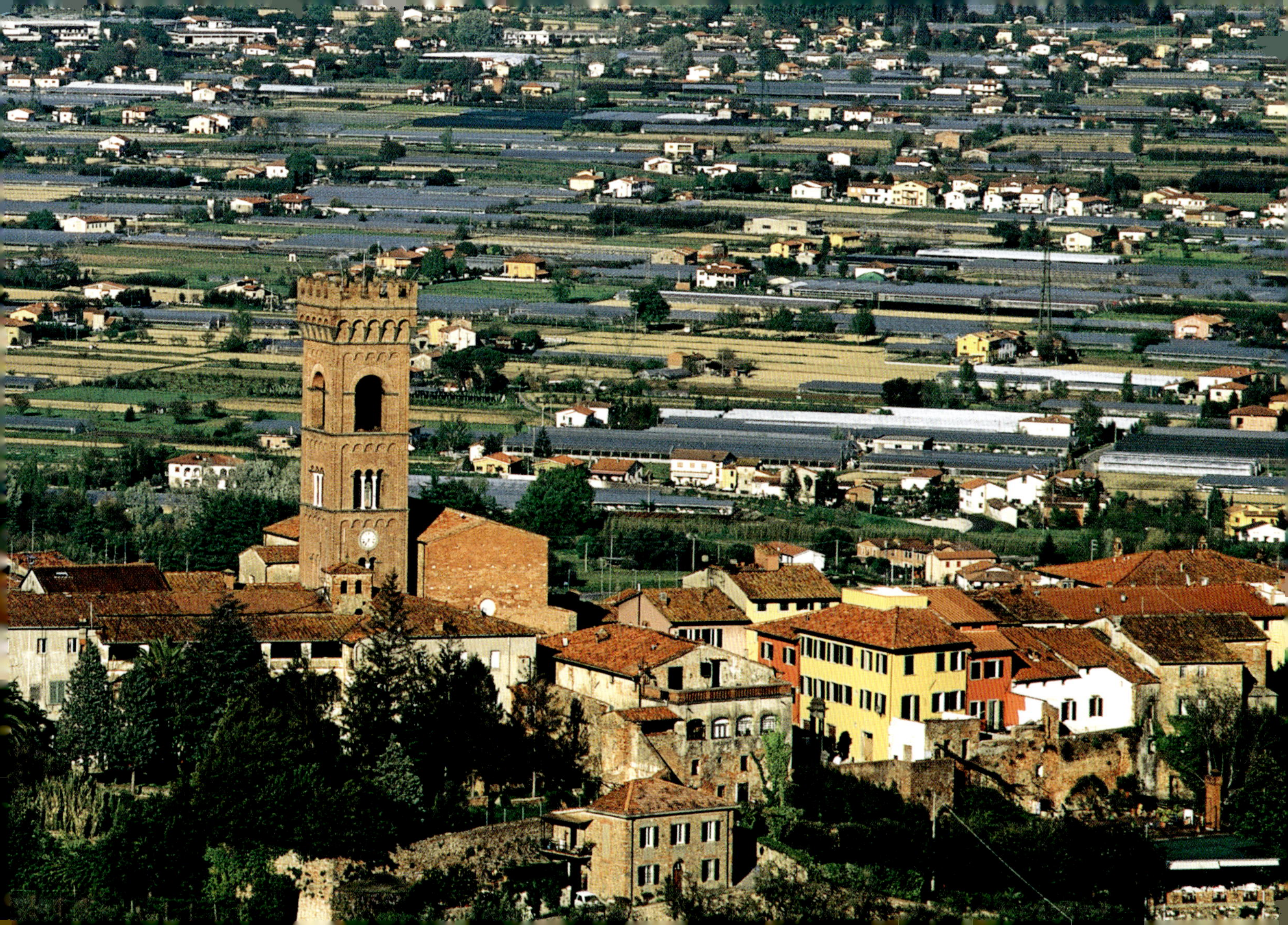

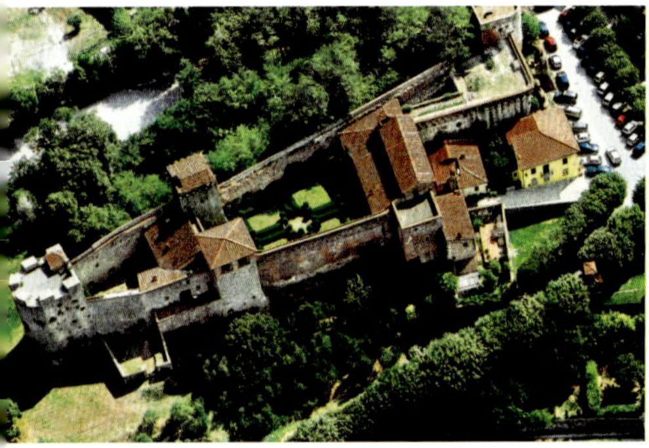

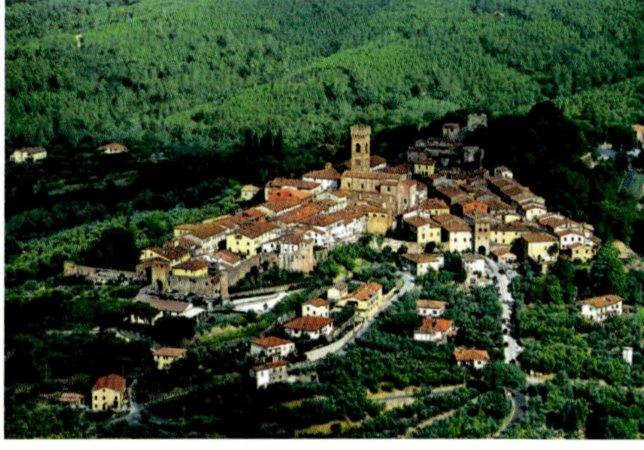

330
Pescia, whose name derives from a mispronunciation of a Lombard word that meant river, has had a notable development due to its production of flowers – for which it is famous worldwide.

331
Despite numerous changes, the center of Pescia, with its ancient buildings, still retains its original form.

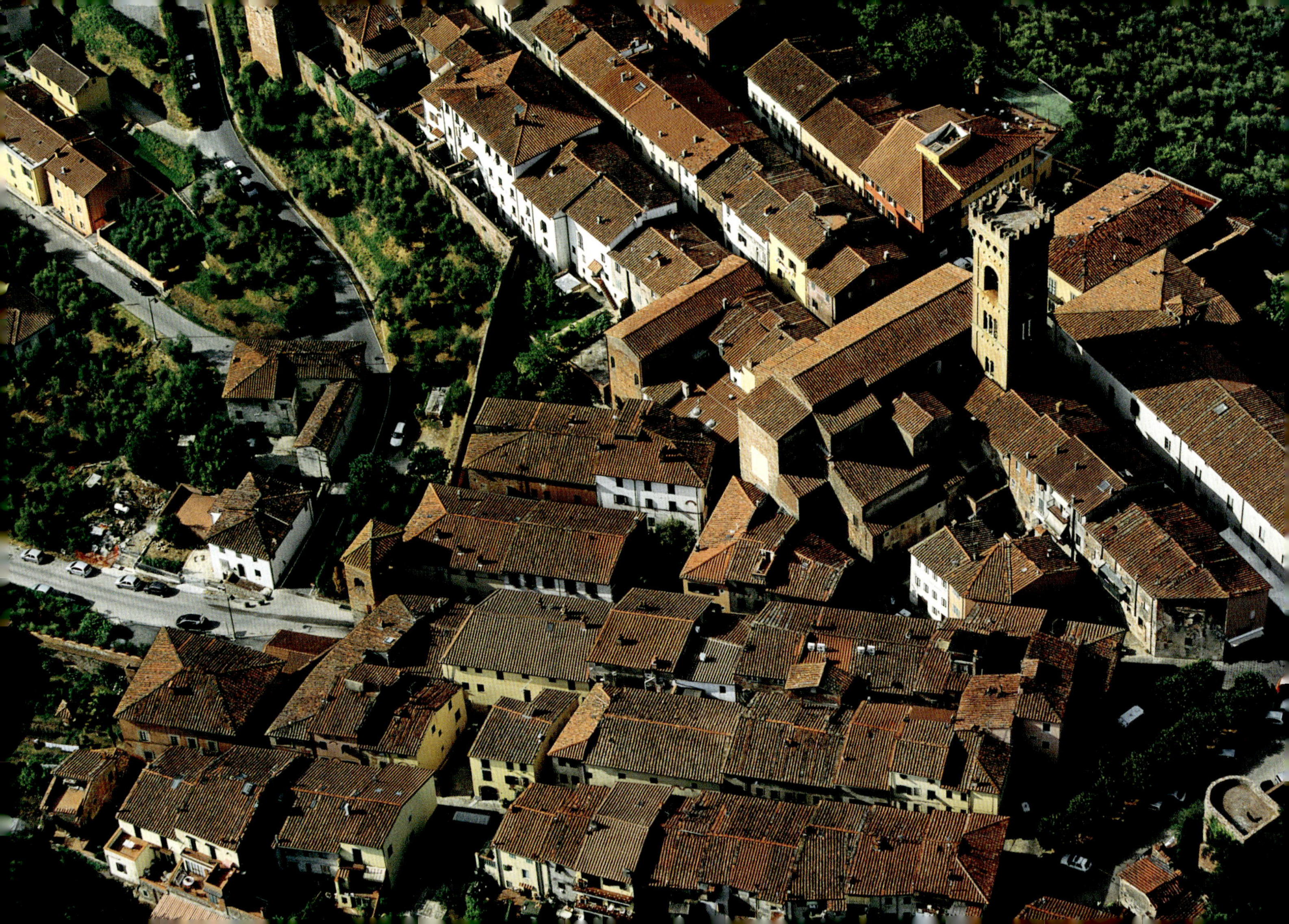

332

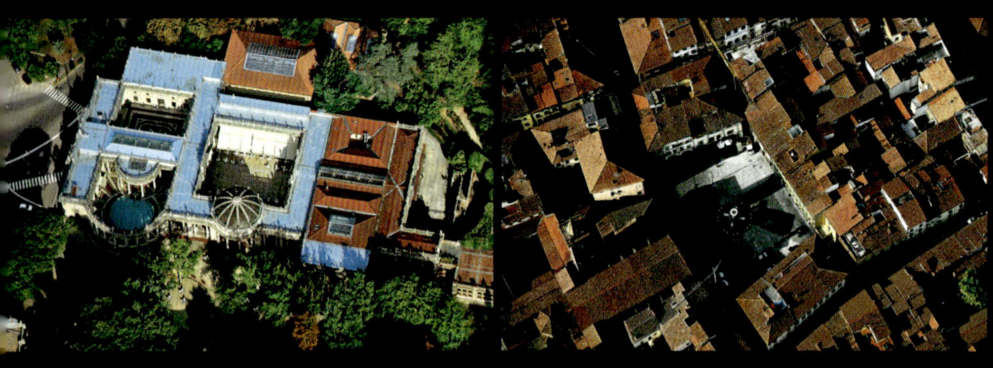

332
Montecatini is considered the pearl among Italian thermal areas with a solid, long-standing therapeutic tradition: in the 1400s, Duke Leopold de' Medici appreciated modern methods for utilizing the mineral waters.

333
The name Certaldo derives from the Latin Cerrus Altus which signifies "hill covered by cerrus trees." The fertile land on which it stands favored the birth and development of this medieval village.

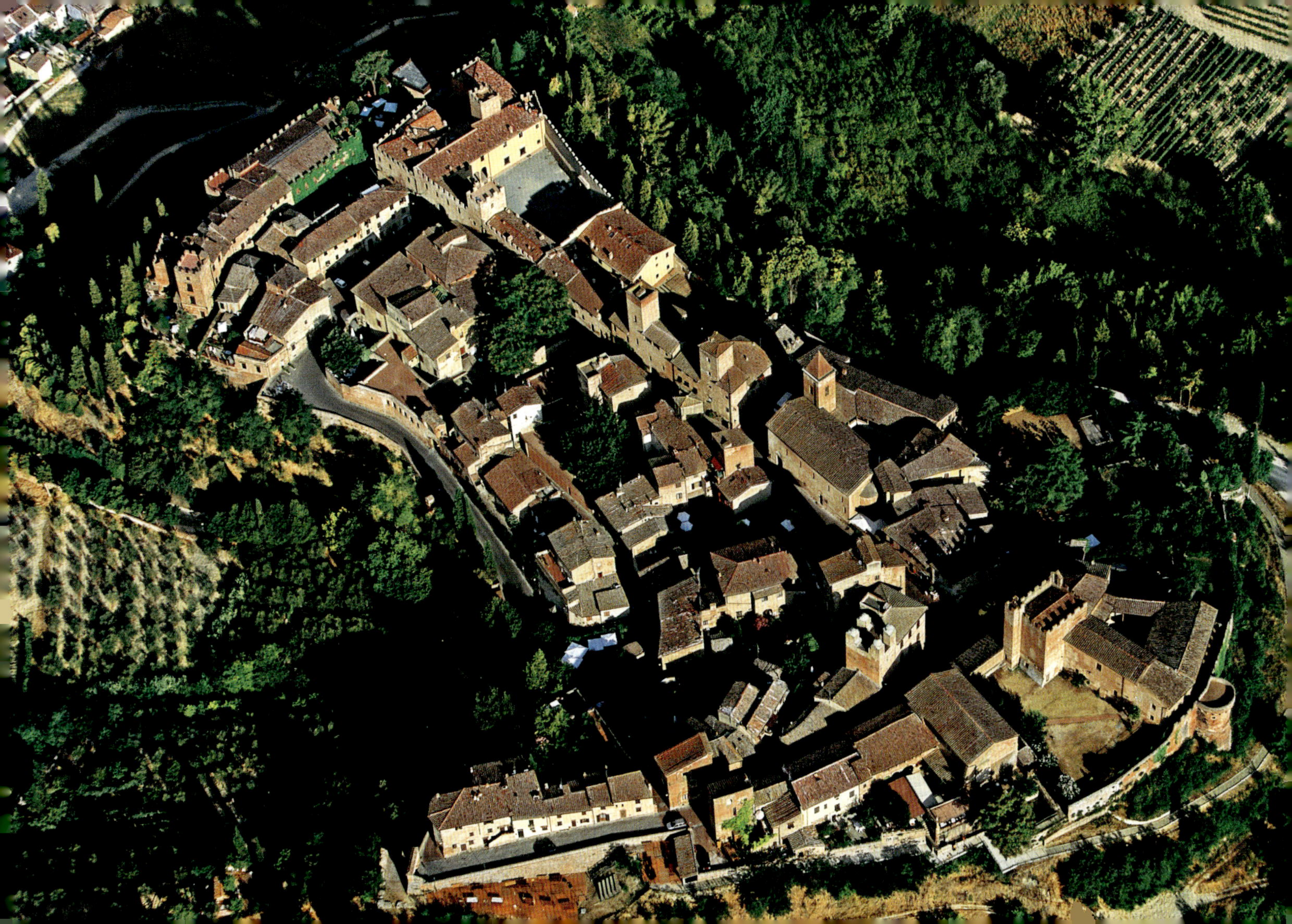

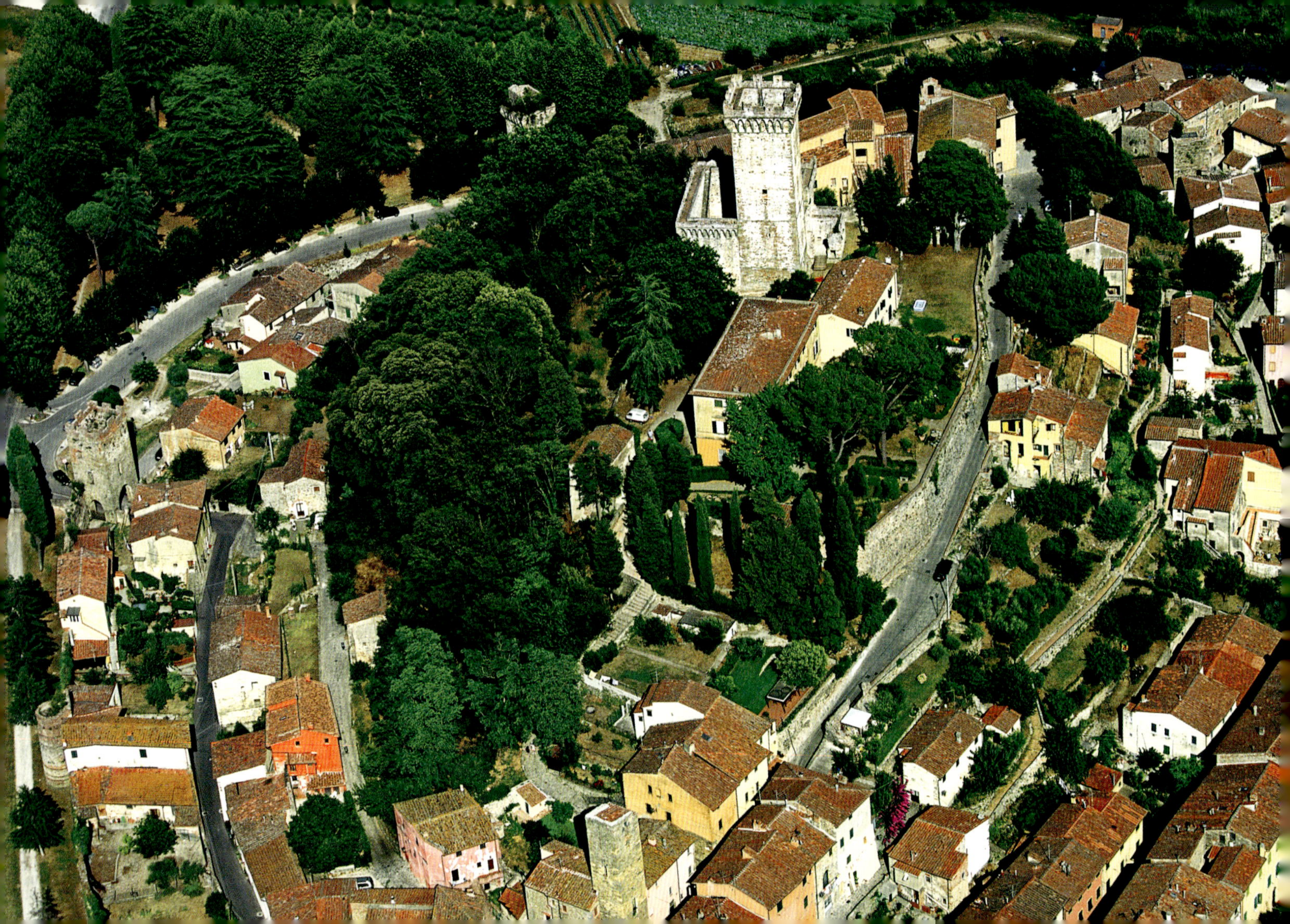

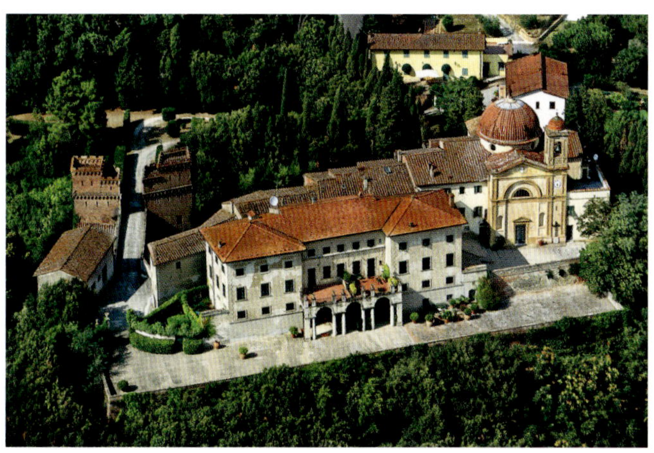

334
The center of Bientina still has noteworthy monuments, like its medieval wall with towers.

335
The village of Forcola is very characteristic; its history dates back to the year 1000.

337

Abbadia San Salvatore is situated on the southeastern side of Mt. Amiata; it owes its name to a Benedictine abbey founded in 743 and suppressed in the 18th century.

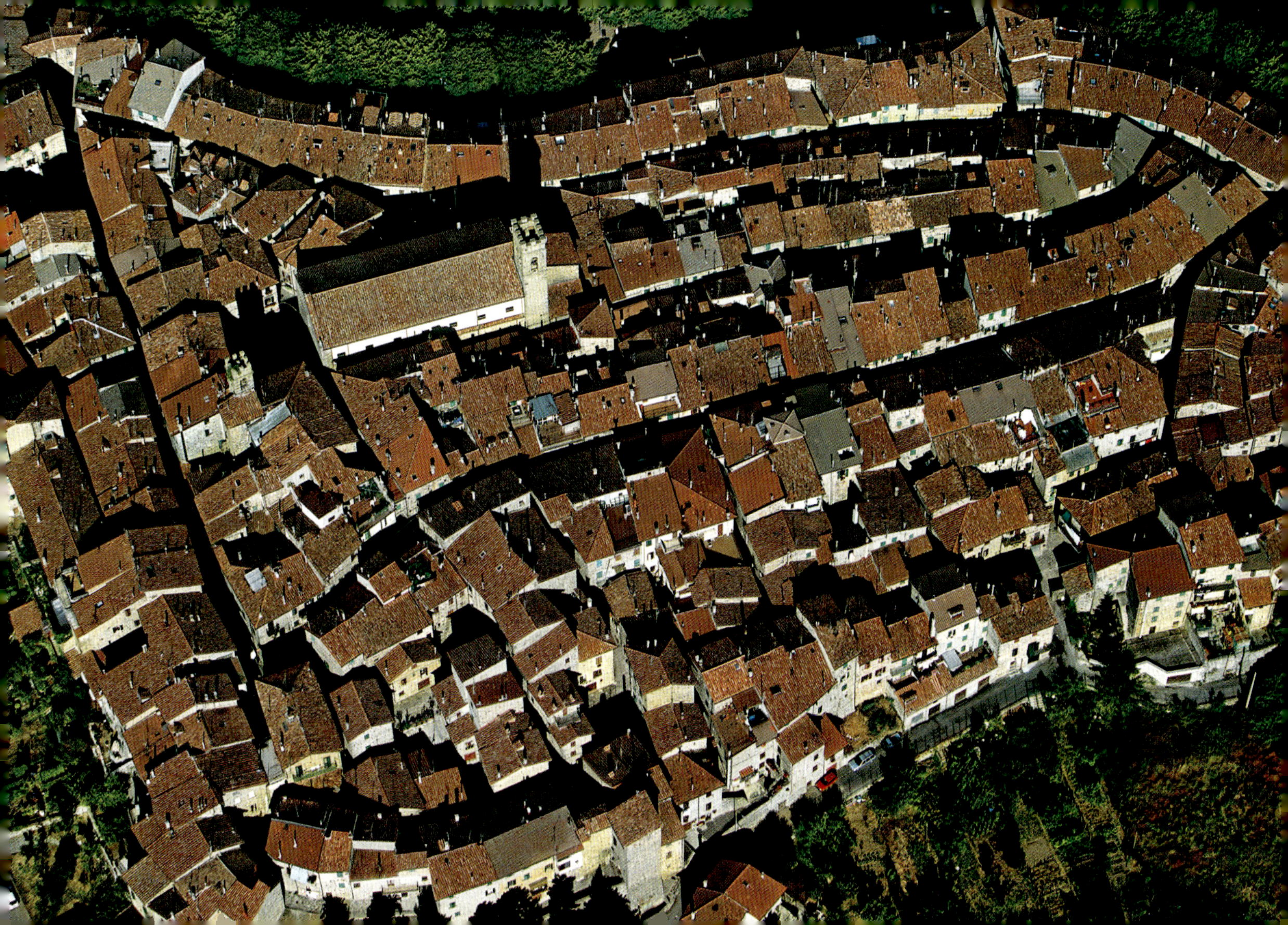

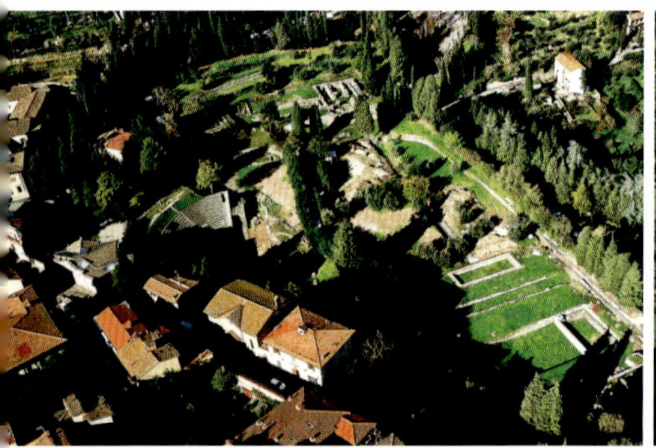

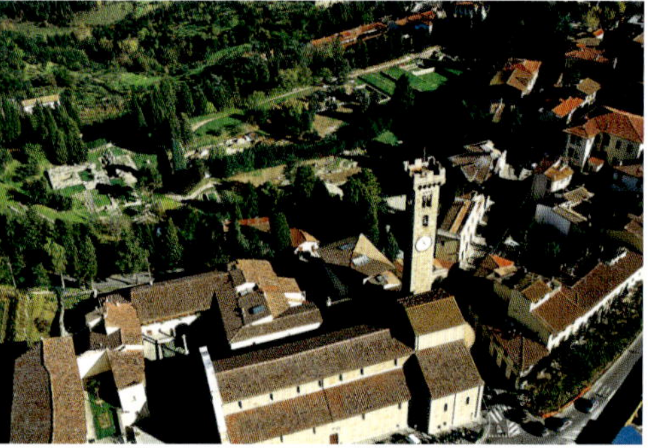

338
Sitting atop a hill that dominates the Arno valley, Fiesole is an ancient center that still retains traces of its Etruscan and Roman heritage.

339
Fiesole's geographic position made it a strategic site for the control of communication routes between central and southern Etruria and the north.

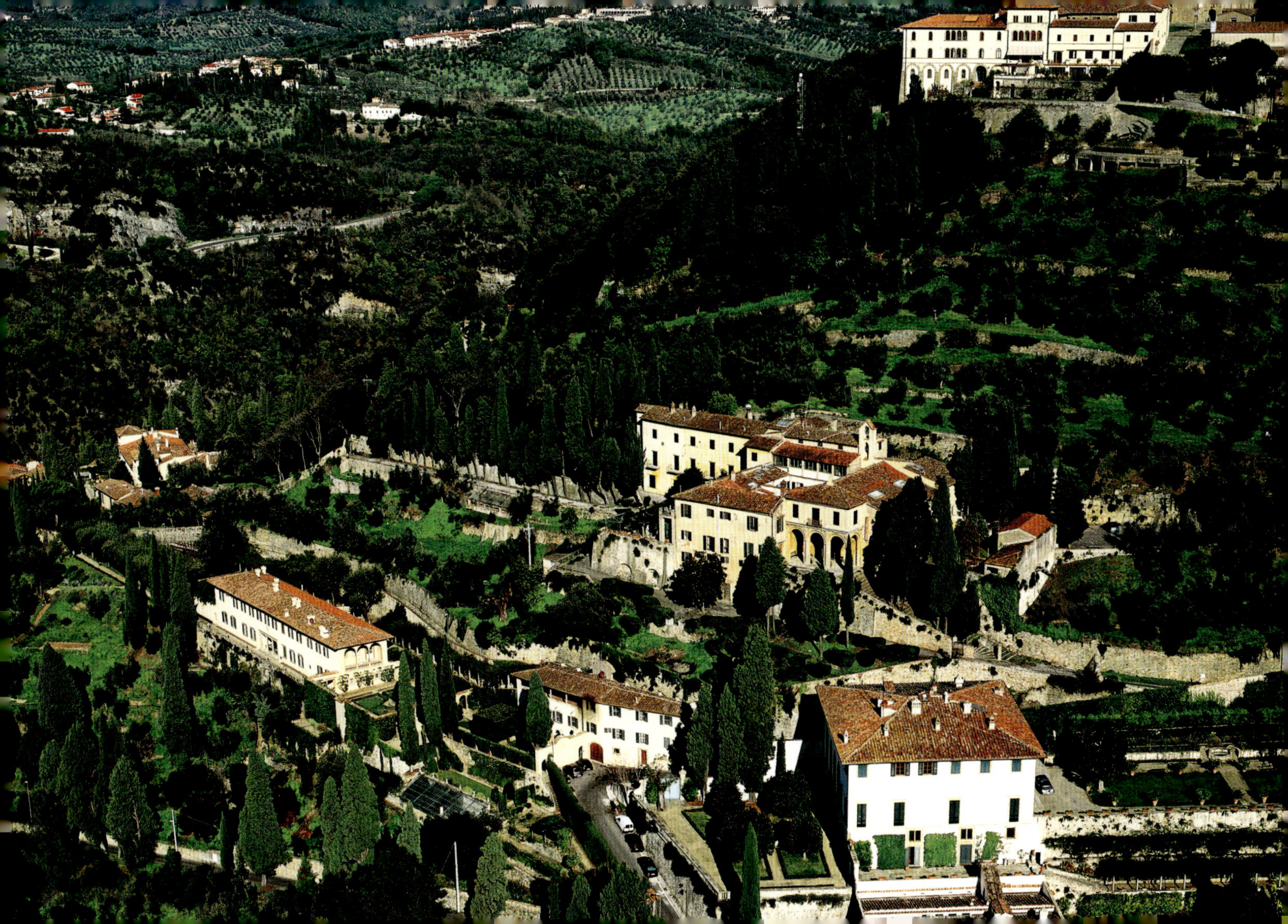

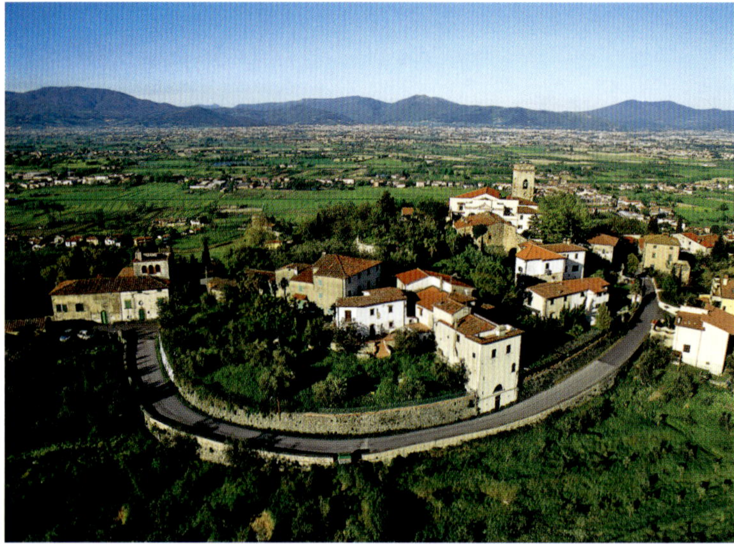

340

The territory around Prato, with its green hills, vineyards and olive groves, offers visitors an evocative panorama.

341

San Miniato is a small city with an important past, located only a few miles from Tuscany's principal artistic cities; for this reason its is called "The city of the XX miles."

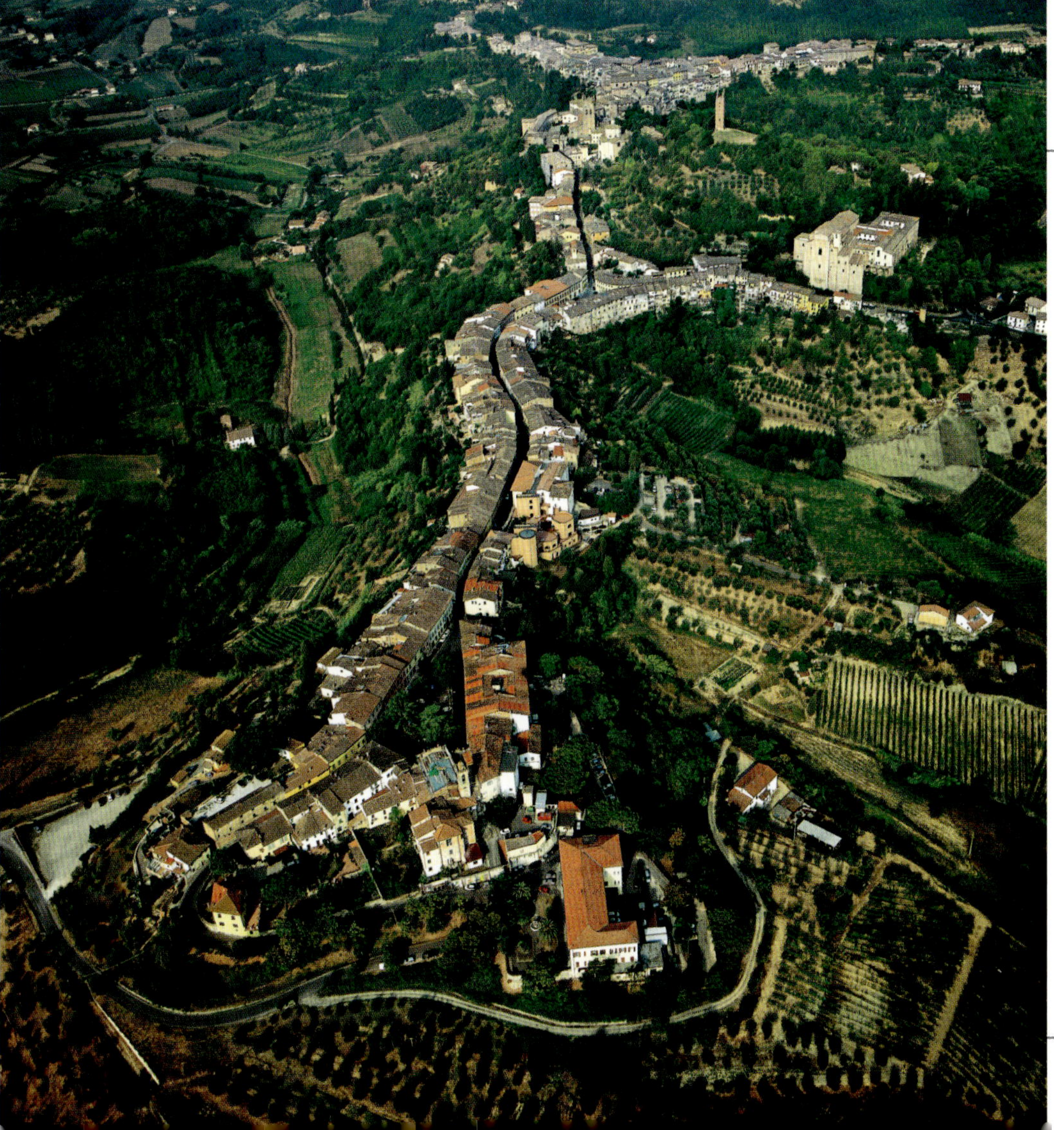

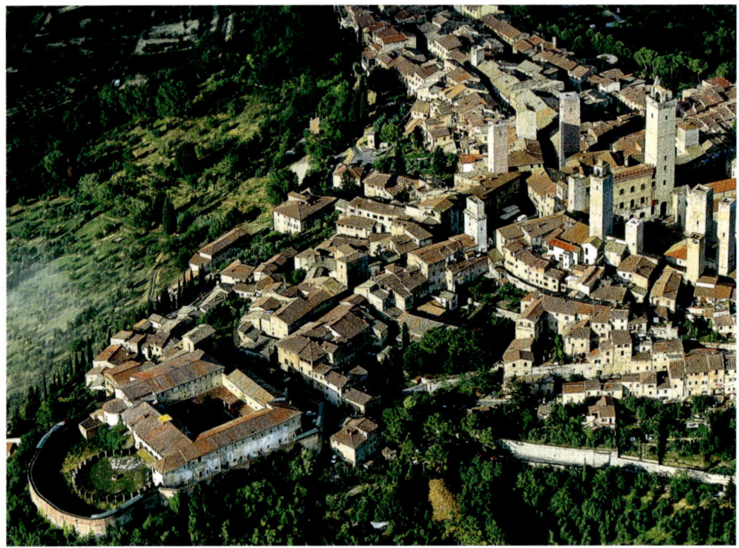

342 and 343

Declared in 1990 by UNESCO to be part of the patrimony of humanity in 1990, San Gimignano is known as "City of Beautiful Towers." However, of the original 72 towers, constructed as symbols of the local aristocrats' wealth, only 14 remain.

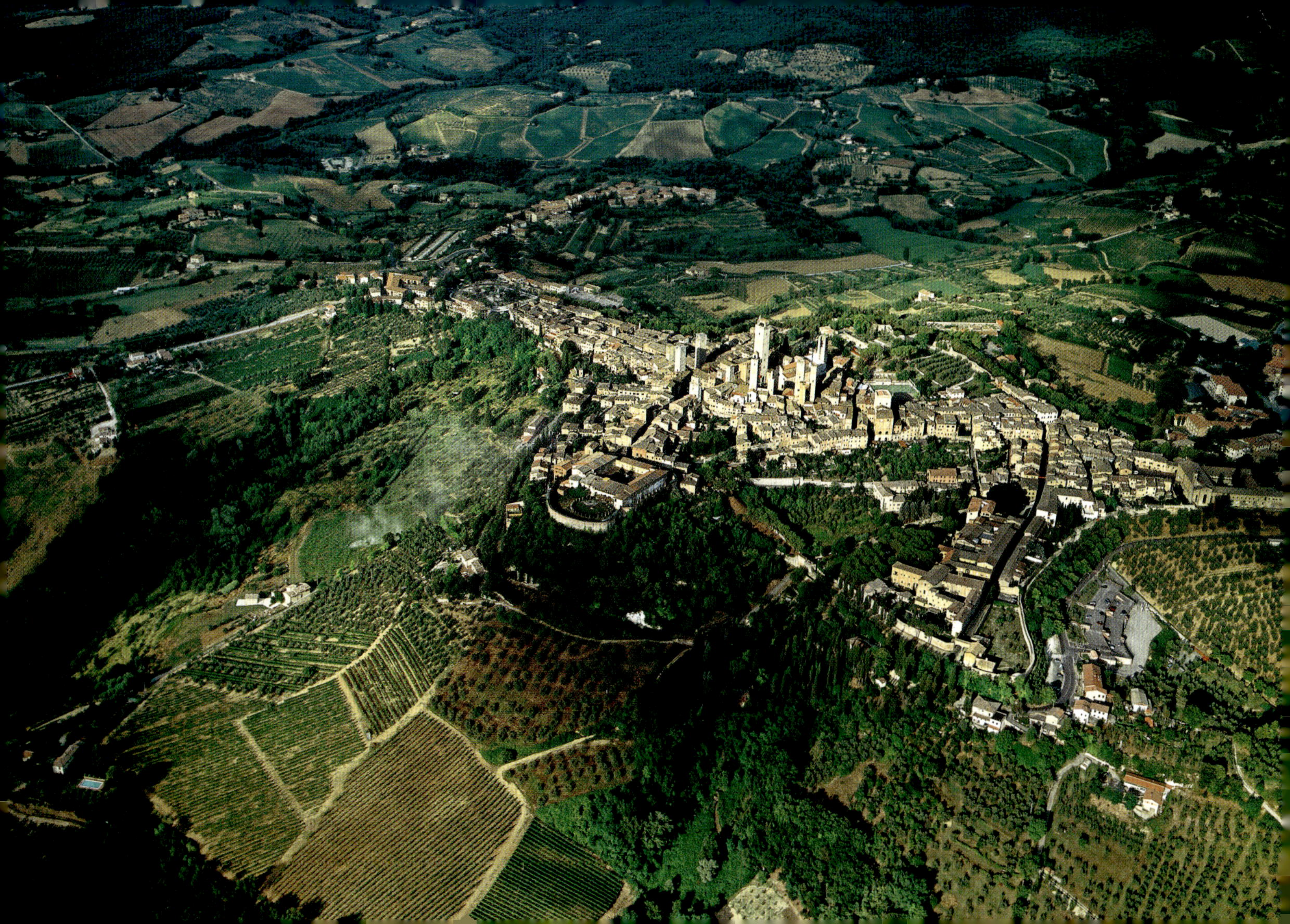

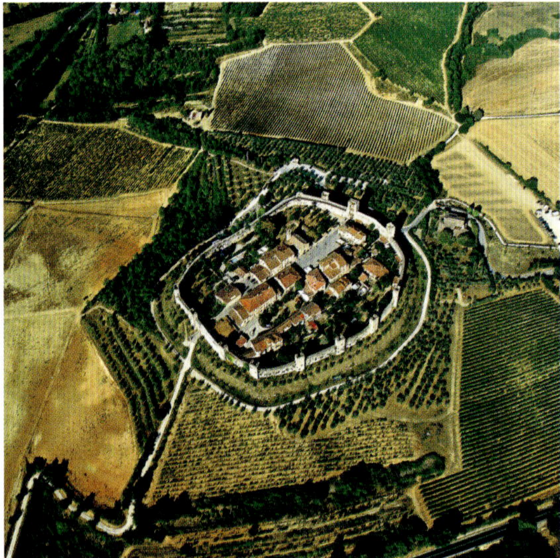

344 and 345

Monteriggioni is famous for its castle, for its emblematic incorruptibility and the crown that rests on the effigy of Italy. Thanks to its walls, the fortress successfully resisted every attempt at siezure for three hundred years.

346-347

The area around Volterra is rich in mineral deposits and offers extraordinary landscapes with small villages perched above forest-bordered canals.

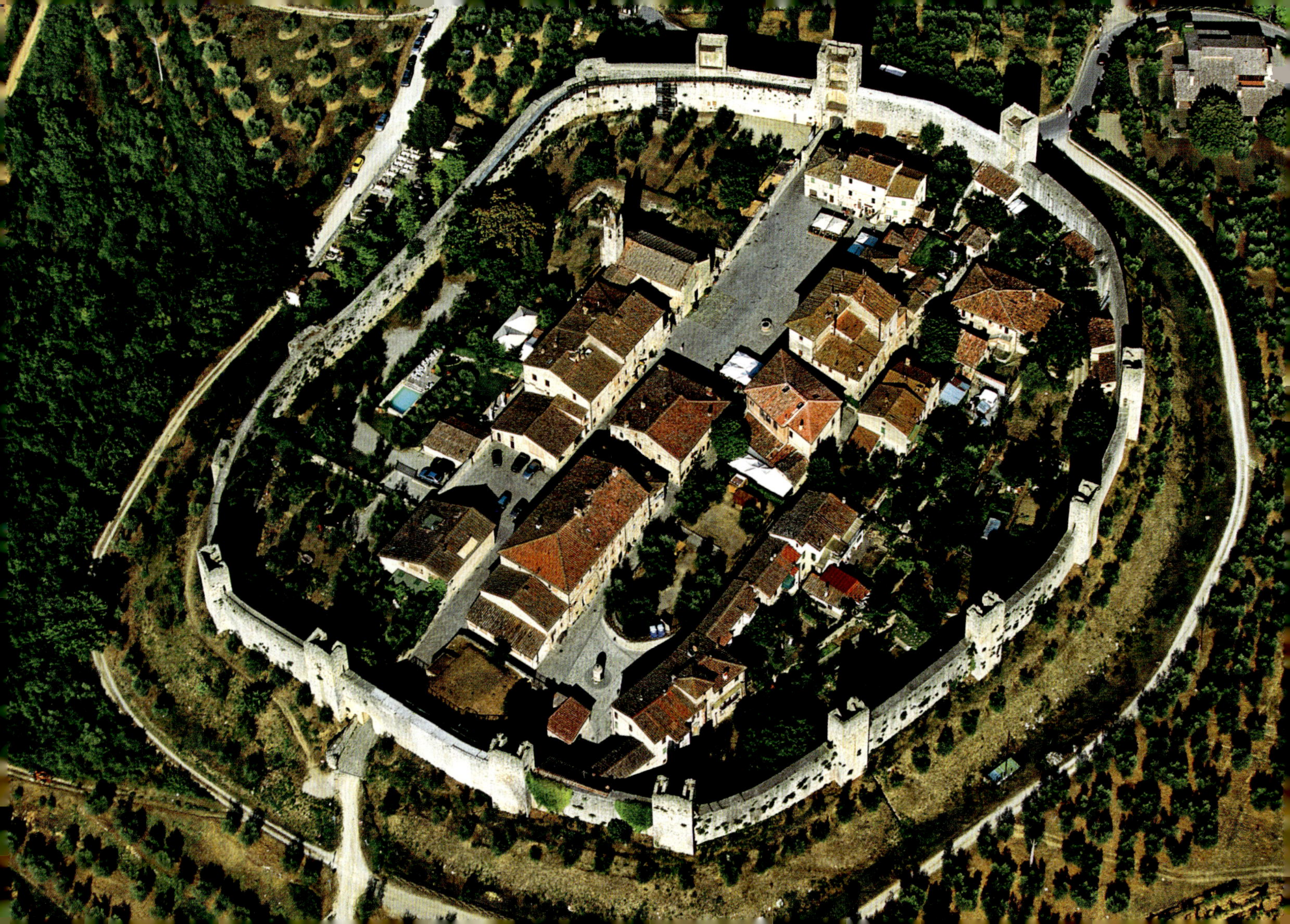

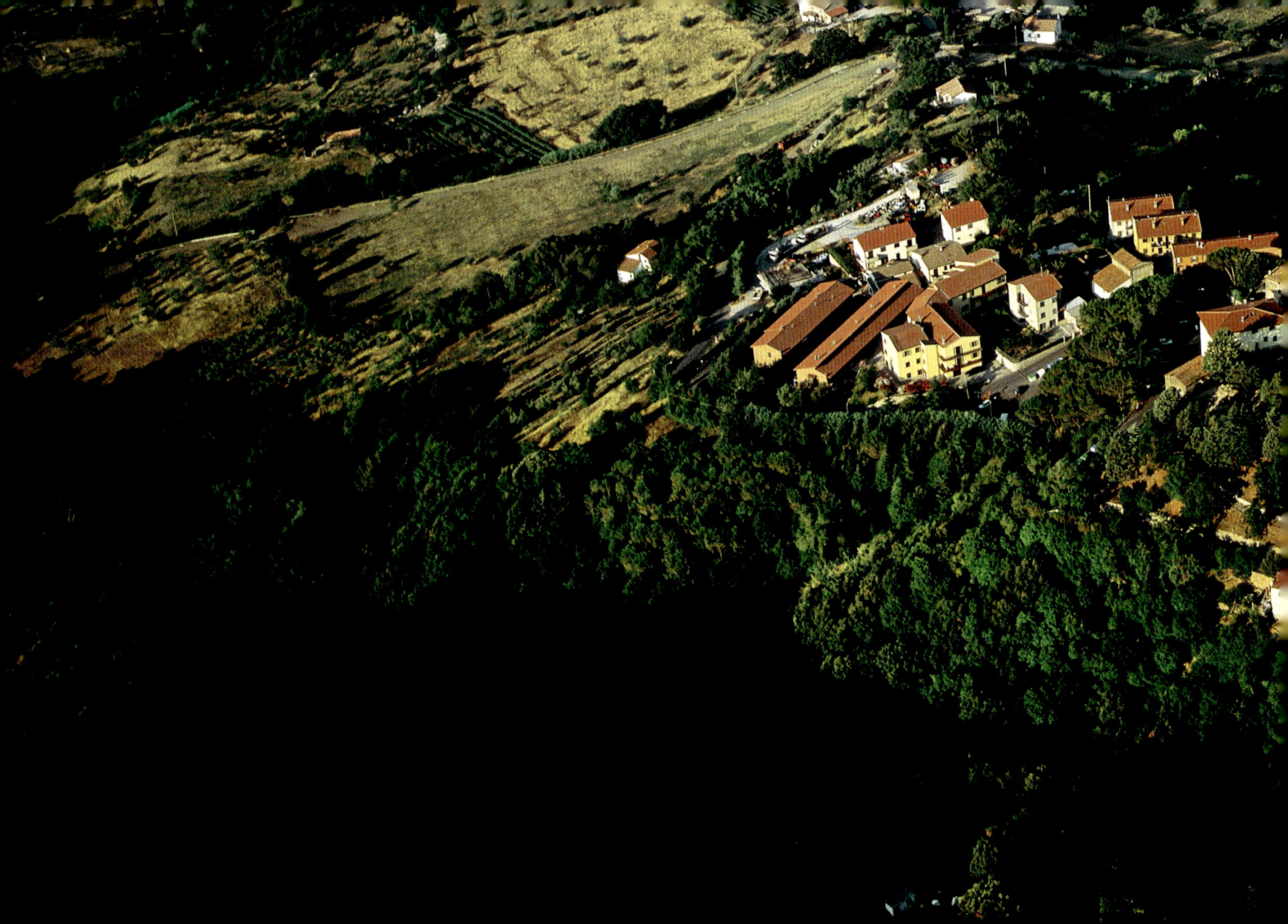

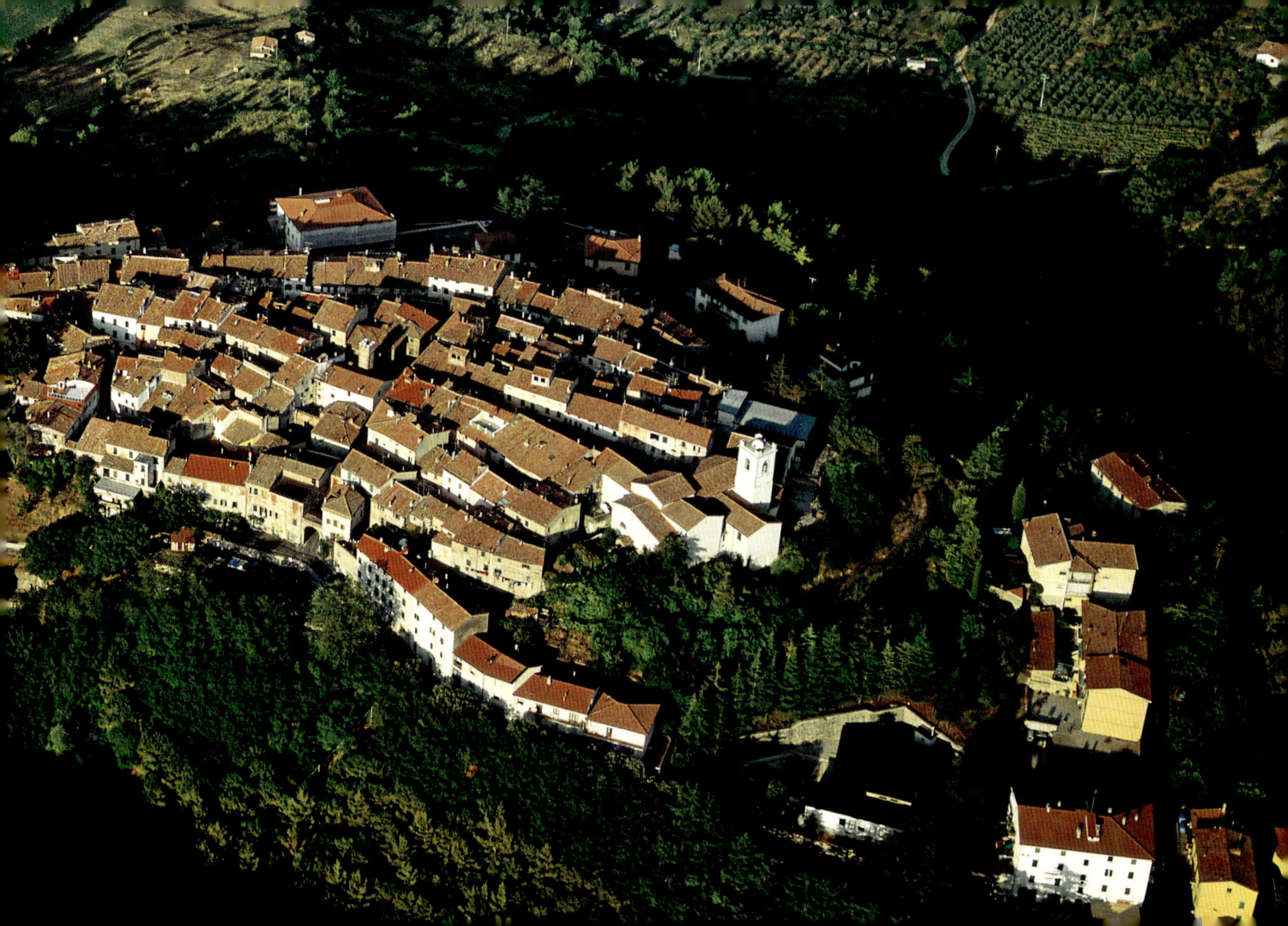

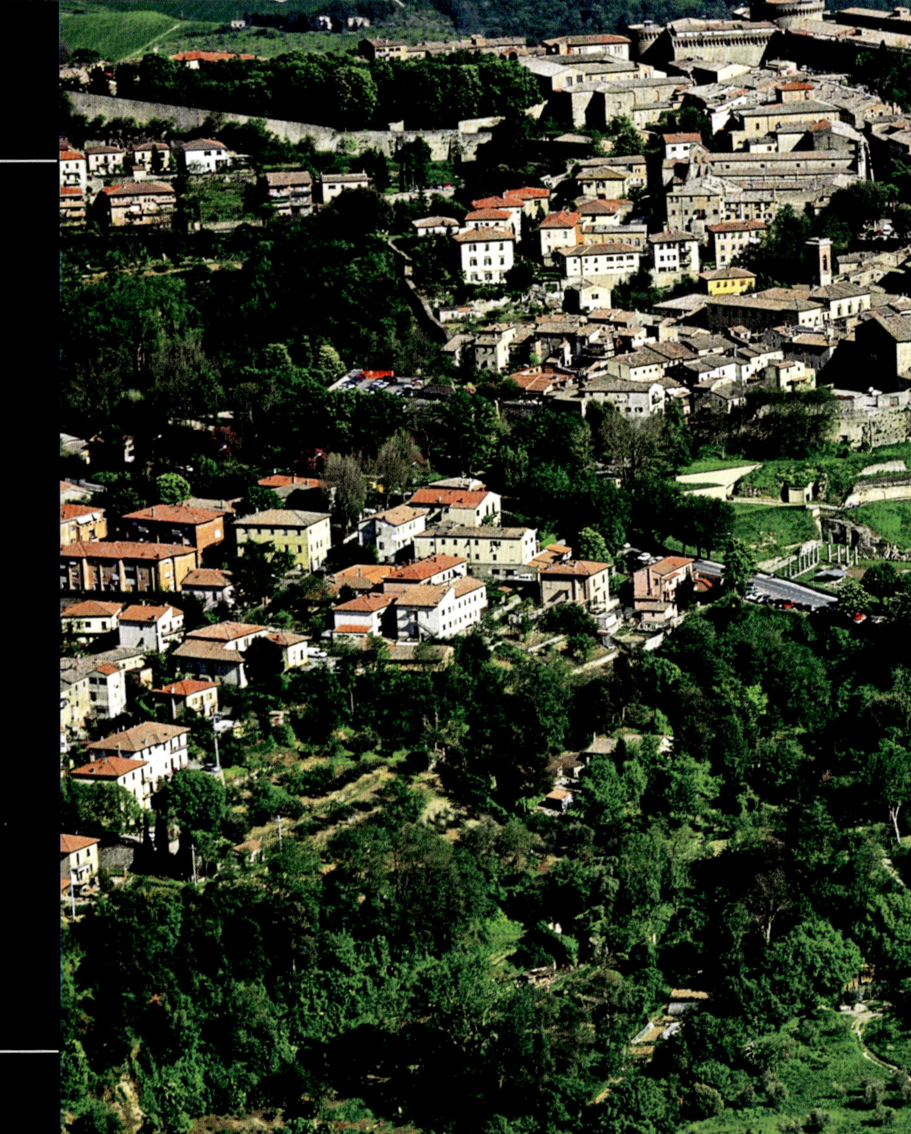

348-349
Volterra's history dates back 3000 years, and the abundance of evidence for this has contributed to making Volterra a unique city of art.

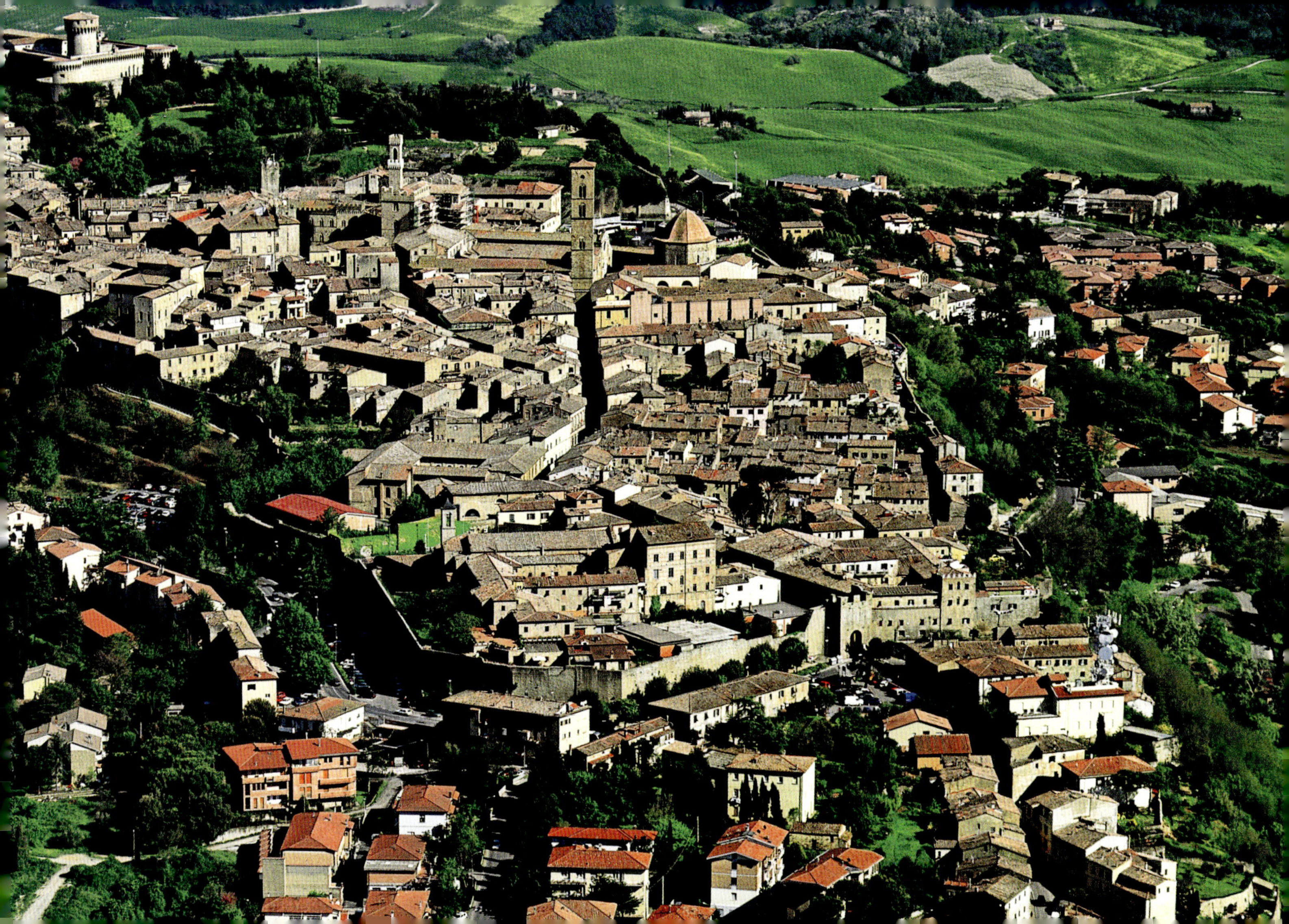

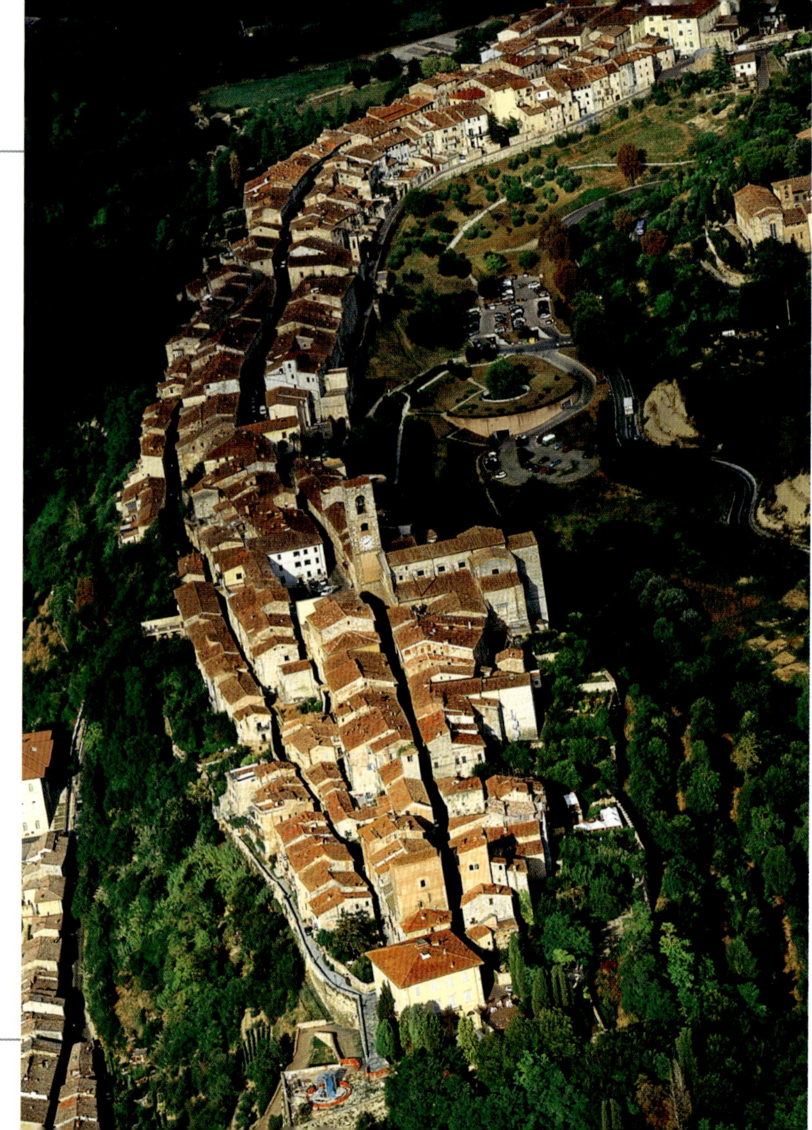

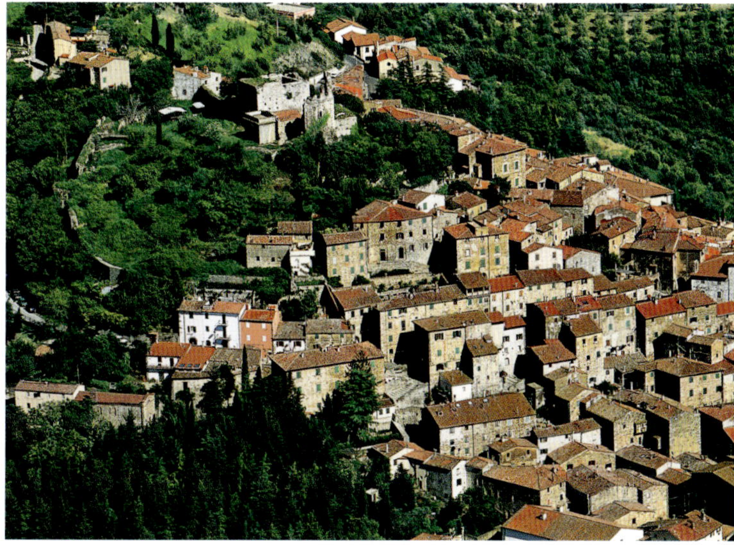

350
The Val d'Elsa, occupying an important strategic position between the Tuscan coast and Siena and Florence, has long been dotted with fortified citadels.

351
The splendid Sienese countryside offers unique scenery, with an infinite number of varied views encompassing villages of every size.

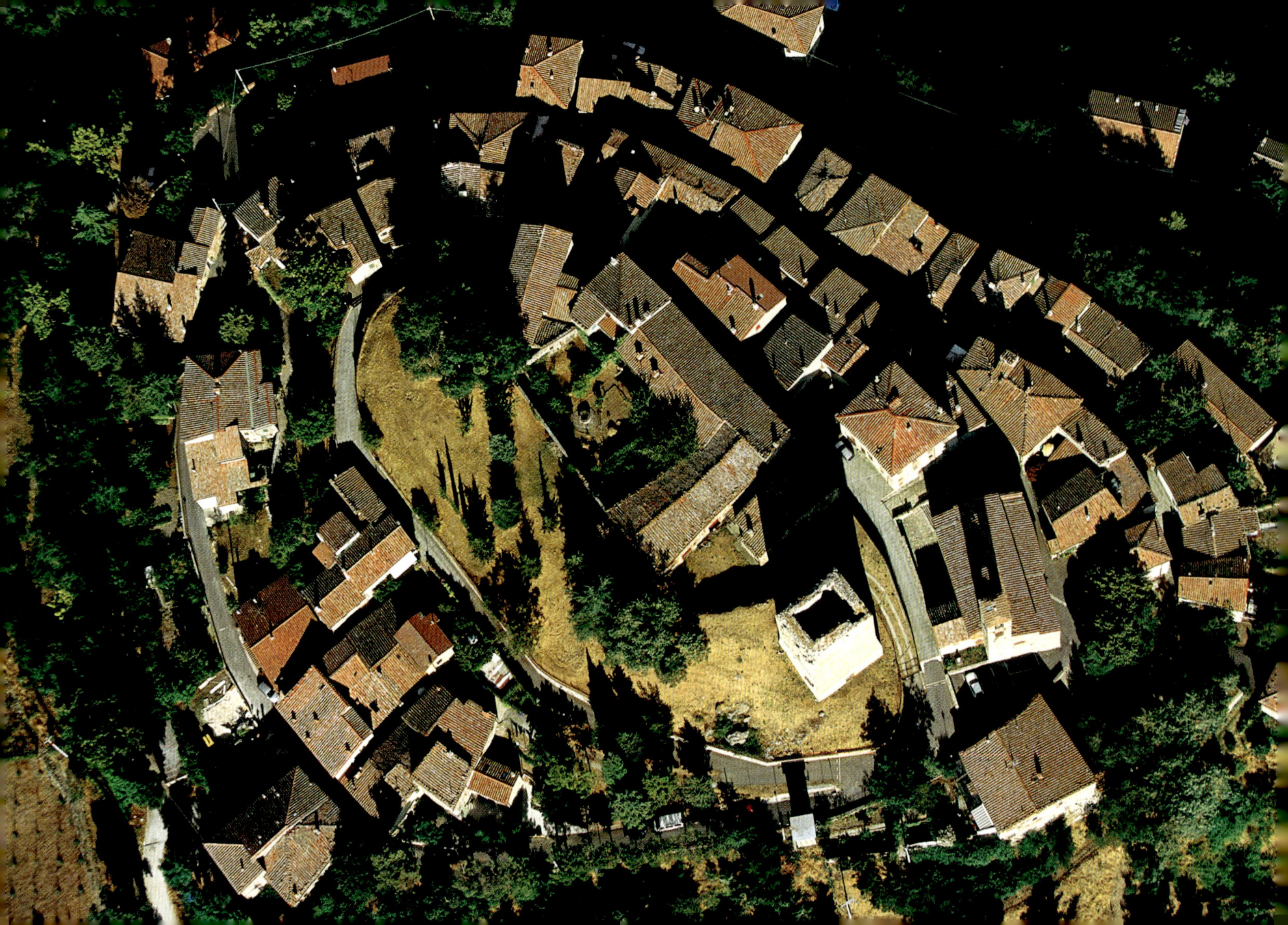

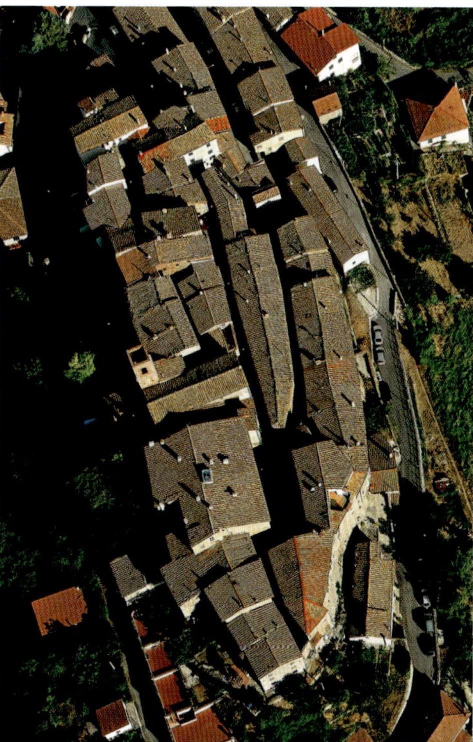

352 and 353

Tuscany's mountain ranges (in this case the Metalliferous Hills) offer terrain often suitable for human habitation. Many areas were cleared, inhabited and walled in ancient times. Most villages and towns date back at least to the medieval era, and they are often clustered around the fortified house of a nobleman, a small castle or a watchtower. In this way, a magnificent urban micronesia arose on the region's hilltops.

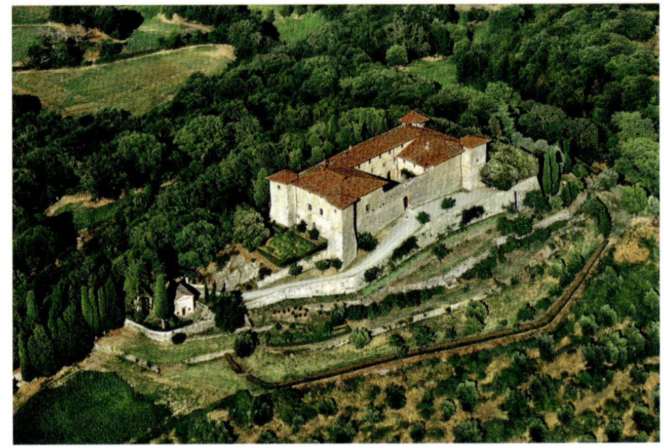

354
The territory of the Metalliferous Hills region extends from Volterra to Massa Marittima and offers wild, evocative scenery, frequently interrupted by medieval fortresses.

355
Pontignano Monastery was built during the first half of the 14th century; Bindo di Falcone, its founder, dedicated it to St. Peter.

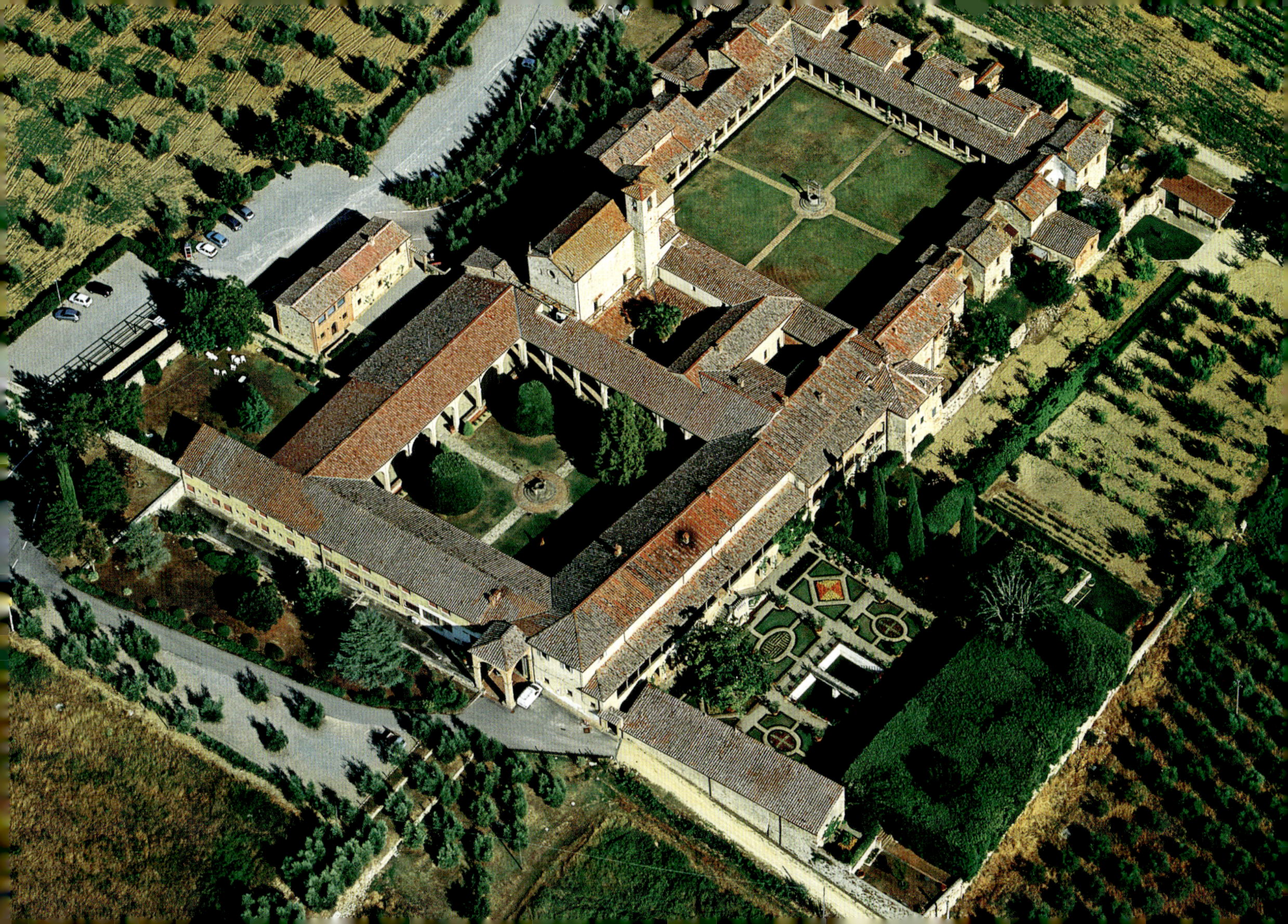

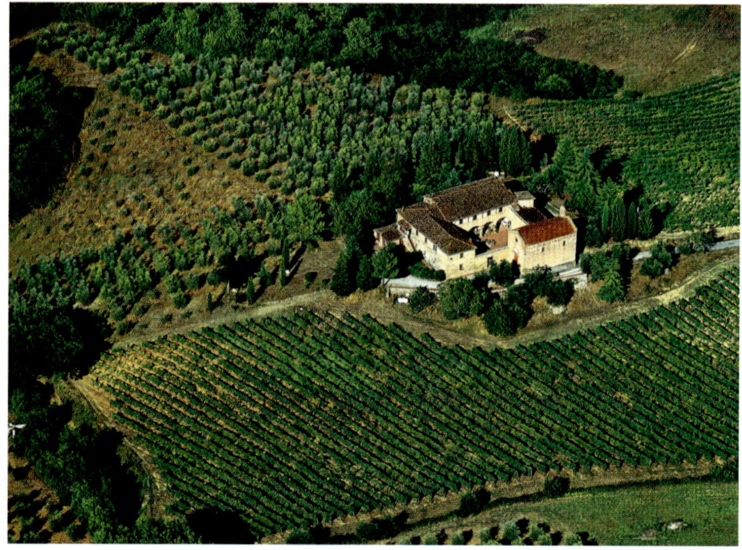

356 and 357

Pontigliano Monastery still retains its original look: renovations undertaken in the Renaissance and later restorations have not altered the balance between religion and nature, on which life in the monastery was based.

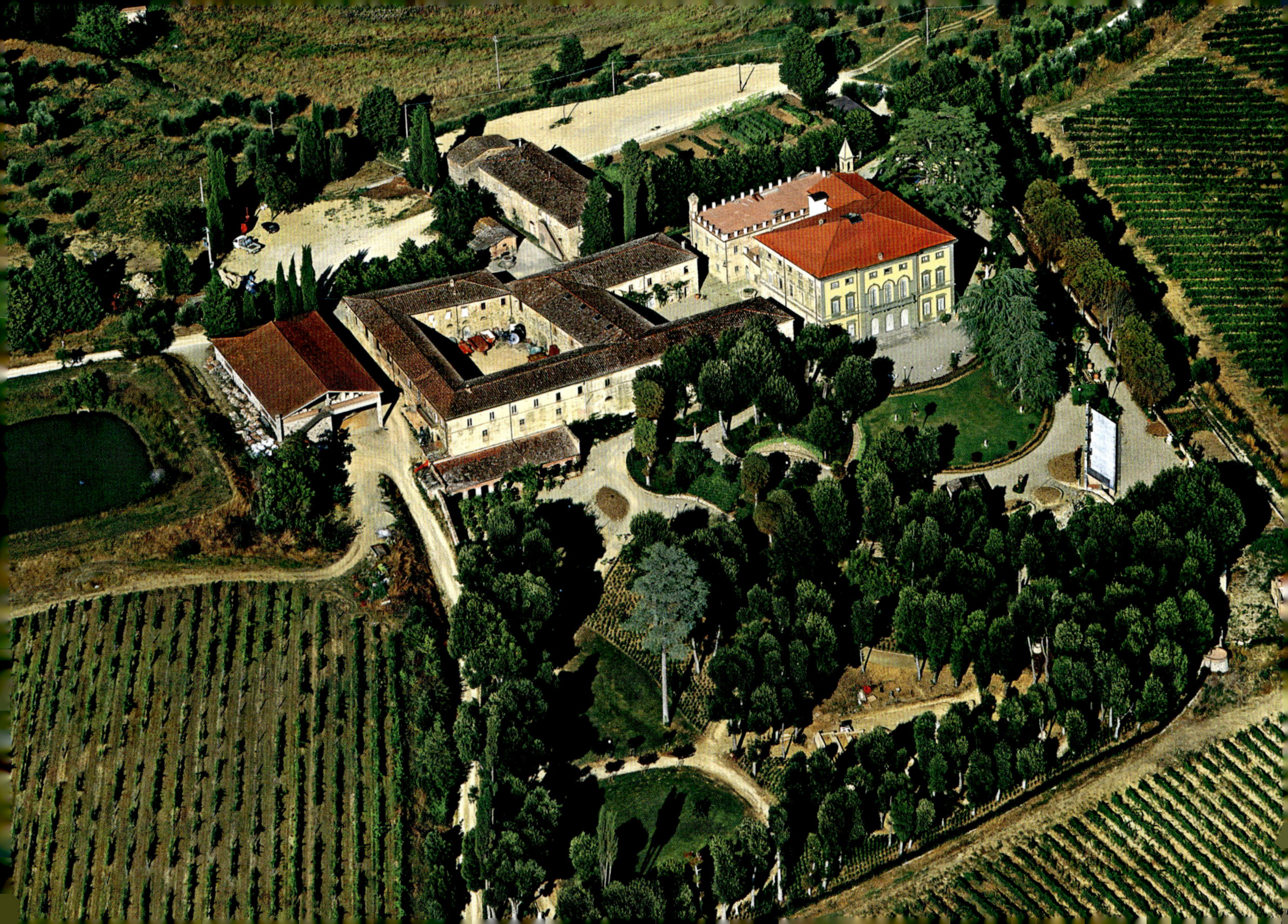

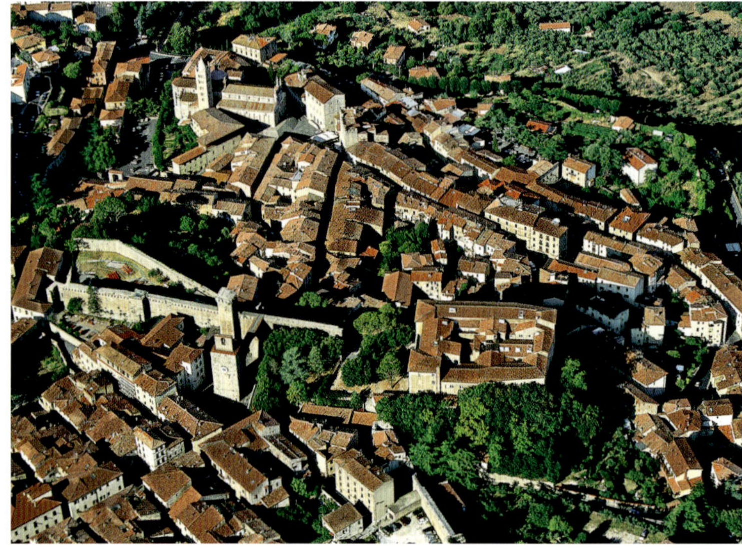

358

Massa Marittima is located in the Metalliferous Hills region, an area of environmental and historical significance.

359

Massa Marittima's San Cerbone Cathedral (right) has been embellished over the centuries by a great variety of building and decorative styles.

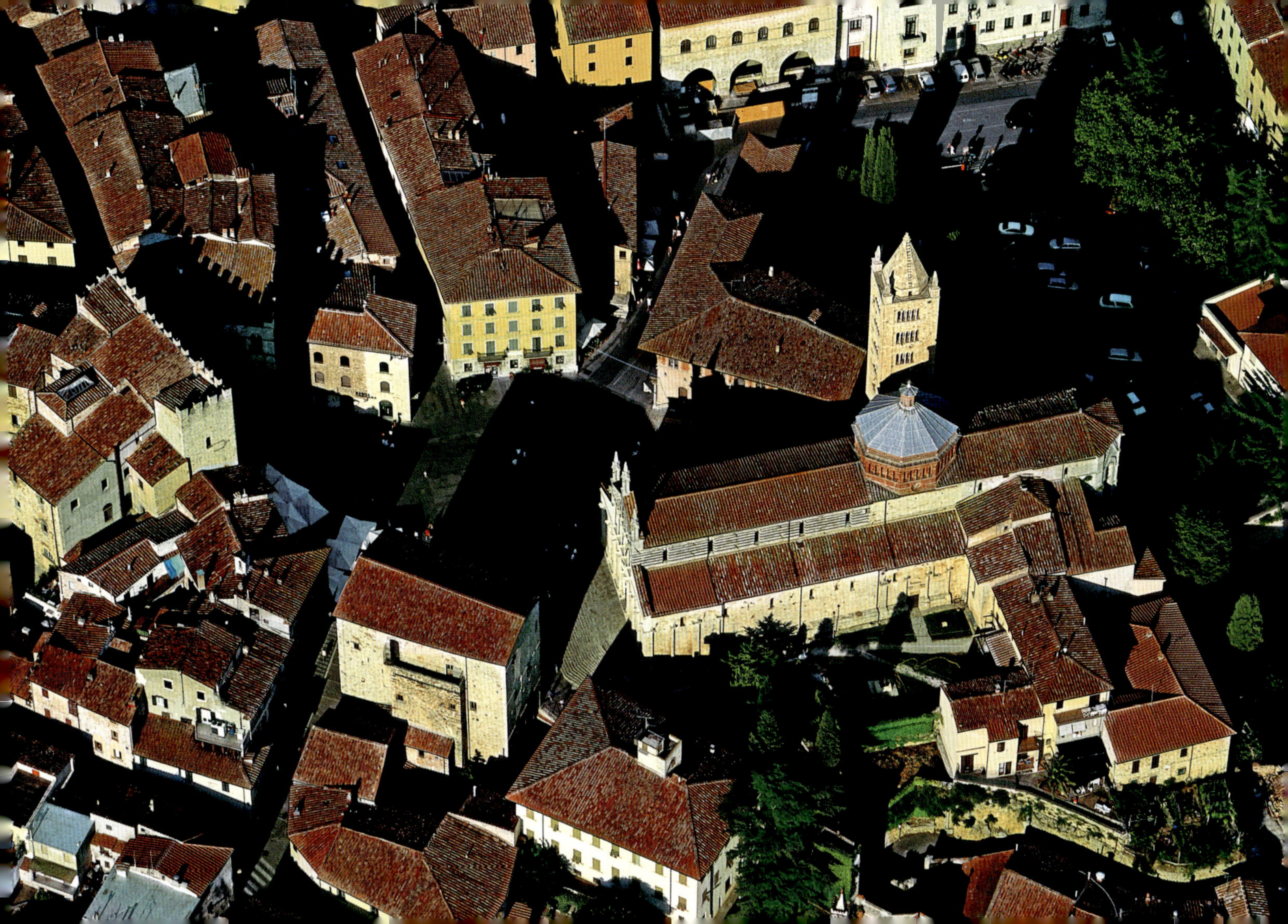

360

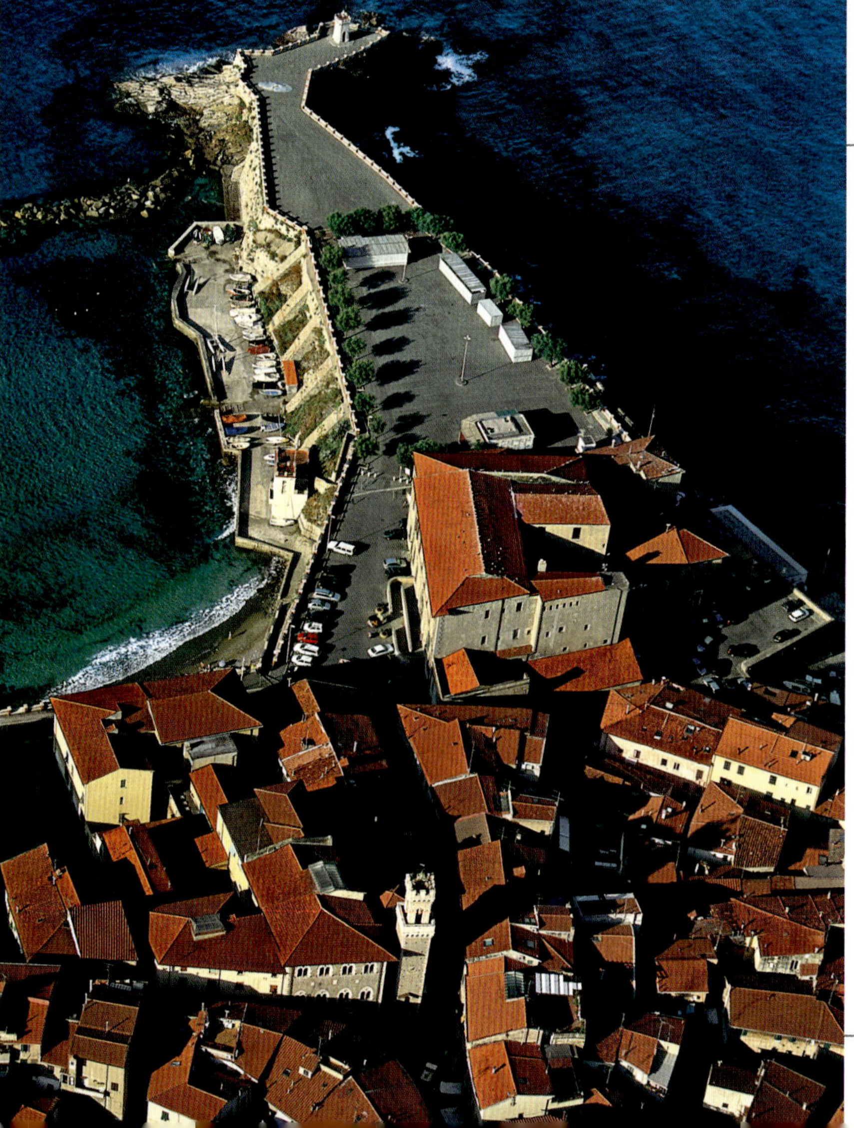

360
Piombino's Piazza Bovio has its origins in the ancient port of Falesia, which dates to the 5th century B. C.

361
Piombino's fortress, which has an 800-hundred-year history, reflects diverse phases of construction.

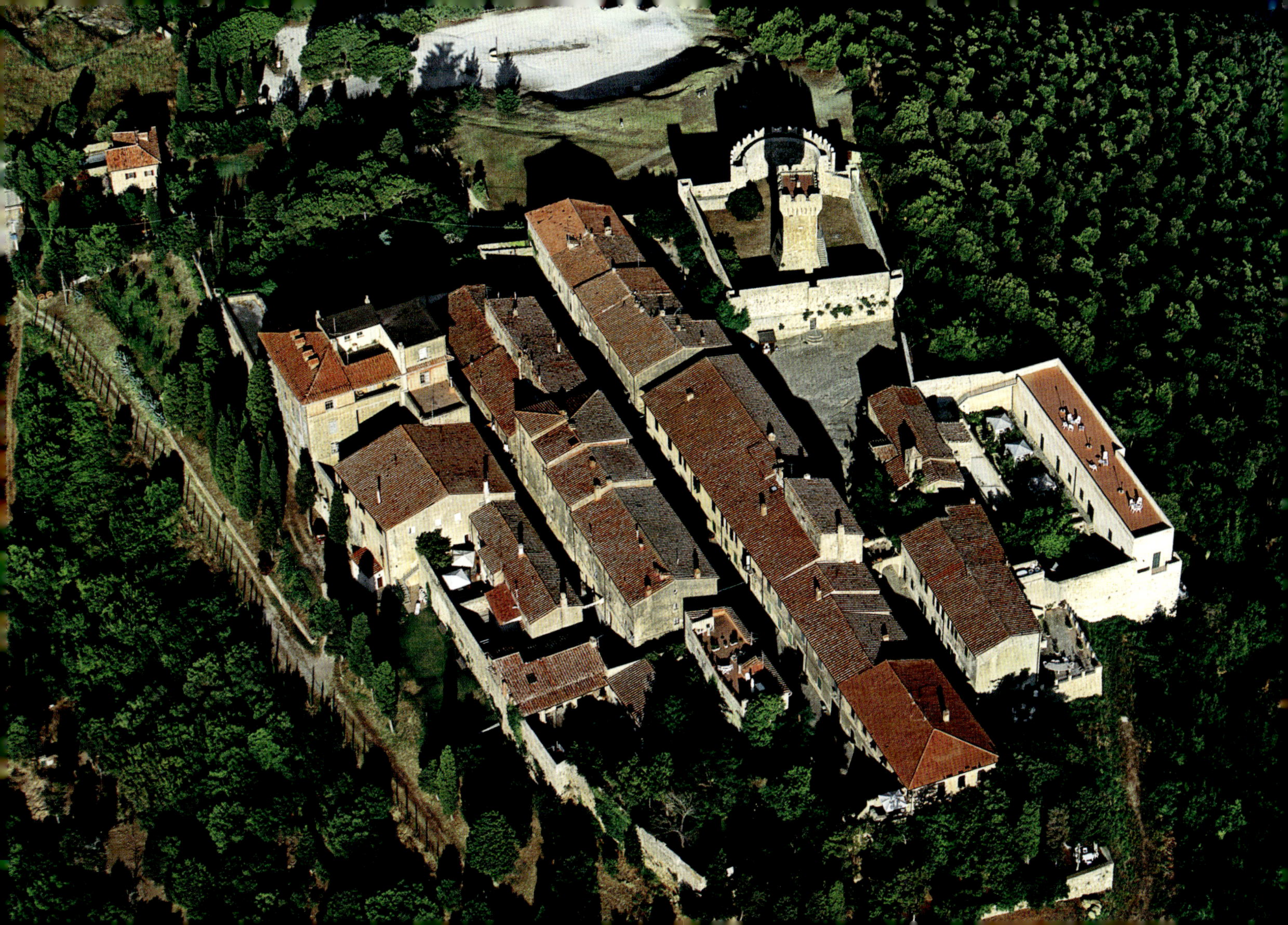

363
The location and shape of Portoferraio's shipyard protect it from the winds; it is among the Mediterranean's safest ports.

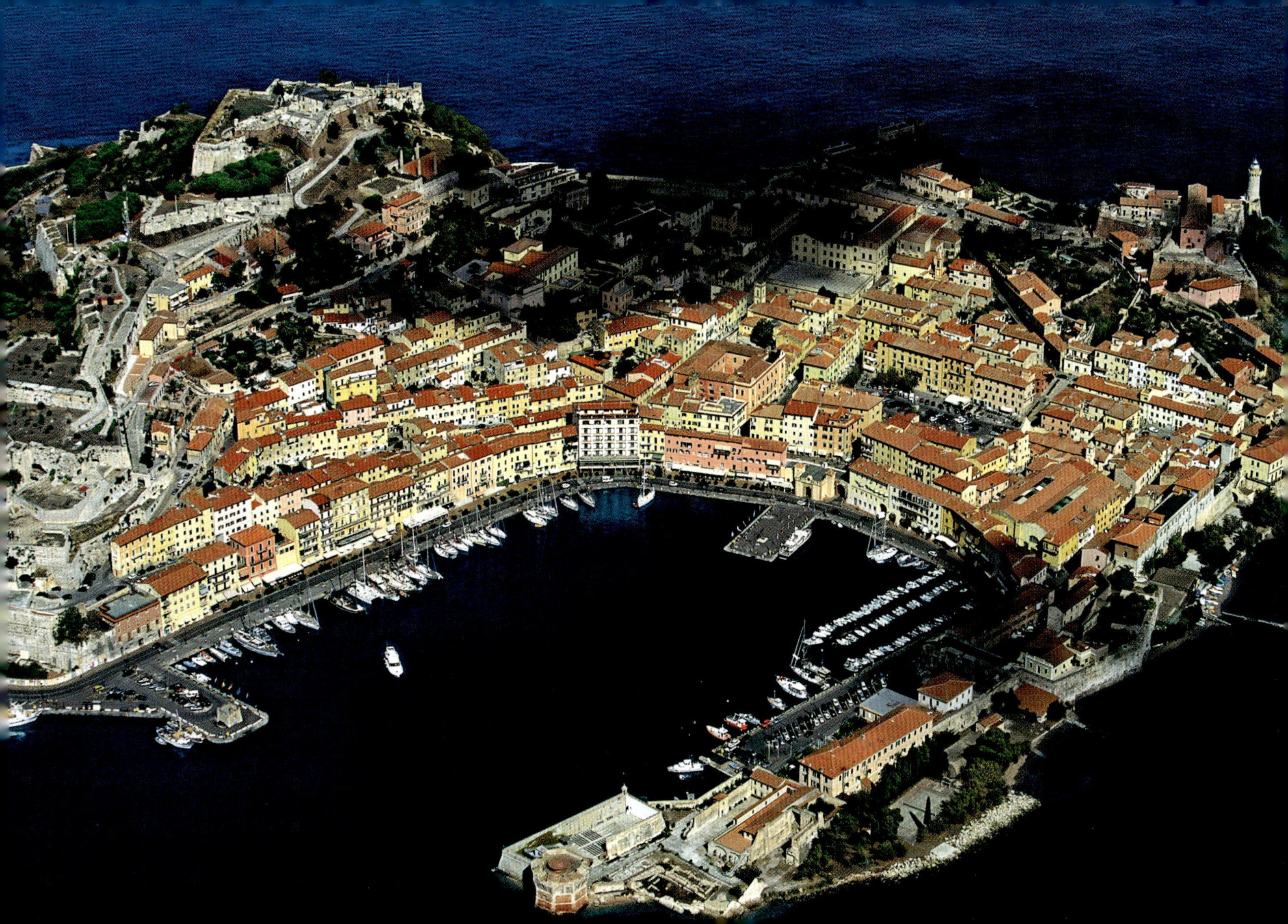

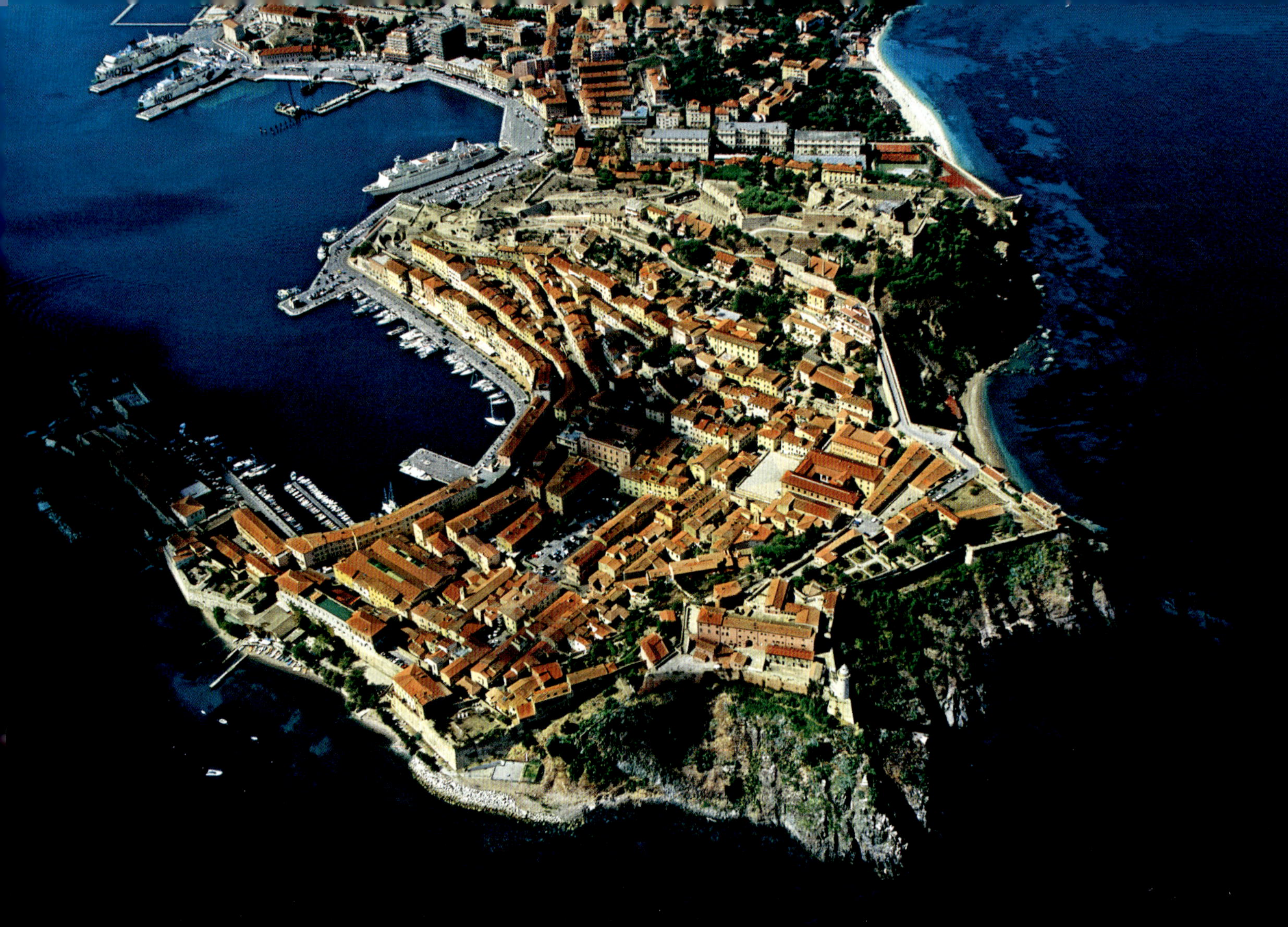

364

Portoferraio possesses some of Elba's most beautiful beaches and seabeds; they have a huge variety of animal and plant life.

365 left

Impressive bastions, still intact, stand at the corners of the wall that surrounds the center of Portoferraio.

365 right

In Roman times, Portoferraio was a principal crossroads for trade going to the West and to Africa.

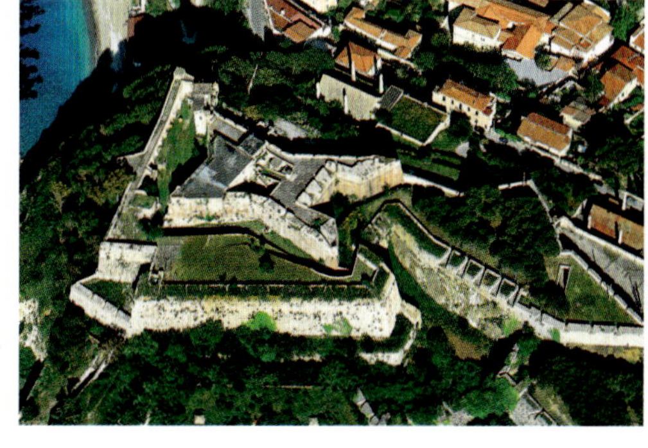

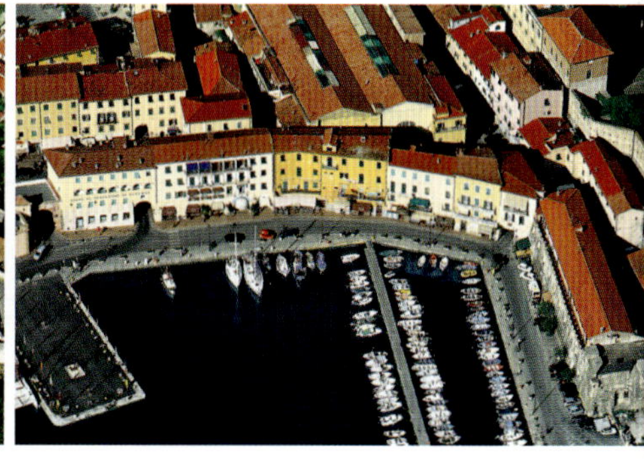

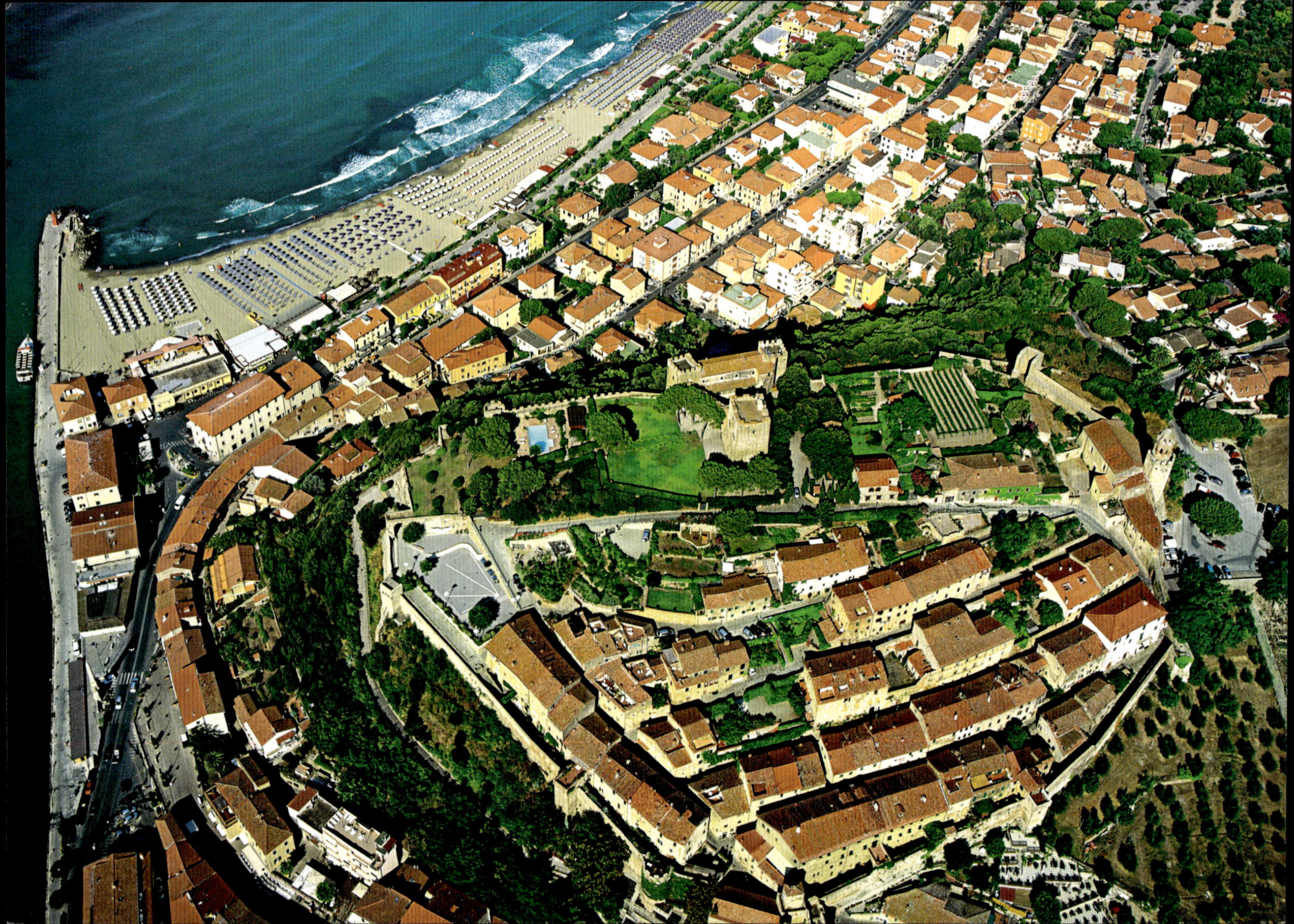

366

Castiglion della Pescaia, true pearl of the Maremma, is proud of its impressive castle of Roman origins, but it owes its fortune to its attractive medieval town plan and buildings..

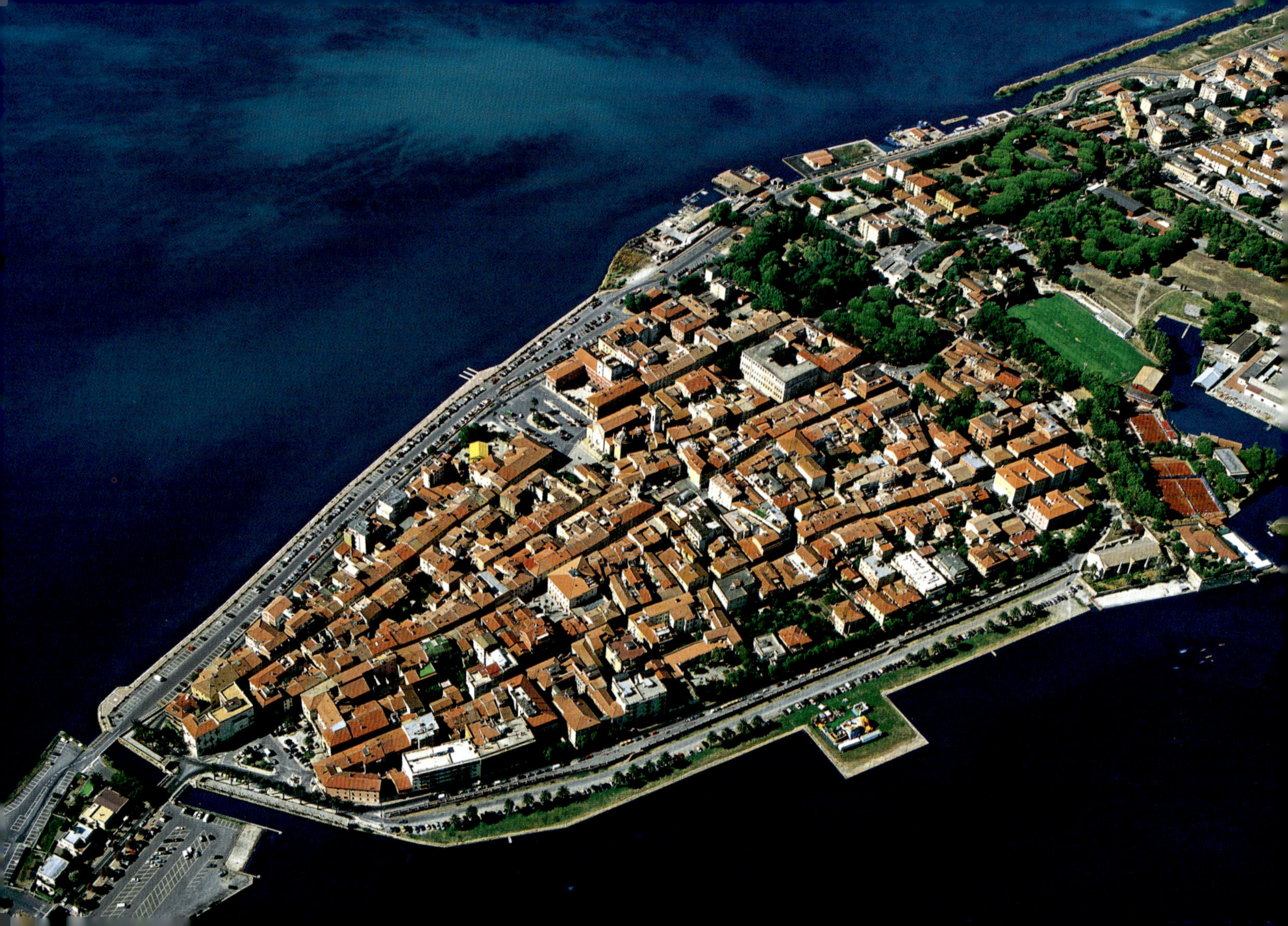

368 and 369

Over the years, Orbetello has become an important tourist center, known for its natural beauty, archeological attractions, and well-designed beach resorts.

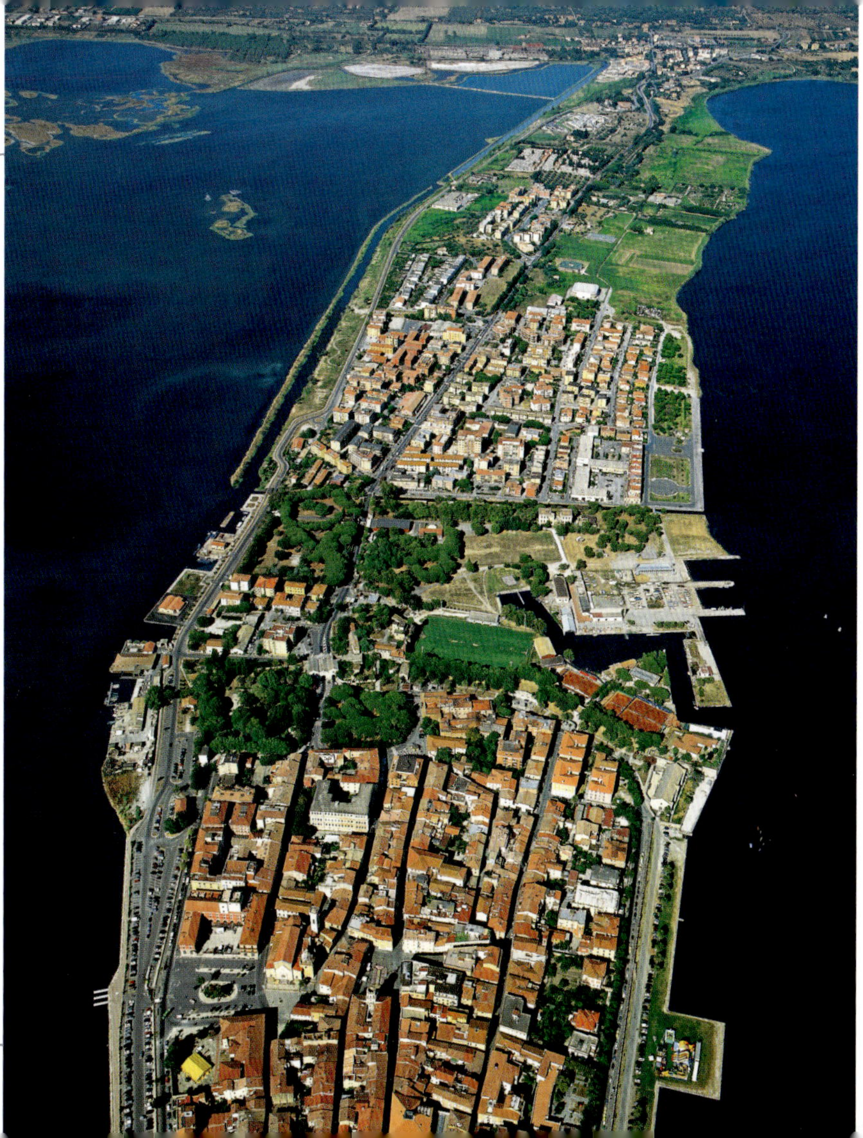

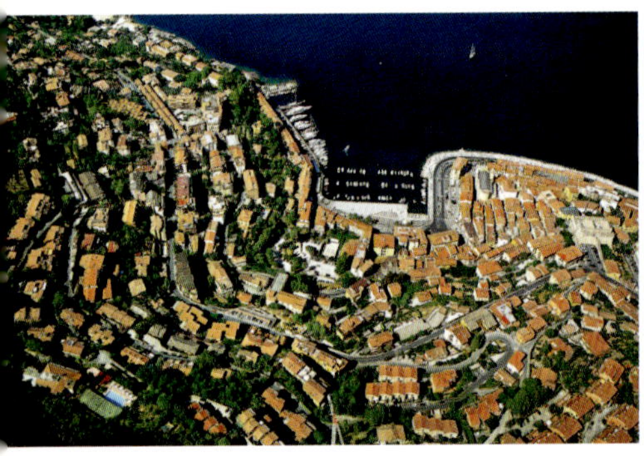

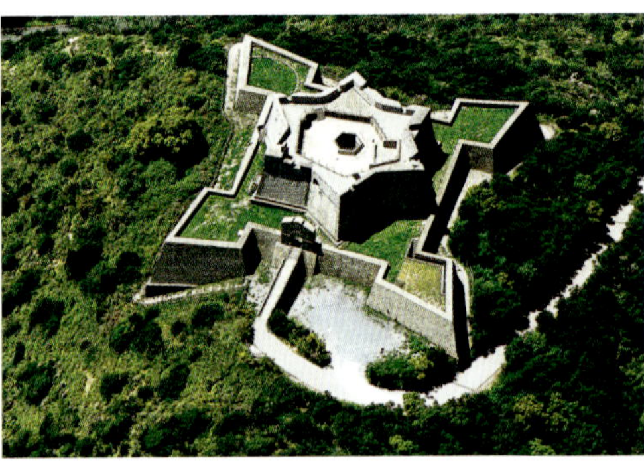

370 left

Enchanting sea resort, Porto Santo Stefano is without a doubt one of the main tourist attractions of Maremma and Tuscany.

370 right

Forte Stella (The Star Fort) rises above Porto Ercole; the citadel takes its name from its hexagonal inner courtyard.

371

Porto Ercole, whose golden beaches attract the rich and the famous, is known as an exclusive tourist spot.

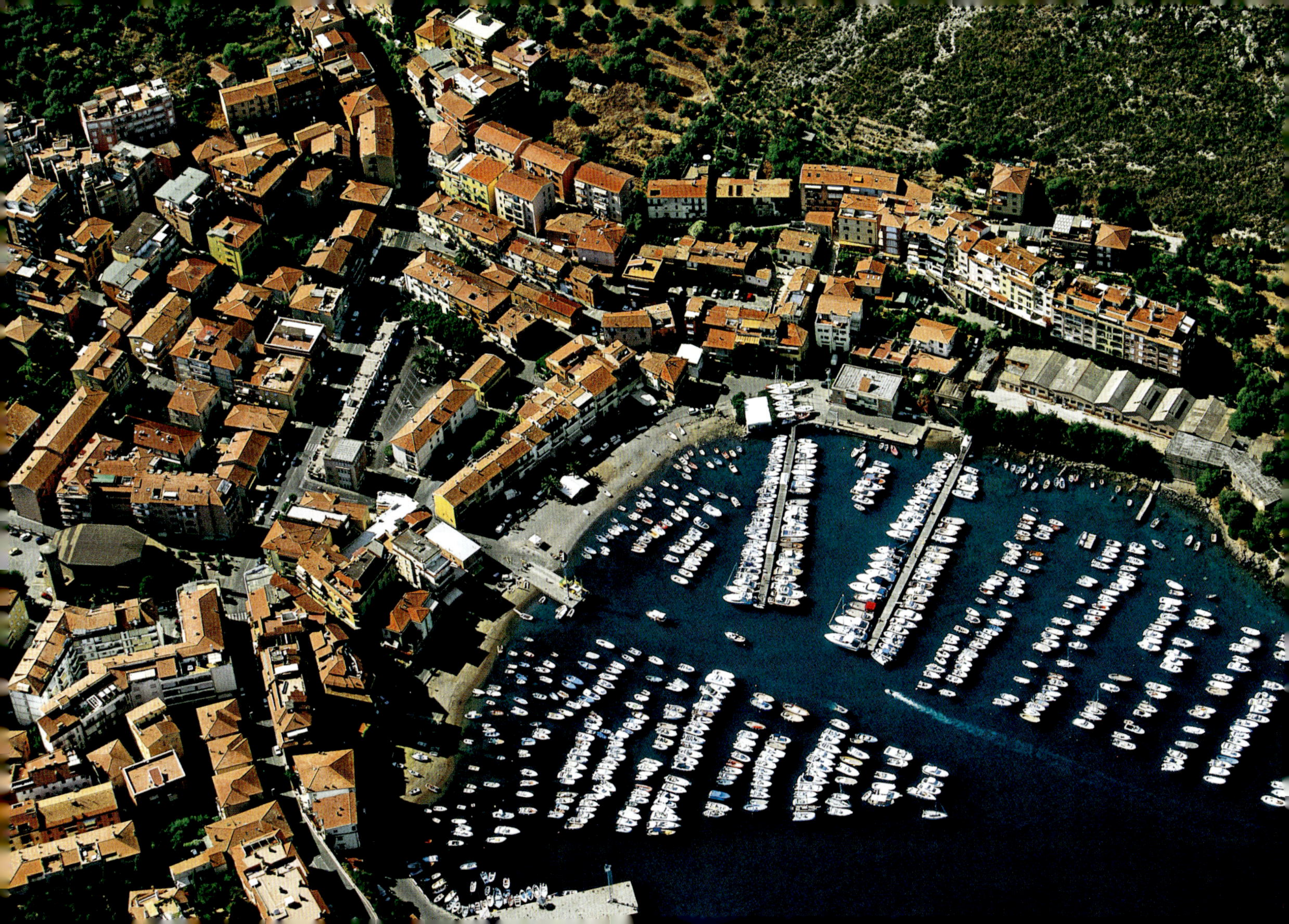

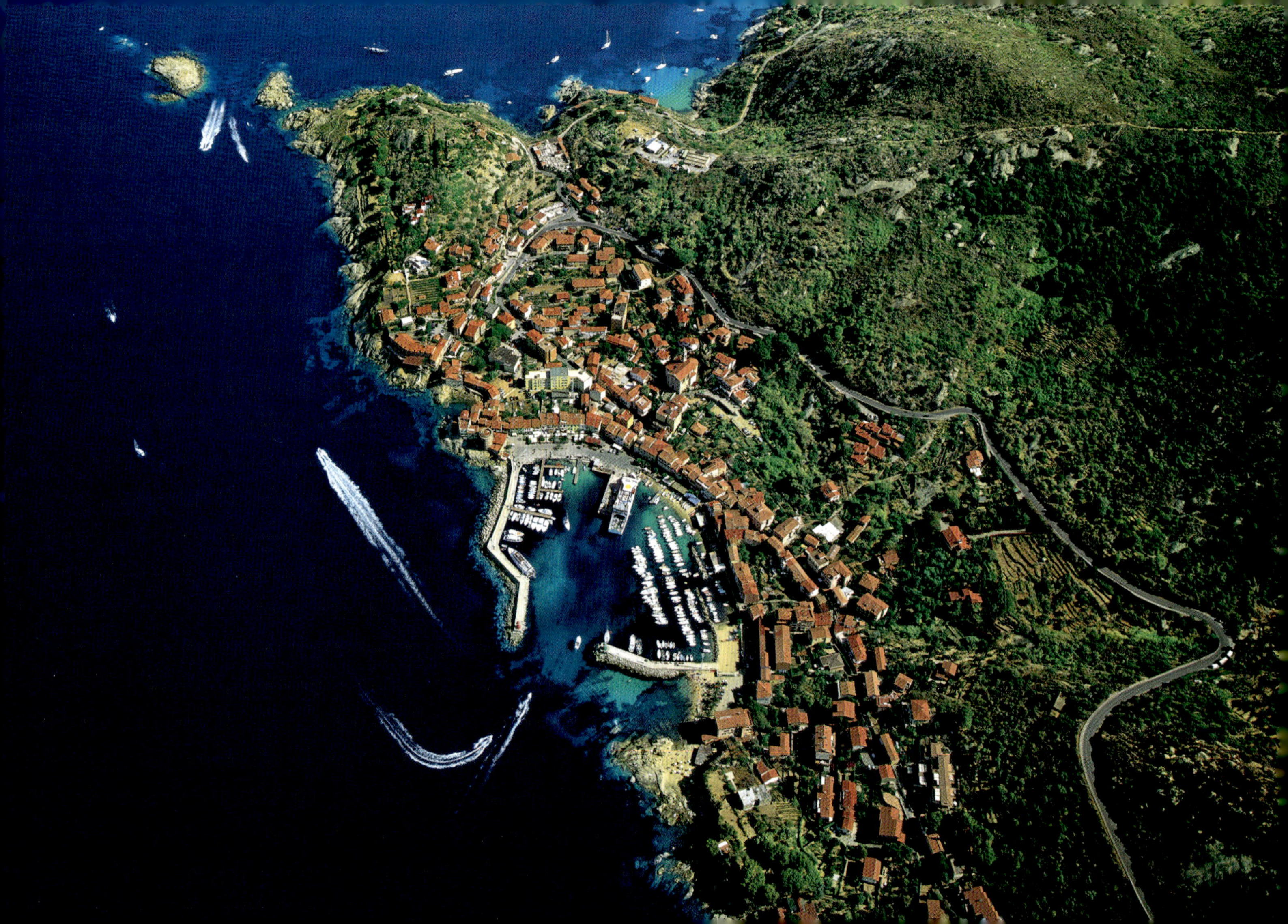

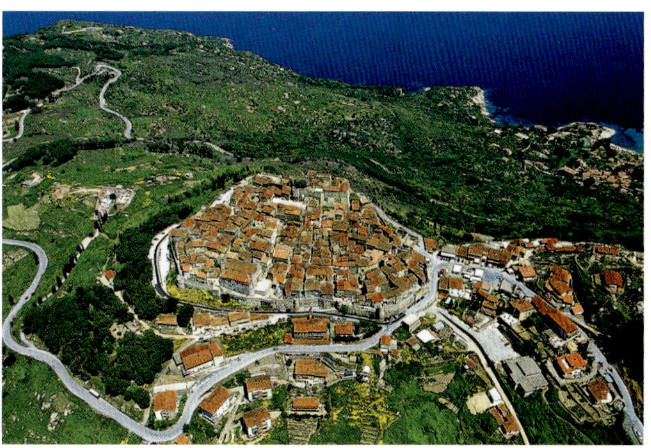

372
Giglio Fortress is a picturesque sea village surrounded by a lush pine forest.

373
Giglio Castle, on a rise of 1475 ft (450 m), and surrounded by an impressive wall, dominates the island.

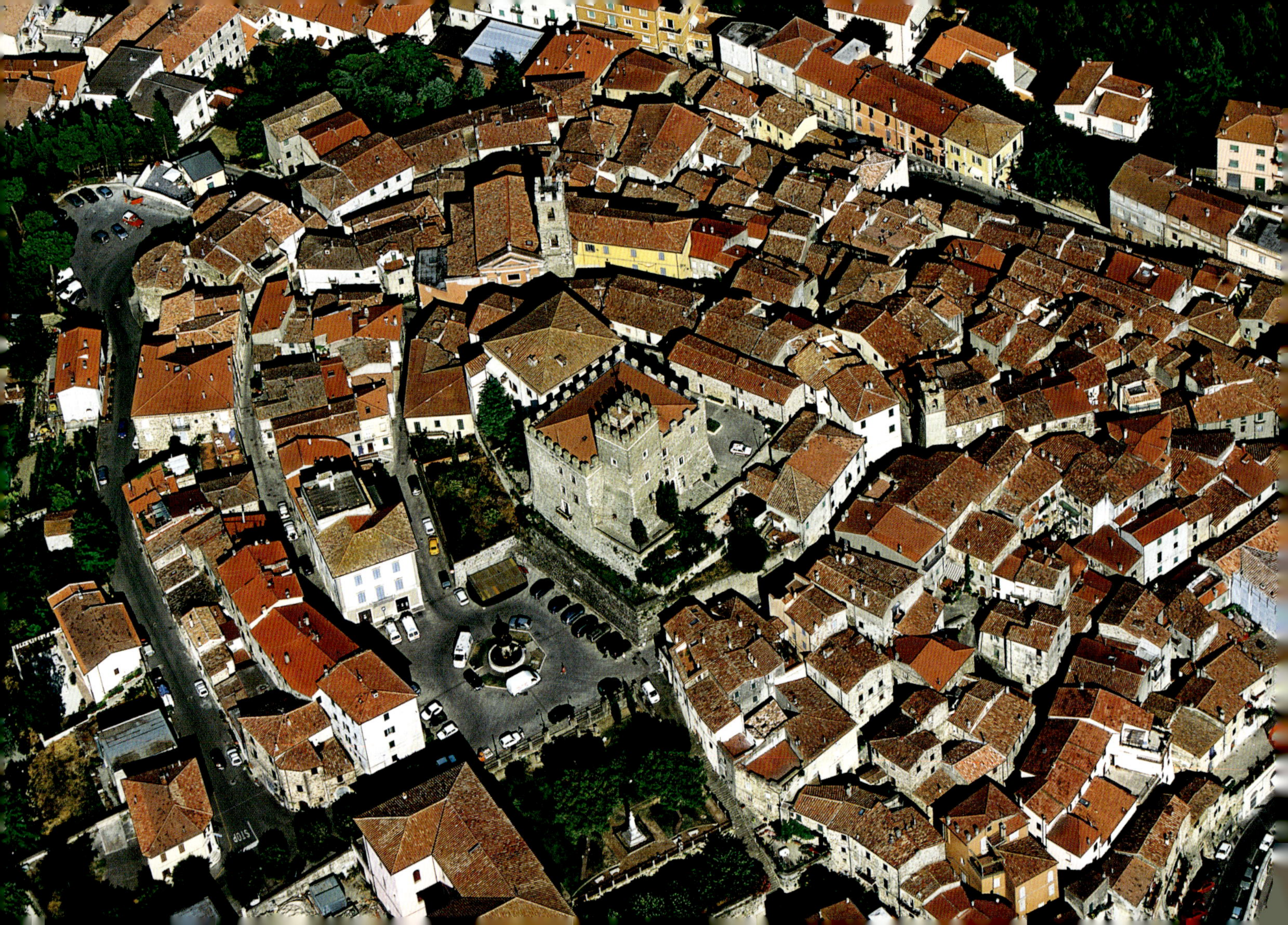

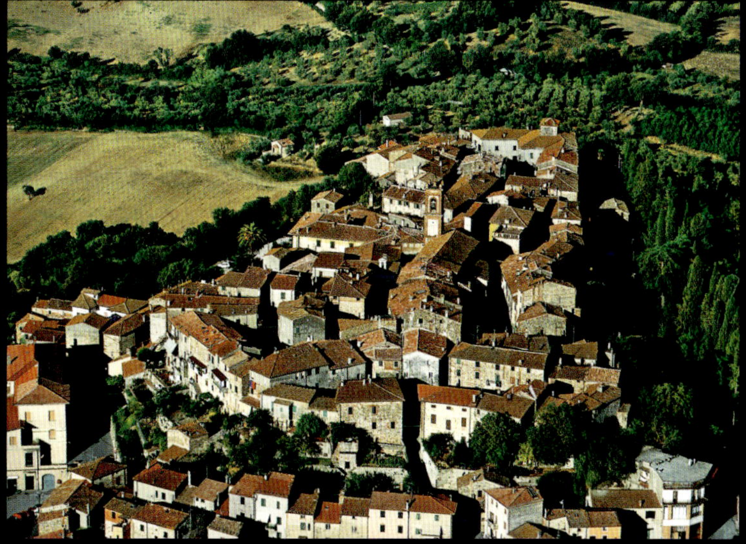

374
Manciano Fortress (center), built by the Aldobrandeschi in the 1200s, is now the seat of the city's municipal authorities.

375
Civitella Marittima, one of the Ardengheschi's oldest estates, is located in forest area crossed by numerous crystalline waterways.

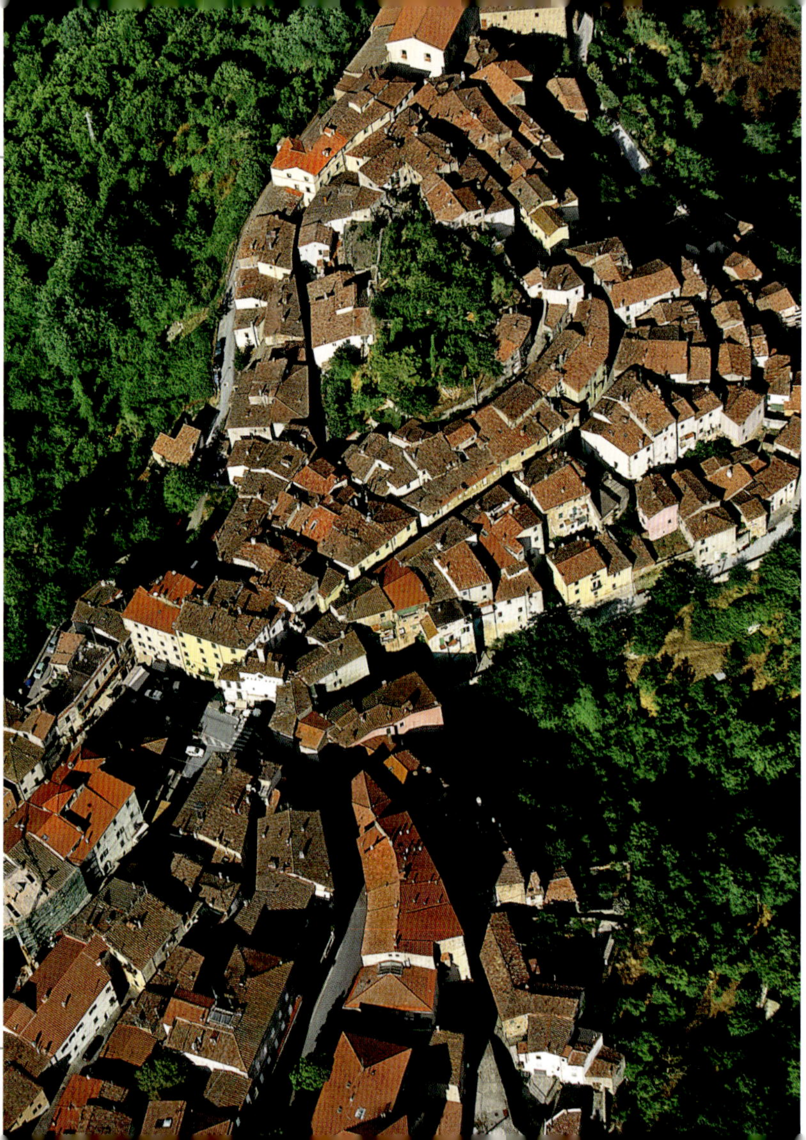

376
Scansano's privileged position, halfway between the coast and Mt. Amiata, has favored human settlements from prehistoric times: the first evidence of habitation dates to the Bronze Age.

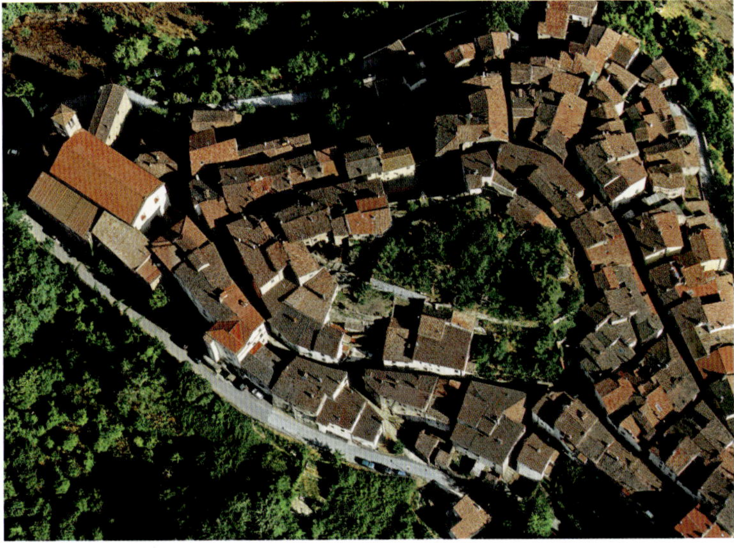

377

In this suggestive image, the garden that occupies one of Scansano's central piazzas seems, from above, to be a green pupil in the middle of a huge eye, suggested by the mosaics of red tiled roofs.

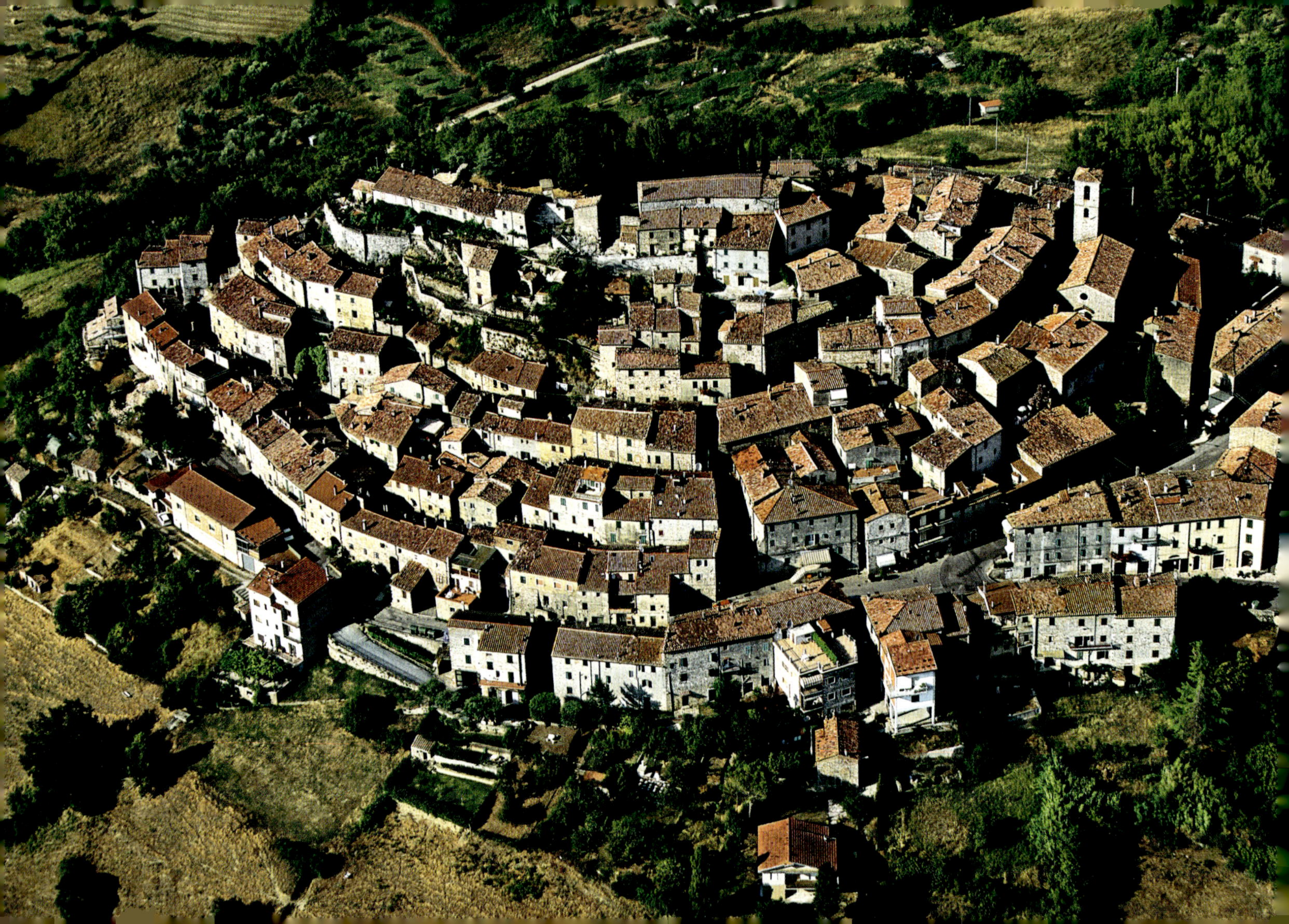

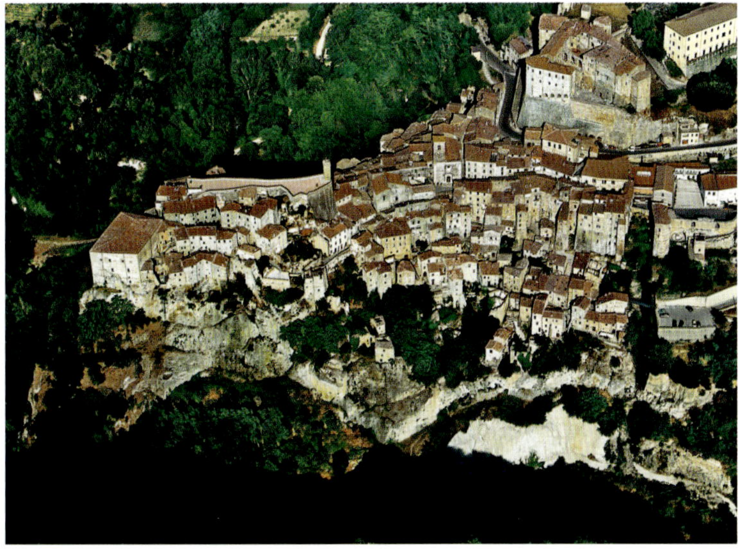

378
Semproniano, gently cradled on the hills of the High Maremma, reveals its semicircular medieval form.

379
Sorano, with its ancient fortifications, arises on the top of a hill of tufo at the extreme southern part of Tuscany, in the area known as "the Etrurian Tufo Zone."

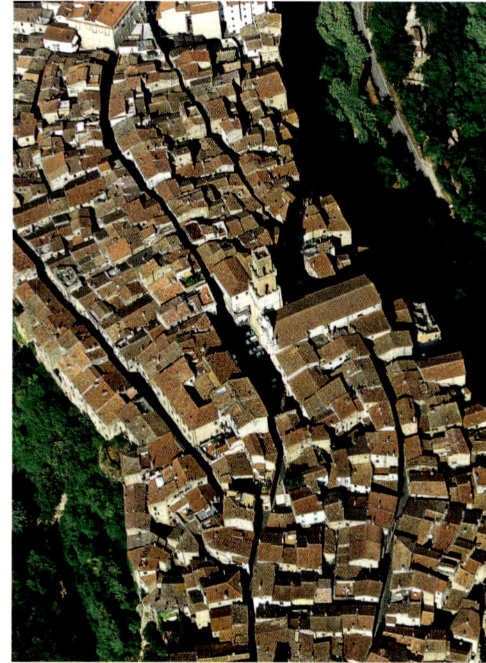

380 and 381

Pitigliano is located on a spur of tufo; its homes still maintain the rock's characteristic color.

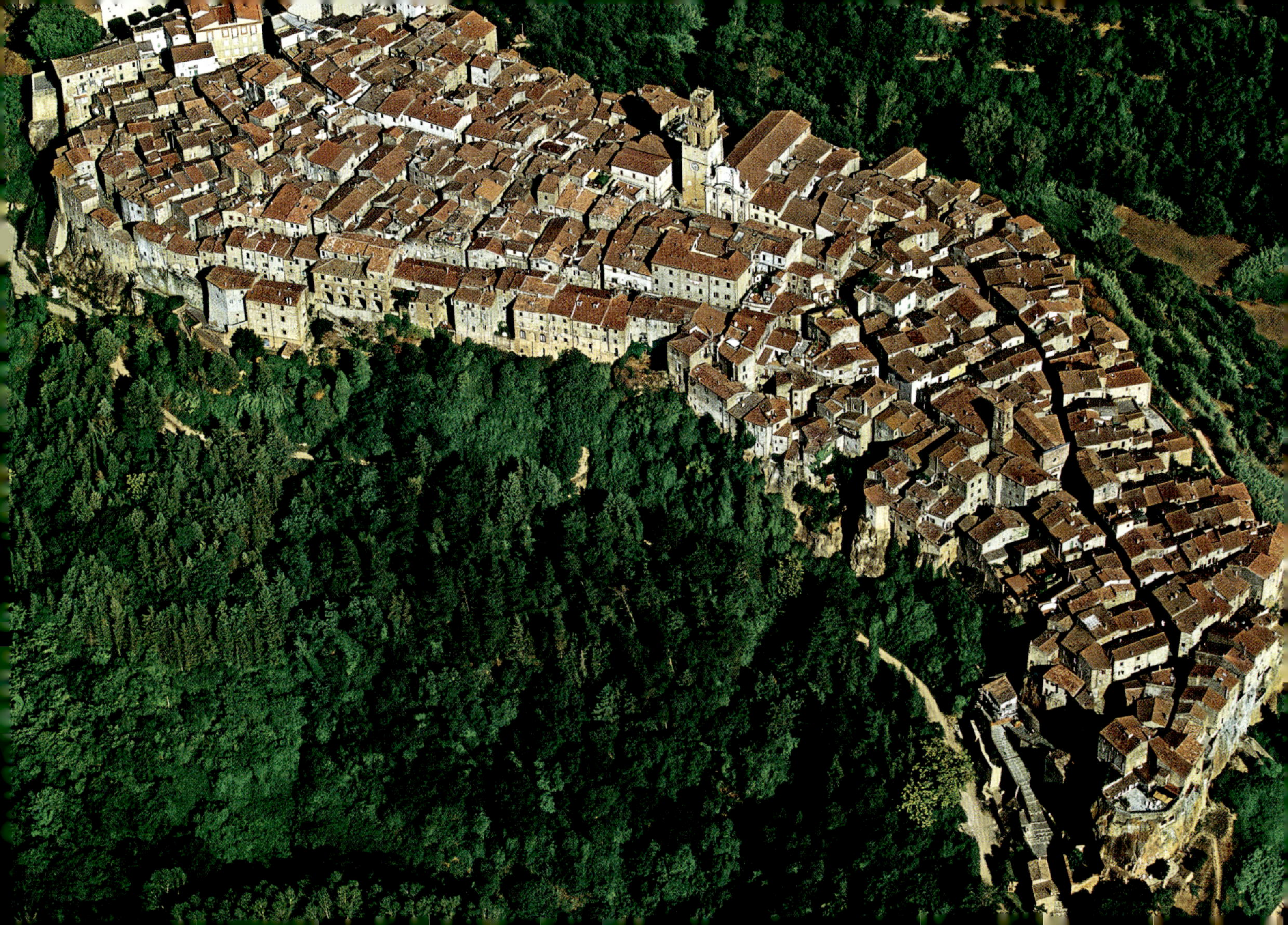

383

Extending over Mt. Amiata's western ridge, Ponticello is an evocative medieval village surrounded by chestnut forests. It has a spectacular view of the Maremma and the Orcia and Ombrone valleys.

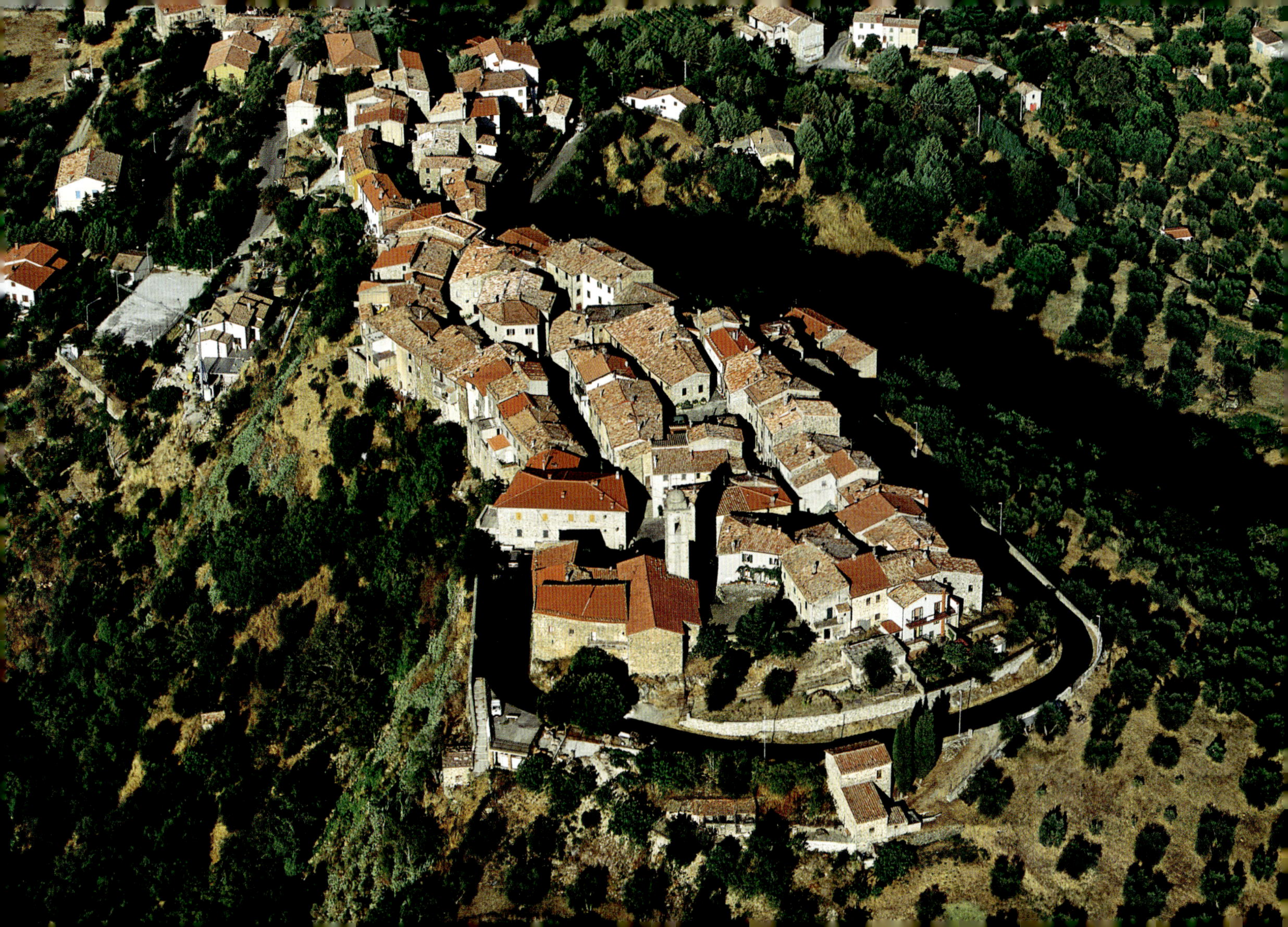

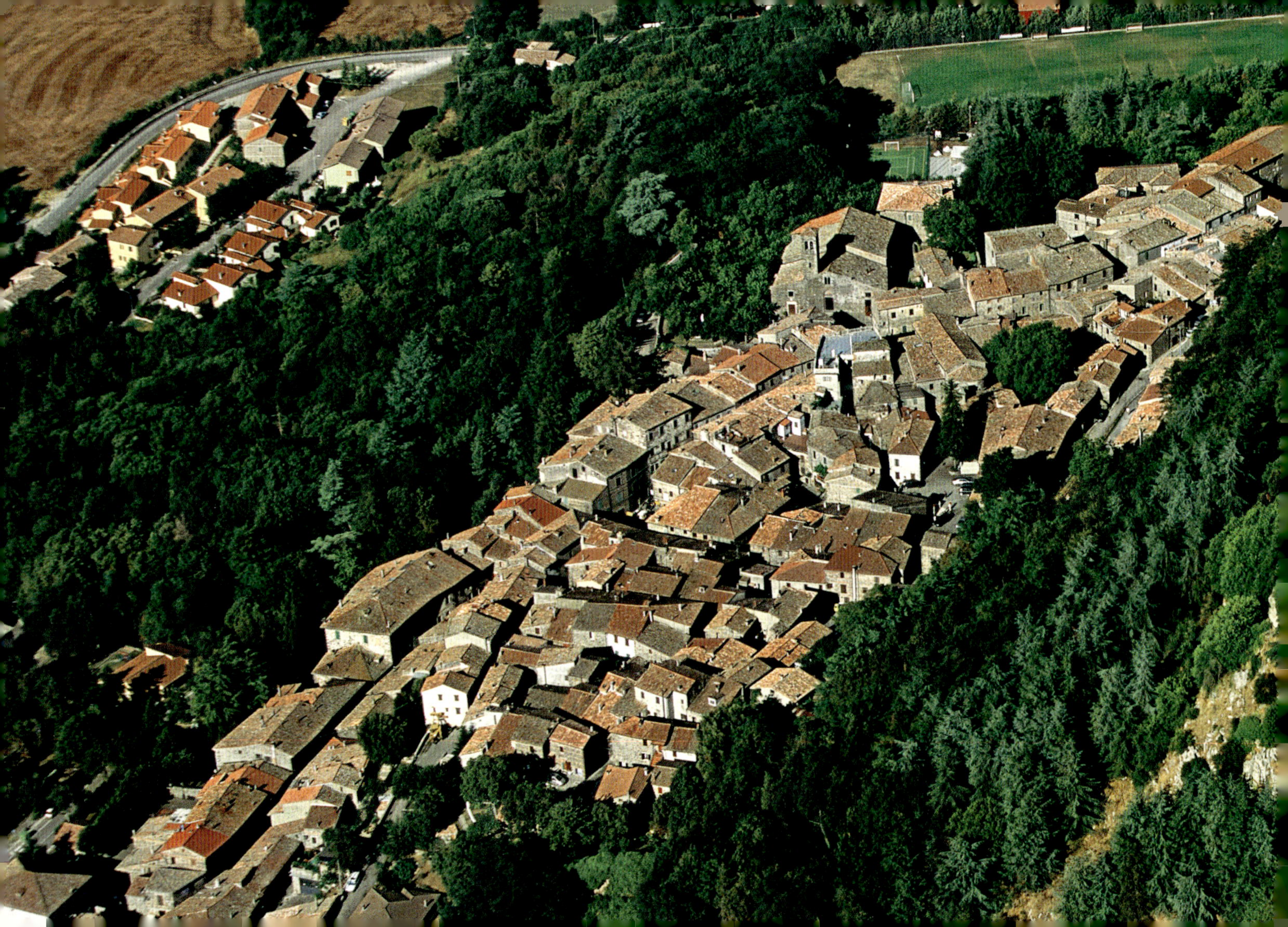

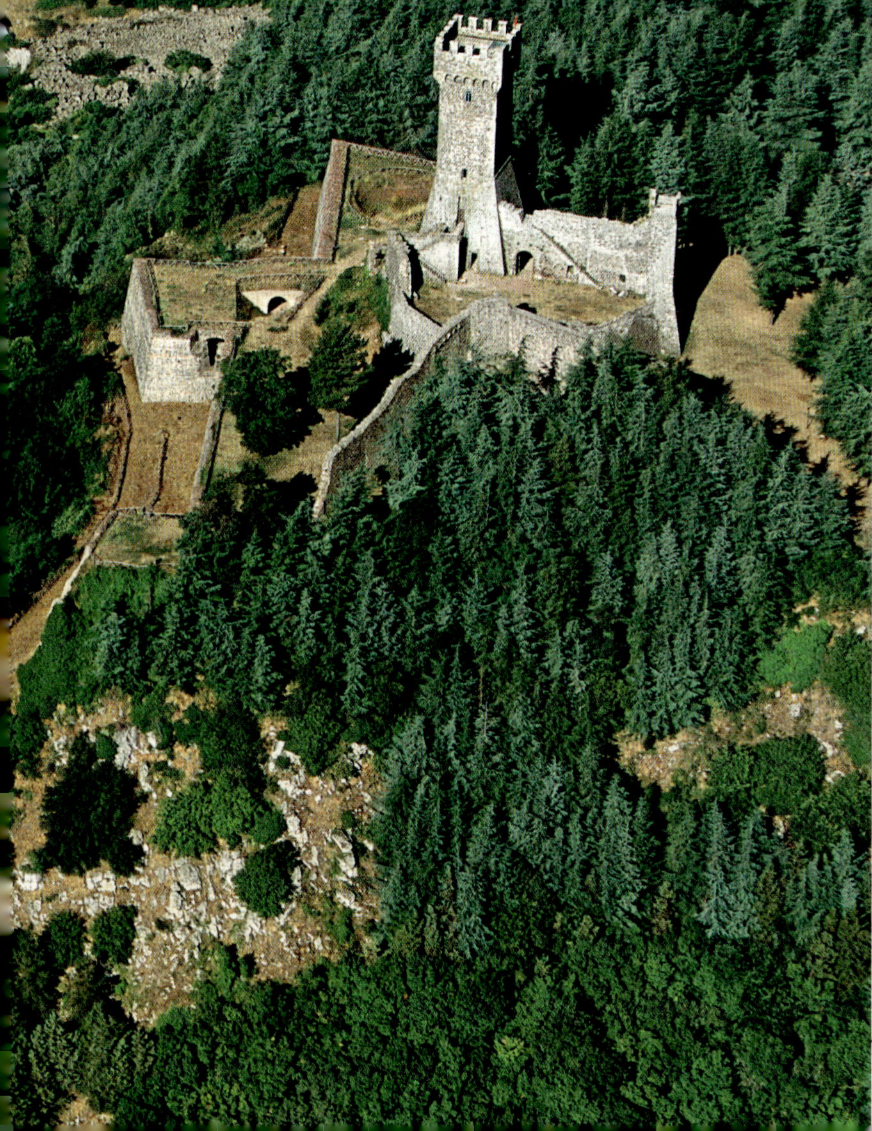

384-385
Given its strategic location, Radicofani fortress (to the right), with its characteristic triangular form, was fought for over the centuries.

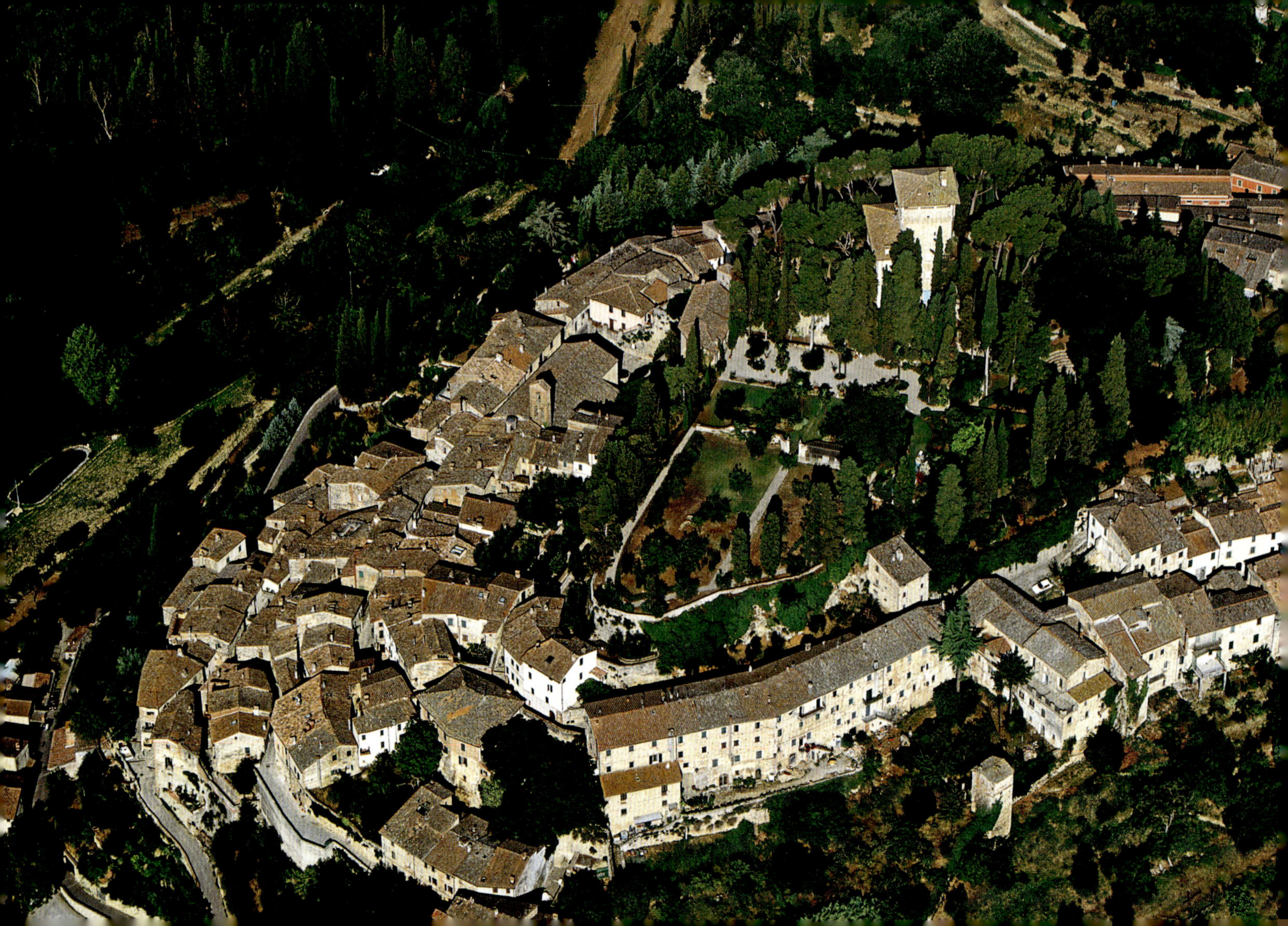

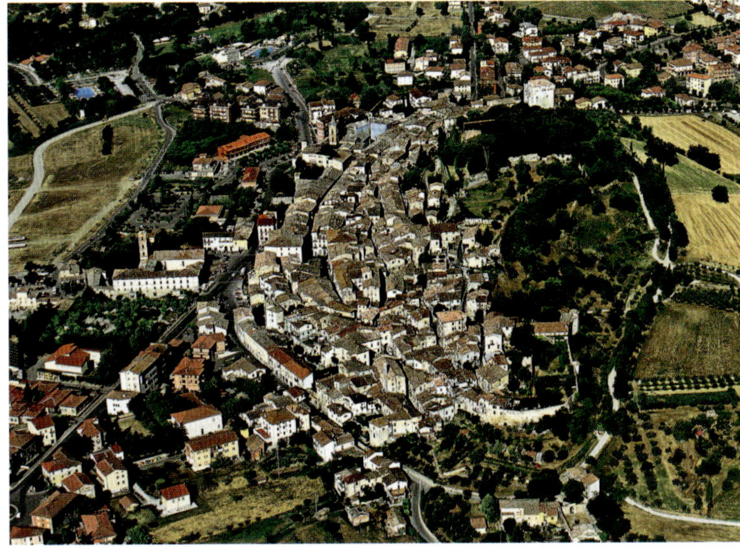

386

With the 13th-century Cetona castle at its center, the medieval village unwinds, its houses built in a spiral around the steep hill.

387

Sarteano occupies a magnificent position amid the gentle Sienese hills, over the Val di Chiana.

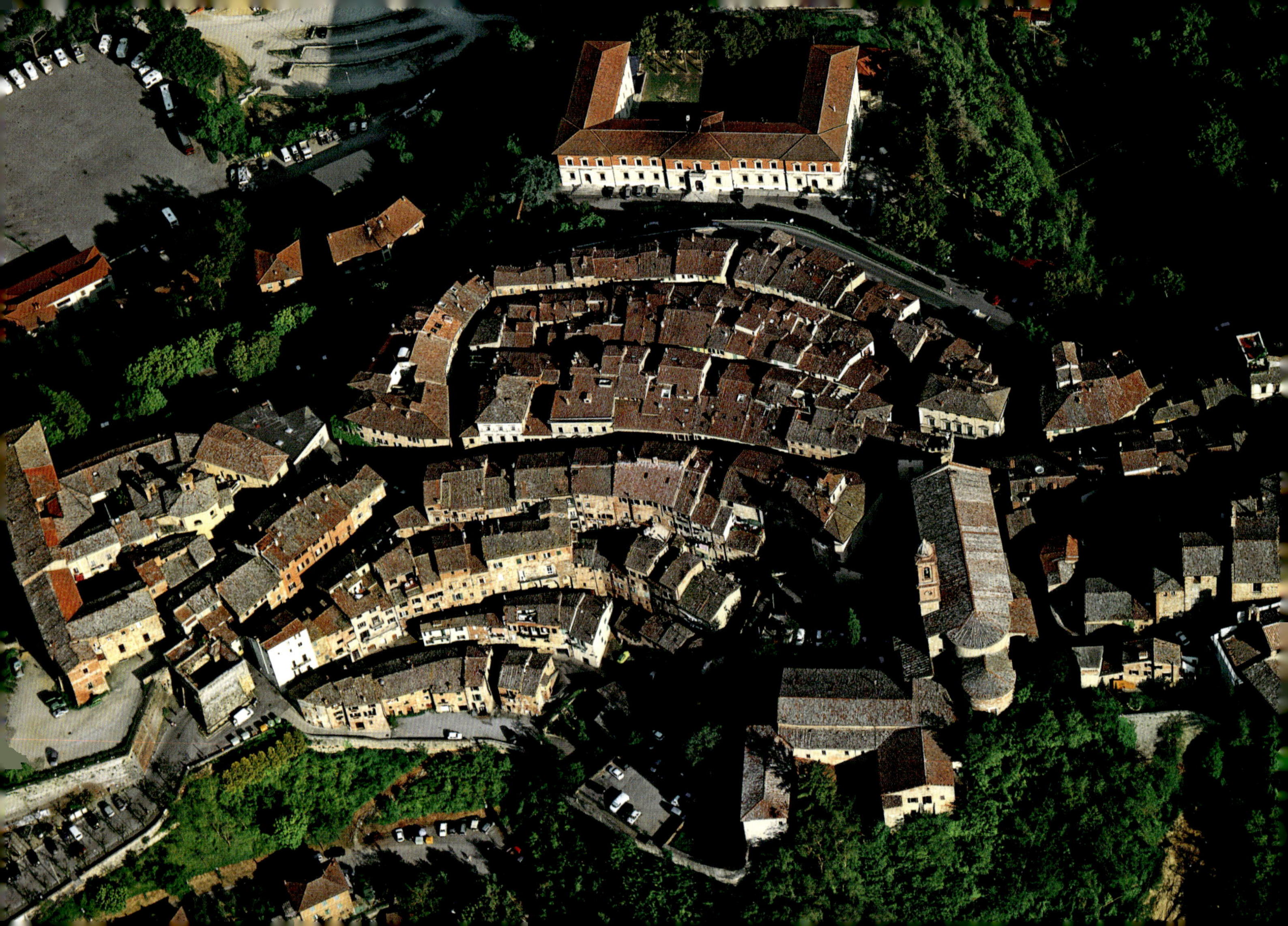

388
Montepulciano, situated on the ridge between Val di Chiana and Val d'Orcia, received its fortified wall in the 16th century. It was designed by Antonio da Sangallo at the request of Duke Cosimo I de' Medici.

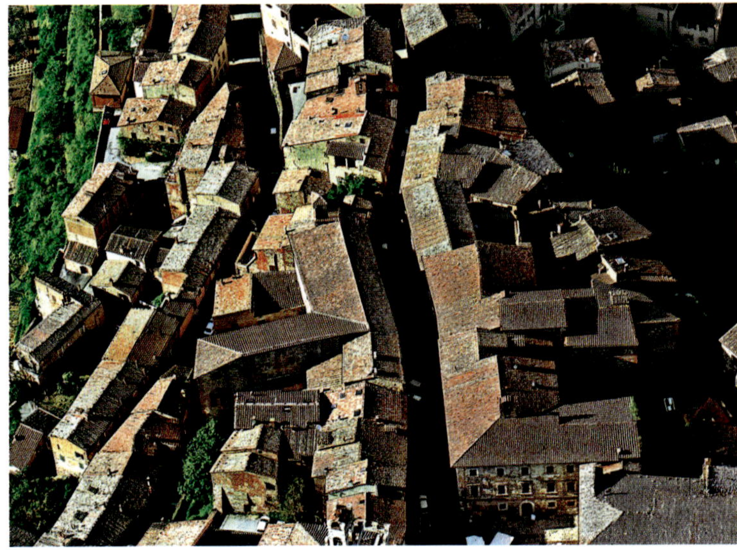

390 and 391

Montepulciano is known not only for its Renaissance buildings and elegant churches but also for one of Tuscany's world-renowned red wines: Vino Nobile.

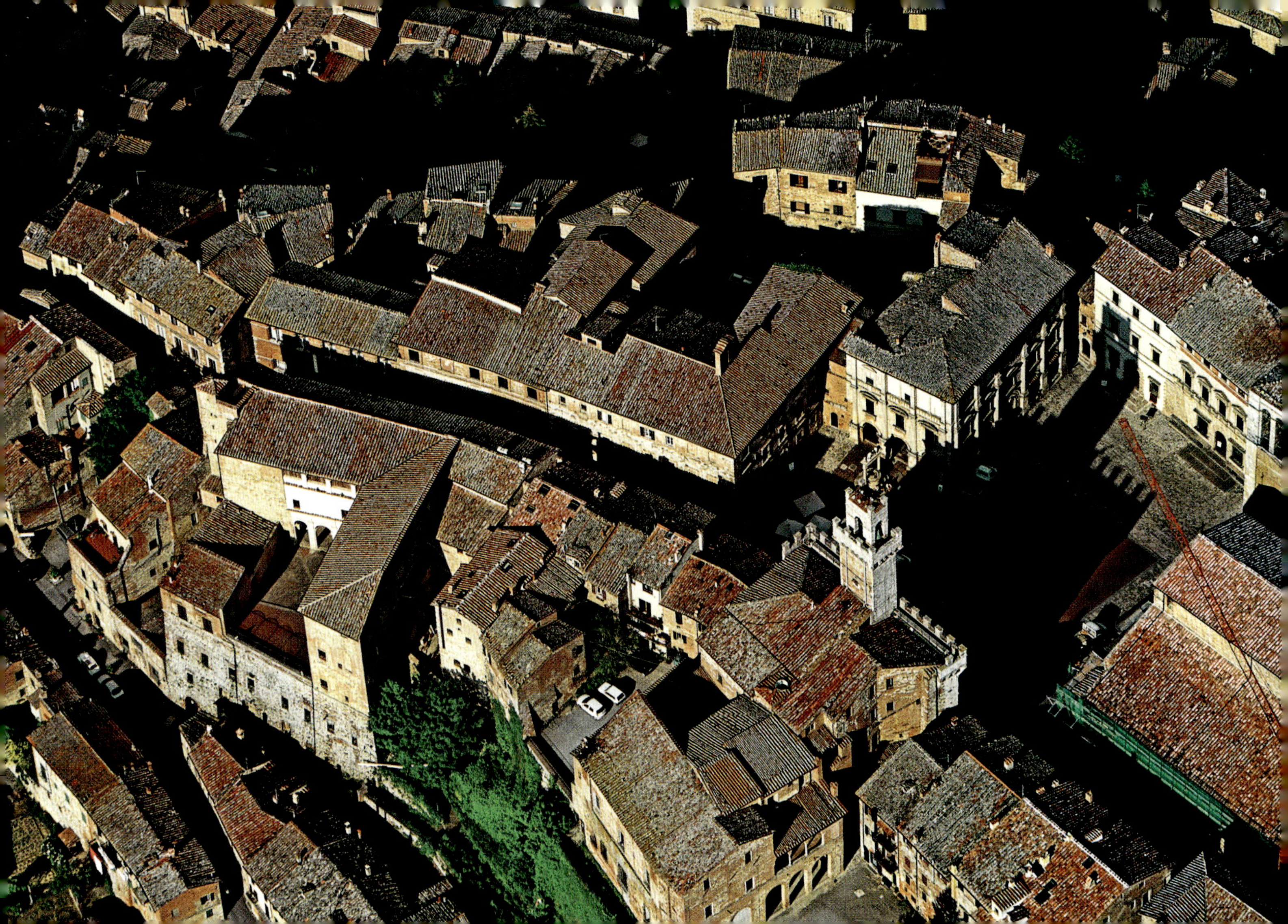

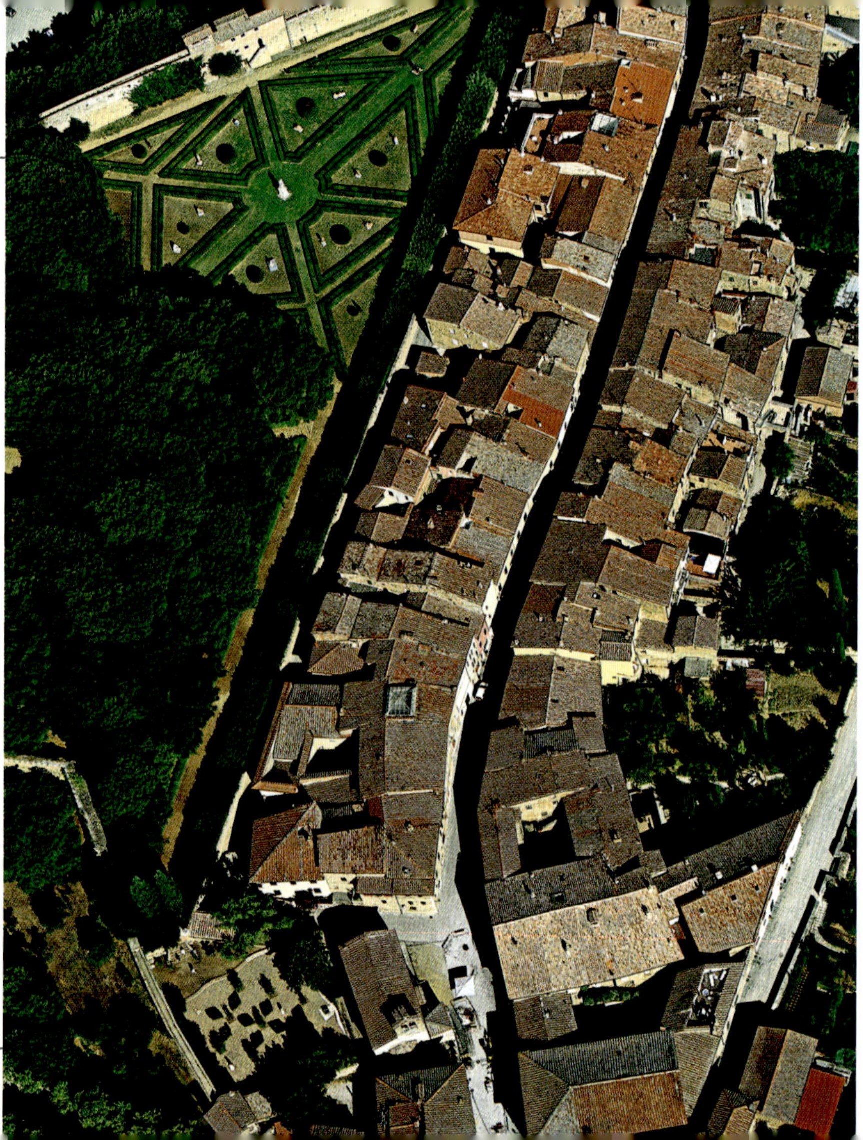

392

San Quirico's Orti Leoni (Leoni Gardens), in the Val d'Orcia, were created around 1580 by the architect Diomede Leoni. They adjoin the city's oldest part.

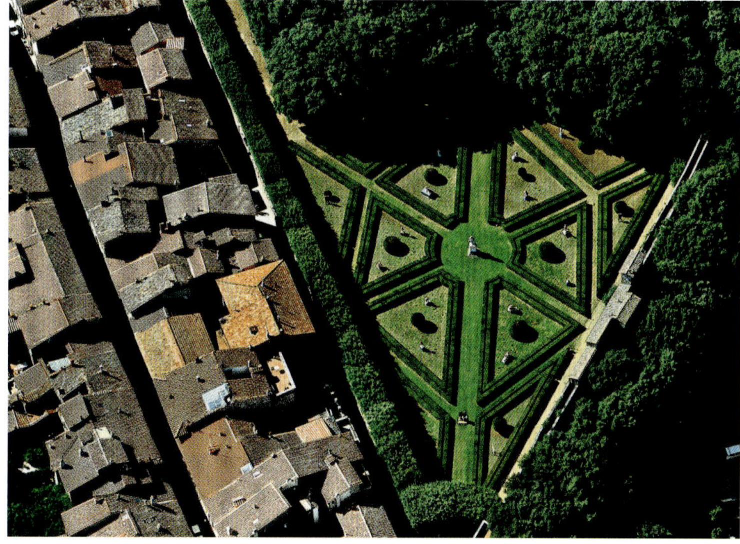

393
This perfectly geometrical box flowerbed, characterizes San Quirico's immense Leoni Gardens, which are surrounded by a dense forest of ancient oaks.

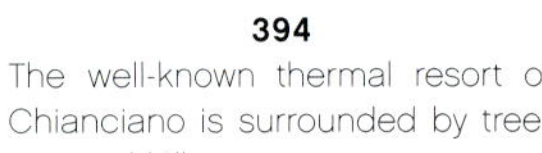

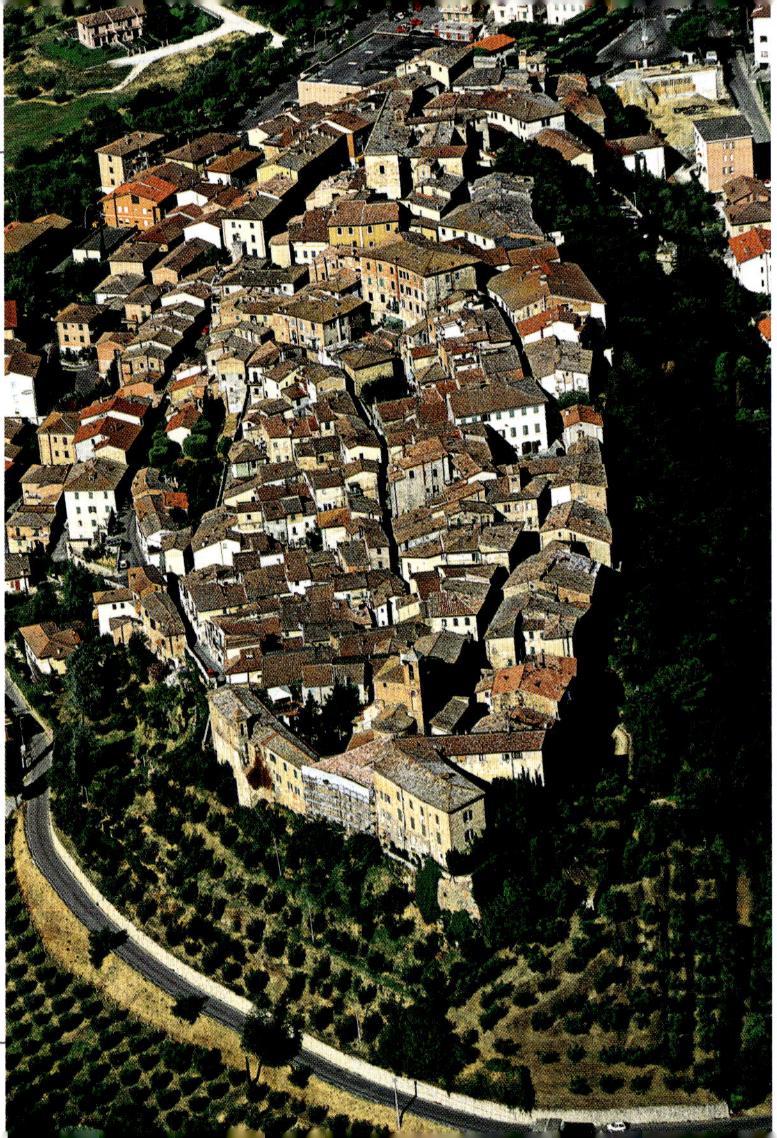

394

The well-known thermal resort of Chianciano is surrounded by tree-covered hills.

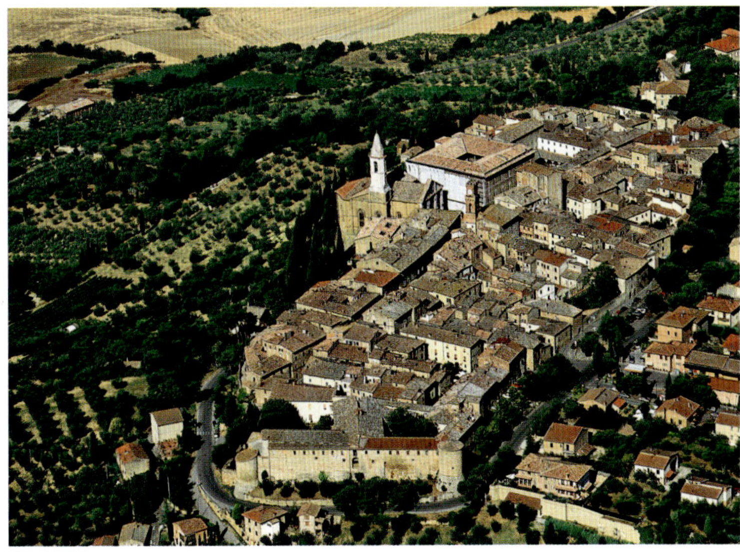

395
Pienza is situated in the beautiful Val d'Orcia. It was the birthplace of Pope Pius II, who completely transformed it to create a perfect renaissance city.

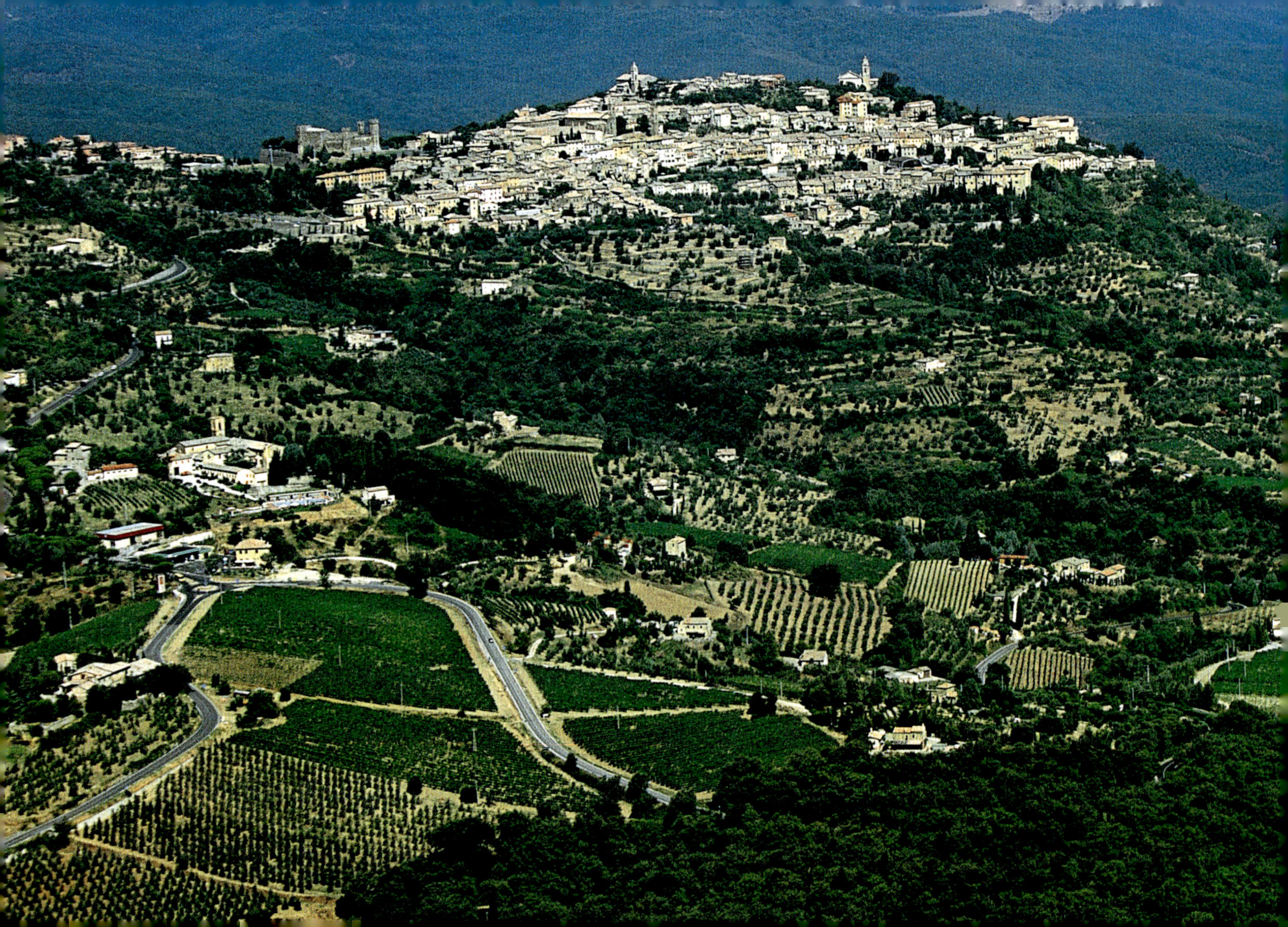

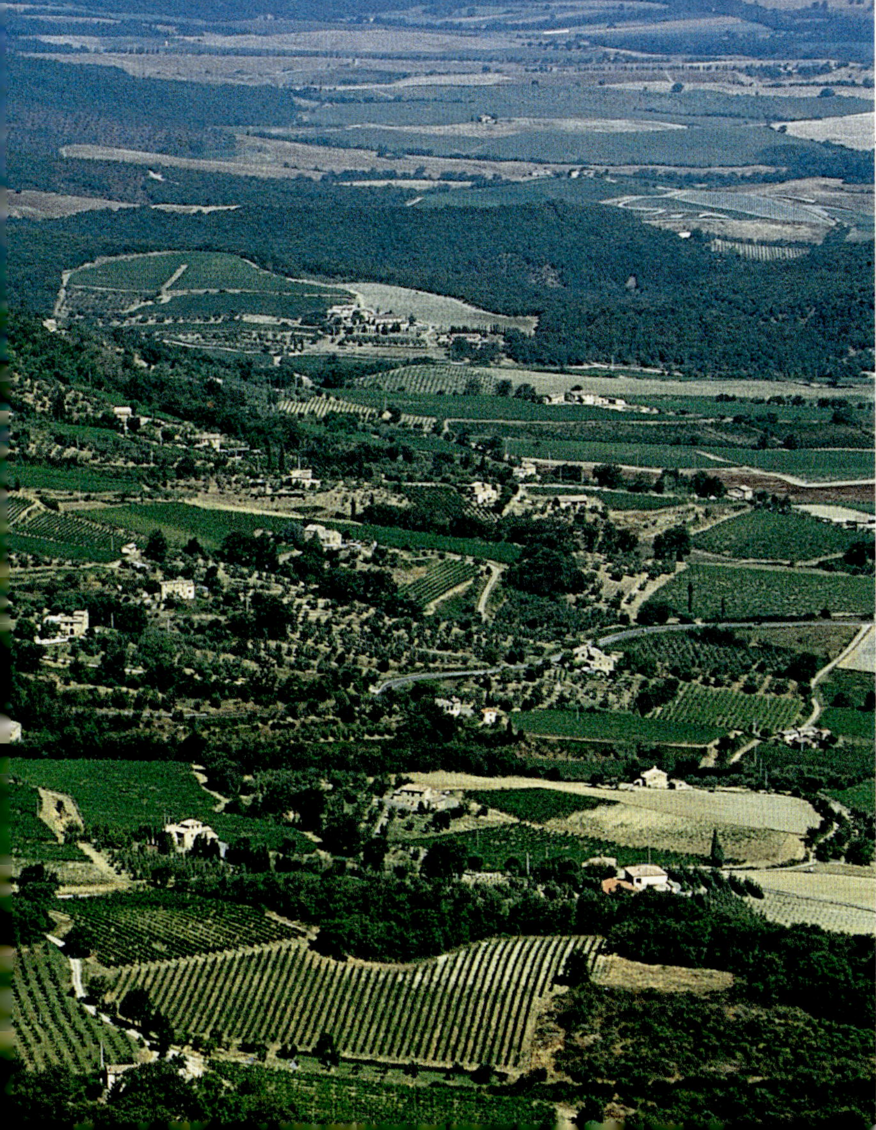

396-397
The hilltop town of Montalcino, with its 14th century fortress, dominates the surrounding countryside.

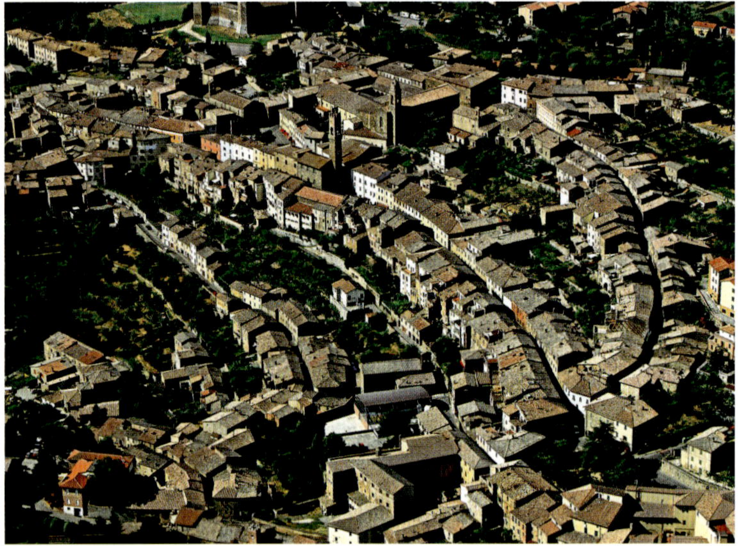

398
Montalcino center reveals the characteristics of a medieval village. Visible is the 14th- century fortress (at top) and the former convent of Sant'Agostino (below).

399
The former convent of Sant' Agostino was built in the 14th century. Today it houses the Diocesan Museum of Sacred Art, and is home to important paintings, sculptures and vases.

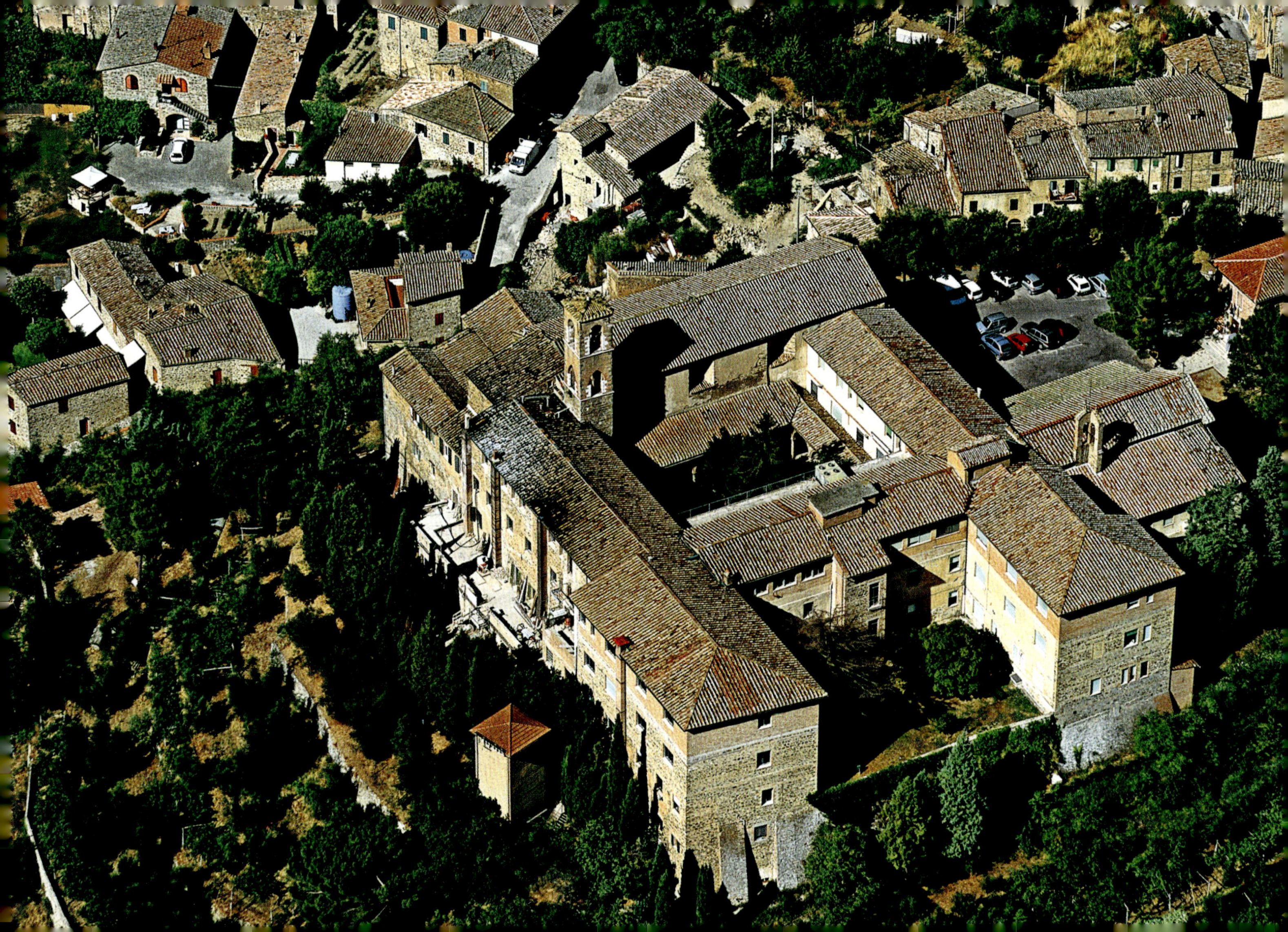

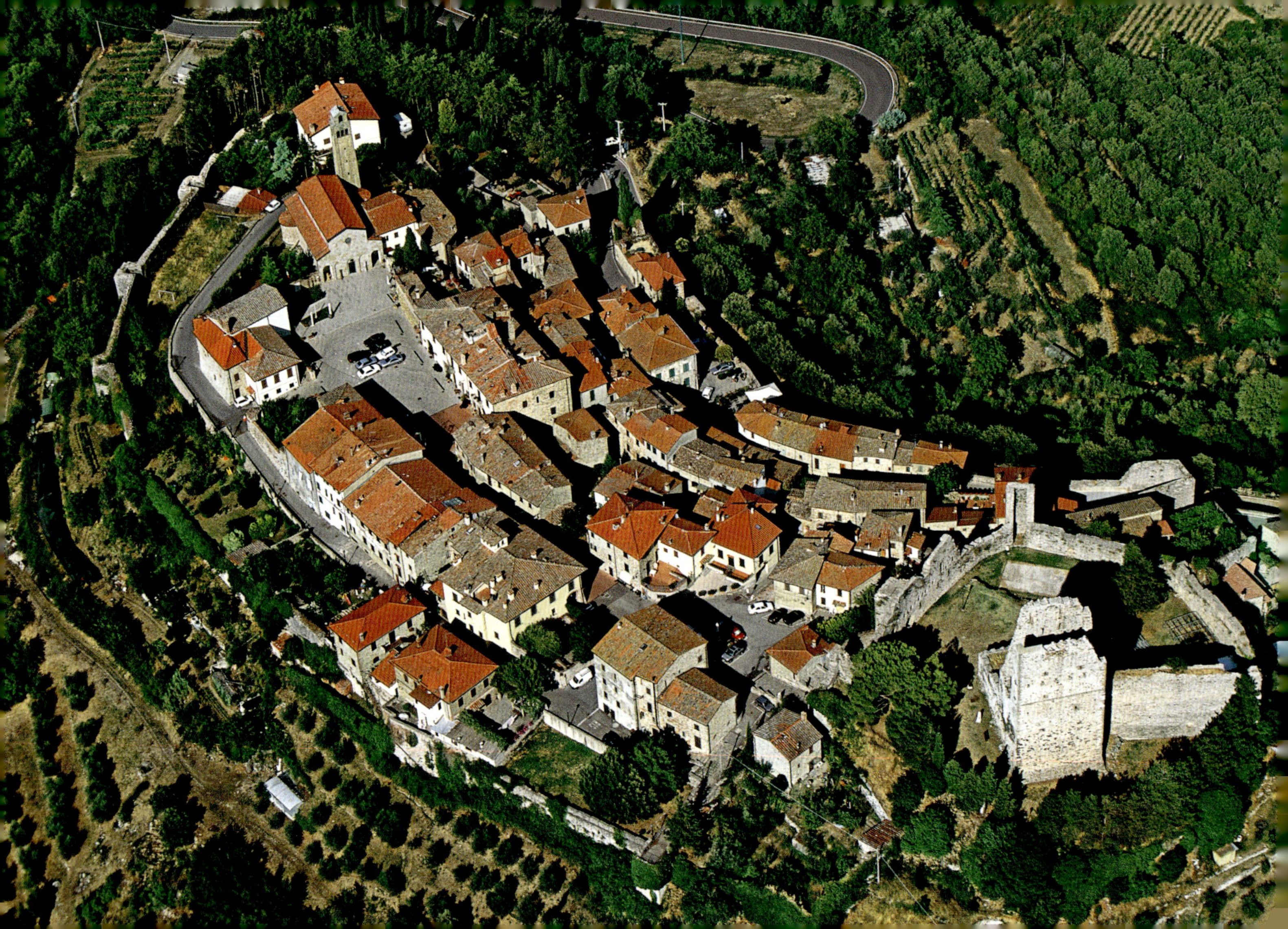

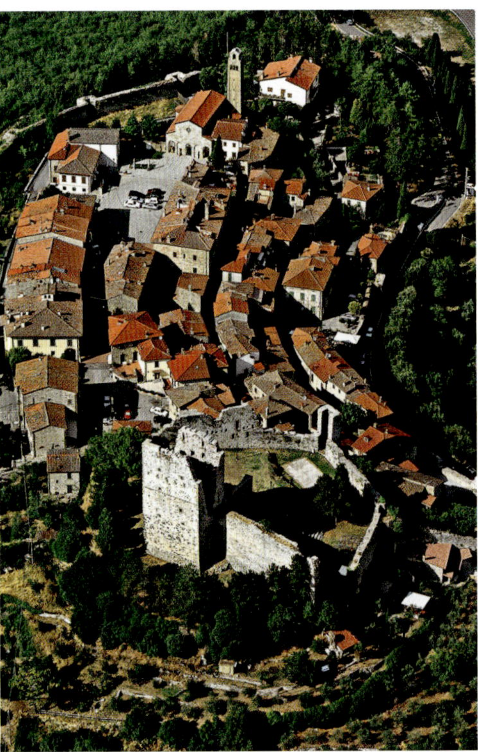

400
Here in the Val di Chiana, the majestic ruins of the 13th-century Civitella fortress, which dates to Lombard times, dominate the nearby village.

401
Civitella's famous fortress is a beautiful example of a walled-in, square medieval castle. It was commissioned by Bishop Guglielmo degli Ubertini of Arezzo.

402-403
Traditionally, Castiglion Fiorentino's origins have always been dated to the medieval era, but recent excavations have brought to light proof of Etruscan settlements.

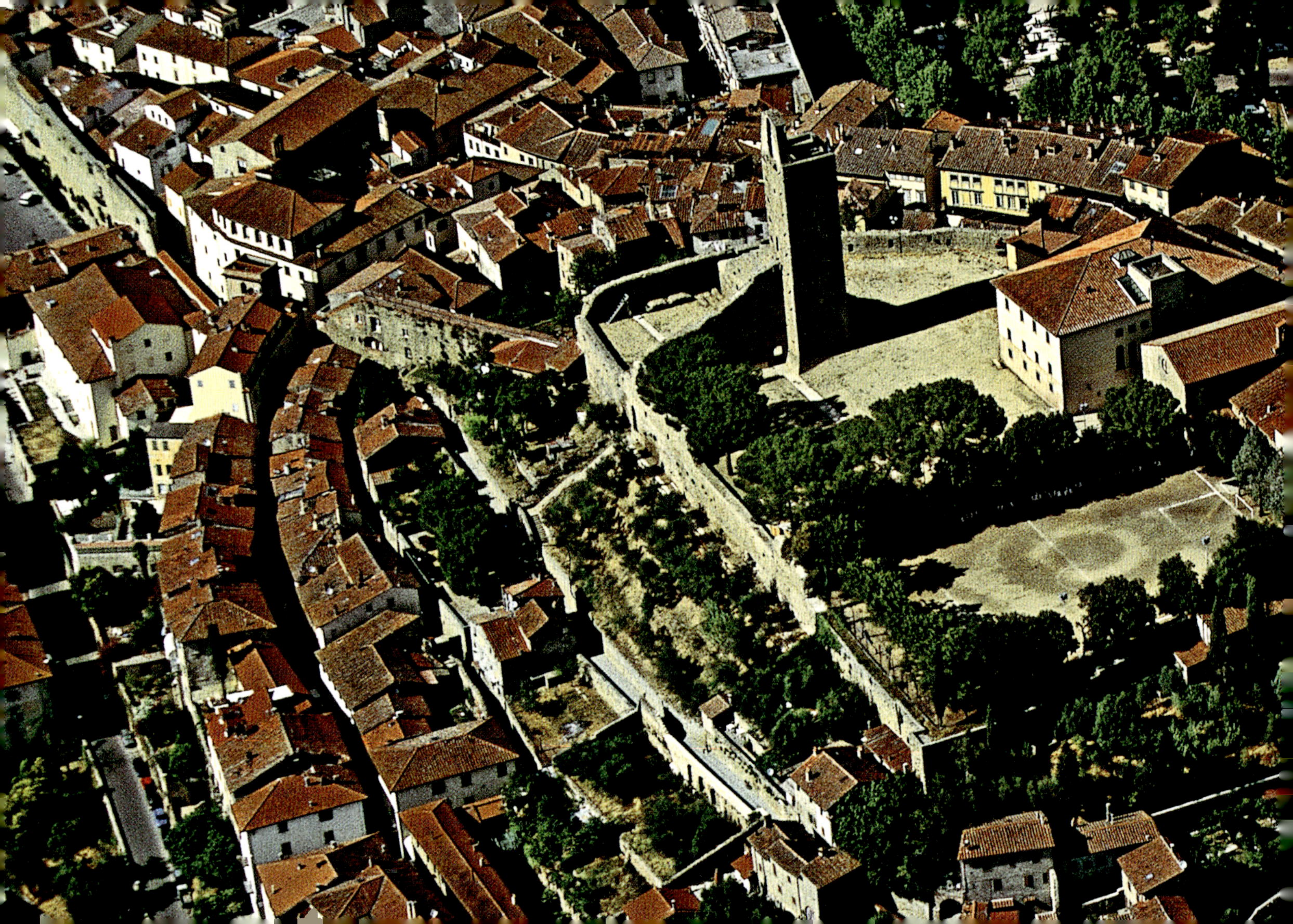

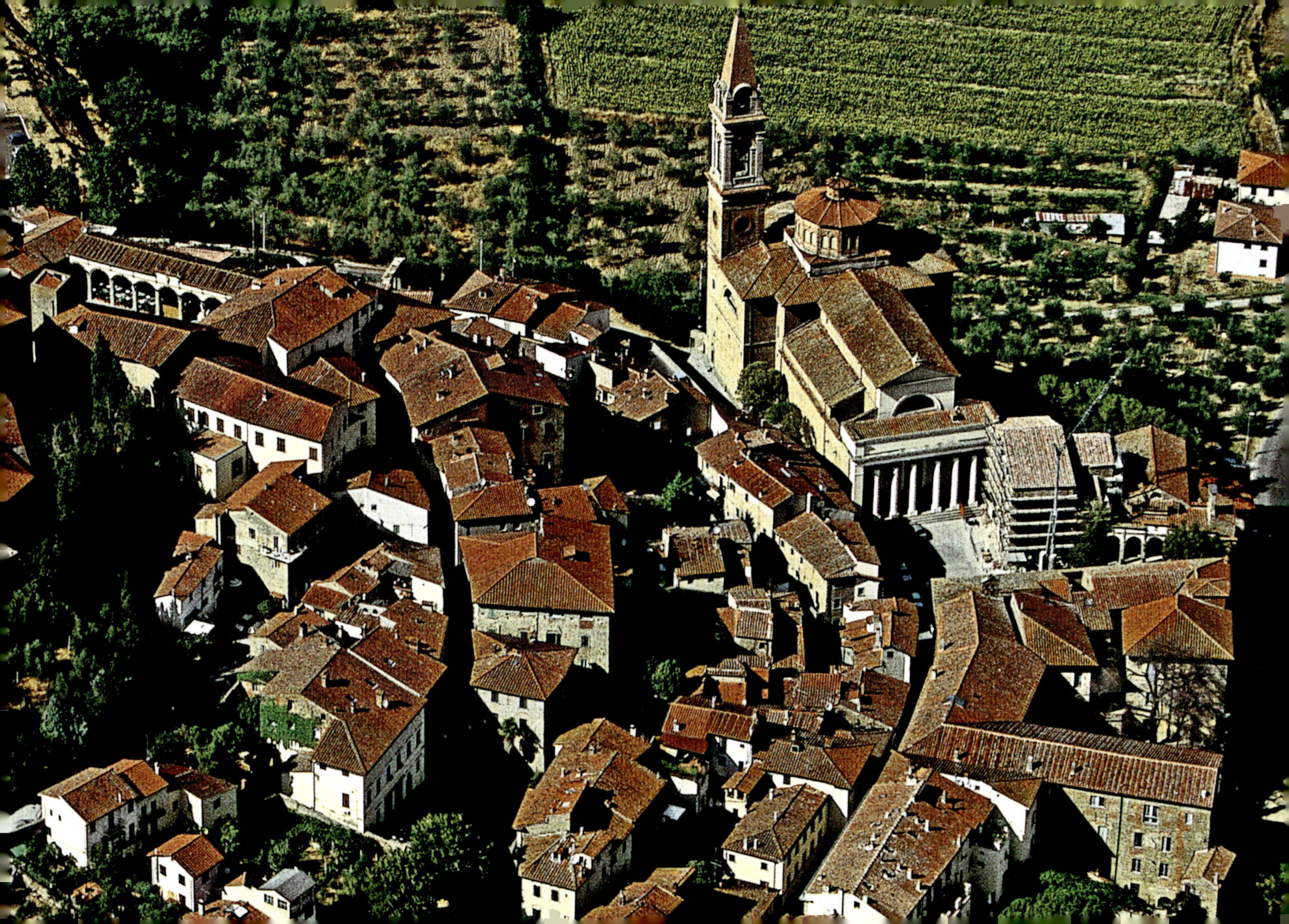

Index

c = caption

Index

Index

Cover
The Cathedral in Florence.

Backcover
Countryside near San Gimignano (Siena).

AT HEART A DEDICATED TUSCAN, BOUND TO HIS NATIVE LAND, THE VAL D'ELSA OF THE SIENESE REGION, **RENATO ROSSI** IS A SCHOLAR OF ANTHROPOLOGY, ARCHAEOLOGY AND ART HISTORY, DISCIPLINES WITH WHICH HE ENRICHED THE HISTORY COURSES HE TOOK AT THE SORBONNE. HE HAS WORKED ON VARIOUS BOOKS ON ANCIENT CIVILIZATIONS AND PUBLISHED, AMONG OTHER THINGS, A SERIES ENTITLED *ATLAS OF THE HISTORY OF MAN*, ALSO PUBLISHED IN FRENCH AND SPANISH (IN CASTILIAN AND CATALAN). HE ALSO COLLABORATED ON THE SERIES "MAN AND THE ENVIRONMENT," WINNER OF THE ANDERSEN AWARD. HE IS THE AUTHOR OF NUMEROUS TEXTS ON CD-ROMS ON HISTORY AND GEOGRAPHY DISTRIBUTED BY THE MAGAZINE *ESPRESSO* AND THE NEWSPAPERS *CORRIERE DELLA SERA* AND *REPUBBLICA*. HIS LATEST WORK, *MIDDLE AGES*, IS NOW BEING PUBLISHED.

Acknowledgments

The Editor wishes to thank Captain Renato Rossi, the Tuscan Aerostatic Association and particularly, Valentino Benvenuti.

Photo Credits

All photographs are by Antonio Attini/Archivio White Star except the following:
Pages 22, 36, 116-117, 118, 119, 151, 194-195, 196, 197, 198, 199, 200, 201, 206, 207, 208, 209, 211, 212, 213, 328-329, 340 Marcello Bertinetti/Archivio White Star - Pagg. 187, 316, 317 Carlo Bonazza - Page 186 Enzo Russo - Pages 35, 68, 121 left and right, 136, 138, 139 Giulio Veggi/Archivio White Star - Cover and backcover Antonio Attini/Archivio White Star

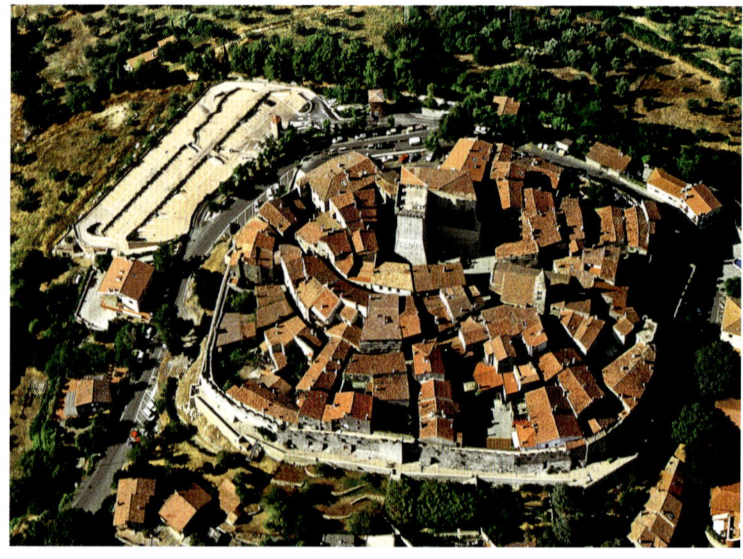

408

Capalbio is one of Tuscany's best fortified cities. Perched on the top of a hill in the heart of the Maremma, it is surrounded by a well-preserved wall.

FLYING HIGH